SIXTH EDITION

Improving Reading Skills

CONTEMPORARY READINGS FOR COLLEGE STUDENTS

Deanne Spears
City College of San Francisco

D0207137

 Higher Education

Boston   Burr Ridge, IL   Dubuque, IA   New York   San Francisco   St. Louis
Bangkok   Bogotá   Caracas   Kuala Lumpur   Lisbon   London   Madrid   Mexico City
Milan   Montreal   New Delhi   Santiago   Seoul   Singapore   Sydney   Taipei   Toronto

For David

The McGraw-Hill Companies

Higher Education

Published by McGraw-Hill, an imprint of The McGraw-Hill Companies, Inc., 1221 Avenue of the Americas, New York, NY 10020. Copyright © 2010, 2004, 2000, 1996, 1992, 1988. All rights reserved. No part of this publication may be reproduced or distributed in any form or by any means, or stored in a database or retrieval system, without the prior written consent of The McGraw-Hill Companies, Inc., including, but not limited to, in any network or other electronic storage or transmission, or broadcast for distance learning.

This book is printed on acid-free paper.

2 3 4 5 6 7 8 9 0 DOC/DOC 0 9

ISBN: 978-007340724-1
MHID: 0-07-340724-0

Editor in Chief: *Michael Ryan*
Publisher: *David S. Patterson*
Director of Development: *Dawn Groundwater*
Sponsoring Editor: *John Kindler*
Editorial Coordinator: *Jesse Hassenger*
Marketing Manager: *Allison Jones*
Production Editor: *Alison Meier*
Media Project Manager: *Ron Nelms*
Design Coordinator: *Laurie Entringer*

Cover Design: *Laurie Entringer*
Interior Design: *Ellen Pettengell*
Photo Research: *Kim Adams*
Production Supervisor: *Louis Swaim*
Production Service: *Anne Draus, Scratchgravel Publishing Services*
Composition: *10/12 Palatino by Macmillan Publishing Solutions*
Printing: *45# New Era Matte Recycled, R. R. Donnelley*
Cover image: *PhotoLink/Getty Images*

Photo Credits
p. 123: © Martin Harvey/Corbis; p. 193: © 2008 D65 Photography/Sue Owrutsky; p. 218: © Susan Van Etten/PhotoEdit; p. 299: © Vincent J. Musi/Aurora Photos; p. 335: © William Thomas Cain/Getty Images; p. 379: © Wolfgang Kaehler/Corbis; p. 401 All: © Chris Jordan, www.chrisjordan.com; p. 443: © Peter Turnley/Corbis; p. 444 All: © Peter Turnley/Corbis

Library of Congress Cataloging-in-Publication Data

Milan Spears, Deanne.
   Improving reading skills : contemporary readings for college students / Deanne Spears.—6th ed.
      p. cm.
   Includes bibliographical references and index.
   ISBN-13: 978-0-07-340724-1 (alk. paper)
   ISBN-10: 0-07-340724-0 (alk. paper)
   1. Reading (Higher education) 2. College readers. 3. Vocabulary. I. Title.
   LB2395.3.M56 2010
   428.4071'1—dc22

                                        2008034955

The Internet addresses listed in the text were accurate at the time of publication. The inclusion of a Web site does not indicate an endorsement by the authors or McGraw-Hill, and McGraw-Hill does not guarantee the accuracy of the information presented at these sites.

www.mhhe.com

About the Author

Deanne Spears is originally from Portland, Oregon, but she considers herself a native Californian, having moved to Los Angeles in the late 1940s when there were still orange groves in the area. She studied comparative literature at the University of Southern California. After teaching reading and composition at City College of San Francisco for many years, she continues to tutor students in reading and to conduct teacher-preparation workshops for the college. Her first passions are reading and studying Italian. Other interests include cooking, hiking, going to the movies, traveling, camping, and exploring the diversity of ethnic food available in the Bay Area. She is married to fellow English teacher and jazz musician David Spears. With David, she is the author of *In Tandem: College Reading and Writing* (2008); she is also the author of *Developing Critical Reading Skills,* Eighth Edition (2009).

Contents

Preface xvi

To the Student xxi

Improving Your Vocabulary 1
  Five Techniques for Acquiring Words 2
  Using Context Clues 7
  Using Print and Online Dictionaries 14

PRACTICE
SELECTION

DAVE BARRY

Tips for Women: How to Have a Relationship with a Guy 23

We're not talking about different wavelengths here. We're talking about different planets, in completely different solar systems. Elaine cannot communicate meaningfully with Roger about their relationship any more than she can meaningfully play chess with a duck. Because the sum total of Roger's thinking on this particular topic is as follows: Huh?

Comprehension Worksheet 33

PART ONE

Getting Started: Practicing the Basics 35
Identifying the Main Idea and Writer's Purpose 36
  The Difference between Fiction and Nonfiction 36
  The Difference between an Article and an Essay 36
  Identifying the Main Idea in Paragraphs 37
  Implied Main Ideas 41
  Thesis Statements in Articles and Essays 43
  Identifying the Writer's Purpose 45

1 PAMELA GRIM

Care in Midair 46

The helicopter took another shaking plunge. As I tried to hold on to the side of the cart, the laryngoscope tumbled out of my hand. I fell after it and caught it as I landed facedown on my seat. This man is going to die now, I thought; no one as sick as he is could survive this. But I would get him reintubated, no matter what.

2 PETE JORDAN

Head Dishwasher? 56

"I'm a dishwasher," I told the guy, "who happens to write." "Well, mister-dishwasher-not-a-writer," he said, "where do you wash dishes?" "Nowhere right now," I said. "This is a tough town for a dishman." "That's 'cause you're too white for the job," he said.

3 JOE ABBOTT

To Kill a Hawk 67

It was the summer of 1971, and a dozen friends and I had driven down the breathtakingly steep and tortuous road into Shelter Cove in southern Humboldt County to camp on the black sand beaches. We were pretty young then, and ill-prepared, and we quickly gobbled our meager food supplies. So I and a couple others went down into the cove to poach abalones among the rocks.

4 ROSE GUILBAULT

School Days 75

"What is that?" Mona scrunched her nose at my doll. "Don't you have a Barbie?" The other girls twittered. What was a Barbie? I wondered. And why was my doll looked down on? I felt embarrassed and quickly stuffed my unworthy toy back into the paper bag. I would not be invited to play with them again.

5 CORNELIA BAILEY

Still Gullah: A Sea Island Sister Struggles to Preserve the Old Ways 85

At age 52 I am the last of a generation to be born, raised and schooled on Sapelo, a little Sea Island off the Georgia coast. I am one of only 74 people left on the island, all of us descendants of West Africans brought here to work the cotton, sugar, rice and tobacco plantations established in the 1800s.

6 JUDITH LEWIS

Walk on the Wilshire Side 94

. . . A few miles west, where Wilshire intersects the fabled retail fantasyland of Rodeo Drive in Beverly Hills, the stares begin. It's not often, in this deeply segregated city, that a small crowd of black and Latino teenagers traipses through these moneyed streets. Women with Botoxed foreheads and surgically stretched cheeks perch at sidewalk café tables, blinking bewilderedly like some odd species of bird.

7 CHARLES FINNEY

The Life and Death of a Western Gladiator 104

The direct rays of the sun could, in a short time, kill him. If the temperature dropped too low he would freeze. Without food he would starve. Without moisture he would die of dehydration. If a man or a horse stepped on him he would be crushed. If anything chased him he could run neither very far nor very fast. Thus it was at the hour of his birth. Thus it would be, with modifications, all his life.

PART TWO Refining the Basics 115

Annotating, Paraphrasing, and Summarizing 116
    Annotating 116
    Paraphrasing 119
    Summarizing 121

8 MARC IAN BARASCH

The Bystander's Dilemma: Why Do We Walk on By? 125

My panhandling talents are nil. Each rejection thuds like a body blow. I can see the little comic-strip thought balloon spring from people's brows—Get a job; I work!

9 CHRIS ROSE

Hell and Back 138

For all of my adult life, I regarded depression and anxiety as pretty much a load of hooey. I never accorded any credibility to the idea that they are medical conditions. Nothing scientific about it. You get sick, get fired, fall in love, get laid, buy a new pair of shoes, join a gym, get religion, seasons change, whatever; you go with the flow, dust yourself off, get back in the game. I thought antidepressants were for desperate housewives and fragile poets.

10 FRANCES MOORE LAPPÉ AND JEFFREY PERKINS

The Two Sides of Fear 152

One spring day not long ago, the two of us hailed a cab in Boston. Noting the driver's strong Russian accent, we asked, "So what do you think of America?" Hesitant at first, he finally blurted out, "You Americans are all afraid." As we approached Harvard Square, two BMWs passed us. "Those people are the most afraid," he said, gesturing at the cars. "They're afraid they'll lose it. In Russia, we feared the KGB. Here, you don't trust anyone. You're all afraid of each other."

11 GEOFFREY COWLEY

The Language Explosion 164

The journey toward language starts not in the nursery but in the womb, where the fetus is continually bathed in the sounds of its mother's voice. Babies just 4 days old can distinguish one language from another. French newborns suck more vigorously when they hear French spoken than when they hear Russian—and Russian babies show the opposite preference.

12 VIRGINIA MORELL

Minds of Their Own 175

For the next 20 minutes, Alex ran through his tests, distinguishing colors, shapes, sizes, and materials (wool versus wood versus metal). He did some simple arithmetic, such as counting the yellow toy blocks among a pile of mixed hues. And, then, as if to offer final proof of the mind inside his bird's brain, Alex spoke up. "Talk clearly!" he commanded, when one of the younger birds Pepperberg was also teaching mispronounced the word green. "Talk clearly!"

13 RICHARD WOLKOMIR

Making Up for Lost Time: The Rewards of Reading at Last 192

But now we try something new, a real-world test: reading the supermarket advertising inserts from a local newspaper. Each insert is a hodgepodge of food pictures, product names and prices. I point to a word and Ken ponders. "C" he says finally. "And it's got those two e's—so that would be 'coffee'!" I point again. He gets "Pepsi." Silently, he sounds out the letters on a can's label. "So that's 'corn,'" he announces.

PART THREE   Tackling More Challenging Prose 207

Making Inferences 208

14 ERIC SCHLOSSER

Fast Food Nation: Behind the Counter 216

At Burger King restaurants, frozen hamburger patties are placed on a conveyor belt and emerge from a broiler ninety seconds later fully cooked. The ovens at Pizza Hut and at Domino's also use conveyor belts to ensure standardized cooking times. The ovens at McDonald's look like commercial laundry presses, with big steel hoods that swing down and grill hamburgers on both sides at once. The burgers, chicken, french fries, and buns are all frozen when they arrive at a McDonald's. The shakes and sodas begin as syrup.

15 STUDS TERKEL

Somebody Built the Pyramids 229

Mike Fitzgerald . . . is a laborer in a steel mill. "I feel like the guys who built the pyramids. Some-body built 'em. Somebody built the Empire State Building, too. There's hard work behind it. I would like to see a building, say the Empire State, with a foot-wide strip from top to bottom and the name of every bricklayer on it, the name of every electrician. So when a guy walked by, he could take his son and say, 'See, that's me over there on the 45th floor. I put that steel beam in.'"

16 VAL PLUMWOOD

Being Prey: Surviving a Crocodile Attack 238

When the whirling terror stopped again I surfaced again, still in the crocodile's grip next to a stout branch of a large sandpaper fig growing in the water. I grabbed the branch, vowing to let the crocodile tear me apart rather than throw me again into that spinning, suffocating hell. For the first time I realized that the crocodile was growling, as if angry.

17 TIM GUEST

Linden Lab's Second Life: Dreamers of the Dream 251

In Second Life, you can walk, or fly, but you can also buy vehicles to travel faster and in higher style. "So people start with the Ferrari, and then after that they think, Well, where could I go from this? How about a floating car?" Only later do they realize they can grow wings.

18 IAN FRAZIER

Dearly Disconnected 263

There was always a touch of seediness and sadness to pay phones, and a sense of transience. Drug dealers made calls from them, and shady types who did not want their whereabouts known, and otherwise respectable people planning assignations, and people too poor to have phones of their own. In the movies, any character who used a pay phone was either in trouble or contemplating a crime.

19 LAWRENCE SHAMES

The Hunger for More 274

Americans have always been optimists, and optimists have always liked to speculate. In Texas in the 1880s, the speculative instrument of choice was towns, and there is no tale more American than this. What people would do was buy up enormous tracts of parched and vacant land, lay out a Main Street, nail together some wooden sidewalks, and start slapping up buildings. . . . The developers would erect a flagpole and name a church, and once the workmen had packed up and moved on, the towns would be as empty as the sky.

20 BILL BRYSON

Lonely Planet 284

In the days of diving suits—the sort that were connected to the surface by long hoses—divers sometimes experienced a dreaded phenomenon known as "the squeeze." This occurred when the surface pumps failed, leading to a catastrophic loss of pressure in the suit. The air would leave the suit with such violence that the hapless diver would be, all too literally, sucked up into the helmet and hosepipe. When hauled to the surface, "all that is left in the suit are his bones and some rags of flesh," the biologist J. B. S. Haldane wrote in 1947, adding for the benefit of doubters, "This has happened."

PART FOUR Mastering Reading about Complex Ideas 297

Patterns of Development 298
    List of Facts or Details 299
    Examples 299
    Reasons—Cause and Effect 300
    Description of a Process 302
    Contrast 302
Transitional Elements 303
    Transitions That Indicate Additional Information Is Coming 304
    Transitions That Introduce Examples or Illustrations 304

Transitions That Show Cause-Effect Connections 305
Transitions That Show Chronological Order or Time Progression 306
Transitions That Show Contrast 306

Some Final Considerations 307

21 **DEBRA J. DICKERSON**

Raising Cain 309

. . . I just mean to say that children primarily meant to me that I'd always be taking care of someone, a fate too many women accept as given. When you grow up a poor black girl in a huge family you spend your life caring for the whole world. Children, I knew, meant that I'd be a human mop and short-order cook forever. . . .

22 **NELSON MANDELA**

Long Walk to Freedom 320

When I was sixteen, the regent decided that it was time that I became a man. In Xhosa tradition, this is achieved through one means only: circumcision. In my tradition, an uncircumcised male cannot be heir to his father's wealth, cannot marry or officiate in tribal rituals. An uncircumcised Xhosa man is a contradiction in terms, for he is not considered a man at all, but a boy.

23 **LYNNE DUKE**

The Picture of Conformity 333

"The next thing is they'll just have cameras everywhere," [Shoshana] Zuboff says. "They'll have software programmed with algorithms, and the algorithms will be able to detect these so-called anomalies. And so you may be distraught because you're flying home to your grandmother's funeral, but the algorithm has detected an anomalous behavior, and the next thing you're being strip-searched by a couple of FBI agents."

24 **DAVID FERRELL**

Badwater: The Ultra-Marathon 347

Every year, two or three dozen elite ultra-marathoners come to Badwater, and every year Badwater beats them down. About a third fail to finish; after 50 miles or 70 miles or 110 miles, the torture exceeds their desire to go on, and they end up rolling away in their cars and minivans, faces covered with wet towels, their bodies stretched out like corpses. For a thin slice of society—zealots who live to train, who measure themselves by their mental toughness—the ultra-marathon is the consummate test of human character.

25 **CARLIN FLORA**

Hello, My Name Is Unique 367

Increasingly, children are also named for prized possessions. In 2000, birth certificates revealed that there were 298 Armanis, 269 Chanels, 49 Canons, 6 Timberlands, 5 Jaguars and 353 girls named Lexus in the U.S.

26 JARED DIAMOND
Easter's End 378

As we try to imagine the decline of [Easter Island's] civilization, we ask ourselves, "Why didn't they look around, realize what they were doing, and stop before it was too late? What were they thinking when they cut down the last palm tree?"

PART FIVE Reading about Issues 393

Persuasive Writing and Opinion Pieces 394
The Principles of Persuasive Writing 394
The Aims of Persuasive Writing 394
How to Read Persuasive Writing 395
Types of Claims 396
Kinds of Evidence 397
The Refutation 398
The Structure of an Argument 400
Bias 400

PRACTICE EDITORIAL
ELIZABETH ROYTE

A Fountain on Every Corner 401

An entire generation of Americans has grown up thinking public faucets equal filth, and the only water fit to drink comes in plastic, factory sealed. It's time to change that perception. . . .

27 CHARLES M. BLOW
Farewell, Fair Weather 405

Just this month, a swarm of tornadoes shredded the central states. California and Florida have been scorched by wildfires, and a crippling drought in the Southeast has forced Georgia to authorize plans for new reservoirs. Who do we have to thank for all this? Probably ourselves.

28 BILL MCKIBBEN
The Environmental Issue from Hell 409

But what makes them [SUVs] such a perfect symbol is the brute fact that they are simply unnecessary. Go to the parking lot of the nearest suburban supermarket and look around: The only conclusion you can draw is that to reach the grocery, people must drive through three or four raging rivers and up the side of a canyon.

29 COURTNEY E. MARTIN
Is the American Dream a Delusion? 415

You know the story: Once upon a time there was a hardworking, courageous young man, born in a poor family, who came to America, put in blood, sweat and tears, and eventually found riches and respect. But knowing the statistics on social mobility and the ever-widening gap between rich and poor, I just can't stomach this "happily ever after" scenario. It is too clean. Real life is full of messy things like racism and the wage gap and child care and nepotism.

30 RUBEN NAVARRETTE
Racial Profiling Is Un-American 421

Now the embattled group is Muslim Americans. In the USA Today/Gallup *poll, 39 percent of Americans said they felt at least some prejudice against Muslims. The same percentage favored requiring Muslims, including those who were U.S. citizens, to carry a special ID to help prevent future terrorist attacks. And 22 percent of respondents said they wouldn't want Muslims as neighbors.*

31 JOHN POMFRET
Two Sides to the Border Fence 426

Legislation passed by Congress mandating the fencing of 700 miles of the U.S. border with Mexico has sparked opposition from an array of land managers, businesspeople, law enforcement officials, environmentalists and U.S. Border Patrol agents as a one-size-fits-all policy response to the nettlesome task of securing the nation's borders.

Paired Editorials—The Fence along the U.S.–Mexican Border 430

32 LUIS ALBERTO URREA
$1.2 Billion Fence Adds Little or No Security 430

On the Mexican side, among much gnashing of teeth, there is a joke that has been circulating the whole time. The gist of it is: Let them put up a fence! They'll hire us to build it! Then, when it's done, we'll run the tourist concessions and the taco stands. Then, when they get tired of it, they'll hire us to tear it down!

33 DUNCAN HUNTER
Building a Wall between Worlds 437

This level of success illustrates that border fencing works. In fact, the San Diego border fence is serving to benefit both sides of the border. As conditions in San Diego County have improved, communities on the Mexican side of the border are no longer at the mercy of the armed gangs and drug smugglers who once roamed and controlled the Tijuana smuggling corridor.

34 PETER TURNLEY
The Line—Photographs from the U.S.–Mexican Border 443

35 Paired Web Sites—Two Scientific Views of Global Warming 446
Union of Concerned Scientists 446
The Heartland Institute 446

PART SIX Reading Textbooks 449

Four Surefire Ways to Get Low Grades 450
Four Suggestions for Making the Most of Your Study Time 453
Applying the SQ3R Study Method to Reading Textbooks 453

36 JOSEPH LOSCO AND RALPH BAKER
Measuring Public Opinion 456
From "Public Opinion—Listening to Citizens," AM GOV—Making Citizenship Meaningful

37 JOSEPH R. DOMINICK, FRITZ MESSERE, AND BARRY L. SHERMAN
The Ratings Process 460
From "Ratings and Audience Feedback," Broadcasting, Cable, the Internet, and Beyond

38 BENJAMIN B. LAHEY
Sleep and Dreams: Conscious while Asleep 468
From "States of Consciousness," Psychology: An Introduction

39 CONRAD PHILLIP KOTTAK
Race 481
From "Ethnicity and Race," Anthropology: The Exploration of Human Diversity

40 SYLVIA S. MADER
Seed Plants, Gymnosperms, and Angiosperms 489
From "Evolution and Diversity of Plants," Biology

Index I-1

Index of Vocabulary Preview Words I-4

Reading Comprehension Progress Chart

Alternate Contents
Arranged by Theme

ADVENTURE

1   **Pamela Grim,** "Care in Midair" 46

6   **Judith Lewis,** "Walk on the Wilshire Side" 94

16   **Val Plumwood,** "Being Prey: Surviving a Crocodile Attack" 238

17   **Tim Guest,** "Linden Lab's Second Life: Dreamers of the Dream" 251

24   **David Ferrell,** "Badwater: The Ultra-Marathon" 347

GENDER ROLES AND GENDER ISSUES

Practice Essay   **Dave Barry,** "Tips for Women: How to Have a Relationship with a Guy" 23

4   **Rose Guilbault,** "School Days" 75

21   **Debra J. Dickerson,** "Raising Cain" 309

RACE AND ETHNICITY

2   **Pete Jordan,** "Head Dishwasher?" 56

4   **Rose Guilbault,** "School Days" 75

5   **Cornelia Bailey,** "Still Gullah: A Sea Island Sister Struggles to Preserve the Old Ways" 85

21   **Debra J. Dickerson,** "Raising Cain" 309

30   **Ruben Navarrette,** "Racial Profiling Is Un-American" 421

31   **John Pomfret,** "Two Sides to the Border Fence" 426

32   **Luis Alberto Urrea,** "$1.2 Billion Fence Adds Little or No Security" 430

33   **Duncan Hunter,** "Building a Wall between Worlds" 437

34   **Peter Turnley,** The Line—Photographs from the U.S.–Mexican Border 443

COMING OF AGE AND INITIATION RITES

3   **Joe Abbott,** "To Kill a Hawk" 67

4   **Rose Guilbault,** "School Days" 75

21   **Debra J. Dickerson,** "Raising Cain" 309

22   **Nelson Mandela,** "Long Walk to Freedom" 320

OUR WORKING LIVES

1   **Pamela Grim,** "Care in Midair" 46

2   **Pete Jordan,** "Head Dishwasher?" 56

5   **Cornelia Bailey,** "Still Gullah: A Sea Island Sister Struggles to Preserve the Old Ways" 85

14   **Eric Schlosser,** "Fast Food Nation: Behind the Counter" 216

15   **Studs Terkel,** "Somebody Built the Pyramids" 229

LANGUAGE AND COMMUNICATION

11   **Geoffrey Cowley,** "The Language Explosion" 164

12   **Virginia Morell,** "Minds of Their Own" 175

13   **Richard Wolkomir,** "Making Up for Lost Time: The Rewards of Reading at Last" 192

18   **Ian Frazier,** "Dearly Disconnected" 263

SCIENCE AND TECHNOLOGY

7   **Charles Finney,** "The Life and Death of a Western Gladiator" 104

18   **Ian Frazier,** "Dearly Disconnected" 263

20   **Bill Bryson,** "Lonely Planet" 284

26   **Jared Diamond,** "Easter's End" 378

Practice Editorial   **Elizabeth Royte,** "A Fountain on Every Corner" 401

27   **Charles M. Blow,** "Farewell, Fair Weather" 405

28   **Bill McKibben,** "The Environmental Issue from Hell" 409

35   Paired Web Sites—Two Scientific Views of Global Warming 446

LIFE LESSONS AND ETHICAL LAPSES

3   **Joe Abbott,** "To Kill a Hawk" 67

8   **Marc Ian Barasch,** "The Bystander's Dilemma: Why Do We Walk On By?" 125

9   **Chris Rose,** "Hell and Back" 138

10   **Frances Moore Lappé and Jeffrey Perkins,** "The Two Sides of Fear" 152

TRENDS IN CONTEMPORARY AMERICAN LIFE

6   **Judith Lewis,** "Walk on the Wilshire Side" 94

10   **Frances Moore Lappé and Jeffrey Perkins,** "The Two Sides of Fear" 152

14   **Eric Schlosser,** "Fast Food Nation: Behind the Counter" 216

17   **Tim Guest,** "Linden Lab's Second Life: Dreamers of the Dream" 251

18   **Ian Frazier,** "Dearly Disconnected" 263

19   **Lawrence Shames,** "The Hunger for More" 274

23   **Lynne Duke,** "The Picture of Conformity" 333

25   **Carlin Flora,** "Hello, My Name Is Unique" 367

29   **Courtney E. Martin,** "Is the American Dream a Delusion?" 415

30   **Ruben Navarrette,** "Racial Profiling Is Un-American" 421

31   **John Pomfret,** "Two Sides to the Border Fence" 426

32   **Luis Alberto Urrea,** "$1.2 Billion Fence Adds Little or No Security" 430

33   **Duncan Hunter,** "Building a Wall between Worlds" 437

34   **Peter Turnley,** The Line—Photographs from the U.S.–Mexican Border 443

SAVING AND DESTROYING THE ENVIRONMENT

5   **Cornelia Bailey,** "Still Gullah: A Sea Island Sister Struggles to Preserve the Old Ways" 85

26   **Jared Diamond,** "Easter's End" 378

Practice Editorial **Elizabeth Royte,** "A Fountain on Every Corner" 401

27   **Charles M. Blow,** "Farewell, Fair Weather" 405

28   **Bill McKibben,** "The Environmental Issue from Hell" 409

35   Paired Web Sites—Two Scientific Views of Global Warming 446

Preface

Once again, it is gratifying to revise *Improving Reading Skills*. Because I have found that students improve more by reading than by reading about techniques and strategies, the sixth edition—like the preceding editions—offers students insightful, engaging, contemporary selections to challenge them and make them want to turn the page. The book's subtitle, *Contemporary Readings for College Students*, reflects the nature of the book. In addition to acquiring skills, students will learn something about the world as they read.

In addition to the readings, the book presents a wide variety of practice exercises to reinforce good reading skills and to help students develop a college-level vocabulary. This basic composition—high-interest contemporary readings and useful exercises—has accounted for the book's past success and remains the guiding principle for this edition. In the brief discussion of the book's important components that follows, users of prior editions will see that most of these components remain the same and that new ones have been incorporated, which I hope will make the book more enjoyable and helpful.

An Overview of the Text

The sixth edition contains 40 reading selections from a variety of media—books, magazines, newspapers, and online sources. The majority are contemporary, representing the kinds of reading students will encounter in their college courses—especially English courses, which require students to read expository and persuasive essays—as well as in their everyday lives after their formal education ends. I want students to see that they are members of a larger community and that reading can be instrumental in helping them fill this role. Reading also provides students with a way to understand the world around them and to search for meaning in their own lives. The book, however, has no particular underlying philosophy, no "ism" to flog. It seeks only to help students to improve their reading comprehension and to read with better concentration and with enjoyment and confidence.

New to this edition is Part Six, Reading Textbooks. In addition to some straightforward advice about coping with the demands of college classes, this section gives students an opportunity to practice college-level reading and analysis with five excerpts from standard college textbooks in various disciplines.

VOCABULARY DEVELOPMENT

This edition continues to stress vocabulary development in the context of each reading. In my experience both teaching and tutoring reading at City College of San Francisco, a weak vocabulary—perhaps even more than poor concentration or lack of interest—is a major stumbling block for many students. Because the interrelationship between comprehension and vocabulary is so strong, intensive emphasis on vocabulary remains an integral part of the text.

To this end, a Vocabulary Preview precedes each selection. Each introduces students to a few words—typically three or four—that they will encounter in the reading. Divided into Word Parts and Word Families, these previews have the twin benefits of teaching the students the meanings of a few important words from the reading and illustrating a systematic way to acquire more new words. Rather than being taught in isolation, the English vocabulary elements that are so useful for developing word recognition—roots, prefixes, and suffixes—are thereby taught in context of the reading. These Vocabulary Preview sections should prove valuable for both native-born students and English-language learners.

Finally, post-reading exercises include two vocabulary activities, the forms of which vary from selection to selection, as a glance through the text will show. This diversity renders the vocabulary exercises more challenging and engaging than repetitive, multiple-choice questions could. Many exercises ask students to locate a word in the paragraph that matches a given definition. Others ask them to show their mastery of the meanings of several words by inserting them into a paragraph correctly. Some exercises ask students to provide variant forms of several of the selection's most important words, and others ask students to write sentences of their own invention using new words.

READING SKILLS

Each of the book's six parts begins with an overview and explanation of various skills necessary for good reading comprehension and analysis. These topics are arranged so that students encounter the most fundamental skills at the beginning of the course before progressing to the next level. Each introduction contains short examples and excerpts to familiarize students with these skills. For example, the introduction to Part One shows students how to locate the main idea in individual paragraphs, the thesis statement in essays, and the writer's purpose. Part Two takes up the skills of annotating, paraphrasing, and summarizing. Part Three presents inference, Part Four gives an overview of the common patterns of development and transitional devices, and Part Five shows students how to read opinion pieces. Finally, Part Six, as noted before, includes some commonsense advice to help students stay out of academic trouble and describes the useful study skills method SQ3R.

Instructors are free to assign these introductory segments in any order that suits their curriculum. Having said this, however, instructors might want to introduce the study skills section (Part Six) early in the course to give students a firm grounding in the first weeks of the semester; in this way, they can put these vital techniques into practice as they read textbooks for their other courses.

READING SELECTIONS

As with earlier editions, I selected the readings using several criteria: They must be well written and relatively easy to understand, especially in Parts One and Two; they must be a reasonable length so that students can complete the reading and accompanying exercises in one sitting; and they must be of sufficient interest to appeal to the most reluctant of readers.

In response to reviewers' suggestions, Parts One and Two now contain more short readings representing quite easy levels. (See the Web site, at *www.mhhe.com/spears*, for word lengths, grade levels, and readability scores.) Following reviewers' preferences and my own subjective tastes and opinions, I have retained a number of readings from the previous edition.

The new readings embrace a wide range of topics. Here are some examples:

- Pete Jordan's humorous and cynical account of looking for work as a dishwasher in New Orleans ("Head Dishwasher?")
- Joe Abbott's heartfelt confession of a youthful indiscretion ("To Kill a Hawk")
- Cornelia Bailey's lament for the slowly dying Gullah culture on Sapelo, a barrier island off the Georgia coast ("Still Gullah: A Sea Island Sister Struggles to Preserve the Old Ways")
- Mark Ian Barasch's experiment with living on the streets of Denver as an exercise in learning compassion ("The Bystander's Dilemma: Why Do We Walk on By?")
- New Orleans journalist Chris Rose's account of his battle with depression ("Hell and Back")
- The strangely absorbing world of online avatars and Second Life as described by Tim Guest ("Linden Lab's Second Life: Dreamers of the Dream")
- An explanation of the limits of the Earth's environment by Bill Bryson ("Lonely Planet")
- Debra J. Dickerson's misgivings about raising her son in the African-American tradition ("Raising Cain")
- Lynne Duke's appraisal of how surveillance cameras in public places are altering human behavior ("The Picture of Conformity")
- An essay about American parents who give their children bizarre names, by Carlin Flora ("Hello, My Name is Unique")

In response to reviewers' suggestions for strengthening the section on opinion pieces, Part Five, Reading about Issues, now begins with a step-by-step explanation of how to read persuasive material using Elizabeth Royte's *New York Times* editorial. In this piece, she argues that cities should build more public water fountains as a way to rid the environment of the ubiquitous plastic water bottle. This selection is carefully annotated to show students how an experienced reader tackles such a piece. Seven persuasive and argumentative readings follow, taking up the issues of climate change, the increasingly illusory American dream for working-class people, and racial profiling. Paired editorials present opposing views of the border fence now being constructed on the U.S.–Mexican border. These editorials are followed and reinforced by Peter Turnley's short photo essay. Part Five ends with an opportunity for students to examine two paired—and competing—Web sites on global warming, one sponsored by the Union of Concerned Scientists, the other by the Heartland Institute.

EXERCISE MATERIAL

The exercises in the sixth edition are more extensive and cover a wider range of skills than those in most other college reading texts. Step by step, each exercise provides students an opportunity to practice their increasing skills at a level appropriate for each reading. By the completion of the course, these exercises will help improve students' comprehension and analytical skills in specific areas such as determining the main idea and writer's purpose; annotating text; writing paraphrases and summaries; comprehending main ideas; distinguishing between main ideas and supporting details; making inferences and drawing conclusions; distinguishing between fact and opinion; analyzing structure; and identifying the meanings of new words in context.

WEB SITE MATERIAL

For help in course planning, instructors who go to the Web site for the book at *www.mhhe.com/spears* will find, for each selection, a brief summary, suggestions for teaching that do not appear in the text, and information on length, readability scores, and reading grade levels.

Changes in the Sixth Edition

For this edition I have incorporated almost without exception the many excellent suggestions made by the reviewers of the previous edition. Here are the most significant ones:

- Increased emphasis on vocabulary development.
- Expanded introductions for each of the book's six parts.
- More easy, short readings, especially in Parts One and Two, and a better balance between multiple-choice and fill-in answers.
- Increased emphasis on annotating, paraphrasing, and summarizing—not just in the introduction to Part Two but also throughout the exercise material in Parts One through Five.
- Suggestions for connecting reading to the World Wide Web, including recommendations for specific Web sites related to a reading's content and also suggestions for further student-initiated research and exploration.
- Paired editorials to give students practice in analyzing opposing viewpoints on current issues. These selections discuss the fence along the border of the United States and Mexico and are accompanied by a reading that provides background information and a photo essay.
- Part 6, Reading Textbooks, offers advice on how to avoid academic trouble along with five textbook excerpts representing these diverse fields: American government, mass media, psychology, anthropology, and biology.

Acknowledgments

I wish to thank all of the reviewers of the sixth edition, who were nearly unanimous in their suggestions about how to improve the book, and I wish to extend my most sincere thanks for their help. If this edition is better than previous ones, it is because of them:

Nancy Bertoglio, American River College
Chandler Clifton, Edmonds Community College
Carolyn Connors, Wor-Wic Community College
Georgia Gaspar, Rio Hondo College
Leona Hunt, Central Florida Community College
Barbara McLay, University of South Florida
Karla Nast, Lone Star College–CyFair
Cathy Seyler, Palm Beach Community College
Katie Smith, Riverside Community College
Teresa Ward, Butte College

Special thanks also go to Joe Abbott, Carolyn Davidson, Jan Rutherford, Jerry Kirsch-Chandler—all of Butte College in Oroville, California. Joe gave me "To Kill a Hawk" to read, and I liked it so much that I included it here; Jerry Kirsch-Chandler gave me several articles on Gullah culture, including the selection by Cornelia Bailey in Part One.

I must also thank Steven Penzinger, formerly of Random House, who believed in my original proposal enough to take a chance on publishing the first edition. John Kindler, my editor at McGraw-Hill, strongly supported the project, and Jesse Hassenger efficiently took care of countless details. Special thanks to Anne Draus of Scratchgravel Publishing Services, who oversaw the production process and shepherded the manuscript through an unusually quick schedule. Carol Lombardi, copy editor for the manuscript, lent a careful eye to everything. To all of them, I am most grateful.

And finally, I must mention my husband, David, who is the master of the plain style and the finer points of grammar and punctuation. He is happy to debate these matters at any time, and if my style has improved at all over the years, it is largely because of him.

Instructors should feel free to send suggestions, comments, or questions via e-mail to me at *dkspears@gmail.com*. I can also be reached through the McGraw-Hill Higher Education Web site at *www.mhhe.com/spears*. I will do my best to answer all correspondence within a day or two.

Deanne Spears
Half Moon Bay, California

To the Student

The Aims of the Text

Your instructor and I hope that you will derive the ultimate benefit from this text: an enjoyment of reading that becomes a lifelong pursuit. Reading well allows you to travel from the comfort of your home, to dream, to escape, to learn, to understand the important issues of the day, to question, and—most crucially for a college student—to think.

This is the sixth edition of *Improving Reading Skills*. Because the book has evolved in many ways—both large and small—in form and content since the first edition, you will benefit from the many changes it has undergone. If you work through the readings diligently and attentively, with your instructor's help you will achieve several goals: better concentration, improved reading comprehension, an advanced level of vocabulary, a knowledge of major word elements, and most important, a way to tie the content of the readings to the outside world. Finally, you can pursue subjects that particularly interest you by accessing relevant Web sites.

The forty selections in this edition are drawn from books, magazines, newspapers, online sources, and college textbooks. All are nonfiction, representing both the reading required in your other college courses (in particular, English courses) and reading material you will encounter throughout the rest of your life. These high-interest readings reflect a variety of topics and writing styles. Some are entertaining; some are informative; some are provocative. Most will give you something to think about—and to write about. The selections are arranged in order of difficulty, which means that as you work through them, you will be able to refine your comprehension, vocabulary, and analytical skills with increasingly more challenging material.

The Structure of the Text

The book is divided into six parts. Each part begins with instruction in a particular reading skill. Since the material moves from simple to moderate to more difficult, the most important skills are taken up first. Each introduction provides you with an opportunity to practice these new skills with short excerpts before going on to the longer readings. For example, Part One begins with a discussion and illustration of main ideas, supporting ideas, and writer's purpose. Building on these fundamental skills, Part Two takes up the interrelated skills of annotating, paraphrasing, and summarizing, and so on. It is worth taking a few minutes to look over the table of contents to see the overall organization of the book.

POST-READING EXERCISES

The exercise material following each reading will help you practice a variety of important reading skills. Taken together, they will help you read more systematically and provide a structure and direction for your reading. Although the types of exercises vary from selection to selection, each skill is reinforced throughout the text as the material becomes more difficult. Further, these exercises break down the process of comprehension and analysis into small, separate steps, so that little by little, you will understand better what to look for when you read, whether you are reading for an academic course or for pleasure.

Each set of exercises always ends with questions for writing or discussion; these ask you to respond to the reading in a short essay or to consider important questions that the selection raises. Take a minute to look over these two sections even if your instructor does not assign them, since they might provide inspiration for essays that you will have to write in other courses.

THE SKILLS YOU WILL LEARN

These are the skills that, apart from vocabulary, you will work on during the term:

- understanding the main idea
- determining the writer's purpose
- distinguishing between main ideas and supporting details
- making accurate inferences
- learning to annotate and to write paraphrases and summaries
- distinguishing between fact and opinion
- analyzing structure; recognizing patterns of development and placement of transitions
- identifying the claim and evidence in editorial (persuasive) writing
- learning to apply a study skills method, SQ3R, to textbook material

EXPLORING ON YOUR OWN: THE WORLD WIDE WEB

The sections called Exploring Related Web Sites provide suggestions if you wish to examine the subject in more detail. In some cases, I provide Web sites for you to explore; in other cases, I suggest how to conduct a search of a particular topic using Google or your favorite search engine. Here I point you in some direction so that if you are particularly intrigued by a selection and want to read more, you can find a starting place. Many of the recommended sites include links to other related sites.

Vocabulary: The Crucial Element

Whether your instructor assigns it or not, be sure to read the introductory material on improving your vocabulary. This section offers useful techniques for acquiring new vocabulary words and introduces you to context clues and to efficient ways to use the dictionary. Good vocabulary is essential for good comprehension skills; if you don't know the meanings of many words a writer uses, it's very difficult to know exactly what he or she is saying.

The best way to improve your vocabulary is to commit yourself during the term to looking up many unfamiliar words that you encounter in your reading. At first this task may seem overwhelming, but as you work through the material, you will see that the job is not as daunting as it might have appeared at first.

The Vocabulary Previews that open each selection in Parts One through Five introduce you to a few words that you will encounter in that selection. These previews discuss Word Parts and Word Families, which will help you decode new words and show you how to break an unfamiliar word into its component parts—prefix, root, and suffix—as an aid to getting at its meaning. Finally, each selection ends with two vocabulary exercises, which give you ample opportunity to learn definitions of important words. As you work through the vocabulary exercises, remember that it is *not* cheating to look up unfamiliar words in the dictionary.

As the weeks go by, you will be pleasantly surprised to find that words you have met in the earlier selections will turn up again in later ones and in your other reading, as well. For example, one student told me that every morning while riding on a San Francisco bus, she had seen an advertisement that used a word previously unfamiliar to her—*nostalgia*. One day she encountered the word in a Vocabulary Preview section, and suddenly the ad made sense to her!

CALCULATING YOUR COMPREHENSION SCORE

The instructions accompanying each set of exercises (Parts One through Four only) ask you to do Exercises A and B without looking back at the selection. Your instructor may allow you to disregard these instructions. Not looking back, however, will force you to read with greater attention and concentration. When you are finished with all the exercises, calculate your comprehension score by counting your correct answers for Exercises A and B according to the formula below.

Since the two questions in Exercise A on determining the main idea and writer's purpose are most crucial, each is worth 2 points, whereas the main-idea questions in Exercise B are each worth 1 point. Your final score will be a percentage of 100. Study this example of a hypothetical student who got both questions in Exercise A correct and four questions in Exercise B correct:

A. No. right ___2___ × 2 = ___4___
B. No. right ___4___ × 1 = ___4___

　　　Total points from A and B ___8___ × 10 = ___80___ percent

Since the selections become progressively more difficult, maintaining a score of 70 percent or higher indicates steady improvement. A chart on which you can keep track of your progress is included at the back of the text.

Finally, to be sure that you get the most out of the text and the course, be sure to ask your instructor for help with anything you do not understand. If you have questions, comments, or suggestions, you can reach me via e-mail at *dkspears@gmail.com* and also through the Web site at *www.mhhe.com/spears*. I will do my best to reply within a day or two.

Deanne Spears

Improving Your Vocabulary

When my students complain in the reading classes I teach that they often have difficulty concentrating and maintaining focus as they read, we discuss the problem at length. Although poor concentration may be the result of many factors—going to school and working at the same time, personal problems, lack of sleep, financial worries—the problem is more often caused by lack of vocabulary. Reading is tedious if there are many unfamiliar words on the page, and having to look up lots of words in the dictionary is time-consuming and discouraging. A weak vocabulary is indeed a significant obstacle to good reading comprehension. Therefore, acquiring new vocabulary words is crucial if you hope to become a better reader. After all, if you do not know what key words on the page mean, you may not understand what a writer is saying.

Acquiring a solid reading vocabulary is a lifelong proposition, and I hope that this text will be of great use as you expand this most necessary of skills. Your goal during the course should be to acquire as many college-level vocabulary words as you can while you read each selection. Your goal after the course ends should be to continue to acquire words as you read in your everyday life.

And acquiring new words will have more benefits besides making you a better reader. Fair or not, people do judge others by their level of vocabulary, and surely as you acquire new words, you can begin to use some of them when you speak. Educated speakers tend to have good vocabularies, and they usually command respect and admiration for this quality. Beware, though. You don't want to come off as pretentious or sound like a walking dictionary.

For these reasons, it is important that you embark on a systematic vocabulary-acquisition program. Several features in this text will help you accomplish this. As you work through the selections, you will learn to identify common prefixes and roots, to break words down into their meaningful parts, and to use context clues to determine the meaning of unfamiliar words. When context clues aren't helpful, you can turn to your dictionary, as even the best readers do from time to time. This introductory portion of the text explores some techniques to increase your *recognition vocabulary*—words you can readily define from both your college and your everyday reading. Everything will work together to give you measurable immediate and long-term results. This introduction discusses these topics:

- Five techniques for acquiring words
- Breaking words down into their component parts
- Using context clues
- Using the dictionary effectively
- Comparing print and online dictionaries

1

As I prepared the selections and the accompanying exercises, I quickly saw that many words from the early selections—actually a surprising number—turned up in subsequent ones. Of course, I did not plan it this way; it just happened. This is the reason I stress that you read the Vocabulary Preview sections preceding each selection, even if your instructor doesn't assign them, and that you work through the two vocabulary exercises after each selection. If you do this conscientiously, not only will your stock of vocabulary words grow, but your reading of the later pieces will be easier and more enjoyable. The thrill of recognition does wonders for one's reading morale. ("I saw the word *clandestine* in the Pete Jordan selection; even better, I remember what it means!")

The single best way to improve your vocabulary is to read a lot. There is no shortcut or substitute for this method. The idea is simple and obvious: The more you read, the more you will be exposed to important vocabulary words. Memorizing long lists of words in isolation or working through vocabulary self-improvement books may fool you into thinking you are learning new words, but their meanings won't stick, and such activities deprive you of encountering words in real writing. The following are a few suggestions for learning new words.

Five Techniques for Acquiring Words

This section introduces some techniques to help you learn new words and retain them better.

TECHNIQUES FOR ACQUIRING WORDS

- Use the Three-Dot Method
- Use Vocabulary Note Cards
- Break New Words Down into Their Component Parts
- Develop an Interest in Etymology
- Subscribe to a Word-of-the-Day Website

USE THE THREE-DOT METHOD

The three-dot method works like this: When you look up a word in the dictionary, make a small dot in pencil next to the entry word. The second time you look it up, make another dot. The third time you look it up, add a third dot, and this time, learn the word! Any word that crops up three times within a short amount of time is obviously an important word that belongs in your permanent and active reading vocabulary.

THE THREE-DOT METHOD

• • • **eu • tha • na • sia** (yōō-thə-nā′zhə, zhē-ə) *n.* The act or practice of ending the life of an individual suffering from a terminal illness or an incurable condition. [Gk., a good death: *eu-*, + *thanatos*, death]

USE VOCABULARY NOTE CARDS (OR KEEP A VOCABULARY NOTEBOOK)

When I studied German in college, our instructor suggested that we use 3″ × 5″ index cards to help us learn important vocabulary words. I did this religiously and found the cards' compact size perfect. Index cards can be easily secured with a rubber band and carried in your backpack, pocket, or purse. I could quickly review vocabulary words that we were to be tested on, sorting through the stack, omitting those I already knew, and concentrating on those that I wasn't so sure of. When the stack of cards became too unwieldy, I organized them into parts of speech (nouns in one stack, verbs in another, and so on), and continued my study.

I can suggest the same method for improving your reading vocabulary. It takes just a minute to write each card, whether you use index cards or a notebook. First, write the word (underline it for emphasis), the context in which it occurred (meaning the original sentence), and if you wish, the part of speech and pronunciation. On the other side, write the definition and etymology. Study this example from Selection 3 by Joe Abbott, "To Kill a Hawk":

Front side of card—word in original context, part of speech, and pronunciation

> . . . the <u>epiphany</u> was in part a result of something that happened the day before
>
> noun
>
> ĭ - pĭf′ə - nē

Reverse side of card—major definitions and the etymology (language from which English word is derived, and its meaning)

> (1) a revelatory manifestation of a divine being
> (2) <u>perception of reality by means of a sudden intuitive realization</u>
> from Greek—"to appear"

Notice that on the reverse side of the card I included two dictionary definitions and underlined the appropriate one for the way the word was used in the original sentence. If your time is limited, just write down the definition that fits the way the word was used. ESL students who are struggling to master the complexities of English vocabulary words might be more interested in learning *variant word forms* (the various forms of the word when other endings are added), as you see on the reverse side of the next card, which comes from Selection 1 by Pamela Grim, "Care in Midair":

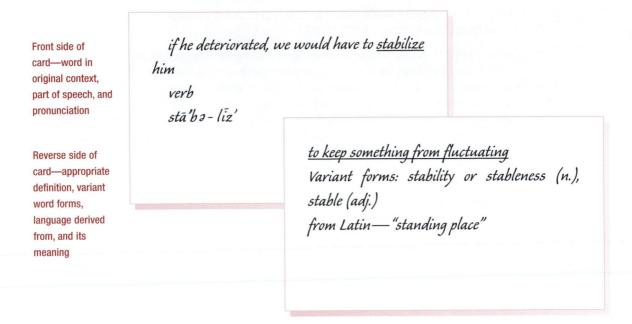

Front side of card—word in original context, part of speech, and pronunciation

if he deteriorated, we would have to stabilize him
verb
stā'bə - līz'

Reverse side of card—appropriate definition, variant word forms, language derived from, and its meaning

to keep something from fluctuating
Variant forms: stability or stableness (n.),
stable (adj.)
from Latin—"standing place"

An alternate method is to write new words in a vocabulary notebook, for example in an inexpensive spiral notebook. Using the notebook means that you can record the words in the order in which they appear, along with the page number where the word appeared in the selection. When you reread the selection, you can easily locate the definitions to refresh your memory in case you can't remember a particular word.

Which words should you write down? You don't want to overwhelm yourself with hundreds of unfamiliar words, so I would suggest—at least at first—noting those words that you have seen before in your reading but that you can't readily define. (This is called your recognition vocabulary.) Because you have seen these words before, they are not completely unfamiliar, and they are probably common enough in adult prose to make them a worthwhile addition to your vocabulary. As your command of new words grows, you can then focus on learning more unusual words.

BREAK NEW WORDS DOWN INTO THEIR COMPONENT PARTS

In Dave Barry's humorous essay that follows this introduction, after a disastrous date with Roger, Elaine calls her closest friend, and as Barry writes, "In *painstaking* detail, they will analyze everything she said and everything he said, going over it time and time again, exploring every word, every expression, and gesture. . . ." Even if you have never seen the word *painstaking*, you can perhaps determine the meaning by separating the two parts of the word and then reversing them: *pains + taking* becomes "taking pains" or "taking great care"—in other words, analyzing the conversation in great detail.

Here is a second example from Selection 3 by Joe Abbott, "To Kill a Hawk." In describing the sudden revelation, or epiphany, that he experienced, Abbot writes:

> . . . even though the thing forgotten was the kind of experience, an epiphany, really, that marks a person's life, a moment which designates an *irrevocable* turning point.

You are probably already familiar with the verb *revoke*, as when one's license is revoked or when some privilege is revoked, in other words, when something is cancelled or taken back. *Irrevocable* (the accent is on the second syllable) can be broken down like this:

ir- (prefix, meaning "not") + *voc-* (root, meaning "to call") + *-able* (suffix, "able to")

Put this all together, and you will get something like this:

a literal definition   not able to be called
a better definition   not able to be cancelled or withdrawn

It's not a perfect definition, since *irrevocable* describes something that can't be taken back, but it's good enough to give you the sense of what Abbott means.

DEVELOP AN INTEREST IN ETYMOLOGY

Etymology refers to the study of word origins, and paying attention to them can be helpful for remembering new words. Something like 60 percent of English words come from Latin and French; another 15 percent derive from Greek, often through Latin, as well. Many words have interesting or unusual origins. Here are two that you will encounter later in this text:

Nemesis, from Selection 7 by Charles Finney, "The Life and Death of a Western Gladiator." Pertaining to Crotalus, the baby rattlesnake that is the subject of the selection, Finney writes: "Most diamondback rattlers do not survive after birth. The roadrunner is one *nemesis* of baby rattlesnakes." *Nemesis* in this context refers to an unbeatable rival, one who causes someone's downfall, or in this case, death. But Nemesis was also the name of the Greek goddess of vengeance, who meted out punishment to those who committed wrongs. Though the meaning of *nemesis* differs from what the classical Greek deity did to people, knowing this etymology may help you remember its contemporary meaning.

Mesmerized, from Selection 13 by Richard Wolkomir, "Making Up for Lost Time: The Rewards of Reading at Last." In describing his own memories of a favorite children's book, Wolkomir says that he was *mesmerized*. The verb *mesmerize* refers to a near-hypnotic state, or in this case, a state of intense enjoyment. *Mesmerism* is named for Friedrich (or Franz) Anton Mesmer (1734–1815), an Austrian doctor who claimed that he could cure diseases by using what he called "animal magnetism," which involved his fixing his eyes on the eyes of an afflicted person. What Mesmer was really doing was hypnotizing his subjects, though at the time, he was considered to be a fraud. So *mesmerism* is the word we use to describe this phenomenon. Again, the derivation of this word may help you remember it when you encounter it again.

If 75 percent of the words in English are derived from Latin, French, and Greek, what of the remaining 25 percent? Many, of course, derive from the original English language, known as Anglo-Saxon. These tend to be the very basic building-block words of the language, words like *sun, moon, walk, boy, daughter, house,* and so on. But many words come from more exotic and unusual languages.

WORDS WITH UNUSUAL ETYMOLOGIES

Arabic	algebra, tariff, alchemy, alkali
Native American languages	canoe, hammock, succotash, moccasin, skunk, chile
Malay	amok (an uncontrolled state)
Tamil	pariah (an outcast)
Alaskan Russian	parka
Hungarian	coach (a type of carriage)
Old Norse	sky, skirt

SUBSCRIBE TO A WORD-OF-THE-DAY WEB SITE

Word-of-the-day Web sites offer a painless and entertaining way to learn new words. Most of them offer the same features: the selected word followed by pronunciation symbols, a definition, a sentence or two using the word, and usually the word's etymology. Here are four word-of-the-day sites to check out. You can visit them each day or, more conveniently, the first two listed in the box below allow you to subscribe (as of summer 2008, each service recommended below is free). Each weekday you receive a new word-of-the-day via e-mail. I have included some recent sample words from each site so that you can decide which site might be most appropriate for your vocabulary level and also for your level of interest.[1]

WORD-OF-THE-DAY WEB SITES

Dictionary.com Word of the Day
http://dictionary.reference.com/wordoftheday
Sample words: garrulous, assuage, xenophobia, diffident, chagrin

Merriam-Webster's Word of the Day
www.merriam-webster.com
Sample words: propagate, detoxify, kangaroo court, colleague, grisly

Yahoo! Education
http://education.yahoo.com/college/wotd
Sample words: abbreviate, criterion, sustain, collaborate, refurbish

OneLook Dictionary Search
www.onelook.com/wotd.shtm
Sample words: plait, homophone, caravan, divisive, ottoman

---

[1]Note that by the time you read this text, one or more of these sites may have moved or expired. If you are unable to locate a particular site, do a search on your favorite search engine to get updated addresses.

Using Context Clues

We begin this section with an exercise called a *cloze test*. Here is a passage from Selection 10 by Frances Moore Lappé and Jeffrey Perkins, "The Two Sides of Fear." Approximately every sixth word has been left out. Your task is to fill in the words that make sense and complete the meaning of the sentence. Be sure to pay attention both to the meaning and to grammar and sentence structure. The subject of this passage is our fear of taking risks.

No wonder we hear the _____ of fear shouting at us _____ pull back

and take no _____. We seem to think that _____ we just retreat into

our private _____, go along, and keep quiet, _____ will be invisible

and safe. _____ there's one big problem. Living _____ fear robs us of

life. _____ beings evolved for something much _____. Our species

would never have _____ it this far if we _____ not by nature curious

problem-_____ and creators—beings who love _____ act, to take risks,

to _____ exuberantly, to aspire to what _____ beyond easy reach.

Here is the passage again, this time with the missing words restored and boldfaced:

No wonder we hear the **voice** of fear shouting at us **to** pull back and take no **risks**. We seem to think that **if** we just retreat into our private **lives**, go along, and keep quiet, **we** will be invisible and safe. **But** there's one big problem. Living **in** fear robs us of life. **Human** beings evolved for something much **better**. Our species would never have **made** it this far if we **were** not by nature curious problem-**solvers** and creators—beings who love **to** act, to take risks, to **live** exuberantly, to aspire to what **lies** beyond easy reach.

Give yourself a point for each answer that matches the correct ones above. Also give yourself a point if you chose *selves* instead of *lives*, *however* instead of *but*, and *is* instead of *lies*. You should consider 12 out 16 correct a very acceptable score.

It's *context* that accounts for your ability to fill in at least some of these words. The word *context* refers to the circumstances or setting, more specifically, to the words and phrases that surround a particular word and that *may* help you figure out its meaning. In the passage about fear above, for example, you used grammatical and context clues to help you choose the right word. For example, the only preposition that works grammatically between *living* and *fear* is *in*. One does not live by fear or live for fear or live to fear. None of these makes any sense in English. And living with fear, which is possible in English, doesn't work in the total context of the passage.

Although the method is not perfect or foolproof, context clues can yield a sufficiently acceptable meaning so that you don't have to look up every unfamiliar word in the dictionary. Consider all the words you've learned since you were a baby. While growing up, you came across new words all the time, and without turning to the dictionary, you figured out their meanings because of the several contexts in which you have encountered them. Babies aren't born with a vocabulary! You learned all the words you know by absorption, by osmosis.

But with a higher level of vocabulary—words that you encounter in your college and adult reading—absorbing their meanings through practice has one major drawback: It takes years to accomplish. And since time is of the essence, you need to develop some shortcuts. When you encounter a new word, first try to break it down into its component parts—prefixes, roots, and suffixes—as you saw in an earlier section. Next, try to use the *context clues* that are briefly described in this section. They are particularly useful when you can get by without a precise dictionary definition.

Here is an example of how using word analysis and context clues together can produce a perfectly acceptable definition. For example, in Selection 7, Charles Finney describes some characteristics of a baby rattlesnake. He writes: "Without moisture, he would die of *dehydration*." The phrase "without moisture" is a helpful context clue. Further, when we break down *dehydration*, into its component parts, we see this:

de- (prefix, meaning "removal of") + *hydra* (root, meaning "water")

a literal definition   the process of removing water
a better definition   loss of water from the body through heat, etc.

Either definition suggests, in this context, that dehydration is a dangerous condition caused by lack of sufficient water.

Of course, if neither breaking the word down nor using context clues produces an adequate definition—and, more important, if you don't understand what the writer is saying, you will have to look it up.

TYPES OF CONTEXT CLUES

To familiarize you with the way these clues work, here are some short excerpts from some of the readings in the text that illustrate each type. Study them carefully. I have identified the author and selection number in each instance and drawn arrows from the context clue to each italicized word.

Synonyms A *synonym* is a word that is close in meaning to the word in question. This is the easiest of the types of context clues to recognize. For example, you have already seen this word from Joe Abbott's selection:

. . . even though the thing forgotten was the kind of experience, an *epiphany*, really, that marks a person's life, a moment which designates an irrevocable turning point.

An *epiphany* means, just as the passage says, an experience that marks a turning point in a person's life. Even if you had never seen the word before, the context tells you its meaning.

Another Synonym Tip Sometimes a writer uses the connecting word *or* to indicate a synonym for an unfamiliar term, especially in scientific material. For example, in

Selection 11, Geoffrey Cowley explains how children learn to speak individual words and to distinguish one word from another. He writes:

> Each of the world's approximately 6,000 languages uses a different assortment of *phonemes*, or distinctive sounds, to build words. As adults, we have a hard time even hearing phonemes from foreign languages.

The term *phonemes* comes from linguistics and is not likely to be in the average reader's vocabulary, so Cowley adds a defining phrase separated with "or." (Note that in most contexts the word *or* indicates a choice, as in "I couldn't decide whether to order pizza or pasta.")

Antonyms An *antonym* is a word that means the opposite of the one you are unsure of. Consider this example: In Selection 11, Geoffrey Cowley discusses the way small children learn first to produce words, then phrases, and finally sentences. He writes:

> Scholars have *bickered* for centuries over how kids accomplish this feat, but most now agree that their brains are wired for the task.

Since *agree* and *bicker* are opposites, we can easily see that *bicker* means the opposite—"to quarrel."

Examples or Series of Details An *example*—a particular instance of something more general—or a cluster of details in a paragraph may reveal the meaning of an unfamiliar word. To describe a diamondback rattlesnake in Selection 7, Charles Finney uses the word *formidable*, followed by these examples, which means that you can define the word on your own:

> At two he was *formidable*. He had grown past the stage where a racer [another kind of snake] or a roadrunner could safely tackle him. He had grown to the size where other desert dwellers—coyotes, foxes, coatis, wildcats—knew it was better to leave him alone.

And a little later, Finney writes:

> He had not experienced death for the simple reason that there had never been an opportunity for anything bigger and stronger than himself to kill him. Now at two, because he was so *formidable*, that opportunity became more and more unlikely.

Both passages include many details supporting the idea that the rattlesnake is stronger and larger than other creatures around him, so you could assume that *formidable* means "impressive" or "arousing fear or dread."

Situation The *situation* or circumstance in which the word is used in may give you a hint as to its meaning. In Selection 9, Marc Ian Barasch describes his experience of living on the streets of Denver for a week as a homeless person as an exercise in compassion. Here is an excerpt:

> It's a different map of the world. Which Starbucks has a security guard who'll let you use the bathroom? How long can you linger in this place or that before you're *rousted*?

Even if you have never seen the word *rousted* before, the situation Barasch describes indicates that to be *rousted* means to be forced out or asked to leave.

Emotion The emotional attitude evident in a passage—its mood—may provide a good enough clue to save you from looking up a word. In "The Environmental Issue from Hell" (Selection 29), Bill McKibben takes up the problem of global warming. He writes:

> So maybe we should think of global warming in a different way—as the great moral crisis of our time, the equivalent of the civil rights movement of the 1960s. Why a moral question? In the first place, no one's ever figured out a more effective way to screw the *marginalized* and poor of this planet than climate change. Having taken their dignity, their resources, and their freedom under a variety of other schemes, we now are taking the very physical ability on which their already difficult lives depend.

Notice McKibben's strong feelings of anger and disapproval. The passage condemns the powerful and expresses sympathy for the poor. Another clue that points to the meaning of *marginalized* is the slang word *screw*. Even more clues lie in the last sentence, "Having taken their dignity, their resources, their freedom . . . " Finally, consider the root of the word *marginalized*: A paper's margins are the edges; similarly, if someone lives on the *margins*, he or she is relegated to the "outer edges" of society. He or she has low social standing. You can infer all this without opening the dictionary.

SUMMARY OF CONTEXT CLUES

- Synonym—a word that means the same or nearly the same
- Antonym—a word that means the opposite or nearly the opposite
- Examples and details—a specific instance or series of details that may reveal a word's meaning
- Situation—the specific circumstances in which a word is used that may help suggest its meaning
- Emotion—the emotional feeling or the mood of the passage

WHEN NOT TO LOOK UP WORDS

Some words simply aren't important enough to look up (unless, of course, you have all the time in the world or are simply curious).[2] For example, in Selection 4, "School Days," Rose Guilbault is describing her feeling of alienation, of being the outsider as a little Latina girl who lives on a farm far away from her mostly Anglo school in King City, California. She is walking home from school feeling dejected. That day all the other little girls had brought their Barbie dolls to school. Not only had they made fun of her non-Barbie doll, but they also teased her because she didn't know what a Barbie was. She writes:

> My mother tried her best to be supportive. Surely she sensed my disaffection when I *trudged* home down the long road, looking weary from another day in the outside world.

You don't have to know precisely what *trudged* means, though the context makes it pretty clear that it's the heavy, plodding way someone walks when he or she is discouraged.

PRACTICE EXERCISES

In this discussion I classified context clues simply to show you the various possibilities. However, when you read, you should only intuit, or be aware, of these types, for there is no particular advantage in being able to identify them. Here are a few exercises—again, short excerpts from selections in the text—giving you an opportunity to practice using context clues with words that are apt to be unfamiliar. Read the example and study the context carefully. In the first space, write your definition of the word—what you think it means. In the second, verify the word's meaning by consulting your dictionary. See how close your definitions are to those in the dictionary.

1. I got out, skirted the sidewalk loafers and reached through a steel gate to knock on the door. A rough-looking mug opened the door and gruffly asked, "Yeah? What d'ya want?" The whole scene felt *clandestine*. . . . (Selection 2, Pete Jordan, "Head Dishwasher?")

   Your definition _____

   Dictionary definition _____

2. To me, modern conveniences are good, but it was our old-fashioned customs and ideas that built such a strong foundation for the people on Sapelo [Island]. Our lives were rich. We were a close-knit, self-sufficient people. But now our old ways are dying, and though I relish many of the modern *amenities* that have come to our island, I feel a heavy sense of loss at the vanishing ways. (Selection 5, Cornelia Bailey, "Still Gullah: A Sea Island Sister Struggles to Preserve the Old Ways")

   Your definition _____

   Dictionary definition _____

---

[2]One measure of this course's success will be your increased desire to satisfy this curiosity, to look up new words because you no longer like not knowing what the writer is saying.

3. "You know, when I first met you, I didn't think you could finish this hike,"
I confess. Kelly shoots me a look of *mock* scorn. "The bangles threw me,"
I explain, pointing to the jingling column of gold on her wrist. "Oh," Kelly
says with a laugh. "I do trail work with my bangles on. I forget that they're
there." (Selection 6, Judith Lewis, "Walk on the Wilshire Side")

Your definition _____

Dictionary definition _____

4. That summer Crotalus [a diamondback rattlesnake] met his first dog. It was
a German shepherd which had been reared on a farm in the Midwest and
there had gained the reputation of being a snake-killer. Black snakes, garter
snakes, pilots, water snakes; it delighted in killing them all. It would seize
them by the middle, *heedless* of their tiny teeth, and shake them violently
until they died. (Selection 7, Charles Finney, "The Life and Death of a
Western Gladiator")

Your definition _____

Dictionary definition _____

5. To find the roots of our fear, let's look back 20,000 years to when our ancestors lived in small tribes, trying to protect themselves and their *vulnerable*
young from animals and other threats bigger and fiercer than they were.
(Selection 10, Frances Moore Lappé and Jeffrey Perkins, "The Two Sides
of Fear")

Your definition _____

Dictionary definition _____

6. I stopped talking to Kelly, my wife. She *loathed* me, my silences, my distance,
my inertia. I stopped walking my dog, so she hated me, too. (Selection 9,
Chris Rose, "Hell and Back")

Your definition _____

Dictionary definition _____

7. Words accrue slowly at first. But around the age of 18 months, children's
abilities explode. Most start acquiring new words at the *phenomenal* rate of
one every two hours. . . . (Selection 11, Geoffrey Cowley, "The Language
Explosion")

Your definition _____

Dictionary definition _____

8. A 1993 U.S. Department of Education report on illiteracy said 21–23 percent
of U.S. adults—about 40 million—read minimally, enough to *decipher* an uncomplicated meeting announcement. . . . I wanted to meet nonreaders because I could not imagine being unable to *decipher* a street sign, or words
printed on supermarket jars, or stories in a book. (Selection 13, Richard
Wolkomir, "Making Up for Lost Time: The Rewards of Reading at Last")

Your definition _____

Dictionary definition _____

9. Regardless of the billions spent on marketing and promotion, all the ads on radio and TV, all the efforts to create brand loyalty, the major chains must live with the unsettling fact that more than 70 percent of fast food visits are "*impulsive*." The decision to stop for fast food is made on the spur of the moment, without much thought. (Selection 14, Eric Schlosser, "Fast Food Nation: Behind the Counter")

   Your definition _____

   Dictionary definition _____

10. Yolanda Leif graphically describes the trials of a waitress in a quality restaurant. They are compounded by her refusal to be *demeaned*. Yet pride in her skills helps her through the night. "When I put the plate down, you don't hear a sound. When I pick up a glass, I want it to be just right. When someone says, 'How come you're just a waitress?' I say, 'Don't you think you deserve being served by me?'" (Selection 15, Studs Terkel, "Somebody Built the Pyramids")

    Your definition _____

    Dictionary definition _____

11. We talked about his clothes. He had bought them himself, from a virtual mall. Fashion, he said, was a great example of how Second Lifers created their world. In the two years since Second Life appeared online, the available outfits had developed from very basic to extremely *sophisticated*, some of the work of successful real-world designers. (Selection 17, Tim Guest, "Linden Lab's Second Life: Dreamers of the Dream")

    Your definition _____

    Dictionary definition _____

12. The speculators, next, would hire people to pass out handbills in the Eastern and Midwestern cities, *tracts* limning the advantages of relocation to "the Athens of the South" or "the new plains Jerusalem." When persuasion failed, the builders might resort to bribery, paying people's moving costs and giving them houses, in exchange for nothing but a pledge to stay until a certain census was taken or a certain inspection made. . . . The speculators' idea, of course, was to *lure* the railroad. (Selection 19, Lawrence Shames, "The Hunger for More")

    Tracts Your definition _____

    Dictionary definition _____

    Lure Your definition _____

    Dictionary definition _____

Using Print and Online Dictionaries

When context clues and breaking down the word aren't enough to give you a word's meaning, you will need to turn to the dictionary. The final section of this part introduces you to specific features of standard college dictionaries; you should study this material closely and refer to it often until you have mastered it. These suggestions show you how best to use this wonderful resource for good results.

First, it is imperative that you have a good, up-to-date dictionary—not some tattered edition you bought at a garage sale or your father's hand-me-down *Webster's* from the 1970s. If you can afford to, invest in your academic future and buy two dictionaries: an unabridged and an abridged version. The word *abridged* means "reduced or condensed." Therefore, an abridged dictionary, usually published in an inexpensive paperback format, is shorter than a complete or *unabridged* dictionary because it does not contain as many words. A standard college edition of an unabridged dictionary generally contains around 175,000 entries. In contrast, my paperback *American Heritage Dictionary* states that it has about 70,000 entries.

Each kind of dictionary has its own advantages. The light weight of the paperback dictionary makes it portable. Unabridged versions, besides containing more words, also contain more complete definitions, etymologies, notes on appropriate usage, and explanations of synonyms. But such a dictionary is heavy to lug around and therefore is better kept at home. Ask your instructor to recommend one, or choose one from this list of the three most widely used dictionaries. Each comes in both an abridged and an unabridged version. In alphabetical order:

> *The American Heritage College Dictionary*
> *The Random House College Dictionary*
> *Webster's New World Dictionary*

THE FEATURES OF A DICTIONARY

No matter which dictionary you choose, all contain the same features. Here is a brief overview of the important ones.

Guide Words *Guide words* are printed in boldface in the top margin of each page; they indicate the first and last words and help you locate words quickly. For example, if you are looking up the word *emulate*, the guide words at the top of the page—which could be *empress* and *enantiomorph*—show you quickly that you're on the right page.

Entry The word *entry* is simply a fancy term for the word that you are looking up. It is printed in boldface type in the left margin; dots separate the syllables, for example:

o • blit • er • ate

Obliterate, therefore, has four syllables.

Pronunciation Symbols *Pronunciation symbols* are printed in parentheses and follow the entry. English has a complicated pronunciation system. Unlike Spanish, for example, in which every letter always has the same sound, English has approximately 75 different sounds but only 26 letters to represent them. A single vowel letter like *a*, for example, can be pronounced seven ways, as in these words: *cat* (ă); *lake* (ā); *bar* (är); *bare* (âr); *part* (är); *law* (ô); and *father* (ä). The pronunciation symbols follow a standardized system to show you how each letter or combination of letters should be pronounced in an unfamiliar word. Ask your instructor for help if you don't know how to pronounce these symbols. In the college edition of *American Heritage Dictionary*, these symbols are printed in the lower-right corner of each *right* page. Other dictionaries print them across the bottom of both pages.

Stress Marks *Stress*, or *accent*, marks are as important as pronunciation symbols for pronouncing words correctly. Referring to the relative degree of loudness of each syllable, stress marks are printed *after* the syllable to be stressed within the pronunciation symbols, as you can see in this word: *solid* (sŏl' ĭd). In this case, the first syllable, *sol*, receives primary stress or emphasis.

English has three kinds of stress. Primary, or heavy stress, is shown by a heavy boldface mark, like this: '. Secondary, or weak stress, is shown by the same mark printed in lighter type, like this: '. Unstressed syllables are often those containing a neutral vowel sound—symbolized by a pronunciation symbol called a *schwa*—which is written like an upside down "e" (ə). For example, the word *magnification* contains all three types of stress:

mgăg'nə-fĭ-kā'shən.

The first syllable takes the secondary stress, the fourth syllable takes the primary stress, and the second and fifth syllables (each with a schwa) are unstressed.

Parts of Speech and Inflected Forms Following the dictionary pronunciation symbols is an abbreviation indicating what part of speech the entry word is. For example, *n.* = noun; *v.* = verb, *adj.* = adjective, *adv.* = adverb, and so forth. As you will see at the end of this section, many words cross over and represent several parts of speech. It's important to know what kind of word (noun, adjective, and so forth) is used in the passage.

Inflected forms—the forms of the word that take inflections or word endings—are also included. Thus, you can look up the proper way to spell the present participle and past tense of a word like *gratify*. In *gratified* (the past tense form), the *y* changes to *i*, and the ending signifying the past tense (*-ed*) is added. In *gratifying* (the present participle), the ending *–ing* is added. Finally, in *gratifies* (the present tense for the third-person form, that is, the form used with "he," "she," or "it") the *y* changes to *i*, and the ending *–es* is added. Similarly, if you want to find the plural of the word *ox*, the dictionary indicates it like this: *n. pl.* oxen. The plural forms of *deer* and *sheep*, however, remain *deer* and *sheep*. The dictionary tells you this, as well.

Order of Definitions The one significant difference in dictionaries is in the order of definitions if a word has more than one meaning. The *American Heritage* and the

Random House college editions follow this system: If a word has multiple senses (two or more meanings, in other words), the central and often the most commonly sought meaning is listed first. Less common senses, older forms, and obsolete senses are listed next. *However*, this does not mean that you should read the first meaning listed and look no farther. The context is crucial in determining which sense best fits a particular word's meaning. This concept will be illustrated in more detail later in this section.

In contrast, the *Merriam-Webster's Collegiate Dictionary* organizes its definitions historically, which means that the earliest sense or senses of a word come first, with more modern senses following. If you are unsure about which method your particular dictionary uses, ask your instructor for help or refer to the early pages of the dictionary, called the *front matter*, where there will be a description of the *Order of Senses* or something similar.

Variant Forms If the word has other grammatical forms, the dictionary will list those after the last definition. If you look up *incorrigible* (an adjective), for example, the dictionary lists as variants *incorrigibility* and *incorrigibleness* (nouns) and *incorrigibly* (adverb).

Etymology A word's *etymology* refers to its linguistic origin, that is, the language from which it came into English. Etymology also refers to the word's history. It is printed in brackets [ ], either before or after the definitions, depending on your dictionary. Some dictionaries abbreviate the language or languages of origin. For example, *OF* indicates Old French, *ME* indicates Middle English, *L* or *Lat* refers to Latin, and *Gk* means Greek. A complete list of those abbreviations can be found in the front matter of your dictionary.

Other Features Some dictionaries include useful drawings in the margins. The *American Heritage* dictionaries (both the college and unabridged editions) are particularly generous in this regard, allowing you to see, for example, the location of El Salvador on a small map of Central America, what a French chateau (castle) looks like, and what Princess Diana looked like, just to cite three random examples from my dictionary. Thus the dictionary goes far beyond being merely a resource for looking up words: It is also a mini-atlas, a biographical index, and a provider of all manner of useful information from the world around you.

SAMPLE DICTIONARY COLUMN

Now that you are familiar with the some of the more important dictionary terminology, reprinted in Figure 1 is one column from the *American Heritage College Dictionary*. Study the arrows to identify the key features discussed above.

CHOOSING THE RIGHT DEFINITION

The tricky part about using the dictionary is determining which sense to use when you are confronted with several meanings. To illustrate this problem, study these two sample paragraphs from two selections you will read. You already saw the

Entries

Pronunciation symbols

Usage note

Variant forms

Etymology

447

Ellesmere Island

eluvium

Guide words

Parts of speech

Definitions

Pronunciation key

Stress marks

chaic. **1.** To remove or carry away to a distance, esp. so as to conceal. **2.** To take (oneself) to a distance. [ME *elongen* < OFr. *esloigner* : *es-*, from (< Lat. *ex-*; see EX-) + *loing*, far (< Lat. *longē*, distant < *longus*, long; see del-¹*).]

e·lon·gate (ĭ-lông′gāt′, ĭ-lŏng′-) *tr. & intr.v.* **-gat·ed, -gat·ing, -gates.** To make or grow longer. —*adj.* or **elongated. 1.** Made longer; extended. **2.** Having more length than width; slender. [LLat. *ēlongāre, ēlongāt-* : Lat. *ē, ex-, ex-* + Lat. *longē*, distant; see ELOIGN.]

e·lon·ga·tion (ĭ-lông′-gā′shən, ĭ-lŏng′-, ē′lông-, ē′lŏng-) *n.* **1.** The act of elongating or the condition of being elongated. **2.** Something that elongates; an extension. **3.** The angular distance between two celestial bodies as seen from Earth.

e·lope (ĭ-lōp′) *intr.v.* **e·loped, e·lop·ing, e·lopes. 1.** To run away with a lover, esp. with the intention of getting married. **2.** To run away; abscond. [Perh. AN *aloper*, to run away from one's husband with a lover < MDu. *ontlopen*, to run away : *ont-*, away from, along; see ant-* + *lopen*, to run.] —e·lope′ment *n.* —e·lop′er *n.*

el·o·quence (ĕl′ə-kwəns) *n.* **1.a.** Persuasive powerful discourse. **b.** The skill or power of using such discourse. **2.** The quality of persuasive powerful expression.

el·o·quent (ĕl′ə-kwənt) *adj.* **1.** Characterized by eloquence. **2.** Vividly or movingly expressive. See Syns at **expressive.** [ME < OFr. < Lat. *ēloquēns, ēloquent-*, pr.part. of *ēloquī*, to speak out. See ELOCUTION.] —el′o·quent·ly *adv.* —el′o·quent·ness *n.*

El Pas·o (păs′ō). A city of extreme W TX on the Rio Grande opposite Ciudad Juárez, Mexico. Pop. 515,342.

El Sal·va·dor (săl′və-dôr′, săl′və-thôr′). A country of Central America on the Pacific; achieved independence from Spain in 1821. Cap. San Salvador. Pop. 4,949,000. —**El Sal′va·dor′i·an** (săl′və-dôr′ē-ən, -dôr′-) *adj. & n.*

else (ĕls) *adj.* **1.** Other; different: *Ask somebody else.* **2.** Additional; more: *anything else.* —*adv.* **1.** In a different or an additional time, place, or manner: *Where else did he go?* **2.** If not; otherwise: *Be careful, or else you will fall.* —**idiom. or else.** Regardless of any extenuating circumstances: *Be there or else!* [ME *elles* < OE. See al-¹*.]

—*Usage Note: Else* is often used redundantly in combination with prepositions such as *but, except,* and *besides: No one else but Sam knew* (omit *else*). • When a pronoun is followed by *else,* the possessive form is generally written thus: *someone else's* (not *someone's else*). Both *who else's* and *whose else* are in use but not *whose else's.* See Usage Notes at **who, whose.**

else·where (ĕls′hwâr′, -wâr′) *adv.* In or to a different or another place: *has property at the shore and elsewhere.*

El·si·nore (ĕl′sə-nôr′, -nōr′). See Helsingør.

El To·ro (tôr′ō). A community of S CA SE of Santa Ana. Pop. 62,685.

el·u·ant (ĕl′yoo-ənt) *n.* A substance used as a solvent in the process of elution. [< Lat. *ēluēns, ēluent-*, pr.part. of *ēluere*, to wash out. See ELUTE.]

el·u·ate (ĕl′yoo-ĭt, -āt′) *n.* The solution of solvent and dissolved matter resulting from elution. [Lat. *ēluere,* to wash out; see ELUTE + -ATE¹.]

e·lu·ci·date (ĭ-loo′sĭ-dāt′) *v.* **-dat·ed, -dat·ing, -dates.** —*tr.* To make clear or plain, esp. by explanation. —*intr.* To give an explanation that clarifies. [LLat. *ēlūcidāre, ēlūcidāt-* : Lat. *ē-, ex-*, intensive pref.; see EX- + Lat. *lūcidus,* bright (< *lūcēre,* to shine; see leuk-*).] —e·lu′ci·da′tion *n.* —e·lu′ci·da′tive *adj.* —e·lu′ci·da′tor *n.*

e·lude (ĭ-lood′) *tr.v.* **e·lud·ed, e·lud·ing, e·ludes. 1.** To evade or escape from, as by daring, cleverness, or skill. **2.** To escape the understanding or grasp of. [Lat. *ēlūdere* : *ē-, ex-, ex-* + *lūdere,* to play (< *lūdus,* play; see leid-*).]

E·lul (ĕl′ool, ĕ-lool′) *n.* The 12th month of the year in the Jewish calendar. [Heb. *'Elūl* < Akkadian *ulūlu, elūlu,* the month Ululu (August/September).]

e·lu·sive (ĭ-loo′sĭv, -zĭv) *adj.* **1.** Tending to elude capture, perception, comprehension, or memory. **2.** Difficult to define or describe. [< Lat. *ēlūsus,* p.part. of *ēlūdere,* to elude. See ELUDE.] —e·lu′sive·ly *adv.* —e·lu′sive·ness *n.*

e·lute (ĭ-loot′) *tr.v.* **e·lut·ed, e·lut·ing, e·lutes.** To extract (one material) from another, usu. by means of a solvent. [< Lat. *ēluere, ēlūt-*, to wash out : *ē-, ex-, ex-* + *-luere,* to wash; see leu(ə)-*.] —e·lu′tion *n.*

e·lu·tri·ate (ĭ-loo′trē-āt′) *tr.v.* **-at·ed, -at·ing, -ates. 1.** To purify, separate, or remove (ore, for example) by washing, decanting, and settling. **2.** To wash away the lighter or finer particles of (soil, for example). [Lat. *ēlutriāre, ēlutriāt-* (< *ēlutrium,* vat, bath < Gk. *ēlutrion,* dim. of *elutron,* tank; see ELYTRON) or *ēlūtriāre* (< *ēlūtor,* one who washes < *ēluere,* to wash out; see ELUTE).] —e·lu′tri·a′tion *n.*

e·lu·vi·ate (ĭ-loo′vē-āt′) *intr.v.* **-at·ed, -at·ing, -ates.** To undergo eluviation.

e·lu·vi·a·tion (ĭ-loo′vē-ā′shən) *n.* The lateral or downward movement of dissolved or suspended material within soil when rainfall exceeds evaporation. [ELUVI(UM) + -ATION.]

e·lu·vi·um (ĭ-loo′vē-əm) *n.* Residual deposits of soil, dust, and rock particles produced by the wind. [NLat. *eluvium* <

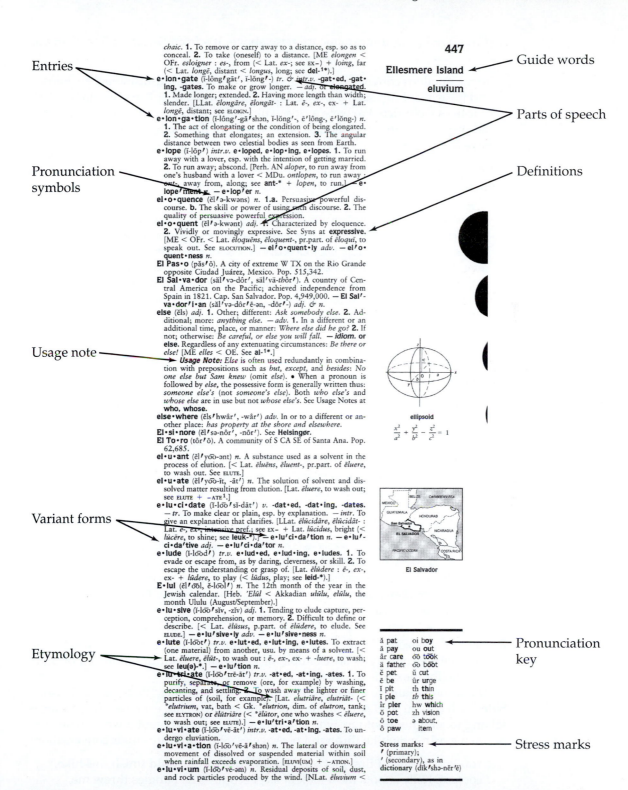

ellipsoid

$$\frac{x^2}{a^2} + \frac{y^2}{b^2} - \frac{z^2}{c^2} = 1$$

El Salvador

ă pat	oi boy
ā pay	ou out
âr care	oo took
ä father	oo boot
ĕ pet	ŭ cut
ē be	ûr urge
ĭ pit	th thin
ī pie	th this
îr pier	hw which
ŏ pot	zh vision
ō toe	ə about,
ô paw	item

Stress marks:
′ (primary);
′ (secondary), as in dictionary (dĭk′shə-nĕr′ē)

Figure 1

first passage in the context clue exercise above. It's from Selection 5 by Cornelia Bailey:

> To me, modern conveniences are good, but it was our old-fashioned customs and ideas that built such a strong foundation for the people on Sapelo [Island]. Our lives were rich. We were a close-knit, self-sufficient people. But now our old ways are dying, and though I *relish* many of the modern *amenities* that have come to our island, I feel a heavy sense of loss at the vanishing ways.

Let's look at the dictionary entries for *relish* and *amenities* one at a time. These definitions are from *The American Heritage College Dictionary:*

> **rel • ish** (rĕl′ĭsh) *n.* **1.** An appetite for something; a strong appreciation or liking; *a relish for luxury.* **2a.** Hearty enjoyment; zest. See synonyms at **zest. b.** Something that lends pleasure or zest. **3a.** A spicy or savory condiment or appetizer, such as chutney or olives. **b.** A condiment of chopped sweet pickle. **4.** The flavor of a food, especially when appetizing. See synonyms at **taste. 5.** A trace or suggestion of a pleasurable quality. —*v.* **–ished, -ish•ing, -ish•es.** —*tr.* **1.** To take keen or zestful pleasure in. **2.** To enjoy the flavor of. **3.** To give spice or flavor to. —*intr.* To have a pleasing or distinctive taste. [Alteration of Middle English *reles,* taste, from Old French, something remaining, from *relaissier,* to leave behind.]

Clearly, this word has many more meanings other than the one we all know—the pickle condiment we put on our hot dogs (definition 3b). Which of the other definitions is appropriate for this context? As Bailey uses *relish* here, it is clearly a verb; it follows the subject of the clause "I." So you can safely skip all the noun definitions. If we skim quickly over the three verb definitions in light of the context, we quickly see that Bailey is not talking about relishing food (appropriate for definitions 2 and 3), which leaves only the first verb definition: She *relished* the amenities that came to Sapelo Island, meaning that she took pleasure in them.

Let's now look at the second word—*amenities*. Again study these dictionary definitions:

> **a • men • i • ty** (ə-mĕn′ĭ-tē, ə - mē′nĭ -) *n. pl.* **–ties 1.** The quality of being pleasant or attractive; agreeableness. **2.** Something that contributes to physical or material comfort. **3.** A feature that increases attractiveness or value, especially of a piece of real estate or a geographic location. **4. amenities** Social courtesies. [Middle English *amenite,* from Old French, from Latin *amoenitas,* from *amoenus,* pleasant.]

Earlier in the selection, Bailey has talked about the coming of electricity to Sapelo Island. Since electricity is an example of an *amenity,* both definitions 2 or 3 are acceptable for the context.

The second example is from Selection 6 by Judith Lewis, "Walk on the Wilshire Side," which you also saw in the preceding context clue exercise. The writer is talking to a high school girl who is wearing some extravagant jewelry while undertaking a 10-mile hike through Los Angeles. She duplicates their conversation:

> "You know, when I first met you, I didn't think you could finish this hike," I confess. Kelly shoots me a look of *mock* scorn. "The bangles threw me,"

I explain, pointing to the jingling column of gold on her wrist. 'Oh," Kelly says with a laugh. "I do trail work with my bangles on. I forget that they're there."

Mock can be four different parts of speech—verb, noun, adjective, and adverb. Study these definitions and then answer the questions below.

---

mock (mŏk) *v.* **mocked, mock•ing, mocks** —*tr.* **1.** To treat with ridicule or contempt, deride. **2a.** To mimic, as in sport or derision. See synonyms at **ridicule**. **b.** To imitate; counterfeit. **3.** To frustrate the hopes of; disappoint. —*intr.* To express scorn or ridicule; jeer: *They mocked at the idea.* —*n.* **1a.** The act of mocking. **b.** Mockery, derision: *said it merely in mock.* **2.** An object of scorn or derision. **3.** An imitation or a counterfeit. —*adj.* Simulated; false; sham: *a mock battle.* —*adv.* In an insincere or pretending manner: *mock sorrowful.* [Middle English *mokken*, from Old French *mocquer.*] —**mock'er** *n.* —**mock'ing•ly** *adv.*

Now answer these questions.

1. As the writer uses the word *mock*, what part of speech is it? _____

2. What definition best fits the way the word is used in context?

    _____

Note that identifying the part of speech, especially when the word has so many grammatical functions, helps you narrow your search and find the correct definition quickly. There is no need to read all definitions, only those that fit the part of speech.

ONLINE EXERCISE

An exercise similar to this one is available online at *www.mhhe.com/spears.* Click on the cover of the book, and go to Student Center.

COMPARING PRINT AND ONLINE DICTIONARIES

Online dictionaries offer a convenient alternative to the traditional print dictionaries. Some Web sites even allow one to interact with a text. When you encounter an unfamiliar word, you simply click on it, and you are taken to the *Merriam-Webster* or *American Heritage Dictionary* site, allowing you to locate the word's meaning without leaving your computer. If you are not reading online, you can use the online version just as you would a traditional print version. These two dictionaries are probably the most popular; the information from both is derived from the print editions, and since both are respectable sources, you can use either with confidence.

TWO ONLINE DICTIONARY SITES

Merriam-Webster's Collegiate Dictionary	*www.merriam-webster.com*
The American Heritage Dictionary of the English Language	*www.bartleby.com/61*

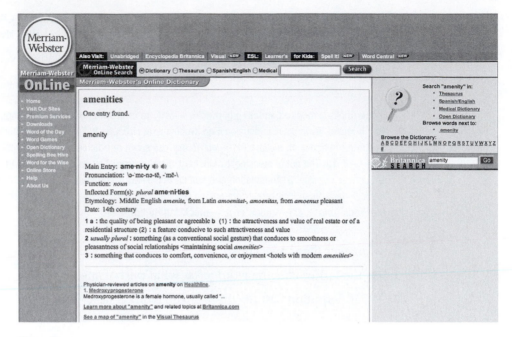

Figure 2

I tested these two sites by looking up both *amenities* and *mock*, two words whose definitions from the print version of *The American Heritage Dictionary* you just saw. The *American Heritage* site provides exactly the same information as the print version does, though, despite my high-speed Internet connection, it took rather a long time to load. The *Merriam-Webster* site required one to scroll down to locate the part of speech for *mock*, and of course, for both, you have to type in the word into the search box. Figure 2 is what the *Merriam-Webster* Web site offers for the word *amenities*.

What are the advantages and disadvantages of print dictionaries versus their online counterparts?

Online Dictionaries—Advantages

- Online dictionaries are undoubtedly more fun to use, and they aren't cluttered with confusing symbols. The print and layout are more readable than the dictionary's small print.
- Most offer links for word-of-the-day information, word games, sites about linguistic history, and so forth. The general information on both sites are free. Subscriptions may be necessary for complete access.
- Both sites offer an auditory pronunciation of words; click on the little microphone, and the word is pronounced for you, an especially useful feature for English-language learners.

Online Dictionaries—Disadvantages

- I found the *Merriam-Webster* site cluttered and not easy to navigate, though one could probably get used to it. The *American Heritage* site required one to scroll down through a list of several expressions containing *mock* before I encountered the single word I wanted.

- Unless you have a superfast connection, these sites may be slow to load. They often carry advertisements for their products or for sponsoring websites, for example, for online booksellers, or they carry distracting banner or pulsating ads.
- In the print version, when you look up the word *chateau*, there is an aerial photo of a French chateau, right in the margin next to the entry. The website doesn't offer photos.
- Except for electronic spellers (like the Franklin models)[3], a computer isn't as portable as a book. Lugging even a compact notebook-style computer around with you is more trouble than carrying a paperback book. Your computer won't work in areas that experience frequent electrical storms or blackouts unless you have a laptop and battery power.

Print Dictionaries—Advantages

- Print dictionaries don't depend on fickle battery power; a paperback edition can be carried around in your backpack or purse.
- Relatively speaking, they cost very little and have withstood the test of time.
- Everything that you need is located in the same place, with no need to click on links or scroll down. Once you become familiar with the layout and the symbols, looking up a word may take less time than typing it in.

Print Dictionaries—Disadvantages

- Even the best print dictionary will need to be replaced from time to time, as new editions are published, to reflect changes in the language, requiring a periodic outlay of money. However, a good hardback dictionary should last you through your college years and beyond.
- Print dictionaries require a little more work to learn to use effectively than online versions.

Perhaps both types have their place, depending on your purpose in reading and on your budget.

To conclude this introduction, this course will have been successful if you find yourself unwilling to be content with a haphazard guess as to a new word's meaning and if you find that with each passing year you find fewer and fewer words to look up. Nothing builds confidence as much as a good reading vocabulary.

---

[3]I am not a big fan of electronic spellers, nor are most English teachers I'm acquainted with. They are expensive, and the definitions are often skimpy and/or misleading. Shop carefully if you want to buy one, by comparing the information provided when you look up a word with the material available from a print dictionary. The Franklin MWS-1840 Speaking Merriam Webster Dictionary and Thesaurus costing about $80 is one of the best. However, the hardbound print *Merriam-Webster Collegiate Dictionary* costs less than $25. The unabridged print edition of *The American Heritage Dictionary* costs $40; the paperback edition is only $6 (prices as of summer 2008).

Practice Selection

What follows is a practice selection in which all the features you'll find throughout this book are explained. Before you begin the readings in Part One, work through this practice selection and complete the exercises following it. Answers are provided at the end for all of the exercises except for the topics for discussion and writing. Explanations of each element are highlighted in color. These explanations will show you how to get the most that you can out of the book, will help you focus and concentrate as you read, and will help you learn what to look for when you read— whether it is assigned essays for your English classes, college textbook material, newspaper or magazine articles, or reading that you do on your own, for pleasure.

Dave Barry has written for the *Miami Herald* since 1983. In 1988 he received a Pulitzer Prize for commentary. Barry's latest book is *Dave Barry's History of the Millennium (So Far)* (2007). In this excerpt reprinted from *Dave Barry's Complete Guide to Guys*, we are introduced to a fictitious couple named Roger and Elaine, who have been dating for six months.

Vocabulary Preview

The Vocabulary Preview introduces you to two or three words in the reading and is divided into two parts. The Word Parts section discusses an important prefix or suffix, and the Word Families section introduces you to a Latin or Greek root that will help you recognize the meanings of other words in the same family.

WORD PARTS

-meter [paragraph 7] As they are driving home, instead of paying attention to what Elaine is saying, Roger checks the *odometer* (pronounced ō - dŏm'- ĭ- tər) and wonders if his car needs an oil change. People often confuse a car's odometer with its speedometer. An odometer measures the distance that a vehicle has traveled, while a speedometer measures the speed at which it is moving.

Odometer joins two Greek word parts: *hodos* ("journey") + *metron* ("measure"). Besides the word *meter* itself (as in a water or gas meter), this Greek word part is attached to other roots referring to instruments that measure all sorts of things, among them *thermometer* (heat), *chronometer* (time), and *barometer* (atmospheric pressure). What do these two words ending in *-meter* mean? Look them up if you are unsure and write their meanings in the space.

Answers
spectrometer: a device that measures wavelengths

hydrometer: an instrument that uses fluid to measure gravity

spectrometer	_____
hydrometer	_____

WORD FAMILIES

Transmission [paragraph 9] Roger also worries about his car's *transmission*. This word is formed by two Latin word parts: the prefix *trans* ("across") and the root *mittere* ("to send"). A car's transmission literally transmits or "sends across" power from the engine to the axle. In English, many other words derive from *mittere*, although the idea of "sending" is lost in some of them, for example, *admission*, *commission*, *permission*, and *submission* ("sending under").

Now the selection: Follow your instructor's suggestions or requirements for reading. Otherwise, use these directions: Read through the selection once; then answer the questions in Exercises A, B, and C. After finishing these, follow the instructions that appear later to complete the assignment.

DAVE BARRY

Tips for Women: How to Have a Relationship with a Guy

Questions to Ask Yourself: Do you know anything about the writer? What does the selection title suggest to you? What do you already know about the subject?

1   Contrary to what many women believe, it's fairly easy to develop a long-term, stable, intimate, and mutually fulfilling relationship with a guy. Of course this guy has to be a Labrador retriever. With human guys, it's extremely difficult. This is because guys don't really grasp what women mean by the term *relationship*.

2   Let's say a guy named Roger is attracted to a woman named Elaine. He asks her out to a movie; she accepts; they have a pretty good time. A few nights later he asks her out to dinner, and again they enjoy themselves. They continue to see each other regularly, and after a while neither one of them is seeing anybody else.

3   And then, one evening when they're driving home, a thought occurs to Elaine, and, without really thinking, she says it aloud: "Do you realize that, as of tonight, we've been seeing each other for exactly six months?"

4   And then there is silence in the car. To Elaine, it seems like a very loud silence. She thinks to herself: Geez, I wonder if it bothers him that I said that. Maybe he's been feeling confined by our relationship; maybe he thinks I'm trying to push him into some kind of obligation that he doesn't want, or isn't sure of.

5   And Roger is thinking: Gosh. *Six months*.

6   And Elaine is thinking: But, hey, *I'm* not sure I want this kind of relationship, either. Sometimes I wish *I* had a little more space, so I'd have time to think about whether I really want us to keep going the way we are, moving steadily toward . . . I mean, where *are* we going? Are we just going to keep seeing each other at this level of intimacy? Are we heading toward *marriage*? Toward *children*? Toward a *lifetime* together? Am I ready for that level of commitment? Do I really even *know* this person?

7   And Roger is thinking . . . so that means it was . . . let's see . . . *February* when we started going out, which was right after I had the car at the dealer's which

means . . . lemme check the odometer . . . *Whoa*! I am *way* overdue for an oil change here.

8   And Elaine is thinking: He's upset. I can see it on his face. Maybe I'm reading this completely wrong. Maybe he wants *more* from our relationship, *more* intimacy, *more* commitment; maybe he has sensed—even before *I* sensed it—that I was feeling some reservations. Yes, I bet that's it. That's why he's so reluctant to say anything about his own feelings: He's afraid of being rejected.

9   And Roger is thinking: And I'm gonna have them look at the transmission again. I don't care *what* those morons say, it's still not shifting right. And they better not try to blame it on the cold weather this time. *What* cold weather? It's eighty-seven degrees out, and this thing is shifting like a goddamn *garbage* truck, and I paid those incompetent thieving cretin bastards *six hundred dollars.*

10   And Elaine is thinking: He's angry. And I don't blame him. I'd be angry, too. God. I feel so *guilty,* putting him through this, but I can't help the way I feel. I'm just not *sure.*

11   And Roger is thinking: They'll probably say it's only a ninety-day warranty. That's exactly what they're gonna say, the scumballs.

12   And Elaine is thinking: Maybe I'm just too idealistic, waiting for a knight to come riding up on his white horse, when I'm sitting right next to a perfectly good person, a person I enjoy being with, a person I truly do care about, a person who seems to truly care about me. A person who is in pain because of my self-centered, schoolgirl romantic fantasy.

13   And Roger is thinking: Warranty? They want a warranty? *I'll* give them a goddamn warranty. I'll take their warranty and stick it right up their . . .

14   "Roger," Elaine says aloud.

15   "What?" says Roger, startled.

16   "Please don't torture yourself like this," she says, her eyes beginning to brim with tears. "Maybe I should never have . . . Oh *God,* I feel so . . ." (*She breaks down, sobbing.*)

17   "What?" says Roger.

18   "I'm such a fool." Elaine sobs. "I mean, I know there's no knight. I really know that. It's silly. There's no knight, and there's no horse."

19   "There's no horse?" says Roger.

20   "You think I'm a fool, don't you?" Elaine says.

21   "No!" says Roger, glad to finally know the correct answer.

22   "It's just that . . . It's that I . . . I need some time," Elaine says.

23   (*There is a fifteen-second pause while Roger, thinking as fast as he can, tries to come up with a safe response. Finally he comes up with one that he thinks might work.*)

24   "Yes," he says.

25   (*Elaine, deeply moved, touches his hand.*)

26   "Oh, Roger, do you really feel that way?" she says.

27   "What way?" says Roger.

28   "That way about time," says Elaine.

29   "Oh," says Roger. "Yes."

30   (*Elaine turns to face him and gazes deeply into his eyes, causing him to become very nervous about what she might say next, especially if it involves a horse. At last she speaks.*)

31 "Thank you, Roger," she says.

32 "Thank *you*," says Roger.

33 Then he takes her home, and she lies on her bed, a conflicted, tortured soul, and weeps until dawn, whereas when Roger gets back to his place, he opens a bag of Doritos, turns on the TV, and immediately becomes deeply involved in a rerun of a tennis match between two Czechoslovakians he has never heard of. A tiny voice in the far recesses of his mind tells him that something major was going on back there in the car, but he is pretty sure there is no way he would ever understand *what*, and so he figures it's better if he doesn't think about it. (This is also Roger's policy regarding world hunger.)

34 The next day Elaine will call her closest friend, or perhaps two of them, and they will talk about this situation for six straight hours. In painstaking detail, they will analyze everything she said and everything he said, going over it time and time again, exploring every word, expression, and gesture for nuances of meaning, considering every possible ramification. They will continue to discuss this subject, off and on, for weeks, maybe months, never reaching any definite conclusions, but never getting bored with it, either.

35 Meanwhile, Roger, while playing racquetball one day with a mutual friend of his and Elaine's, will pause just before serving, frown, and say: "Norm, did Elaine ever own a horse?"

36 We're not talking about different wavelengths here. We're talking about different *planets*, in completely different *solar systems*. Elaine cannot communicate meaningfully with Roger about their relationship any more than she can meaningfully play chess with a duck. Because the sum total of Roger's thinking on this particular topic is as follows:

37 *Huh?*

38 Women have a lot of trouble accepting this. Despite millions of years of over-whelming evidence to the contrary, women are convinced that guys must spend a certain amount of time thinking about the relationship. How could they not? How could a guy see another human being day after day, night after night, sharing countless hours with this person, becoming physically intimate—how can a guy be doing these things and *not* be thinking about their relationship? This is what women figure.

39 They are wrong. A guy in a relationship is like an ant standing on top of a truck tire. The ant is aware, on a very basic level, that something large is there, but he cannot even dimly comprehend what this thing is, or the nature of his involvement with it. And if the truck starts moving, and the tire starts to roll, the ant will sense that something important is happening, but right up until he rolls around to the bottom and is squashed into a small black blot, the only distinct thought that will form in his tiny brain will be, and I quote.

40 *Huh?*

41 Which is exactly what Roger will think when Elaine explodes with fury at him when he commits one of the endless series of petty offenses, such as asking her sister out, that guys are always committing in relationships because they have virtually no clue that they are in one.

42 "How *could* he?" Elaine will ask her best friends. "What was he thinking?"

43   The answer is, He *wasn't* thinking, in the sense that women mean the word. He can't: He doesn't have the appropriate type of brain. He has a guy brain, which is basically an analytical, problem-solving type of organ. It likes things to be definite and measurable and specific. It's not comfortable with nebulous and imprecise relationship-type concepts such as *love* and *need* and *trust.* If the guy brain has to form an opinion about another person, it prefers to form that opinion based on something concrete about the person, such as his or her earned-run average.

44   So the guy brain is not well-suited to grasping relationships. But it's good at analyzing and solving mechanical problems. For example, if a couple owns a house, and they want to repaint it so they can sell it, it will probably be the guy who will take charge of this project. He will methodically take the necessary measurements, calculate the total surface area, and determine the per-gallon coverage capacity of the paint; then, using his natural analytical and mathematical skills, he will apply himself to the problem of figuring out a good excuse not to paint the house.

45   "It's too humid," he'll say. Or: "I've read that prospective buyers are actually attracted more to a house with a lot of exterior dirt." Guys simply have a natural flair for this kind of problem-solving. That's why we always have guys in charge of handling the federal budget deficit.

46   But the point I'm trying to make is that, if you're a woman, and you want to have a successful relationship with a guy, the Number One Tip to remember is:

1. Never assume that the guy understands that you and he have a relationship.

47   The guy will not realize this on his own. You have to plant the idea in his brain by constantly making subtle references to it in your everyday conversation, such as:

- "Roger, would you mind passing me a Sweet 'n' Low, inasmuch as we have a relationship?"
- "Wake up, Roger! There's a prowler in the den and we have a relationship. You and I do, I mean."
- "Good news, Roger! The gynecologist says we're going to have our fourth child, which will serve as yet another indication that we have a relationship!"
- "Roger, inasmuch as this plane is crashing and we probably have only about a minute to live, I want you to know that we've had a wonderful fifty-three years of marriage together, which clearly constitutes a relationship."

48   Never let up, women. Pound away relentlessly at this concept, and eventually it will start to penetrate the guy's brain. Some day he might even start thinking about it on his own. He'll be talking with some other guys about women, and, out of the blue, he'll say, "Elaine and I, we have, ummm . . . We have, ahhh . . . We . . . We have this *thing.*"

49   And he will sincerely mean it. ✳

From Dave Barry, *Dave Barry's Complete Guide to Guys.* © 1995 by Dave Barry. Reprinted by permission of Random House, Inc.

Exercises

Do not refer to the selection for Exercises A–C unless your instructor directs you to do so.

The first two exercises measure your overall comprehension.

A. DETERMINING THE MAIN IDEA AND PURPOSE

Choose the best answer.

_____ 1. The main idea of the selection is that men and women

    a. are interested in different activities.
    b. think and communicate on completely different wavelengths.
    c. should date for a long time before they begin to think about a long-term commitment.
    d. are not clear about what they want from relationships with the opposite sex.

Exercise A asks you to identify the writer's main idea and purpose. Part One will help you with this. For now, see how well you can do on your own.

_____ 2. With respect to the main idea, the writer's purpose is to

    a. explain why so many relationships fail.
    b. criticize men and women for not understanding the opposite sex.
    c. entertain the reader with an amusing story.
    d. poke fun at men and women's styles of communicating.

Exercise B measures how well you understand the main ideas in the supporting paragraphs. It is not meant to be tricky but meant to determine how well you understand the important ideas in the selection.

B. COMPREHENDING MAIN IDEAS

Choose the correct answer.

_____ 1. According to Barry, guys have trouble understanding what women mean by the term

    a. *commitment.*
    b. *marriage.*
    c. *communication.*
    d. *relationship.*

_____ 2. Roger and Elaine, the couple in this hypothetical story, have been seeing each other for exactly

    a. six weeks.
    b. six months.
    c. a year.
    d. six years.

_____ 3. After several moments of silence, when Elaine tells Roger "there's no horse," he

    a. knows exactly what she is referring to.
    b. thinks she is crazy.
    c. was also thinking about a horse.
    d. has no idea what she is talking about.

Note: The answers appear after the question groups. For the balance of the selections, the answers appear in the Annotated Instructor's Edition only.

_____ 4. Barry states that men have trouble communicating about relationships and that women

    a. have trouble accepting this.
    b. have exactly the same problem.
    c. understand men's feelings well.
    d. want to find sensitive men who will share their ideas about relationships.

_____ 5. Barry describes men's brains as

    a. analytical and problem-solving.
    b. incapable of thinking about two thoughts at the same time.
    c. well-equipped to understand relationship terms like *love* and *need*.
    d. poorly suited to solving mechanical problems, preferring to seek expert advice.

_____ 6. Barry humorously advises a woman who wants to have a relationship with a guy to

    a. choose a guy who enjoys the same activities as she does.
    b. nag and criticize him for his insensitivity until she finally wears him down.
    c. give up the idea as hopeless and just accept his inability to understand.
    d. plant the idea in his brain by constantly making subtle references to it.

ANSWERS TO EXERCISES A AND B

Now check your answers. If you disagree with an answer, ask your instructor for an explanation.

A. Determining the Main Idea and Purpose

1. b   **2.** d

B. Comprehending Main Ideas

1. d   **2.** b   **3.** d   **4.** a   **5.** a   **6.** d

COMPREHENSION SCORE

Next, you can figure out your comprehension score.

Score your answers for Exercises A and B as follows:

A. No. right _____ × 2 = _____
B. No. right _____ × 1 = _____
Total points from A and B _____ × 10 = _____ percent

This sequencing exercise gives you practice in seeing how sentences in a paragraph must be arranged to produce a logical discussion.

C. SEQUENCING

The sentences from the selection's opening paragraph have been scrambled. Read the sentences and choose the sequence that puts them back into logical order. Do not refer to the original selection.

    1. With human guys, it's extremely difficult. **2.** Contrary to what many women believe, it's fairly easy to develop a long-term, stable, intimate, and mutually fulfilling relationship with a guy. **3.** This is because guys don't really grasp what women mean by the term *relationship.* **4.** Of course this guy has to be a Labrador retriever.

_____ Which of the following represents the correct sequence for these sentences?

 a. 1, 3, 2, 4
 b. 2, 4, 1, 3
 c. 3, 4, 1, 2
 d. Correct as written.

You may refer to the selection as you work through the remaining exercises.

D. INTERPRETING MEANING

Write your answers to these questions in your own words.

Now read the selection again and circle words you don't know and can't figure out from the context. Then look up the words you circled. Now complete the remaining exercises.

1. Barry's humor in this piece relies on *overstatement,* sometimes called *hyperbole* (hī-pûr′ bə-lē) or deliberate exaggeration for effect. Here is one example: Barry states in paragraph 36, "We're not talking about different wavelengths here. We're talking about different *planets,* in completely different *solar systems.*" Look through the selection and find two other examples of overstatement.

 _____

 _____

Exercise D asks you to go beyond the surface ideas. Later you will be asked to study the structure and organization of particular selections.

2. From Elaine's response in paragraph 18 about there being no knight and no horse, what has occurred in her thinking process?

 _____

 _____

3. Barry writes in paragraphs 36 and 37 that the sum total of Roger's thinking on the subject of his and Elaine's relationship is *"Huh?"* What does this response mean?

 _____

 _____

Exercise E tests your understanding of some of the most important words in the selection. Since you have looked up the words you didn't know, you should be able to complete this section quickly.

4. At the end of paragraph 48, what is Barry poking fun at when Roger says, "Elaine and I, we have, ummm . . . We have, ahhh . . . We . . . We have this *thing.*"

 _____

 _____

E. UNDERSTANDING VOCABULARY

Choose the best definition according to an analysis of word parts or the context.

_____ **1.** this level of *intimacy* [paragraphs 6 and 8]:

 a. privacy
 b. long-term commitment

     c. closeness, familiarity
     d. friendship

_____ 2. in *painstaking* detail [34]:

     a. simple
     b. exaggerated
     c. sketchy
     d. extremely careful

_____ 3. *nuances* of meaning [34]:

     a. slight variations
     b. intentions
     c. direct expressions
     d. examinations

_____ 4. every possible *ramification* [34]:

     a. interpretation
     b. consequence
     c. use of the imagination
     d. cause or reason

_____ 5. pound away *relentlessly* [48]:

     a. harshly
     b. angrily
     c. persistently
     d. politely

> Exercise F varies from selection to selection. This one asks you to consider forms of words that are in the same family but have endings that change their grammatical function. (That is, they are *inflected* forms.) If you aren't sure which form to use, try reading the sentence out loud and inserting each choice to see which one "sounds right," or consult your dictionary for further help.
>
> Now check answers. Any wrong answers? Ask your instructor for an explanation.

F. USING VOCABULARY

In parentheses before each sentence are some inflected forms of words from the selection. Study the context and the sentence. Then write the correct form in the space provided.

1. (*commit, commitment*) Roger and Elaine's imaginary dialogue suggests that neither of them is ready for a _____.

2. (*incompetence, incompetent, incompetently*) Roger is convinced that the mechanic who worked on his car was guilty of dishonesty and _____.

3. (*pettiness, petty, pettily*) A guy like Roger can never understand why a woman would make a big deal out of something _____ like asking Elaine's sister out.

4. (*subtlety, subtle, subtly*) Barry suggests that a woman can instill the idea of having a relationship by _____ referring to the concept in her everyday conversation.

ANSWERS TO EXERCISES C–F

C. Sequencing

b

D. Interpreting Meaning

1. Here are some possible answers: Roger watches a tennis match between two unknown Czech players, rather than contemplate what went on between him and Elaine in the car [paragraph 33]. Roger commits a "petty offense" by asking Elaine's sister out [paragraph 41]. A guy figures out calculations for painting a house and then devises excuses for not doing the job [paragraphs 44–45].
2. Elaine's mistake is assuming that Roger, in his silence, is thinking about the same thing as she is.
3. "Huh?" means that Roger has no idea what Elaine is talking about.
4. Barry means that men have difficulty even saying the word *relationship* perhaps because it may imply a commitment they are not yet ready to make.

E. Understanding Vocabulary

1. c **2.** d **3.** a **4.** b **5.** c

F. Using Vocabulary

1. commitment **2.** incompetence **3.** petty **4.** subtly

G. TOPICS FOR DISCUSSION

1. Aside from Barry's observation that guys' brains are different from women's, what might be some other reasons that men have difficulty talking about relationships and abstract concepts like *love* and *need* and *commitment*?
2. Is Barry being fair to men? to women?

H. TOPICS FOR WRITING

1. Write an imaginary dialogue between Roger and Elaine that represents your past experience in a relationship. The situation is this: Elaine wants to have a relationship with Roger, and she wants him to make a commitment, but Roger isn't so sure that he's ready to make this leap.
2. Barry's essay deals with the different communication styles used by men and women. Choose another activity that men and women do differently—for example, cooking, studying, shopping, or watching television—and write an essay describing these differences.

Exploring Related Web Sites

- A collection of Dave Barry's recent *Miami Herald* columns can be found at:

  www.miamiherald.com/living/columnists/dave_barry

- Dr. John Gray's well-known 1992 book, *Men Are from Mars, Women Are from Venus*, examines the differences between men and women in terms

---

Whether or not your instructor assigns these questions, you should look the questions over in Exercise G. They ask you to respond to what you read and to extend your thinking, perhaps to similar situations in your own life. One of the topics might be the perfect choice for a paper in your composition class.

of communication styles, emotional needs, and other concepts relevant our relationships with the opposite sex. This Wikipedia article provides a good overview of the book's scope and content (note that you must input the capital letters as shown). If this information interests you, you might read the book.

www.en.wikipedia.org/wiki/Men_Are_From_Mars,_Women_Are_From_Venus

On the next page is a Comprehension Worksheet for those who wish to have an alternative to the text's multiple-choice questions. The page can easily be duplicated for use with any of the text selections.

Comprehension Worksheet

1. Author's name and title of the selection: _____

_____

2. Topic of the selection (What or who is it about?): _____

3. Main idea (What is the main point of the selection?): _____

_____

_____

4. Purpose (Why did the writer write it?): _____

_____

5. Supporting ideas (List two or three points that support the main point.):

   a. _____

   b. _____

   c. _____

6. Evaluation (What was your reaction to the selection? Why do you feel this way?):

_____

_____

7. Does your experience and/or observation correspond to the ideas expressed in the selection? Explain. _____

_____

8. What other information would you like to have on this subject? _____

_____

PART ONE

Getting Started: Practicing the Basics

Identifying the Main Idea and Writer's Purpose

Before beginning this section, be sure to read "To the Student" at the beginning of the book. This short introduction previews the book's organization and content and explains what you should accomplish during the term. Each introduction to the book's six parts discusses a particular skill or set of skills that will make you a better reader; these skills are organized by order of importance. In Part One you will work on the following areas—the most important ones in the course:

- Learning the difference between fiction and nonfiction prose
- Finding the main idea in paragraphs, whether stated or implied
- Locating thesis statements in articles and essays
- Identifying the writer's purpose

THE DIFFERENCE BETWEEN FICTION AND NONFICTION

Writing comes in three types: prose, poetry, and drama. This book is concerned with *prose*—ordinary writing that consists of words grouped into sentences and sentences grouped into paragraphs—just like the print that you are reading on this page. *Prose* is further divided into two types: nonfiction and fiction.

Your college textbooks are nonfiction; the daily newspaper is nonfiction; magazine articles are nonfiction, and so are the readings in this book. Nonfiction writing discusses real people with real problems and real events in their lives, real issues and ways to resolve them, real events in the world and their consequences. The novel you take with you to read at the beach is fiction. Simply put, nonfiction is writing that is real, whereas fiction is writing that is imaginative. This chart lists some common types of nonfiction.

COMMON TYPES OF NONFICTION

- Articles in magazines and newspapers
- Autobiographies and biographies
- Books on history, politics, social problems, and so on
- Editorials or opinion pieces
- Material on websites (information sites, blogs, and the like)
- Essays
- Memoirs and journals
- Textbooks

THE DIFFERENCE BETWEEN AN ARTICLE AND AN ESSAY

Two important types of nonfiction are *essays* and *articles*. In this book—as well as in many of your other classes—you will read both. The difference between an essay and an article is a little tricky, and the distinction is not always clear, especially because many magazines publish both.

Probably the easiest way to understand the difference is to think of an article as being more contemporary; that is, it deals with *current* issues and problems. An essay, on the other hand, tends to be *universal* in scope because it offers the writer's perceptions on age-old problem that affect all cultures, all humans. An essay is also more literary, more open in its form, and more enduring. Selection 8 in Part Two, "The Bystander's Dilemma: Why Do We Walk on By?" by Marc Ian Barasch, is an article. It was published in *Utne*, a magazine for a mass audience, but more important, it deals with a contemporary question—why do we ignore the homeless? Not every country has as serious a homeless problem as many American cities do, so the problem is not universal.

But Selection 26 by Jared Diamond in Part Four, "Easter Island," is an essay. Its structure is formal, and the discussion has significance far beyond the boundaries of the island that lies off the coast of Chile. The future of mankind is at stake because, as Diamond eloquently concludes, we are ruining the environment.

But these distinctions may not be worth making, and I urge you not to worry about whether a particular piece of prose is an essay or an article. What *is* important to remember is that essays and articles should be called "essays" and "articles," *not* "stories," which refer properly only to fiction, writing that is imaginative or invented.

IDENTIFYING THE MAIN IDEA IN PARAGRAPHS

With those important definitions out of the way, we now turn to the comprehension skill that is at the heart of everything in your college career—how to locate the main idea of what you're reading. Let's say that you have just seen *No Country for Old Men*, the 2007 movie made by Joel and Ethan Coen that won an Oscar for Best Picture in 2008. The next day your friend asks you what the movie was about and whether she should rent it. You say something like this:

> The movie takes place in rural West Texas, and it's about violence and greed and what they do to people. Josh Brolin plays Llewelyn Moss, a local guy who stumbles upon the site of a drug deal that has gone terribly wrong and who steals $2 million that he finds there. A psychopathic killer named Anton Chigurh is on the trail of the missing money, and he kills anyone who gets in his way with a terrible kind of gun that I've never seen before. As the crimes escalate and become more violent, Sheriff Ed Tom Bell, who is played by Tommy Lee Jones, investigates these crimes.

What have you just done? In these four sentences you have stated the main point of a two-hour movie, in other words, what it's about. And based on this summary, your friend can decide if she wants to rent it or not.

In your college reading, finding the main idea, of course, is a little more difficult. There is no trailer to show you the highlights, no friend to summarize for you, no annotations in the margins, and no way of asking the writer what he or she means. All you have are print and paper, so it's up to you to work through the words and sentences and make sense of it all. Step-by-step, this book—its readings and exercises—will help you make sense of what you're reading and give you the practice to perfect your reading skills.

Consider this simple diagram of a typical paragraph:

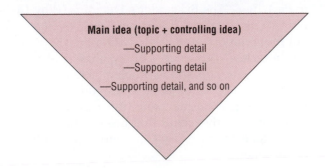

Main idea (topic + controlling idea)
—Supporting detail
—Supporting detail
—Supporting detail, and so on

This diagram suggests that the typical paragraph moves from a general statement (the main idea) to the supporting details or reinforcing points. This is why the triangle is printed with the larger side at the top. Here is a supporting paragraph from a selection that appears in Part Three—"Fast Food Nation: Behind the Counter" by Eric Schlosser. Notice how the structure of the paragraph matches the diagram above. The main idea is printed in boldface.

> **Teenagers have long provided the fast food industry with the bulk of the workforce.** The industry's rapid growth coincided with the baby-boom expansion of that age group. Teenagers were in many ways the ideal candidates for these low-paying jobs. Since most teenagers still lived at home, they could afford to work for wages too low to support an adult, and until recently, their limited skills attracted few other employers. A job at a fast food restaurant became an American rite of passage, a first job soon left behind for better things. The flexible terms of employment in the fast food industry also attracted housewives who needed extra income. As the number of baby-boom teenagers declined, the fast food chains began to hire other marginalized workers: recent immigrants, the elderly, and the handicapped.

The first sentence represents the main idea of the paragraph, which consists of the *topic* and a *controlling idea*. The topic—the fast food industry—is restricted to the controlling idea—the popularity of a large teenage workforce. Notice that the sentences following the first one all explain and back up Schlosser's point—the *reasons* that the fast food industry relied so heavily on teenagers for its workforce.

As you will see in the reading selections in this text, paragraphs are the building blocks of an essay. As the writer moves through the discussion, each paragraph makes a point, though as you will see later, some paragraphs have *implied* (unstated) main ideas. Further, the point has to be supported, developed, and backed up. No idea is so good on its own that it can stand undefended.

Another way to visualize the main idea of a paragraph is to imagine an umbrella that covers everything beneath it, as you see in this diagram:

Main idea

Supporting details

Occasionally in the exercises following the selections in this text, you will be asked to choose a title for a paragraph. This kind of question is just another way of asking you to identify the topic and the controlling idea—what the writer wants us to understand about the topic. Here, for example, are four titles for the paragraph that you just read. Which one best represents what the paragraph is about? Which is the "umbrella" statement?

1. "Types of Workers in Fast Food Restaurants"
2. "Teenagers: Ideal Workers in the Fast Food Industry"
3. "Good Jobs for Teenagers"
4. "Why Fast Food Restaurants Are Popular"

In a typical exercise like this, some titles will be incorrect because they are too broad, too narrow, irrelevant, or trivial. The correct title, or umbrella, will include all the essential elements. For the Schlosser paragraph, number 1 is inaccurate, since Schlosser does not discuss in detail types of workers; number 3 is too general; and number 4 is off topic. Only number 2 includes Schlosser's main point.

Let's practice with one more paragraph. This one is from an article that appears in Part Two. The title is "Minds of Their Own" by Virginia Morell, which appeared in *National Geographic*. Alex, mentioned in the last sentence, was an African gray parrot who learned to "speak" English. Study the annotations (notes) in the left margin as you read the paragraph. Then answer the questions that follow.

skills associated
with intelligence

these skills don't
exist only in
humans

(1) Certain skills are considered key signs of higher mental abilities: good memory, a grasp of grammar and symbols, self-awareness, understanding others' motives, imitating others, and being creative. (2) Bit by bit, in ingenious experiments, researchers have documented these talents in other species, gradually chipping away at what we thought made human beings distinctive while offering a glimpse of where our own abilities came from. (3) Scrub jays know that other jays are thieves and that stashed food can spoil; sheep can recognize faces; chimpanzees use a variety of tools to probe termite mounds

Examples of
intelligence in
various species
of animals

and even use weapons to hunt small mammals; dolphins can imitate human postures; the archerfish, which stuns insects with a sudden blast of water, can learn how to aim its squirt simply by watching an experienced fish perform the task. (4) And Alex the parrot turned out to be a surprisingly good talker.

Which of the following best represents the main idea of the passage?

1. Animals are smarter than humans in many respects.
2. Our intelligence derives from animal behavior.
3. Animal species display complex mental abilities similar to those in humans.
4. Self-awareness and creativity are two essential kinds of mental abilities present in both humans and animal species.

Which of the following would be the best title for this paragraph?

1. "Humanlike Mental Abilities in Animals"
2. "Animal Research"
3. "Who Is Smarter—Animals or Humans?"
4. "Ingenious Experiments with Animals"

The answers are 3 and 1, respectively.

Notice that the main idea in this paragraph is followed by a series of logical statements—first, that scientific research allows us to recognize mental abilities in animals, and second, a list of representative animal species and various behaviors that indicate these mental abilities. The sentences work together to form a coherent and unified discussion that is relatively easy to follow. Let's look at the structure of this paragraph in another way. Study this diagram:

> Skills associated with mental abilities—good memory, grasp of grammar and symbols, and so on.
>> Researchers have devised experiments to show how these abilities are present in animals.
>>> Examples of various animal species' behaviors that reflect these mental abilities (scrub jays, sheep, chimps, dolphins, archerfish, and Alex the parrot).

This diagram shows that the paragraph moves from the very general to the more specific so that the specific supporting details both prove and reinforce the central point.

Some words of caution: You may have been taught that you should look for a topic sentence in a paragraph and that it usually is the first sentence. Unfortunately, this advice is misleading. A writer is under no obligation to make your reading experience easy, and few professional writers structure their paragraphs according to a formula. Some do, but many don't. This advice gets students into trouble when they encounter college-level and other adult prose because so many paragraphs in the essays you will read don't have topic sentences. This is especially evident in newspaper articles, where the narrow-column format requires short paragraphs to create a readable format.

In essays or articles, the main idea of supporting paragraphs can appear in the second or third sentence, in the middle of the paragraph, or even at the end. And some paragraphs do not have a main idea. In this case, the supporting statements suggest the main idea, which you have to state for yourself. Consider these two questions as ways to help you either locate or state the main idea of what you read:

- What's the point of what I'm reading?
- What is the *single* most important idea that the writer wants me to come away with?

If you can come up with a single sentence—certainly no more than two—that answers these questions, then you will make significant gains in your reading. Read the next paragraph and, as before, answer the questions that follow. The passage is from an article called "Hello, My Name Is Unique" by Carlin Flora, originally published in *Psychology Today*. The subject is naming children. The word *iconoclastic* in sentence 3 means going against tradition or convention.[1]

(1) No one can predict whether a name will be consistent with a child's or a teen's view of herself. (2) The name could be ethnic, unique or white-bread, but if it doesn't reinforce her sense of self, she will probably be unhappy with it and may even feel alienated from parents or peers because of it. (3) An Annika with iconoclastic taste will be happy with her name, but a Tallullah who longs for a seat at the cheerleaders' table may feel that her name is too weird.

Which of the following best represents the main idea of the passage?

1. Unique or unusual names will reinforce a child's sense of self.
2. Weird names have become more popular in recent years.
3. A child may be unhappy with an unusual name if it doesn't reinforce her sense of self.
4. Parents should be careful when naming their children.

Which of the following would be the best title for this paragraph?

1. "One's Name and One's Sense of Self"
2. "Iconoclastic Names"
3. "New Fads in Naming Children"
4. "How Names Can Make Us Feel Alienated"

The answers are 3 and 1 respectively. In this paragraph the second part of the second sentence represents the writer's main idea. The first sentence simply introduces the subject but does not actually represent what the writer wants us to understand about the relationship between a child's name and his or her sense of self.

IMPLIED MAIN IDEAS

Not all paragraphs are as helpfully structured as the two you have been working with. Some paragraphs present only the supporting details, which require the

---

[1] From Greek, an *iconoclast* refers literally to one who destroys traditional religious images, now to one who goes against tradition (icon + smasher).

reader to determine the main idea for herself. In this type of paragraph, the main idea is *implied*—meaning that the supporting details *suggest* the main point without saying it directly. Read this passage from Eric Schlosser's article in Section 14. This time, write your own notes in space provided in the right margin.

At Burger King restaurants, frozen hamburger patties are placed on a conveyer belt and emerge from a broiler ninety seconds later fully cooked. The ovens at Pizza Hut and at Domino's also use conveyer belts to ensure standardized cooking times. The ovens at McDonald's look like commercial laundry presses, with big steel hoods that swing down and grill hamburgers on both sides at once. The burgers, chicken, french fries, and buns are all frozen when they arrive at a McDonald's. The shakes and sodas begin as syrup. At Taco Bell restaurants the food is "assembled," not prepared. The guacamole isn't made by workers in the kitchen; it's made at a factory in Michoacán, Mexico, then frozen and shipped north. The chain's taco meat arrives frozen and precooked in vacuum-sealed plastic bags. The beans are dehydrated and look like brownish corn flakes. The cooking process is simple. "Everything's add water," a Taco Bell employee told me. "Just add hot water."

What is Schlosser's main point? What do all of these details add up to? Although there is no specific main-idea sentence—it is implied, not stated—there are plenty of supporting details. Ask yourself what all of these details about fast food being frozen, packaged, precooked, and "prepared" by just adding hot water add up to. Write your answer here:

_____

_____

Here is one possibility. Your sentence, of course, may be worded differently, but it should contain the same elements as this one:

> Most of the food served in fast food restaurants is frozen, and it is assembled and cooked with hardly any human intervention.

In other words, the food is assembled, not prepared or cooked, just as any other factory product is. Bicycles are assembled, computers are assembled, and Big Macs and Whoppers are assembled, too.

Whether it is stated or implied, the writer's point must nonetheless be supported with details, examples, stories, anecdotes (little stories), definitions of unfamiliar terms, explanations, analysis—whatever way the writer can best back up his or her point. The trick is to separate the main point from these supporting ideas. Part Four examines these various types of support; you might want to read it even before your instructor assigns it.

THESIS STATEMENTS IN ARTICLES AND ESSAYS

Articles and essays are both composed of individual paragraphs linked together in the same way a chain is linked together to produce a sustained piece of writing that may be a single page to 20 or more pages. Whatever the length, the writer of an article has in mind a focus or a point, which, like the main idea of a paragraph, may be stated or implied. This main idea is called the *thesis* or *thesis statement*. In your composition classes, you are probably familiar with the concept of a thesis. After all, your essay has to be about something. A writer may place the thesis near the beginning of the essay, in the middle, or at the end, but usually it comes somewhere near the beginning. In addition, a thesis might be two sentences, though rarely more than that.

To practice locating the thesis, here are the first four paragraphs from "Hello, My Name Is Unique," a passage from which you read earlier in this section. Three words that might be unfamiliar to you are defined here:

bard (paragraph 1)	a poet
idiosyncratic (paragraph 3)	unusual or peculiar to a particular individual
monikers (paragraph 4)	names

After you read these four paragraphs, underline the sentence that you think probably represents the thesis for the entire article.

1 Proper names are poetry in the raw, said the bard W. H. Auden. "Like all poetry, they are untranslatable." Mapping your name onto yourself is a tricky procedure indeed. We exist wholly independently of our name, yet they alone represent us on our birth certificates and gravestones.

2 Would a Rose by any other name be just as sweet-tempered? Does Orion feel cosmically special? Psychologists, parents and the world's Oceans, Zanes and Timothys are divided on the extent to which first names actually matter.

You Named Him *What*?

3 Today's parents seem to believe they can alter their child's destiny by picking the perfect—preferably idiosyncratic—name. (Destiny, incidentally, was the ninth most popular name for girls in New York City last year.) The current crop of preschoolers includes a few Uniques, with uncommonly named playmates like Kyston, Payton and Sawyer. From Dakota to Heaven, Integrity to Serenity, more babies are being named after places and states of mind. Names with alternative spellings are on the upswing, like Jaxon, Kassidy, Mikayla, Jazmine and Nevaeh (Heaven spelled backward), as are mix-and-match names such as Ashlynn and Rylan.

4 "For the first time in history, the top 50 names account for less than 50 percent of boys born each year, and for less than 40 percent of girls," says Cleveland Kent Evans, professor of psychology at Bellevue University in Nebraska and author of *Unusual and Most Popular Baby Names*. Evans believes that our homogeneous strip-mall culture fosters the desire to nominally distinguish our children. He cites a boom in unique names dating to the late 1980s but says the taste for obscure monikers developed in the 1960s, when parents felt less obligated to keep certain names in the family.

Two possibilities exist for the thesis—the third sentence of paragraph 2 or the first sentence of paragraph 3. Here is a paraphrase of these two candidates for the thesis:

> 1. People disagree about the degree to which first names really matter. (paragraph 2)
> 2. Today's parents seem to think that they can influence a child's destiny by picking the perfect name, preferably an unusual one. (paragraph 3)

Which is the better choice? If you consider the details that follow the second example in the box above, it appears that the writer, Carlin Flora, is going to explore the idea that parents are increasingly choosing idiosyncratic names. A careful reading of the entire selection, which you will do later in this book, bears this out. The writer is concerned with the impact of unusual names on our personalities. The writer mentions the fact that psychologists, parents, and people with unusual names disagree over the matter only as a lead-in to the thesis. Notice, too, that a caption used in the article, "Can Names Alter Our Self-Perception?" bears this out.

IDENTIFYING THE WRITER'S PURPOSE

Although he or she may not be aware of it when opening a new document on the computer screen, every writer has in mind some *purpose*, the intention or the reason he or she is going to the trouble of writing. The ancient Greeks taught that literature had three aims: to please, to instruct, and to persuade. What exactly did they mean?

THE WRITER'S PURPOSE IN CLASSICAL TERMS
• **To please:** to delight, entertain, amuse, give pleasure to, describe, paint a picture in words
• **To instruct:** to teach, show, inform, examine, expose, analyze, criticize
• **To persuade:** to convince, change one's mind, influence, argue, recommend, give advice to

Sometimes it is hard to see an exact distinction between "instructing" and "persuading" since the very act of "instructing" us about something that needs to be changed might also "convince" us of the need for that change. For example, in the passage about the mental abilities of various species of animals, the writer is clearly informing us (instructing), but there is also an implied or secondary purpose—to persuade us not only that these abilities exist but that they are marvelous in their own right. Maybe we humans aren't as distinctive as we think we are.

Another example of how a writer may have overlapping purposes can be seen in the Practice Essay by Dave Barry, "Tips for Women: How to Have a Relationship with a Guy." Barry humorously explores the difficulties men and women have talking to each other. Obviously, his purpose is, at least in part, to entertain. But what other purpose might he have? Because Barry pokes fun at men for their inability to commit to a relationship and at women for exhaustingly analyzing every little thing that happens between a man and a woman, his purpose seems more to instruct than to persuade. He is pointing out our differences, not trying to reform us or make us change our ways. Besides, what writer, discussing the age-old battle of the sexes, could ever accomplish that!

As you complete the exercises following the readings in Parts One through Four, the second question always asks you to choose the writer's purpose. In this case, choose the *primary* purpose and do not concern yourself with overlapping purposes.

PAMELA GRIM

Care in Midair

Pamela Grim is an emergency medical physician and research scientist in Cleveland, Ohio. Several of her pieces (such as this one) have appeared in an ongoing series called "Vital Signs" published in Discover *magazine. In addition, she has published a book describing her medical experiences,* Just Here Trying to Save a Few Lives: Tales of Life and Death from the ER *(2000). "Care in Midair" narrates a harrowing helicopter flight she took while trying to save the life of a critically ill patient who was being transported to a larger hospital. In a biographical sketch accompanying this piece, Grim writes, "In the ER, you never know if you've done the right thing. You come home and think, 'Should I have done this? Should I have done that?' In my stories, I am not the hero."*

Vocabulary Preview

WORD PARTS

Micro- [paragraph 3] The helicopter pilot had to speak to the medical crew through his helmet's *microphone* because of the helicopter's noise. The prefix *micro-* came into English from Latin, although it was originally a Greek prefix. Indicating smallness, it is attached to many words to form compounds. In this case *microphone* is derived from *micro-* ("small") + *phonos* ("sound" or "voice"). Other words beginning with *micro-* include *microbiology, microscope,* and *microorganism.*

WORD FAMILIES

Circulatory [paragraph 7] Mr. Prodham, the critically ill subject of this article, suffered from a collapse of his *circulatory* system, referring to the circular movement of blood through the human body. This word comes from the Latin root *circus* ("circle") and the related prefix *circum-* ("around"). In addition to *circus,* a word that derives from the fact that a circus takes place inside a ring, English contains a multitude of words in this family, among them:

circuit	a closed circular line around an object or area
circuitous	taking a roundabout, out-of-the way course
circumference	the boundary line around a circle
circumnavigate	to go around, as in to circumnavigate the globe
circumlocution	using an unnecessary number of words, to "talk around" a subject (*circum-* + *loqui* ["to speak"])

Other words you will need to know:

intubation   the process of inserting a breathing tube into a patient's throat
extubation   the process of removing this breathing tube

PAMELA GRIM

Care in Midair

1   We were at 2,000 feet and dropping fast. The flight nurse and I fumbled with our harnesses, preparing to jump out. I was the helicopter physician on duty, and we were rushing to pick up a critically ill patient in a small hospital about 150 miles away. We had to move; the weather was closing in.

2   Skip, the pilot, canted the helicopter toward one of the hospital parking lots. We were to unload hot—that meant we had to jump out with our equipment just as the helicopter touched down and run like crazy through the propeller wash and rotary roar. Already the guards at the hospital entrance were being hit by the wind from the props. Their coats were blown open, and one of them lost his hat.

3   "You have 20 minutes," said Skip as he jockeyed us down. He couldn't just say it, of course; he had to use his helmet's microphone. The rotary blades made too much noise. All our monitor equipment for the patient had to be electronic with visual output only. Our regular stethoscopes were useless.

4   The helicopter struts touched down with a bounce. "Go," Skip shouted through his mike.

5   I opened my door, grabbed two of the monitors and ducked out. Venetra, the flight nurse, was right behind me.

6   The attending physician had already told us about the patient. It was a heart-breaking case. Two weeks earlier Kevin Prodham had had a massive heart attack. Since then he'd had every complication known: blood clots, sepsis, renal failure, liver failure. Most patients would never survive this, but Mr. Prodham was only 42. He'd been a healthy, active businessman until two weeks ago. "He has kids in grade school," one of the nurses told me as we headed for the intensive care unit.

7   I winced when I saw him. He looked like a drowned man, bloated from the collapse of his circulatory system. He was on a ventilator, with leads and monitors and probes going everywhere.

8   Venetra began setting up the monitoring equipment while I flipped through the patient's chart. For the past 24 hours, his oxygen saturation had been less than 70 percent. His blood pressure, despite medication, had gone south early this morning and stayed there. He was comatose; tests of his liver functions were nearly incompatible with life, and he probably should have started dialysis the week before. This man was close to dying.

9   I checked my watch. We had about 15 minutes. First we had to switch all the pumps and monitors from the hospital equipment to our specially designed "helicopter proof" ones. Because the helicopter was not pressurized, the pumps

had to operate at varying ambient pressures. And they all had to have visual alarms because we couldn't hear anything. Then we had to move the patient over to the helicopter gurney and disconnect him from the ventilator. The hospital staff had already inserted a breathing tube into his airway; throughout the flight we would have to pump air into his lungs manually, using a device called an Ambu bag.

10   I was worried about the weather, though—within five minutes, I was signaling Venetra. We were taking too much time. She ignored me; a slipup with an IV line or a pump set at the wrong speed could destroy any other attempt to save this man's life.

11   Finally we were ready. We trundled down the hallways. The patient's wife did not let go of his hand until we reached the door.

12   It was colder now, and the sky looked thin and gray. Maybe the wind had picked up, but with the helicopter going, it was hard to tell.

13   We slid the patient into the back of the helicopter. He was a big man, and tall. His feet stuck out over the end of the gurney, nearly tickling Skip's ears. We would have to do everything back here, and if he deteriorated, we'd have to stabilize him. That meant IVs, chest tubes, central lines—all difficult procedures on the ground, much less at a thousand feet and 140 mph. But I had faith in Skip. He had trained as a military pilot in Southeast Asia. In Vietnam, he told us, there were only two kinds of helicopter pilots: good ones and dead ones.

14   We took our places for liftoff. I buckled myself into a seat by the patient's head. Skip contacted base. "This is Air Transport One," he said. "We are lifting off at 4:33. Four souls on board."

15   "Souls." Skip always said that. I patted our patient, hoping his soul was still connected to his body.

16   We lifted off. I could feel the helicopter slip sideways with the gusting wind, recover, then slip again. We kept rising and then leveling off. Rain started pricking at the windows. The thunderclouds looked ominous.

17   The ride seemed to be getting bouncier. I sat pumping the Ambu bag, trying to keep my balance.

18   Skip came on the intercom: "I'm going up another 500 feet. It should be smoother up there. How's the patient?"

19   "Alive," I said.

20   "Barely," Venetra added.

21   "You guys buckled in?" Skip asked, and as he did, a gust of wind hit the helicopter. I fell against the window as the entire helicopter swung sideways. I ended up looking straight down at the farm fields 1,500 feet below. It was the last view I saw of the ground. We were enfolded in a cloud of gray mist. Then we ascended and just as quickly dropped back down. Venetra and I were being tossed around like little dolls.

22   We swung sideways again, so far askew that the helicopter blades were almost directly to my right. "We can't stay aloft like this," I thought in the second we hung that way. With another gust we were righted. I had been in the bumpy helicopter before, but it was never anything like this.

23   It was worse than any roller coaster. The downs weren't like those of going down a hill; they were those of dropping from some great height. As I reached

out to hold on to the leather strap above me, I realized my hands were shaking.

24 "Should we go back?" I yelled at Skip through the intercom. There was a long pause. Skip must have contacted base with us out of the circuit. Finally he came back on. "That's a negative. Base states weather worse behind us."

25 I was struggling to pump the Ambu bag to breathe for the patient, but I kept being thrown back into the window. Then the patient showed the only sign of life I saw during the whole trip. He coughed. As he did, the Ambu bag collapsed in my hand. The patient had extubated himself.

26 "We lost the airway," I yelled to Venetra through the microphone. Unless we quickly slipped in a breathing tube, he could suffocate in minutes.

27 This had happened to me once before. We ended up landing in a cornfield long enough for me to get a new endotracheal tube in. I wasn't going to risk an intubation in the air that day, and then the helicopter was a rock compared with how it felt now.

28 "Skip, Skip," I shouted into my microphone. "The patient's extubated himself. Can we land for a few minutes?"

29 There was a long pause. "That's a negative, doctor. Weather conditions do not permit." Skip had never called me "doctor" before.

30 Venetra had unstrapped herself; she wedged her knees under the patient cart and prepared Mr. Prodham for a second intubation.

31 Now I had to get out of my seat belt. As I reached for my buckle I realized I was scared—not just nervous, but deep-in-my-bones frightened. It took an act of conscious will for me to open that metal clasp. Immediately, I was airborne and then slammed down to the left, against a small cabinet. I was too scared to know whether I'd been hurt. I inched my way to the head of the cart and groped for the box containing the intubation equipment. I grabbed a laryngoscope—the tool we use for introducing the breathing tube into the airway. As I did so we made another ascent—gentler this time, but still enough to spill the contents of the box everywhere.

32 "Give me a tube," I said to Venetra. She groped around on the floor, looking for the right size. She found one and handed it to me. I opened up the laryngoscope and slid it into the patient's mouth. I tried to get the tongue up and out of the way. My heart sank along with the next sickening drop of the helicopter—I had forgotten how bloated with water the patient was. His tongue nearly filled his whole mouth. How was I going to see?

33 I looked up at Venetra. She looked green.

34 "I'm airsick," she said. "I'm going to throw up."

35 "Well, don't do it on the patient."

36 She grabbed a bag out of the closet and stuck her head inside.

37 The helicopter took another shaking plunge. As I tried to hold on to the side of the cart, the laryngoscope tumbled out of my hand. I fell after it and caught it as I landed facedown on my seat.

38 This man is going to die now, I thought; no one as sick as he is could survive this. But I would get him reintubated, no matter what. I righted myself and edged back to the front of the cart.

39 Then Venetra was holding the Ambu bag, ready. I snapped open the laryngoscope and slid the blade into the patient's mouth. Please, I said to myself. Please.

40   I saw for a moment all the landmarks—the epiglottis and beyond to the vocal cords. At least I could see past the tongue.

41   The helicopter lunged again, and the patient's face rolled away. As I tried to pull him back into place, I thought of a helicopter crash I'd seen in Colorado—the doctor in the back with two shattered hips. I knew those injuries. And I could see in the wreckage up front the pilot and the nurse hanging limply in their harnesses. I could hear the wind coming through the shattered glass and see those two figures sway. They had pushed the weather—trying to reach an unstable patient in some far-off clinic.

42   The helicopter bucked again, but this time the movement worked for me. I was flung forward, my hand jerking up, and the tube, as if of its own accord, slipped into place cleanly, right between the vocal cords and down into the airway.

43   My first thought was, Maybe there is a God.

44   I straightened up. "I'm in," I shouted to Venetra. "I saw it."

45   We dropped again. I struggled to hold the tube in place. We may be about to die, I told myself, but this man will not lose this endotracheal tube.

46   Another ascent and then the rain stopped. For a moment our flight became steady and fairly quiet. Then came a pounding on the roof and walls of the helicopter. It sounded like someone was beating the helicopter with a baseball bat.

47   "What *is* that?" I shouted at Venetra.

48   "Hail," she said. "That's hail."

49   We sat there, wedged in place, while all around us the metal seemed alive with the force of pounding rocks. I looked back down at my patient. I had no way to listen for breathing sounds, so I had to trust that the tube was in place. As I pumped air, it seemed his color was better. His pulse stayed rock steady at 75.

50   Suddenly the helicopter lit up as if it were on fire. An explosion, I thought. We've exploded. Then I thought, that can't be, I'm still alive. I looked out the window.

51   "Lightning," Venetra said.

52   The intercom buzzed again. "Hang on," Skip shouted to us. "I think we're through the worst of it." And then, as suddenly as it started, the helicopter stopped bouncing around and settled into its customary glide. We broke free from the gray clouds, and the helicopter filled with evening sunlight.

53   The patient's heart rate was 75.

54   When we landed, Skip stepped out of the helicopter, looking shaken and pale. He stood at the edge of the helicopter pad, smoking a cigarette, his head bowed, as if in prayer. When he looked up at me, he was wearing the same expression I had seen on doctors who had just lost patients they didn't expect to lose.

55   "I pushed the weather," he muttered as I patted his shoulder. "I can't believe how I pushed the weather."

56   "Well, we made it," I told him. "It's a happy ending. . . ."

57   And there was another happy ending. Mr. Prodham responded to therapy, the liver failure reversed itself, and his kidneys perked up enough for him not to need dialysis. I stopped by the ICU every day to see how he was doing. His wife

was always sitting there, holding his hand. One day I found her alone in the waiting room, crying because her husband was doing well enough to be taken off the ventilator.

58   "It's a miracle," she said, gripping my hand. "All this has been a miracle."

59   "Yes, yes," I said, squeezing her hand in return. I didn't tell her that during our wild ride I saw no evidence of a miracle. Just fear, hard work, and—well—maybe a little divine nudge to the elbow during the intubation.

60   Or maybe that's not true. Maybe something did hint at the miraculous. It was at the end of the flight, after we had cleared the clouds. First it was sunset, but as we flew east the sunlight disappeared, and it was nearly night when we got back to the city. We were flying at about 1,000 feet, and at that height you could see the grid of streets below, lined with dollhouses and marked by streetlights. The lights were laid out before us, brighter and brighter until they formed a solid mass of light that edged the black ocean. The skyscrapers were to the north and they, too, were marked out only by light. The real buildings, the steel and concrete, were as insubstantial as the night.

61   As I gazed out across the city, I wondered if Vietnam felt like this: you rode like bats out of hell, through the land of death and destruction, suffering everywhere you looked, until at some moment, after you broke free from the ground fire, you'd see as you looked all around you how beautiful the night sky was. ✳

From Pamela Grim, "Care in Midair," *Discover* Magazine, November 1998. Reprinted by permission of the author.

Exercises

Do not refer to the selection for Exercises A–C unless your instructor directs you to do so.

A. DETERMINING THE MAIN IDEA AND PURPOSE

Choose the best answer.

_____ 1. The main idea of the selection is that
   a. working as a helicopter physician is a difficult job, especially during a storm.
   b. physicians and their crews must sometimes care for their patients under difficult conditions.
   c. physicians risk their lives every day rescuing sick patients.
   d. the writer and her crew faced an enormous challenge trying to save a man's life during a terrifying helicopter ride.

_____ 2. With respect to the main idea, the writer's purpose is to
   a. defend her actions during the flight.
   b. relate her fears and triumphs by telling a story of a medical crisis.
   c. describe her medical training and experience.
   d. describe the bravery and skill emergency physicians possess.

B. COMPREHENDING MAIN IDEAS

Choose the correct answer.

_____ 1. Grim and her helicopter crew had only 20 minutes to get the sick patient into the helicopter because the

    a. weather was bad and getting worse.
    b. emergency room team was ending its shift.
    c. patient was near death.
    d. helicopter needed routine maintenance.

_____ 2. Mr. Prodham was suffering primarily from a collapse of his

    a. respiratory system.
    b. kidneys.
    c. circulatory system.
    d. liver.

_____ 3. The writer and Venetra, the flight nurse, had unusual difficulty trying to stabilize the patient during the flight because

    a. he was uncooperative.
    b. they did not have sufficient training to save such a critically ill patient.
    c. the weather was turbulent, making the helicopter bounce around wildly.
    d. the equipment wasn't functioning properly.

_____ 4. Grim says that this particular helicopter ride was worse than

    a. any other helicopter ride she had been on.
    b. a roller coaster ride.
    c. taking a parachute jump.
    d. a scary amusement park ride.

_____ 5. The most terrifying and the most dangerous part of the flight occurred when

    a. the crew had to reinsert the patient's breathing tube.
    b. the patient's blood pressure dropped quickly.
    c. hailstones hit the helicopter.
    d. lightning struck the helicopter.

_____ 6. Throughout the ordeal and despite her obvious fear, Grim exhibited one overriding emotion or feeling:

    a. a faith that God or some higher being would intervene and save them with a miracle.
    b. a strong determination to save the patient's life.
    c. a lack of confidence in her medical skills.
    d. a feeling of impending doom.

COMPREHENSION SCORE

Score your answers for Exercises A and B as follows:

A. No. right _____ × 2 = _____

B. No. right _____ × 1 = _____

Total points from A and B _____ × 10 = _____ percent

C. SEQUENCING

These sentences from one paragraph in the selection have been scrambled. Read the sentences and choose the sequence that puts them back into logical order. Do not refer to the original selection.

> **1** It sounded like someone was beating the helicopter with a baseball bat. **2** Another ascent and then the rain stopped. **3** Then came a pounding on the roof and walls of the helicopter. **4** For a moment our flight became steady and fairly quiet.

_____ Which of the following represents the correct sequence for these sentences?

    a. 1, 3, 2, 4
    b. 2, 4, 3, 1
    c. 2, 3, 4, 1
    d. Correct as written

You may refer to the selection as you work through the remaining exercises.

D. INTERPRETING MEANING

Write your answers for these questions in your own words.

1. See paragraphs 6 and 8. What is the overall effect on the human body when the circulatory system collapses? _____

2. What does Skip, the pilot, mean when he tells the crew that in Vietnam, "there were only two kinds of helicopter pilots: good ones and dead ones"?

_____

3. In paragraph 41 Grim describes another medical crew whose helicopter had crashed when the pilot had "pushed the weather." Skip later uses the same phrase in paragraph 55. What does it mean? _____

_____

E. UNDERSTANDING VOCABULARY

Look through the paragraphs listed below and find a word that matches each definition. Refer to the dictionary if necessary. An example has been done for you.

Ex. cringed in pain [paragraph 7] _____winced_____

1. unconscious, lacking alertness [8] _____

2. surrounding, encircling [9] _____

3. threatening, menacing [16] _____

4. at an angle, crookedly [22] _____

5. voluntary action, done on its own [42—phrase] _____

6. lacking substance or reality [60] _____

F. USING VOCABULARY

Write the correct inflected form of the base word (in parentheses) in each of the following sentences. Be sure to add the appropriate ending to fit the grammatical requirements of the sentence. Refer to your dictionary if necessary.

1. (*circulatory*—use a noun) The _____ of blood in the human body affects the functioning of every other organ.

2. (*incompatibility*—use an adjective) The patient's poor liver function was

   _____ with life.

3. (*stabilize*—use an adjective) Despite the wild gyrations of the helicopter, Grim

   and her co-worker were able to keep the patient's condition _____.

4. (*ascent*—use a verb) As the helicopter _____, the medical equipment fell out of the box.

G. TOPICS FOR DISCUSSION

1. What are some of the ways in which Grim makes her narrative suspenseful?
2. How would you describe Grim's suitability for emergency medicine? What qualities does she embody? Do you agree with her statement quoted in the headnote to the selection that she is not a hero?

H. TOPICS FOR WRITING

1. Write a paragraph recounting the many dangerous elements Grim and the others in the helicopter encountered during this mission.
2. How would you describe the writer's suitability for emergency medicine? What qualities does she embody? How are you made aware of these qualities in the selection? Write a paragraph or two answering these questions.
3. If you have ever been in a situation where someone's life was in danger and you had to intervene in some way, write about that experience. Be sure to include details about the exact circumstances: what happened to the victim, how you responded, and your emotional state before, during, and after the intervention.

Exploring Related Web Sites

- This site offers a comprehensive review of Pamela Grim's book, *Just Here Trying to Save a Few Lives* and also shows how these real-life stories of life in the ER are different from a television series like *ER*. In the Search box, type "Pamela Grim."

  www.lahey.org

- Frank Huyler is another physician who practices emergency medicine in Albuquerque, New Mexico. His collection of short essays, *The Blood of Strangers,* contains a behind-the-scenes look at what working in an ER is really like. One of the essays from this book has been published online by *Lost* magazine. It describes the ER staff's attempts to save a pilot who was badly burned when his plane crashed into a box canyon in Colorado.

  www.lostmag.com/issue13/burn.php

2

PETE JORDAN

Head Dishwasher?

Pete Jordan describes himself as a dishwasher who happens to write. A few years ago, he embarked on a quest: He vowed to wash dishes in every state in the United States and to write about the experience. And so for 12 years, from 1989 to 2001, he traveled the country, "dishing"—getting dishwasher jobs and recording his impressions in an underground zine that he founded and on "This American Life," a public radio program. His articles have now been collected in a book titled Dishwasher *(2007). Using an informal style, Jordan comments on entry-level jobs, working conditions in restaurants, and the work ethic in America. This excerpt from the book chronicles his dishwashing life in New Orleans, before 2005's devastating Hurricane Katrina. Jordan now lives in Amsterdam, where he continues to write while working as a bicycle mechanic.*

Vocabulary Preview

WORD PARTS

bene- [paragraph 3] English contains many so-called loan words from Latin that begin with the prefix *bene-*, which means "well." The adjective *beneficial* describes an action that promotes a favorable result, in other words, something good. The noun *beneficiary* refers to the person who receives this outcome. A *benefactor* is a person who helps another. Four other words beginning with this prefix are *benefit*, *benevolence* ("wishing well"), *benediction* ("good saying"), and *benign*, often used to describe something harmless, for example, a tumor or a cyst.

WORD FAMILIES

sensibilities [paragraph 21] The word *sensibilities* means sensitivity or receptiveness to outside impressions, whether pleasant or unpleasant. The base of this word comes from the Latin verb *sentire*, "to feel." You can see these roots in the following words in this family: *sensitive, sensuous, sensational, sentiment, sensory,* and *sensible*. But even though these words come from the same root and all pertain to sense or to the senses, they are not exact synonyms. You should check a dictionary if you are unsure of the word's exact meaning.

Other Words You Will Need to Know Jordan uses three slang terms for dishwashing— "dishing," "pearl diving," and "suds buster."

PETE JORDAN

Head Dishwasher?

1 In New Orleans, I hoped to dish in a stereotypical place. So I explored the French Quarter and scoured the windows of every Cajun-y and Creole-y restaurant for *"Plongeur* Wanted" signs. Not seeing any work advertised in the French Quarter, I took to walking into places and asking for applications. No one showed any interest in hiring me, though. But then again, I suppose I didn't show much interest in *being* hired. Restaurant managers sought enthusiastic desperation in their applicants, a *"please* hire me" expression on their faces. In my case, whenever my application was reviewed, I usually slouched in a chair and yawned and scratched. Not even the creative list of references on my application—a circus midget, a retired pederast, a future astronaut and even the southern Indiana judo champion—caught their attention.

2 While pounding the pavement looking for work, I covered a lot of ground and saw a lot of the city. The architecture of so many of the old shotgun shack houses in both well-heeled and decrepit neighborhoods was captivating. But what held my attention even closer were those neighborhoods' sidewalks. In a lot of areas, the pavement was uneven, pushed up by tree roots and/or from decades of neglect (that is, where there *were* sidewalks and not just dirt paths). If a stroller wasn't careful, he could (or in my case—*did*) trip and land on his face.

3 Because I was so busy watching where my feet were stepping, my eyes were diverted from searching for The Sign or seeing the passing houses. But the diversion proved beneficial—it helped to hone my coin-finding skills. Pay phones, newspaper machines and especially the sidewalks of the nation were awash in currency if one was patient enough to look for it. My burgeoning skills—like being able to distinguish between a nickel and a slug from fifty feet off—came in handy. In fact, they were so useful, they helped me find change *eleven days* straight.

4 But my coin-finding luck remained better than my job-finding luck.

5 "This is Pete." Cheryl said, introducing me to some guy at a party she dragged me to. "Pete's a writer."

6 "Oh yeah, what do you write?" he asked.

7 "Well, I'm *not* a writer," I said.

8 "He's a writer who happens to wash dishes," Cheryl said.

9 I didn't agree. An air-conditioner repairman who complains about a restaurant's crappy eats is not a food critic; he's an air-conditioner repairman. A schoolteacher who allows her husband to snap nude photos of her is not a porn star; she's a schoolteacher. And a dishwasher who writes about washing dishes is not a writer; he's a dishwasher—and a damn proud one.

10 "I'm a dishwasher," I told the guy, "who happens to write."

11 "Well, mister-dishwasher-not-a-writer," he said, "where do you wash dishes?"

12 "Nowhere right now," I said. "This is a tough town for a dishman."

13   "That's 'cause you're too *white* for the job," he said. He claimed that at every place in New Orleans that he'd worked as a waiter, whites waited and blacks dished.

14   "That's a myth," I said. "Any place that needs its dishes washed will hire any willing dope to do it—regardless of race."

15   He claimed it was racist of me to want to dish in New Orleans.

16   "You're taking a job away from a black person," he said.

17   If, according to his theory, certain jobs were for whites and certain ones for blacks, by eschewing my "white job" (as a banker or lawyer or whatever) to work a "black job," wouldn't I be freeing up my "white job" for a black person?

18   Racism, I told him, was assuming that shitty jobs should be reserved for blacks.

19   Regardless, it would take more than rumors about racism to keep me out of the sinks. After canvassing the town proved fruitless, I stooped to combing the newspaper classifieds. But each time I answered an ad, I found two or three other (usually black) job seekers already there, filling out applications. I never got hired.

20   There were other classified ads for dish jobs out in Metairie, the suburb bordering New Orleans to the west. Not long before, Metairie had distinguished itself by electing the ass-wipe David Duke—former Ku Klux Klan grand poobah—to a seat in the Louisiana House of Representatives. Oddly enough, it was dishwashing that turned Duke into a racist. In his autobiography, he described watching a dishwasher at a coffeehouse in Delhi, India, in 1971:

> Cleanliness was not one of his finer points, for he looked as though he moonlighted as a gravedigger. Crusty black dirt trimmed the tips of his long fingernails; the lighter spots on his face and neck, on closer inspection, turned out to be streaks where sweat had washed off some layers of muck. After hundreds of swabbings from the same filthy water, his dishrag resembled what I imagined were mummy wrappings.

21   Duke's dainty sensibilities were so offended that by the end of the day, he had a revelation: "It was at that point that I realized who I am. I am an Aryan."

22   Looking at all the openings listed in Metairie, I had to wonder, Did I really want to try to dish out in a place that had elected a well-known bigot to office?

23   Well, the question was moot; I didn't want a job located farther than I could comfortably commute by foot or by bike. And there was no way I was walking or cycling out to Metairie every day. Especially since I was already within walking distance of hundreds of New Orleans restaurants.

24   Besides, I remained confident I could find a job in town. After all, when Levon Helm, drummer of The Band, quit Bob Dylan's first electric tour in 1965 because he was tired of the audiences' booing, he fled to New Orleans and got a job dishing at The Court of Two Sisters restaurant. (Never mind that he was fired after a day and a half when he was caught eating an entrée.) And when Alex Chilton (of the Box Tops and Big Star fame) dropped out of the music scene, he also wound up dishing in the Quarter. If those two white boys could do it, why couldn't I?

25   My faith began to waver. After all, there was that time in San Diego several years before when I had searched high and low for dish work. At a couple

restaurants that flew The Sign, the managers wouldn't even give me an application. In fact, they both offered me instead a position as a *waiter*! And not one, but two boss-guys straight out told me they only hired Mexicans to wash their dishes. One explained he had "less trouble with them"—meaning it was easier to keep them in their place. Raises and promotions were neither asked for nor offered. But because I was white, it was assumed I'd skip out on them within weeks, when a better opportunity came along.

26 Well, it was true—I would've skipped out within weeks. But it wouldn't have had anything to do with better opportunities, just the same opportunity in some other restaurant in some other town.

27 Then it happened. I got a call from a chef at a restaurant in the French Quarter. When I'd handed him an application the week before, he'd shown no interest in hiring me, despite my concerted effort to not yawn or scratch (the slouching was unavoidable). Now he was saying to come in, that he had a job for me.

28 As I trekked down to Decatur Street, I was pumped with excitement. The naysayers and myth-perpetuators were going to be proven wrong. A white man *could* find a dish job in New Orleans.

29 In his office at the huge restaurant, the chef grinned as if he was as thrilled as I was about the job.

30 "You'll be in charge of the other dishwashers—six to ten of them on any given night," he said.

31 I didn't understand.

32 "You'll be head dishwasher," he explained.

33 *Head* dishwasher? Me? I barely managed to be the head of myself, let alone heading anyone else. Besides, as a suds buster who hated authority, was I really expected to push around my fellow workers?

34 I was stunned silent.

35 The shock continued as he gave me a brief tour of the dishrooms located on two different floors. Indeed, all the other dishers were black. Why hadn't he promoted one of them? They obviously knew the setup better than I did. Instead, he hired a white guy to be the head of a bunch of black guys.

36 "Yeah, this'll work out great," he said as he glanced at my application again. "You say you're a hard worker, so this'll be a good job for you."

37 That socked me like a punch in the gut. Never in my life—not in the deepest darkest moments of sarcasm, not as a practical joke and especially not as a story line on an application—had I ever called myself "a hard worker." If anything, I took great pains to never sell myself as a hard worker. This dude was clearly delusional.

38 Still, it *was* a dish job. Deeply confused, I said nothing. As I left, the chef told me to return the next afternoon at five o'clock to begin head-dishwashing.

39 The following day was spent agonizing over what to do. Still desperate to dish in New Orleans—to make Louisiana state #14 in my quest—and in need of cash to get traveling again, here was my opportunity. As five o'clock approached, I started walking—not to the Quarter, though. Instead, I wandered through Mid-City, resuming my search for the all-important window signs. And it was a good walk. That liberating feeling of discarding a job, I discovered, could be achieved without even ever gaining it. Then, to top it off, in three

different spots along a one-block stretch of South Carrollton Avenue, I picked up nine coins—37 cents total. Not too shabby!

40   A couple days later, a listing appeared in the want ads of the *Times-Picayune:*

Dishwashers wanted for one-day jobs
Cash $$$ paid per day

41   Now *that* was the gig for me. I was so impatient to get started that instead of hoofing it, I bummed a ride from Cheryl. When we pulled up to the listed address, Cheryl looked at the seedy characters in front of the building. They were lounging on the sidewalk and drinking brown-bagged booze.

42   "You're not about to sell your plasma, are you?" she asked.

43   "No," I said. "At least I don't think so."

44   I got out, skirted the sidewalk loafers and reached through a steel gate to knock on the door. A rough-looking mug opened the door and gruffly asked, "Yeah? What d'ya want?"

45   The whole scene felt clandestine, so I said, "The newspaper ad sent me."

46   "Oh, all right." His scowl softened. "C'mon in."

47   He unlocked the gate, introduced himself as Terry and led me into the office. He explained that this was where companies involved in shady work like asbestos removal found their cheap labor. Now the operation was expanding its labor pool to crack the dishwashing market. Since us dishers often shook off our jobs without notice, this place was assembling a crew of dishmen. Now jilted employers would have a place to pick up last-minute replacements. As the hopeful laborers waited for job assignments, they hung around in the hiring hall and out on the curb.

48   The plan was captivating. I could already see my role: the on-call, troubleshooting pearl diver—wherever and whenever dishes needed washing, I'd be there (though, inevitably, I'd be late).

49   It reminded me of the scene in Charles Bukowski's book *Factotum.* The author's alter ego, Henry Chinaski, gets hired at a downtown Los Angeles employment office to answer the phone and hire the dishwashers. On his first day, he needs four dishwashers from among the forty bums waiting outside the office. So he throws four pennies in the air. Whoever retrieves a penny, gets a job. Then, as Bukowski writes:

> Bodies jumped and fell, clothing ripped, there were curses, one man screamed, there were several fistfights. Then the lucky four came forward, one at a time, breathing heavily, each with a penny.

50   "Where do you need me today?" I asked.

51   "Nowhere," Terry said, "We need to sign on the dishwashers first before we can start offering to hire them out."

52   In the meantime, he said, he could assign me other jobs. I gave Terry—word for word—the same reply I'd overheard another dishing applicant give only minutes earlier:

53   "Nah, none of that heavy labor stuff for me, just dishwashing."

54   The next morning, I awoke full of confidence from having found a job. But the thought of sitting around a hiring hall wasn't nearly as enticing as the prospect

of poking around a place I hadn't yet explored. While considering whether New Orleans could ever serve as my permanent home, I figured—if so—it'd be fun to live near a ferry route. So I caught the Jackson Avenue ferry across the Mississippi River to Gretna. The town, with its runty cottages, was pleasant. But it was too quaint to justify living in just to ride a ferry every day. I didn't get around to calling the hiring hall until late in the afternoon. Terry answered and reminded me that in order to be hired out, I had to either be at the hall in person or I had to call in the morning.

55   "And no," he said. "There ain't no dishwashing jobs yet."

56   The next morning I caught the Algiers ferry across to the neighborhood of Algiers. Though it was sleepier than even the most drowsy of New Orleans neighborhoods, its ferry sailed straight to the French Quarter. So it won my vote for most-likely-place-for-me-to-live-in-New-Orleans because it was just a short ferry ride from so many potential dish jobs.

57   After my venture into Algiers, I called Terry. He yelled at me, "Look! You ain't gonna get any jobs by calling in the afternoon!"

58   My morning-time strolls and late-afternoon check-ins persisted one more day. That last time I called, Terry didn't bother answering my question. Upon hearing my voice, he hung up. My career as the on-call, troubleshooting pearl diver was over before I was ever called upon to shoot a single trouble.

59   Now I was really in a pickle. As summer neared and the punishing New Orleans humidity increased, I became hell-bent to get out of town. But I had no money for a bus ticket. So, to pick up some cash lickety-split, I guinea-pigged it. At a research clinic, drugs were put in my mouth and in my veins as doctors and nurses sat around to see if I'd get a fever. I was one of the lucky ones; there were no reactions to note. I survived the placebo with enough dough to get myself moving.

60   Cheryl, her boyfriend and everyone else I knew in town rubbed it in. This white boy still hadn't dished in New Orleans. Louisiana wouldn't be conquered state #14 after all.

61   I left town defeated. ✳

Exercises

Do not refer to the selection for Exercises A–C unless your instructor directs you to do so.

A. DETERMINING THE MAIN IDEA AND PURPOSE

Choose the best answer.

_____   **1.** The main idea of the selection is that

    a. racism is a persistent problem in the restaurant industry.

    b. it's a myth that certain jobs in New Orleans' restaurants are reserved only for blacks.

<ol start="3" type="a" style="list-style-type: none;">
<li>**c.** dishwashing is a low-paying job suitable for transients who want plenty of free time to do their own thing.</li>
<li>**d.** the writer was ultimately defeated in his quest to get a job washing dishes in New Orleans, confirming the idea that these jobs are generally reserved for blacks.</li>
</ol>

_____ **2.** The writer's purpose is to

- **a.** describe his experiences looking for various dishwashing jobs in New Orleans.
- **b.** describe the conditions for entry-level workers in New Orleans.
- **c.** examine relations between whites and blacks in the New Orleans restaurant industry.
- **d.** argue for increased oversight of the restaurant industry concerning wages and working conditions.

B. COMPREHENDING MAIN IDEAS

Choose the correct answer.

_____ **1.** Initially, Jordan wasn't hired for dishwashing jobs because he

- **a.** didn't demonstrate sufficient enthusiasm or desperation.
- **b.** had no experience.
- **c.** was a convicted pedophile.
- **d.** had compiled a poor employment record.

_____ **2.** While searching for a job as a dishwasher, Jordan amused himself with a diversion—

- **a.** panhandling for spare change.
- **b.** watching people's reactions when he asked for job.
- **c.** picking up spare change on the street or in pay phones.
- **d.** inventing creative references for his job applications.

_____ **3.** Jordan learned that dishwashers in New Orleans generally

- **a.** must sign on with a crew because absenteeism among dishwashers is so high.
- **b.** are either black or Mexican, making it difficult for whites to get these jobs.
- **c.** must have experience, preferably in a large hospital or in the military.
- **d.** have little opportunity for advancement to become busboys or waiters.

_____ **4.** Jordan recounts the story of Levon Helm, drummer for The Band, who was fired from his dishwashing job at The Court of Two Sisters restaurant because he

- **a.** was caught stealing money from the cash register.
- **b.** was accused of making racist comments to his fellow employees.
- **c.** came to work stoned.
- **d.** was caught eating an entrée.

_____ **5.** When Jordan was called in to apply for a job at a French Quarter restaurant, he

   a. wasn't hired because he had too much experience and therefore would have to be paid more.
   b. wasn't hired because he didn't have any experience.
   c. was immediately offered the job of head dishwasher overseeing a crew of black dishwashers.
   d. was promised a job that later was rescinded.

_____ **6.** After answering a newspaper ad and talking to Terry, the hiring agent, Jordan learned that the operation was going to supply laborers to employers who wanted

   a. cheap labor to do shady work like removing asbestos.
   b. a crew of dishwashers available to replace those who failed to show up for work.
   c. illegal immigrants who were willing to work for low wages and no benefits.
   d. all of the above.
   e. only a and b.

COMPREHENSION SCORE

Score your answers for Exercises A and B as follows:

A. No. right _____ × 2 = _____

B. No. right _____ × 1 = _____

Total points from A and B _____ × 10 = _____ percent

C. SEQUENCING

These sentences from one paragraph in the selection have been scrambled. Read the sentences and choose the sequence that puts them back into logical order. Do not refer to the original selection.

1 Indeed, all the other dishers were black. **2** Instead, he hired a white guy to be the head of a bunch of black guys. **3** The shock continued as he gave me a brief tour of the dishrooms located on two different floors. **4** Why hadn't he promoted one of them? **5** They obviously knew the setup better than I did.

_____ Which of the following represents the correct sequence for these sentences?

   a. 3, 1, 4, 5, 2
   b. 1, 3, 2, 5, 4
   c. 3, 2, 4, 1, 5
   d. Correct as written.

You may refer to the selection as you work through the remaining exercises.

D. LOCATING SUPPORTING DETAILS

For each main idea stated here, find one relevant detail that supports it.

1. Some of the New Orleans neighborhoods that Jordan walked through were

   decrepit. _____

2. Jordan thought that taking a job as a dishwasher would not be racist; in fact,

   he would be helping a black job seeker because . . . _____

   _____

For each main idea stated here, find two relevant details that support it.

3. At one restaurant, described in paragraph 25, Jordan was offered a job as a
   waiter. The bosses told him that they hired only Mexicans as dishwashers

   because they were "less trouble" meaning that . . . _____

   _____

4. Jordan never returned to the restaurant whose chef had hired him as head

   dishwasher because . . . _____

   _____

You may refer to the selection as you work through the remaining exercises.

E. INTERPRETING MEANING

Where appropriate, write your answers to these questions in your own
words.

1. When Jordan uses the word "creative" to describe his list of job references
   (circus midget, retired pederast, judo champion, etc.), what does he mean?

   _____

2. Why does Jordan object to being called a writer? (See paragraphs 5–10.)

   _____

   _____

3. In paragraphs 20–21, Jordan recounts how David Duke, the former KKK
   leader, became an "Aryan," meaning in this context a white racist. What

   made Duke come to this realization? _____

   _____

4. Why, above all, did Jordan want a job dishwashing so badly in New Orleans?

   (See paragraph 39.) _____

   _____

5. Look again at the excerpt from Charles Bukowski's book *Factotum*, mentioned in paragraph 49. What does the quotation tell us about dishwashing jobs for the bums looking for a job? Why did Henry Chinaski throw pennies

in the air to choose four workers? _____

_____

_____

F. UNDERSTANDING VOCABULARY

Look through the paragraphs listed below and find a word that matches each definition. Refer to a dictionary if necessary. An example has been done for you.

Ex. moved, switched, redirected [paragraphs 2–3] _____ diverted _____

1. growing and flourishing [2–3] _____

2. avoiding, shunning [17–19] _____

3. surveying, thoroughly examining [17–19] _____

4. irrelevant and insignificant because the situation has already been decided [23–24] _____

5. those who take a pessimistic view of things or deny them [27–33] _____

6. those who prolong or continue believing in an idea [27–33] _____

7. disreputable, squalid, shabby [41–45] _____

8. concealed, done in secret, to hide something illegal [45–48] _____

9. those whose employees didn't show up [47–49] _____

10. enticing, attractive [48–49] _____

11. a Latin phrase (two words) meaning a second self [49–50] _____

12. an inactive substance used in a medical experiment, sugar pill [59–60] _____

G. LANGUAGE ANALYSIS—UNDERSTANDING SLANG

Jordan uses several informal and slang words and phrases. Consider these examples in their context and then write the meaning of each in the space provided. The paragraph number where each occurs is included.

1. to pound the pavement [paragraph 2] _____

2. a well-heeled neighborhood [2]

3. to skip out on [25]   _____

4. pumped [28]   _____

5. to top it off [39]   _____

_____

_____

6. gig [41]   _____

7. brown-bagged booze [41]   _____

8. in a pickle [59]   _____

9. lickety-split [59]   _____

10. guinea-pigged it [59]   _____

_____

H. TOPICS FOR DISCUSSION

1. Why was it so difficult for Jordan to get a job, as a white, washing dishes in New Orleans?

2. To what degree are certain jobs in your community dominated by members of a particular ethnic or immigrant group? To what extent is this simply a matter of self-selection—meaning that members of a particular group flock to jobs where others like them have gone before? To what extent is it a subtle form of racism?

I. TOPICS FOR WRITING

1. Write a short narrative in which you describe an unsuccessful job search.

2. What's the worst job you have ever had? Write a short essay describing the job itself (duties, working conditions, and so on), including the specific reasons that it was so unpleasant.

Exploring Related Web Sites

- Read more about Pete Jordan and dishwashing jobs at his Web site:

  www.dishwasherpete.com

- This financial blog has lots of commentary on entry-level jobs as well as other subjects pertaining to Target and Wal-Mart.

  http://allfinancialmatters.com/2008/03/24/an-interesting-piece-on-target/ #comment-260418

3

JOE ABBOTT

To Kill a Hawk

Joe Abbott is a native of northern California's Humboldt County, the setting for the events that are described in this narrative retrospective. Before becoming a full-time reading teacher at Butte College in northern California, Abbott was actively involved with environmental groups, including the Año Nuevo Interpretive Association. (Año Nuevo, north of Santa Cruz, California, is home to a large population of elephant seals.) This article was first published in the Chico News and Review. *Abbott writes this about his piece: "I believe there are no issues more pressing than environmental concerns. In our confinement on this lonely and small planet we have to learn to live with the other species that share our existence, and must learn whether our purposes are altruistic or selfish—because it is increasingly apparent that our fates are inexorably connected. 'To Kill a Hawk' explains how I came to that belief."*

Vocabulary Preview

WORD PARTS

ir-, irrevocable [paragraph 3] The prefix *-ir* is a variant of two more common prefixes that indicate negation, *un-* and *in-*. *Ir-* is used to make words beginning with the letter *r* negative, as in *irrevocable, irrational,* and *irresponsible. Irrevocable* is pronounced with the accent on the second syllable: ĭ-rĕv′ə-kə-bəl. Difficult words like this one are more accessible if you learn to break them down, like this:

ir- ("not") + *voc* ("to call") + able (able to) = not able to be called back, not able to be reversed

WORD FAMILIES

cogn-, recognition [paragraph 14] When he saw the redtail hawk shot, Abbott experienced a shock of *recognition,* something that he had always known existed. The root of this noun is *cogn-,* from the Latin verb *cognoscere,* meaning "to know." Thus, when we recognize something, literally we know it again. Here are some other examples of words in this family:

cognitive	the mental process by which knowledge is acquired
cognizant	being aware, fully informed, conscious
precognition	knowing something before it happens
incognito	a person who does not want to be recognized

You will meet the word *connoisseur* in Selection 6. Based on the information provided above, if someone is a food connoisseur, what does that mean? _____

_____

Other words you will need to know:

poaching   illegally taking fish or game, either by trespassing or by killing more than is legally allowed.
gastropods   abalone are a prized type of shellfish found along the California coast. Like snails and limpets, abalone are *gastropods*, from Latin *gastro-* ("stomach") and *pod* ("foot" or "footlike"), so called because their means of locomotion is this muscular foot.

JOE ABBOTT

To Kill a Hawk

1   So now we have revelation: ex-CIA agent claims Earth First! has engaged genetic scientists for development of a doomsday virus to rid the planet of pesky Homo sapiens infestation. It's an interesting story, although it would be more interesting to locate someone who believed anything these guys said anymore.

2   But the question of spook veracity aside, I recently spent an evening rereading (spiritual founder of Earth First!) Edward Abbey's *Desert Solitaire.* In the chapter "Serpents of Paradise," I came across an intriguing line: " . . . I'd rather kill a man than a snake," Abbey wrote. This struck a familiar tone for me, so I reached for something else I recently read, Robinson Jeffers' selected poems.

3   Sure enough, I found something in the poem "Hurt Hawks." Jeffers wrote: "I'd sooner, except for the penalties, kill a man than a hawk." A fine poem, as fine as Abbey's desert essays. But such a curious sentiment. As I compared these lines, they reminded me of something I'd forgotten, even though the thing forgotten was the kind of experience, an epiphany, really, that marks a person's life, a moment which designates an irrevocable turning point.

4   The epiphany was in part the result of something that happened the day before. It was summer of 1971, and a dozen friends and I had driven down the breathtakingly steep and tortuous road into Shelter Cove in southern Humboldt County to camp on the black sand beaches. We were pretty young then, and ill-prepared, and we quickly gobbled our meager food supplies. So I and a couple others went down into the cove to poach abalones among the rocks. The tide was ebbing and we didn't have to swim too much in the cold water, and since in those days abalone were a cinch to find before the season opened, we nabbed thirty in an hour or so.

5   Of course thirty abalone is meat enough for sixty people, not a dozen, and because we had no refrigeration and despite stuffing ourselves, gorging on the tasty butter-fried gastropods, most of the abalone went to waste. Since we had no way of preserving them, we buried the lot.

6   I had grown up a hunter and a fisherman, and I suppose I knew a little about the maintenance of fish or animal populations. I mean I'd killed for fun before without regret, yet when I left camp early the next morning I felt some remorse about those wasted abalones.

7   My girlfriend and I had just climbed above a coastal fog on the steep Shelter Cove road in her car, had almost reached the crest where the road forked for the King's Range and Redway, when I noticed a big redtail puffed against the damp and chill of the morning. He was perched atop a huge roadside pine and, although I've always liked to watch hawks despite having shot a couple for no reason, I didn't slow or stop because I didn't want to disturb him. Perhaps I thought a hawk deserves a morning sunning to warm his hollow bones. More likely I identified with the predator.

8   But as we crested the mountain we came upon a red Dodge convertible (I've never forgotten) with two men in it, the passenger standing on his seat. He had a rifle scoped on the redtail.

9   I don't know why the moment touched me. To that point in my life I pretty much thought that whatever anybody else did to an animal was his own business. I stomped the brakes, the tires scrunching to a stop in the gravel. And for some reason I leaned on the horn—anything, to frighten the bird. For a moment it was almost as if I were the bird, that somehow our two fates were intertwined in a way I could not explain. It was like watching somebody hurt someone you love. I still can't explain the suddenness of it.

10   I pressed harder on the horn, but there was no sound. No, my girlfriend's horn hadn't worked for months. I had forgotten.

11   I don't know what the guy must have thought. Perhaps he believed I stopped so I'd not disturb his shot. For a long time (or maybe it seemed that way) the guy scoped the hawk while we just sat there, transfixed on the horrible inevitability of the moment. And then he fired.

12   Writing of such a moment, I realize that it perhaps inspires, even for the most sensitive persons, only a momentary disgust for the senseless act. One hawk of the thousands shot yearly. And this incident occurred so long ago.

13   But at that moment I experienced anger and sadness. Strange emotions for someone convinced that the beasts were on the planet so that humankind might hunt them down. The driver threw the convertible into gear and the two peeled away in a swirl of gravel and dust. I left the car idling in the dirt road and walked back to the cliff alongside the great pine. Looking down the bank I couldn't see the redtail. But I knew he'd been hit; grey fluff still drifted in the chill windless air.

14   Imagine the downy feathers hanging in air a few thousand feet above the ocean, above the steep tawny cliffs descending to the fog-shrouded beach where the abalones rotted in the black sand. Imagine me as I stood on the high cliff, stood looking for the big redtail, the bird no more to lift into the stiff afternoon wind off the ocean as the sun burned over the manzanita and pine-crested heights, the great mountains of the King's Range. Imagine behind my eyes something changing at that moment, a realization of the enormity not of the two men's sin but of my own; the recognition of something I had never suspected although it had ever been before me.

15   And then imagine how I could suddenly have seen those two men in that convertible disappear, heard their tires scramble in the pea gravel as the red convertible in one terrible moment hung in air over the long steep cliffs, heard the men's screams as the car plunged. . . .

16   Rather kill a man than a hawk or snake? I choose to kill none. Yet that morning long ago, for those few moments, without regret I could have heard that car roll down those canyons. I could understand many things that are perhaps as ugly as the death of that redtail. ✳

Joe Abbott, "To Kill a Hawk" from *Chico News and Review* (August 1991). Copyright © 1991 by Joe Abbott. Reprinted with the permission of the author.

Exercises

Do not refer to the selection for Exercises A–C unless your instructor directs you to do so.

A. DETERMINING THE MAIN IDEA AND PURPOSE
Choose the best answer.

_____ 1. The main idea of the selection is that, for the writer, the death of the hawk meant

    a. the end of his adolescence and the beginning of adulthood.

    b. an epiphany or revelation that killing an animal for sport or fun is a senseless, stupid act.

    c. a recognition human and animal lives are equally sacred.

    d. a much worse act than his and his friends' illegal poaching of abalone.

_____ 2. The writer's purpose is to

    a. argue for stricter laws against poaching fish and game, especially of prized species like abalone.

    b. describe how beauty and cruelty are often intertwined in nature.

    c. relate a narrative to show the folly of youth and inexperience.

    d. describe an incident of cruelty and selfishness that forever transformed his thinking.

B. COMPREHENDING MAIN IDEAS
Choose the correct answer.

_____ 1. At the beginning of the selection, Abbott refers to a poem by Robinson Jeffers called "Hurt Hawk," which contains the phrase,

    a. "I'd sooner kill a man than a hawk."

    b. "I'd rather kill a snake than a hawk."

    c. "I'd rather die than kill a hawk."

    d. "I'd sooner kill a hawk than a man."

_____ **2.** Abbott relates that the abalone along the Humboldt coast were easy to catch because

    a. they moved slowly and therefore were easy targets.
    b. they were brightly colored and therefore easy to spot.
    c. the season hadn't opened yet so they were plentiful.
    d. they came onto the beach to spawn.

_____ **3.** Since Abbott and his friends had no way of preserving the extra abalone, they

    a. gave them to another group of campers on the beach.
    b. threw them back into the ocean.
    c. fed them to the seagulls.
    d. buried them in the sand.

_____ **4.** Abbott writes that while he was growing up, he

    a. used to fish and hunt.
    b. was a vegetarian.
    c. believed that hunting and fishing were unethical.
    d. studied animal ecology and management of animal populations.

_____ **5.** After watching the driver of the car taking aim to shoot the hawk, Abbott

    a. decided to report the man for illegal hunting.
    b. searched in vain for the bird in order to save it.
    c. felt as if his fate and the bird's fate were somehow intertwined.
    d. pushed the car with its occupants over the cliff.

_____ **6.** Ultimately, the incident of the shooting of the redtail hawk represented the shock of recognition, namely that their poaching of abalone the day before was

    a. ethically quite different from the man's shooting the hawk.
    b. as ugly and enormous a sin as the man's shooting the hawk.
    c. much worse than the man's shooting the hawk because it was done out of ignorance.
    d. not as morally wrong as the man's shooting the hawk because they needed the food.

COMPREHENSION SCORE

Score your answers for Exercises A and B as follows:

A. No. right _____ × 2 = _____

B. No. right _____ × 1 = _____

Total points from A and B _____ × 10 = _____ percent

C. SEQUENCING

These sentences from one paragraph in the selection have been scrambled. Read the sentences and choose the sequence that puts them back into logical order. Do not refer to the original selection.

1 One hawk of the thousands shot yearly. **2** And this incident occurred so long ago. **3** Writing of such a moment, I realize that it perhaps inspires, even for the most sensitive persons, only a momentary disgust for the senseless act.

_____ Which of the following represents the correct sequence for these sentences?

    a. 3, 2, 1
    b. 1, 3, 2
    c. 3, 1, 2
    d. Correct as written.

You may refer to the selection as you work through the remaining exercises.

D. DISTINGUISHING BETWEEN MAIN IDEAS AND SUPPORTING DETAILS

Label the following statements from the selection as follows: MI if it represents a _main idea_ and SD if it represents a _supporting detail_.

_____ **1.** The epiphany that Abbott experienced was the result of the preceding day's poaching incident.

_____ **2.** The group camped on the black sand beaches and ate their meager food supply.

_____ **3.** The group poached 30 abalone they found among the rocks, but since they had no way to preserve those they didn't need, they buried them.

_____ **4.** Although Abbott had grown up hunting and fishing, he felt some degree of remorse for the wasted abalone.

E. INTERPRETING MEANING

Where appropriate, write your answers to these questions in your own words.

1. What is the connection between Edward Abbey's line in "Serpents of Paradise"

and the line in Robinson Jeffers's poem (see paragraphs 2–3)?_____

_____

2. In paragraph 3, Abbott uses the word "epiphany" to describe the moment that changes his life. Consult a dictionary and then write a definition in your

own words. _____

3. What hint of a change occurs in Abbott's thinking in paragraph 6 as a result of the poaching incident? _____

4. Why was the sight of the man's scoping the redtail hawk and his subsequent shooting of it so terrible for the writer to witness? _____

_____

_____

F. UNDERSTANDING VOCABULARY

Look through the paragraphs listed below and find a word that matches each definition. Refer to a dictionary if necessary. An example has been done for you.

Ex. truthfulness [paragraphs 1–2]   _____veracity_____

1. Judgment Day [1–2]   _____

2. unable to be reversed [2–3]   _____

3. arousing curiosity and interest [2–3]   _____

4. a sudden revelation or realization [3–4]   _____

5. twisting, winding, bending [4]   _____

6. stuffing with food, devouring greedily [4–5]   _____

7. reached the top of [7–8]   _____

8. motionless, with amazement, fear, terror, etc. [11–12] _____

G. USING VOCABULARY

In parentheses before each sentence are some inflected forms of words from the selection. Study the context and the sentence. Then write the correct form in the space provided.

1. (*reveal, revelation, revelatory*) Abbott experienced an intense epiphany, a sudden _____ as he watched the man shoot the redtail hawk.

2. (*remorse, remorseful, remorsefully*) After the poaching incident, Abbott contemplated the significance of what he and his friends had done with _____.

3. (*prey, predator, predation, predatory*) Redtail hawks are birds of _____.

4. (*inevitable, inevitably, inevitability*) The worst part about watching the shooting of the hawk was that its death was _____.

5. (*inspire, inspiring, inspired, inspiration*) For the writer, the two incidents— poaching the abalone and the death of the hawk—were intertwined, _____ horror and disgust.

H. TOPICS FOR DISCUSSION

1. Why doesn't Abbott try to justify their poaching of the abalone by saying that their food supplies were meager and that they would run out of food?
2. What is going through the writer's mind as he watches the hawk's feathers floating in the air high above the ocean?

I. TOPICS FOR WRITING

1. Write a narrative essay in which you explain the circumstances leading to an epiphany of your own.
2. Abbott seems to suggest that these intertwined experiences on that day on the Humboldt County coast changed his thinking about hunting and fishing. Write an essay in which you examine your own thoughts about hunting and fishing—for sport, not for the survival of a family.

Exploring Related Web Sites

- Poaching is an enormous problem in Africa, where both subsistence farmers and commercial poachers illegally hunt animals on the world's endangered species list, for example, elephants, lions, tigers, certain types of antelope, and rhinoceros. Here is one Web site devoted to discussing this issue:

  www.myacreofafrica.org

- What laws against poaching exist in your state? Is poaching a problem where you live? Read about this issue and its effect on your state's environment and animal population. Using Google or your favorite search engine, type in the following:

  poaching laws, name of state (Example: poaching laws, Iowa)

- California abalone is a prized delicacy. Abalone meat costs well over $60 per pound, and it is almost impossible to find in stores. Skin divers hunt for abalone off the coast of California, and the laws are strict about how many abalone can be legally taken. Here is a beginning Web site with lots of information about this mollusk delicacy:

  http://en.wikipedia.org/wiki/Abalone

ROSE GUILBAULT

School Days

Rose Castillo Guilbault was born in Mexico and later immigrated with her family to the United States, where they settled near King City, a small farming town in California's Salinas Valley, known as the lettuce capital of the world. Guilbault has had a varied journalistic career both in print and television. Currently, she is vice president of Corporate Communications and Publishing for the California State Automobile Association. This excerpt is from her recent book, Farmworker's Daughter: Growing Up Mexican in America *(2005), which recounts her memories of growing up in Nogales, Mexico, and King City, California, from a bicultural perspective.*

Vocabulary Preview

WORD PARTS

This selection contains three useful word parts—two prefixes and one suffix. Prefixes and suffixes are parts of words that can't stand alone. A prefix is attached to the beginning of a root; it affects or changes the meaning of the root. A suffix, on the other hand, is attached to the end of a root and usually changes the word's grammatical part of speech, as you will see in these three examples:

em- [paragraph 9] This prefix signifies "becoming" or "causing to be." Thus, the word *empowered* means "causing one to have power." Sometimes this prefix is spelled *en-*, depending on the first letter of the root word. You can easily determine the meaning of these words by just looking at the root following the prefix: *encourage, entrap, enliven, embitter*.

sub- [paragraph 45] The prefix *sub-* from the Latin means "under" and *conscious* means "aware." Therefore, one's *subconscious* is a partial sort of awareness because it is submerged below full consciousness. This prefix is easy to recognize in words like *submarine* ("under the ocean") or *subplot* ("a secondary plot"), but it is less easy to detect in other words. Look up the following four words in the dictionary and write their meanings in the space provided. If "under" is clearly suggested, write "yes" next to the definition. If not, write "no."

subterranean _____

subjugate _____

subordinate _____

subjective _____

_____

-ish [paragraph 3] In describing her complaints as "childish," Guilbault means that they were immature in the sense of being foolish or silly. This word ends with the useful suffix *-ish*, or "having the qualities or characteristics of"—referring to the root word. Thus, *childish* means having the qualities of a child, in a negative sense, whereas *childlike* means having the qualities of a child, but in a positive sense. Some other words with the prefix *-ish* are *sheepish, sluggish,* and *mannish*. This particular suffix changes the root noun into an adjective.

WORD FAMILIES

assimilation [paragraph 5] The process of assimilation refers to the gradual adoption by a minority group of the customs of the prevailing culture. The root *similar* is in the middle of this word, meaning "same" (from the Latin root *similes*, "like"). Thus, when one becomes assimilated into American society, he or she becomes "like" an American. Besides the obvious word *similar*, here are some other words with this root. Write their meaning in the space provided. Check a dictionary if you are unsure.

simile _____

facsimile _____

verisimilitude _____

ROSE GUILBAULT

School Days

1   I hated school. I hated leaving home every day. Home was safe, warm, and constant, without the conflicts I had to endure in the outside world. But I couldn't tell my mother that. She was so full of optimism.

2   "Oh, you're going to learn so many things. American schools are the best in the world! You'll be so smart because you'll know two languages." Her face shone with enthusiasm when she said these things, and I didn't want to dampen her spirits.

3   Her words suppressed my childish complaints. But even if I had dared share my feelings with her, I didn't yet have the vocabulary to explain the bigger issues that were the real source of pain, nor would I understand them myself for years to come. At six years of age, I lived in a world of confusion—the language, the kids, the culture spun around me like a vortex. Within one year I had moved away from family and the stability of a routine to a foreign country with a

foreign language. Then we moved from town and our newly established relationships with friends and neighbors to an isolated farm where I had to readjust again and, now, school.

4   Each day presented challenges and I had to sort through them by myself. Even if I wanted to ask for help, what exactly would I ask for? Help me understand what the teacher is saying, or stop the kids from treating me like an oddball?

5   I intuitively knew that the person I leaned on for everything—my mother—would not be able to help me. She relied heavily on her own experiences as a basis of understanding the world, and just as the Wizard of Oz had nothing in his bag for Dorothy, she had nothing to smooth this assimilation for me. Once I stepped outside my door, I was all alone and had to fend for myself. The only thing I feared more than school was disappointing my mother, so I hid my anxieties.

6   Every morning, she walked me the full two miles to the school bus stop and stayed with me until the bus arrived. The boss's boys walked by themselves and stood on the opposite side of the road, not talking to us while we waited. It set the tone for a curious relationship. They weren't unfriendly, but neither were they forthcoming. Their whole family couldn't decide whether to treat us as subordinate employees or as neighbors.

7   I was glad to have my mother with me. Cattle roamed on one side of the road and the bulls liked to bellow and chase us along the fence. Their snorting and hoofing terrified me.

8   Leaving my mother and boarding the bus brought up still more fears. The big yellow bus was filled with high school kids who were to be dropped off first before we continued to the elementary school. The older kids laughed at me, and I couldn't understand most of what was being said. They'd often not let me sit next to them, stacking schoolbooks alongside empty seats when they saw me approach. I learned to automatically walk quickly to the back and sit by myself. I found all of this confusing and humiliating.

9   At school things were no better. The teacher's instructions would wash over me like a wave; I heard the sounds but didn't understand their purpose. But eventually, slowly and unexpectedly the English language revealed itself to me. Every new word and every new definition was like lifting a layer of film from my eyes, giving me clarity to see the world around me. Words empowered me and I pursued their secrets assiduously. At home all I had was an ancient English/Spanish dictionary my father had used to teach himself English, but its tiny print and archaic language did more to obscure meaning than shed light on it. I actually learned more from the grocery store–bought encyclopedias, which I read cover to cover one summer. By the end of first grade I was scholastically on track: I knew the alphabet, wrote in block print, and could read the "Dick and Jane" books. By second grade, my English was much improved. My interest in books also heightened with the acquisition of a library card, and it helped that the library was conveniently located across the street from San Lorenzo Elementary School. I loved the feel and smell of hardbound books at the library. I delighted in sitting quietly, trying to decipher the mysteries between their pages, mainly by interpreting the illustrations.

10   But for all my struggles in the classroom, my greatest challenges occurred on the playground. The girls talked about things I knew the words for but had no point of reference on. They talked about birthday parties with cake and games like pin the tail on the donkey and musical chairs, barbecues with hot dogs and root beer, and toys I'd never heard of.

11   One day Mona said we should bring our dolls to play with at recess. I wanted desperately to fit in, so I stuffed an old baby doll—the only doll I owned—into a paper bag.

12   "Why are you taking that paper bag to school?" my mother asked.

13   I knew she wouldn't understand why I'd want to take my doll, so I fibbed. "The teacher asked us to bring our dolls."

14   My mother raised an eyebrow but chose not to pursue the matter.

15   At recess, the other girls all pulled out their dolls. It made me want to laugh out loud—they'd all brought the very same one! I proudly pulled out my baby doll. Nobody had one like her!

16   "What is that?" Mona scrunched her nose at my doll. "Don't you have a Barbie?"

17   The other little girls twittered. What was a Barbie? I wondered. And why was my doll looked down on? I felt embarrassed and quickly stuffed my unworthy toy back into the paper bag. I would not be invited to play with them again. Nor would I be invited to Mona's or any of the other girls' birthday parties.

18   And that's why I hated school. Cultural gaffes were far more difficult to overcome than language gaps. I felt like an outsider, and I would not be able to shake that sense of alienation throughout my school years in King City.

19   My mother tried her best to be supportive. Surely she sensed my disaffection when I trudged home down the long road, looking weary from another day in the outside world.

20   "My teacher Mrs. Lewis doesn't like me," I confided once. "I'm always in trouble because she says I talk too much."

21   "Do you?" my mother asked gently.

22   "No. I just answer the girl next to me, but I get in trouble, not her."

23   The following week my mother insisted I take a tray of homemade enchiladas to Mrs. Lewis. I had to carry them on the school bus wrapped in a brown grocery bag. Even the high school kids couldn't hide their curiosity.

24   "What's in the bag?" they asked over and over.

25   I was mortified. What would they think if I told them I was taking food for my teacher? I'd seen some kids bring apples, but never an entree!

26   I refused to talk and huddled in the corner of the bus by myself, clutching my package.

27   "She's a retard," a high school boy said disgustedly. And that, mercifully, stopped the questions.

28   Once we reached the grammar school I nervously walked straight to my classroom, avoiding the playground. I arrived breathless. Anxious thoughts popped into my head. What if Mrs. Lewis was disgusted and threw the dish into the trash can. Or worse, acted superior and asked, "What is this? Does your family actually eat this?" I would not be able to bear it if Mrs. Lewis expressed any form of rejection toward my mother's offering. I would simply never go to school again!

29   "Why, what's this? It's not time to come in yet." Mrs. Lewis looked up from her desk when she heard me close the door.

30   "My mother sent you this." I thrust the package in front of me.

31   She put on the glasses that hung from a gold chain and often rested on her ample bosom, and strode toward me. Mrs. Lewis was plump but moved quickly.

32   She took the wrinkled package and unwrapped it carefully on her desk.

33   "Enchiladas!" she cried out. "I love enchiladas! How did your mother know?"

34   I shrugged happily. How *did* my mother know?

35   "Bless her heart," Mrs. Lewis clapped her hands together. "Homemade enchiladas!"

36   From that day I can honestly say I was treated differently. Mrs. Lewis was more patient and attentive after the gift.

37   But not all situations could be solved with homemade enchiladas. I wanted my mother to be a part of the classroom culture. I wanted her to be like the popular kids' mothers, to be a room mother so I would fit in with my classmates. But she couldn't because she didn't drive or speak English. Another teacher suggested she make cupcakes for classroom celebrations instead. I thought this presented a great opportunity to be accepted by the class. I had observed how kids whose mothers made cupcakes were given special stature by the others.

38   It didn't work out quite so easily, though.

39   "I don't know what a cupcake is," my mother said, perplexed.

40   "It's like a little cake. But it's in a wrapper," I tried to explain.

41   "I can make empanadas for your party. They're probably similar," she offered.

42   Now, I knew there was no similarity between empanadas and cupcakes other than their both being desserts, but my mother insisted I ask my teacher if she could bring them. I had a bad feeling about it, but I went ahead and asked anyway.

43   "Oh no, dear," Mrs. Steussy demurred. "The children only eat American things. Have her bring cupcakes."

44   Mama learned to make cupcakes by deciphering a recipe from her new Betty Crocker cookbook. The other mothers baked theirs in colored papers or pretty tinfoil cups and decorated them with candy and little umbrellas or flags or plastic figures identifying the occasion. If it was St. Patrick's Day, the cupcakes were green with little leprechauns on top. For St. Valentine's Day, white-frosted cupcakes would be decorated with red candy hearts and coordinated red foil cups.

45   But my mother's cupcakes never turned out like the other mothers'. Hers looked like pale muffins haphazardly spread with a glob of thin, runny white frosting (made from C&H confectioner's sugar and not Fluffy Frosting Mix). My classmates looked at the box lined with wax paper instead of colored tinfoil like the others and whispered "yuck." A knot formed in my throat and I silently swore I'd never ask my mother to make anything for class ever again. It was the beginning of a subconscious effort to keep my private life and school life separate. If the other kids didn't know about my home life, they would assume I was like them. I could be American at school just like everybody else. And as long as anyone who really mattered never came to my house—which was not difficult since we lived way out in the country—they'd never know the truth. ✳

Exercises

Do not refer to the selection for Exercises A–C unless your instructor directs you to do so.

A. DETERMINING THE MAIN IDEA AND PURPOSE

Choose the best answer.

_____ 1. The main idea of the selection is the writer's discovery that

    a. assimilation is much more than simply learning a new language and customs.

    b. she learned to assimilate at school but to keep her private life at home invisible and separate.

    c. humiliation and rejection were painful but necessary first steps on the road to becoming assimilated.

    d. her mother's encouragement and support helped her to endure the alienation she first experienced at school.

_____ 2. The writer's purpose is to

    a. complain about the lack of support young immigrant children receive at school.

    b. suggest ways that immigrant children can successfully conquer their fears and sense of alienation.

    c. criticize her parents for not doing more to help her fit in better.

    d. relate her experiences and feelings of rejection, alienation, and accommodation as she tried in vain to become accepted.

B. COMPREHENDING MAIN IDEAS

Choose the correct answer.

_____ 1. When Guilbault announced that she hated school, she said her mother expressed

    a. similar fears and uncertainties.

    b. optimism and encouragement.

    c. indifference and lack of interest.

    d. feelings of conflict and ambivalence.

_____ 2. On the school bus, the high school students

    a. welcomed her and asked her to sit with them.

    b. moved their seats when they saw her get on the bus.

    c. laughed at her and refused to let her share their seats.

    d. helped her with her homework and taught her new English words.

_____ 3. As she describes her status as a recent immigrant, Guilbault's greatest challenges lay

    a. in the classroom.

    b. at home, with her parents.

      c. on the school bus.

      d. on the playground.

_____ **4.** Guilbault's feelings of being an outsider, of being alienated were particularly reinforced

      a. when the other girls laughed at her doll.

      b. when the other children made fun of her English.

      c. at birthday parties where she didn't understand the games.

      d. when her teacher refused to give her extra help with her studies.

_____ **5.** Mrs. Lewis, Guilbault's teacher, reacted to the gift of homemade enchiladas with

      a. genuine pleasure.

      b. false pleasure.

      c. repugnance, disgust.

      d. curiosity.

_____ **6.** A final humiliating experience occurred when Guilbault's mother

      a. made empanadas for the class.

      b. made cupcakes for the class.

      c. invited some of her daughter's classmates home for a party.

      d. came to school to help in the classroom.

COMPREHENSION SCORE

Score your answers for Exercises A and B as follows:

A. No. right _____ × 2 = _____

B. No. right _____ × 1 = _____

Total points from A and B _____ × 10 = _____ percent

C. SEQUENCING

These sentences from one paragraph in the selection have been scrambled. Read the sentences and choose the sequence that puts them back into logical order. Do not refer to the original selection.

    1 The only thing I feared more than school was disappointing my mother, so I hid my anxieties. **2** She relied heavily on her own experiences as a basis of understanding the world, and just as the Wizard of Oz had nothing in his bag for Dorothy, she had nothing to smooth this assimilation for me. **3** I intuitively knew that the person I leaned on for everything—my mother—would not be able to help me. **4** Once I stepped outside my door, I was all alone and had to fend for myself.

_____ Which of the following represents the correct sequence for these sentences?

      a. 1, 3, 2, 4

      b. 3, 2, 4, 1

    c. 4, 3, 2, 1
    d. Correct as written

You may refer to the selection as you work through the remaining exercises.

D. LOCATING SUPPORTING DETAILS

For the main idea stated here, find details that support it: "Guilbault faced many unpleasant things when she boarded the school bus each day." [paragraph 8] The second and last ones have been done for you.

1. _____

2. She couldn't understand what the older kids were saying.

3. _____

4. _____

5. She sat by herself in the back of the bus.

E. UNDERSTANDING VOCABULARY

Look through the paragraphs listed below and find a word that matches each definition. Refer to a dictionary if necessary. An example has been done for you.

Ex. put an end to, curtailed [paragraphs 2–3]   _____ suppressed _____

 1. depress, diminish [2–3]   _____

 2. to manage by oneself, without help [phrase 5–6]   _____

 3. read, interpret, figure out [9]   _____

 4. diligently, persistently [9]   _____

 5. conceal, hide [9]   _____

 6. giggled [17–18]   _____

 7. clumsy social mistakes [17–19]   _____

 8. describing an experience of humiliation, shame [23–26]   _____

 9. filled with confusion, bewilderment; puzzled [38–42]   _____

10. objected, voiced opposition to [42–44]   _____

F. USING VOCABULARY

In parentheses before each sentence are some inflected forms of words from the selection. Study the context and the sentence. Then write the correct form in the space provided.

1. (*intuition, intuitively*) From simple ＿＿＿＿＿＿ Guilbault learned at an early age that she would have to rely only on herself, and not her mother, to become accepted.

2. (*stability, stable, stabilize*) Guilbault describes the difficulty she experienced moving from a ＿＿＿＿＿＿ and secure environment to one of confusion and alienation.

3. (*anxiety, anxious, anxiously*) Guilbault was particularly ＿＿＿＿＿＿ every morning when she boarded the school bus.

4. (*acquire, acquisition, acquisitive*) When she was able to ＿＿＿＿＿＿ a library card, Guilbault turned to reading for both learning and comfort.

5. (*rely, reliance, reliable*) In her quest to fit in, Guilbault realized early that she had to ＿＿＿＿＿＿ only on herself.

6. (*mercy, merciful, mercifully*) ＿＿＿＿＿＿, Guilbault's teacher accepted the homemade enchiladas with evident pleasure.

G. TOPICS FOR DISCUSSION

1. Guilbault feels an obvious conflict and ambivalence toward her mother and her supportive efforts. What do you think about this conflict? Does Guilbault's realization that she has to go it alone in her quest to assimilate seem cruel or merely realistic?
2. Guilbault is now middle-aged, meaning that her account is set a generation ago. Do immigrant children today face the same cruelty and hostility that Guilbault describes? What cultural factors today suggest that acceptance would be easier?

H. TOPICS FOR WRITING

1. What makes assimilation for immigrants so difficult? Go through the selection again, this time annotating (making notes in the margins) suggested answers to this question. Then write a short essay summarizing what Guilbault has to say about this problem.
2. If you have a friend, relative, or co-worker who has recently immigrated, interview him or her about the kinds of obstacles and problems the person encountered upon arrival. Then write a short essay discussing them. Include the measures the person took to overcome these difficulties.

Exploring Related Web Sites

- It used to be said that America is a melting pot, a nation of immigrants. More recently, some cultural historians have begun to describe America as being more of a salad bowl, where each individual component (ethnic group) is part of a whole but retains its individual cultural traits. What questions are important to consider concerning immigration and assimilation? Begin with these three Web sites to read various points of view.

Thomas M. Sipos, "A Nation of Assimilated Immigrants"

www.enterstageright.com/archive/articles/0605/0605immigrant.htm

Russell Roberts, "Immigration and Assimilation"

www.cafehayek.typepad.com/hayek/2006/05/immigration_and.html

Samuel P. Huntington, "Reconsidering Immigration: Is Mexico a Special Case?"

www.cis.org/articles/2000/back1100.html

- Explore what people have to say about the subject on various blogs. On the home page at Google, click on "more," pull down to "Blogs," type in "immigration" and "assimilation."

5 Still Gullah: A Sea Island Sister Struggles to Preserve the Old Ways

Cornelia Bailey is a resident of Sapelo Island, a barrier island off the coast of Georgia. Sapelo is one of the last enclaves of Gullah culture, an African-American culture that has existed on Georgia's Sea Islands for over 200 years. The Gullahs are descendants of West African slaves, many of whom were Muslim. Today their culture blends Christian and Islamic religious beliefs. Because these islands are relatively isolated from the mainland, Gullah culture has survived, but now second-home and industrial development are threatening their way of life. Bailey describes herself as a "griot," an African word referring to the tribal historian who, as she writes, keeps "the oral history of the tribe, as it [has been] passed down for thousands of years." In this spirit, Bailey is the author of God, Dr. Buzzard, and the Bolito Man *(2000), a memoir about growing up on the island and about Gullah culture, which is sometimes called Geechee culture. Along with her husband, Bailey conducts tours of the island and teaches visitors about the island's history and culture. This article first appeared in* Essence *magazine.*

Vocabulary Preview

contra- [paragraph 4] The word *contradictions* is derived from the prefix *contra-* ("against") and the Latin verb *dicere* ("to say"). Thus, when someone contradicts us, he or she says the opposite of what we say, in other words, speaks against. Here are some other words beginning with this prefix:

contraindicate	an indication of the inadvisability of something, usually of a particular drug with a medical condition
contraception	a means of preventing pregnancy
contravene	to act counter to, to violate an order or decision

What do these two words mean?

contrarian _____

contraband (and give an example) _____

_____

WORD FAMILIES

vivid [paragraph 3] The adjective *vivid* means brilliant or perceived as bright and distinct. When Bailey refers to the *vivid* greens of Sapelo Island, she uses the word in the sense of having intensely bright colors. The word derives from the Latin verb *vivere* ("to live"), and this root can be seen in these related words: *vivacious* ("full of spirit or life"); *vivify* ("to give life to"), and *vivisection* ("the practice of doing medical research on live animals"). A related Latin root is the noun *vita*, meaning "life," which you can see in the words *vital* ("necessary for life"), *vitality*, and *vitamin*.

CORNELIA BAILEY

Still Gullah: A Sea Island Sister Struggles to Preserve the Old Ways

1   At age 52 I am the last of a generation to be born, raised and schooled on Sapelo, a little Sea Island off the Georgia coast. I am one of only 74 people left on this island, all of us descendants of West Africans brought here to work the cotton, sugar, rice and tobacco plantations established in the 1800's. Today my life is a blend of the old and the new ways. I live on a dirt road in a wooden house that my husband and I built 24 years ago, and my 94-year-old papa still makes his own cast nets for fishing. I can drive a horse as well as a car. I can use a garden hoe as well as a tiller, and I can cook better on a woodstove than an electric one, which isn't all that surprising when you consider that we didn't get electricity on Sapelo until 1967.

2   To me, modern conveniences are good, but it was our old-fashioned customs and ideas that built such a strong foundation for the people on Sapelo. Our lives were rich. We were a close-knit, self-sufficient people. But now our old ways are dying, and though I relish many of the modern amenities that have come to our island, I feel a heavy sense of loss at the vanishing ways.

3   You might not notice the changes at first. On the surface, Sapelo seems much as it always was. White and red oleander trees, live oaks, cedars, myrtles and wide, tall Georgia pines form a thick green canopy over paved and unpaved roads. Everywhere you look on this 16,000-acre, 12-mile-long island, you see a profusion of green. Vivid greens, soft greens, forest greens—thick grass and foliage and every type of wildflower kissing the sides of old wooden houses with welcoming wraparound porches set here and there on the landscape. Deer and possum and raccoon still roam our backyards. And all over the island, the air is quiet, bathed in a hush you can see *and* feel, the kind of hush God must have intended when creating Sapelo.

4   But if you look beyond the wild natural beauty of the place, you might notice something different in the people. You will see the proud stance as well as the angry walk, the easy smile as well as the hard frown, the serenity of island life as well as the travails. All the contradictions in our lives are visible in the faces and postures of our people—the old people who don't want our ways to change and the young people who do. And yet, even the young ones understand our tradition and take pride in our heritage and the way it connects us to the past.

5   My own ancestors came to Sapelo in the 1790's, arriving with the French who fled Haiti with their slaves after the revolution that ended slavery there. Others of our ancestors may have come even before that. Captured by the Portuguese in Sierra Leone, they may have been brought to the Sea Islands as early as the mid-1600's to work on plantations that subsequently failed. The rest of us came after a White planter named Thomas Spalding bought the southern portion of the island in 1802 and imported enslaved Blacks from the West Indies and Golas from West Africa to work his fields. The name Gullah is derived from these Gola people.

6   After slavery ended, our ancestors stayed on, carving out a life that was rich in the culture of the Gola tribe. Today we make our baskets in much the same way that they still do in West Africa. We sing Mende songs and share superstitions and folklore that are astonishingly similar to those in Sierra Leone. But some of the old traditions have diminished. My parents' generation fished the Atlantic, hunted for wild game and planted peanuts, corn, watermelon, okra, pumpkin, beans, sweet potatoes and peas—anything that they could dry and preserve in jars.

7   That was how our families lived until the R. J. Reynolds Co. bought land for a family retreat here back in 1933. Then slowly life on Sapelo began to change. Most of our men went to work maintaining the grand Reynolds mansion. They had to rise before dawn to plant and plow their fields, and they fished by the light of the stars. But our old ways persisted for a long while. I can still smell the sweat of our men as they walked behind oxen, horses and mules, turning the soil of vegetable patches before heading off to do their salaried work. While they were gone, our women fished at Raccoon Bluff with a cane pole and drop line from a *bateau* (boat), trusting in the Lord because they sure couldn't swim. Then the men would go out at night, holding aloft a *flambeau* (lighted torch) as they cast for alligators with a long pole and a giant hook.

8   We did everything for ourselves. I can still hear my grandmother's voice as she called my sister home from gathering firewood. And the fun we used to have when night fell! I remember, as a child, sitting in the corner come Friday or Saturday night and watching with delight as Papa and his friends drank moonshine and danced the Buzzard Lope, a pantomime of enslaved Africans in the fields, forbidden by overseers to attend to the fallen among them. The Buzzard Lope told a sad story, and yet our ancestors had taken their pain and turned it into something easier to tolerate—the rousing, hand-clapping, foot-stomping rhythm of a dance. While Papa and his friends whirled and gestured and clapped in our living room, some of the other men made music by blowing combs and playing guitars. Others beat time by doing the soft shoe, the tap dance, each one trying to outdo the other's moves.

9   Sometimes the men would get like this on weeknights too. Even when Papa finished work late, some of the men would follow him home to a hot supper, then they'd make music and dance. And we kids would get out of bed just to watch them. The next day we'd go outside and try our best to imitate Papa's steps and the sound of that comb!

10   Papa would sing to us once in a while around the house, but the truth is, he wasn't much on singing. So mostly he'd just sit and tell us stories while he built his homemade nets and fox traps or cooked hominy grits. Papa and Mama provided for us the best they could. We had alligator dishes along with pork greens some days. We had game birds and shore birds—wild turkey and gannet. We had fish and turtle of all kinds. And deer, squirrel, rabbit, raccoon and possum.

Some days Papa had to poach on the big plantation for food. Some days we feasted. Some days we had only the vegetables we raised in our fields.

11   But even on the lean days, life was simple and good. I remember Papa showing us how to take the bladder from a fresh-killed hog, roll it in warm ashes until it was thin, and then blow it up: our first balloon! Or he'd show us how to make a whistle from a spent [empty] seashell or whittle a toy to play with. Other times, he'd bring home a pocket full of kumquats from around the Reynolds mansion.

12   Those days of my childhood were the best, when Sapelo was home to some 600 people and was described as a paradise by the Black families that lived here. But where is that paradise now? First the Reynolds plantation closed down in 1970. After that the state moved in to establish a wildlife refuge on the Reynolds land, and the University of Georgia in Athens located a marine institute on the island. But even though the state-run wildlife refuge and the marine lab were hiring, employment fell off. More and more of our people began catching the three-times-daily ferry to the town of Meridian on the Georgia coast to find work. Soon our children began to attend school on the mainland as well, and when they finished high school, they found jobs there too.

13   Bit by bit our communities dispersed, so that now there is only one main settlement here—Hog's Hummock in the south. Our churches have only a handful of worshipers left, and our organizations such as the Farmers Alliance are gone. We grow few crops and hardly hunt game on the island any more. Instead we catch the ferry to the mainland to do our supermarket and other shopping. There are no more weeknight meetings in local prayer houses, no more hot-supper evenings at which young people meet, and few boys and girls to giggle in the dark with only the stars and the crickets and a chorus of frogs for company.

14   But we cannot let our culture just dwindle like our population. We have to tell our young people the old stories, show them our dances and teach them our crafts so that they will be able to pass the culture on to their children. That is why, since 1995, we have held an annual festival called Cultural Day on the third Saturday of September, in the hope that the people of Sapelo, living here and on the mainland, will bring their traditional baskets, their handmade nets and their family recipes and stories, and share Gullah culture with a new generation. That is also why we welcome visitors to the island. They can rent mobile homes or stay in a Hog's Hummock guest house not far from the dock. Although there is no visitor's center here, state tourist centers on nearby St. Simons Island or in the towns of Meridian and Savannah can offer information on what to do in Sapelo. For starters, you might try an old-fashioned mule tour run by my own son, Maurice Bailey. Of course, plants and trees and wildlife abound, and those of us left on Sapelo enjoy demonstrating our local crafts and cooking.

15   In these ways, we do our best to preserve what life was like in the old days. We can never forget that we who remain *are* Sapelo Island, connected to one another by the spirit of the place and by the ancestors who made a home here. We are bound by the high tide and the rich earth, by the gossip and the dances, by smoked mullets and the taste of fresh-dug sweet potatoes cooked in hot ashes, and the buzzing of gnats on a cool, sea-smelling night. ✳

Cornelia Bailey, "Still Gullah: A Sea Island Sister Struggles to Preserve the Old Ways" from *Essence* (February 1998). Copyright © 1998. Reprinted with the permission of the author.

Exercises

Do not refer to the selection for Exercises A–C unless your instructor directs you to do so.

A. DETERMINING THE MAIN IDEA AND PURPOSE

Choose the best answer.

_____ **1.** The main idea of the selection is that

 a. the lives of residents of Sapelo Island are nearly unchanged from the way they were nearly 200 years ago.
 b. Sapelo Island is a vacation paradise, but its rapid development by people building second homes will likely destroy those very features that make it so pleasant.
 c. the few remaining residents of Sapelo Island have continued the old traditions while adopting some new ways, though their culture is in danger of dying out.
 d. young people are abandoning Sapelo Island, meaning that there is almost no hope of the older traditions and culture surviving.

_____ **1.** The writer's purpose is to

 a. encourage readers to include Sapelo Island in their vacation plans to Georgia.
 b. explain the history and culture of the Gullahs on Sapelo Island and lament the changes that are threatening their culture.
 c. relate narratives about her childhood on Sapelo Island as a way of keeping Gullah culture alive for its residents.
 d. examine the historical roots of the Gullah people, the ancestors of Sapelo Island's current residents.

B. COMPREHENDING MAIN IDEAS

Choose the correct answer.

_____ **1.** According to Bailey's introduction, the number of residents on Sapelo today is only

 a. 15.
 b. 74.
 c. 150.
 d. about 1,000.

_____ **2.** Upon first glance, Sapelo Island doesn't appear to have changed much because

 a. the people still live as they did 200 years ago.
 b. the island doesn't have any modern features like electricity or public transit.
 c. the houses have never been remodeled.
 d. the vegetation is lush, and the atmosphere is quiet.

_____ 3. The culture on Sapelo Island is African-American, and the inhabitants are descendants of people who were

    a. former slaves from West Africa and Haiti.
    b. escaped slaves from other Southern states.
    c. slaves freed after the end of the American Civil War.
    d. brought from East Africa to work on plantations.

_____ 4. Bailey describes an essential contradiction for the residents of Sapelo Island, namely

    a. the presence of newcomers from the mainland who are threatening the traditional ways of the native residents.
    b. the lack of jobs on the island in contrast to the various employment opportunities on the Georgia mainland.
    c. the tension between the old people who don't want the island's ways to change and the young people who do.
    d. the introduction of mass-produced goods and food and the old ways of making things by hand.

_____ 5. According to the writer, the most significant change to Sapelo Island came with

    a. the end of the Civil War.
    b. the arrival of electricity and other amenities.
    c. the building of a family retreat by members of the Reynolds family.
    d. the construction of a tourist compound that attracted mainlanders.

_____ 6. The employment situation on Sapelo Island became difficult, and the result is that many residents

    a. have no work at all.
    b. take a ferry from the island to work and buy groceries on the mainland.
    c. struggle to feed their families by tending small gardens and by hunting.
    d. go to mainland schools to learn new job skills in technology and tourism.

COMPREHENSION SCORE

Score your answers for Exercises A and B as follows:

A. No. right _____ × 2 = _____
B. No. right _____ × 1 = _____
Total points from A and B _____ × 10 = _____ percent

C. SEQUENCING

These sentences from one paragraph in the selection have been scrambled. Read the sentences and choose the sequence that puts them back into logical order. Do not refer to the original selection.

1 And yet, even the young ones understand our tradition and take pride in our heritage and the way it connects us to the past. **2** All the contradictions in our lives are visible in the faces and postures of our people—the old people who don't want our ways to change and the young people who do. **3** You will see the proud stance as well as the angry walk, the easy smile as well as the hard frown, the serenity of island life as well as the travails. **4** But if you look beyond the wild natural beauty of the place, you might notice something different in the people.

_____ Which of the following represents the correct sequence for these sentences?

    a. 4, 3, 2, 1
    b. 2, 3, 1, 4
    c. 4, 1, 3, 2
    d. Correct as written.

You may refer to the selection as you work through the remaining exercises.

D. INTERPRETING MEANING

Where appropriate, write your answers to these questions in your own words.

1. What is the dominant impression of Sapelo Island from the writer's description in paragraph 3? _____

2. What is the central contradiction evident in life on Sapelo Island as the writer describes it? _____

3. What are two reasons that the island residents used music, song, pantomime, and storytelling, according to what the writer suggests in paragraphs 8 and 10? _____

_____

4. What is the writer's purpose in paragraphs 14–15? _____

_____

E. UNDERSTANDING VOCABULARY

Choose the best definition according to an analysis of word parts or the context.

_____ **1.** I *relish* many of the modern amenities [paragraph 2]

    a. develop
    b. appreciate
    c. find distasteful
    d. use regularly

_____ 2. the modern *amenities* [2]

   a. customs, ways
   b. traditional handicrafts
   c. social courtesies
   d. things that contribute to personal comfort

_____ 3. the proud *stance* [4]

   a. sense of discouragement or dejection
   b. attitude or position of someone standing
   c. expression of emotion or feeling
   d. method of dealing with outsiders

_____ 4. the serenity of the island life as well as the *travails* [4]

   a. peacefulness, tranquility
   b. lack of economic opportunity
   c. difficult, painful work or effort
   d. tensions, emotional anxieties

_____ 5. even on the *lean* days [11]

   a. normal
   b. hottest
   c. preferred
   d. meager

_____ 6. our communities *dispersed* [13]

   a. grew wealthier
   b. grew in number
   c. scattered
   d. disappeared

_____ 7. we cannot let our culture just *dwindle* [14]

   a. be reduced until almost nothing remains
   b. be forgotten
   c. be neglected
   d. be taken advantage of or exploited

_____ 8. plants and trees and wildlife *abound* [14]

   a. area available for observing
   b. exist in great numbers
   c. are dying off dramatically
   d. are almost extinct

F. USING VOCABULARY

In parentheses before each sentence are some inflected forms of words from the selection. Study the context and the sentence. Then write the correct form in the space provided.

1. (*profusion, profuse, profusely*) On Sapelo Island a large variety of native trees

   like live oaks and Georgia pines grow _____.

2. (*contradict, contradiction, contradictory*) The residents of Sapelo Island face

   many _____ elements in their daily lives.

3. (*diminish, diminishment, diminished*) Bailey laments the fact that the old

   traditional island ways are beginning to _____.

4. (*tolerate, tolerance, tolerant, tolerantly*) From the pantomimes and stories, island

   residents learned the art of _____—the necessity of taking something
   painful and making it easier to accept.

5. (*imitate, imitations, imitative*) After witnessing an evening of music, storytelling,

   drinking, and dancing, the children would practice their _____
   of the adults' gestures.

G. TOPICS FOR DISCUSSION

1. On balance, would you say that Bailey is optimistic or pessimistic about saving Gullah culture? What factors threaten its survival? What measures, aside from increased tourism, would help to ensure its survival?
2. What cultural characteristics, as Bailey describes them, does she find admirable in the residents of Sapelo Island?

H. TOPICS FOR WRITING

1. If you have visited an unusual place, write a short essay describing its physical appearance and any unusual practices that the residents take part in.
2. If you are fortunate enough to have a grandmother or grandfather who is living (or perhaps a great-grandparent), interview him or her about the way life was, say, 50 years ago. Then write an essay summarizing his or her memories.

Exploring Related Web Sites

- As Bailey writes in this article, keeping Gullah culture alive is important to the island residents. Here is one online story to read concerning a different Sea Island, St. Helena Island:

  "Unique Gullah/Geechee Culture at Risk"

  http://archives.cnn.com/2002/fyi/news/02/13/gullah/index.html

- A short video on sweetgrass baskets that are made by Gullah women near Charleston, South Carolina, is titled "Preserving the Sweetgrass Basket Tradition" and is available at this address:

  http://basketmakers.com/topics/bymaterial/sweetgrass/sweetgullahindex.htm

  Scroll down to "Basket-Weaving Is Threatened in South Carolina." Then click on "multimedia slide show."

Walk on the Wilshire Side

Freelance writer Judith Lewis writes on environmental issues. This article was originally published in Sierra, *the Sierra Club's bimonthly magazine devoted to environmental issues. If you are unfamiliar with the geography of Los Angeles, here are some useful facts. The sprawling city covers 466 square miles and includes a population of nearly 4 million, sandwiched between mountains and the ocean. This area forms the Los Angeles Basin. The five-county area that constitutes greater Los Angeles has a population of 20 million. The city itself is bisected by Wilshire Boulevard, which runs west from the downtown area 13 miles to the Pacific Ocean, ending near the Santa Monica Pier. In this article, Lewis writes about an urban program to help students connect with their city by walking the length of Wilshire.*

Vocabulary Preview

WORD PARTS

bi- and other numerical prefixes [paragraph 5] English contains a large number of Latin and Greek prefixes referring to numbers. One of them is *bi-*, meaning "two." *Sierra* magazine is a *bimonthly*, which means it is published every two months. The walk down Wilshire Boulevard is a *biannual* event, so it takes place every two years. Other words that begin with the prefix *bi-* include *bifocals* (a type of glasses with two different lenses), *bisect* (to cut into two parts), and *bisexual* (relating to both sexes).

Here are some other common Latin and Greek prefixes indicating number and some words illustrating them:

half	*semi-* (semisweet, semicircle); *hemi-* (hemisphere)
one	*uni-* (unicycle, unison, unicorn)
two	*duo-* (duet, dual)
three	*tri-* (tricycle, trimester, triplets, trident)
ten	*deca-* (decade, decathlon, decimal)

WORD FAMILIES

credentials [paragraph 19] Public school teachers need a *credential* before they are allowed to teach. A *credential* is a certificate giving them the authority to do so. The root of this word is the Latin verb *credere* ("to put trust in," "to believe"). In other words, one supposedly can trust people with credentials because they are certified as qualified to do what they do. Other words with the root *cred-* include the following:

creed	a system of religious beliefs
credibility	believability
credulity	gullibility; a disposition to believe too readily
incredible	describing something that is unbelievable
incredulous	describing someone who is unbelieving or skeptical
credit	belief or confidence in the truth of something; confidence in one's ability to repay a debt in the future

JUDITH LEWIS

Walk on the Wilshire Side

1   The early-morning sun glints off the skyscrapers of downtown Los Angeles. Mar'cel Stribling, a 19-year-old senior at gritty Crenshaw High School in South Los Angeles, stands on the steps of a gleaming white office tower, making up rhymes. "I don't wanna be nothing like Kanye West," he shouts. "I just want to tell you I'm the best."

2   Muthoni Gaciku, 14, rolls her eyes and goes back to chatting with her friend Wendy Velasco, 15, about her future career. "I want to be a food connoisseur," states the tiny Gaciku, a recent Kenyan immigrant, shifting back and forth in her pigtails and cropped pants. "That way, I can eat all the time."

3   A couple of steps behind them, Renee Kelly leans against the office building smiling, talking to no one. With her square-tipped, French-manicured finger-nails, bejeweled sunglasses, and thick black hair twisted and tucked neatly under a black baseball hat, she looks poised and glamorous—but hardly prepared for the journey ahead: a 13-mile hike along Wilshire Boulevard, the avenue that splits sprawling Los Angeles down the center, connecting downtown to the Pacific Ocean. I ask her if she knows what she's in for. "I did it three years ago," she says, "so let's see if I still got it. I'm middle-aged now."

4   Kelly is 19.

5   She and 17 other students and recent graduates of Crenshaw High School got up before dawn for this biannual event for the school's Eco Club/Venture Crew. Other outings, like the five-day backpacking trip in Yosemite National Park, may offer more in the way of communion with nature. But traversing the all-concrete length of Wilshire Boulevard has its special allure—especially in a city where no one walks. "Three years ago, we did it in the rain," says Bill Vanderberg, the Eco Club's adviser and Crenshaw's dean of students. "I said, 'I'm never doing this again.' But the kids never stopped talking about it. They just never stopped bugging me."

6   From its downtown source to its terminus at the Santa Monica Pier, in its meanderings through Koreatown to the eight-lane swath it cuts through swanky Westside, Wilshire connects Los Angeles far more than touristy Sunset or Hollywood Boulevards do. Walking it is a proclamation of freedom for kids

from the neighborhoods that surround Crenshaw. Because of the strife and stray bullets of warring gangs, few venture far from their home turf, and fewer still do so on foot. It pains Vanderberg, who grew up in the suburbs of New York City. Most of his early outdoor adventures, he recalls, were urban ones: "We'd get up and hit the street and walk as far as we could just to see where it went. These kids can't do that, ever."

7   Crenshaw's dropout rate is twice the already high L.A. average, and violence in the communities surrounding the campus is common. "I saw these kids with their worlds closing in on them," Vanderberg says. "I wanted them to see what else is out there." Trips to the mountains offer access to open space; the Wilshire hike gives teens access to their own diverse hometown.

8   "Here are the rules," Vanderberg declares as the group assembles. "No CD players, no iPods, and no headphones. We're out here to hear the sounds of the city and talk to each other, not to check out and get through it.

9   "And learn how to cross the street," he adds. "In California, people just walk and don't bother to look. I'm from New York. In New York, we look, no matter what the light says."

10   Our starting point is the Metro Red Line rail station at Western Avenue. A little after 8:30 a.m., we set out. Gaciku and Velasco walk arm in arm, running to stay at the front of the squad, where Stribling continues his high-decibel rap, now boasting of his unflagging energy. "I'm in JROTC," he tells me. "I can walk for *days*."

11   I'm feeling the same. I happen to live on Wilshire Boulevard and considered myself on intimate terms with its landmarks. But now distances familiar to me from long, dull drives shatter into scores of small discoveries. I spot storefronts and building facades I never knew were there, and the blocks melt away. When we hit Highland Avenue at 10:00 a.m., Vanderberg calls for a break. We're smack in the heart of Los Angeles, just shy of the historic Miracle Mile—a segment of Wilshire designed for early automobile traffic, replete with art deco high-rises and streamlined moderne office towers. I'm astonished: I've never walked from Western to Highland. It never occurred to me that I could.

12   Lumbering Escalades and Excursions are trapped in asphalt between traffic lights. We blend in easily here, but a few miles west, where Wilshire intersects the fabled retail fantasyland of Rodeo Drive in Beverly Hills, the stares begin. It's not often, in this deeply segregated city, that a small crowd of black and Latino teenagers traipses through these moneyed streets. Women with Botoxed foreheads and surgically stretched cheeks perch at sidewalk café tables, blinking bewilderedly like some odd species of bird. I half expect security guards to roll up and ask what we're doing here. Stribling stops rapping long enough to stare in a window at a $3,000 pair of socks. "They better have a lifetime warranty!" he declares.

13   By noon we clear Beverly Hills, and what was a pleasantly cool day becomes oppressively hot. Vanderberg takes out the map: three long miles to the sea. "This is going to be the tough hour," he confides to me. "It's been four hours already, and we've got some complaints coming in about feet."

14   In fact, except for Vanderberg himself, the only one who looks undisturbed by the journey is Renee Kelly. As I limp along next to her, I notice that her hair

remains smooth and neat, her lips still glossy, and her smile as fresh and relaxed as it was when we began.

15   "You know, when I first met you, I didn't think you could finish this hike," I confess.

16   Kelly shoots me a look of mock scorn.

17   "The bangles threw me," I explain, pointing to the jingling column of gold on her wrist.

18   "Oh," Kelly says with a laugh. "I do trail work with my bangles on. I forget that they're there."

19   Kelly, the daughter of Jamaican parents who never took her camping, earned her outdoors credentials three years ago on a camping trip to Death Valley. She was in tenth grade and not doing well. "I was fed up with school and about to drop out," she says. "I was going through things." The trip wasn't easy. "It was freezing cold. The wind was snapping in our faces, our tents blew down, and everything broke. All our cars got stuck in the mud." But she got to throw herself off the high, forgiving slopes of the Eureka Dunes and saw the precipitous, snow-capped Panamint Mountains rising high above the salty flats at Badwater.[1] A world apart from fast-food drive-ins and strip malls opened up, and Kelly saw a future for herself in it. "I realized that if I wanted to go on more trips, I had to show up at school more," she says. "So I did."

20   Kelly graduated last year and now studies nursing at Los Angeles Trade Technical College, with plans to be a park ranger.

21   As Vanderberg folds up the map, he looks down sternly at one girl's slip-on tennies. "Where are your socks?" he demands.

22   "I'm not answering," says 18-year-old Maria Diego, batting long, mascara-coated eyelashes. Diego was last year's Eco Club vice president, and she's spent the whole day walking with her friend Karla Rivera, 17. The two have known each other since elementary school but only became friends on a club backpacking trip. "And now we're 'Diego-Rivera'!" chirps Rivera.

23   "I got close to Mr. Vanderberg because I wasn't a real good student and I had to go and talk to him a lot," says Diego. The Yosemite trip was her first, and she found it exhausting. "And at the end, I looked back and realized I'd done something I thought I could never do."

24   Did it improve her schoolwork?

25   "For a while," Diego says, looking down at her inadequately shod feet. "I got off track again this year."

26   In fact, Diego had dropped out of school the previous year and only squeaked out a diploma in December after completing a series of courses in night school. Sometimes a walk in the woods—or a walk down the length of Wilshire Boulevard—is just what it is; it's not a panacea, and it's not going to turn every teenager around. "We're here to introduce kids to the outdoors," Vanderberg says, "not to perform miracles on everyone."

---

[1]Badwater, the lowest point in the Western Hemisphere, is the subject of Selection 25, Part Four. It's the beginning point of the Badwater Marathon, a yearly event in Death Valley, California. (Ed.)

27 Lots of kids come to Eco Club events but don't attend the meetings, Vanderberg says. Others come out once and never return, with no explanation. "But they still had an experience they never had before," he insists. The Eco Club shouldn't have to justify itself, Vanderberg argues, by saving every academic career. "It's enough when we just get one," he says.

28 At 1:30 p.m., we hit Lincoln Boulevard, which divides the rest of Los Angeles from what everyone knows as the Beach. With nine blocks left, Diego and Rivera start running into the ocean breeze. Vanderberg shouts at them to slow down, but it's no use. When we cross Ocean Avenue and hit the soft dirt of the walking path, Gaciku jumps into the air and lets out a whoop. Stribling announces loudly that he could walk the whole thing again. Kelly, gold earrings sparkling, camera swinging calmly from her wrist, just beams a broad, quiet smile. ✳

Judith Lewis, "Walk on the Wilshire Side," *Sierra* (May–June 2007). Copyright © 2007 by Judith Lewis. Reprinted with the permission of the author.

Exercises

Do not refer to the selection for Exercises A–C unless your instructor directs you to do so.

A. DETERMINING THE MAIN IDEA AND PURPOSE

Choose the best answer.

_____ 1. The main idea of the selection is that for students and former students at Crenshaw High School, the walk down Wilshire Boulevard represents

    a. a chance to escape from the dull monotony of classroom instruction for a day.

    b. a way for them to explore the city that they already know well from a different perspective.

    c. a proclamation of freedom, allowing them to see beyond the violence in their neighborhoods, if only for a day.

    d. a panacea or cure-all for students in danger of dropping out.

_____ 2. The writer's purpose is to

    a. describe the origins of the walk and the reasons it was established.

    b. show other teachers how to go about setting up such a walk.

    c. caution students about the implications of dropping out of school.

    d. relate the events of one particular walk and its positive effects on the participants.

B. COMPREHENDING MAIN IDEAS

Choose the correct answer.

_____ 1. The walk down Wilshire is sponsored by Crenshaw High School's
   a. Sierra Club chapter.
   b. Eco Club/Venture Crew.
   c. science department.
   d. Outdoor Education/Yosemite Institute.

_____ 2. The special allure of the Wilshire walk for these students is
   primarily that it
   a. offers a chance to commune with nature.
   b. is open only to the best students in the school, and competition
      is fierce.
   c. allows them to see Beverly Hills, Santa Monica, and the Pacific
      Ocean.
   d. is unusual—a very different activity from what they are accus-
      tomed to.

_____ 3. Bill Vanderberg, the dean of students at Crenshaw High School,
   originally sponsored the walk because he wanted to
   a. duplicate a similar program from his days as a student in
      New York.
   b. show students that there is something else for them besides the
      violence in their communities.
   c. show students how the other half (more affluent people) live.
   d. stop the dropout rate at the school from becoming even
      worse.
   e. only a and b.
   f. a, b, and c.

_____ 4. When the group reaches Rodeo Drive, the famous luxury shopping
   street in Beverly Hills, the students discover that people on the
   street and in the outdoor cafes
   a. are staring at them because minorities are unusual in this
      area.
   b. have called the police to report suspicious activity.
   c. are amazed to see such a large group of people actually
      walking.
   d. are amused by the way these young people are dressed.

_____ 5. For Kelly, the daughter of Jamaicans, life changed after
   a. a camping trip to Death Valley.
   b. a hiking trip in Yosemite.
   c. she dropped out of school and couldn't find a job.
   d. she entered the nursing program at Los Angeles Trade Technical
      College.

_____ **6.** For Maria Diego, the backpacking trip to Yosemite she made the year before

    a. represented a chance to be at one with nature for the first time.

    b. showed her the importance of staying in school and studying hard.

    c. made her realize that she wanted to study outdoor education in college.

    d. gave her a sense of accomplishment, since she finished something she never thought she would be able to do.

COMPREHENSION SCORE

Score your answers for Exercises A and B as follows:

A. No. right _____ × 2 = _____

B. No. right _____ × 1 = _____

Total points from A and B _____ × 10 = _____ percent

C. SEQUENCING

These sentences from one paragraph in the selection have been scrambled. Read the sentences and choose the sequence that puts them back into logical order. Do not refer to the original selection.

    1 She [Kelly] and 17 other students and recent graduates of Crenshaw High School got up before dawn for this biannual event for the school's Eco Club/Venture Crew. **2** Other outings, like the five-day backpacking trip in Yosemite National Park, may offer more in the way of communion with nature. **3** But traversing the all-concrete length of Wilshire Boulevard has its special allure—especially in a city where no one walks.

_____ Which of the following represents the correct sequence for these sentences?

    a. 2, 1, 3

    b. 3, 2, 1

    c. 2, 3, 1

    d. Correct as written.

You may refer to the selection as you work through the remaining exercises.

D. LOCATING SUPPORTING DETAILS

For the main idea stated here from paragraphs 6 and 7, find relevant details that support it. The first and third ones have been done for you.

    Walking the length of Wilshire Boulevard gives these students unusual opportunities.

1. It's a proclamation of freedom.

2. _____

3. Vanderberg wanted to duplicate what he had experienced growing up in New York.

4. _____

5. _____

E. UNDERSTANDING VOCABULARY

Choose the best definition according to an analysis of word parts or the context.

_____ 1. a food *connoisseur* [paragraph 2]

    a. critic
    b. server
    c. expert
    d. writer

_____ 2. *traversing* the all-concrete length of [5]

    a. crossing, traveling over
    b. examining, investigating
    c. driving along
    d. trespassing on

_____ 3. its special *allure* [5]

    a. significance
    b. benefit
    c. opportunity
    d. attraction

_____ 4. its *meanderings* through Koreatown [6]

    a. proceeding in a straight line
    b. passing through little streets and alleys
    c. following a winding course
    d. looping around in a circle

_____ 5. his *unflagging* energy [10]

    a. tireless, never-ending
    b. contagious
    c. impressive
    d. enviable

_____ 6. *replete* with art-deco high-rises [11]

    a. crowded
    b. decorated lavishly
    c. ruined esthetically
    d. abundantly supplied

_____ **7.** a look of *mock* scorn [16]

    a. hateful
    b. pretend
    c. pure
    d. humorous

_____ **8.** the *precipitous,* snow-capped Panamint Mountains [19]

    a. extremely steep
    b. hazy and indistinct in the distance
    c. friendly, welcoming
    d. craggy, rocky

_____ **9.** he looks down *sternly* [21]

    a. full of surprise
    b. reluctantly
    c. severely
    d. worriedly

F. USING VOCABULARY

From the following list of vocabulary words, choose a word that fits in each blank according to both the grammatical structure of the sentence and the context. Use each word in the list only once. Do not change the form of the word.

facades	swanky	urban
terminus	gleaming	biannual
intersects	traverse	meanders

During this _____ walk, the students _____ the city of Los Angeles along Wilshire Boulevard. First the street _____ through Koreatown. As the students walk along the Miracle Mile, they see that the exterior parts of the high-rises, called _____, are _____ in the sunlight. In Beverly Hills, Wilshire _____ with the _____ shopping area of Rodeo Drive. Further west, the _____ of Wilshire Boulevard is in Santa Monica where it meets the Pacific Ocean. These lucky students from Crenshaw High see their _____ environment from an entirely new perspective.

G. TOPICS FOR DISCUSSION

1. Comment on the students described in the article. What do they have in common, aside from their enthusiasm about going on this walk? In what ways does this biannual event appeal to them?

2. Before you read this article, what were your impressions of Los Angeles—whether from your reading or from the media? What impressions of the city does this article convey to the reader? How do these impressions accord with your earlier thoughts?
3. What programs to prevent high school students from dropping out exist in your community? How do they work? Are they effective?

H. TOPICS FOR WRITING

1. Consider question 3 above. If you are familiar with a program in your community to keep high school students from dropping out, describe the way it works, its appeal, and its effectiveness.
2. What are some reasons that high school students choose to drop out before graduating? Using information from your own experience, reading, and/or observation, write an essay exploring these reasons. Offer some suggestions or solutions if possible in your conclusion.

Exploring Related Web Sites

- Read this background article that accompanied a television news story on ABC:

    http://abcnews.go.com/US/story?id=2667532

- How does your state fare? Locate the most recent high school dropout statistics that you can find online. Start by typing in this phrase in the search box in Google or your favorite search engine:

    name of state, high school dropout rates (Example: Georgia, high school dropout rates)

7 CHARLES FINNEY

The Life and Death of a Western Gladiator

In this fictional account Charles Finney describes the life cycle of Crotalus, a diamondback rattlesnake, one of the most feared yet splendid creatures that inhabit the western United States. This article first appeared in Harper's.

Vocabulary Preview

WORD PARTS

De- [paragraph 3] The prefix *de-* refers to the removal of something. Therefore, *dehydration* means the process of removing water. Here is how the word is broken down:

de- ("removal of") + *hydr* ("water") + *-ation*.

Incidentally, new words ending with the common noun suffix *-tion* will be easy to pronounce if you remember that the primary accent or stress mark always occurs on the syllable just *before* the suffix: dē-hī-drā´ shən. Some other words with the prefix *de-*:

defoliate	to remove vegetation
deoxygenate	to remove oxygen from a substance, like water
depilatory	to remove hair from (*de-* + *pilus* ["hair"])

What do these two words mean?

desegregate   _____

deflate   _____

WORD FAMILIES

somnolent [paragraph 13] As he lies in his cave, Crotalus becomes *somnolent*, or sleepy. From the Latin word *somnus*, English has a few words in this family that refer to sleep, in addition to sleep aid products like Sominex.

somnolence	sleepy
insomnia	the inability to sleep
insomniac	one who suffers from insomnia

If a woman is a somnambulist, what does she do? _____

CHARLES FINNEY

Life and Death of a Western Gladiator

1   He was born on a summer morning in the shady mouth of a cave. Three others were born with him, another male and two females. Each was about five inches long and slimmer than a lead pencil.

2   Their mother left them a few hours after they were born. A day after that his brother and sisters left him also. He was all alone. Nobody cared whether he lived or died. His tiny brain was very dull. He had no arms or legs. His skin was delicate. Nearly everything that walked on the ground or burrowed in it, that flew in the air or swam in the water or climbed trees was his enemy. But he didn't know that. He knew nothing at all. He was aware of his own existence, and that was the sum of his knowledge.

3   The direct rays of the sun could, in a short time, kill him. If the temperature dropped too low he would freeze. Without food he would starve. Without moisture he would die of dehydration. If a man or a horse stepped on him he would be crushed. If anything chased him he could run neither very far nor very fast.

4   Thus it was at the hour of his birth. Thus it would be, with modifications, all his life.

5   But against these drawbacks he had certain qualifications that fitted him to be a competitive creature of this world and equipped him for its warfare. He could exist a long time without food or water. His very smallness at birth protected him when he most needed protection. Instinct provided him with what he lacked in experience. In order to eat he first had to kill; and he was eminently adapted for killing. In sacs in his jaws he secreted a virulent poison. To inject that poison he had two fangs, hollow and pointed. Without that poison and those fangs he would have been among the most helpless creatures on earth. With them he was among the deadliest.

6   He was, of course, a baby rattlesnake, a desert diamondback, named *Crotalus atrox* by the herpetologists Baird and Girard and so listed in the *Catalogue of North American Reptiles* in its issue of 1853. He was grayish brown in color with a series of large dark diamond-shaped blotches on his back. His tail was white with five black cross-bands. It had a button on the end of it.

7   Little Crotalus lay in the dust in the mouth of his cave. Some of his kinfolk lay there too. It was their home. That particular tribe of rattlers had lived there for scores of years.

8   The cave had never been seen by a white man.

9   Sometimes as many as two hundred rattlers occupied the den. Sometimes the numbers shrunk to as few as forty or fifty.

10   The tribe members did nothing at all for each other except breed. They hunted singly; they never shared their food. They derived some automatic degree of safety from their numbers, but their actions were never concerted toward using their numbers to any end. If an enemy attacked one of them, the others did nothing about it.

11   Young Crotalus's brother was the first of the litter to go out into the world and the first to die. He achieved a distance of fifty feet from the den when a Sonoran racer, four feet long and hungry, came upon him. The little rattler, despite his poison fangs, was a tidbit. The racer, long skilled in such arts, snatched him up by the head and swallowed him down. Powerful digestive juices in the racer's stomach did the rest. Then the racer, appetite whetted, prowled around until it found one of Crotalus's little sisters. She went the way of the brother.

12   Nemesis of the second sister was a chaparral cock. This cuckoo, or roadrunner as it is called, found the baby amid some rocks, uttered a cry of delight, scissored it by the neck, shook it until it was almost lifeless, banged and pounded it upon a rock until life had indeed left it, and then gulped it down.

13   Crotalus, somnolent in a cranny of the cave's mouth, neither knew nor cared. Even if he had, there was nothing he could have done about it.

14   On the fourth day of his life he decided to go out into the world himself. He rippled forth uncertainly, the transverse plates on his belly serving him as legs.

15   He could see things well enough within his limited range, but a five-inch-long snake can command no great field of vision. He had an excellent sense of smell. But, having no ears, he was stone deaf. On the other hand, he had a pit, a deep pock mark between eye and nostril. Unique, this organ was sensitive to animal heat. In pitch blackness, Crotalus, by means of the heat messages recorded in his pit, could tell whether another animal was near and could also judge its size. That was better than an ear.

16   The single button on his tail could not, of course, yet rattle. Crotalus wouldn't be able to rattle until that button had grown into three segments. Then he would be able to buzz.

17   He had a wonderful tongue. It looked like an exposed nerve and was probably exactly that. It was forked, and Crotalus thrust it in and out as he traveled. It told him things that neither his eyes nor his nose nor his pit told him.

18   Snake fashion, Crotalus went forth, not knowing where he was going, for he had never been anywhere before. Hunger was probably his prime mover. In order to satisfy that hunger he had to find something smaller than himself and kill it.

19   He came upon a baby lizard sitting in the sand. Eyes, nose, pit, and tongue told Crotalus it was there. Instinct told him what it was and what to do. Crotalus gave a tiny one-inch strike and bit the lizard. His poison killed it. He took it by the head and swallowed it. Thus was his first meal.

20   During his first two years, Crotalus grew rapidly. He attained a length of two feet; his tail had five rattles on it and its button. He rarely bothered with lizards any more, preferring baby rabbits, chipmunks, and round-tailed ground squirrels. Because of his slow locomotion he could not run down these agile little things. He had to contrive instead to be where they were when they would pass. Then he struck swiftly, injected his poison, and ate them after they died.

21   At two he was formidable. He had grown past the stage where a racer or a roadrunner could safely tackle him. He had grown to the size where other desert

dwellers—coyotes, foxes, coatis, wildcats—knew it was better to leave him alone.

22   And, at two, Crotalus became a father, his life being regulated by cycles. His cycles were plantlike. The peach tree does not "know" when it is time to flower, but flower it does because its cycle orders it to do so.

23   In the same way, Crotalus did not "know" when it was time for young desert diamondback rattlers to pair off and breed. But his cycle knew.

24   He found "her" on a rainy morning. Crotalus's courtship at first was sinuous and subtle, slow and stealthy. Then suddenly it became dynamic. A period of exhaustion followed. Two metabolic machines had united to produce new metabolic machines.

25   Of that physical union six new rattlesnakes were born. Thus Crotalus, at two, had carried out his major primary function: he had reproduced his kind. In two years he had experienced everything that was reasonably possible for desert diamondback rattlesnakes to experience except death.

26   He had not experienced death for the simple reason that there had never been an opportunity for anything bigger and stronger than himself to kill him. Now, at two, because he was so formidable, that opportunity became more and more unlikely.

27   He grew more slowly in the years following his initial spurt. At the age of twelve he was five feet long. Few of the other rattlers in his den were older or larger than he.

28   He had a castanet of fourteen segments. It had been broken off occasionally in the past, but with each new molting a new segment appeared.

29   His first skin-shedding back in his babyhood had been a bewildering experience. He did not know what was happening. His eyes clouded over until he could not see. His skin thickened and dried until it cracked in places. His pit and his nostrils ceased to function. There was only one thing to do and that was to get out of that skin.

30   Crotalus managed it by nosing against the bark of a shrub until he forced the old skin down over his head, bunching it like the rolled top of a stocking around his neck. Then he pushed around among rocks and sticks and branches, literally crawling out of his skin by slow degrees. Wriggling free at last, he looked like a brand new snake. His skin was bright and satiny, his eyes and nostrils were clear, his pit sang with sensation.

31   For the rest of his life he was to molt three or four times a year. Each time he did it he felt as if he had been born again.

32   At twelve he was a magnificent reptile. Not a single scar defaced his rippling symmetry. He was diabolically beautiful and deadly poison.

33   His venom was his only weapon, for he had no power of constriction. Yellowish in color, his poison was odorless and tasteless. It was a highly complex mixture of proteids, each in itself direly toxic. His venom worked on the blood. The more poison he injected with a bite, the more dangerous the wound. The pain rendered by his bite was instantaneous, and the shock accompanying it was profound. Swelling began immediately, to be followed by a ghastly oozing. Injected directly into a large vein, his poison brought death quickly, for the victim died when it reached his heart.

34   At the age of twenty Crotalus was the oldest and largest rattler in his den. He was six feet long and weighed thirteen pounds. His whole world was only about a mile in radius. He had fixed places where he avoided the sun when it was hot and he was away from his cave. He knew his hunting grounds thoroughly, every game trail, every animal burrow.

35   He was a fine old machine, perfectly adapted to his surroundings, accustomed to a life of leisure and comfort. He dominated his little world.

36   The mighty seasonal rhythms of the desert were as vast pulsations, and the lives of the rattlesnakes were attuned to them. Spring sun beat down, spring rains fell, and, as the plants of the desert ended their winter hibernations, so did the vipers in their lair. The plants opened forth and budded; the den "opened" too, and the snakes crawled forth. The plants fertilized each other, and new plants were born. The snakes bred, and new snakes were produced. The desert was repopulated.

37   In the autumn the plants began to close; in the same fashion the snake den began to close, the reptiles returned to it, lay like lingering blossoms about its entrance for a while, then disappeared within it when winter came. There they slept until summoned forth by a new spring.

38   Crotalus was twenty years old. He was in the golden age of his viperhood.

39   But men were approaching. Spilling out of their cities, men were settling in that part of the desert where Crotalus lived. They built roads and houses, set up fences, dug for water, planted crops.

40   They homesteaded the land. They brought new animals with them—cows, horses, dogs, cats, barnyard fowl.

41   The roads they built were death traps for the desert dwellers. Every morning new dead bodies lay on the roads, the bodies of the things the men had run over and crushed in their vehicles.

42   That summer Crotalus met his first dog. It was a German shepherd which had been reared on a farm in the Midwest and there had gained the reputation of being a snake-killer. Black snakes, garter snakes, pilots, water snakes; it delighted in killing them all. It would seize them by the middle, heedless of their tiny teeth, and shake them violently until they died.

43   This dog met Crotalus face to face in the desert at dusk. Crotalus had seen coyotes aplenty and feared them not. Neither did the dog fear Crotalus, although Crotalus then was six feet long, as thick in the middle as a motorcycle tire, and had a head the size of a man's clenched fist. Also this snake buzzed and buzzed and buzzed.

44   The dog was brave, and a snake was a snake. The German shepherd snarled and attacked. Crotalus struck him in the underjaw; his fangs sank in almost half an inch and squirted big blobs of hematoxic poison into the tissues of the dog's flesh.

45   The shepherd bellowed with pain, backed off, groveled with his jaws in the desert sand, and attacked again. He seized Crotalus somewhere by the middle of his body and tried to flip him in the air and shake him as, in the past, he had shaken slender black snakes to their death. In return, he received another poison-blurting stab in his flank and a third in the belly and a fourth in the eye as the terrible, writhing snake bit wherever it could sink its fangs.

46   The German shepherd had enough. He dropped the big snake and in sick, agonizing bewilderment crawled somehow back to his master's homestead and died.

47   The homesteader looked at his dead dog and became alarmed. If there was a snake around big enough to kill a dog that size, it could also kill a child and probably a man. It was something that had to be eliminated.

48   The homesteader told his fellow farmers, and they agreed to initiate a war of extermination against the snakes.

49   The campaign during the summer was sporadic. The snakes were scattered over the desert, and it was only by chance that the men came upon them. Even so, at summer's end, twenty-six of the vipers had been killed.

50   When autumn came the men decided to look for the rattlers' den and execute mass slaughter. The homesteaders had become desert-wise and knew what to look for.

51   They found Crotalus's lair, without too much trouble—a rock outcropping on a slope that faced the south. Cast-off skins were in evidence in the bushes. Bees flew idly in and out of the den's mouth. Convenient benches and shelves of rock were at hand where the snakes might lie for a final sunning in the autumn air.

52   They killed the three rattlers they found at the den when they first discovered it. They made plans to return in a few more days when more of the snakes had congregated. They decided to bring along dynamite with them and blow up the mouth of the den so that the snakes within would be sealed there forever and the snakes without would have no place to find refuge.

53   On the day the men chose to return nearly fifty desert diamondbacks were gathered at the portals of the cave. The men shot them, clubbed them, smashed them with rocks, Some of the rattlers escaped the attack and crawled into the den.

54   Crotalus had not yet arrived for the autumn rendezvous. He came that night. The den's mouth was a shattered mass of rock, for the men had done their dynamiting well. Dead members of his tribe lay everywhere. Crotalus nosed among them, tongue flicking as he slid slowly along.

55   There was no access to the cave any more. He spent the night outside among the dead. The morning sun warmed him and awakened him. He lay there at full length. He had no place to go.

56   The sun grew hotter upon him and instinctively he began to slide toward some dark shade. Then his senses warned him of some animal presence near by; he stopped, half coiled, raised his head and began to rattle. He saw two upright figures. He did not know what they were because he had never seen men before.

57   "That's the granddaddy of them all," said one of the homesteaders. "It's a good thing we came back." He raised his shotgun. *

From Charles Finney, "The Life and Death of a Western Gladiator." Reprinted by permission of Barthold Fles, Literary Agent.

Exercises

Do not refer to the selection for Exercises A and B unless your instructor directs you to do so.

A. DETERMINING THE MAIN IDEA AND PURPOSE

Choose the best answer.

_____ 1. The main idea of the selection is that
   a. the life of a diamondback rattlesnake is harsh.
   b. Crotalus was well suited to survive in his environment until civilization intruded.
   c. diamondback rattlesnakes are a threat to human settlements.
   d. diamondback rattlesnakes can adapt to even the most hostile environment because of their strong instinct to survive.

_____ 2. The writer's purpose in telling the story of Crotalus is to
   a. encourage the reader to learn more about rattlesnakes.
   b. persuade the reader that rattlesnakes are important to the environment.
   c. describe those physical characteristics of the rattlesnake that enable it to survive so well.
   d. inform and make the reader sympathetic to the rattlesnake's life cycle and behavior.

B. COMPREHENDING MAIN IDEAS

Choose the correct answer.

_____ 1. In describing the baby stage in a rattlesnake's life, Finney emphasizes its
   a. dependence on its mother.
   b. well-developed killing instinct.
   c. deadly effect on its victims.
   d. helplessness and susceptibility to danger.

_____ 2. According to the selection, rattlesnakes
   a. hunt in groups.
   b. have a well-organized and complex society.
   c. must be taught to hunt by adults.
   d. live solitary lives except for breeding.

_____ 3. This particular group of rattlesnakes described in the selection lived in
   a. an abandoned farmhouse.
   b. a den or cave.
   c. a large underground cavern.
   d. a quarry.

_____ **4.** The rattlesnake "senses" the presence of other animals by using its

   a. pit.
   b. mouth.
   c. eyes.
   d. ears.

_____ **5.** Rattlesnakes molt or shed their skin

   a. once a year.
   b. twice a year.
   c. three or four times a year.
   d. three or four times in a normal life span.

_____ **6.** After the homesteaders found the rattlesnakes, they decided to

   a. alert the authorities.
   b. begin a campaign to decrease their numbers.
   c. exterminate them.
   d. move them to a more isolated location.

COMPREHENSION SCORE

Score your answers for Exercises A and B as follows:

A. No. right _____ × 2 = _____

B. No. right _____ × 1 = _____

Total points from A and B _____ × 10 = _____ percent

You may refer to the selection as you work through the remaining exercises.

C. RECOGNIZING SUPPORTING DETAILS

Place an X in the space for each statement that *directly* supports this main idea from the selection: "[H]e had certain qualifications that fitted him to be a competitive creature of this world and equipped him for its warfare."

1. _____   The direct rays of the sun could, in a short time, kill him.

2. _____   Without moisture he would die of dehydration.

3. _____   He could exist a long time without food or water.

4. _____   He was eminently adapted for killing by means of the virulent poison contained in sacs in his jaws.

5. _____   To inject that poison he had two fangs, hollow and pointed.

6. _____   Without that poison and those fangs he would have been the most helpless creature on earth.

D. INTERPRETING MEANING

Write your answers for these questions in your own words.

1. Read paragraph 2 and explain why the survival rate of baby rattlesnakes is so low. _____

2. What single characteristic mentioned in paragraph 5 makes a rattlesnake more deadly than all other creatures on earth? _____

3. In paragraphs 22–25, what does Finney say is the main impetus for Crotalus to reproduce? _____

4. Aside from the danger the snakes presented to children and livestock, what are *two* reasons that the homesteaders were so determined to destroy the

   rattlesnake population? _____

   _____

   _____

5. Did Crotalus survive the homesteaders' assault? How do you know? _____

   _____

   _____

E. UNDERSTANDING VOCABULARY

Look through the paragraphs listed below and find a word that matches each definition. Refer to the dictionary if necessary. An example has been done for you.

Ex. changes, alterations [paragraphs 3–4]   _____modifications_____

1. actively poisonous, toxic [5]   _____

2. an unbeatable rival or opponent [12–13]   _____

3. sleepy [12–13]   _____

4. to plan cleverly, devise, scheme [20]   _____

5. active, forceful, energetic [24]   _____

6. awesome in strength, intimidating [26]   _____

7. dreadful, horrible [33]   _____

8. thorough, deep, pervasive [33–34]   _____

9. confusion, complete puzzlement [45–46]   _____

10. shelter or protection from danger [51–52]   _____

F. USING VOCABULARY

In parentheses before each sentence are some inflected forms of words from the selection. Study the context and the sentence. Then write the correct form in the space provided.

1. (*formidableness, formidability, formidable, formidably*) Because of Crotalus's

   _____ size and strength, it became less likely that another animal could kill him.

2. (*bewilderment, bewilder, bewildered*) Crotalus felt _____ the first time he shed his skin.

3. (*symmetry, symmetrical, symmetrically*) As an adult rattlesnake, Crotalus's

   body was an example of perfect _____.

4. (*domination, dominated, dominant, dominantly*) Crotalus was _____ over that particular tribe of snakes.

5. (*sporadic, sporadically*) At first the homesteaders carried out their

   extermination campaign _____.

G. TOPICS FOR DISCUSSION

1. Why does Finney delay identifying Crotalus as a rattlesnake until paragraph 6?
2. Look up the meaning of the *chronological* in the dictionary. Then explain the connection between this word and the way Finney organizes his ideas.
3. Look again through paragraphs 1–8. Most of the sentences are short and simple. What do sentences like this lend to the story?

H. TOPICS FOR WRITING

1. On separate paper, write a short summary of the physical changes Crotalus underwent throughout his life, from his birth to adulthood.
2. Describe the life cycle of an animal or organism that you have observed or studied.
3. An imbalance between the native organisms in an environment is a common problem today. Sometimes these imbalances are a result of human interference with the population; sometimes they have natural causes. For example, in the West, the native deer population has grown to a point where the environment can often no longer support it, mainly because the numbers of the deer's natural predators—mountain lions and bobcats—are declining. Investigate and report on an ecological imbalance in your area.

Exploring Related Web Sites

Further information, including photographs, about diamondback rattlers of the American Southwest can be found at these sites. The first one is sponsored by the San Diego Natural History Museum.

www.sdnhm.org/fieldguide/herps/crot-atr.html

www.biopark.org/Catrox.html

http://whozoo.org/AnlifeSS2001/mindpapr/MP_WesternDiamondback.html

www.californiaherps.com/snakes/pages/c.atrox.html

PART TWO

Refining the Basics

Annotating, Paraphrasing, and Summarizing

The skills you will learn in Part Two follow directly from the work you did in Part One—finding main ideas and locating supporting details. The three skills you will learn here—annotating, paraphrasing, and summarizing—are not only extraordinarily useful for college students but also for anyone who must understand, absorb, remember, and condense information from the printed page. The following diagram summarizes and defines them:

Annotating	A study and comprehension skill, which includes: Writing notes in the margin of a text, circling words you don't know, noting questions to ask, and otherwise interacting with the text
Paraphrasing	A comprehension and writing skill, which includes: Putting a writer's words into your own words without leaving anything important out, similar to translating
Summarizing	A comprehension and writing skill, which includes: Writing a passage that condenses a writer's ideas by identifying only the main points and omitting unimportant supporting details

What is the relationship among these three skills? Annotating is the first step both to good comprehension and to writing a successful summary; paraphrasing is a preliminary step necessary to produce a good summary. Finally, both paraphrasing and summarizing show you and your instructor how well you have understood what you read and how accurately you can convey the ideas in your own words.

ANNOTATING

College students often complain about having a bad memory because they claim not to remember a lot of what they read. But I think that the source of this problem lies elsewhere. The culprit may not be a bad memory, but *passive reading*. Rather than being actively involved with the material, a passive reader is an optimist. She reads the text once, hoping to get the full meaning without doing the hard work that good comprehension requires.

It's almost impossible for a reader—even a very experienced reader—to get the full meaning and to remember what's important after one only reading. (I am referring here specifically to your college reading assignments, where good comprehension is required, not to the kind of casual reading you do in popular magazines, in the daily paper, or online.) Nothing is more frustrating to a student than to complete an assigned essay for his English class and then to be forced to admit that he doesn't remember much of what he read.

Students whom I tutor each week tell me that they often don't understand much of what they read—a quite different problem from not remembering.

When students tell me that they have read an essay three times and still don't get it, the more likely culprit is that they haven't bothered to look up unfamiliar vocabulary words. I always gently remind them that they could read an essay 50 times and, unless they know what the words on the page mean, they'll never get it. If this problem sounds familiar to you, now would be a good time to review the section at the beginning of the text on vocabulary improvement techniques.

As for the student who can't remember what he just read, he has wasted a lot of valuable time, requiring him to read the assignment again, and perhaps even a third time. It is much less likely that you will lose focus or that you will get distracted if you get into the habit of annotating the text. This means that while you read, you write notes in the margins.

You already have seen this process demonstrated in the introduction to Part One, where you identified main and supporting ideas. This next section explains and demonstrates the process of annotating in more detail. Throughout the text, you will have many opportunities to practice this skill, and your instructor may require you to practice annotating beyond the exercises in this book.

How to Annotate Annotating is sometimes called reading with a pencil in your hand. (And using a pencil is a good idea, so that you can erase your notes later, if you want to.) If you can't bear to mark up your text because you want to sell the book back after the course ends, then make a photocopy of the assignment. This will allow you to mark it up as much as you want.

Note, too, that annotating is not the same as highlighting the words with a yellow or pink Magic Marker. Many students rely on these markers as a study aid while they read their textbook assignments; reading instructors, however, generally discourage this practice. Such marks only tell you that the material will be important to learn—some day! As such, highlighting is a *passive* activity. And my students tell me that because they are uncertain what to highlight, they end up highlighting too much. Over-highlighting makes the pages look colorful to be sure, but it is not an efficient way to get and to retain the main points.

Careful annotating, in contrast, allows you both to read *actively* and to pull out the essential ideas at the same time. Here are some suggestions for good annotations. Study them before you continue on to study the models that follow.

TECHNIQUES FOR ANNOTATING	
Main ideas	Jot down little phrases in your own words, restating the main ideas.
Phrases or sentences that you don't understand	Put a question mark in the margin.
Vocabulary words that are unfamiliar to you	Circle them in the text.
Questions to ask in class	Write in the margin and mark with a clear symbol of your own devising.
Ideas that you disagree with	Write a star or some other symbol in the margin.

To illustrate this process, consider a brief excerpt from Selection 12 that appears in this section of the text, Virginia Morell's "Minds of Their Own," which discusses animal intelligence, cognition, and use of language. Read the passage first; then study the annotations.

Dolphins—social animals
Experiments in Hawaii
tested for cognitive abilities
**Why are dolphins called "cosmopolitan"?

In the late 1960s a cognitive psychologist named Louis Herman began investigating the cognitive abilities of bottlenose dolphins. Like humans, dolphins are highly social and (cosmopolitan,) living in subpolar to tropical environments worldwide; they're highly vocal; and they have special sensory skills, such as echolocation. By the 1980s Herman's cognitive studies were focused on a group of four young dolphins—Akeakamai, Phoenix, Elele, and Hiapo—at the Kewalo Basin Marine Mammal Laboratory in Hawaii. The dolphins were curious and playful, and they transferred their sociability to Herman and his students.

Louis Herman— experimented to see how complex dolphin brains are
**What does he mean by "flower" in this sense?

"In our work with the dolphins, we had a guiding philosophy," Herman says, "that we could bring out the full (flower) of their intellect, just as educators try to bring out the full potential of a human child. Dolphins have these big, highly complex brains. My thought was, 'OK, so you have this pretty brain. Let's see what you can do with it.'"

Hand-and-arm signals represented basic grammar Dolphins did well, showed that they understood grammar

To communicate with the dolphins, Herman and his team invented a hand- and arm-signal language, complete with a simple grammar. For instance, a pumping motion of the closed fists meant "hoop," and both arms extended overhead (as in jumping jacks) meant "ball." A "come here" gesture with a single arm told them to "fetch." Responding to the request "hoop, ball, fetch," Akeakamai would push the ball to the hoop. But if the word order was changed to "ball, hoop, fetch," she would carry the hoop to the ball. Over time she could interpret more grammatically complex requests, such as "right, basket, left, Frisbee, in," asking that she put the Frisbee on her left in the basket on her right. Reversing "left" and "right" in the instruction would reverse Akeakamai's actions. Akeakamai could complete such requests the first time they were made, showing a deep understanding of the grammar of the language.

Here are the next five paragraphs from this discussion of dolphins' cognitive abilities for you to practice with. Remember to keep your notes brief (don't write in complete sentences), and to circle unfamiliar words. Since students must often use annotating to prepare writing assignments, for the purposes of this exercise, assume that you must write an essay explaining dolphin intelligence. Annotate the passage with this subject in mind.

"They're a very vocal species," Herman adds. "Our studies showed that they could imitate arbitrary sounds that we broadcast into their tank, an ability that may be tied to their own need to communicate. I'm not saying they have a dolphin language. But they are capable of understanding the novel instructions that we convey to them in a tutored language; their brains have that ability.

"There are many things they could do that people have always doubted about animals. For example, they correctly interpreted, on the very first occasion, gestured instructions given by a person displayed on a TV screen behind an underwater window. They recognized that television images were representations of the real world that could be acted on in the same way as in the real world."

They readily imitated motor behaviors of their instructors too. If a trainer bent backward and lifted a leg, the dolphin would turn on its back and lift its tail in the air. Although imitation was once regarded as a simpleminded skill, in recent years cognitive scientists have revealed that it's extremely difficult, requiring the imitator to form a mental image of the other person's body and pose, then adjust his own body parts into the same position—actions that imply an awareness of one's self.

"Here's Elele," Herman says, showing a film of her following a trainer's directions. "Surfboard, dorsal fin, touch." Instantly Elele swam to the board and, leaning to one side, gently laid her dorsal fin on it, an untrained behavior. The trainer stretched her arms straight up, signaling "Hooray!" and Elele leaped into the air, squeaking and clicking with delight.

"Elele just loved to be right," Herman said, "And she loved inventing things. We made up a sign for 'create' which asked a dolphin to create its own behavior."

One final word: Keep your annotations neat and brief. You don't want to clutter up the margins with too many notes or with words that you can't read in a few weeks. Annotate only the main idea and important supporting details, not unimportant or reinforcing details.

PARAPHRASING

Next we turn to paraphrasing, a skill that I often use in both my reading and composition classes. Paraphrasing helps you to focus and to read accurately. As you will recall from the introduction to this section, *paraphrasing* means restating the writer's words in your own words. It is useful both to test comprehension and to clarify meaning. When you paraphrase, you to go through the passage one sentence at a time, rewriting and changing the words into your own words as much as possible, without changing the meaning of the original. That's the hard part. Also it is perfectly all right if your paraphrase turns out to be longer than the original. To write a successful paraphrase, consider the suggestions below:

TECHNIQUES FOR PARAPHRASING
• Substitute a synonym (a word that means the same) for a key word in the original.
• An exception to the above: Don't strain to find a synonym for major words. Call a dolphin a *dolphin*, not a marine cetacean mammal.
• Omit very unimportant ideas if your instructor allows this.
• Combine ideas when possible.
• Maintain the flavor and level of formality of the original passage.
• Do not inject your own ideas or opinions.

First read the following passage, which comes from Selection 7 in Part One by Charles Finney, "The Life and Death of a Western Gladiator." Then study the paraphrase and compare it with the original. See if you can identify each of the techniques from the box above.

Original Passage

At twelve he was a magnificent reptile. Not a single scar defaced his rippling symmetry. He was diabolically beautiful and deadly poison.

His venom was his only weapon, for he had no power of constriction. Yellowish in color, his poison was colorless and tasteless. It was a highly complex mixture of proteids, each in itself direly toxic. His venom worked on the blood. The more poison he injected with a bite, the more dangerous the wound. The pain rendered by his bite was instantaneous, and the shock accompanying it was profound. Swelling began immediately, to be followed by a ghastly oozing. Injected directly into a large vein, his poison brought death quickly, for the victim died when it reached his heart. (121 words)

Paraphrase

By the time he turned 12, he was a most impressive snake. He had no scars from fighting, he was beautiful in a very scary way, and the poison in his bite was lethal.

Because he was not a constrictor, he killed his victims with his venom, which was yellowish with no smell or taste. Composed of a complex of incredibly toxic proteids, his venom poisoned the blood, and the more venom he injected into a wound, the more dangerous it was. His victim suffered immediate pain, shock, and swelling. And if the snake injected the venom into a large vein, the victim died as soon as it reached its heart. (111 words)

Here are two short passages for you to practice with. The first is paragraph 26 from "Life and Death of a Western Gladiator."

Original Passage

He had not experienced death for the simple reason that there had never been an opportunity for anything bigger and stronger than himself to kill him. Now, at two, because he was so formidable, that opportunity became more and more unlikely. (41 words)

Write your paraphrase here:

The second is a bit longer—paragraph 4 from Rose Guilbault's selection "School Days."

Original Passage

I intuitively knew that the person I leaned on for everything—my mother—would not be able to help me. She relied heavily on her own experiences as a basis of understanding the world, and just as the Wizard of Oz had nothing in his bag for Dorothy, she had nothing to smooth this assimilation for me. Once I stepped outside my door, I was all alone and had to fend for myself. The only thing I feared more than school was disappointing my mother, so I hid my anxieties. (90 words)

Write your paraphrase here:

_____

_____

_____

_____

_____

_____

_____

_____

_____

_____

SUMMARIZING

Summarizing—the last skill—is the culmination of the other two skills: Before you can write a summary, you must first annotate the text; the summary-writing process requires you to paraphrase important points but also to eliminate minor supporting details. The point of writing a summary is to convey only the most important information, so you have to develop a feel for what to save and what to drop. This process sounds harder than it really is. When one paints a room, he or she has to spend more time preparing the surface than actually painting it. Writing a summary is the same. It just takes good preparation and practice.

First, study the chart below, which lists the techniques for summarizing. You may use them all, or you may decide that some work better than others. Before you begin, I suggest making a photocopy of the selection you are summarizing so that you can annotate it easily.

TECHNIQUES FOR SUMMARIZING

- Read the selection and circle unfamiliar words.
- Read the selection again, annotate it, and look up circled words.
- Underline important phrases and sentences and cross out unimportant material.
- Copy the notes from your margins onto a piece of paper or type them into a computer. Leave plenty of space between your notes from each paragraph.
- Review your notes. Add or delete information as needed.
- Rewrite the selection, condensing where you can. Substitute your own words for the writer's, where possible, and add transitions to show the relationship between ideas.
- Read through your summary and check for accuracy. Be sure you don't introduce your own ideas or opinions.

Now study this short example, which comes from Selection 11, "The Language Explosion" by Geoffrey Cowley. Pay particular attention to the crossed out words and phrases.

Original Passage

~~The journey toward~~ language starts ~~not in the nursery but~~ in the womb, where the fetus is ~~continually~~ bathed in the sounds of its mother's voice. Babies just 4 days old can distinguish one language from another. ~~French newborns suck more vigorously when they hear French spoken than when they hear Russian—and Russian babies show the opposite preference.~~ At first, ~~they notice only~~ general rhythms and melodies. But newborns ~~are also~~ sensitive to speech sounds, ~~and they~~ home in quickly on the ones that matter. (86 words)

Summary

A baby listens to its mother's language in the womb. Even at 4 days, babies can distinguish their mother's language from another. Initially, they hear only general rhythms, but soon they focus on the sounds of their native language. (39 words)

A rule of thumb is that a summary should be about 25 percent of the original length. The sample summary above is longer than 25 percent, but that is because we are working with only a single paragraph with very few ideas to omit. In longer passages, as you will see in the next section, there will be more information to cut.

Forcing yourself to limit a summary to an arbitrary number of words is an intellectually rigorous and challenging exercise. It requires you to think about what to save and what to omit, how to keep the meaning of the original, using the fewest possible words, and how not to distort the meaning. The trick to writing a good summary is to see the difference between main ideas and supporting details. Crossing out unnecessary words and phrases, as demonstrated above, allows you more easily to see what is essential to save and what can be safely eliminated.

For further practice in summarizing, here is a mini-essay from *Discover* magazine. Its subject is a strange one—monkeys that eat charcoal. The original passage is around 325 words long, so try to keep your summary between 80 and 100 words.[1]

---

[1]You can count your words manually or, in Microsoft Word, you can select "Word Count" from the "Tools" menu.

Original Passage

Monkeys in Zanzibar eat charcoal to neutralize toxins in their diet. ("A Briquette a Day," *Discover*)

The human population of Zanzibar, a Tanzanian island off the East African coast, doubles every 15 years or so. The island's red colobus monkeys, however, are dwindling as their habitats are destroyed for firewood and timber. But some monkeys have found a way to coexist with humans: they snack on charcoal.

Thomas Struhsaker, a zoologist at Duke University, has been studying the effects of selective logging on rain forest wildlife in eastern Africa. A Tanzanian biologist told him about the monkeys' charcoal habit in 1981. Over the years, as the human population grew, Struhsaker noticed that the monkeys ate more and more charcoal. "Each animal," he says, "eats about five grams a day."

The monkeys live in an area with almond, mango, and other exotic fruit trees. The leaves of these trees are rich in protein but also contain toxic compounds like tannic acids. Most animals avoid the leaves. But charcoal has a well-known ability to absorb toxins—it is

Summary

_____

_____

_____

_____

_____

_____

_____

_____

_____

_____

_____

_____

_____

_____

_____

_____

_____

_____

_____

_____

_____

_____

_____

_____

_____

_____

used as a poison control agent, and in Europe people use it in liquid form as a digestive aid. When a monkey eats charcoal after chomping on leaves, its meal goes down a little easier. The charcoal selectively holds on to large tannic acid molecules, allowing them to pass through the body while smaller nutritious proteins are absorbed by the gut.

The monkeys snatch charcoal from kilns and also nibble on charred wood and tree stumps. Struhsaker isn't sure how they acquired the habit. "There must be a quick effect so they can learn by association," he says. Baby monkeys, at least, learn from imitating their mothers, and the mothers themselves may have learned from eating soil containing charcoal particles.

"These are pretty clever animals," says Struhsaker. "They've picked up a habit that allows them to exploit a resource to an extent that was not possible before." Despite this adaptation, red colobus populations are still shrinking in Zanzibar, even in nature reserves, where speeding cars take a large toll. "If they put the potholes back in the road, or built speed bumps, I think the reserve animals would be fine."

"A Briquette a Day," *Discover* Magazine, July 1998. Reprinted by permission.

8

MARC IAN BARASCH

The Bystander's Dilemma: Why Do We Walk on By?

Marc Ian Barasch, a former editor for Psychology Today, *studied literature, philosophy, and film at Yale University. A practicing Buddhist, Barasch has written a book titled* Field Notes on the Compassionate Life: A Search for the Soul of Kindness. *The book is about empathy, altruism, and compassion—an exploration into human conduct based on acting from unselfish motives and with sensitivity to others' problems. This selection was adapted from the book and was later reprinted in a magazine titled* Greater Good, *published by the Center for the Development of Peace and Well-Being at the University of California, Berkeley. In the essay, which I have slightly condensed, Barasch examines the "bystander's dilemma"—why we often fail to come to the aid of someone in trouble. In this excerpt, Barasch describes his experiment—what it is like to panhandle on the streets of Denver.*

Vocabulary Preview

WORD PARTS

em- [paragraph 18] Used to form verbs from adjectives, the prefix *em-* indicates "becoming" or "causing to be." *Empower,* therefore, means "causing one to have power." The prefix can also be spelled *en-,* depending on the initial letter of the root word. Here are some other examples of words beginning with this prefix:

encourage	to cause to be courageous, to give courage to
entrap	to cause (someone) to be trapped
enliven	to give life to, make more lively or energetic

What do these words mean? Check a dictionary if necessary.

embellish	_____
enlighten	_____
embroil	_____

equi- [17] When we *equivocate,* we use language that avoids making a clear statement or that misleads, from Latin *equi-* ("equal") + *voc-* ("to call"). In other words, equivocation involves saying two things at the same time rather than being decisive.

Some other words that begin with this prefix, signifying either equal or equality, are these:

equivalent   having equal value
equity   the state of being fair and impartial
equilibrium   state of balance due to the equal action of opposing forces

If your house is equidistant from your college and your place of work, what does

that mean? _____

**WORD
FAMILIES**

potent [paragraph 2] The homeless often smell bad, or as Barasch says, their smell is *potent* because it intrudes so strongly on passersby. *Potent* means "powerful," derived from the Latin root *potens*, or "power." Here are two other words in this family:

impotent   the opposite of potent, often referring to a man who is incapable of sexual activity
potential   having the power or capacity for future development

What is a potentate? _____

MARC IAN BARASCH

The Bystander's Dilemma: Why Do We Walk on By?

1   It was one of those small encounters that lodges in the mind like a pebble in the shoe: A few years ago, walking back from the market at dusk, I heard a muffled keening coming from a pile of discarded coats on the sidewalk 20 yards ahead. The sound became more intense as I approached, a kind of Doppler effect, until I made out a man about my age, wrapped in layers of outerwear, loudly demanding a handout. I gave him a dollar and, for good measure, dug into my bag for an apple. But my conscience was hardly appeased.

2   Street people. The homeless. Truth be told, most of us find them an annoyance. They barge into public space (sometimes their smell, supernally potent, intrudes first), interrupting our train of thought or flow of conversation. Haven't they brought this on themselves in some way (in some way *we* clearly haven't)? Why don't they get a job, bootstrap themselves out of purgatory? We avert our eyes, feign sudden deafness, sidestep them as they sprawl at our feet. We're as eager to cross paths with them as we would be with Marley's Ghost.[1]

---

[1] Jacob Marley, or Marley's Ghost, a character in Charles Dickens's *A Christmas Carol,* appears before Ebenezer Scrooge at the beginning of the novel to warn him. Scrooge thinks that the ghost is merely a figment of his imagination. (Ed.)

3   That I had barely helped the man had a sting of irony, as I'd just begun re-searching a new book on empathy, altruism, and compassion. Browsing for quotes, I'd stumbled on *Works of Love*, a tome by the alternately cranky and transcendent 19th century philosopher Søren Kierkegaard,[2] whose moral scolding had instantly gotten under my skin. When he mocked that person who is "never among the more lowly"; who "will go about with closed eyes . . . when he moves around in the human throng"; and jeered the existential snob who "thinks he exists only for the distinguished, that he is to live only in the alliance of their circles," well . . . I couldn't pretend I didn't know whom he was talking about.

4   In fact, I was anticipating a rather gala break in my writing schedule: a trip to Cannes and then on to a farmhouse in glorious Provence, an offer from a jetsetting filmmaker buddy I could hardly refuse.

5   But then another invitation had suddenly cropped up in the same calendar slot, this one from a group called the Zen Peacemaker Order, to go on what they called a "street retreat." With the back of my neck still prickling under Kierkegaard's gaze (to say nothing of my editor's), I decided to stay on the ground. Literally. The retreat rules were simple: Hit the pavement unbathed and unshaven, without money or change of clothes, joining for the better part of a week the ranks of those whom life had kicked to the curb. A sojourn in the land of *ain't got nothin', got nothin' to lose* might, I thought, pierce my bystander's armor. . . .

BEARING WITNESS

6   The street retreats are the brainchild of Bernie Glassman. A bearded, portly for-mer aerospace engineer ordained as a Buddhist *roshi*,[3] Bernie had been looking for ways to integrate spiritual practice with compassionate social action. Some-time in the 1980s, he decided to spend a few months walking aimlessly around the inner-city Bronx neighborhood that abutted his meditation center, hanging out, talking with people in his cannily receptive way, listening to their problems. Out of this had grown, as naturally and prolifically as a zucchini patch, a sprawling multimillion-dollar social organization serving the rebuked and the scorned.

7   First there was the Greyston Bakery, which employed people just getting out of prison or off the street. The business grew, eventually snagging a contract to make brownies for Ben and Jerry's Ice Cream. But it soon came smack up against the endemic problems of the neighborhood. People missed work because of drug problems. Batches of dough were ruined because employees lacked basic math skills to measure ingredients or the reading skills to decipher labels on cans. But each problem had suggested, after trial and error, its own solution. The Greyston Mandala that emerged from Bernie's first street-scuffing walka-bout now trains, employs, houses, and provides health services to hundreds of the formerly marginal, as well as offering care and housing to people with AIDS on the site of a former Catholic nunnery.

---

[2] Søren Kierkegaard (1813–1855) was a Danish philosopher and thinker, often called the father of exis-tentialism. He advocated a passionate commitment to others and taking responsibility for one's own actions while rejecting traditional rationalism. (Ed.)
[3] In Zen Buddhism a *roshi* is a spiritual leader. (Ed.)

8   When Bernie's 55th birthday rolled around, rather than resting on his laurels, he decided to spend a few days sitting homeless on the steps of the Capitol, figuring out what next to do with his life. During what turned out to be Washington, D.C.'s coldest, snowiest week in half a century, he dreamed up the multifaith Peacemaker Order, a spiritual path based on just bearing witness and seeing what happened.

9   "When we bear witness," he wrote, when we become the situation— homelessness, poverty, illness, violence, death—then right action arises by itself. We don't have to worry about what to do. We don't have to figure out solutions ahead of time. . . . It's as simple as giving a hand to someone who stumbles, or picking up a child who has fallen on the floor."

10   You could say, Witness, *schmitness*.[4] Fine for Bernie, with his track record of weaving straw into gold. But if he hadn't recommended it, I'd be hard put to justify my week of taking to the streets in a bum costume, as if I and my fellow retreatants didn't have somewhere better to go. What I had to tell myself was, at least for this interlude, there would be no "better," and no worse.

THE HAUNTED STREET

11   And so I find myself living on the streets of Denver, dressed in ratty, stinking clothes, a toothbrush in my pocket and a week's worth of stubble on my cold-reddened cheeks. I'm hoping to discover some way to be a little less full of myself; to see if more kindness might arise if I persuade Mr. Ego to move out for a week.

12   But what I find arising is my innate irritability. I can be impatient, and homelessness involves lots of waiting: waiting for a soup kitchen to open, then waiting for your number to be called for a meal; waiting for the rain or snow to let up, or for a cop to stop looking your way. It's a different map of the world: Which Starbucks has a security guard who'll let you use the bathroom? How long can you linger in this place or that before you're rousted? It's pretty much a stray dog's life, sniffing for a bone to gnaw, a tree to piss on, knowing nobody wants you, wary of the company you keep.

13   And what to make of my new company? My friend Søren K.,[5] in his tough-old-bird fashion, argued against harboring any delusions that "by loving some people, relatives and friends, you would be loving the neighbor." No, he squawked, the real point is "to frighten you out of the beloved haunts of preferential love." Most of my new neighbors *are* haunted. Life has failed them, or they've failed it. A tall, stringy young man with lank, black-dyed hair, tattooed like a Maori, tells me, "If you see Sherry, tell her Big John's back from Oklahoma." His eyes have the jittery glint of crank, each pupil a spinning disco ball, fitfully sparkling. An alcoholic Indian vet yanks open his shirt to show me his scars—the roundish puckers from shrapnel, the short, telegraphic dashes from ritual piercing at a Sun Dance—weeping over a life he no longer wants.

---

[4] "Witness, schmitness" is an example of a Yiddish expression in which one says a word and then repeats it, but this time changing the first consonant to "sch." The phrase thus dismisses the idea. (Ed.)
[5] Søren Kierkegaard. (Ed.)

14 An angry-looking man approaches me to ask—to demand—that I give him a plastic fork, purpose unknown. When I demur, he stalks over to the dumpster and scrabbles through it unproductively.

15 "I'm sorry," I say.

16 "I'll just *bet* you are," he snarls, then raises both middle fingers, staring into my eyes with cold fury.

17 I can't say I'm pleased to meet him, but WWKD: What Would Kierkegaard Do?[6] "Root out all equivocation and fastidiousness in loving them!" *Sir, yessir.* The Buddhist sage Atisha recommended a prayer upon encountering those folks who mess with our minds: *When I see beings of a negative disposition, or those oppressed by negativity or pain, may I, as if finding a treasure, consider them precious.*

18 Every cerebral word of this homily is *not* running through my head as I step toward my new neighbor with a little faux-nod of appreciation, hoping he hasn't stashed a ball-peen hammer in his coat. But he backs away, lips curled, then turns and runs, pursued by some host of invisibles. At least, I tell myself, I've managed to become more curious about him than repulsed, mindful that the more I amp up my judgment of others, the more I empower that ogre of criticism that grinds my own bones to make its bread. Really, I don't know how these guys drove their lives into the ditch, or how to winch them out. I try to stay present, feeling my heart's systole and diastole, its sympathies opening, closing, opening, closing.

THE DEBT OF LOVE

19 I'm willing to practice extending those sympathies to my street neighbors. But I'm not nearly as enthusiastic about doing what the Zen Peacemaker Order refers to as "begging practice." The thought horrifies me. Sure, I've done that high-class begging known as fundraising, palm outstretched for checks written out to high-minded projects. But I've always felt it was worth the other person's while; there were good deeds to show for it. Here on the street I, the beggar, have nothing to offer the beggee. There is no mutual exchange, just an imbalance of boons. I'm a walking bundle of needs, and it galls me.

20 Besides, it isn't easy to get those needs met. Faces turn to stone at my plea for food money. Eyes flicker sideways, ahead to the middle distance, to the ground, anywhere but the empty space where I'm standing. The Confucians of the Sung Dynasty compared not feeling compassion for a stranger to not feeling that your own foot's caught fire, and too many of us seem to have gone numb. (I think of an acquaintance of mine, a much-awarded designer of leafy town squares in the New Urbanist style. "Of course," he once said to me ruefully, "the more open space, the bigger the quotient of 'bummage.'")

21 Bummage I am. I supplicate downtown pedestrians, dauntingly busy on their way from here to there, clutching purses and shopping bags and cell phones and lovers' waists. I recognize the filmy bubble of self-concept that surrounds them, that protective aura of specialness. How often do most of us secretly say to ourselves that we're smarter, stronger, taller, more charming than average; have

---

[6] A play on a common question asked by Christians: WWJD? or What Would Jesus Do? (Ed.)

a cooler job, a more lovely spouse, more accomplished children; that we are (somehow) more spiritual, even more selfless? Anything is grist for the mill of selfhood versus otherness, of the gourmet-flavored me versus plain-vanilla everyone else. I, too, have achieved my differentiation at some cost and considerable effort; even here, hugging the ground, I resist inhabiting the same universe as the full-time failures.

22   But I'm already there in one respect: My panhandling talents are nil. Each rejection thuds like a body blow. I can see the little comic-strip thought balloon spring from people's brows— *Get a job; I work!* It occurs to me to just forget it. Though we've agreed that during the week we'd each scrape up $3.50 for the bus fare home, throwing any extra into the kitty for the homeless shelter, I think, *Why put myself through it? I'll send a check when I get home.*

23   But I'm hungry *now.* I'm also starting to realize that there's more to "begging practice" than meets the eye. Roshi Bernie Glassman has explained it with disarming simplicity: "When we don't ask, we don't let others give. When we fear rejection, we don't let generosity arise." I realize that the street, much like a meditation cushion, has put my issues on parade, and this begging routine's got them goose-stepping smartly past the reviewing stand. There's the Humiliation Battalion. The Fear of Rejection Brigade. The Undeserving Auxiliary. And of course, the Judgment Detachment—for I find I'm even judging my potential donors (are *they* good enough to give *me* a dollar?).

24   My profound reluctance to ask passersby for help feels not unlike my aversion to calling friends when I'm needful in other ways, those times when I'm feeling sad, lost, lonely, bereft. I prize autonomy; I'm overly proud of it. I don't *want* to owe people for my well-being. Or just maybe I don't want to owe them my love. I wonder suddenly if I'm not rejecting gratitude itself, that spiritual 3-in-1 oil said to open the creakiest gate around the heart? Aren't we all in debt—to our parents, teachers, friends, and loved ones—for our very existence?

25   But dear Søren Kierkegaard thought even *this* was a crock. Sure, he said, we think the person who is loved owes a debt of gratitude to the one who loves them. There is an expectation that it should be repaid in kind, on installment, "reminiscent," he says sarcastically, "of an actual bookkeeping arrangement." Instead, he turns the whole thing on its head: "No, the one who loves runs into debt; in feeling himself gripped by love, he feels this as being in an infinite debt. Amazing!"

26   *Amazing.* It is his most radical proposition: We owe those who elicit love from us for allowing us to be overfilled with the stuff. We owe a debt to those who suffer because they draw forth our tenderness. (Do I think that by avoiding others' suffering, I can hoard my stash of good feelings and not get bummed out? The "helper's high" phenomenon suggests the opposite: It's giving that turns on the juice, taps us into the infinite current.) Giving and taking start to seem less like zero-sum transactions than some universal love-circuitry, where what goes around not only comes around but comes back redoubled.

27   Still, "How'd you like to enter into Kierkegaard's infinite debt of love?" is not going to win Year's Best Panhandling Line. I ask a stylish young guy—*No War: Not in Our Name* button on his fawn-colored coat, canvas messenger bag in muted gray—if he can spare a little change for food. He calls out chidingly over

his shoulder, "I don't give *on the street.*" Fair enough. But the bank building's LED thermometer reads 25 degrees, and the sun still hasn't gone down. I haven't had dinner. Sleeping on the street is a frigid proposition, and body heat requires calories. Then I realize I'm judging him and everyone else, defeating the whole purpose of the exercise. I make a point to mentally bless all comers and goers.

28   I approach a bearded guy in a fringed suede jacket. He declines, but hangs around as if waiting for someone. A few minutes later, hearing me unsuccessfully petition a half dozen more people, he comes over and hands me two dollars, cautioning *sotto voce*, "Don't tell anyone I gave it to you," as if worried I'd alert a Fagin's gang of accomplices.[7]

29   I've now streamlined my pitch: "I'm sleeping on the street tonight, I'm hungry. I wonder if you could help me out at all?" Most people's eyes still slam down like steel shutters over a storefront at closing time, but then, ". . . Could you help me out?" and a man who's just passed me with a curt *No* pivots abruptly, yanked like a puppet by his heartstrings, and walks back with a green bill. "On second thought, I can." And I see in that moment how much more effort it takes to resist the raw tug of each other's existence.

30   I strike out another 20 or 30 times before a crisp-looking gent crosses my palm with silver. "Thanks so much, it's chilly out tonight," I mumble, surprised after so many averted gazes. "It *is* cold," he says sympathetically, and those three words restore my faith.

SMALL CHANGE

31   A week later, back home again, I'm delighted to be sleeping in my own bed. Bathed, shaved, fed, dressed, I take a walk on the mall with a friend. He looks at me askance as I press a dollar into a panhandler's palm and then, seeing how browbeaten the man looks, peel off another two and chat with him for a while.

32   I'm trying to become insufferably virtuous, I tell my friend. How am I doing?

33   Great, he replies, you're getting on my nerves.

34   These days, I give money to the people with cardboard signs who stake out corners on trafficked streets, remembering when I was stranded once on the highway, having to scare up a ride with my own magic-markered plea. One guy comes up to the window to recite his story as my car idles at a light. He's a former truck driver with a neck injury, he says, saving up for surgery. He seems utterly sincere, though I'm not sure that matters: I know he must have his reasons. I hand him a bill and drive off. Then, feeling suddenly touched, I circle the block and cut recklessly through two lanes of traffic to give him another. "For your medical fund," I yell, practically hurling a tenner at him to beat the light. "God bless you, you and your family," he yells after me; and yes, I think, he's for real, and yes, I also think, how Dickensian: *Oh, kind sir.* But I also mentally thank him for helping me sink deeper into that debt that swallows all others and makes them small—small, and of no consequence.

35   I won't claim I've evolved that much. Not in a week or two; not in a few months. Sure, I help out, sometimes, at the local soup kitchen; kick in for the

---

[7]Another reference to a Dickens novel, in this case *Oliver Twist*. Fagin is a criminal who recruits little boys and teaches them to be thieves and pickpockets. (Ed.)

anti-homelessness coalition. But I do feel as if my inner pockets have been turned inside out, shaking loose some small change in my life. I've developed an ineluctable soft spot. I can't help but notice the people at the margins, the ones who used to be the extras in my movie. Knowing a little of how they feel makes me an easy touch. The money I give out sometimes mounts up, 20, 30 bucks a month, unburdening the wallet, filling the heart's purse. Until I figure out what I can do to really change things—or until the world becomes a different place—this feels better than okay. ✳

Marc Ian Barasch, "The Bystander's Dilemma: Why Do We Walk on By?" from *Greater Good* (Fall/Winter 2006–2007). Reprinted with the permission of the author.

Exercises

Do not refer to the selection for Exercises A–C unless your instructor directs you to do so.

A. DETERMINING THE MAIN IDEA AND PURPOSE

Choose the best answer.

_____ 1. The main idea of the selection is that

    a. homelessness is an endemic, persistent problem in American cities.

    b. there is a great deal of disagreement among social thinkers and philosophers about how we should respond to the homeless.

    c. for the writer, panhandling for a week gave him a new perspective and newfound compassion for the homeless.

    d. street retreats are a novel way to integrate spiritual practice with compassionate social action.

_____ 2. With respect to the presence of the homeless in his community, the writer's purpose is to

    a. discuss various methods that communities have used to deal with the issue.

    b. describe his search for both a philosophic and a practical response to them.

    c. explain the philosopher Søren Kierkegaard's thinking about compassion.

    d. urge cities and municipal governments to establish more programs to help them.

B. COMPREHENDING MAIN IDEAS

Choose the correct answer.

_____ 1. Barasch's encounter with a homeless man who asked for money was ironic because

    a. he was researching a book on compassion at the time.

    b. he had recently been homeless himself.

     c. he had never thought much about the homeless problem before.

     d. he had never given money to panhandlers before.

_____ **2.** The purpose of the street retreat sponsored by the Zen Peacemaker Order was to

     a. teach people a workable and compassionate response to the homeless by following the thinking of Søren Kierkegaard.

     b. sponsor job training programs and improved accommodations for the homeless.

     c. ask participants to panhandle and live on the streets for a week.

     d. offer religious services for the homeless.

_____ **3.** Bernie Glassman's project, the Greyston Bakery, was unusual because it

     a. was immediately successful, far beyond what anyone expected.

     b. was the first project to be sponsored by Buddhists.

     c. made ice cream for Ben & Jerry's.

     d. gave former prisoners and homeless people an opportunity for employment.

_____ **4.** The philosophic idea behind Bernie Glassman's project, sponsored by the Peacemaker Order, is to "bear witness," which means that participants

     a. actually become the situation and experience homelessness firsthand.

     b. observe and record their impressions of what they see.

     c. figure out solutions to a problem and then apply them.

     d. give money to the homeless without asking them what it will be used for.

_____ **5.** Barasch observes that the daily life of a homeless person is filled with lots of

     a. waiting.

     b. encounters with angry citizens who tell him or her to get a job.

     c. small joys that make life a bit less miserable.

     d. time for pondering life's larger issues.

_____ **6.** Because of Barasch's experience on the streets of Denver, he now

     a. talks to panhandlers and learns their stories before deciding whether to give money.

     b. notices people who live on the margins and often gives them money.

     c. refuses to hand out money to those who can't get their lives together.

     d. hands out pamphlets telling panhandlers where they can get help.

COMPREHENSION SCORE

Score your answers for Exercises A and B as follows:

A. No. right _____ × 2 = _____
B. No. right _____ × 1 = _____

Total points from A and B _____ × 10 = _____ percent

C. SEQUENCING

These sentences from one paragraph in the selection have been scrambled. Read the sentences and choose the sequence that puts them back into logical order. Do not refer to the original selection.

1 Sometime in the 1980s, he decided to spend a few months walking aimlessly around the inner-city Bronx neighborhood that abutted his meditation center, hanging out, talking with people in his cannily receptive way, listening to their problems. **2** A bearded, portly former aerospace engineer ordained as a Buddhist *roshi*, Bernie had been looking for ways to integrate spiritual practice with compassionate social action. **3** Out of this had grown, as naturally and prolifically as a zucchini patch, a sprawling multimillion-dollar social organization serving the rebuked and the scorned. **4** The street retreats are the brainchild of Bernie Glassman.

_____ Which of the following represents the correct sequence for these sentences?

    a. 1, 3, 2, 4
    b. 2, 1, 3, 4
    c. 4, 2, 1, 3
    d. Correct as written.

You may refer to the selection as you work through the remaining exercises.

D. LOCATING SUPPORTING DETAILS

For the main ideas from the selections paraphrased here, find two relevant details that support each one.

1. The Greyston Bakery employed people newly released from prison or trying to find a new life off the streets. However, it soon came smack up against the endemic problems of the neighborhood. [paragraph 7]

    a. _____

    b. _____

2. The writer recognized the "filmy bubble of self-concept" that surrounds the people on the street, that "protective aura of specialness." [paragraph 21]

    a. _____

    _____

    b. _____

    _____

E. INTERPRETING MEANING

1. Look again at the quotations Barasch cites from the philosopher Søren Kierkegaard in paragraph 3. Explain in your own words what they mean.

   _____

   _____

2. In paragraph 20, Barasch cites the opinion of an acquaintance, an urban designer, who observes the following: "the more open space, the bigger the quotient of 'bummage.'" What does he mean, and why would this be the case? _____

   _____

3. Paragraphs 25 and 26 present what Barasch calls a "radical proposition"— that "we owe a debt to those who suffer because they draw forth our tenderness." What exactly does he mean? _____

   _____

F. UNDERSTANDING VOCABULARY

Look through the paragraphs listed below and find a word that matches each definition. Refer to a dictionary if necessary. An example has been done for you.

Ex. soothed, relieved [paragraphs 1–2]   _____appeased_____

1. a place of suffering for those in disgrace [2–3]   _____

2. identification with another's situation or feelings [3] _____

3. temporary stay, brief period of residence [5]   _____

4. cleverly, shrewdly [6–7]   _____

5. describing those who live on the edges of society or at the lower limits of social acceptability [7–8]   _____

6. prevalent or established in a particular area [7–8]   _____

7. inborn, natural, inherent [11–12]   _____

8. on guard, watchful [11–12]   _____

9. excessively scrupulous or sensitive [17–18]   _____

10. French for fake, false [18—here used as part of a compound word]   _____

11. irritates, annoys, exasperates [19–20]   _____

12. discouragingly, dismayingly [21–22]   _____

13. deprived, abandoned, lacking what is needed [24–25]   _____

14. bring or draw out [26]

_____

15. disapprovingly, reproachfully [27]

_____

G. USING VOCABULARY

Here are some words from the selection. Write an original sentence using each word that shows both that you know how to use the word and what it means.

1. *avert* [paragraph 2] _____

_____

2. *interlude* [10] _____

_____

3. *nil* [22] _____

_____

4. *autonomy* [24] _____

_____

5. *streamlined* [29] _____

_____

H. ANNOTATING EXERCISE

The title of the essay, "The Bystander's Dilemma" refers to a situation that involves two or more unfavorable alternatives. What exactly was the dilemma that Barasch confronted when homeless people panhandled him for money? What dilemma did he experience when he panhandled himself? Look through the essay again and annotate the essay, but this time making notes only on those portions of the essay that pertain to this concept.

I. TOPICS FOR DISCUSSION

1. Consider again the subtitle of this selection. Why *do* we just walk on by?
2. To what extent do you think Barasch's opinion changed to compassion because of his own experience on the street? If you don't routinely give spare change to panhandlers, how much do you think your attitude would change if you had to panhandle for a week?
3. Does one have the "right" to be homeless, to refuse shelter? This question involves civil liberties, and it has been a thorny one that many communities have been dealing with, with varying degrees of success. If streets are considered "public," that is, if they belong to the people, does that fact include the right to live on them?
4. Barasch cites the thinking of Danish philosopher Søren Kierkegaard in his revised response to the homeless and in his newfound empathy toward their plight. How do you respond to the homeless, specifically to their panhandling (assuming that this is a common occurrence in your community)? Do you

give them money or not? Do you listen to their stories? Whatever your usual reaction, what is the philosophical basis for it?

J. TOPICS FOR WRITING

1. What was your attitude toward the homeless before reading this article? Examine your thinking in some depth. Has this article in any way changed your thinking? If a homeless person were to come up to you on the street today and ask you for a dollar or some spare change (for whatever reason), what would you do? Write an essay setting forth your attitudes and your explanations for them.

2. To what extent is homelessness a problem in your community? Do some investigation, either by making firsthand observations or by reading about the issue in your local newspaper. If it is a problem, what factors contribute to it? If it is not a problem, what factors contribute to its absence? Write a short paper presenting your findings.

Exploring Related Web Sites

- An advocacy group for the homeless supports various social policies in cities across the country. Read about their activities at this Web site:

    www.nationalhomeless.org

- A symposium on the bystander's dilemma was published in the Fall/Winter 2006–2007 issue of *Greater Good* magazine, including the article above along with six other essays. One of them deals with the increasing problem of bullying in schools.

    http://greatergood.berkeley.edu/greatergood/archive/2006fallwinter

- A five-day gathering in Seattle in April 2008 was titled Seeds of Compassion. The event featured the Dalai Lama, who convened with researchers, policy makers, and teachers to discuss ways to teach children to be compassionate. Learn more about this event by starting at this Web site.

    www.seedsofcompassion.org

    If you want more information, type in "seeds of compassion" in the search box of your favorite search engine.

9

Hell and Back

Chris Rose is a native of Washington, D.C. After graduating from the University of Wisconsin, he joined the Washington Post *as a news clerk. In 1984 he moved to the New Orleans* Times-Picayune *to cover crime and politics. Throughout his career at the newspaper, he has also covered the culture and economics of New Orleans as well as the jazz and nightlife scene. After Hurricane Katrina in 2005, he began to cover the devastation that resulted from the storm, writing about his adopted city as it struggled to put itself back together. In 2006, Rose and several of his newspaper colleagues won the Pulitzer Prize for Public Service for their coverage of Katrina and its effects on the residents of the city. But the storm did more than destroy houses; it also affected the psyches of the inhabitants. In this selection from the* Times-Picayune, *Rose chronicles the depression that threatened to destroy him.*

Vocabulary Preview

WORD PARTS

mal- [paragraphs 43, 44, and 61] Rose uses three words beginning with the prefix *mal-*, which means either "bad" or "ill." *Malevolence* (paragraph 43) means malicious or evil behavior (from *mal-* + *volens* ["to wish"]). Next, Rose refers to his depression as a *malady*, an illness (paragraph 44). Finally, *malaise* (paragraph 61) means a general feeling of unease or depression. Here are three more words beginning with this prefix:

malice	the desire to harm others, ill will
malign	to speak badly of others
malnutrition	poor nutrition

What do these two words mean? Consult a dictionary if you are unsure.

malignant _____

malaria _____

WORD FAMILIES

sympathy, empathy [paragraphs 11 and 45] The words *sympathy* and *empathy* stem from the Latin root *-pathy* or *pathos*, meaning "emotions" or "feelings." When we experience sympathy, we literally feel the same feelings as another, from *sym-* ("same") and *-pathy*. *Empathy* means identification with another's feelings, but it is stronger than *sympathy* because it suggests that one has undergone the same experience. With sympathy, one simply understands the feelings another is experiencing without necessarily having experienced the same thing.

To complicate matters, from the Greek, the root *patho-* means "disease" or "suffering." Hence, a *pathologist* is one who studies the nature and causes of disease. Usually the context will indicate which meaning is intended.

CHRIS ROSE

Hell and Back

1   I pulled into the Shell station on Magazine Street, my car running on fumes. I turned off the motor. And then I just sat there.

2   There were other people pumping gas at the island I had pulled into and I didn't want them to see me, didn't want to see them, didn't want to nod hello, didn't want to interact in any fashion.

3   Outside the window, they looked like characters in a movie. But not my movie. I tried to wait them out, but others would follow, get out of their cars and pump and pay and drive off, always followed by more cars, more people. How can they do this, as if everything is normal, I wondered. Where do they go? What do they do?

4   It was early August, and two minutes in my car with the windows up and the air conditioner off was insufferable. I was trapped, in my car and in my head. So I drove off with an empty tank rather than face strangers at a gas station.

5   Before I continue, I should make a confession. For all of my adult life, I regarded depression and anxiety as pretty much a load of hooey. I never accorded any credibility to the idea that they are medical conditions. Nothing scientific about it. You get sick, get fired, fall in love, get laid, buy a new pair of shoes, join a gym, get religion, seasons change, whatever; you go with the flow, dust yourself off, get back in the game. I thought antidepressants were for desperate housewives and fragile poets.

6   I no longer feel that way. Not since I fell down the rabbit hole myself and enough hands reached down to pull me out. One of those hands belonged to a psychiatrist holding a prescription for antidepressants. I took it. And it changed my life. Maybe saved my life.

7   This is the story of one journey, my journey, to the edge of the post-Katrina abyss, and back again. It is a story with a happy ending—at least so far.

8   I had already stopped going to the grocery store weeks before the Shell station meltdown. I had made every excuse possible to avoid going to my office because I didn't want to see anyone, didn't want to engage in small talk, Hey, how's the family?

9   My hands shook. I had to look down when I walked down steps, holding the banister to keep steady. I was at risk every time I got behind the wheel of a car; I couldn't pay attention.

10   I lost 15 pounds, and it's safe to say I didn't have a lot to give. I stopped talking to Kelly, my wife. She loathed me, my silences, my distance, my inertia. I stopped walking my dog, so she hated me, too.

11   I stopped answering phone calls and e-mails. I maintained limited communication with my editors to keep my job at the New Orleans *Times-Picayune*, but I started missing deadlines anyway. My editors cut me slack. There's a lot of slack being cut in this town now. A lot of legroom, empathy, and forgiveness.

12   I tried to keep an open line of communication with my kids, but it was still slipping away. My two oldest, 7 and 5, began asking, "What are you looking at, Daddy?"

13   The thousand-yard stare. I couldn't shake it. Boring holes into the house behind my back yard. Daddy is a zombie. That was my movie: *Night of the Living Dead*. Followed by *Morning of the Living Dead*, followed by *Afternoon* . . .

14   My darkness first became visible during fall of 2005. As the days of covering Hurricane Katrina's aftermath turned into weeks, which turned into months, I began taking long walks, miles and miles, late at night, one arm pinned to my side, the other waving in stride.

15   I had crying jags and other "episodes." One day, while the city was still mostly abandoned, I passed out on the job, fell face first into a tree, snapped my glasses in half, gouged a hole in my forehead, and lay unconscious on the side of the road for an entire afternoon. You might think that would have been a wake-up call, but it wasn't. Instead, as I had with everything else that was happening to me, I wrote a column about it, trying to make it sound funny.

16   My wife and kids spent the last four months of 2005 at my parents' home in Maryland. Until Christmas I worked, and lived, completely alone. Even when my family finally returned, I spent the next months driving endlessly through bombed-out neighborhoods. I met legions of people who appeared to be dying from sadness, and I wrote about them.

17   I was receiving thousands of e-mails in reaction to my stories in the paper, and most of them were more accounts of death, destruction, and despondency by people from around south Louisiana. I am pretty sure I possess the largest archive of personal Katrina stories, little histories that would break your heart.

18   I guess they broke mine.

19   I never considered seeking treatment. I was afraid medication might alter my emotions to a point of insensitivity, lower my antenna to where I could no longer feel the acute grip that Katrina and the flood have on the city's psyche.

20   Talk about "embedded"[1] journalism; this was the real deal.

21   As time wore on, the toll at home worsened. I declined all dinner invitations that my wife wanted desperately to accept, something to get me out of the house, get my feet moving. I let the lawn and weeds overgrow and didn't pick up my dog's waste. I rarely shaved or bathed. I stayed in bed as long as I could, as often as I could.

---

[1]A reference to an earlier usage: During the American invasion of Iraq that begin in March 2003, dozens of print and television journalists were "embedded" with American troops, living with them and writing their experiences for the readers back home. (Ed.)

22   I don't drink anymore, so the nightly self-narcolepsy that so many in this community employ was not an option. And I don't watch TV, so I developed an infinite capacity to just sit and stare. I'd noodle around on the piano, read weightless fiction, and reach for my kids, always, trying to hold them, touch them, kiss them. Tell them I was still here.

23   But I was disappearing fast, slogging through winter and spring and grinding to a halt by summer. I was a dead man walking. I had never been so scared in my life.

24   That summer, with the darkness clinging to me like humidity, my stories in the *Times-Picayune* moved from gray to brown to black. Readers wanted stories of hope, inspiration, and triumph, something to cling to; I gave them anger and sadness and gloom. They started e-mailing me, telling me I was bringing them down when they were already down enough.

25   This one, August 21, from a reader named Molly: "I recently became worried about you. I read your column and you seemed so sad. And not in a fakey-columnist kind of way."

26   This one, August 19, from Debbie Koppman: "I'm a big fan. But I gotta tell ya—I can't read your columns anymore. They are depressing. I wish you'd write about something positive."

27   There were scores of e-mails, maybe hundreds. I lost count. Most were kind, solicitous even; strangers invited me over for a warm meal. But this one, on August 14, from a reader named Johnny Culpepper, stuck out: "Your stories are played out, Rose. Why don't you just leave the city; you're not happy, you bitch and moan all the time. Just leave or pull the trigger and get it over with." I'm sure he didn't mean it literally, but truthfully, I thought it was funny. I showed it around to my wife and editors.

28   Three friends of mine had, in fact, killed themselves in the past year and I had wondered what that was like. I rejected it, but, for the first time, I understood why they did it. Hopeless, helpless, and unable to function. A mind shutting down and taking the body with it. A pain not physical but not of my comprehension, and always there, a buzzing fluorescent light. No way out, I thought. Except there was.

29 I don't need to replay the early days of trauma for you here. You know what I'm talking about. Whether you were in south Louisiana or somewhere far away, in a shelter or at your sister's house, whether you lost everything or nothing, you know what I mean.

30   Maybe my case is more extreme because I immersed myself in the horror and became a full-time chronicler of sorrowful tales—an audience for other people's pain. There is no such thing as leaving it behind at the office when a whole city takes the dive.

31   Then again, my case is less extreme than that of the first responders, the doctors, nurses, and emergency medical technicians, and certainly anyone who got trapped in the Dome or the Convention Center or worse—in the water, in attics, and on rooftops. In some cases, stuck in trees.

32   I've got nothing on them. How the hell do they sleep at night?

33 　　None of it made sense. My personality has always been marked by insouciance and laughter, the seeking of adventure. I am the class clown, the life of the party, the bon vivant. I have always felt like I was more alert and alive than anyone in the room.

34 　　In the measure of how one made out in the storm, my life was cake. My house, my job, and my family were all fine. My career was gangbusters, all manner of awards and attention. A book with great reviews and stunning sales, full auditoriums everywhere I was invited to speak, appearances on television and radio, and the overwhelming support of readers who left gifts, flowers, and cards on my doorstep, thanking me for my stories.

35 　　I had become a star of a bizarre constellation. No doubt about it, disasters are great career moves for people in my line of work. So why the hell was I so miserable? This is the time of my life, I told myself. I am a success. I have done good things.

36 　　To no avail.

37 　　I changed the message on my phone to say: "This is Chris Rose. I am emotionally unavailable at the moment. Please leave a message." I thought this was hilarious. Most of my friends recognized it as a classic cry for help. My editor, my wife, my dad, my friends, and strangers on the street who recognized me from my picture in the paper had been telling me for a long time: You need to get help.

38 　　I didn't want help. I didn't want medicine. And I sure as hell didn't want to sit on a couch and tell some guy with glasses, a beard, and a degree from Dartmouth about my troubles.

39 　　Everybody's got troubles. I needed to stay the course, keep on writing, keep on telling the story of New Orleans. I needed to do what I had to do, the consequences be damned, and what I had to do was dig further and further into what has happened around here—to the people, my friends, my city, the region.

40 　　Lord, what an insufferable mess it all is. I'm not going to get better, I thought. I'm in too deep.

41 In his book *Darkness Visible: A Memoir of Madness*, which is the best literary guide to depression that I have found, William Styron recounts his descent into and recovery from depression. One of the biggest obstacles, he says, is the term itself, what he calls "a true wimp of a word."

42 　　He traces the medical use of the term to a Swiss psychiatrist named Adolf Meyer, who, Styron says, "had a tin ear for the finer rhythms of English and therefore was unaware of the semantic damage he had inflicted by offering 'depression' as a descriptive noun for such a dreadful and raging disease.

43 　　"Nonetheless, for over 75 years the word has slithered innocuously through the language like a slug, leaving little trace of its intrinsic malevolence and preventing, by its very insipidity, a general awareness of the horrible intensity of the disease when [it is] out of control."

44 　　He continues: "As one who has suffered from the malady in extremis yet returned to tell the tale, I would lobby for a truly arresting designation. 'Brainstorm,' for instance, has unfortunately been preempted to describe,

somewhat jocularly, intellectual inspiration. But something along these lines is needed.

45   "Told that someone's mood disorder has evolved into a storm—a veritable howling tempest in the brain . . . even the uninformed layman might display sympathy rather than the standard reaction that 'depression' evokes, something akin to 'So what?' or 'You'll pull out of it' or 'We all have bad days.'"

46   Styron is a helluva writer. His words were my life. I was having one serious brainstorm. Hell, it was a brain hurricane, Category 5. But what happens when your despair starts bleeding over into the lives of those around you? What happens when you can't get out of your car at the gas station even when you're out of gas? (Man, talk about the perfect metaphor.)

47   Then last summer, a colleague of mine at the newspaper took a bad mix of medications and went on a violent driving spree, an episode that ended with his pleading with the cops who surrounded him with guns drawn to shoot him.

48   He had gone over the cliff. And I thought to myself: If I don't do something, I'm next.

49   The first visit to my psychiatrist, who asked not to be identified for this story, was August 15, 2006. I told him I had doubts about his ability to make me feel better. I pled guilty to skepticism. I'm no Tom Cruise[2]; psychiatry is fine, I thought. For other people.

50   My very first exchange with my doctor had a morbidly comic element to it. At least, I thought so. Approaching his office, I had noticed a dead cat in his yard. Freshly dead, with flies just beginning to gather around the eyes. My initial worry was that some kid who loves this cat might see it, so I said to him, "Before we start, do you know about the cat?"

51   Yes, he told me. It was being taken care of. Then he paused and said, "Well, you're still noticing the environment around you. That's a good sign."

52   The analyst in him had kicked in, but the patient in me was still resisting. In my lifelong habit of damping down serious discussions with sarcasm, I said to him: "Yeah, but what if the dead cat was the only thing I saw? What if I didn't see or hear the traffic or the trees or the birds or anything else?"

53   I crack myself up. I see dead things. Get it?

54   Yeah, neither did he.

55   We talked for an hour. He told me he wanted to talk to me three or four times before he made a diagnosis and prescribed any medication. When I came home from that first visit without a prescription, my wife was despondent and my editor enraged. To them, it was plain to see I needed something, anything, and fast.

56   Unbeknownst to me, my wife immediately wrote a letter to my doctor, pleading with him to put me on something. Midway through my second session, I must have convinced him as well because he pulled out some samples of a drug called Cymbalta.

---

[2]The actor Tom Cruise, a member of the Church of Scientology, made headlines when he denounced psychiatry and standard treatments for depression on the *Oprah Winfrey Show*.

57   He said it could take a few weeks to kick in. Best case, four days. Its reaction time would depend on how much body fat I had; the more I had, the longer it would take. That was a good sign for me. By August, I had become a skeletal version of my pre-K self.

58   Before I left that second session, he told me to change the message on my phone, that "emotionally unavailable" thing. Not funny, he said.

59   I began taking Cymbalta on August 24, a Thursday. Since I had practically no body fat to speak of, the drug kicked in immediately. That whole weekend, I felt like I was in the throes of a drug rush: mildly euphoric, but also leery of what was happening inside me. I felt off balance. But I felt better, too. I told my wife this, but she was guarded. My long-standing gloom had cast such a pall over our relationship that she took a wait-and-see attitude.

60   By Monday, the dark curtain had lifted almost entirely. The despondence and incapacitation vanished, just like that, and I was who I used to be: energetic, sarcastic, playful, affectionate, and alive.

61   I started talking to Kelly about plans for the kids at school, extracurricular activities, weekend vacations. I had not realized until that moment that while I was stuck in my malaise, I had had no vision of the future whatsoever. It was almost like not living.

62   Kelly came around. We became husband and wife again. We became friends. It felt like a come-to-Jesus experience. It felt like a miracle. But it was just medicine, plain and simple.

63   I asked my doctor to tell me exactly what was wrong with me so I could explain it in this story. I still don't really understand it, the science of depression, the actions of synapses, transmitters, blockers, and stimulants. *The Diagnostic and Statistical Manual of Mental Disorders*, psychiatry's chief handbook, practically doubles in size every time it's reprinted, filled with newer and clearer clinical trials, research, and explanations.

64   But here's my doctor's take: The amount of cortisol, a hormone produced in response to chronic stress, increased to dangerous levels in my brain. The overproduction was blocking the transmission of serotonin and norepinephrine, neurotransmitters that mediate messages between nerves in the brain. This communication system is the basic source of all mood and behavior.

65   My brain was literally shorting out. The cells were not communicating properly. Chemical imbalances were dogging the work of my neurotransmitters, my electrical wiring. A real and true physiological deterioration had begun.

66   I had a disease. This I was willing to accept (grudgingly, since it ran against my lifelong philosophy of self-determination). I pressed my doctor: What is the difference between sad and depressed? How do you know when you've crossed over?

67   "Post-traumatic stress disorder is bandied about as a common diagnosis in this community, but I think that's probably not the case," he told me. "What people are suffering from here is what I call Katrina syndrome— marked by sleep disturbance, recent memory impairment, and increased irritability.

68   "Much of this is totally normal. . . . But when you have the thousand-yard stare, when your ability to function is impaired, then you have gone from 'discomfort' to 'pathologic.' If you don't feel like you can go anywhere or do anything—or sometimes, even move—then you are sick."

69   And that was me. And if that is you, let me offer some unsolicited advice, something that you've already been told a thousand times by people who love you, something you really ought to consider listening to this time: Get help.

70   I hate being dependent on a drug. Hate it more than I can say. But if the alternative is a proud stoicism in the face of sorrow accompanied by prolonged and unspeakable despair—well, I'll take dependence.

71   Today, I can take my kids to school in the morning and mingle effortlessly with the other parents. Crowds don't freak me out. I'm not tired all day, every day. I love going to the grocery store. I can pump gas. I notice the smell of night-blooming jasmine and I play with my kids and I clean up after my dog.

72   The only effect on my writing I have noticed is that the darkness lifted. I can still channel anger, humor, and irony, the three speeds I need on my editorial stick shift.

73   And I'm not the only one who senses the change. Everyone sees the difference, even readers. I'm not gaunt. I make eye contact. I can talk about the weather, the Saints, whatever. It doesn't have to be so dire, every word and motion.

74   Strange thing is this: I never cry anymore. Ever.

75   I cried every day from August 29, 2005, until August 24, 2006—360 days straight. And then I stopped. Maybe the extremes of emotion have been smoothed over, but, truthfully, I've shed enough tears for two lifetimes. Even at the Saints' *Monday Night Football* game, a moment that weeks earlier would have sent me reeling into spasms of open weeping, I held it together. A lump in my throat, to be sure, but no prostration anymore.

76   It's my movie now. I am part of the flow of humanity that clogs our streets and sidewalks, taking part in and being part of the community and its growth. I have clarity, and oh, what a vision it is.

77   I am not cured, not by any means. Clinical trials show Cymbalta has an 80 percent success rate after six months, and as I write this, I'm just two months in. I felt a backwards tilt recently—the long stare, the pacing, it crept in one weekend—and it scared me so badly that I went to my doctor and we agreed to increase the strength of my medication.

78   Before Katrina, I would have called somebody like me a wuss. Not to my face. But it's what I would have thought, this talk of mood swings and loss of control, all this psychobabble and hope-dope. What a load of crap. Get a grip, I would have said.

79   And that's exactly what I did, through a door that was hidden from me, but that I was finally able to see. I have a disease. Medicine saved me. I am living proof.

80   Emphasis on living. ✶

Exercises

Do not refer to the selection for Exercises A–C unless your instructor directs you to do so.

A. DETERMINING THE MAIN IDEA AND PURPOSE

Choose the best answer.

_____ 1. The main idea of the selection is that

    a. the writer's immersing himself in the sad stories resulting from Katrina led to a nearly crippling bout with depression.

    b. the instances of depression in New Orleans multiplied exponentially as a result of Katrina's devastation.

    c. for the writer, everyone else's troubles were more important than dealing with his own mental health.

    d. the writer believed that seeking treatment for depression only indicated a form of psychological weakness that he refused to give in to.

_____ 2. The writer's purpose is to

    a. compare his experiences with depression and recovery with those that other New Orleans residents endured as a result of Hurricane Katrina.

    b. describe a nightmarish journey, from his confrontation with depression to his gradual recovery.

    c. examine current psychological theories about the origin of depression.

    d. examine the experiences he and so many other Katrina victims underwent in the days following the hurricane.

B. COMPREHENDING MAIN IDEAS

Choose the correct answer.

_____ 1. One of the earliest manifestations of Rose's depression was his inability to

    a. complete his usual newspaper assignments.

    b. eat.

    c. sleep.

    d. interact with others.

_____ 2. Rather than engage in life's usual activities, Rose says that he essentially became

    a. darkness visible.

    b. a dead man walking.

    c. a television addict.

    d. bedridden.

_____ 3. As a result of his newspaper columns about the hurricane's aftermath, Rose received

    a. thousands of accounts of death and destruction from newspaper readers.

    b. a warning from his newspaper editors to make his stories more optimistic.

    c. hundreds of suggestions for how he could help himself recover.

    d. solace and relief that made him forget about his own troubles.

_____ 4. Rose rejected psychiatric help at first because

    a. he was embarrassed about his feelings and also afraid of what others would think.

    b. he couldn't afford treatment and was ashamed to admit it.

    c. everyone has troubles; he just needed to keep on writing.

    d. he didn't trust psychiatrists because he thought they were no better than quacks.

_____ 5. Rose quotes William Styron who says that the word _depression_ does not do justice to the intensity of the disease and its effects on the sufferer. He says that a better term might be

    a. malevolence of the spirit.

    b. brainstorm.

    c. whirlwind.

    d. psychological abyss.

_____ 6. Ultimately, what saved Rose from his crippling affliction was

    a. an antidepressant called Cymbalta prescribed by a psychiatrist.

    b. his wife's understanding and support.

    c. his sense of humor.

    d. a dose of serotonin.

COMPREHENSION SCORE

Score your answers for Exercises A and B as follows:

A. No. right _____ × 2 = _____

B. No. right _____ × 1 = _____

Total points from A and B _____ × 10 = _____ percent

C. SEQUENCING

These sentences from one paragraph in the selection have been scrambled. Read the sentences and choose the sequence that puts them back into logical order. Do not refer to the original selection.

    1 That summer, with the darkness clinging to me like humidity, my stories in the _Times-Picayune_ moved from gray to brown to black. **2** Readers wanted stories of hope, inspiration, and triumph, something to cling to; I gave them anger and sadness and gloom. **3** They started e-mailing me, telling me I was bringing them down when they were already down enough.

_____ Which of the following represents the correct sequence for these sentences?

a. 3, 2, 1

b. 2, 3, 1

c. 1, 3, 2

d. Correct as written.

You may refer to the selection as you work through the remaining exercises.

D. IDENTIFYING SUPPORTING DETAILS

Place an X beside each statement that *directly* supports this main idea from the selection: Rose's depression manifested itself in some serious ways emotionally before he finally sought help from a psychiatrist.

1. _____ He stopped going to the grocery store and went to his office as little as possible.

2. _____ His hands shook, and he walked unsteadily.

3. _____ He tried to keep an open line of communication with his children.

4. _____ He developed a "thousand-yard stare."

5. _____ He read William Styron's account of his depression, *Darkness Visible.*

6. _____ He rarely shaved or bathed and stayed in bed as long as he could.

7. _____ He kept his sense of humor, even though it was dark.

8. _____ His stories were relentlessly gloomy and filled with anger and sadness.

E. UNDERSTANDING VOCABULARY

Choose the best definition according to an analysis of word parts or the context.

_____ **1.** A lot of legroom, *empathy,* and forgiveness [paragraph 11]

    a. suffering

    b. identification with another's experience

    c. intense feeling of sorrow

    d. emotional distance or detachment

_____ **2.** *legions* of people [16]

    a. multitudes, large numbers

    b. various groups or classes

    c. urban residents

    d. army soldiers

_____ **3.** more accounts of death and *despondency* [17]

    a. destruction, damage

    b. flooding, deluge

    c. bravery, courage

    d. depression, dejection

_____ **4.** the star of a *bizarre* constellation [35]

    a. brightly shining

    b. difficult to comprehend

    c. strange, odd
    d. crowded, overflowing

_____ **5.** slithered *innocuously* [43]

    a. harmfully
    b. harmlessly
    c. quietly
    d. without notice

_____ **6.** to describe, somewhat *jocularly* [44]

    a. jokingly, humorously
    b. accurately, precisely
    c. colorfully, vividly
    d. critically, unsympathetically

F. USING VOCABULARY

From the following list of vocabulary words, choose a word that fits in each blank according to both the grammatical structure of the sentence and the context. Use each word in the list only once. Do not change the form of the word. (Note that there are more words than blanks.)

abyss	inertia	empathy	toll
bizarre	innocuously	solicitous	leery
euphoric	malaise	credibility	immersed

1. Rose writes that as he _____ himself in the sad stories from Katrina survivors, he descended into an _____ that he couldn't escape from.

2. His readers wrote him _____ letters, but the archive of sad stories had taken its _____ on him emotionally; he suffered from an _____ and from a _____ that he could not shake off.

3. _____ of psychiatrists, he placed no _____ in the idea that depression was a medical condition that could be cured by medication.

G. PARAPHRASING EXERCISE

1. Here are some sentences from paragraph 19 in the selection. Write your paraphrase in the space provided, but change the first-person pronoun "I" to third-person "he."

Original Passage

I never considered seeking treatment. I was afraid medication might alter my emotions to a point of insensitivity, lower my antenna to where I could no longer feel the acute grip that Katrina and the flood have on the city's psyche.

Your Paraphrase

_____

_____

_____

_____

_____

2. These sentences to paraphrase are from paragraph 30.

Original Passage	Your Paraphrase
Maybe my case is more extreme because I immersed myself in the horror and became a full-time chronicler of sorrowful tales—an audience for other people's pain. There is no such thing as leaving it behind at the office when a whole city takes the dive.	_____ _____ _____ _____ _____

H. SUMMARIZING EXERCISE

Write a summary of paragraphs 41–43 in the space below. The passage is approximately 150 words long, so your summary should be about 35 or 40 words.

_____

_____

_____

I. TOPICS FOR DISCUSSION

1. Aside from his eventual decision to get help, what positive characteristics does Rose exhibit in his chronicle that seem to have helped him weather his depression without committing suicide?
2. Hurricane Katrina was a terrible natural disaster, one of the worst in American history. From what Rose writes, and from other sources, why did this particular natural disaster so strongly affect the nation's psyche?

J. TOPICS FOR WRITING

1. If you have experience with someone suffering from depression, write a short chronicle tracing the person's bout with the illness—including symptoms, emotional and physical effects, and the ramifications of the disease on those around him or her.
2. Do some research on an illness or medical condition that has afflicted a member of your family. Use both print and online sources. Then write an essay summarizing the information you have gathered. Include a discussion of causes, symptoms, and treatment.

Exploring Related Web Sites

- Photographs of Hurricane Katrina's impact on New Orleans are widely available online. Go to Google, click on "images," and then type in "Katrina photographs."
- If you want more information about depression—its symptoms and available treatment—do an online search or begin your study with this informative and authoritative Web site:

    www.nimh.nih.gov/health/topics/depression/index.shtml

FRANCES MOORE LAPPÉ AND JEFFREY PERKINS

The Two Sides of Fear

Frances Moore Lappé has had a lifetime interest in social change. She is best known for her 1971 landmark book, Diet for a Small Planet. *Jeffrey Perkins is the cofounder of curious minds (the lower-case letters are correct), a nonprofit Boston group that sponsors workshops to show people how to redirect their lives and help them confront their fears. This excerpt comes from their recent book,* You Have the Power: Choosing Courage in a Culture of Fear *(2004). It was reprinted in* Utne, *the alternative magazine devoted to social and cultural issues.*

Vocabulary Preview

WORD PARTS

re- [paragraphs 12, 22, and 23] In the selection, Lappé and Moore use four words beginning with the prefix *re-: rethink, redirect, reinterpret,* and the unusual *re-rechannel.* This prefix conveys the idea of a repeated action. Therefore, to *rethink* means simply to think again or to think in a different way. However, not all words beginning with *re-* have this meaning: *Reconsider, reimburse, recalculate,* and *regenerate* do, but *register, regulate, residence,* and *rebuke* ("to scold") do not. Strip away the prefix and see if the root can stand alone. If it can, then the prefix likely has the meaning discussed.

What do these three words mean?

rehydrate   _____

rejuvenate   _____

revitalize   _____

WORD FAMILIES

primal [paragraph 22] From the Latin root *primus* ("first"), *primal* refers either to first in importance or to first in time. This common root is at the heart of many English words, among them: *primary* (the early grades in school, of great importance, or a preliminary election); *primer* (a child's first reading book); and *prime minister* (the top political leader, for example, in Britain and Canada).

What does a primatologist study? _____

Sometimes celebrities—typically actresses and singers—are called *prima donnas*. What does this phrase mean, and what language does it derive from? _____

_____

_____

dictatorial [paragraph 23] A *dictator* is an absolute ruler who tells people what to do and how to think. *Dictatorial* is the adjective form derived from the noun. Both come from the Latin root verb *dicere* ("to speak" or "to say"). Here are some other words in this family:

predict	to tell before, to foretell
diction	choice of words in speaking or writing
verdict	a jury's decision (*veir* ["true"] + *dicere*)
benediction	a blessing (*bene-* ["well"] + *dicere*)

What is a contradiction? What does it have to do with saying or speaking?

_____

FRANCES MOORE LAPPÉ AND JEFFREY PERKINS

The Two Sides of Fear

1   One spring day not long ago, the two of us hailed a cab in Boston. Noting the driver's strong Russian accent, we asked, "So what do you think of America?"

2   Hesitant at first, he finally blurted out, "You Americans are all afraid."

3   As we approached Harvard Square, two BMWs passed us. "Those people are the most afraid," he said, gesturing at the cars. "They're afraid they'll lose it. In Russia, we feared the KGB. Here, you don't trust anyone. You're all afraid of each other."

4   The philosopher behind the wheel that morning seemed to peer right into the heart of our nerve-jangled nation. A terror alert system that never drops below yellow reminds us that in this new "permanent war" since 9/11 we can expect attacks at any moment. Hospital entrances now sternly warn: "Do not enter if exposed to anthrax." (As if we'd even know!) Potential killers swarm around us: airplanes, errant asteroids, ozone holes, and possible poison gas. Meanwhile, sudden layoffs, shaky retirement funds, and a staggering national deficit all conspire to make us feel we're one pink slip away from losing our homes and our futures.

5   No wonder we heed the voice of fear shouting at us to pull back and take no risks. We seem to think that if we just retreat into our private lives, go along, and keep quiet, we'll be invisible and safe. But there's one big problem. Living in fear robs us of life. Human beings evolved for something much better. Our species never would have made it this far if we were not by nature curious problem-solvers and creators—beings who love to act, to take risks, to live exuberantly, to aspire to what lies beyond easy reach.

6   We see the cost of denying our true nature all around us these days, beginning with our bewilderment over how we've ended up creating a world so few of us

desire. After all, no sane person wakes up wanting more children to die of hunger, yet today almost 17,000 starving children will die. Few actually plot to spoil the environment, yet such damage is all around us. Almost no one yearns for more violence, yet the past 100 years have been the bloodiest in human history.

7   Our world has slipped out of whack with our common dreams for one reason: We don't believe we have the power to create the world we really want. And what lies at the root of this acquiescence? Fear. The fear of being different, and the fear of the unknown. Together, these ancient human impulses harden around us into the status quo. They keep us trapped, afraid to listen to our hearts and pursue our dream of a better life.

8   To find the roots of fear, let's look back 20,000 years to when our ancestors lived in small tribes, trying to protect themselves and their vulnerable young from animals and other threats bigger and fiercer than they were. By then, humans had learned their evolutionary lessons well: On our own, we were toast. Banishment from the tribe meant certain death.

9   But what if we happen to be in a new stage of human evolution, one in which our inherited responses to fear are not life-preserving, but life-threatening? This is precisely our thesis. In a moment when the new hypertribe of global corporate culture is destroying the very essentials of life, following the pack has become dangerous: What used to mean life now means death—for our spirits, and ultimately for our planet.

10   To reverse the ruination of the planet, we clearly have to *do* something different today, which is a way of saying we must walk into the unknown. And we must *be* different as well, which means we have to risk separating ourselves from others. If we accept that our fear is simply a hardwired, biological response, we're powerless. Instead, we have to realize that it's our *ideas* about fear that are all-important. How we view fear can shut us down. But viewed in a different way, fear can also open us up, allowing us to discover our power to create the world we want.

11   Consider the *Apollo 13* story. Hurtling through space after an onboard explosion in 1970, the three astronauts were able to save themselves because they'd spent years learning not to freeze up in a crisis, but to think—in fact to nimbly *re*think. When all energy had to be shut down in the main craft, they turned the lunar landing craft into a temporary home. Sticking with the original plan would have killed them.

12   This little craft may be the perfect symbol of our need now to rethink our own situation before it is too late. Can we redirect the power of our fear toward survival? The very sensation of fear is useful. It's telling us that we're in a moment when positive action is necessary to repair our own life-support system. Either we raise our understanding of our own wiring and improve our use of it, or we hurtle on to destruction.

13   To understand how deeply fear affects us, it's critical to grasp how fear is being fomented today. Consider George W. Bush's speeches surrounding the Iraq war. As reported by Madeleine K. Albright in the journal *Foreign Affairs*, sometimes his words were downright chilling. "At some point we may be the only ones left," Bush said shortly before the war and "that's okay with me." In another

speech, Bush made 44 consecutive statements referring to the crisis and future catastrophic repercussions—a major presidential swing toward fear-inducing rhetoric. Hearing such talk, it's easy to ignore signs that the world may actually be getting less dangerous, according to Joseph Cirincione of the Carnegie Endowment for International Peace. Fewer nuclear weapons dot the planet today than 15 years ago, he notes, as well as fewer biological and chemical weapons, even fewer missile-delivery systems.

14   We're also hit daily with scary media messages—from images of violence in the world's hot spots to advertisers playing on our fears of everything from riding in small cars to crime. The trouble is, this fear-hype blinds us to the threats we *should* be addressing, like global warming and the industrial contamination of life's key resources. We lose sleep worrying that our children might be kidnapped, molested, or struck down in a Columbine-style massacre, though these risks are actually very low. On the other hand, in *The Culture of Fear*, author Barry Glassner notes that every year, 5,000 children and adolescents show up in emergency rooms with work-related injuries, most of which could have been avoided by enforcing simple safety rules.

15   This is the paradox of modern fear—so pervasive and so misplaced. It helps us to understand why French philosopher Patrick Viveret calls fear the "emotional plague of our planet." We're clearly being *made* to fear. Fear is a time-honored form of control.

16   A first step toward freedom is to crack one driver of our fear: the myth of scarcity. The belief that there's never enough to go around keeps us on a competitive treadmill, afraid to listen to our own hearts. If we see ourselves as isolated egos competing against other egos, we can't seriously discuss a future that's good for all. Democracy itself becomes suspect in a culture that assumes that greedy egoists will always turn the democratic process to their own selfish ends. This shrunken view of our nature, pushed into high gear since the greed-is-good 1980s, is destructive in two ways. It denies both our innate gifts for problem solving and our need for connection.

17   In contrast, it appears that the pleasures of cooperating are imbedded in our very cells. As reported in 2002, researchers at Emory University in Atlanta used magnetic resonance imaging to watch brain responses in women playing Prisoner's Dilemma, a game that explores whether participants will cooperate or act selfishly in the pursuit of personal gain. The way people play the game is often cited as "proof" of how deeply self-interested we tend to be, but the scientists were surprised when the MRI scans told a different story. Rather than lighting up most brightly during acts of selfishness—or in response to such acts—the brain areas linked to pleasure and reward responded most intensely when players cooperated. It turns out that cooperation is fun.

18   Thus, the reason many people feel trapped, even despairing, about the state of our world, is *not* what we assumed: It's not just a shaky economy or suicide bombers or ecological meltdown. It's that *we've been forced to deny who we are*. To reclaim our true natures, we have to be willing to step into the unknown, encounter conflict, and take the chance that we'll lose standing in the eyes of our peers.

19   Again, these are the ancient risks we've evolved to abhor. But there will always be people who defy the norm, whose worst fear is to live without

passion or authenticity. When she was asked if she was afraid about traveling into space, Mae Jemison, the first black female astronaut, put it bluntly: "Not at all," she said. "In fact, I told my parents that if I died they should never feel bad for me. I am doing what I love." Fear of death often pales when life is lived fully.

20   We're convinced that it's possible for all of us to live with that passion, to fulfill our twin needs for deeper meaning and genuine connection. But first we need a new concept of fear that allows us to see it as a sign to step forward. In other words, fear at certain critical junctures can mean *go*.

21   Our future may depend on whether we can make this radical shift in our inherited view of fear. Rather than warning us that something is wrong, fear can also mean that something is just right—that we're doing precisely what is true to our deepest wisdom.

22   Fortunately, we human beings do not have to be prisoners of our primal responses to fear. We have also evolved a complex consciousness that allows us to look at ourselves with some objectivity. We can use that skill to reinterpret fear as *a source of energy*. The question is, how can we reroute that power to our advantage?

23   One answer can be found in the life of the Reverend Timothy Njoya, a Presbyterian pastor in Nairobi who for years has been a leading critic of Kenya's dictatorial government. After being threatened repeatedly for preaching his pro-democracy message, Njoya, a slight and agile man, found seven armed assailants at his door one night. In telling the story, he playfully acted out what happened after his attackers sliced off his fingers and slashed open his belly. Lying on the floor, certain he was dying, he began giving his attackers his most treasured belongings. His generosity so moved his assailants that they rushed him to the hospital. His ability to re-rechannel the energy of his fear saved his life.

24   How could anyone not respond to such brutality with sheer terror and aggression?

25   "Fear is an energy that comes from inside us, not outside," he answered. "It's neutral. So we can channel it into fear, paranoia, or euphoria, whatever we choose." Njoya used the example of a lion as it confronts both predators and prey. In either case, what it senses first is fear, he said. But instead of lunging blindly, the lion recoils, pauses, and focuses its energies before it springs.

26   "We can do the same," he added. "We can harness our would-be fears, harmonize our energies, and channel them into courage."

27   We may be the first humans who can look at how our biology serves us—or does not serve us. We then face a choice. We can respond in the old, inherited ways, or we can see fear simply as information and energy to be used for our own creative ends. Indeed, whether we can achieve this radical shift in our view of fear may ultimately determine our future. ✻

Exercises

Do not refer to the selection for Exercises A–C unless your instructor directs you to do so.

A. DETERMINING THE MAIN IDEA AND PURPOSE

Choose the best answer.

_____ **1.** The main idea of the selection is that

    a. the media have created an atmosphere of fear that threatens to paralyze us and to destroy our freedom.

    b. human beings have always been fearful, but in the contemporary world, there is so much to be fearful of that it is no wonder we are constantly afraid.

    c. our inherited responses to fear have trapped us and threaten not only our lives and spirits but the planet itself.

    d. we see the cost of denying our true natures all around us in the form of warfare, famine, and violence.

_____ **2.** The writers' purpose is to

    a. show the origins of fear throughout human history, especially during the last century.

    b. teach us how to confront fears in our daily lives.

    c. argue that politicians deliberately exploit our fears for their own selfish interests.

    d. persuade us to walk into the unknown and to view fear in a different way.

B. COMPREHENDING MAIN IDEAS

Choose the correct answer.

_____ **1.** The philosophic Russian cab driver in Boston told the writers that in his view, Americans

    a. are afraid of each other and don't trust others any more.

    b. have much to be afraid of after the terrorist attacks of 2001.

    c. are too tied to their material possessions and live by shallow values.

    d. have no idea what it is like to live under a dictatorship.

_____ **2.** The writers say that our fear makes us live invisibly, and that this ultimately

    a. destroys our chance for personal happiness.

    b. results in our keeping a constant lookout for signs of danger.

    c. robs us of life.

    d. means that we are safe but no longer curious about the world around us.

_____ 3. The writers trace the history of fear, saying that 20,000 years ago, our ancestors, who lived in small tribes, had to be fearful because

    a. there was even more violence in the world then than there is today.

    b. the tribes fought with each other, requiring our ancestors to choose their allies carefully.

    c. there were threats from dangerous animals.

    d. one person alone could not survive without the protection of other tribe members.

    e. all of the above.

    f. only c and d.

_____ 4. The writers refer to a new hypertribe that they say is destroying the very essence of life—namely

    a. terrorism and the sponsors of the War on Terror.

    b. those who wage war.

    c. global corporate culture.

    d. the threat of nuclear weapons.

_____ 5. Ultimately, the writers' point about fear is that we must view it in a different way, by which they mean we must

    a. view fear as a way to open us up and to create the kind of world we really want.

    b. reject deliberate appeals to fear like terrorist alerts or anthrax warnings.

    c. pay attention to our natural instincts for survival and yield to fear only when it is healthy.

    d. embrace pacifism and demand an end to violence around the world as the only sensible solution.

_____ 6. An experiment using magnetic resonance imaging (MRI) at Emory University in 2002 recorded brain responses to women playing Prisoner's Dilemma. The experiment showed that the women's brains responded most intensely when they were

    a. afraid.

    b. acting selfishly.

    c. cooperating.

    d. undergoing intense conflict.

COMPREHENSION SCORE

Score your answers for Exercises A and B as follows:

A. No. right _____ × 2 = _____

B. No. right _____ × 1 = _____

Total points from A and B _____ × 10 = _____ percent

C. SEQUENCING

These sentences from the concluding paragraph have been scrambled. Read the sentences and choose the sequence that puts them back into logical order. Do not refer to the original selection.

1 We can respond in the old, inherited ways, or we can see fear simply as information and energy to be used for our own creative ends. **2** We may be the first humans who can look at how our biology serves us—or does not serve us. **3** We then face a choice. **4** Indeed, whether we can achieve this radical shift in our view of fear may ultimately determine our future.

_____ Which of the following represents the correct sequence for these sentences?

    a. 1, 3, 2, 4
    b. 4, 1, 3, 2
    c. 2, 3, 1, 4
    d. Correct as written.

You may refer to the selection as you work through the remaining exercises.

D. IDENTIFYING SUPPORTING DETAILS

Place an X beside each statement that _directly_ supports this main idea from the selection: There are many ways that fear is generated in us as a means of control.

1. _____ President George W. Bush constantly alluded to threats to our way of life in countless speeches concerning the Iraq war.

2. _____ The media give us scary images that appeal to our sense of fear.

3. _____ There are fewer nuclear weapons today than there were 15 years ago.

4. _____ Barry Glassner wrote a book called _The Culture of Fear_.

5. _____ The media publishes images that make us afraid to drive small cars.

6. _____ We are afraid that our children will be molested or kidnapped.

E. INTERPRETING MEANING

Write your answers to these questions in your own words.

1. Examine the discussion in paragraphs 5–8 carefully. Do you see any contradictions in the writers' discussion of the sources of our fear? _____

_____

_____

2. What is the connection between the ruination of the planet (presumably from global warming) and fear? (See paragraphs 9–10.) _____

_____

3. What is the central point that the writers make in their recounting of the *Apollo 13* story? (See paragraphs 11–12.) _____

_____

4. According to the writers, why shouldn't we worry, for example, about nuclear weapons and strangers abducting our children? _____

_____

_____

5. Aside from what the writers call "the global corporate culture," what are some other agents of fear in our society today? _____

_____

_____

F. DISTINGUISHING BETWEEN FACT AND OPINION

For each of the following statements from the selection, write F if the statement represents a factual statement that can be verified or O if the statement represents the writers' or someone else's subjective interpretation. The first two are done for you.

___O___ 1. The past 100 years have been the bloodiest in human history.

___F___ 2. The *Apollo 13* astronauts saved themselves from certain disaster because they had been trained not to freeze up.

_____ 3. Our world is out of whack with our dreams because today we don't believe that we have the power to create the world we really want.

_____ 4. If safety rules were properly enforced, there would not be so many injuries to children and adolescents, according to Barry Glassner in *The Culture of Fear*.

_____ 5. The paradox of modern life is that we're made to fear as a form of control.

_____ 6. The experiment conducted at Emory University was intended to watch brain responses to impulses of selfishness and cooperation.

_____ 7. People feel trapped because we have been forced to deny our true natures.

_____ 8. The experience of Mae Jemison, the first black female astronaut, shows that one is not afraid when doing what one loves and living life fully.

G. UNDERSTANDING VOCABULARY

Look through the paragraphs listed below and find a word that matches each definition. Refer to a dictionary if necessary. An example has been done for you.

Ex. going astray, wayward [paragraph 4]   _____errant_____

1. pay attention to [5]   _____

2. out of balance, not functioning correctly
    [7—phrase]   _____

3. forced exile, expulsion [8–9]   _____

4. generated, spread [13]   _____

5. speaking or writing that uses persuasive
    techniques [13]   _____

6. an apparent or seeming contradiction [15–16]   _____

7. spread throughout, diffuse [15–16]   _____

8. detest, strongly dislike, loathe [18–19]   _____

9. original, from the first order [22–23]   _____

10. a state of intense happiness or well-being [25–26]   _____

H. USING VOCABULARY

Write the correct inflected form of the base word (in parentheses) in each of the following sentences. Be sure to add the appropriate ending to fit the grammatical requirements of the sentence. Refer to your dictionary if necessary.

1. (*bewilderment*—use an adjective) Most of us are _____ because we have no idea why the world is so different from the one we would like to live in.

2. (*vulnerable*—use a noun) Our ancestors' _____ to real physical dangers made them necessarily afraid.

3. (*destruction*—use an adjective) Our disregard for saving the planet from _____ behavior will have serious consequences if we don't change our ways.

4. (*catastrophic*—use a singular noun) Bush alluded to certain _____ concerning the threat from terrorists.

5. (*competitive*—use a verb) Our drive to _____ has turned us into a society of greedy egoists.

6. (*dictatorial*—use a noun) According to Timothy Njoya, the Presbyterian minister, Kenya was an example of a _____.

I. PARAPHRASING EXERCISE

1. Here are some sentences from paragraph 7 from the selection. Write a paraphrase of them in the space provided.

Original Passage

Our world has slipped out of whack with our common dreams for one reason: We don't believe we have the power to create the world we really want. And what lies at the root of this acquiescence? Fear. The fear of being different, and the fear of the unknown.

Your Paraphrase

_____

_____

_____

_____

_____

_____

2. These sentences are from paragraph 16. Again write your paraphrase in the space provided.

Original Passage

A first step toward freedom is to crack one driver of our fear: the myth of scarcity. The belief that there's never enough to go around keeps us on a competitive treadmill, afraid to listen to our own hearts. If we see ourselves as isolated egos competing against other egos, we can't seriously discuss a future that's good for all.

Your Paraphrase

_____

_____

_____

_____

_____

_____

J. TOPICS FOR DISCUSSION

1. Read the first few paragraphs again. The writers list several things that have aroused fear in us—terrorism warnings, anthrax scares, job layoffs, airplane crashes. In the body of the article, do they reconcile the reality of these modern-day elements with their suggestion to open ourselves up to a new way of looking at fear? Are they saying that we should not be afraid of these all-too-real possibilities, or something else altogether?
2. Just how seriously can you take the writers' assertion that our current fears are an inherited relic that evolved from our ancestors? What other factors might account for the state of the world (war, violence, famine, and so forth)?

3. Lappé and Moore carefully examine the philosophic repercussions of our fear. What would have strengthened their discussion? Specifically, what *concrete* lessons do we learn from their analysis—practical solutions that we could implement in our daily lives?

4. In paragraph 16 the writers allude to the myth of scarcity, which apparently keeps us on a consumer treadmill. But today there is no shortage of BMWs or electronic toys. What keeps us buying? What might be some other reasons that Americans consume so much—far beyond their basic requirements?

K. TOPICS FOR WRITING

1. The competitive treadmill is one theme in this article. Examine your own competitive instincts with regard to material possessions. Do you feel the constant need to acquire more because, as the writers say, there is a myth of scarcity? Or are there other motives feeding this impulse? Do you think carefully about purchases that you make and your reasons for doing so? Write an essay in which you address these questions, perhaps focusing on one recent purchase—the real reasons and rationalizations you devised before purchasing it.

2. The writers blame the media for bombarding us with scary messages—kidnappings, molestations, Columbine-style massacres. As I write this, a recent wave of freeway shootings in Southern California and a string of takeover robberies at Oakland restaurants have raised the fear level in the area. Examine one incident currently in the news and follow the media's coverage of it—both in print and on television (or on news Web sites). To what extent has the media taken an isolated incident and turned it into a trend—thereby exacerbating our fears? Follow the story for a few days, and then report on your findings.

Exploring Related Web Sites

- A Web site that gives information about Lappé and Perkins' book, *You Have the Power*, also contains several links, including one for Jeff Perkins' curious minds organization in Boston and another for Frances Moore Lappé's Small Planet Institute.

  http://purevisual.com/clients/courage/resources.html

- The Diderot effect is a phenomenon associated with consumerism and buying behavior. Do a search using Google or your favorite search engine and read about this trait.

11

GEOFFREY COWLEY
The Language Explosion

Geoffrey Cowley received his undergraduate degree in English from Lewis and Clark College in Portland, Oregon, and a master's degree in English from the University of Washington. His formal interest in language dates back to graduate school when he studied linguistics. Now Newsweek's *senior editor for health and medicine, Cowley covers medical research, fitness trends, and health policy issues. "The Language Explosion" examines the step-by-step process by which very young children acquire language.*

Vocabulary Preview

WORD PARTS

-fy [paragraph 9] According to Cowley, children possess certain skills that *simplify* the process of learning language. The verb *simplify* ("to make simple") ends with the suffix *-fy,* (which means "to cause to become" or "to make"). This suffix comes at the end of many common verbs, among them *codify, pacify, modify,* and *satisfy.* What do these verbs mean? Check a dictionary if you need help determining the meaning of their roots.

deify   _____

liquefy   _____

stupefy   _____

WORD FAMILIES

Linguist [paragraph 3] The words *linguist* and *psycholinguist* appear throughout this selection. A linguist studies language. Both *linguist* and *language* originally derive from the Latin root *lingua-,* or "tongue." And in fact, some people use the word *language* and *tongue* interchangeably. Here are four other words in this family:

linguistics	the study of languages
linguaphile	one who loves language (*lingua-* + *philos* ["love"])
linguine	a type of Italian pasta, so-called because the broad, flat strands are thought to resemble little tongues
lingo	an unfamiliar or specialized vocabulary of a particular field

GEOFFREY COWLEY

The Language Explosion

1   Barry is a pixie-faced 3-year-old who can't yet draw a circle or stack his blocks in a simple pattern. There is little chance he will ever live independently. He may never learn to tie his own shoes. Yet Barry is as chatty and engaging a person as you could ever hope to meet. He knows his preschool classmates—and their parents—by name. When he wakes his mom in the morning, he strokes her cheek and tells her how beautiful she is. Then he asks her how she slept. Barry has Williams syndrome, a rare congenital disorder caused by abnormalities on chromosome 7. Children with the condition share an array of distinctive traits, including weak hearts, elfin faces and extremely low IQs. But they're unusually sociable, and often display an extraordinary feeling for language. Ask a Williams child to name an animal, says Dr. Ursula Bellugi of the Salk Institute's Laboratory for Cognitive Neuroscience, and you may get a fanciful discourse on yaks, koalas or unicorns.

2   If we learned language in the same way that we learn to add, subtract or play cards, children like Barry would not get much beyond hello and goodbye. Nor, for that matter, would normal toddlers. As anyone who has struggled through college French can attest, picking up a new language as an adult is as simple as picking up a truck. Yet virtually every kid in the world succeeds at it—and without conscious effort. Children attach meanings to sounds long before they shed their diapers. They launch into grammatical analysis before they can tie their shoes. And by the age of 3, most produce sentences as readily as laughter or tears.

3   Scholars have bickered for centuries over how kids accomplish this feat, but most now agree that their brains are wired for the task. Like finches or sparrows, which learn to sing as hatchlings or not at all, we're designed to acquire certain kinds of knowledge at particular stages of development. Children surrounded by words almost always become fluent by 3, whatever their general intelligence. And people deprived of language as children rarely master it as adults, no matter how smart they are or how intensively they're trained. As MIT linguist Steven Pinker observes in his acclaimed 1994 book *The Language Instinct*, "Language is not a cultural artifact that we learn the way we learn to tell time or how the federal government works. It is a distinct piece of [our] biological makeup." Whether they emerge speaking Spanish, Czech or Hindi, kids all acquire language on the same general schedule. And as a growing body of research makes clear, they all travel the same remarkable path.

SOUND

4   The journey toward language starts not in the nursery but in the womb, where the fetus is continually bathed in the sounds of its mother's voice. Babies just 4 days old can distinguish one language from another. French newborns suck

more vigorously when they hear French spoken than when they hear Russian—and Russian babies show the opposite preference. At first, they notice only general rhythms and melodies. But newborns are also sensitive to speech sounds, and they home in quickly on the ones that matter.

5   Each of the world's approximately 6,000 languages uses a different assortment of phonemes, or distinctive sounds, to build words. As adults, we have a hard time even hearing phonemes from foreign languages. The French don't notice any real difference between the *th* sounds in *thick* and *then*—and to most English speakers, the vowel in the French word *tu* (*ee* through rounded lips) is just another *oo*. Researchers have found that month-old infants register both of those distinctions and countless others from the world's languages. But at 6 and 10 months, they start to narrow their range. They grow oblivious to foreign phonemes while staying attuned to whatever sounds the speakers around them are using.

6   Acquiring a set of phonemes is a first step toward language, but just a baby step. To start decoding speech, you have to recognize words. And as anyone listening to a foreign conversation quickly discovers, people don't talk one . . . word . . . at . . . a . . . time. Real-life language—even the melodious "parentese" that parents use with infants—consists mainly of nonstopstreamofsound. So how do babies suss out the boundaries? Long before they recognize words, says Peter Jusczyk, a cognitive scientist at Johns Hopkins University, they get a feel for how their language uses phonemes to launch syllables. By the time they're 7 months old, American babies are well accustomed to hearing *t* joined with *r* (as in *tram*) and *c* with *l* (as in *clam*), but they've been spared combinations like *db*, *gd*, *kt*, *ts* and *ng*, all of which occur in other languages. And once they have an ear for syllables, word boundaries become less mysterious. *Ten / groaning / deadbeats / are / cleaning / a / train on / blacktop* makes acoustic sense in English even if you don't know the words. *Te / ngroanin / gdea / dbea / tsare / cleani / nga / traino / nbla / cktop* isn't an option.

7   As children start to recognize and play with syllables, they also pick up on the metrical patterns among them. French words tend to end with a stressed syllable. The majority of English words—and virtually all of the *mommy-daddy-doggie* diminutives that parents heap on children—have the accented syllable up front. Until they're 6 months old, American babies are no more responsive to words like *bigger* than they are to words like gui*tar*. But Jusczyk has found that 6- to 10-month-olds develop a clear bias for words with first-syllable accents. They suck more vigorously when they hear such words, regardless of whether they're read from lists or tucked into streams of normal speech. The implication is that children less than a year old hear speech not as a blur of sound but as a series of distinct but meaningless words.

MEANING

8   By their first birthday, most kids start linking words to meanings. Amid their streams of sweet, melodic gibberish, they start to name things—ball, cup, bottle, doggie. And even those who don't speak for a while often gesture to show off

their mastery of the nose, eyes, ears, and toes. These may seem small steps; after all, most 1-year-olds are surrounded by people who insist on pointing and naming every object in sight. But as Pinker observes, making the right connections is a complicated business. How complicated? Imagine yourself surrounded by people speaking a strange language. A rabbit runs by, and someone shouts, "*Gavagai!*" What does the word mean? "Rabbit" may seem the obvious inference, but it's just one of countless logical alternatives. *Gavagai* could refer to that particular creature, or it could have a range of broader meanings, from "four-legged plant eater" to "furry thing in motion." How do kids get to the right level of generalization? Why don't they spend their lives trying to figure out what words like "rabbit" mean?

9   Because, says Stanford psychologist Ellen Markman, they come to the game with innate mental biases. Markman has shown that instead of testing endless hypotheses about each word's meaning, kids start from three basic assumptions. First, they figure that labels refer to whole objects, not parts or qualities. Second, they expect labels to denote classes of things (cups, balls, rabbits) rather than individual items. Third, they assume that anything with a name can have only one. These assumptions don't always lead directly to the right inference ("I'm not a noying," Dennis the Menace once told Mr. Wilson, "I'm a cowboy"). But they vastly simplify word learning. In keeping with the "whole object" assumption, a child won't consider a label for "handle" until she has one for "cup." And thanks to the "one label per object" assumption, a child who has mastered the word *cup* never assumes that *handle* is just another way of saying the same thing. "In that situation," says Markman, "the child accepts the possibility that the new word applies to some feature of the object."

10   Words accrue slowly at first. But around the age of 18 months, children's abilities explode. Most start acquiring new words at the phenomenal rate of one every two hours—and for the first time, they start combining them. Children don't all reach these milestones on exactly the same schedule; their development rates can vary by a year or more, and there's no evidence that late talkers end up less fluent than early talkers. But by their second birthdays, most kids have socked away 1,000 to 2,000 words and started tossing around two-word strings such as "no nap," "all wet," or "bottle juice."

GRAMMAR

11   Once kids can paste two words together, it's not long before they're generating sentences. Between 24 and 30 months, "no nap" may become "I don't want nap," and "bottle juice" may blossom into "I want juice." When kids hit that stage, their repertoires start expanding exponentially. Between 30 and 36 months, most acquire rules for expressing tense (*walk* versus *walked*) and number (*house* versus *houses*), often overextending them to produce statements like "I bringed home three mouses." They also start using "function words"—the *somes, woulds, whos, hows* and *afters* that enable us to ask either "Do you like milk?" or "Would you like some milk?"

12   More fundamentally, they discover that words can have radically different meanings depending on how they're strung together. Even before children start combining words on their own, most know the difference between "Big Bird is tickling Cookie Monster" and "Cookie Monster is tickling Big Bird." That awareness marks the zenith of language development. A chimp can learn to label things, and a high-powered computer can process more information in a minute than any person could handle in a lifetime. But neither a chimp nor a mainframe is any match for a runny-nosed 3-year-old when it comes to reporting who did what to whom. When a chimp with a signboard signals "Me banana you banana you," chances are he wants you to give him one, but the utterance could mean almost anything. Three-year-olds don't talk that way. The reason, most linguists agree, is that natural selection has outfitted the human brain with software for grammatical analysis. As MIT linguist Noam Chomsky realized more than 30 years ago, the world's languages all build sentences from noun phrases ("The big dog") and verb phrases ("ate my homework"). And toddlers who have never heard of grammar identify them effortlessly.

13   To confirm that point, psycholinguists Stephen Crain and Mineharu Nakayama once invited 3-, 4- and 5-year-olds to interview a talking "Star Wars" doll (Jabba the Hutt). With a child at his side, one researcher would pull out a picture and suggest asking Jabba about it. For example: "Ask Jabba if the boy who is unhappy is watching Mickey Mouse." You can't compose the right sentence—"Is the boy who is unhappy watching Mickey Mouse?"—unless you recognize *the-boy-who-is-unhappy* as a single noun phrase. As Chomsky would have predicted, the kids got it right every time.

14   If children's minds were open to all the possible relationships among words, they would never get very far. No one could memorize 140 million sentences, but a kid who masters 25 common recipes for a noun phrase can produce more than that number from scratch. Too much mental flexibility would confine children. Pinker observes: "innate constraints set them free." Not everyone is blessed with those constraints. Kids with a hereditary condition known as Specific Language Impairment, or SLI, never develop certain aspects of grammar, despite their normal IQs. But those are rare exceptions. Most kids are so primed for grammatical rules that they'll invent them if necessary.

15   Consider hearing adults who take up American Sign Language so they can share it with their deaf children. They tend to fracture phrases and leave verbs unconjugated. Yet their kids still become fluent, grammatical signers. "Children don't need good teachers to master language," says Elissa Newport, a cognitive scientist at the University of Rochester. "They pick up whatever rules they can find, and sharpen and extend them." That, according to University of Hawaii linguist Derek Bickerton, is why the crude pidgins that crop up in mixed-language communities quickly evolve into fully grammatical creoles. When language lacks a coherent grammar, children create one.

16   That's not to say language requires no nurture. Children raised in complete silence grow deaf to grammar. "Chelsea," whose correctable hearing problem

went untreated until she was 31, eventually learned enough words to hold a job in a vet's office. Yet her expressive powers have never surpassed those of a chimp with a signboard. She says things like "The woman is bus the going" or "I Wanda be drive come." Fortunately, Chelsea is a rare exception. Given even a few words to play with, most kids quickly take flight. "You don't need to have left the Stone Age," Pinker says. "You don't need to be middle class." All you need to be is young. ✻

Geoffrey Cowley "The Language Explosion," *Newsweek*, Spring-Summer 1997, Special Edition. © 1997, Newsweek, Inc. All right reserved. Reprinted by permission.

Exercises

Do not refer to the selection for Exercises A and B unless your instructor directs you to do so.

A. DETERMINING THE MAIN IDEA AND PURPOSE

Choose the best answer.

_____ **1.** The main idea of the selection is that

    a. no matter what language they speak, children all acquire language following the same remarkable path.

    b. children who are not exposed to language as infants rarely master it well.

    c. linguists disagree about the way children acquire language.

    d. further research must be done before linguists can know exactly how children acquire language.

_____ **2.** The writer's purpose is to

    a. summarize recent research on child language acquisition.

    b. show parents how to help their children learn to speak earlier.

    c. convince parents to spend more time talking to their newborn babies.

    d. explain the stages a child goes through on his or her way to acquiring language.

B. COMPREHENDING MAIN IDEAS

Choose the correct answer.

_____ **1.** Small children who have been deprived of language

    a. never learn to speak.

    b. rarely master it as adults.

    c. must attend special schools and be taught by specially trained teachers.

    d. show signs of mental and physical retardation.

_____ 2. According to the article, children are designed to acquire certain kinds of knowledge at particular stages of development. This language acquisition usually occurs between

    a. before birth to age three.
    b. ages one to two.
    c. ages four to six.
    d. ages seven to nine.

_____ 3. An important step in a baby's language development is the ability to

    a. reproduce sounds she hears.
    b. distinguish phonemes that make up syllables and identify word boundaries.
    c. recognize that sounds are merely symbols for things in the real world.
    d. accept sounds from their own language and reject sounds that are from foreign languages.

_____ 4. According to Stanford psychologist Ellen Markman, a child learns to attach meaning to words by

    a. testing a whole set of theories about the meaning of each word he hears.
    b. figuring out for himself by process of deduction what each word means.
    c. learning to speak each word independently before connecting it to its meaning.
    d. following the assumption that a label refers to a whole object and not to its parts or qualities.

_____ 5. The sentence "I bringed home three mouses" shows that the child

    a. has not learned correct grammar.
    b. is connecting phonemes that make sense.
    c. is employing common rules to express time and number in her sentences.
    d. has no flexibility in the way she expresses herself.

_____ 6. When a child produces the sentences "Big Bird is tickling Cookie Monster" and "Cookie Monster is tickling Big Bird," it is a sign that he

    a. is showing a capacity for grammatical analysis.
    b. has learned that sentences are different from two-word phrases.
    c. cannot clearly indicate who did what to whom.
    d. recognizes that all the things in the world around him have names.

COMPREHENSION SCORE

Score your answers for Exercises A and B as follows:

A. No. right _____ × 2 = _____
B. No. right _____ × 1 = _____

Total points from A and B _____ × 10 = _____ percent

You may refer to the selection as you work through the remaining exercises.

C. DISTINGUISHING BETWEEN MAIN IDEAS
AND SUPPORTING DETAILS

Label the following statements from the selection as follows: MI if it represents a *main idea* and SD if it represents a *supporting detail.*

1. _____   The journey toward language starts not in the nursery but in the womb, where the fetus is continually bathed in the sounds of its mother's voice.

2. _____   Babies just 4 days old can distinguish one language from another.

3. _____   French newborns suck more vigorously when they hear French spoken than when they hear Russian.

4. _____   Russian babies show the opposite preference.

5. _____   At first, they notice only general rhythms and melodies.

6. _____   But newborns are also sensitive to speech sounds, and they home in quickly on the ones that matter.

D. INTERPRETING MEANING

Write your answers for these questions in your own words.

1. From the selection as a whole, state *two* important points Cowley makes

   about the way a child acquires language. _____

   _____

   _____

2. From paragraphs 2 and 3, what does Cowley mean when he says that "picking up a new language as an adult is as simple as picking up a truck"?

   _____

3. In paragraph 3, what does the writer mean in the first sentence when he says

   that children's brains are "wired" for the task of learning language? _____

   _____

4. What point is Cowley trying to make in paragraph 9 when he quotes Dennis the Menace telling Mr. Wilson, "I'm not a noying. I'm a cowboy"? _____

_____

_____

5. Read paragraph 10 again. If the 18-month child of a friend or relative were not acquiring words at the phenomenal rate Cowley cites—one word every two hours—what advice would you give the parents? _____

_____

_____

_____

E. UNDERSTANDING VOCABULARY

Look through the paragraphs listed below and find a word that matches each definition. An example has been done for you.

Ex. irregularities, conditions that are not normal
[paragraph 1]   _____abnormalities_____

1. assert, confirm, substantiate [2]   _____

2. quarreled, argued about, disagreed [3]   _____

3. completely unmindful of, lacking conscious
   awareness of [5]   _____

4. choice, alternative [6]   _____

5. nonsense talk, babble [8]   _____

6. inborn, natural, present at birth [9 and 14]   _____

7. complete lists of skills and talents, entire
   vocabulary [11]   _____

8. the highest point, apex, pinnacle [12]   _____

F. USING VOCABULARY

In parentheses before each sentence are some inflected forms of words from the selection. Study the context and the sentence. Then write the correct form in the space provided.

1. (*abnormality, abnormal, abnormally*) Williams syndrome is caused by an

   _____ chromosome 7, which results in weak hearts and low IQ.

2. (*fluency, fluent, fluently*) Most children develop complete _____ in their native language by the age of three.

3. (*deprivation, deprived, depriving, deprivable*) Babies who are routinely

   _____ of hearing language rarely master it later in life.

4. (*vigor, vigorous, vigorously*) Researchers note that even very small babies suck

   more _____ when they hear their own language than when they hear
   a foreign language.

5. (*simplification, simplify, simple, simply*) The innate biases that children bring to

   their learning of language allow them to _____ the process.

G. ANNOTATING EXERCISE

In the left margin, annotate paragraphs 8 and 9.

H. SUMMARIZING EXERCISE

1. Write a summary of paragraph 9 in the space below. The paragraph is
   approximately 175 words long, so your summary should be around 45 words.

   _____

   _____

   _____

   _____

I. TOPICS FOR DISCUSSION

1. What factors make a child's acquisition of language so phenomenal?
2. The opening paragraph describes the language abilities of Barry, a little boy
   with Williams syndrome, and the concluding paragraph describes the language abilities of Chelsea, whose correctable hearing problem went untreated
   until adulthood. Why does Cowley use these two people to open and close
   the essay?
3. In paragraph 12, Cowley gives an example of a chimpanzee sentence,
   "Me banana you banana you." What point does this example support?

J. TOPICS FOR WRITING

1. If you are acquainted with a child younger than three—a brother or sister,
   nephew or niece, a neighbor's child, or perhaps your own child—observe the
   child for an hour as he or she goes about playing, listen to the child's speech,
   and take notes. When you're finished with your observations, write a short
   report in which you evaluate the child's speech in relation to the stages of
   development Cowley explains in the article.
2. Judging from what you read in this article, what advice would you give to the
   parents of a newborn? Write a short essay summarizing your advice.

3. If you are studying a foreign language in college or if you studied one in high school, write an essay in which you contrast your efforts to learn to speak the language with the seemingly effortless way that children acquire their native language. What specific problems did you encounter? What factors make studying a language as an adult so incredibly difficult?

Exploring Related Web Sites

- These two sites provide general information about language acquisition in children.

  "Mama Teached Me Talk!" *www.facstaff.bucknell.edu/rbeard/acquisition.html*

  www.Isadc.ore/info/ling-faqs.com

  This site, sponsored by the Linguistic Society of America, provides links with FAQs (Frequently Asked Questions).

- This site offers a wealth of suggestions for parents, including message boards, academic skill builders, information on nutrition, and a host of other topics relating to raising a child.

  www.familyeducation.com

12 VIRGINIA MORELL
Minds of Their Own

Alex, an African gray parrot; Betsy, a border collie; and Maya, a bottlenose dolphin—these diverse creatures demonstrate a remarkable facility for language, challenging the usual human claims of superiority in this regard. Virginia Morell is a science writer from Oregon who writes frequently for National Geographic, *where this article was originally published.*

Vocabulary Preview

WORD PARTS

-ize [digitized (paragraph 27); categorize (paragraph 37); synchronize (paragraph 81)] The suffix *-ize* is one of the most common verb endings in English. Its most common meaning is "to come to be" or "to make into" added to the root noun or adjective. Thus, *digitized* means "to make digital," *categorize* means "to put into categories," and *synchronize* means to "make something happen at the same time." To determine a meaning of a verb ending with *-ize*, simply drop off the ending and identify the meaning of the root. Here is an interesting word ending with the suffix *-ize*. What does it mean? Consult a dictionary if necessary.

bowdlerize _____

_____

_____

WORD FAMILIES

chron- [paragraph 81] As you saw in the preceding section, *synchronize* refers to several actions that occur at the same time. The root *chron-*, from Greek *khronos*, means "time." The prefix *syn-* means "same." Thus, when put together, the word means, literally "same" + "time" + "make." Other words containing the root *chron-* are *chronicle*, a record of the times; *chronological* (time order); and *chronometer* (a very precise type of watch).

Sometimes people develop a chronic cough. What does this mean? _____

_____

VIRGINIA MORELL

Minds of Their Own

1   In 1977 Irene Pepperberg, a recent graduate of Harvard University, did something very bold. At a time when animals still were considered automatons, she set out to find what was on another creature's mind by talking to it. She brought a one-year-old African gray parrot she named Alex into her lab to teach him to reproduce the sounds of the English language. "I thought if he learned to communicate, I could ask him questions about how he sees the world."

2   When Pepperberg began her dialogue with Alex, who died last September at the age of 31, many scientists believed animals were incapable of any thought. They were simply machines, robots programmed to react to stimuli but lacking the ability to think or feel. Any pet owner would disagree. We see the love in our dogs' eyes and know that, of course, Spot has thoughts and emotions. But such claims remain highly controversial. Gut instinct is not science, and it is all too easy to project human thoughts and feelings onto another creature. How, then, does a scientist prove that an animal is capable of thinking—that it is able to acquire information about the world and act on it?

3   "That's why I started my studies with Alex," Pepperberg said. They were seated—she at her desk, he on top of his cage—in her lab, a windowless room about the size of a boxcar, at Brandeis University. Newspapers lined the floor; baskets of bright toys were stacked on the shelves. They were clearly a team—and because of their work, the notion that animals can think is no longer so fanciful.

4   Certain skills are considered key signs of higher mental abilities: good memory, a grasp of grammar and symbols, self-awareness, understanding others' motives, imitating others, and being creative. Bit by bit, in ingenious experiments, researchers have documented these talents in other species, gradually chipping away at what we thought made human beings distinctive while offering a glimpse of where our own abilities came from. Scrub jays know that other jays are thieves and that stashed food can spoil; sheep can recognize faces; chimpanzees use a variety of tools to probe termite mounds and even use weapons to hunt small mammals; dolphins can imitate human postures; the archerfish, which stuns insects with a sudden blast of water, can learn how to aim its squirt simply by watching an experienced fish perform the task. And Alex the parrot turned out to be a surprisingly good talker.

5   Thirty years after the Alex studies began, Pepperberg and a changing collection of assistants were still giving him English lessons. The humans, along with two younger parrots, also served as Alex's flock, providing the social input all parrots crave. Like any flock, this one—as small as it was—had its share of drama. Alex dominated his fellow parrots, acted huffy at times around Pepperberg, tolerated the other female humans, and fell to pieces over a male assistant who dropped by for a visit. ("If you were a man," Pepperberg said, after noting Alex's aloofness toward me, "he'd be on your shoulder in a second, barfing cashews in your ear.")

6   Pepperberg bought Alex in a Chicago pet store. She let the store's assistant pick him out because she didn't want other scientists saying later that she'd deliberately chosen an especially smart bird for her work. Given that Alex's brain was the size of a shelled walnut, most researchers thought Pepperberg's interspecies communication study would be futile.

7   "Some people actually called me crazy for trying this," she said. "Scientists thought that chimpanzees were better subjects, although, of course, chimps can't speak."

8   Chimpanzees, bonobos, and gorillas have been taught to use sign language and symbols to communicate with us, often with impressive results. The bonobo Kanzi, for instance, carries his symbol-communication board with him so he can "talk" to his human researchers, and he has invented combinations of symbols to express his thoughts. Nevertheless, this is not the same thing as having an animal look up at you, open his mouth, and speak.

9   Pepperberg walked to the back of the room, where Alex sat on top of his cage preening his pearl gray feathers. He stopped at her approach and opened his beak.

10   "Want grape," Alex said.

11   "He hasn't had his breakfast yet," Pepperberg explained, "so he's a little put out."

12   Alex returned to preening, while an assistant prepared a bowl of grapes, green beans, apple and banana slices, and corn on the cob.

13   Under Pepperberg's patient tutelage, Alex learned how to use his vocal tract to imitate almost one hundred English words, including the sounds for all of these foods, although he calls an apple a "ban-erry."

14   "Apples taste a little bit like bananas to him, and they look a little bit like cherries, so Alex made up that word for them," Pepperberg said.

15   Alex could count to six and was learning the sounds for seven and eight.

16   "I'm sure he already knows both numbers," Pepperberg said. "He'll probably be able to count to ten, but he's still learning to say the words. It takes far more time to teach him certain sounds than I ever imagined."

17   After breakfast, Alex preened again, keeping an eye on the flock. Every so often, he leaned forward and opened his beak: "Ssse . . . won."

18   "That's good, Alex," Pepperberg said. "Seven. The number is seven."

19   "Ssse . . . won! Se . . . won!"

20   "He's practicing," she explained. "That's how he learns. He's thinking about how to say that word, how to use his vocal tract to make the correct sound."

21   It sounded a bit mad, the idea of a bird having lessons to practice, and willingly doing it. But after listening to and watching Alex, it was difficult to argue with Pepperberg's explanation for his behaviors. She wasn't handing him treats for the repetitive work or rapping him on the claws to make him say the sounds.

22   "He has to hear the words over and over before he can correctly imitate them," Pepperberg said, after pronouncing "seven" for Alex a good dozen times in a row. "I'm not trying to see if Alex can learn a human language," she added. "That's never been the point. My plan always was to use his imitative skills to get a better understanding of avian cognition."

23   In other words, because Alex was able to produce a close approximation of the sounds of some English words, Pepperberg could ask him questions about a bird's basic understanding of the world. She couldn't ask him what he was thinking about, but she could ask him about his knowledge of numbers, shapes, and colors. To demonstrate, Pepperberg carried Alex on her arm to a tall wooden perch in the middle of the room. She then retrieved a green key and a small green cup from a basket on a shelf. She held up the two items to Alex's eye.

24   "What's same?" she asked.

25   Without hesitation, Alex's beak opened: "Co-lor,"

26   "What's different?" Pepperberg asked.

27   "Shape," Alex said. His voice had the digitized sound of a cartoon character. Since parrots lack lips (another reason it was difficult for Alex to pronounce some sounds, such as *ba*), the words seemed to come from the air around him, as if a ventriloquist were speaking. But the words—and what can only be called the thoughts—were entirely his.

28   For the next 20 minutes, Alex ran through his tests, distinguishing colors, shapes, sizes, and materials (wool versus wood versus metal). He did some simple arithmetic, such as counting the yellow toy blocks among a pile of mixed hues.

29   And, then, as if to offer final proof of the mind inside his bird's brain, Alex spoke up. "Talk clearly!" he commanded, when one of the younger birds Pepperberg was also teaching mispronounced the word green. "Talk clearly!"

30   "Don't be a smart aleck," Pepperberg said, shaking her head at him. "He knows all this, and he gets bored, so he interrupts the others, or he gives the wrong answer just to be obstinate. At this stage, he's like a teenage son; he's moody, and I'm never sure what he'll do."

31   "Wanna go tree," Alex said in a tiny voice.

32   Alex had lived his entire life in captivity, but he knew that beyond the lab's door, there was a hallway and a tall window framing a leafy elm tree. He liked to see the tree, so Pepperberg put her hand out for him to climb aboard. She walked him down the hall into the tree's green light.

33   "Good boy! Good birdie," Alex said, bobbing on her hand.

34   "Yes, you're a good boy. You're a good birdie." And she kissed his feathered head.

35   He was a good birdie until the end, and Pepperberg was happy to report that when he died he had finally mastered "seven."

36   Many of Alex's cognitive skills, such as his ability to understand the concepts of same and different, are generally ascribed only to higher mammals, particularly primates. But parrots, like great apes (and humans), live a long time in complex societies. And like primates, these birds must keep track of the dynamics of changing relationships and environments.

37   "They need to be able to distinguish colors to know when a fruit is ripe or unripe," Pepperberg noted. "They need to categorize things—what's edible, what isn't—and to know the shapes of predators. And it helps to have a concept of numbers if you need to keep track of your flock, and to know who's single and who's paired up. For a long-lived bird, you can't do all of this with instinct; cognition must be involved."

38   Being able mentally to divide the world into simple abstract categories would seem a valuable skill for many organisms. Is that ability, then, part of the evolutionary drive that led to human intelligence?

39   Charles Darwin, who attempted to explain how human intelligence developed, extended his theory of evolution to the human brain: Like the rest of our physiology, intelligence must have evolved from simpler organisms, since all animals face the same general challenges of life. They need to find mates, food, and a path through the woods, sea, or sky—tasks that Darwin argued require problem-solving and categorizing abilities. Indeed, Darwin went so far as to suggest that earthworms are cognitive beings because, based on his close observations, they have to make judgments about the kinds of leafy matter they use to block their tunnels. He hadn't expected to find thinking invertebrates and remarked that the hint of earthworm intelligence "has surprised me more than anything else in regard to worms."

40   To Darwin, the earthworm discovery demonstrated that degrees of intelligence could be found throughout the animal kingdom. But the Darwinian approach to animal intelligence was cast aside in the early 20th century, when researchers decided that field observations were simply "anecdotes," usually tainted by anthropomorphism. In an effort to be more rigorous, many embraced behaviorism, which regarded animals as little more than machines, and focused their studies on the laboratory white rat—since one "machine" would behave like any other.

41   But if animals are simply machines, how can the appearance of human intelligence be explained? Without Darwin's evolutionary perspective, the greater cognitive skills of people did not make sense biologically. Slowly the pendulum has swung away from the animal-as-machine model and back toward Darwin. A whole range of animal studies now suggest that the roots of cognition are deep, widespread, and highly malleable.

42   Just how easily new mental skills can evolve is perhaps best illustrated by dogs. Most owners talk to their dogs and expect them to understand. But this canine talent wasn't fully appreciated until a border collie named Rico appeared on a German TV game show in 2001. Rico knew the names of some 200 toys and acquired the names of new ones with ease.

43   Researchers at the Max Planck Institute for Evolutionary Anthropology in Leipzig heard about Rico and arranged a meeting with him and his owners. That led to a scientific report revealing Rico's uncanny language ability: He could learn and remember words as quickly as a toddler. Other scientists had shown that two-year-old-children—who acquire around ten new words a day—have an innate set of principles that guides this task. The ability is seen as one of the key building blocks in language acquisition. The Max Planck scientists suspect that the same principles guide Rico's word learning, and that the technique he uses for learning words is identical to that of humans.

44   To find more examples, the scientists read all the letters from hundreds of people claiming that their dogs had Rico's talent. In fact, only two—both border collies—had comparable skills. One of them—the researchers call her Betsy—has a vocabulary of more than 300 words.

45   "Even our closest relatives, the great apes, can't do what Betsy can do—hear a word only once or twice and know that the acoustic pattern stands for something," said Juliane Kaminski, a cognitive psychologist who worked with Rico and is now studying Betsy. She and her colleague Sebastian Tempelmann had come to Betsy's home in Vienna to give her a fresh battery of tests. Kaminski petted Betsy, while Tempelmann set up a video camera.

46   "Dogs' understanding of human forms of communication is something new that has evolved,"Kaminski said, "something that's developed in them because of their long association with humans." Although Kaminski has not yet tested wolves, she doubts they have this language skill. Maybe these collies are especially good at it because they're working dogs and highly motivated, and in their traditional herding jobs, they must listen very closely to their owners."

47   Scientists think that dogs were domesticated about 15,000 years ago, a relatively short time in which to evolve language skills. But how similar are these skills to those of humans? For abstract thinking, we employ symbols, letting one thing stand for another. Kaminski and Tempelmann were testing whether dogs can do this too.

48   Betsy's owner—whose pseudonym is Schaefer—summoned Betsy, who obediently stretched out at Schaefer's feet, eyes fixed on her face. Whenever Schaefer spoke, Betsy attentively cocked her head from side to side.

49   Kaminski handed Schaefer a stack of color photographs and asked her to choose one. Each image depicted a dog's toy against a white background—toys Betsy had never seen before. They weren't actual toys; they were only images of toys. Could Betsy connect a two-dimensional picture to a three-dimensional object?

50   Schaefer held up a picture of a fuzzy, rainbow-colored Frisbee and urged Betsy to find it. Betsy studied the photograph and Schaefer's face, then ran into the kitchen, where the Frisbee was placed among three other toys and photographs of each toy. Betsy brought either the Frisbee or the photograph of the Frisbee to Schaefer every time.

51   "It wouldn't have been wrong if she'd just brought the photograph," Kaminski said. "But I think Betsy can use a picture, without a name, to find an object. Still, it will take many more tests to prove this."

52   Even then, Kaminski is unsure that other scientists will ever accept her discovery because Betsy's abstract skill, as minor as it may seem to us, may tread all too closely to human thinking.

53   Still, we remain the inventive species. No other animal has built skyscrapers, written sonnets, or made a computer. Yet animal researchers say that creativity, like other forms of intelligence, did not simply spring from nothingness. It, too, has evolved.

54   "People were surprised to discover that chimpanzees make tools," said Alex Kacelnik, a behavioral ecologist at Oxford University, referring to the straws and sticks chimpanzees shape to pull termites from their nests. "But people also thought, 'Well, they share our ancestry—of course they're smart.' Now we're finding these kinds of exceptional behaviors in some species of birds. But we don't have a recently shared ancestry with birds. Their evolutionary history is

very different; our last common ancestor with all birds was a reptile that lived over 300 million years ago.

55 "This is not trivial," Kacelnik continued. "It means that evolution can invent similar forms of advanced intelligence more than once—that it's not something reserved only for primates or mammals."

56 Kacelnik and his colleagues are studying one of these smart species, the New Caledonian crow, which lives in the forests of that Pacific island. New Caledonian crows are among the most skilled of tool-making and tool-using birds, forming probes and hooks from sticks and leaf stems to poke into the crowns of the palm trees, where fat grubs hide. Since these birds, like chimpanzees, make and use tools, researchers can look for similarities in the evolutionary processes that shaped their brains. Something about the environments of both species favored the evolution of tool-making neural powers.

57 But is their use of tools rigid and limited, or can they be inventive? Do they have what researchers call mental flexibility? Chimpanzees certainly do. In the wild, a chimpanzee may use four sticks of different sizes to extract the honey from a bee's nest. And in captivity, they can figure out how to position several boxes so they can retrieve a banana hanging from a rope.

58 Answering that question for New Caledonian crows—extremely shy birds— wasn't easy. Even after years of observing them in the wild, researchers couldn't determine if the birds' ability was innate, or if they learned to make and use their tools by watching one another. If it was a genetically inherited skill, could they, like the chimps, use their talent in different, creative ways?

59 To find out, Kacelnik and his students brought 23 crows of varying ages (all but one caught in the wild) to the aviary in his Oxford lab and let them mate. Four hatchlings were raised in captivity, and all were carefully kept away from the adults, so they had no opportunity to be taught about tools. Yet soon after they fledged, all picked up sticks to probe busily into cracks and shaped different materials into tools. "So we know that at least the bases of tool use are inherited," Kacelnik said. "And now the question is, what else can they do with tools?"

60 Plenty. In his office, Kacelnik played a video of a test he'd done with one of the wild-caught crows, Betty, who had died recently from an infection. In the film, Betty flies into a room. She's a glossy-black bird with a crow's bright, inquisitive eyes, and she immediately spies the test before her: a glass tube with a tiny basket lodged in its center. The basket holds a bit of meat. The scientists had placed two pieces of wire in the room. One was bent into a hook, the other was straight. They figured Betty would choose the hook to lift the basket by its handle.

61 But experiments don't always go according to plan. Another crow had stolen the hook before Betty could find it. Betty is undeterred. She looks at the meat in the basket, then spots the straight piece of wire. She picks it up with her beak, pushes one end into a crack in the floor, and uses her beak to bend the other end into a hook. Thus armed, she lifts the basket out of the tube.

62 "This was the first time Betty had ever seen a piece of wire like this," Kacelnik said. "But she knew she could use it to make a hook and exactly where she needed to bend it to make the size she needed."

63   They gave Betty other tests, each requiring a slightly different solution, such as making a hook out of a flat piece of aluminum rather than a wire. Each time, Betty invented a new tool and solved the problem. "It means she had a mental representation of what it was she wanted to make. Now that," Kacelnik said, "is a major kind of cognitive sophistication."

64   This is the larger lesson of animal cognition research: It humbles us. We are not alone in our ability to invent or plan or to contemplate ourselves—or even to plot and lie.

65   Deceptive acts require a complicated form of thinking, since you must be able to attribute intentions to the other person and predict that person's behavior. One school of thought argues that human intelligence evolved partly because of the pressure of living in a complex society of calculating beings. Chimpanzees, orangutans, gorillas, and bonobos share this capacity with us. In the wild, primatologists have seen apes hide food from the alpha male or have sex behind his back.

66   Birds, too, can cheat. Laboratory studies show that western scrub jays can know another bird's intentions and act on that knowledge. A jay that has stolen food itself, for example, knows that if another jay watches it hide a nut, there's a chance the nut will be stolen. So the first jay will return to move the nut when the other jay is gone.

67   "It's some of the best evidence so far of experience projection in another species," said Nicky Clayton in her aviary lab at Cambridge University. "I would describe it as, 'I know that you know where I have hidden my stash of food, and if I were in your shoes I'd steal it, so I'm going to move my stash to a place you don't know about.'"

68   This study, by Clayton and her colleague Nathan Emery, is the first to show the kind of ecological pressures, such as the need to hide food for winter use, that would lead to the evolution of such mental abilities. Most provocatively, her research demonstrates that some birds possess what is often considered another uniquely human skill: the ability to recall a specific past event. Scrub jays, for example, seem to know how long ago they cached a particular kind of food, and they manage to retrieve it before it spoils.

69   Human cognitive psychologists call this kind of memory "episodic memory" and argue that it can exist only in a species that can mentally travel back in time. Despite Clayton's studies, some refuse to concede this ability to the jays. "Animals are stuck in time," explained Sara Shettleworth, a comparative psychologist at the University of Toronto in Canada, meaning that they don't distinguish among past, present, and future the way humans do. Since animals lack language, she said, they probably also lack "the extra layer of imagination and explanation" that provides the running mental narrative accompanying our actions.

70   Such skepticism is a challenge for Clayton. "We have good evidence that the jays remember the what, where, and when of specific caching events, which is the original definition of episodic memory. But now the goalposts have moved." It's a common complaint among animal researchers. Whenever they find a mental skill in a species that is reminiscent of a special human ability, the human cognition scientists change the definition. But the animal researchers

may underestimate their power—it is their discoveries that compel the human side to shore up the divide.

71   "Sometimes the human cognitive psychologists can be so fixed on their definitions that they forget how fabulous these animal discoveries are," said Clive Wynne of the University of Florida, who has studied cognition in pigeons and marsupials. "We're glimpsing intelligence throughout the animal kingdom, which is what we should expect. It's a bush, not a single-trunk tree with a line leading only to us."

72   Some of the branches on that bush have led to such degrees of intelligence that we should blush for ever having thought any animal a mere machine.

73   In the late 1960s a cognitive psychologist named Louis Herman began investigating the cognitive abilities of bottlenose dolphins. Like humans, dolphins are highly social and cosmopolitan, living in subpolar to tropical environments worldwide; they're highly vocal; and they have special sensory skills, such as echolocation. By the 1980s Herman's cognitive studies were focused on a group of four young dolphins—Akeakamai, Phoenix, Elele, and Hiapo—at the Kewalo Basin Marine Mammal Laboratory in Hawaii. The dolphins were curious and playful, and they transferred their sociability to Herman and his students.

74   "In our work with the dolphins, we had a guiding philosophy," Herman says, "that we could bring out the full flower of their intellect, just as educators try to bring out the full potential of a human child. Dolphins have these big, highly complex brains. My thought was, 'OK, so you have this pretty brain. Let's see what you can do with it.'"

75   To communicate with the dolphins, Herman and his team invented a hand- and arm-signal language, complete with a simple grammar. For instance, a pumping motion of the closed fists meant "hoop," and both arms extended overhead (as in jumping jacks) meant "ball." A "come here" gesture with a single arm told them to "fetch." Responding to the request "hoop, ball, fetch," Akeakamai would push the ball to the hoop. But if the word order was changed to "ball, hoop, fetch," she would carry the hoop to the ball. Over time she could interpret more grammatically complex requests, such as "right, basket, left, Frisbee, in," asking that she put the Frisbee on her left in the basket on her right. Reversing "left" and "right" in the instruction would reverse Akeakamai's actions. Akeakamai could complete such requests the first time they were made, showing a deep understanding of the grammar of the language.

76   "They're a very vocal species," Herman adds. "Our studies showed that they could imitate arbitrary sounds that we broadcast into their tank, an ability that may be tied to their own need to communicate. I'm not saying they have a dolphin language. But they are capable of understanding the novel instructions that we convey to them in a tutored language; their brains have that ability.

77   "There are many things they could do that people have always doubted about animals. For example, they correctly interpreted, on the very first occasion, gestured instructions given by a person displayed on a TV screen behind an underwater window. They recognized that television images were representations of the real world that could be acted on in the same way as in the real world."

78   They readily imitated motor behaviors of their instructors too. If a trainer bent backward and lifted a leg, the dolphin would turn on its back and lift its tail in the air. Although imitation was once regarded as a simpleminded skill, in recent years cognitive scientists have revealed that it's extremely difficult, requiring the imitator to form a mental image of the other person's body and pose, then adjust his own body parts into the same position—actions that imply an awareness of one's self.

79   "Here's Elele," Herman says, showing a film of her following a trainer's directions. "Surfboard, dorsal fin, touch." Instantly Elele swam to the board and, leaning to one side, gently laid her dorsal fin on it, an untrained behavior. The trainer stretched her arms straight up, signaling "Hooray!" and Elele leaped into the air, squeaking and clicking with delight.

80   "Elele just loved to be right," Herman said. "And she loved inventing things. We made up a sign for 'create,' which asked a dolphin to create its own behavior."

81   Dolphins often synchronize their movements in the wild, such as leaping and diving side by side, but scientists don't know what signal they use to stay so tightly coordinated. Herman thought he might be able to tease out the technique with his pupils. In the film, Akeakamai and Phoenix are asked to create a trick and do it together. The two dolphins swim away from the side of the pool, circle together underwater for about ten seconds, then leap out of the water, spinning clockwise on their long axis and squirting water from their mouths, every maneuver done at the same instant. "None of this was trained," Herman says, "and it looks to us absolutely mysterious. We don't know how they do it—or did it."

82   He never will. Akeakamai and Phoenix and the two others died accidentally four years ago. Through these dolphins, he made some of the most extraordinary breakthroughs ever in understanding another species' mind—a species that even Herman describes as "alien," given its aquatic life and the fact that dolphins and primates diverged millions of years ago. "That kind of cognitive convergence suggests there must be some similar pressures selecting for intellect," Herman said. "We don't share their biology or ecology. That leaves social similarities— the need to establish relationships and alliances superimposed on a lengthy period of maternal care and longevity—as the likely common driving force."

83   "I loved our dolphins," Herman says, "as I'm sure you love your pets. But it was more than that, more than the love you have for a pet. The dolphins were our colleagues. That's the only word that fits. They were our partners in this research, guiding us into all the capabilities of their minds. When they died, it was like losing our children."

84   Herman pulled a photograph from his file. In it, he is in the pool with Phoenix, who rests her head on his shoulder. He is smiling and reaching back to embrace her. She is sleek and silvery with appealingly large eyes, and she looks to be smiling too, as dolphins always do. It's an image of love between two beings. In that pool, at least for that moment, there was clearly a meeting of the minds. ✳

Exercises

Do not refer to the selection for Exercises A–C unless your instructor directs you to do so.

A. DETERMINING THE MAIN IDEA AND PURPOSE

Choose the best answer.

_____ **1.** The main idea of the selection is that

    a. scientists do not accept the concept that animals can think abstractly and use language intelligently; the animals in these studies have just been well trained.

    b. only humans are able to use true language; animals merely imitate sounds without understanding their meaning.

    c. current research on animals suggests that the roots of knowledge are deep and that limited forms of intelligence exist throughout the animal kingdom.

    d. current animal research has chipped away at the idea that human beings are the only creatures who are intelligent and who can use language.

_____ **2.** The writer's purpose is to

    a. offer reasons to support the proposal that more definitive research on animal intelligence needs to be conducted.

    b. summarize research on animal intelligence using illustrations from several species.

    c. convince the reader that animals are just as intelligent as human beings, if not more so.

    d. describe the controversy over experiments using animals.

B. COMPREHENDING MAIN IDEAS

Choose the correct answer.

_____ **1.** One significant problem facing researchers like Irene Pepperberg in her work with Alex, the African gray parrot, is that

    a. it's easy to project human thought and feelings onto creatures, making it necessary to devise research carefully.

    b. other scientists criticize these experiments, making it difficult to get the scientific community to take them seriously.

    c. funding for projects using animals is limited.

    d. animal-rights groups like PETA[1] object to research on animals.

[1]People for the Ethical Treatment of Animals

_____ 2. Morell mentions five skills that are key signs of higher mental abilities, all of which are demonstrated in the animals cited in the articles. Which one was *not* mentioned?

    a. a grasp of grammar and symbols
    b. self-awareness
    c. the ability to reproduce human speech
    d. being creative
    e. understanding others' motives
    f. imitating others

_____ 3. Pepperberg's experiments with Alex, the African gray parrot, were specifically intended to investigate

    a. parrot behavior in flocks.
    b. whether or not birds are intelligent.
    c. his ability to manipulate symbols using a communication board.
    d. interspecies communication—whether a human can converse with a bird.

_____ 4. Remarkably, Alex could distinguish between

    a. sameness and difference between colors and shapes.
    b. consonants and vowels in spoken words.
    c. the humans and other parrots that make up his flock.
    d. quantities of objects.

_____ 5. Betsy the border collie, who has been studied for her language ability, not only has a vocabulary of 300 words, but can also

    a. fetch an item she has never seen before.
    b. herd a large group of animals and keep them under control.
    c. match a photograph of an object with the actual object.
    d. think abstractly, just as humans do.

_____ 6. Scientists theorize that some birds have developed the mental ability to deceive, which probably stems from the

    a. competition for space in which to roam.
    b. innate tendency to be mischievous and to play games.
    c. need to compete with other deceptive creatures.
    d. need to hide food to get them through the winter.

COMPREHENSION SCORE

Score your answers for Exercises A and B as follows:

A. No. right _____ × 2 = _____
B. No. right _____ × 1 = _____

Total points from A and B _____ × 10 = _____ percent

C. SEQUENCING

These sentences from one paragraph in the selection have been scrambled. Read the sentences and choose the sequence that puts them back into logical order. Do not refer to the original selection.

1 Laboratory studies show that western scrub jays can know another bird's intentions and act on that knowledge. **2** So the first jay will return to move the nut when the other jay is gone. **3** Birds, too, can cheat. **4** A jay that has stolen food for itself, for example, knows that if another jay watches it hide a nut, there's a chance the nut will be stolen.

_____ Which of the following represents the correct sequence for these sentences?

    a. 1, 3, 4, 2
    b. 3, 4, 2, 1
    c. 3, 1, 4, 2
    d. Correct as written.

You may refer to the selection as you work through the remaining exercises.

D. DISTINGUISHING BETWEEN MAIN IDEAS AND SUPPORTING DETAILS

Label the following sentences from one paragraph in the selection as follows: MI if it represents a *main idea* and SD if it represents a *supporting detail*.

1. _____ Charles Darwin, who attempted to explain how human intelligence developed, extended his theory of evolution to the human brain.

2. _____ Like the rest of our physiology, intelligence must have evolved from simpler organisms, since all animals face the same general challenges of life.

3. _____ They need to find mates, food, and a path through the woods, sea, or sky—tasks that Darwin argued require problem-solving and categorizing abilities.

4. _____ Indeed, Darwin went so far as to suggest that earthworms are cognitive beings because, based on his close observations, they have to make judgments about the kinds of leafy matter they use to block their tunnels.

5. _____ He hadn't expected to find thinking invertebrates and remarked that the hint of earthworm intelligence "has surprised me more than anything else in regard to worms."

E. DISTINGUISHING BETWEEN FACT AND OPINION

For each of the following paraphrased statements from the selection, write F if the statement represents a factual statement that can be verified or O if the statement represents the writer's or someone else's subjective interpretation. The first one is done for you.

1. ___0___ Dogs' understanding of human communication was a matter of evolution.

2. _____ Dogs' understanding of human communication developed because of their long association with humans.

3. _____ Wolves may not have the same language skills as dogs.

4. _____ Juliane Kaminski, a cognitive psychologist, has not yet tested wolves to determine their language capabilities.

5. _____ Border collies are especially good at understanding human language because they're working dogs.

6. _____ Herding breeds like border collies must listen carefully to their owners as they perform their traditional herding tasks.

F. INTERPRETING MEANING

Where appropriate, write your answers to these questions in your own words.

1. _____ Read paragraph 4 again. How is the main idea developed?
   a. a series of examples
   b. definitions of key terms
   c. a discussion of comparisons, or similar ideas
   d. classification into specific categories

2. Look at paragraph 6 again. Why didn't Irene Pepperberg herself pick out

   Alex at the pet store? _____

   _____

3. From the information presented in paragraphs 12–14, what is remarkable

   about the word that Alex used to describe an apple? _____

   _____

4. What is the most important finding that emerged from the experiments with New Caledonian crows like Betty, as described in paragraphs 59–63?_____

   _____

5. _____ Which of the following *best* represents the conclusion of the selection as a whole?
   a. "Gut instinct is not science, and it is all too easy to project human thoughts and feelings onto another creature." [paragraph 2]
   b. "Being able mentally to divide the world into simple abstract categories would seem a valuable skill for many organisms." [paragraph 31]

    c. "A whole range of animal studies now suggest that the roots of cognition are deep, widespread, and highly malleable." [paragraph 41]

    d. "This is the larger lesson of animal cognition research: It humbles us. We are not alone in our ability to invent or plan or to contemplate ourselves—or even to plot and lie." [paragraph 64]

G. UNDERSTANDING VOCABULARY

Look through the paragraphs listed below and find a word that matches each definition. Refer to a dictionary if necessary. An example has been done for you.

Ex. unreal, existing only in the imagination [paragraphs 2–3]   <u>   fanciful   </u>

  1. marked by inventive skill and imagination [4]   <u>   </u>

  2. touchy, irritated, offended [5–6]   <u>   </u>

  3. quality of being reserved or remote, distant [5–6]   <u>   </u>

  4. the mental process of knowing, including reasoning [22–23]   <u>   </u>

  5. attributed, assigned [36–37]   <u>   </u>

  6. spoiled, contaminated [39–40]   <u>   </u>

  7. capable of being shaped, formed, or changed [40–41]   <u>   </u>

  8. inborn, natural [43 and 58]   <u>   </u>

  9. unnaturally keen and perceptive; eerie [43]   <u>   </u>

10. a false name, used to protect one's identity [47–48]   <u>   </u>

11. of little significance or value [54–55]   <u>   </u>

12. ascribe, relate to a source [64–65]   <u>   </u>

H. USING VOCABULARY

Write the correct inflected form of the base word (in parentheses) in each of the following sentences. Be sure to add the appropriate ending to fit the grammatical requirements of the sentence. Refer to your dictionary if necessary.

  1. (*category*—use a verb) Animals are intelligent because they _____ objects in the real world, such as food.

  2. (*anthropology*—use another noun, plural in form) _____ in Leipzig, Germany, have studied Rico's amazing and unnerving ability to acquire language.

3. (*synchronize*—use a noun) One observation scientists have made about

   dolphin behavior is the _____ of their movements.

4. (*mispronunciation*—use a verb) Alex sometimes _____ words, which was understandable since parrots don't have lips, making some sounds difficult to produce.

5. (*demonstrate*—use an adverb) Having studied earthworms in some depth,

   Charles Darwin was able _____ to show degrees of intelligence in the animal world.

I. SUMMARIZING EXERCISE

Write a summary of paragraphs 38-41 in the space below. The passage is approximately 350 words long, so your summary should be about 75 words.

_____

_____

_____

_____

_____

_____

J. TOPICS FOR DISCUSSION

1. What is anthropomorphism? Have the scientists who conducted the various studies described in the selection guarded against this problem, and if so, how?
2. Why are some cognitive scientists so skeptical of animal researchers' findings about animal intelligence and animals' ability to use language?
3. Why are research experiments on crows, dolphins, parrots, and dogs like those described in this selection important? What myths and misconceptions have they overturned?

K. TOPICS FOR WRITING

1. Watch either of the two videos listed in Exploring Related Web Sites on YouTube. Then write a short essay summarizing what you observed. Choosing either Alex or Skidboot, discuss his behavior as it reveals his cognitive skills.
2. If you have an animal of your own, write a short essay in which you assess your pet's intelligence, using examples from your own observation of its behavior. Show that the animal's behavior suggests the use of cognitive skills.

Exploring Related Web Sites

- Alex the African gray parrot died unexpectedly in September 2007, but you can see Alex in action in many videos available on YouTube. Here is one:

  www.youtube.com/watch?v=R6KvPN_Wt8I

- Australian cattle dogs, also known as Queensland heelers, are an extremely intelligent breed of herding dogs. Watch a video of the amazing Skidboot, who was owned by a rancher named David Hartwig in Quinlan, Texas. After you watch the video listed below, think about whether the dog is simply performing tricks or whether his actions suggest a higher intelligence. (Skidboot eventually went blind; he died in March 2007.)

  www.youtube.com/watch?v=P2BfzUIBy9A

13 Making Up for Lost Time: The Rewards of Reading at Last

Richard Wolkomir graduated in 1964 from Syracuse University, where he received a bachelor's degree in American studies with a minor in journalism. After working as a writer-editor for the McGraw-Hill Publishing Company in New York City, he moved to Vermont, where he currently lives. A winner of many awards for his writing, Wolkomir has written extensively for Reader's Digest, National Geographic, *and the* Smithsonian Magazine, *where this selection was first published. In it he recounts his experience helping Ken Adams, a 64-year-old Vermont farmer.*

Vocabulary Preview

WORD PARTS

Animal adjectives: -ine [paragraph 9] Wolkomir recounts a book he loved as a child about a mouse, Peter Churchmouse, who has a *feline* friend, a rectory cat. The English adjective suffix *-ine* is added to many Latin roots referring to animals. They can describe either an animal or behavior associated with a particular animal. *Feline* (Latin root *felis*, "cat"), then, refers either to the animal itself or to behavior that is "catlike." Some other words with this suffix are *canine* (referring to a dog, from *canis*); *lupine* (describing a wolf, from *lupus*); *equine* (referring to a horse, from *equus*); and *serpentine* (serpentlike, obviously from *serpent*). What animals do these adjectives refer to? Check a dictionary if you are unsure.

leonine _____   porcine _____

bovine _____   piscine _____

WORD FAMILIES

Illiteracy [paragraph 43] When the writer decided to help Ken Adams, a 64-year-old illiterate Vermont farmer, learn how to read, he was overwhelmed with the magnitude of the task. Adams's experience illustrates the sad situation of many students who "fall through the cracks." Branded a slow learner by his teachers in his one-room schoolhouse, Adams was passed along year after year and received little help from either his family or his teachers. Yet, as Wolkomir finds out, Adams is anything but slow: He is a whiz at fixing mechanical things and, despite his obvious handicap, he tackles learning to read with diligence and good humor.

Illiteracy is a serious problem, even in a country as affluent as the United States; indeed, Wolkomir cites statistics that 40 percent of American adults read at a very low level of proficiency. The prefix *il-* means "not, " and *literacy* refers to the ability to read and write, from the Latin root *littera* ("letter"). English has many words in this family, among them: *literal*, *literature*, and *obliterate* ("to destroy completely so as not to leave a trace"), from *ob-* ("off" or "away from") + *littera*.

RICHARD WOLKOMIR

Making Up for Lost Time: The Rewards of Reading at Last

1   I decide simply to blurt it out. "Ken?" I ask. "Why didn't you learn to read?" Through the Marshfield community center's window, I see snowy fields and the Vermont village's clapboard houses. Beyond, mountains bulge. "I was a slow learner," Ken says. "In school they just passed me along, and my folks told me I wasn't worth anything and wouldn't amount to anything."

2   Ken Adams is 64, his hair white. He speaks Vermontese, turning "I" into "Oy," and "ice" into "oyce." His green Buckeye Feeds cap is blackened with engine grease from fixing his truck's transmission, and pitch from chain-sawing pine logs. It is 2 degrees below zero outside on this December afternoon; he wears a green flannel shirt over a purple flannel shirt. He is unshaven, weather reddened. He is not a tall man, but a lifetime of hoisting hay bales has thickened his shoulders.

3   Through bifocals, Ken frowns at a children's picture book, *Pole Dog*. He is studying a drawing: an old dog waits patiently by a telephone pole, where its owners abandoned it. He glares at the next pictures. Cars whizzing by. Cruel

Richard Wolkomir (right) helps Ken Adams with a reading lesson.
Source: © 1999 Sue Owrutsky

people tormenting the dog. "Looks like they're shootin' at him, to me!" he announces. "Nobody wants an old dog," he says.

4   Ken turns the page. "He's still by the pole," he says. "But there's that red car that went by with those kids, ain't it?" He turns the page again. The red car has stopped to take the old dog in, to take him home. "*Somebody* wants an old dog!" Ken says. "Look at that!"

5   This is my first meeting with Ken. It is also my first meeting with an adult who cannot read.

6   I decided to volunteer as a tutor after a librarian told me that every day, on the sidewalks of our prim little Vermont town, I walk by illiterate men and women. We are unaware of them because they can be clever at hiding their inability to read. At a post office counter, for instance, when given forms to fill out, they say, "Could you help me with this? I left my glasses home."

7   Ken Adams is not alone in his plight. A 1993 U.S. Department of Education report on illiteracy said 21–23 percent of U.S. adults—about 40 million—read minimally, enough to decipher an uncomplicated meeting announcement. Another 25–28 percent read and write only slightly better. For instance, they can fill out a simple form. That means about *half* of all U.S. adults read haltingly. Millions, like Ken Adams, hardly read at all.

8   I wanted to meet nonreaders because I could not imagine being unable to decipher a street sign, or words printed on supermarket jars, or stories in a book. In fact, my own earliest memory is about reading. In this memory, in our little Hudson River town, my father is home for the evening from the wartime lifeboat factory where he is a foreman. And he has opened a book.

9   "Do you want to hear about Peter Churchmouse?" my father asks. Of course! It is my favorite, from the little library down the street. My father reads me stories about children lost in forests. Cabbage-stealing hares. A fisherman who catches a talking perch. But my favorite is Peter Churchmouse, a small but plucky cheese addict who befriends the rectory cat. Peter is also a poet, given to reciting original verse to his feline friend during their escapades. I cannot hear it enough.

10   My father begins to read. I settle back. I am taking a first step toward becoming literate—I am being read to. And although I am only 2, I know that words can be woven into tales.

11   Now, helping Ken Adams learn to read, I am re-entering that child's land of chatty dogs and spats-wearing frogs. Children's books—simply worded, the sentences short—are perfect primers, even for 60-year-olds who turn the pages with labor-thickened fingers and who never had such books read to them when they were children.

12   "Do you remember what happened from last time?" asks Sherry Olson, of Central Vermont Adult Basic Education, who tutors Ken an hour and a half each week.

13   I have volunteered as Sherry's aide. My work requires too much travel for me to be a full-fledged tutor. But I am actually relieved, not having sole responsibility for teaching an adult to read. That is because—when I think about it—I don't know how I read myself. I scan a printed page; the letters magically reveal

meaning. It is effortless. I don't know how I do it. As for teaching a man to read from scratch, how would I even begin?

14 Sherry, a former third-grade teacher, gives me hints, like helping Ken to learn words by sight so that he doesn't have to sound out each letter. Also, we read stories so Ken can pick out words in context. Ken reads Dr. Seuss rhyming books and tales about young hippopotamuses helping on the family farm. At the moment, we are reading a picture book about Central American farmers who experience disaster when a volcano erupts.

15 "The people had to move out, and put handkerchiefs over their noses!" Ken says, staring at the pages. He starts to read: "They . . . prayed? . . . for the . . . fire? . . ." "Yes, that's right, fire," Sherry says. "They prayed for the fire to . . . go out?" "That word is 'stop,'" Sherry says.

16 I listen carefully. A few sessions ahead, it will be my turn to try teaching. "They prayed for the fire to *stop*," Ken says, placing a thick forefinger under each word. "They watched from the s . . ." "Remember we talked about those?" Sherry says. "When a word ends in a silent *e,* what does that silent *e* do to the vowel?" "It makes it say itself," Ken says. "So what's the vowel in *s-i-d-e?*" she asks. "It's *i,* and it would say its own name,'" Ken says, pronouncing it "oy." "So that would be 'side.'" "Good," Sherry says.

17 Ken reads the sentence: "They watched from the side of the hill!" He sounds quietly triumphant. "They-uh," he says, in backcountry Vermontese. "That's done it."

18 After the session, I stand a few minutes with Ken in the frozen driveway. He has one foot on the running board of his ancient truck, which he somehow keeps going. He tells me he was born in 1931 into a family eking out an existence on a hardscrabble farm. His trouble in school with reading is puzzling, because Ken is intelligent.

19 For instance, he says he was late today because he had to fix his truck. And now he launches into a detailed analysis of the transmission mechanisms of various species of trucks. Also, during the tutoring session, we played a game that required strewing word cards upside down on a table and remembering their locations. Ken easily outscored both Sherry and me in this exercise.

20 Ken described himself as a "slow learner," but clearly he is not slow. Sherry has told me he probably suffers from a learning disability. People with these perceptual disorders experience difficulties such as seeing letters reversed. Although their intelligence may actually be above average, learning to read is difficult for them. They need individual tutoring.

21 "It was a one-room school, with eight grades, so I didn't get much attention there," Ken tells me. "It was just the same as the folks at home were doing when they kicked me along through the grades, and when you got to be 16, that's when they kicked you out."

22 After he left school, he left home. "Then you knock around, one farm to another," he says. "I'd get $15 a week, and room and board." Besides farming, he worked in bobbin mills and sawmills and granite quarries. "Then I was at a veneer mill in Bradford," he says. "After that I was caretaker at a farm for six years until I had to give it up because I had heart attacks."

23 Now he subsists on a $400-a-month Social Security disability pension plus $90 a month in food stamps. He lives alone in a farmhouse he built himself more than 25 years ago, five miles up a mountain dirt road. He earns money for his medicines by cutting firewood, haying, digging postholes with his tractor, snowplowing and cutting brush. "I'm doing odds-and-ends jobs where you can take your time, because the doctor told me I have to stop whenever I feel I need to rest," he says.

24 He cannot afford electricity from the power company, but he gets what current he needs, mostly for lights, by—ingeniously—drawing it from car batteries. To recharge the batteries, he hooks them up in his truck for a day. He also can charge them with a diesel generator. He waits until prices dip to buy fuel for his generator and tractor. "I've got a few maples around my house," he tells me. "I'll find a rusted-out evaporator, fix it up and make syrup—there's always a few things I can do, I guess."

25 I ask how he's managed all these years, not reading. He says his bosses did the reading for him. And now a Marshfield couple, lifelong friends, help him read his mail and bills and notices. But they are entering their 80s. "Now I've got to learn to read myself, as a backup," Ken says.

26 To find out more about what illiteracy does to people like Ken, I telephoned the U.S. Department of Education and spoke with the Deputy Secretary, Madeleine Kunin. She told me that only 3–5 percent of adult Americans cannot read at all. "But literacy is a moving target," she said. "We figure the 40 million who do read, but at the lowest proficiency levels, have difficulty handling some of the tasks they need to hold a job today." Kunin, a former Vermont governor, cited that state's snowplow drivers: "Now they have computers attached, and they need a high school degree just to drive a snowplow."

27 Ken arrives for his next session in a dark mood. It turns out his tape recorder, used for vocabulary practice, is broken. "I can't fix it because the money's all gone for this month," he says. "I had to go to the doctor, and that's $30, and it was $80 for the pills, and they keep going up." He says one of his prescriptions jumped from $6.99 to $13 in two months. "I don't know if I'll keep taking them," he says. Illiteracy has condemned Ken to a lifetime of minimum-wage poverty.

28 He brightens reading a story. It is about a dog, John Brown, who deeply resents his mistress's new cat. Ken stumbles over a word. "Milk?" Sherry and I nod. "Go and give her some milk," Ken reads, then pauses to give us a dispatch from the literacy front: "I was trying to figure that out, and then I see it has an *i*," he says.

29 My own first attempt at solo tutoring finally comes, and I am edgy. Sherry has wryly admonished Ken, "You help Richard out." I show him file cards, each imprinted with a word for Ken to learn by sight. He is supposed to decipher each word, then incorporate it in a sentence. I write his sentence on the card to help him when he reviews at home. Ken peers at the first word. "All," he says, getting it easily. He makes up a sentence: "We all went away."

30 "That's right," I say. Maybe this won't be so hard after all. I write Ken's sentence on the card for him. Then I flip another card. Ken peers at it, his face working as he struggles with the sounds. "As," he says.

31   During our last session, he confused "as" and "at." Now he has it right. So he has been doing his homework.

32   "As we went down the road, we saw a moose," Ken says, composing a sentence. That reminds him that the state recently allowed moose hunting, game officials arguing that moose have become so plentiful they cause highway accidents. "Yesterday, I come around a turn and there was *ten* moose, a big male and females and young ones," Ken says. "They shouldn't be shooting those moose—they ain't hurting anyone, and it ain't the moose's fault if people don't use their brakes."

33   I flip another card. "At!" Ken says, triumphing over another of our last session's troublemakers. "We are at the school." But the next word stumps him. It is "be." I put my finger under the first letter. "What's that sound?" I ask. When he stares in consternation, I make the sound "buh." But Ken is blocked. He can't sound out the next letter, even though he has often done it before. "Eeeee," I say, trying to help. "Now put the two sounds together."

34   Ken stares helplessly at the word. I am beginning to understand the deep patience needed to tutor a man like Ken, who began these sessions a year before, knowing the alphabet but able to sound out only a few words. "Buh . . . eeee," I say, enunciating as carefully as I can. "Buh . . . eeee," Ken repeats. Abruptly, his forehead unfurrows. "Oh, that's *'be,'*" he says. "Be—We should be splitting wood!"

35   "Was that what you were doing before the tutoring session?" I ask, to give us both a break. "Nope, plowing snow with my tractor for my friend who broke off his ankle," Ken says.

36   That is arresting information. When I ask what happened, Ken says his octogenarian friend was chain-sawing cherry trees when a bent-back branch lashed out, smashing his lower leg. Ken, haying a field, saw his friend ease his tractor down from the mountainside woodlot, grimacing in agony, working the tractor's pedals with his one good foot.

37   Ken himself once lost his grip on a hay bale he was hoisting. A twig poking from the bale blinded his right eye. Now learning to read is doubly difficult because his remaining eye often tires and blurs. These grim country stories of Ken's make my worries—delayed flights, missed appointments—seem trivial. I flip another card: "But." "Bat," Ken says cautiously. "Buh . . . uh . . . tuh," I prompt. "But," he finally says. "I would do it, but I have to go somewhere else."

38   I write Ken's sentence on the card and he reads it back. But he stumbles over his own words, unable to sound out "would." I push down rising impatience by remembering the old man in the woods, crawling toward his tractor, dragging that smashed leg.

39   Finally, I put away the cards, glad to be done with them. Tutoring can be frustrating. Why are even easy words sometimes so hard to get? Now we look at a puzzle. On one side it has pictures of various automobile parts. On the other side are printed the parts' names. The idea is to match the pictures and the names. Before I can start asking Ken to try sounding out big terms like "connecting rod," he points to one of the drawings. It looks to me like deer antlers. "Carburetor?" I guess. "Exhaust manifold," Ken says.

40   "What's this one?" I inquire. For all I know, it might be something Han Solo is piloting through hyperspace. "Starter," Ken says. It seems to me he is gloating a little. He points again. "Camshaft?" I ask. Ken corrects me. "Crankshaft," he says, dryly.

41   It is a standoff. I know the printed words. Ken knows the actual objects to which the words refer. "When I was a kid," he tells me, "I bought an old '35 truck. Sometimes it had brakes and sometimes it didn't. I was probably 17. It made lots of smoke, so mosquitoes never bothered me. But one day I got sick of it. I put it under a pine tree and I hoisted the engine up into the tree to look at it. The pressure plate weren't no good. And the fellow showed me how to fix it."

42   That reminds Ken of a later episode. "One time we had to get the hay in, but the baler was jammed. We had the guys from the tractor place, but they could not fix it. Finally I asked the old guy for some wrenches and I adjusted it, and I kept on adjusting, and after that it worked perfectly. I just kept adjusting it a hair until I had it. And then we were baling hay!" No wonder Ken's bosses were happy to do his reading for him. Even so, in our late 20th-century wordscape, illiteracy stymies people like him. And working with Ken has me puzzled: Why do so many people fail to learn to read?

43   I telephoned an expert, Bob Caswell, head of Laubach Literacy International, a nonprofit organization that trains tutors worldwide. He told me many non-readers, like Ken Adams, suffer from perceptual reading disorders. But there are other reasons for illiteracy, and it is by no means confined to any one part of the population.

44   "People think adult nonreaders are mainly poor, urban minorities, but 41 percent are English-speaking whites," Caswell said, adding that 22 percent are English-speaking blacks, 22 percent are Spanish-speaking, and 15 percent are other non-English speakers. More than half of nonreading adults live in small town and suburbs. Caswell cited U.S. Department of Labor figures that put illiteracy's annual national cost at $225 billion in workplace accidents, lost productivity, unrealized tax revenues, welfare and crime. One big reason for this whopping problem is *parents* who read poorly.

45   Well over a third of all kids now entering public schools have parents who read inadequately, he said. "Everywhere we find parents who *want* to read to their kids, but can't," he added. "And a child with functionally illiterate parents is twice as likely to grow up to be functionally illiterate."

46   But as I met some of Ken Adams's fellow students, I discovered all sorts of causes for being unable to decipher an English sentence. For instance, I met a woman who had escaped from Laos to Connecticut knowing only Laotian. She learned enough English watching *Sesame Street* ("Big Bird and all that," she told me), and later from being tutored, to become a citizen.

47   I also met a man in his 30s who worked on a newspaper's printing press. He could not spell the simplest words. He said it was because, at age 10, he had begun bringing alcohol to school in peanut-butter jars. After his son was

born, he turned to Alcoholics Anonymous and mustered the courage to seek tutoring.

48   I met another man who had dropped out of school in frustration. Not until he tried to enlist in the military did he discover he was nearly deaf. The operator of a creamery's cheese-cutting machine told me he never learned to read because his family had been in a perpetual uproar, his mother leaving his father seven times in one year. And I met a farm wife, 59, who rarely left her mountaintop. But now, with tutoring she was finally learning to read, devouring novels— "enjoyment books," she called them.

49   In central Vermont, these struggling readers receive free tutoring from nonprofit Adult Basic Education offices, each employing a few professionals, like Sherry Olson, but relying heavily on armies of volunteers, like me. Other states have their own systems. Usually, the funding is a combination of federal and state money, sometimes augmented with donations. Mostly, budgets are bare bones.

50   Many states also rely on nonprofit national organizations, like Laubach Literacy Action (Laubach International's U.S. division) and Literacy Volunteers of America, both headquartered in Syracuse, New York, to train volunteers. Laubach's Bob Caswell told me that, nationwide, literacy services reach only 10 percent of adult nonreaders. "Any effort is a help," he said.

51   Help has come late for Ken Adams. Reviewing his portfolio, I found the goals he set for himself when he began: "To read and write better. And to get out and meet people and develop more trust." Asked by Sherry to cite things that he does well, he had mentioned "fixing equipment, going to school and learning to read, trying new things, telling stories, farming." He remembered being in a Christmas play in second grade and feeling good about that. And he remembered playing football in school: "They would pass it to me and I'd run across the goal to make a score." He mentioned no fond family memories. But he had some good moments. "I remember the first time I learned to drive a tractor," he had said. "We were working in the cornfields. I was proud of that." And a later notation, after he had several months of tutoring, made me think of Ken living alone in his hand-built farmhouse on ten acres atop the mountain. "I like to use recipes," he said. "I use them more as I learn to read and write better. I made Jell-O with fruit, and I make bean salad. I feel good I can do that."

52   In our tutoring sessions, between bouts with the vocabulary cards, Ken tells me he was the oldest of four children. When he was small, his father forced him to come along to roadside bars, and then made Ken sit alone in the car for hours. Ken remembers shivering on subzero nights. "He always said I'd never amount to nothing," Ken says.

53   I ask Ken, one day, if his inability to read has made life difficult. He tells me, "My father said I'd never get a driver's license, and he said nobody would ever help me." Ken had to walk five miles down his mountain and then miles along highways to get to work. "And," he recalls, "I was five years in the quarries in

Graniteville—that was a long way." Sometimes he paid neighbors to drive him down the mountain. "They said the same as my father, that I'd never get a license," he says. "They wanted the money."

54   It was not until he was 40 years old that he applied for a license. He had memorized sign shapes and driving rules, and he passed easily. "After I got my license I'd give people a ride down myself," he says. "And they'd ask, 'How much? And I'd always say, 'Nothing, not a danged thing!'"

55   To review the words he has learned, Ken maintains a notebook. On each page, in large block letters, he writes the new word, along with a sentence using the word. He also tapes to each page a picture illustrating the sentence, as a memory aid. To keep him supplied with pictures to snip, I bring him my old magazines. He is partial to animals. He points to one photograph, a black bear cub standing upright and looking back winsomely over its shoulder. "That one there's my favorite," Ken says. And then he tells me, glowering, that he has seen drivers swerve to intentionally hit animals crossing the road. "That rabbit or raccoon ain't hurting anyone," he says.

56   We start a new book, *The Strawberry Dog.* Ken picks out the word "dog" in the title. "That dog must eat strawberries," he says. "I used to have a dog like that. I was picking blackberries. Hey, where were those berries going? Into my dog!"

57   We read these books to help Ken learn words by sight and context. But it seems odd, a white-haired man mesmerized by stories about talkative beavers and foppish toads. Yet, I find myself mesmerized, too. The sessions are reteaching me the exhilaration I found in a narrative as a child, listening to my father read about Peter Churchmouse. Our classes glide by, a succession of vocabulary words—"house," "would," "see"—interwoven with stories about agrarian hippopotamuses and lost dogs befriended.

58   One afternoon it is my last session with Ken. We have wrestled with words through a Christmas and a March sugaring, a midsummer haying, an October when Ken's flannel shirts were specked with sawdust from chain-sawing stove logs. Now the fields outside are snowy; it is Christmas again.

59   My wife and I give Ken a present that she picked out. It is bottles of jam and honey and watermelon pickles, nicely wrapped. Ken quickly slides the package into his canvas tote bag with his homework. "Aren't you going to open it? Sherry asks. "I'll open it Christmas day," Ken says. "It's the only present I'll get." "No, it isn't," she says, and she hands him a present she has brought.

60   And so we begin our last session with Ken looking pleased. I start with a vocabulary review. "Ignition coil," Ken says, getting the first card right off. He gets "oil filter," too. He peers at the next card. "Have," he says. And he reads the review sentence: "Have you gone away?"

61   He is cruising today. When I flip the next card, he says "There's that 'for.'" It is a word that used to stump him. I turn another card. He gets it instantly. "But." He gets "at," then another old nemesis, "are." I ask him to read the card's review sentence. "Are we going down . . . street?" he says. He catches himself. "Nope. That's down*town*!"

62   I am amazed at Ken's proficiency. A while ago, I had complained to my wife that Ken's progress seemed slow. She did some math: one and half hours of tutoring a week, with time off for vacations and snowstorms and truck breakdowns, comes to about 70 hours a year. "That's like sending a first grader to school for only 12 days a year," she said. And so I am doubly amazed at how well Ken is reading today. Besides, Sherry Olson has told me that he now sounds out—or just knows—words that he never could have deciphered when he began. And this reticent man has recently read his own poems to a group of fellow tutees—his new friends—and their neighbors at a library get-together.

63   But now we try something new, a real-world test: reading the supermarket advertising inserts from a local newspaper. Each insert is a hodgepodge of food pictures, product names and prices. I point to a word and Ken ponders. "C" he says finally. "And it's got those two *e's*—so that would be 'coffee'!" I point again. He gets "Pepsi." Silently, he sounds out the letters on a can's label. "So that's 'corn,'" he announces. He picks out "brownies." This is great. And then, even better, he successfully sounds out the modifier: "Fudge," he says. "They-uh!"

64   We're on a roll. But now I point to the page's most tortuous word. Ken starts in the middle again, "ta?" I point my finger at the first letters. "Po," he says, unsure. As always when he reads, Ken seems like a beginning swimmer. He goes a few strokes. Flounders.

65   Po-ta . . . ," Ken says. He's swum another stroke. "To," he says, sounding out the last syllable. "Po-ta-to, po-ta-to—Hey, that's potato!" He's crossed the pond. "Ken!" I say. "Terrific!" He sticks out his chin. He almost smiles. "Well, I done better this time," he says. "Yup, I did good." ✳

From Richard Wolkomir, "Making Up for Lost Time: The Rewards of Reading at Last," *Smithsonian*, August 1996. © 1996 Richard Wolkomir. Reprinted by permission of the author.

Exercises

Do not refer to the selection for Exercises A and B unless your instructor directs you to do so.

A. DETERMINING THE MAIN IDEA AND PURPOSE

Choose the best answer.

_____ **1.** The main idea of the selection is that

    a. illiteracy is the most difficult problem American educators face today.

    b. learning to read as an adult is a tedious but rewarding activity.

    c. teaching an illiterate adult is a frustrating process that requires time, profound patience, and understanding.

    d. adult illiterates can never master reading skills they should have learned as children.

_____ **2.** The writer's purpose is to

    a. urge teachers to do a better job of teaching children to read.

    b. criticize the nation's teachers for passing students along, thereby dooming them to illiteracy and underemployment.

    c. explain the difficulties and triumphs one illiterate adult experienced as he learned to read.

    d. promote adult literacy programs and encourage the reader to volunteer in these programs.

B. COMPREHENDING MAIN IDEAS

Choose the correct answer.

_____ **1.** According to a U.S. Department of Education report on illiteracy and another report cited in the selection, only 3 to 5 percent of adult Americans are completely illiterate; however, the number of adult Americans who read haltingly or minimally is around

    a. 10 percent.

    b. 25 percent.

    c. 40 percent.

    d. 50 percent.

_____ **2.** Wolkomir finds that the most appropriate materials for teaching an adult learner like Ken Adams are

    a. the daily newspaper and supermarket ads.

    b. children's books.

    c. books on subjects that the student is interested in.

    d. comic books.

_____ **3.** Ken Adams displays a special talent for

    a. fixing household appliances.

    b. fixing trucks and other mechanical things.

    c. cooking.

    d. building houses and barns.

_____ **4.** According to Sherry Olson, the primary reading tutor, Ken Adams' difficulty with learning to read as a child was probably the result of

    a. brain damage at birth.

    b. his own unwillingness to do his schoolwork.

    c. his elementary teachers' incompetence.

    d. a perceptual reading disorder.

_____ **5.** Bob Caswell of Laubach Literacy International reports that adult nonreaders are

    a. not confined to any one segment of the population.

    b. generally urban minorities.

    c. unwilling to take the necessary steps to learn to read.

    d. people who live on farms, where reading is not a necessary skill.

_____ **6.** One particular problem for more than a third of children now entering public schools is that they may fall behind because

    a. their school districts have cut budgets drastically.

    b. their parents are themselves functionally illiterate and can't help them much.

    c. their classrooms are understaffed.

    d. their instructors can't agree on the best method to teach reading.

COMPREHENSION SCORE

Score your answers for Exercises A and B as follows:

A. No. right _____ × 2 = _____

B. No. right _____ × 1 = _____

Total points from A and B _____ × 10 = _____ percent

You may refer to the selection as you work through the remaining exercises.

C. LOCATING SUPPORTING DETAILS

For each main idea stated here, find and write down two supporting details.

1. Sherry, Ken Adams's primary tutor, gives the writer tips on how to go about helping Ken learn to read. [paragraph 14]

    a. _____

    b. _____

2. Ken Adams says that he was a "slow learner," but clearly he is not slow. [paragraph 19]

    a. _____

    b. _____

D. LOCATING INFORMATION

Where appropriate, write your answers for these questions in your own words.

1. From paragraph 13, what are the two descriptive words (adjective or adverb) that Wolkomir uses to describe his own reading process? _____

2. From the selection as a whole and specifically from paragraph 21, what are two reasons that Ken Adams's teachers didn't recognize his difficulty and help him? _____

_____

_____

3. From paragraph 26, what is Madeleine Kunin's main point about literacy and the workforce? _____

_____

4. Look again at paragraphs 36 and 37 in which the writer cites "grim country stories." What is the significance of the chain saw accident for the writer mentioned in paragraph 38? _____

_____

5. Briefly list three benefits that Ken Adams will derive from learning to read.

_____

_____

_____

E. INTERPRETING MEANING

Write your answers for these questions in your own words.

1. In paragraphs 8–10, Wolkomir describes his own fond memories of reading. How does he account for his love of reading? _____

2. What is the purpose of the statistics cited in paragraphs 7 and 26? _____

_____

3. Look again at paragraphs 46–48. Write the sentence that states the main idea for this section. _____

_____

4. For the writer, what does helping Ken Adams learn to read teach him about reading? _____

F. UNDERSTANDING VOCABULARY

Choose the best definition according to an analysis of word parts or the context.

_____ 1. not alone in his *plight* [paragraph 7]
  a. bad state
  b. alienation
  c. lack of education
  d. unhappiness

_____ 2. I *scan* a printed page [13]
  a. read carefully
  b. open
  c. glance over
  d. study intensely

_____ **3.** by *ingeniously* drawing it [24]

     a. tightly

     b. with inventive skill

     c. slowly and carefully

     d. intelligently

_____ **4.** Sherry has *wryly admonished* Ken [29]

     a. harshly criticized

     b. cautiously suggested

     c. humorously warned

     d. subtly reminded

_____ **5.** he stares in *consternation* [33]

     a. fear and anxiety

     b. uncertainty and bewilderment

     c. amazement and delight

     d. confidence and self-assurance

_____ **6.** this *reticent* man [62]

     a. restrained, reserved

     b. outspoken, blunt

     c. honest, open

     d. shy, timid

G. USING VOCABULARY

From the following list of vocabulary words, choose a word that fits in each blank according to both the grammatical structure of the sentence and the context. Do not change the form of the word. (Note that there are more words than blanks.)

augmented	context	trivial	exhilaration
enunciated	mesmerized	nemesis	reticent
primers	triumph	eking	sole

1. The writer _____ each word carefully when working with Ken

Adams; the difficulties Adams faces make him realize how _____ some of his own concerns are.

2. It is clear that Adams feels both a sense of _____ and of

_____ from making such good progress.

3. Adams life has been difficult: _____ out an existence on his Social

Security pension _____ by food stamps.

4. Despite the fact that Adams is reading children's stories, he appears to be

_____ by them, and the easy stories allow him to figure out words

from the _____.

H. ANNOTATING EXERCISE

Go through the article and place a star next to any piece of information that supports this idea: Illiteracy presents serious obstacles for the adults who can't read.

I. TOPICS FOR DISCUSSION

1. How would you characterize Ken Adams from what you have read?
2. Why is it so difficult to teach an adult to read? What are the special obstacles that Wolkomir encountered in his tutoring sessions with Ken Adams? What might be some other obstacles that he didn't include in his essay?

J. TOPICS FOR WRITING

1. Using Ken Adams as the central example, write a paragraph or two in which you summarize the plight of illiterate adults.
2. Do you remember learning to read? Write a short paper describing your first experiences learning to read. Who taught you? Was it pleasurable or frustrating? To what extent have your childhood experiences affected your attitude toward reading as an adult?

Exploring Related Web Sites

- An updated report with many links on the state of literacy in the United States is available at this site sponsored by the National Institute for Literacy:

   www.nifl.gov

- If you would like to volunteer to help someone learn to read, or if you know someone who needs help reading, the Web site for ProLiteracy Worldwide lists various literacy programs in the United States:

   www.literacyvolunteers.org

   Click on "Find a Literacy Program Near You." Then click on either "Volunteer!" or "Need Help?" Enter your state or zip code, and you will see a list of programs available in your area.

PART THREE

Tackling More Challenging Prose

Making Inferences

Look carefully at this cartoon:

"I thought it was pretty good, for a book."

What can you conclude about the little boy from his remarks? The cartoonist does not tell us the boy's attitude toward books. He suggests or implies it, and from what he implies, we *infer*. This means that we draw a conclusion by reading into his remark—the boy probably prefers to play video games or watch television than read a book. Notice the comma before "for a book," which emphasizes the boy's usual lack of interest in reading books. You will practice making inferences like this with many of the readings in the next two parts of the text.

Let's say that on a cloudy winter day you are driving and you approach a narrow mountain road. Suddenly, you notice that all of the cars coming toward you have their headlights on, and you wonder why. One possibility is that the cars are part of a funeral procession. Another is that they are driving in an area in which headlights are required during the day (such as on narrow or windy roads or in daylight test zones) and that all the drivers forgot to turn off their lights. A third is that they have just emerged from dense fog. Which of these conclusions is accurate? (Any one of them could be true, of course, but one is *probably* more accurate than the other two.)

Usually the cars in a funeral procession have identifying signs on their windshields. And it would be unlikely that every single driver forgot to turn off the lights at the end of the narrow or windy section of road or at the end of a test zone.

So the most likely possibility is that a patch of dense fog lies ahead. And, of course, if you reached the patch of dense fog as you proceed up the mountain, this inference would be confirmed by observation and experience.

What process is involved here? When you make an *inference*, you draw a conclusion, not from something you actually know, but rather from what you know to be true from experience. We know from experience that, even in daylight, sensible drivers often turn on their lights when driving through dense fog.

As this example shows, we make inferences in the real world all the time. Here is another situation in which you'd be likely to make inferences: Suppose you live next door to a family named Sullivan. One morning you observe that the Sullivans' newspapers are piling up at their front door. From this fact, you might infer three things: (1) They are away on vacation; (2) they forgot to cancel their newspaper delivery; and (3) they forgot to ask someone to pick the papers up so as not to attract burglars.

These conclusions are *logical*; that is, they derive from the facts based on our experience in the world. However, they may not actually *be* true. The Sullivans may have been called away on a family emergency and simply were too distraught to remember that the newspapers would pile up. Perhaps they are all stricken with the flu and are unable to get out. A more far-fetched inference might be that they have all been murdered, and no one has detected the crime yet.

In the absence of any other information, however, the first set of three inferences stated earlier are more likely to be accurate. This is the important point about inferences: They are statements more of *probability* than of fact.

When you make an inference, in reading or in real life, you draw a logical conclusion, not from something you actually know, but rather from what you know to be true from experience. In reading, this process is called "reading between the lines," drawing a logical conclusion from what the writer suggests but does not explicitly state.

Many of my students find the inference questions in the text to be among the most challenging of the exercises. The emphasis on drawing accurate inferences will ensure that you can become a more proficient reader. Making inferences means that you can move beyond literal or surface comprehension to gain deeper meanings, to see connections that the writer wants you to see. Making good inferences also reinforces the thinking process that lies beneath the syntax of the subject, and extends your understanding of that subject. The reader who understands only the surface meaning of what he or she reads misses a lot.

In some of the inference sections in the remainder of the book, you will be asked to write a sentence or two in your own words stating an appropriate inference that you can draw from a particular passage. However, in most of the selections in Parts Three and Four, you will be asked to train your mind to categorize inferences in a rational way. You will be asked to label statements from the text using this key: Y (Yes), N (No), or CT (Can't Tell). Study the information in the following box to understand the differences between these answer choices:

LABELING INFERENCES

Y   A "yes" answer means that the inference is *probably accurate*. It states something that the
writer's words actually imply or suggest.

N   A "no" answer means that the inference is *probably inaccurate*, either because it shows a
misreading or a distortion of the writer's words, or because one part of the inference
statement is accurate but another part is not, making the whole statement not accurate.

CT A "can't tell" answer means that *you can't be sure one way or the other* if the inference is
logical or accurate. The writer does not mention anything that would allow you to draw such
a conclusion, or the conclusion exists outside the selection in something else you have read
or have other knowledge of. In other words, you "can't tell" from *this* particular passage.

Before we look at some sample inference questions, let us examine the difference between N and CT in more detail. Think about this statement:

Blue is a color, and north is a quality.

Is this an accurate statement? The first part is fine, but north is a direction, not a
quality. It's the same with inferences. In a complicated inference containing two
ideas, if one idea is accurate and the other is not, mark it N. CT, on the other hand,
means just that—you simply can't tell. To return to our earlier headlight example,
if only one car coming toward you has its headlights on, you wouldn't have
enough information to make an inference. (Some people prefer to drive with their
lights on during the day, especially on narrow, curvy roads, but this is not a generalization about all drivers that you can make from your driving experience.)

Let us start with a simple example from one of the readings from Part Two—
"The Bystander's Dilemma: Why Do We Walk on By?" by Marc Ian Barasch. In
this paragraph the writer is describing the Greyston Bakery program, which
Bernie Glassman started for homeless people in an attempt to give them jobs.
Barasch writes this:

The business grew, eventually snagging a contract to make brownies for
Ben and Jerry's Ice Cream. But it soon came smack up against the endemic
problems of the neighborhood. People missed work because of drug
problems. Batches of dough were ruined because employees lacked basic
math skills to measure ingredients or the reading skills to decipher labels
on cans.

Now consider these inferences. Mark them Y, N, or CT, as instructed above.

1. _____   Greyston Bakery was fortunate to get a contract from Ben &
Jerry's.

2. _____   Lack of education is one reason that homeless people have trouble
holding down jobs.

3. _____   The bakery workers' drug problems caused more problems than
their lack of reading and math skills.

4. _____ The problems in the neighborhood where Greyston Bakery was located were temporary and could have easily been remedied with better funding and more social programs.

5. _____ The bakery never really got off the ground.

6. _____ Greyston Bakery eventually shut down.

Now compare your answers with these:

1. Y   **2.** Y   **3.** CT   **4.** N   **5.** N   **6.** CT

Here is an explanation of the answers:

- Question 1 should be marked Y. The verb "snagged" suggests that the contract with Ben & Jerry's was a positive development for the bakery.
- Similarly, question 2 is accurate because Barasch points to poor reading and math skills at two reasons that the bakery got into difficulty; its workers' inability to do simple math or to follow written instructions disrupted production.
- Question 3 is a good example of a statement that should be marked CT. Barasch does not indicate whether the workers' drug problems or their poor academic skills were equally to blame or whether one problem was worse than the other. We simply don't know because he doesn't provide any details.
- Question 4 is an inaccurate inference. The word "endemic" suggests that the drug and academic problems were prevalent and entrenched, therefore not easily solved.
- Question 5 stems from a misreading of the passage: The bakery must have been doing something right to get the initial contract to make brownies.
- And finally, question 6 is another example of a "can't tell" situation since Barasch does not reveal the bakery's fate. Perhaps changes were made and the bakery is doing just fine.

When doing the inference exercises, don't make wild guesses. Always return to the selection, read the appropriate passage again, and think about the writer's words and what they suggest. To help you work through the exercises and to strengthen your understanding of what you read, consider these suggestions:

HOW TO MAKE ACCURATE INFERENCES

- Look up the meanings of any unfamiliar words and consider the definitions in context.
- Think about the possibilities of interpretation by examining the writer's words and phrases.
- Look carefully at the way the statement is worded. Then return to the passage and locate the pertinent passage. Test the statement for accuracy.
- Remember that inferences are *statements of probability*, not facts. They proceed from facts, but they are not facts themselves.
- If you are in doubt about an answer, ask your instructor for help or for further clarification.

In order to make reliable inferences, you need to pay close attention to the passage. First, look up the meaning of any unfamiliar words. You can't interpret a passage accurately if you don't know what the writer is saying. For example, in the passage above, Barasch describes the neighborhood's problems as "endemic." Although you can probably get his general meaning without knowing the exact definition of "endemic," you might not make the connection between the bakery's troubles and these problems (drugs and poor educational skills). There is a big difference between temporary, easily solved problems and endemic ones that are entrenched and not easily solved.

If you are unsure about an answer, ask your instructor for help or for further clarification. If your college has a reading laboratory where tutoring is available, you might avail yourself of its services. Finally, remember that good readers may sometimes disagree over the answers because inferences are not always black and white. That's what makes them fun and challenging.

Let's look at some additional examples from two selections you have already read. This one is from Selection 7 in Part One—"The Life and Death of a Western Gladiator," by Charles Finney. In the passage, Finney is describing the characteristics of Crotalus, a young diamondback rattlesnake:

[1] He could see things well enough within his limited range, but a five-inch-long snake can command no great field of vision. [2] He had an excellent sense of smell. [3] But, having no ears, he was stone deaf. [4] On the other hand, he had a pit, a deep pock mark between eye and nostril. [5] Unique, this organ was sensitive to animal heat. [6] In pitch blackness, Crotalus, by means of the heat messages recorded in his pit, could tell whether another animal was near and could also judge its size. [7] That was better than an ear.

Mark the following inferences Y, N, or CT.

1. _____ Rattlesnakes are nearly blind.

2. _____ The "pit," the rattlesnake's main sensing device, is used to detect the presence of potential victims and enemies.

3. _____ No other species of snake possesses a pit like the diamondback rattlesnake.

4. _____ Rattlesnakes locate their prey by smelling them, even from great distances.

5. _____ A rattlesnake is seriously handicapped by not being able to hear.

Question 1 should be marked N. Notice these words in the first sentence: "can command no great field of vision." Although the snake can't see very far, he is certainly not "nearly blind." So this is an inaccurate inference. Question 2 should be marked Y. It shows an accurate understanding of what the "pit" is and what it is used for—to locate the presence of other animals, whether they represent a potential threat or that night's dinner.

To answer question 3, you have to think carefully about what the word "unique" in sentence 5 means—"one of a kind." But it's not clear how Finney is using this word; it is ambiguous, capable of two possible interpretations. Does he mean that the rattlesnake's pit is unique to diamondback rattlesnakes or that the pit is unique compared to a snake's other sense organs? It's hard to tell, so in this case CT is a safe answer.

Question 4 should be marked N. Look again at Finney's words in light of how the statement is worded: He writes in sentence 5 that the pit is "sensitive to animal heat," which doesn't involve smell. So this statement is an example of misreading. Question 5 is tricky, but it too should be marked N. Again, his words suggest that his being "stone deaf" is not a terrible handicap. You can figure out this answer by considering the contrasting phrase in sentence 4, "on the other hand," and also the last sentence, "That [the pit] was better than an ear."

Here is a slightly longer and more challenging practice passage from Geoffrey Cowley's article, "The Language Explosion," Selection 11 in Part Two:

[1] More fundamentally, they [little children] discover that words can have radically different meanings depending on how they're strung together. [2] Even before children start combining words on their own, most know the difference between "Big Bird is tickling Cookie Monster" and "Cookie Monster is tickling Big Bird." [3] That awareness marks the zenith of language development. [4] A chimp can learn to label things, and a high-powered computer can process more information in a minute than any person could handle in a lifetime. [5] But neither a chimp nor a mainframe [computer] is any match for a runny-nosed 3-year-old when it comes to reporting who did what to whom. [6] When a chimp with a signboard signals "Me banana you banana you," chances are he wants you to give him one, but the utterance could mean almost anything. [7] Three-year-olds don't talk that way. [8] The reason, most linguists agree, is that natural selection has outfitted the human brain with software for grammatical analysis. [9] As MIT linguist Noam Chomsky realized more than 30 years ago, the world's languages all build sentences from noun phrases ("The big dog") and verb phrases ("ate my homework"). [10] And toddlers who have never heard of grammar identify them effortlessly.

This time, write your answer in the space provided. Then below each answer, write a brief explanation of why you marked each one as you did and identify the phrase or sentence that led you to your answer. Be sure to refer back to the excerpt before completing the exercise.

1. _____ The human brain is inferior to the "brain" of a mainframe computer.

Explanation: _____

_____

_____

2. _____ The chimpanzee's words like "Me banana you banana you" are both incomprehensible and ungrammatical.

Explanation: _____

_____

_____

3. _____ The chimpanzee's words like "Me banana you banana you" were simple for the chimpanzee to produce.

Explanation: _____

_____

4. _____ Chimpanzees' brains lack the software for grammatical analysis that is innate in humans.

Explanation: _____

_____

_____

_____

5. _____ The term *grammar* in this context means, simply, a way to connect one's thoughts meaningfully.

Explanation: _____

_____

6. _____ The sentence "Cookie Monster is tickling Big Bird" consists of a noun phrase and a verb phrase.

Explanation: _____

_____

_____

7. _____ One must study grammar in order to speak correctly, no matter what language environment one is raised in.

Explanation: _____

_____

_____

8. _____ The world's languages are more alike structurally than one might imagine.

Explanation: _____

_____

This process shows you the importance of rereading the relevant sentence or sentences carefully. In my experience, students may make significant mistakes in their reading because they read inattentively or, more often, they go off wildly into their own interpretation based on their experience or based on an erroneous understanding of what the author has said. If you diligently undertake to follow the recommendations discussed in this chapter, you will find that your reading comprehension will not only be more accurate; it will also reflect a depth of understanding that superficial comprehension of only the main points cannot provide.

14

ERIC SCHLOSSER

Fast Food Nation: Behind the Counter

Eric Schlosser's best-selling book Fast Food Nation: The Dark Side of the All-American Meal, *has become an almost instant classic. Schlosser, a correspondent for the* Atlantic Monthly, *investigated McDonald's, Burger King, Taco Bell, Kentucky Fried Chicken, and other fast food chains in the tradition of an old-fashioned muckraker. (A muckraker is a journalist who thoroughly investigates and exposes misconduct, usually in a particular industry.) In looking at the "dark side" of the fast food industry, Schlosser shows how the fast food industry has permanently changed potato production in Idaho and the beef industry in Iowa and has contributed both to urban sprawl throughout the country and a decline in Americans' nutritional health. In this selection, Schlosser uses the city of Colorado Springs as the backdrop for a behind-the-scenes look at how a typical McDonald's operates.*

Vocabulary Preview

WORD PARTS

Automated [paragraph 4] The word *automated* refers to machinery or equipment that runs by itself, without human intervention or control. (Schlosser alludes to automated site selection software programs and robotic drink machines.) *Automatic* combines the Greek prefix *auto-* ("self") + *-matos* ("willing"). Many other words in English begin with *auto-,* among them *automobile* (self-moving) and *autopsy* (a medical examination of a corpse to determine the cause of death (from *auto-* + *opsis* ["sight"], or literally, "a seeing for oneself"). What do these words mean? Consult a dictionary if you are unsure.

automaton	_____
autocracy	_____
autonomy	_____
autograph	_____

WORD FAMILIES   **Demographic [paragraph 4]** McDonald's Corporation employs commercial satellites to provide information about future *demographic* growth in order to locate new restaurants near areas with a growing population. The word *demographic* combines two Greek roots: *demos* ("people") + *graphos* ("writing"), though this etymology does not yield a particularly helpful definition. The adjective *demographic* actually refers to characteristics of human population, from *demography*, the study of human population size, growth, and related subjects. Other words that come from *demos* include *democracy* ("rule of the people") and *demagogue*, "a political leader who gains power by stirring up people's prejudices."

ERIC SCHLOSSER

Fast Food Nation: Behind the Counter

1   Despite all the talk in Colorado about aerospace, biotech, computer software, telecommunications, and other industries of the future, the largest private employer in the state today is the restaurant industry. In Colorado Springs, the restaurant industry has grown much faster than the population. Over the last three decades the number of restaurants has increased fivefold. The number of chain restaurants has increased tenfold. In 1967, Colorado Springs had a total of twenty chain restaurants. Now it has twenty-one McDonald's.

2   The fast food chains feed off the sprawl of Colorado Springs, accelerate it, and help set its visual tone. They build large signs to attract motorists and look at cars the way predators view herds of prey. The chains thrive on traffic, lots of it, and put new restaurants at intersections where traffic is likely to increase, where development is heading but real estate prices are still low. Fast food restaurants often serve as the shock troops of sprawl, landing early and pointing the way. Some chains prefer to play follow the leader: when a new McDonald's opens, other fast food restaurants soon open nearby on the assumption that it must be a good location.

3   Regardless of the billions spent on marketing and promotion, all the ads on radio and TV, all the efforts to create brand loyalty, the major chains must live with the unsettling fact that more than 70 percent of fast food visits are "impulsive." The decision to stop for fast food is made on the spur of the moment, without much thought. The vast majority of customers do not set out to eat at a Burger King, a Wendy's, or a McDonald's. Often, they're not even planning to stop for food—until they see a sign, a familiar building, a set of golden arches. Fast food, like the tabloids at a supermarket checkout, is an impulse buy. In order to succeed, fast food restaurants must be seen.

4   The McDonald's Corporation has perfected the art of restaurant site selection. In the early days Ray Kroc flew in a Cessna to find schools, aiming to put new restaurants nearby. McDonald's later used helicopters to assess regional growth patterns, looking for cheap land along highways and roads that would lie at the heart of future suburbs. In the 1980s, the chain became one of the world's leading purchasers of commercial satellite photography, using it to predict sprawl

from outer space. McDonald's later developed a computer software program called Quintillion that automated its site-selection process, combining satellite imagery with detailed maps, demographic information, CAD drawings, and sales information from existing stores. "Geographic information systems" like Quintillion are now routinely used as site-selection tools by fast food chains and other retailers. As one marketing publication observed, the software developed by McDonald's permits businessmen to "spy on their customers with the same equipment once used to fight the cold war."

5   The McDonald's Corporation has used Colorado Springs as a test site for other types of restaurant technology, for software and machines designed to cut labor costs and serve fast food even faster. Steve Bigari, who owns five local McDonald's, showed me the new contraptions at his place on Constitution Avenue. It was a rounded, postmodern McDonald's on the eastern edge of the city. The drive-through lanes had automatic sensors buried in the asphalt to monitor the traffic. Robotic drink machines selected the proper cups, filled them with ice, and then filled them with soda. Dispensers powered by compressed carbon dioxide shot out uniform spurts of ketchup and mustard. An elaborate unit emptied frozen french fries from a white plastic bin into wire-mesh baskets

for frying, lowered the baskets into hot oil, lifted them a few minutes later and gave them a brief shake, put them back into the oil until the fries were perfectly cooked, and then dumped the fries underneath heat lamps, crisp and ready to be served. Television monitors in the kitchen instantly displayed the customer's order. And advanced computer software essentially ran the kitchen, assigning tasks to various workers for maximum efficiency, predicting future orders on the basis of ongoing customer flow.

6   Bigari was cordial, good-natured, passionate about his work, proud of the new devices. He told me the new software brought the "just in time" production philosophy of Japanese automobile plants to the fast food business, a philosophy that McDonald's has renamed Made for You. As he demonstrated one contraption after another—including a wireless hand-held menu that uses radio waves to transmit orders—a group of construction workers across the street put the finishing touches on a new subdivision called Constitution Hills. The streets had patriotic names, and the cattle ranch down the road was for sale.

THROUGHPUT

7   Every Saturday Elisa Zamot gets up at 5:15 in the morning. It's a struggle, and her head feels groggy as she steps into the shower. Her little sisters, Cookie and Sabrina, are fast asleep in their beds. By 5:30, Elisa's showered, done her hair, and put on her McDonald's uniform. She's sixteen, bright-eyed and olive-skinned, pretty and petite, ready for another day of work. Elisa's mother usually drives her the half-mile or so to the restaurant, but sometimes Elisa walks, leaving home before the sun rises. Her family's modest townhouse sits beside a busy highway on the south side of Colorado Springs, in a largely poor and working-class neighborhood. Throughout the day, sounds of traffic fill the house, the steady whoosh of passing cars. But when Elisa heads for work, the streets are quiet, the sky's still dark, and the lights are out in the small houses and rental apartments along the road.

8   When Elisa arrives at McDonald's, the manager unlocks the door and lets her in. Sometimes the husband-and-wife cleaning crew are just finishing up. More often, it's just Elisa and the manager in the restaurant, surrounded by an empty parking lot. For the next hour or so, the two of them get everything ready. They turn on the ovens and grills. They go downstairs into the basement and get food and supplies for the morning shift. They get the paper cups, wrappers, cardboard containers, and packets of condiments. They step into the big freezer and get the frozen bacon, the frozen pancakes, and the frozen cinnamon rolls. They get the frozen hash browns, the frozen biscuits, the frozen McMuffins. They get the cartons of scrambled egg mix and orange juice mix. They bring the food upstairs and start preparing it before any customers appear, thawing some things in the microwave and cooking other things on the grill. They put the cooked food in special cabinets to keep it warm.

9   The restaurant opens for business at seven o'clock, and for the next hour or so, Elisa and the manager hold down the fort, handling all the orders. As the place starts to get busy, other employees arrive. Elisa works behind the counter. She takes orders and hands food to customers from breakfast through lunch. When she finally walks home, after seven hours of standing at a cash register,

her feet hurt. She's wiped out. She comes through the front door, flops onto the living room couch, and turns on the TV. And the next morning she gets up at 5:15 again and starts the same routine.

10   Up and down Academy Boulevard, along South Nevada, Circle Drive, and Woodman Road, teenagers like Elisa run the fast food restaurants of Colorado Springs. Fast food kitchens often seem like a scene from *Bugsy Malone,* a film in which all the actors are children pretending to be adults. No other industry in the United States has a workforce so dominated by adolescents. About two-thirds of the nation's fast food workers are under the age of twenty. Teenagers open the fast food outlets in the morning, close them at night, and keep them going at all hours in between. Even the managers and assistant managers are sometimes in their late teens. Unlike Olympic gymnastics—an activity in which teenagers consistently perform at a higher level than adults—there's nothing about the work in a fast food kitchen that requires young employees. Instead of relying upon a small, stable, well-paid, and well-trained workforce, the fast food industry seeks out part-time, unskilled workers who are willing to accept low pay. Teenagers have been the perfect candidates for these jobs, not only because they are less expensive to hire than adults, but also because their youthful inexperience makes them easier to control.

11   The labor practices of the fast food industry have their origins in the assembly line systems adopted by American manufacturers in the early twentieth century. Business historian Alfred D. Chandler has argued that a high rate of "throughput" was the most important aspect of these mass production systems. A factory's throughput is the speed and volume of its flow—a much more crucial measurement, according to Chandler, than the number of workers it employs or the value of its machinery. With innovative technology and the proper organization, a small number of workers can produce an enormous amount of goods cheaply. Throughput is all about increasing the speed of assembly, about doing things faster in order to make more.

12   Although the McDonald brothers had never encountered the term "throughput" or studied "scientific management," they instinctively grasped the underlying principles and applied them in the Speedee Service System. The restaurant operating scheme they developed has been widely adopted and refined over the past half century. The ethos of the assembly line remains at its core. The fast food industry's obsession with throughput has altered the way millions of Americans work, turned commercial kitchens into small factories, and changed familiar foods into commodities that are manufactured.

13   At Burger King restaurants, frozen hamburger patties are placed on a conveyor belt and emerge from a broiler ninety seconds later fully cooked. The ovens at Pizza Hut and at Domino's also use conveyor belts to ensure standardized cooking times. The ovens at McDonald's look like commercial laundry presses, with big steel hoods that swing down and grill hamburgers on both sides at once. The burgers, chicken, french fries, and buns are all frozen when they arrive at a McDonald's. The shakes and sodas begin as syrup. At Taco Bell restaurants the food is "assembled," not prepared. The guacamole isn't made by workers in the kitchen; it's made at a factory in Michoacán, Mexico, then frozen and shipped north. The chain's taco meat arrives frozen and precooked in

vacuum-sealed plastic bags. The beans are dehydrated and look like brownish corn flakes. The cooking process is fairly simple. "Everything's add water," a Taco Bell employee told me. "Just add hot water."

14   Although Richard and Mac McDonald introduced the division of labor to the restaurant business, it was a McDonald's executive named Fred Turner who created a production system of unusual thoroughness and attention to detail. In 1958, Turner put together an operations and training manual for the company that was seventy-five pages long, specifying how almost everything should be done. Hamburgers were always to be placed on the grill in six neat rows; french fries had to be exactly 0.28 inches thick. The McDonald's operations manual today has ten times the number of pages and weighs about four pounds. Known within the company as "the Bible," it contains precise instructions on how various appliances should be used, how each item on the menu should look, and how employees should greet customers. Operators who disobey these rules can lose their franchises. Cooking instructions are not only printed in the manual, they are often designed into the machines. A McDonald's kitchen is full of buzzers and flashing lights that tell employees what to do.

15   At the front counter, computerized cash registers issue their own commands. Once an order has been placed, buttons light up and suggest other menu items that can be added. Workers at the counter are told to increase the size of an order by recommending special promotions, pushing dessert, pointing out the financial logic behind the purchase of a larger drink. While doing so, they are instructed to be upbeat and friendly. "Smile with a greeting and make a positive first impression," a Burger King training manual suggests. "Show them you are GLAD TO SEE THEM. Include eye contact with the cheerful greeting."

16   The strict regimentation at fast food restaurants creates standardized products. It increases the throughput. And it gives fast food companies an enormous amount of power over their employees. "When management determines exactly how every task is to be done . . . and can impose its own rules about pace, output, quality, and technique," the sociologist Robin Leidner has noted, "[it] makes workers increasingly interchangeable." The management no longer depends upon the talents or skills of its workers—those things are built into the operating system and machines. Jobs that have been "de-skilled" can be filled cheaply. The need to retain any individual worker is greatly reduced by the ease with which he or she can be replaced.

17   Teenagers have long provided the fast food industry with the bulk of its workforce. The industry's rapid growth coincided with the baby-boom expansion of that age group. Teenagers were in many ways the ideal candidates for these low-paying jobs. Since most teenagers still lived at home, they could afford to work for wages too low to support an adult, and until recently, their limited skills attracted few other employers. A job at a fast food restaurant became an American rite of passage, a first job soon left behind for better things. The flexible terms of employment in the fast food industry also attracted housewives who needed extra income. As the number of baby-boom teenagers declined, the fast food chains began to hire other marginalized workers: recent immigrants, the elderly, and the handicapped.

18   English is now the second language of at least one-sixth of the nation's restaurant workers, and about one-third of that group speaks no English at all. The proportion of fast food workers who cannot speak English is even higher. Many know only the names of the items on the menu; they speak "McDonald's English."

19   The fast food industry now employs some of the most disadvantaged members of American society. It often teaches basic job skills—such as getting to work on time—to people who can barely read, whose lives have been chaotic or shut off from the mainstream. Many individual franchisees are genuinely concerned about the well-being of their workers. But the stance of the fast food industry on issues involving employee training, the minimum wage, labor unions, and overtime pay strongly suggests that its motives in hiring the young, the poor, and the handicapped are hardly altruistic. ✱

Exercises

Do not refer to the selection for Exercises A and B unless your instructor directs you to do so.

A. DETERMINING THE MAIN IDEA AND PURPOSE

Choose the best answer.

_____ **1.** The main idea of the selection is that

   a. the restaurant industry is the largest private employer in Colorado.

   b. McDonald's Corporation has perfected the process of selecting sites and standardizing every aspect of its restaurant operations.

   c. Colorado Springs is McDonald's test site for designing restaurant technology, for software, and for machines designed to cut labor costs.

   d. McDonald's is particularly successful because of its regimented approach to hiring and training workers and its standardized menu.

_____ **2.** The writer's purpose is to

   a. argue that the reader should not patronize McDonald's or other fast food restaurants.

   b. criticize fast food restaurants for putting independent restaurants out of business.

   c. examine some common business practices McDonald's employs that the average person might not be aware of.

   d. investigate the hiring, training, and salary practices McDonald's uses with its largely teenage workforce.

B. COMPREHENDING MAIN IDEAS

Choose the correct answer.

_____ 1. McDonald's and other fast food chains prefer to situate new restaurants

   a. in established neighborhoods with high population density.
   b. near areas of high traffic where land is still cheap and where future suburbs will develop.
   c. in inner-city neighborhoods where there is a source of cheap labor.
   d. along heavily traveled interstates and other major highways.

_____ 2. Despite all the money fast food companies spend on marketing, promotion, and advertising, most customers eat at such restaurants because

   a. the food is cheap, filling, and good.
   b. fast food restaurants are everywhere and are therefore hard not to patronize.
   c. they see a sign or a familiar building and stop in on impulse.
   d. they can eat a meal in a relatively short period of time.

_____ 3. To select new restaurant sites, McDonald's currently

   a. employs satellite photography and a computer software program.
   b. follows the lead of other fast food restaurants and locates stores near other existing establishments.
   c. takes customer surveys to find out where diners would like new restaurants to be built.
   d. chooses areas close to schools to achieve a ready-made customer base.

_____ 4. The philosophy underlying the automated systems that make McDonald's restaurants run more productively originated in

   a. the Japanese automobile industry.
   b. the American automobile industry.
   c. Silicon Valley technology firms.
   d. McDonald's corporate headquarters.

_____ 5. As used in the fast food industry, the term _throughput_ refers to

   a. the number of customers who order their food at a fast food restaurant's drive-through window.
   b. increasing the speed of assembly and doing every step faster to produce more in a given time.
   c. shortening the amount of time customers eat their meals inside the restaurant, thus ensuring faster customer turnover and higher profits.
   d. shortening the number of items on a restaurant's menu so that fewer employees are needed to assemble the food.

6. Ultimately, Schlosser emphasizes two chief characteristics of fast food restaurants and their operations, namely

a. efficiency and high quality.
b. good career opportunities and fringe benefits.
c. standardization and regimentation.
d. genuine friendliness and a desire to serve.

COMPREHENSION SCORE

Score your answers for Exercises A and B as follows:

A. No. right _____ × 2 = _____

B. No. right _____ × 1 = _____

Total points from A and B _____ × 10 = _____ percent

You may refer to the selection as you work through the remaining exercises.

C. IDENTIFYING SUPPORTING DETAILS

Place an X in the space for each sentence from the selection that *directly* supports this main idea: "Teenagers have long provided the fast food industry with the bulk of its workforce."

1._____ [Workers] are instructed to be upbeat and friendly.

2._____ A McDonald's kitchen is full of buzzers and flashing lights that tell employees what to do.

3._____ Instead of relying upon a small, stable, well-paid, and well-trained workforce, the fast food industry seeks out part-time, unskilled workers who are willing to accept low pay.

4._____ Teenagers have been the perfect candidates for these jobs, not only because they are less expensive to hire than adults, but also because their youthful inexperience makes them easier to control.

5._____ The industry's rapid growth coincided with the baby-boom expansion of that age group [teenagers].

6._____ Since most teenagers still lived at home, they could afford to work for wages too low to support an adult, and until recently, their limited skills attracted few other employers.

7._____ A job at a fast food restaurant became an American rite of passage, a first job soon left behind for better things.

8._____ The flexible terms of employment in the fast food industry also attracted housewives who needed extra income.

9._____ As the number of baby-boom teenagers declined, the fast food chains began to hire other marginalized workers: recent immigrants, the elderly, and the handicapped.

10._____ English is now the second language of at least one-sixth of the nation's restaurant workers, and about one-third of that group speaks no English at all.

D. MAKING INFERENCES

For each of these statements write Y (yes) if the inference is an accurate one, N (no) if the inference is an inaccurate one, and CT (can't tell) if the writer does not give you enough information to make an inference one way or another.

1. _____ Since most customers stop at a fast food restaurant on impulse, it is important that its signs be conspicuous from the street. [paragraph 2]

2. _____ McDonald's is not the only fast food business to use geographic information systems; most of the other chains employ the same technology. [paragraph 2]

3. _____ Foreign countries welcome McDonald's outlets in their countries as symbols of American efficiency and progress. [essay as a whole]

4. _____ *Throughput* means that fast food outlets can save money by reducing labor costs. [paragraphs 11–12]

5. _____ Fast food chains prefer to hire teenagers to staff their restaurants because they are more energetic and more enthusiastic about work than are older workers. [paragraph 17]

E. INTERPRETING MEANING

Where appropriate, write your answers for these questions in your own words.

1. Read paragraph 2 again. What purpose is served by Schlosser's use of these words: "predators," "prey," and "shock troops"? _____

   _____

   What do these phrases suggest about his point of view? _____

   _____

2. _____ Read paragraph 4 again. A good title for this paragraph would be
   a. "Restaurant Locations."
   b. "Uses for Commercial Satellite Photography."
   c. "How McDonald's Selects New Sites."
   d. "Site Selection Tools."

3. In your own words, state the main point of paragraph 5. _____

   _____

   _____

   Now list three important supporting details for that point. _____

   _____

   _____

4. In paragraph 8 Schlosser uses the word "frozen" six times. Why? _____

   _____

5. In relation to the selection as a whole, how does the writer characterize Elisa

   Zamot's typical workday at McDonald's? _____

   _____

6. Paragraph 13 consists only of several examples but no stated main idea.
   Based on the many details in the paragraph, what is Schlosser's point?

   _____

   _____

F. UNDERSTANDING VOCABULARY

Choose the best definition according to an analysis of word parts or the context.

_____ 1. to *assess* regional growth patterns [paragraph 4]

   a. evaluate
   b. consider
   c. estimate
   d. research

_____ 2. *demographic* information [4]: The study of

   a. the relationship between advertising and profits
   b. natural resources
   c. political systems
   d. human population

_____ 3. her family's *modest* townhouse [7]

   a. crowded, cramped
   b. plain, not showy
   c. well-lived in, comfortable
   d. untidy, messy

_____ 4. a much more *crucial* measurement [11]

   a. commonly accepted
   b. difficult to calculate
   c. accurate, precise
   d. critical, very important

_____ 5. with *innovative* technology [11]

   a. newly introduced
   b. sophisticated, complicated
   c. valuable, costly
   d. superior, outstanding

_____ 6. the *ethos* of the assembly line [12]

   a. unique design
   b. atmosphere, environment
   c. fundamental value, character
   d. purpose, function

_____ **7.** the strict _regimentation_ [16]: characterized by

    a. haphazard order

    b. military power

    c. careful, thoughtful planning

    d. uniformity, rigid order

_____ **8.** its motives . . . are hardly _altruistic_ [19]

    a. beneficial

    b. unselfish

    c. questionable

    d. genuine

G. USING VOCABULARY

From the following list of vocabulary words, choose a word that fits in each blank according to both the grammatical structure of the sentence and the context. Use each word in the list only once. Do not change the form of the word. (Note that there are more words than blanks.)

accelerate	computerized	efficiency	marginalized
automated	cordial	flexible	obsession
coincided	declined	franchises	predators

1. One of Schlosser's primary complaints is that fast food companies like

   McDonald's _____ urban sprawl because they regard cars and

   their passengers the way _____ look at prey.

2. Because every aspect of food "assembly" at a typical McDonald's is both

   _____ and _____, they operate at maximum

   efficiency.

3. Fast food chains like to hire teenagers because their hours fit into the outlets'

   _____ work schedules, but they are increasingly hiring

   _____ workers like recent immigrants, the elderly, and the

   handicapped.

H. ANNOTATING EXERCISE

Assume that you are preparing an essay on this topic: Based on the evidence in the selection, explain the particular ways in which the jobs at a typical McDonald's have been "deskilled." Annotate the relevant sections of Schlosser's essay in the left margin.

I. SUMMARIZING EXERCISE

Write a summary of the section of the selection that comprises paragraphs 7–10. This section is approximately 650 words long, so your summary should be about 150 words.

J. TOPICS FOR DISCUSSION

1. On balance, how would you characterize Schlosser's opinion of McDonald's hiring practices?
2. Schlosser paints a rather grim picture of McDonald's and its fast food counterparts. What are some positive features that fast food restaurants have brought to American culture?

K. TOPICS FOR WRITING

1. Write a short essay in which you summarize Schlosser's ideas about the effect fast food chain restaurants have on a community. Now write a second paragraph in which you examine the effects a particular fast food restaurant has had on your community. You might want to consider traffic patterns, eating habits, or employment matters.
2. Do you eat at fast food restaurants regularly? If so, what are their attractions? If not, why not? Write an essay addressing this question and explaining your reasoning.
3. What is your definition of fine dining? Write an essay in which you address this term, being sure to include a description of the perfect restaurant, including ambience (atmosphere), service, decor, quality of food, and price. Refer to the characteristics of a specific restaurant as you write your description.

Exploring Related Web Sites

With all the discussion about the obesity epidemic in the United States, it's important for consumers to be able to evaluate the nutritional quality of what they eat, particularly for readers with children. Check out these Web sites for five popular fast food companies. Which ones give the most complete nutritional information about the food served at their establishments? Which site provides the easiest access to this information? Can you locate information on such statistics as grams of fat, grams of sodium, and whether transfat is used in preparing their french fries?

McDonald's	*www.mcdonalds.com*
Burger King	*www.burgerking.com*
In-N-Out Burger	*www.inandout.com*
Jack in the Box	*www.jackinthebox.com*
Kentucky Fried Chicken	*www.kfc.com*

15

Somebody Built the Pyramids

Louis "Studs" Terkel (1912–2008) was a writer, radio personality, and disk jockey, but he was best known as a social historian. Over the years Terkel published several books of taped interviews, among them Division Street: America *(1967), about his beloved city of Chicago;* Hard Times: An Oral History of the Great Depression in America *(1976); and* Working: People Talk About What They Do All Day and How They Feel About What They Do *(1974).*

Even though this selection was published over 35 years ago, the attitudes these workers display about their jobs resonate with modern workers, who if anything, experience even more stress, loss of identity, and lack of recognition than do the workers cited here. This essay was originally titled "Here Am I, a Worker" and appeared in Capitalism: The Moving Target. *Many of the workers interviewed in this piece appear in* Working, *cited above.*

Vocabulary Preview

WORD PARTS

anti- [paragraph 14] Terkel writes that modern workers feel like *antiheroes*. The prefix *anti-* when attached to words in English means "against" or "in opposition to." You can see this meaning in common words like *antiwar*, *anti-American*, and *antislavery*. In the case of *antihero*, the word refers to a modern hero, one who lacks the qualities of a traditional hero. In the spaces below, write three more words that begin with this common prefix and their meanings.

_____

_____

_____

WORD FAMILIES

anonymous [paragraph 1] One of the common complaints of modern workers is that they feel *anonymous*, literally "having no name or identity." It comes from the Greek: *an-* ("without") + *nomen* ("name"). Other words in English with the root *nym* or *nomen* are *noun* (a grammatical term for a word that is the name of something), *synonym* (words with the same meaning), and *homonym* (words that

229

sound the same but that have different spellings and meanings). What do these words mean? Check your dictionary if necessary.

antonym   _____

nominate   _____

nominal   _____

nom de plume   _____

STUDS TERKEL

Somebody Built the Pyramids

1   In our society (it's the only one I've experienced, so I cannot speak for any other) the razor of necessity cuts close. You must make a buck to survive the day. You must work to make a buck. The job is often a chore, rarely a delight. No matter how demeaning the task, no matter how it dulls the senses or breaks the spirit, one *must* work or else. Lately there has been a questioning of this "work ethic," especially by the young. Strangely enough, it has touched off profound grievances in others, hitherto silent and anonymous.

2   Unexpected precincts are being heard from in a show of discontent by blue collar and white. Communiqués are alarming concerning absenteeism in auto plants. On the evening bus the tense, pinched faces of young file clerks and elderly secretaries tell us more than we care to know. On the expressways middle-management men pose without grace behind their wheels, as they flee city and job.

3   In all, there is more than a slight ache. And there dangles the impertinent question: Ought there not be another increment, earned though not yet received, to one's daily work—an acknowledgement of a man's *being*?

4   Steve Hamilton is a professional baseball player. At 37 he has come to the end of his career as a major-league pitcher. "I've never been a big star. I've done about as good as I can with the equipment I have. I played with Mickey Mantle and with Willie Mays. People always recognize them. But for someone to recognize me, it really made me feel good. I think everybody gets a kick out of feeling special."

5   Mike Fitzgerald was born the same year as Hamilton. He is a laborer in a steel mill. "I feel like the guys who built the pyramids. Somebody built 'em. Somebody built the Empire State Building, too. There's hard work behind it. I would like to see a building, say The Empire State, with a foot-wide strip from top to bottom and the name of every bricklayer on it, the name of every electrician. So when a guy walked by, he could take his son and say, 'See, that's me over there on the 45th floor. I put that steel beam in.' Picasso can point to a painting. I think I've done harder work than Picasso, and what can I point to? Everybody should have something to point to."

6   Sharon Atkins is 24 years old. She's been to college and acridly observes: "The first myth that blew up in my face is that a college education will get you a worthwhile job." For the last two years she's been a receptionist at an advertising

agency. "I didn't look at myself as 'just a dumb broad' at the front desk, who took phone calls and messages. I thought I was something else. The office taught me differently."

7 Among her contemporaries there is no such rejection; job and status have no meaning. Blue collar or white, teacher or cabbie, her friends judge her and themselves by their beingness. Nora Watson, a young journalist, recounts a party game, Who Are You? Older people respond with their job titles: "I'm a copy writer," "I'm an accountant." The young say, "I'm me, my name is so-and-so."

8 Harry Stallings, 27, is a spot welder on the assembly line at an auto plant. "They'll give better care to that machine than they will to you. If it breaks down, there's somebody out there to fix it right away. If I break down, I'm just pushed over to the other side till another man takes my place. The only thing the company has in mind is to keep that line running. A man would be more eager to do a better job if he were given proper respect and the time to do it."

9 You would think that Ralph Grayson, a 25-year-old black, has it made. He supervises twenty people in the audit department of a large bank. Yet he is singularly discontented. "You're like a foreman on an assembly line. Or like a technician sitting in a computer room watching the machinery. It's good for a person who enjoys that kind of job, who can dominate somebody else's life. I'm not too wrapped up in seeing a woman, 50 years old—white, incidentally—get thrown off her job because she can't cut it like the younger ones.

10 "I told management she was a kind and gentle person. They said 'We're not interested in your personal feelings. Document it up.' They look over my appraisal and say: 'We'll give her about five months to shape up or ship out.'"

11 The hunger persists, obstinately, for pride in a man's work. Conditions may be horrendous, tensions high, and humiliations frequent, yet Paul Dietch finds his small triumphs. He drives his own truck, interstate, as a steel hauler. "Every load is a challenge. I have problems in the morning with heartburn. I can't eat. Once I off-load, the pressure is gone. Then I can eat anything. I accomplished something."

12 Yolanda Leif graphically describes the trials of a waitress in a quality restaurant. They are compounded by her refusal to be demeaned. Yet pride in her skills helps her through the night. "When I put the plate down, you don't hear a sound. When I pick up a glass, I want it to be just right. When someone says, 'How come you're just a waitress?' I say, 'Don't you think you deserve being served by me?'"

13 Peggy Terry has her own sense of pride and beauty. Her jobs have varied with geography, climate, and the ever-felt pinch of circumstance. "What I hated worst was being a waitress, the way you're treated. One guy said, 'You don't have to smile, I'm gonna give you a tip anyway.' I said, 'Keep it, I wasn't smiling for a tip.' Tipping should be done away with. It's like throwing a dog a bone. It makes you feel small."

14 Ballplayer. Laborer. Receptionist. Assembly-line worker. Truck driver. Bank official. Waitress. What with the computer and all manner of automation, add scores of hundreds of new occupations and, thus, new heroes and antiheroes to Walt Whitman's old anthem. The sound, though, is no longer melodious. The desperation is unquiet.

15   Perhaps Nora Watson has put her finger on it. She reflects on her father's work. He was a fundamentalist preacher, with whom she had been profoundly at odds.

16   "Whatever, he was, he was. It was his calling, his vocation. He saw himself as a core resource of the community. He liked his work, even though his family barely survived, because that was what he was supposed to be doing. His work was his life. He himself was not separate and apart from his calling. I think this is what all of us are looking for, a calling, not just a job. Most of us, like the assembly-line worker, have jobs that are too small for our spirit. Jobs are not big enough for people."

17   Does it take another, less competitive, less buck-oriented society to make one match the other? ✳

Studs Terkel, "Somebody Built the Pyramids" from *Capitalism: The Moving Target*, edited by Leonard Silk. Copyright © 1974 by Studs Terkel. Used by permission of Random House, Inc.

Exercises

Do not refer to the selection for Exercises A and B unless your instructor directs you to do so.

A. DETERMINING THE MAIN IDEA AND PURPOSE

Choose the best answer.

_____ 1. The main idea of the selection is that

    a. working may be demeaning in today's competitive society.

    b. workers want more respect and recognition for their efforts.

    c. workers have rejected the traditional American work ethic.

    d. automation and computerization have disrupted the American workplace.

_____ 2. The writer's purpose is to

    a. explain his own attitudes toward work and working.

    b. examine the attitudes and concerns of various workers toward their jobs.

    c. criticize American corporate leaders for providing poor treatment and pay.

    d. recommend ways that American workers can improve their working lives.

B. COMPREHENDING MAIN IDEAS

Choose the correct answer.

_____ 1. Terkel states that for the workers he interviewed, a work ethic means that

    a. work builds character and makes us stronger.

    b. only those who work hard and endure unhappiness will be assured of rewards.

c. one must know the difference between right and wrong and act accordingly.

d. one must work no matter how demeaning the job is.

_____ **2.** As an example of worker discontent, Terkel offers a single example. Which one?

a. the high number of people receiving unemployment compensation.

b. the high number of people who frequently change jobs.

c. the problem of absenteeism in auto plants.

d. the extreme fatigue American workers suffer from.

_____ **3.** Terkel suggests that workers need "another increment," by which he means

a. an acknowledgement of one's being.

b. profit sharing and regular bonuses for a job well done.

c. higher status and prestige.

d. one's name on a plaque recognizing one's contribution to the finished product.

_____ **4.** Sharon Atkins, the ad agency receptionist, learned a hard lesson, namely that

a. a college education doesn't guarantee a person a worthwhile job.

b. she was hired for her looks, not for her talents or abilities.

c. no one in the office respected her skills or knowledge.

d. her job was boring and senseless.

_____ **5.** What Ralph Grayson, the black supervisor in a bank, most dislikes about his job is

a. having to monitor his workers to be sure they're doing their jobs.

b. his employer's indifference to illness or other personal problems.

c. having to evaluate and perhaps threaten to fire an older woman who isn't as productive as some of the younger workers.

d. the laziness and inefficiency he must tolerate from the workers he supervises.

_____ **6.** All of the workers whom Terkel quotes complain that their jobs fail to give them

a. respect and a feeling of self-worth.

b. a decent wage and generous benefits.

c. health insurance.

d. job security and a chance for advancement.

COMPREHENSION SCORE

Score your answers for Exercises A and B as follows:

A. No. right _____ × 2 = _____
B. No. right _____ × 1 = _____

Total points from A and B _____ × 10 = _____ percent

You may refer to the selection as you work through the remaining exercises.

C. LOCATING INFORMATION

Despite their complaints, it is evident that the workers Terkel interviewed show pride in their work and in doing a good job. For each of these people below, look through the paragraph cited and locate the specific information that reinforces this idea.

1. Mike Fitzgerald, steel mill laborer [paragraph 5] _____

   _____

   _____

2. Paul Dietch, truck driver [paragraph 11] _____

   _____

   _____

3. Yolanda Leif, waitress [paragraph 12] _____

   _____

   _____

D. INTERPRETING MEANING

Write your answers to these questions in your own words.

1. At the end of paragraph 1, Terkel writes that young workers in the 1970s were questioning the work ethic and making their grievances known, ending by saying that these grievances were "hitherto silent and anonymous." What

   does this phrase mean? _____

   _____

   _____

2. What does Mike Fitzgerald, the steel mill worker, mean when he says "I feel

   like the guys who built the pyramids. Somebody built 'em"? _____

   _____

   _____

   _____

3. Look again at paragraph 7. What difference does Terkel see in older workers and younger workers in the way they see themselves? _____

_____

_____

E. UNDERSTANDING VOCABULARY

Choose the best definition according to an analysis of word parts or the context.

_____ 1. the *impertinent* question [paragraph 3]

    a. not displaying good manners, disrespectful
    b. irrelevant, not concerned with the subject
    c. unimportant, trivial
    d. unanswerable, debatable

_____ 2. the hunger *persists* [11]

    a. increases, gets worse
    b. cannot be satisfied
    c. continues, endures
    d. needs to be documented

_____ 3. the hunger persists, *obstinately* [11]

    a. unconsciously
    b. invisibly
    c. unfortunately
    d. stubbornly

_____ 4. Leif *graphically* describes [12]

    a. reluctantly, hesitatingly
    b. boldly, courageously
    c. vividly, realistically
    d. angrily, showing a temper

_____ 5. they are *compounded* [12]

    a. added to, made more important
    b. made less convincing
    c. demeaned, degraded
    d. mixed up, confused with

F. USING VOCABULARY

From the following list of vocabulary words, choose a word that fits in each blank according to both the grammatical structure of the sentence and the context. Use each word in the list only once. Do not change the form of the word. (Note that there are more words than blanks.)

acridly   demeaning   grievance   profound
anonymous   discontent   myth   whether

The most common _____ of these workers is that their jobs are

_____, that their jobs are too small for their spirit. There is a feeling

that their achievements are not recognized, _____ they are blue-

collar workers or white-collar workers. The _____ seems to be es-

pecially _____ with workers who make a building or a monument

that will last for hundreds of years but who still remain _____.

G. TOPICS FOR DISCUSSION

1. Is there any evidence that Terkel has preconceived ideas about work and attitudes toward work? In other words, do the ideas expressed by the workers he interviewed always match his ideas that work is demeaning and that among workers, "job and status have no meaning"? See in particular paragraphs 4–6.
2. Terkel's essay was published in the mid-1970s, nearly 40 years ago. Based on your firsthand knowledge and/or observation, do today's workers feel more fulfilled than those Terkel describes in this piece or do they exhibit the same discontent that he records?
3. If you were to play the party game, "Who Are You?" how would you identify yourself? How would your parents? Is the concept of self the same or different for these generations?

H. TOPICS FOR WRITING

1. In the conclusion Terkel discusses the disconnect between our spirits and our jobs, ending with a rhetorical question, one asked for effect: "Does it take another, less competitive, less buck-oriented society to make one match the other?" Write a short essay in which you address this question and how to remedy the situation.
2. Terkel's essay is centered on the observation that 1970s workers felt a discontent in their lives, that their jobs didn't give them a sense of being. Interview several people whom you are acquainted with about their jobs and their feelings about the work they do. Present your findings in a short essay that you organize around a central impression. Use their ideas as support for this impression.
3. Write a short essay in which you describe your ideal job.

Exploring Related Web Sites

- Joanne B. Ciulla, professor of leadership and ethics at the University of Richmond, has updated the modern concept of work ethic based on her experience teaching college students. Titled "The Work Ethic, in a Modern Guise" and published on July 1, 2007, this somewhat humorous article is available online at the following address:

  www.nytimes.com/2007/07/01/business/yourmoney/01pre.html?_r=1&oref=slogin

- Jared Sandberg, a columnist for the *Wall Street Journal*, wrote a recent column titled "A Modern Conundrum: When Work's Invisible, So Are Its Satisfactions," (February 19, 2008), which bears out exactly what Terkel says in the selection. You can read the full article at this address:

  http://s.wsj.net/article/SB120338000214975633.html

- The pyramids of Egypt (including the Great Pyramid at Giza) are the last of the Seven Wonders of the Ancient World to survive. When Mike Fitzgerald laments that the names of the thousands of Egyptian slaves who built the pyramids are lost in history because no one commemorated their efforts, we might want to learn more about the pyramids' history—how they were constructed, what they were used for, and so on. Do a search using your favorite search engine to locate pictures and information about these structures. Here is one site to get you started:

  http://touregypt.net/construction

16 Being Prey: Surviving a Crocodile Attack

Val Plumwood (1939–2008) was an Australian ecofeminist intellectual and a pioneer of environmental philosophy. She dedicated her career to what is sometimes described as ecological humanities, including work to preserve biodiversity and to control deforestation. Formerly Australian Research Council Fellow at the Australian National University, she also taught at North Carolina State University, the University of Montana, and the University of Sydney. The incident described in this narrative excerpt occurred in February 1985 near the city of Darwin in Kakadu National Park, located on the northern coast of Australia. The article was originally published in a different form in Travelers' Tales *(1999) and was included in* Best Science and Nature Writing 2001.

Vocabulary Preview

WORD PARTS

-ity (noun suffix) Five words in this selection illustrate this common noun suffix. (A prefix, you will remember, is a word part that comes at the beginning of a word that often indicates meaning. A suffix is a word part added to the end of a root, which makes the root into another part of speech. In other words, suffixes commonly indicate grammatical part of speech rather than convey meaning.) The noun suffix *-ity* is added to adjectives to form abstract nouns that express a state or condition. In paragraph 10, then, *subjectivity* means "the condition of being subjective," and *timidity* in paragraph 3 means "the state of being timid." The selection also contains the words *integrity*, *eternity*, and *capacities* (the latter is the plural spelling).

WORD FAMILIES

Aquatic [paragraph 2] Plumwood writes that "the crocodile was a symbol of the power and integrity of this place and the incredible richness of its *aquatic* habitats." *Aqua* can refer both to the color blue-green (like the sea), or simply to water. Other examples of words in the family using this root are *aquaplane*, *aquarium*, *aqueous* (an adjective meaning "watery"), and *aqueduct*, (a system for transporting water, *aqua* + *ducere* ["to lead"]).

TWO OTHER IMPORTANT WORDS

Aboriginal and indigenous [paragraphs 2 and 5] *Aboriginal*, when capitalized, refers to the *indigenous* or original inhabitants of Australia. When written in lower case, *aboriginal* refers to any original inhabitants of a particular region, for example, the Ainu of Japan or the Indians of North and South America. Both words are of Latin origin: *Aboriginal* comes from the prefix *ab-* + *origine* ("beginning"), and *indigenous* derives from the Latin root *indigina*, "a native."

VAL PLUMWOOD

Being Prey: Surviving a Crocodile Attack

1   In the early wet season, Kakadu's paperbark wetlands are especially stunning, as the water lilies weave white, pink, and blue patterns of dreamlike beauty over the shining thunderclouds reflected in their still waters. Yesterday, the water lilies and the wonderful bird life had enticed me into a joyous afternoon's idyll as I ventured onto the East Alligator Lagoon for the first time in a canoe lent by the park service. "You can play about on the backwaters," the ranger had said, "but don't go onto the main river channel. The current's too swift, and if you get into trouble, there are the crocodiles. Lots of them along the river!" I followed his advice and glutted myself on the magical beauty and bird life of the lily lagoons, untroubled by crocodiles.

2   Today, I wanted to repeat that experience despite the drizzle beginning to fall as I neared the canoe launch site. I set off on a day trip in search of an Aboriginal rock art site across the lagoon and up a side channel. The drizzle turned to a warm rain within a few hours, and the magic was lost. The birds were invisible, the water lilies were sparser, and the lagoon seemed even a little menacing. I noticed now how low the 14-foot canoe sat in the water, just a few inches of fiberglass between me and the great saurians,[1] close relatives of the ancient dinosaurs. Not long ago, saltwater crocodiles were considered endangered, as virtually all mature animals in Australia's north were shot by commercial hunters. But after a decade and more of protection, they are now the most plentiful of the large animals of Kakadu National Park. I was actively involved in preserving such places, and for me, the crocodile was a symbol of the power and integrity of this place and the incredible richness of its aquatic habitats.

3   After hours of searching the maze of shallow channels in the swamp, I had not found the clear channel leading to the rock art site, as shown on the ranger's sketch map. When I pulled my canoe over in driving rain to a rock outcrop for a hasty, sodden lunch, I experienced the unfamiliar sensation of being watched. Having never been one for timidity, in philosophy or in life, I decided, rather than return defeated to my sticky trailer, to explore a clear, deep channel closer to the river I had traveled along the previous day.

[1]*Saurians* refers to Sauria, the suborder of reptiles including lizards, crocodiles, and alligators. The Greek root is *sauros* or "lizard." (Ed.)

Map of Australia with location of Kakadu National Park

4   The rain and wind grew more severe, and several times I pulled over to tip water from the canoe. The channel soon developed steep mud banks and snags. Farther on, the channel opened up and was eventually blocked by a large sandy bar. I pushed the canoe toward the bank, looking around carefully before getting out in the shallows and pulling the canoe up. I would be safe from crocodiles in the canoe—I had been told—but swimming and standing or wading at the water's edge were dangerous. Edges are one of the crocodile's favorite food-capturing places. I saw nothing, but the feeling of unease that had been with me all day intensified.

5   The rain eased temporarily, and I crossed a sandbar to see more of this puzzling place. As I crested a gentle dune, I was shocked to glimpse the muddy waters of the East Alligator River gliding silently only 100 yards away. The channel had led me back to the main river. Nothing stirred along the riverbank, but a great tumble of escarpment cliffs up on the other side caught my attention. One especially striking rock formation—a single large rock balanced precariously on a much smaller one—held my gaze. As I looked, my whispering sense of unease turned into a shout of danger. The strange formation put me sharply in mind of

two things: of the indigenous Gagadgu owners of Kakadu, whose advice about coming here I had not sought, and of the precariousness of my own life, of human lives. As a solitary specimen of a major prey species of the saltwater crocodile, I was standing in one of the most dangerous places on earth.

6   I turned back with a feeling of relief. I had not found the rock paintings, I rationalized, but it was too late to look for them. The strange rock formation presented itself instead as a telos[2] of the day, and now I could go, home to trailer comfort.

7   As I pulled the canoe out into the main current, the rain and wind started up again. I had not gone more than five or ten minutes down the channel when, rounding a bend, I saw in midstream what looked like a floating stick—one I did not recall passing on my way up. As the current moved me toward it, the stick developed eyes. A crocodile! It did not look like a large one. I was close to it now but was not especially afraid; an encounter would add interest to the day.

8   Although I was paddling to miss the crocodile, our paths were strangely convergent. I knew it would be close, but I was totally unprepared for the great blow when it struck the canoe. Again it struck, again and again, now from behind, shuddering the flimsy craft. As I paddled furiously, the blows continued. The unheard of was happening; the canoe was under attack! For the first time, it came to me fully that I was prey. I realized I had to get out of the canoe or risk being capsized.

9   The bank now presented a high, steep face of slippery mud. The only obvious avenue of escape was a paperbark tree near the muddy bank wall. I made the split-second decision to leap into its lower branches and climb to safety. I steered to the tree and stood up to jump. At the same instant, the crocodile rushed up alongside the canoe, and its beautiful, flecked golden eyes looked straight into mine. Perhaps I could bluff it, drive it away, as I had read of British tiger hunters doing. I waved my arms and shouted, "Go away!" (We're British here.) The golden eyes glinted with interest. I tensed for the jump and leapt. Before my foot even tripped the first branch, I had a blurred, incredulous vision of great toothed jaws bursting from the water. Then I was seized between the legs in a red-hot pincer grip and whirled into the suffocating wet darkness.

10   Our final thoughts during near-death experiences can tell us much about our frameworks of subjectivity. A framework capable of sustaining action and purpose must, I think, view the world "from the inside," structured to sustain the concept of a continuing, narrative self; we remake the world in that way as our own, investing it with meaning, reconceiving it as sane, survivable, amenable to hope and resolution. The lack of fit between this subject-centered version and reality comes into play in extreme moments. In its final, frantic attempts to protect itself from the knowledge that threatens the narrative framework, the mind can instantaneously fabricate terminal doubt of extravagant proportions: *This is not really happening. This is a nightmare from which I will soon awake.* This desperate delusion split apart as I hit the water. In that flash, I

---

[2] *Telos* is a word of Greek origin meaning "the end result of a goal-oriented process." The word also appears in paragraph 22 on page 244. (Ed.)

glimpsed the world for the first time "from the outside," as a world no longer my own, an unrecognizable bleak landscape composed of raw necessity, indifferent to my life or death.

11   Few of those who have experienced the crocodile's death roll have lived to describe it. It is, essentially, an experience beyond words of total terror. The crocodile's breathing and heart metabolism are not suited to prolonged struggle, so the roll is an intense burst of power designed to overcome the victim's resistance quickly. The crocodile then holds the feebly struggling prey underwater until it drowns. The roll was a centrifuge of boiling blackness that lasted for an eternity, beyond endurance, but when I seemed all but finished, the rolling suddenly stopped. My feet touched bottom, my head broke the surface, and coughing, I sucked at air, amazed to be alive. The crocodile still had me in its pincer grip between the legs. I had just begun to weep for the prospects of my mangled body when the crocodile pitched me suddenly into a second death roll.

12   When the whirling terror stopped again I surfaced again, still in the crocodile's grip next to a stout branch of a large sandpaper fig growing in the water. I grabbed the branch, vowing to let the crocodile tear me apart rather than throw me again into that spinning, suffocating hell. For the first time I realized that the crocodile was growling, as if angry. I braced myself for another roll, but then its jaws simply relaxed; I was free. I gripped the branch and pulled away, dodging around the back of the fig tree to avoid the forbidding mud bank, and tried once more to climb into the paperbark tree.

13   As in the repetition of a nightmare, the horror of my first escape attempt was repeated. As I leapt into the same branch, the crocodile seized me again, this time around the upper left thigh, and pulled me under. Like the others, the third death roll stopped, and we came up next to the sandpaper fig branch again. I was growing weaker, but I could see the crocodile taking a long time to kill me this way. I prayed for a quick finish and decided to provoke it by attacking it with my hands. Feeling back behind me along the head, I encountered two lumps. Thinking I had the eye sockets, I jabbed my thumbs into them with all my might. They slid into warm, unresisting holes (which may have been the ears, or perhaps the nostrils), and the crocodile did not so much as flinch. In despair, I grabbed the branch again. And once again, after a time, I felt the crocodile jaws relax, and I pulled free.

14   I knew I had to break the pattern; up the slippery mud bank was the only way. I scrabbled for a grip, then slid back toward the waiting jaws. The second time I almost made it before again sliding back, braking my slide by grabbing a tuft of grass. I hung there, exhausted. *I can't make it,* I thought. *It'll just have to come and get me.* The grass tuft began to give away. Flailing to keep from sliding farther, I jammed my fingers into the mud. This was the clue I needed to survive. I used this method and the last of my strength to climb up the bank and reach the top. I was alive!

15   Escaping the crocodile was not the end of my struggle to survive. I was alone, severely injured, and many miles from help. During the attack, the pain from the injuries had not fully registered. As I took my first urgent steps, I knew something was wrong with my leg. I did not wait to inspect the damage but took off away from the crocodile toward the ranger station.

16   After putting more distance between me and the crocodile, I stopped and realized for the first time how serious my wounds were. I did not remove my clothing to see the damage to the groin area inflicted by the first hold. What I could see was bad enough. The left thigh hung open, with bits of fat, tendon, and muscle showing, and a sick, numb feeling suffused my entire body. I tore up some clothing to bind the wounds and made a tourniquet for my bleeding thigh, then staggered on, still elated from my escape. I went some distance before realizing with a sinking heart that I had crossed the swamp above the ranger station in the canoe and could not get back without it.

17   I would have to hope for a search party, but I could maximize my chances by moving downstream toward the swamp edge, almost two miles away. I struggled on, through driving rain, shouting for mercy from the sky, apologizing to the angry crocodile, repenting to this place for my intrusion. I came to a flooded tributary and made a long upstream detour looking for a safe place to cross.

18   My considerable bush[3] experience served me well, keeping me on course (navigating was second nature). After several hours, I began to black out and had to crawl the final distance to the swamp's edge. I lay there in the gathering dusk to await what would come. I did not expect a search party until the following day, and I doubted I could last the night.

19   The rain and wind stopped with the onset of darkness, and it grew perfectly still. Dingoes[4] howled, and clouds of mosquitoes whined around my body. I hoped to pass out soon, but consciousness persisted. There were loud swirling noises in the water, and I knew I was easy meat for another crocodile. After what seemed like a long time, I heard the distant sound of a motor and saw a light moving on the swamp's far side. Thinking it was a boat, I rose up on my elbow and called for help. I thought I heard a faint reply, but then the motor grew fainter and the lights went away. I was as devastated as any castaway who signals desperately to a passing ship and is not seen.

20   The lights had not come from a boat. Passing my trailer, the ranger noticed there was no light inside it. He had driven to the canoe launch site on a motorized trike and realized I had not returned. He had heard my faint call for help, and after some time, a rescue craft appeared. As I began my 13-hour journey to Darwin Hospital, my rescuers discussed going upriver the next day to shoot a crocodile. I spoke strongly against this plan: I was the intruder, and no good purpose could be served by random revenge. The water around the spot where I had been lying was full of crocodiles. That spot was under six feet of water the next morning, flooded by the rains signaling the start of the wet season.

21   In the end I was found in time and survived against many odds. A similar combination of good fortune and human care enabled me to overcome a leg infection that threatened amputation or worse. I probably have Paddy Pallin's incredibly tough walking shorts to thank for the fact that the groin injuries were not as severe as the leg injuries. I am very lucky that I can still walk well and have lost few of my previous capacities. The wonder of being alive after being held—quite literally—in the jaws of death has never entirely left me. For the first

[3] "Bush" here refers to the Australian bush, the vast area of the country that is not settled. (Ed.)
[4] Dingoes are wild dogs native to Australia. (Ed.)

year, the experience of existence as an unexpected blessing cast a golden glow over my life, despite the injuries and the pain. The glow has slowly faded, but some of that new gratitude for life endures, even if I remain unsure whom I should thank. The gift of gratitude came from the searing flash of near-death knowledge, a glimpse "from the outside" of the alien, incomprehensible world in which the narrative of self has ended.

22   . . . [T]he story of the crocodile encounter now has, for me, a significance quite the opposite of that conveyed in the master/monster narrative. It is a humbling and cautionary tale about our relationship with the earth, about the need to acknowledge our own animality and ecological vulnerability. I learned many lessons from the event, one of which is to know better when to turn back and to be more open to the sorts of warnings I had ignored that day. As on the day itself, so even more to me now, the telos of these events lies in the strange rock formation, which symbolized so well the lessons about the vulnerability of humankind I had to learn, lessons largely lost to the technological culture that now dominates the earth. In my work as a philosopher, I see more and more reason to stress our failure to perceive this vulnerability, to realize how misguided we are to view ourselves as masters of a tamed and malleable nature. . . . ✱

From Val Plumwood, *Traveler's Tales.* © 1999 by Val Plumwood. Reprinted by permission of the author.

Exercises

Do not refer to the selection for Exercises A–C unless your instructor directs you to do so.

A. DETERMINING THE MAIN IDEA AND PURPOSE

Choose the best answer.

_____ 1. The main idea of the selection is that
    a. surviving a near-death crocodile attack gave the writer a glimpse into an incomprehensible part of nature and of human life.
    b. crocodiles are fiercely dangerous creatures who prey on humans who venture into their waters.
    c. the writer's experience in the Australian bush was useful when she encountered a crocodile.
    d. in confronting her crocodile attacker, the writer learned that human endurance and the will to triumph can conquer every peril in nature.

_____ 2. The writer's purpose is to
    a. describe an exotic location in a faraway place.
    b. tell a frightening story that gave the writer a new perspective on life.

    c. present an account of the writer's experience as a naturalist.

    d. observe and describe a powerful creature in its own environment.

B. COMPREHENDING MAIN IDEAS

Choose the correct answer.

_____ **1.** Before the writer set off in a canoe to explore, the park ranger at Kakadu National Park told her not to

    a. venture into the main river channel.

    b. stay out in the water too long.

    c. climb onto the channel's muddy banks.

    d. be afraid of the park's crocodiles.

_____ **2.** When the writer crossed the sandbar to see the place from a closer view, she initially felt both

    a. wonder and delight.

    b. unease and fear of danger.

    c. anxiety and panic.

    d. curiosity and a desire to see more.

_____ **3.** When the writer first encountered the crocodile, she says that it resembled a

    a. partially submerged log.

    b. strange rock formation.

    c. dark shadow in the water.

    d. floating stick.

_____ **4.** Plumwood writes that, when faced with danger, it is human nature to

    a. alter reality by doubting that the danger is real.

    b. feel terrified by the reality of the situation.

    c. feel intimately connected to the reality of the situation.

    d. adopt a purely objective point of view.

_____ **5.** After the crocodile attacked the first two times, the writer was able to escape the crocodile's grasp by

    a. scrambling back into her canoe and paddling furiously.

    b. climbing to safety on the muddy bank away from the water.

    c. leaping into the branches of a nearby tree growing in the water.

    d. hitting the crocodile on the head with her canoe paddle.

_____ **6.** As a result of her near-death experience, Plumwood

    a. decided to investigate potential dangers before setting off on such an adventure again.

    b. promised to seek the advice of experts before starting off on a dangerous journey.

    c. sustained lifelong crippling serious injuries to her leg.

    d. felt gratitude for the gift of life.

COMPREHENSION SCORE

Score your answers for Exercises A and B as follows:

A. No. right _____ × 2 = _____
B. No. right _____ × 1 = _____
Total points from A and B _____ × 10 = _____ percent

C. SEQUENCING

These sentences from one paragraph in the selection have been scrambled. Read the sentences and choose the sequence that puts them back into logical order. Do not refer to the original selection.

1 I did not wait to inspect the damage but took off away from the crocodile toward the ranger station. **2** Escaping the crocodile was not the end of my struggle to survive. **3** As I took my first urgent steps, I knew something was wrong with my leg. **4** During the attack, the pain from the injuries had not fully registered. **5** I was alone, severely injured, and many miles from help.

_____ Which of the following represents the correct sequence for these sentences?
  a. 4, 3, 1, 5, 2
  b. 5, 3, 4, 1, 2
  c. 2, 5, 4, 3, 1
  d. 3, 5, 2, 4, 1
  e. Correct as written.

You may refer to the selection as you work through the remaining exercises.

D. IDENTIFYING SUPPORTING DETAILS

Place an X in the space for each sentence from the selection that *directly* supports this main idea: "Few of those who have experienced the crocodile's death roll have lived to describe it."

1. _____ It is, essentially, an experience beyond words of total terror.

2. _____ The crocodile's breathing and heart metabolism aren't suited to prolonged struggle.

3. _____ The roll is an intense burst of power designed to overcome the victim's resistance quickly.

4. _____ The crocodile then holds the feebly struggling prey underwater until it drowns.

5. _____ I prayed for a quick finish and decided to provoke it by attacking it with my hands.

6. _____ After putting more distance between me and the crocodile, I stopped and realized for the first time how serious my wounds were.

E. MAKING INFERENCES

For each of these statements write Y (yes) if the inference is an accurate one, N (no) if the inference is an inaccurate one, and CT (can't tell) if the writer does not give you enough information to make an inference one way or another.

1. _____ Plumwood was an experienced canoeist. [article as a whole]

2. _____ The writer got into trouble and encountered crocodiles because the ranger's sketch of the waterways was wrong. [paragraph 3]

3. _____ If Plumwood had asked the Aboriginal Gagadgu owners of Kakadu Park for advice, they would undoubtedly have told her not to venture into the waterways in a canoe. [paragraph 5]

4. _____ When Plumwood awaited "what would come" after the attack, she is referring to certain death. [paragraph 18]

5. _____ Apart from the fact that Plumwood didn't want the crocodile that attacked her killed, the particular crocodile would have been difficult to identify. [paragraph 20]

F. INTERPRETING MEANING

Where appropriate, write your answers for these questions in your own words.

1. _____ Which of the following sentences from the selection *best* represents the main idea?
   a. "As a solitary specimen of a major prey species of the saltwater crocodile, I was standing in one of the most dangerous places on earth."
   b. "Our final thoughts during near-death experiences can tell us much about our frameworks of subjectivity."
   c. "I struggled on, through driving rain, shouting for mercy from the sky, apologizing to the angry crocodile, repenting to this place for my intrusion."
   d. "The gift of gratitude came from the searing flash of near-death knowledge, a glimpse 'from the outside' of the alien, incomprehensible world in which the narrative of self has ended."

2. The first part of the essay establishes a mood that strongly contrasts with the mood after the attack. What contrasts in emotion are suggested?

   _____ and _____

3. Paragraph 10 is quite difficult. Study it carefully and also read the last sentence of the selection, which repeats the same idea. To help you, first what do the words "inside" and "outside" refer to in the phrases "from the inside"

   and "from the outside." _____

   _____

   _____

4. _____   A good title for paragraph 11 would be
   a. "Experiencing Total Terror."
   b. "Why Crocodiles Kill."
   c. "An Unbelievable Experience."
   d. "Crocodile Behavior."

5. Look through paragraph 11 and 12 again. List three phrases that convey the
   intense violence of the crocodile's attack. _____

   _____

   _____

G. UNDERSTANDING VOCABULARY

Look through the paragraphs listed below and find a word that matches
each definition. Refer to a dictionary if necessary. An example has been done for
you.

Ex. threatening, frightening [paragraph 2]   ____menacing____

 1. the state of being whole and unimpaired [2]:   _____

 2. natural environments, surroundings [2]:   _____

 3. an intricate network, a labyrinth [3]:   _____

 4. soggy, full of water [3]:   _____

 5. referring to native inhabitants [5]:   _____

 6. not inclined to believe [9]:   _____

 7. agreeable, open to [10]   _____

 8. make up, invent [10]:   _____

 9. gloomy, offering little hope [10]   _____

10. overwhelmed, nearly destroyed [19]:   _____

H. USING VOCABULARY

Here are some words from the selection. Write an original sentence using each
word that shows both that you know how to use the word and what it means.

1. *precariously* _____

2. *rationalized* _____

3. *delusion* _____

4. *repenting* _____

I. PARAPHRASING EXERCISE

Write a paraphrase of the last four sentences of the article in paragraph 21, starting at "The wonder of being alive . . ." _____

_____

_____

_____

_____

_____

J. SUMMARIZING EXERCISE

1. Write a sentence summarizing paragraph 10. _____

_____

_____

_____

2. Write a sentence summarizing paragraph 21. _____

_____

_____

K. TOPICS FOR DISCUSSION

1. Go to a good unabridged dictionary, in the library if necessary, and look up the meaning of the Greek word *hubris*. To what extent do Plumwood's actions reflect this concept?
2. What are some devices that the writer uses to maintain interest and to create suspense and terror in the reader?

L. TOPICS FOR WRITING

1. Write a short narrative in which you describe an experience where you felt, as Plumwood did, "total terror." It does not have to be an incident as harrowing as a crocodile attack, but everyone has felt intense fear at one time or another.
2. What kind of person did Val Plumwood reveal herself to be from the description of her near-death experience in Australia? Write a character sketch in which you discuss her traits, being sure to provide evidence from the narrative to support your characterizations.

Exploring Related Web Sites

- End the confusion over the difference between crocodiles and alligators by checking relevant Web sites. Using Google or your favorite search engine, type in "alligators and crocodiles, differences" in the search box. You will find several relevant sites.
- Information about Kakadu National Park, including photographs, are available at these two sites. The first is the park's official website.

  www.environment.gov.au/parks/kakadu

  http://goaustralia.about.com/library/weekly/aa111799.htm

17

Linden Lab's Second Life: Dreamers of the Dream

Tim Guest is a British journalist who writes for the New York Times, *the* Guardian, *and* Vogue, *among other publications. His first book was* My Life in Orange: Growing Up with the Guru *(2004) about growing up with his mother, who was a devotee of Bhagwan Rashneesh, a mystical cult leader. The book from which this reading comes is titled* Second Lives: A Journey Through Virtual Worlds *(2007). This selection focuses on Linden Lab's Web site, Second Life, where participants can join a virtual community. The site is immensely popular throughout the world, especially in South Korea, but increasingly in the United States as well.*

Vocabulary Preview

WORD PARTS

pre- [paragraph 11] Guest describes the various furnishings and clothing available online to Second Life residents, among them a *prefabricated* virtual beach house. The word *prefabricate* means "to make or manufacture in advance," meaning that the virtual beach house is manufactured in a factory before it is later assembled on-site.

The prefix *pre-* means "before," and it is attached to dozens of English roots, for example, *prerequisite*, *prelude*, and *pretext*. A *prerequisite* is a requirement that must be completed as a condition of something undertaken later; for example, in most colleges Economics 1A would be a prerequisite to Economics 1B. A *prelude* is an "introductory performance or action that precedes the main event." It comes from the Latin: *pre-* + *ludere* ("to play"). And finally, a *pretext* is an "ostensible or professed purpose used as an excuse." In this word, the meaning of the prefix is somewhat obscured. What do these words beginning with *pre-* mean? Of the six, which two begin with *pre-* but have little or no connection with "before"?

prearrange _____

precede _____

precarious _____

precursor _____

premonition _____

pretense _____

251

**WORD
FAMILIES**

renovation [paragraph 5]; innovations [paragraph 14] At the heart of *renovation* and *innovation* is the Latin root *novus*, meaning "new." To *renovate* means, literally, "to make new again," as when one renovates a kitchen or a bathroom. *Innovations* refer to things that are newly introduced. The word *novel* as a noun means a type of fictional book and as an adjective means "new," as in a novel idea. (In the eighteenth century, the novel was considered a new form of writing.) The French word *nouveau* comes from the same root and in English means new and different, especially concerning fashion. What do these three words mean? Look them up in a dictionary if you are unsure.

novelty _____

novice _____

nova _____

_____

TIM GUEST

Linden Lab's Second Life: Dreamers of the Dream

1   In July 2007, there were 7.7 million registered Second Life accounts. Back in May 2005, when I first visited Linden Lab, Second Life was home to just twenty-five thousand people.

2   Linden Lab was a small start-up company, named after the address of its first San Francisco offices, 333 Linden Street. Philip Rosedale,[1] the CEO, had begun the business with his own capital, along with investors and entrepreneurs who had made fortunes from such tech companies as Lotus, Xerox, eBay, and Yahoo. When I visited, there were thirty or so employees. Most people in the real world had never heard of Second Life, but to Linden Lab employees, it was everything.

3   What made Second Life different from most virtual worlds was that Linden Lab sculpted only the landscape. Apart from some core elements (such as Orientation Island), everything was made by the residents. For Linden Lab, this was a coup. It avoided the immense effort and huge start-up cost required to build the contents of the world; they just laid out the territory, and let the inhabitants fill it.

4   This ability to create and to shape objects at will was the notion that first captivated Rosedale. He had always loved to build things, but, even as a child, he had been frustrated by the limitations of the real world. In fourth grade, Philip built his first computer from a kit. In eighth grade, he bought a retractable garage door motor, climbed into his attic, and sawed a hole in the ceiling so that when he pushed a button his bedroom door would slide up, *Star Trek* style, into

---

[1] Philip Rosedale stepped down as CEO of Linden Labs in April 2008 but remains its chairman; he was succeeded by Mark Kingdon.

A scene from Second Life

the attic. It wasn't easy, though, to shape an entire universe according to his dreams. "I would imagine some neat thing and then try to build it in the real world, and it was rather difficult," he told me. "You run into problems like abrasion and friction and the fact that you can't just cut things." That year, frustrated by his growing ambitions, Rosedale began to yearn for a "magical machine," a super-technical tool belt that would let him build whatever he wanted, without worrying about all the real-world practical limitations that stood between him and his imagination.

5   By June 1999—after putting himself through college with the profits from his own software company—Philip decided that what he wanted wasn't the ability to change the real world, but to conquer it and replace it with something better: a virtual world with no barrier between thought and action. He left his position as chief technology officer of RealNetworks, which had bought out his video streaming software, and joined forces with an old colleague to form Linden Lab. Their vision was a renovation of Philip's childhood dream: a world where people could build whatever they liked, and become whoever they wanted.

6   Right from the beginning of online worlds, the players were quicker than the developers to recognize the possibilities in their new virtual lives. The designers of EverQuest were stunned when they discovered players were getting married online. In The Sims Online, you can combine objects, but not create new ones, and the residents worked hard to overcome this limitation. In one case, a group of Sims residents decided they wanted a piano, so they built one out of a desk and chairs, with cigars for piano keys. Linden Lab decided to harness that creative force and allow its users to build literally anything they liked. Compared to the amusement-park atmosphere of other games, where missions and goals are laid out like set rides—the same experience for everyone—this world would

be more like a public park, with a minimum of rules. Linden Lab would create the physics, design the interface, and invent the basic ownership guidelines, and with luck, a whole virtual society would emerge. Linden Lab christened its world "Second Life," for what they saw as its unique benefit. "We agonized over the name," Philip told me. "We got into this classic marketing thing, where you talk about features and benefits. So the feature is a distributed computing environment in which you can build anything, but the benefit is a Second Life."

7   I met Philip at Linden Lab's latest real-world office, near the North Beach area of San Francisco: a gray stone-walled, high-ceilinged, loft-style building, with thirty or so desks grouped together in clover-like fours, with huge, high-spec PCs on each. On the wall were pinups that looked like holiday destinations—a Japanese temple, a tropical island—but were, of course, pictures of places in Second Life. The atmosphere was part cutting-edge start-up tech company, and part hardcore gaming café. (To our right, one employee was busy blow-drying his painted fantasy figurines.)

8   When Linden Lab employees first joined the company, they were given new virtual names. Many were already Second Life residents, and they kept their original selves, but for all official work, they used their "Linden" avatar. So, for example, Philip Rosedale's virtual self was called Philip Linden. In Second Life, as in most virtual worlds, each character's name is displayed above his or her virtual head, so that in Second Life, when you meet one of the world's creators, you know right away who it is.

9   I had met John Linden, another Linden Lab employee, inside Second Life, but not Philip. Philip Rosedale's Second Life self looked much like his real-world body—cropped blond hair, wide blue eyes. The real Philip had a wide mouth, and blond hair, and when he grew excited, his eyes widened. When he talked about Second Life, he grew excited a lot.

10   We sat at his desk, and Philip logged in. His other persona, Philip Linden, appeared on-screen. He hadn't been online for a few days, he explained. His last visit to Second Life had been for the wedding of two longtime Second Life residents, Mash Mandala and Baccara Rhodes. (The wedding was so well attended, Philip explained, that the server nearly crashed; to reduce the number of objects the server had to handle, the bride asked everyone to remove their hair.) Philip's avatar was still hovering beside the virtual chapel, dressed to the virtual nines: a tux and white bow tie, red virtual rose pinned to his virtual breast.

11   We talked about his clothes. He had bought them himself, from a virtual mall. Fashion, he said, was a great example of how Second Lifers created their world. In the two years since Second Life appeared online, the available outfits had developed from very basic to extremely sophisticated, some the work of successful real-world designers. Much of the in-world Second Life content that is for sale is also advertised outside the world, on websites such as http://shop.onrez.com, where you can use your real-world credit card, or in some cases even your cellphone, to buy virtual haute couture that is delivered directly to you online (with, of course, no shipping charges). Philip showed me a few garments—skirts, garters, gowns—and pointed out the complex visual tricks: realistic-looking effects that had surprised even Linden Lab employees. Residents can also shop

inside Second Life itself; they can take a virtual stroll through one of the many virtual malls, hand over their virtual cash, and receive outfits from automated machines that let them try before they buy. It's not just clothes; you can buy vehicles—a virtual Ferrari will set you back 800 Linden Dollars, or about $2.40 in real money. You can buy accessories (a virtual Apple Blueberry iBook goes for 200 Linden Dollars), and, of course, there's the largest market: property. (A pre-fabricated virtual beach house goes for 1,800 Linden Dollars, about 6 real dollars, but that's before you've bought the land to put it on.)

12   Philip showed me maps of the Second Life landmass as it grew: from the virtual equivalent of around 140 acres, in March 2002, to around 11,200 acres when I visited the world in early 2004. Demand for virtual land was so high, Philip said, they were adding 160 acres a week.

13   And all this was exactly what they had hoped for. They would never have had the resources to create such a complex world themselves, but because of the free-form nature of Second Life, they didn't have to. Buildings, vehicles, clothing, even custom-made gestures—a dance, a wave, a different kind of laugh—all designed by residents, are at the center of most Second Life activity and trade.

14   As an example, Philip gave me a tour of third-party websites, run by Second Life residents, which sold virtual clothes. At these sites, with names like 2ndlook, you could input your credit card details and purchase a pair of socks (twenty cents), a ball gown (forty cents), or a furry bear suit (two dollars). (I asked if Second Life experienced fashion trends. Philip didn't have the figures, but from what I had already seen in virtual worlds, hemlines went up, and they stayed up. In Second Life, where perfect body shapes were the norm, people had it, and they flaunted it.) He took me through a gallery of images of community-made dresses; they looked as varied and as fashionable as those from the pages of *Vogue*. Philip explained how fast they had seen fashions evolve in Second Life, in a kind of arms race between designers for innovations that would attract virtual business. Early clothes were just 3-D shapes, but soon designers learned to make their dresses look like real cloth. At the time of my visit, the latest fashion was for hand-sculpted dresses, with carefully modeled creases and folds. The open attitude to currency exchange had created a whole virtual economy. Residents worked—as designers, event managers, pet manufacturers, hug makers, even virtual strippers—to earn Linden Dollars. "The market is getting very competitive," Philip told me. "There's money to be made." At the time of my visit, twenty or so Second Life residents sold enough virtual clothes, property, and animations to exchange their virtual profit for U.S. dollars and live off the result.

15   "All this really incredible stuff is coming from the community," Philip said. "I think that one of the surprises with Second Life is the degree to which people do tend to want to rebuild the world that they know. So people's first purpose is to make an avatar that looks like them, and their second one is to have a luxury car, or a house on a cliff, overlooking the ocean, built with wood, and with high ceilings. People first rebuild the world that they know, and only then do they defy it or experiment with it." Philip took travel as an example. In Second Life, you can walk, or fly, but you can also buy vehicles to travel faster and in higher

style. "So people start with the Ferrari, and then after that they think, Well, where could I go from this? How about a floating car?" Only later do they realize they can grow wings. (Philip told me how, when they first opened their world to residents, they began with twenty people in 140 virtual acres; each one immediately built a virtual house, even though there was not yet any virtual rain.)

16   "We're trying to create an environment where any kind of stuff can happen. It's their world," Philip told me. He turned to his screen and showed me a Web page: Online photo albums captured Second Life residents' favorite virtual moments. Someone called Kit Calliope rode a giant green dragon; there was an arty shot of a flock of flying metal bubbles; someone else was dressed up as a cartoon squirrel. (The poster of the picture asked, "Is this the cutest squirrel in the world?") Philip likened Second Life to Burning Man, the festival in Black Rock, Nevada. Once a year, for eight days, around forty thousand visitors build a fantasy town on the dry plain of an ancient lakebed to create a place where almost anything goes. Inside his virtual world, Philip Rosedale hoped for the same freedom of expression, the same abandon of day-to-day concerns.

17   Above Philip, a beautiful woman with fairy wings looked down and waved. Philip grew animated. In the new digital frontier, he told me, people were *nice*. "I'm actually pretty introverted. I was a really nerdy kid and definitely not gregarious," he told me. To illustrate the friendliness inside virtual worlds, Philip imagined a situation where, in a strange place, he saw a beautiful woman. "In real life if I came out of the subway in Paris or New York or London, and I saw some beautiful woman, I wouldn't just go walk over to her. Yet in Second Life, you do that almost instantly."

18   "I don't know if the general public understands the fundamental love Linden Lab has for the community," Philip said. "When residents see a Linden, they think. They have god powers. They could delete me. But it's not like that." He laughed. "Well, we *can* delete them—but we don't. We are more like custodians. We make sure the trees grow, the land remains, the ocean flows. We're not so much gods—we're groundskeepers."

19   To Philip, the world of Second Life was a triumph of self over other, an opportunity to improve on the real. "Second Life is a world which is perhaps in many ways identical to the world we live in, but, in a number of significant ways, better." *

Postscript: In April 2008, it was reported that Linden Labs is contemplating a public offering to sell shares in the company to the public; however, as the writer of the technology blog listed below says, Linden Labs may not be doing as well as the company claims. Apparently, the number of actual users is much less than the number of people who have downloaded the software, and the site has had a lot of technical problems. For further information, see *http://www.sfgate.com/cgi-bin/ article.cgi?f=/c/a/2008/04/23/BUV910A2I1.DTL&hw=linden+labs&sn=004&sc=589.*

Exercises

Do not refer to the selection for Exercises A and B unless your instructor directs you to do so.

A. DETERMINING THE MAIN IDEA AND PURPOSE

Choose the best answer.

_____ 1. The main idea of the selection is that Second Life is

    a. a game where people compete with each other to acquire the most property and material possessions.

    b. an example of the new digital frontier that allows people to interact in virtual worlds.

    c. a social networking site where people can meet others who share their interests.

    d. a virtual world where people can build whatever they want and become whatever they want.

_____ 2. The writer's purpose is to

    a. give instructions so that the reader can create his or her own virtual world in Second Life.

    b. trace the history and purpose of Second Life and discuss some of its unique features.

    c. express admiration for Second Life and present reasons that readers should join this virtual world.

    d. express criticism for Second Life and present reasons that readers should avoid joining this virtual world.

B. COMPREHENDING MAIN IDEAS

Choose the correct answer.

_____ 1. Second Life is different from other online virtual worlds in one respect, namely that it

    a. lays out the territory and lets the inhabitants fill it with whatever they want.

    b. does not charge any money to join or to maintain an avatar on the site.

    c. offers a wide range of environments to live in and characters to adopt.

    d. is entirely designed and maintained by members who pay a fee to join.

_____ 2. Philip Rosedale, the CEO of Second Life, above all wanted to create a new virtual world where there would be no limitations on

    a. the money and property that one could accumulate.

    b. the number of people who could participate.

       c. one's imagination or dreams.

       d. the number of virtual identities that participants could take on.

_____ 3. Guest compares Second Life, as its designers envisioned it, to

       a. a vast supermarket where one can buy anything he or she desires.

       b. an amusement park with set rides.

       c. a club with many rules and regulations to ensure that everything works in an orderly fashion.

       d. a public park with only a minimum of rules.

_____ 4. One online wedding of two Second Life residents was so well attended that the server almost crashed, requiring the virtual guests to

       a. take off all their virtual clothes.

       b. take back their virtual wedding gifts.

       c. take off their virtual hair.

       d. not eat any virtual food at the virtual reception.

_____ 5. Guest mentions several kinds of virtual items that one can buy at online malls to enhance one's Second Life existence. Which one of the following was *not* included?

       a. property

       b. college degrees

       c. vehicles

       d. clothing

       e. prefabricated houses

       f. accessories like an Apple iBook

_____ 6. Rosedale emphasizes that, above all, Second Life is successful and takes little work to maintain because

       a. the residents themselves do all the work and design almost everything.

       b. investors have funded the company generously.

       c. the company has incredibly sophisticated and powerful computers and servers to handle the traffic the site generates.

       d. it exists only in cyberspace and therefore isn't real.

COMPREHENSION SCORE

Score your answers for Exercises A and B as follows:

A. No. right _____ × 2 = _____

B. No. right _____ × 1 = _____

Total points from A and B _____ × 10 = _____ percent

You may refer to the selection as you work through the remaining exercises.

C. LOCATING SUPPORTING DETAILS

For the main idea stated here, find relevant details that support it: Unlike The Sims Online, Second Life does not erect limitations for its residents as they create their new virtual lives. [paragraph 6] The second and last ones have been done for you.

1. _____

2. Second Life residents worked hard to overcome the limitations of the Sims site and harnessed their creative energy.

3. _____

4. _____

5. _____

6. The name "Second Life" offers the benefit of having a second life.

D. DISTINGUISHING BETWEEN FACT AND OPINION

For each of the following statements from the selection, write F if the statement represents a factual statement that can be verified or O if the statement represents the writer's or someone else's subjective interpretation.

1. _____ What made Second Life different from most virtual worlds was that Linden Lab employees sculpted only the landscape.

2. _____ Apart from some core elements (such as Orientation Island), everything was made by the residents.

3. _____ For Linden Lab, this was a coup.

4. _____ It avoided the immense effort and huge start-up cost required to build the contents of the world; they just laid out the territory, and let the inhabitants fill it.

5. _____ Linden Lab christened its world "Second Life."

6. _____ Linden Lab employees consider having a second life a unique benefit.

E. MAKING INFERENCES

For each of these statements write Y (yes) if the inference is an accurate one, N (no) if the inference is an inaccurate one, or CT (can't tell) if the writer does not give enough information to make an inference one way or another.

1. _____ According to the information in paragraph 1, Second Life became very popular almost immediately after only two years of operation.

2. _____ The investors and entrepreneurs who began the start-up that became Linden Lab had a lot of technological experience before establishing the company. [paragraph 2]

3. _____ The reason that Linden Lab's employees let the virtual residents of Second Life create the contents of their world is that they were underfunded; they hadn't raised enough money to do the job themselves. [paragraphs 3 and 6]

4. _____ Second Life is more popular and has more members than the two rival virtual worlds, The Sims Online and EverQuest. [paragraph 6]

5. _____ Residents who want to buy virtual clothes for their virtual selves must shop only at online malls owned by Second Life. [paragraph 11]

6. _____ Second Life is so popular that it is adding 160 acres a week to its landmass, so much that eventually it will run out of space. [paragraph 12]

F. UNDERSTANDING VOCABULARY

Look through the paragraphs listed below and find a word that matches each definition. Refer to a dictionary if necessary. An example has been done for you.

Ex. those who organize and operate new businesses
[paragraphs 2–3]   ___entrepreneurs___

1. carried out or simulated by means of a computer
[3, 5, and elsewhere]   _____

2. triumph, brilliantly executed strategy [3–4]   _____

3. attracted, fascinated [4]   _____

4. renewal, making new again [5–6]   _____

5. bring under control and utilize effectively [5–6]   _____

6. astonished, amazed [5–6]   _____

7. gave a name to something new [5–6]   _____

8. a virtual second self, an imaginary persona
[8, 10, and throughout]   _____

9. typical or standard model or pattern [14]   _____

10. exhibited or shown in a flashy manner [14]   _____

11. sociable, enjoying the company of others [17–18]   _____

12. characterized by interest or preoccupation in
oneself [17–18]   _____

G. USING VOCABULARY

In parentheses before each sentence are some inflected forms of words from the selection. Study the context and the sentence. Then write the correct form in the space provided.

1. (*renovate, renovated, renovation*) The intention of Second Life is to give

   residents a chance to create a different life, a _____ version of one's real life.

2. (*retract, retraction, retractable*) Philip Rosedale, the CEO of Second Life, always enjoyed building things when he was a child, for example a door that could

    _____ into the attic.

3. (*prefabricate, prefabricated, prefabrication*) In Second Life it's possible to buy a

    _____ virtual beach house to put on your virtual beachfront property.

4. (*innovate, innovated, innovative, innovation*) Virtual clothing designers compete

    with each other to create _____ designs to attract virtual customers.

5. (*animate, animated, animation, animatedly*) Philip Rosedale talked

    _____ when he discussed the new digital frontier.

H. PARAPHRASING EXERCISE

Here are three sentences from the selection. Write a paraphrase of each in the space provided.

1. Philip decided that what he wanted wasn't the ability to change the real world, but to conquer it and replace it with something better: a virtual world

    with no barrier between thought and action. [paragraph 5] _____

    _____

    _____

    _____

2. Philip's avatar was still hovering beside the virtual chapel, dressed to the

    virtual nines. . . . [paragraph 10] _____

    _____

3. In Second Life, where perfect body shapes were the norm, people had it, and

    they flaunted it. [paragraph 14] _____

    _____

I. ANNOTATING EXERCISE

Assume that you are preparing an essay on the first topic in section K below. Annotate the relevant sections of Guest's essay in the left margin.

J. TOPICS FOR DISCUSSION

1. How would you describe Guest's point of view toward virtual worlds in general and toward Second Life in particular? Is he neutral, or is his stance

evident in his description of how Second Life works and what benefits it confers on its players?

2. Look through the selection again. What is the source for most of the information Guest provides about Second Life?

3. Apparently, the residents of Second Life are quite enthralled with their virtual lives. Do you see any danger in this absorption—for example, creating an avatar that represents a person with ideal physical and emotional characteristics, attending a virtual wedding, or buying a prefabricated virtual beach house? Is such an activity a waste of time, or in fact, is it a whole new way of interpreting one's own identity?

4. One of the chapters in Guest's book on Second Life deals with sex in virtual communities. If you create an avatar that has virtual sex online with another avatar, have you cheated on your boyfriend, girlfriend, partner, or spouse?

K. TOPICS FOR WRITING

1. Write a short essay in which you explain and summarize the unique experience and benefits of participating in online virtual worlds as Guest describes them.

2. Have you ever joined a virtual community such as Second Life? If so, write an essay in which you explain your reasons for doing so. If not, explain why you would not be interested in such an activity.

3. Read paragraphs 13–16 again carefully. Do you see a fundamental irony in the sorts of lives the residents create for themselves and in the conception Philip Rosedale envisions for Second Life? Write a paragraph responding to this question: What really seems to be governing the lives of Second Life residents as they create their virtual existences?

Exploring Related Web Sites

- If you are unfamiliar with online virtual worlds like Second Life, you can see for yourself some of its features at their home page. You must install the software to see all of its features, but you can access blogs, tutorials, and other basic information about how this community works without registering. Here is the address:

  http://secondlife.com

- Guest mentions a Web site where Second Lifers can buy virtual haute couture (high fashion) for their online avatars. The address provided in paragraph 11 is listed again here. At the home page click on "apparel" in the menu bar. Notice how curvaceous and yet skinny the female avatars' bodies are.

  http://shop.onrez.com

18 Dearly Disconnected

IAN FRAZIER

Ian Frazier writes both humorous and serious nonfiction. After graduating from Harvard, he wrote for a magazine in Chicago; then in 1974 he joined the staff of the New Yorker *magazine where he writes feature articles, humorous pieces, and material for "The Talk of the Town." In 1982, he moved to Montana and began doing research for one of his best-known books,* Great Plains *(1984). Among his other books are* On the Rez *(2000) and* Gone to New York: Adventures in the City *(2005). Currently he lives in New York City. This article was originally published in* Mother Jones.

Vocabulary Preview

WORD PARTS

tele- [paragraph 10] In Selection 9 by Chris Rose, you were introduced to the root -*pathy* meaning "feeling" (as in *sympathy* and *empathy*). *Telepathy* contains the same root, but as with most prefixes, when the Greek prefix *tele-* is added to this root, it completely changes the definition. Meaning "literally at a distance," *telepathy* refers to communication other than what occurs between the usual five senses—in other words, the odd sensation that you can sometimes feel what another is thinking or feeling even though you are apart. *Tele-* precedes many new, usually technical words, in English. Here are a few (besides the obvious *television* and *telescope*):

telegram	communication transmitted by wire; from *tele-* + *graphos* ("writing")
teleconference	a conference held among people in different locations
telemarketing	marketing or selling goods over the telephone, literally at a distance

What is a TelePrompter? _____

_____

WORD FAMILIES

mater- [paragraph 8] From the Latin root *mater-* ("mother") comes a family of words in English. (The masculine version is *pater-*.) Some common words stemming from *mater-* are *maternal*, *maternity*, *matrimony*, and *matricide* (the killing of one's mother). Consider these two words. What do they have to do with "mother"? Refer to your dictionary if necessary.

matrilineal _____

alma mater _____

IAN FRAZIER

Dearly Disconnected

1   Before I got married I was living by myself in an A-frame cabin in northwestern Montana. The cabin's interior was a single high-ceilinged room, and at the center of the room, mounted on the rough-hewn log that held up the ceiling beam, was a telephone. I knew no one in the area or indeed the whole state, so my entire social life came to me through that phone. The woman I would marry was living in Sarasota, Florida, and the distance between us suggests how well we were getting along at the time. We had not been in touch for several months; she had no phone. One day she decided to call me from a pay phone. We talked for a while, and after her coins ran out I jotted the number on the wood beside my phone and called her back. A day or two later, thinking about the call, I wanted to talk to her again. The only number I had for her was the pay phone number I'd written down.

2   The pay phone was on the street some blocks from the apartment where she stayed. As it happened, though, she had just stepped out to do some errands a few minutes before I called, and she was passing by on the sidewalk when the phone rang. She had no reason to think that a public phone ringing on a busy street would be for her. She stopped, listened to it ring again, and picked up the receiver. Love is pure luck; somehow I had known she would answer, and she had known it would be me.

3   Long afterwards, on a trip to Disney World in Orlando with our two kids, then aged six and two, we made a special detour to Sarasota to show them the pay phone. It didn't impress them much. It's just a nondescript Bell Atlantic pay phone on the cement wall of a building, by the vestibule. But its ordinariness and even boringness only make me like it more; ordinary places where extraordinary events have occurred are my favorite kind. On my mental map of Florida that pay phone is a landmark looming above the city it occupies, and a notable, if private, historic site.

4   I'm interested in pay phones in general these days, especially when I get the feeling that they are about to go away. Technology, in the form of sleek little phones in our pockets, has swept on by them and made them begin to seem antique. My lifelong entanglement with pay phones dates me; when I was young they were just there, a given, often as stubborn and uncongenial as the curbstone underfoot. They were instruments of torture sometimes. You had to feed them fistfuls of change in those pre-phone-card days, and the operator was a real person who stood maddeningly between you and whomever you were trying to call. And when the call went wrong, as communication often does, the pay phone gave you a focus for your rage. Pay phones were always getting smashed up, the receivers shattered to bits against the booth, the coin slots jammed with chewing gum, the cords yanked out and unraveled to the floor.

5   You used to hear people standing at pay phones and cursing them. I remember the sound of my own frustrated shouting confined by the glass walls of a phone booth—the kind you don't see much anymore, with a little ventilating fan in the ceiling that turned on when you shut the double-hinged glass door. The

noise that fan made in the silence of a phone booth was for a while the essence of romantic, lonely-guy melancholy for me. Certain specific pay phones I still resent for the unhappiness they caused me, and others I will never forgive, though not for any fault of their own. In the C concourse of the Salt Lake City airport there's a row of pay phones set on the wall by the men's room just past the concourse entry. While on a business trip a few years ago, I called home from a phone in that row and learned that a friend had collapsed in her apartment and was in the hospital with brain cancer. I had liked those pay phones before, and had used them often; now I can't even look at them when I go by.

6   There was always a touch of seediness and sadness to pay phones, and a sense of transience. Drug dealers made calls from them, and shady types who did not want their whereabouts known, and otherwise respectable people planning assignations, and people too poor to have phones of their own. In the movies, any character who used a pay phone was either in trouble or contemplating a crime. Pay phones came with their own special atmospherics and even accessories sometimes—the predictable bad smells and graffiti, of course, as well as cigarette butts, soda cans, scattered pamphlets from the Jehovah's Witnesses, and single bottles of beer (empty) still in their individual, street-legal paper bags. Mostly, pay phones evoked the mundane: "Honey, I'm just leaving. I'll be there soon." But you could tell that a lot of undifferentiated humanity had flowed through these places, and that in the muteness of each pay phone's little space, wild emotion had howled.

7   Once, when I was living in Brooklyn, I read in the newspaper that a South American man suspected of dozens of drug-related contract murders had been arrested at a pay phone in Queens. Police said that the man had been on the phone setting up a murder at the time of his arrest. The newspaper story gave the address of the pay phone, and out of curiosity one afternoon I took a long walk to Queens to take a look at it. It was on an undistinguished street in a middle-class neighborhood, by a florist's shop. By the time I saw it, however, the pay phone had been blown up and/or firebombed. I had never before seen a pay phone so damaged; explosives had blasted pieces of the phone itself wide open in metal shreds like frozen banana peels, and flames had blackened everything and melted the plastic parts and burned the insulation off the wires. Soon after, I read that police could not find enough evidence against the suspected murderer and so had let him go.

8   The cold phone outside a shopping center in Bigfork, Montana, from which I called a friend in the West Indies one winter when her brother was sick; the phone on the wall of the concession stand at Redwood Pool, where I used to stand dripping and call my mom to come and pick me up; the sweaty phones used almost only by men in the hallway outside the maternity ward at Lenox Hill Hospital in New York; the phone by the driveway of the Red Cloud Indian School in South Dakota where I used to talk with my wife while priests in black slacks and white socks chatted on a bench nearby; the phone in the old woodpaneled phone booth with leaded glass windows in the drugstore in my Ohio hometown—each one is as specific as a birthmark, a point on earth unlike any other. Recently I went back to New York City after a long absence and tried to find a working pay phone. I picked up one receiver after the next without

success. Meanwhile, as I scanned down the long block, I counted half a dozen or more pedestrians talking on their cell phones.

9   It's the cell phone, of course, that's putting the pay phone out of business. The pay phone is to the cell phone as the troubled and difficult older sibling is to the cherished newborn. People even treat their cell phones like babies, cradling them in their palms and beaming down upon them lovingly as they dial. You sometimes hear people yelling on their cell phones, but almost never yelling at them. Cell phones are toylike, nearly magic, and we get a huge kick out of them, as often happens with technological advances until the new wears off. Somehow I don't believe people had a similar honeymoon period with pay phones back in their early days, and they certainly have no such enthusiasm for them now. When I see a cell-phone user gently push the little antenna and fit the phone back into its brushed-vinyl carrying case and tuck the case inside his jacket beside his heart, I feel sorry for the beat-up pay phone standing in the rain.

10   People almost always talk on cell phones while in motion—driving, walking down the street, riding on a commuter train. The cell phone took the transience the pay phone implied and turned it into VIP-style mobility and speed. Even sitting in a restaurant, the person on a cell phone seems importantly busy and on the move. Cell-phone conversations seem to be unlimited by ordinary constraints of place and time, as if they represent an almost-perfect form of communication whose perfect state would be telepathy.

11   And yet no matter how we factor the world away, it remains. I think this is what drives me so nuts when a person sitting next to me on a bus makes a call from her cell phone. Yes, this busy and important caller is at no fixed point in space, but nevertheless I happen to be beside her. The job of providing physical context falls on me; I become her call's surroundings, as if I'm the phone booth wall. For me to lean over and comment on her cell-phone conversation would be as unseemly and unexpected as if I were in fact a wall; and yet I have no choice, as a sentient person, but to hear what my chatty fellow traveler has to say.

12   Some middle-aged guys like me go around complaining about this kind of thing. The more sensible approach is just to accept it and forget about it, because there's not much we can do. I don't think that pay phones will completely disappear. Probably they will survive for a long while as clumsy old technology still of some use to those lagging behind, and as a backup if ever the superior systems should temporarily fail. Before pay phones became endangered I never thought of them as public spaces, which of course they are. They suggested a human average; they belonged to anybody who had a couple of coins. Now I see that, like public schools and public transportation, pay phones belong to a former commonality our culture is no longer quite so sure it needs.

13   I have a weakness for places—for old battlefields, car-crash sites, houses where famous authors lived. Bygone passions should always have an address, it seems to me. Ideally, the world would be covered with plaques and markers list-ing the notable events that occurred at each particular spot. A sign on every pay phone would describe how a woman broke up with her fiance here, how a young ballplayer learned that he had made the team. Unfortunately, the world itself is fluid, and changes out from under us; the rocky islands that the pilot Mark Twain was careful to avoid in the Mississippi are now stone outcroppings

in a soybean field. Meanwhile, our passions proliferate into illegibility, and the places they occur can't hold them. Eventually pay phones will become relics of an almost-vanished landscape, and of a time when there were fewer of us and our stories were on an earlier page. Romantics like me will have to reimagine our passions as they are—unmoored to earth, like an infinitude of cell-phone messages flying through the atmosphere. ✳

Ian Frazier, "Dearly Disconnected" from *Mother Jones* (January–February 2000). Copyright © 2000 by the Foundation for National Progress. Reprinted with permission.

Exercises

Do not refer to the selection for Exercises A–C unless your instructor directs you to do so.

A. DETERMINING THE MAIN IDEA AND PURPOSE

Choose the best answer.

_____ 1. The main idea of the selection is that

    a. pay phones used to be as much of a fixture on American city streets as sidewalks and lampposts.

    b. cell phones have a distinct advantage over pay phones because of their mobility and ease of use.

    c. the pay phone, a venerable public institution, is now practically an antique, almost put out of business by cell phones.

    d. the pay phone has always been associated with slightly illicit elements, like making drug deals and arranging lovers' trysts.

_____ 2. The writer's purpose is to

    a. lament the passing of the pay phone and describe some of his connections with them in the past.

    b. put forth reasons that pay phones should be protected as a symbol of an earlier form of communication.

    c. put forth reasons that pay phones are superior to cell phones.

    d. show how technology has changed the fabric of American culture.

B. COMPREHENDING MAIN IDEAS

Choose the correct answer.

_____ 1. Frazier recounts the story of how a pay phone played an important part in his relationship with the woman whom he eventually married, specifically because

    a. she called him every day in Montana from a pay phone in Florida.

    b. he lost touch with her for several months because he lost the pay phone number where he could reach her.

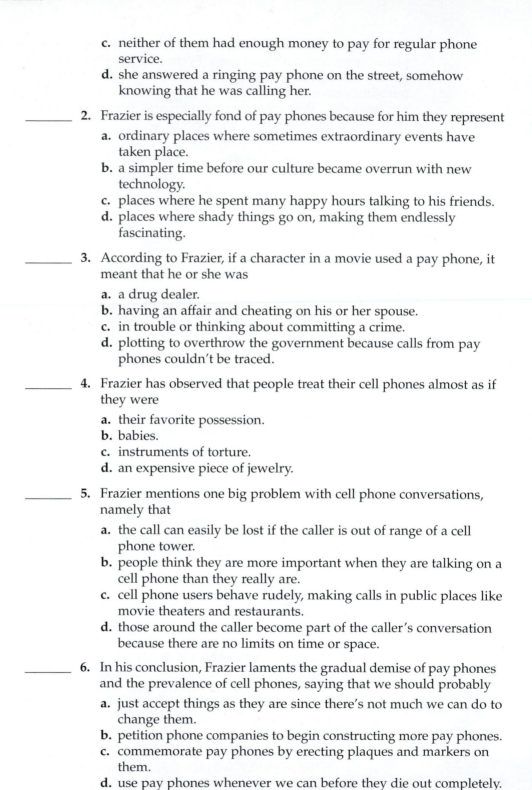

    c. neither of them had enough money to pay for regular phone service.

    d. she answered a ringing pay phone on the street, somehow knowing that he was calling her.

_____ **2.** Frazier is especially fond of pay phones because for him they represent

    a. ordinary places where sometimes extraordinary events have taken place.

    b. a simpler time before our culture became overrun with new technology.

    c. places where he spent many happy hours talking to his friends.

    d. places where shady things go on, making them endlessly fascinating.

_____ **3.** According to Frazier, if a character in a movie used a pay phone, it meant that he or she was

    a. a drug dealer.

    b. having an affair and cheating on his or her spouse.

    c. in trouble or thinking about committing a crime.

    d. plotting to overthrow the government because calls from pay phones couldn't be traced.

_____ **4.** Frazier has observed that people treat their cell phones almost as if they were

    a. their favorite possession.

    b. babies.

    c. instruments of torture.

    d. an expensive piece of jewelry.

_____ **5.** Frazier mentions one big problem with cell phone conversations, namely that

    a. the call can easily be lost if the caller is out of range of a cell phone tower.

    b. people think they are more important when they are talking on a cell phone than they really are.

    c. cell phone users behave rudely, making calls in public places like movie theaters and restaurants.

    d. those around the caller become part of the caller's conversation because there are no limits on time or space.

_____ **6.** In his conclusion, Frazier laments the gradual demise of pay phones and the prevalence of cell phones, saying that we should probably

    a. just accept things as they are since there's not much we can do to change them.

    b. petition phone companies to begin constructing more pay phones.

    c. commemorate pay phones by erecting plaques and markers on them.

    d. use pay phones whenever we can before they die out completely.

COMPREHENSION SCORE

Score your answers for Exercises A and B as follows:

A. No. right _____ × 2 = _____

B. No. right _____ × 1 = _____

Total points from A and B _____ × 10 = _____ percent

C. SEQUENCING

These sentences from one paragraph in the selection have been scrambled. Read the sentences and choose the sequence that puts them back into logical order. Do not refer to the original selection.

1 Long afterwards, on a trip to Disney World in Orlando with our two kids, then aged six and two, we made a special detour to Sarasota to show them the pay phone. **2** It didn't impress them much. **3** It's just a nondescript Bell Atlantic pay phone on the cement wall of a building, by the vestibule. **4** But its ordinariness and even boringness only make me like it more; ordinary places where extraordinary events have occurred are my favorite kind. **5** On my mental map of Florida that pay phone is a landmark looming above the city it occupies, and a notable, if private, historic site.

_____ Which of the following represents the correct sequence for these sentences?

    a. 5, 1, 3, 4, 2
    b. 3, 2, 5, 4, 1
    c. 1, 5, 2, 4, 3
    d. 5, 1, 4, 2, 3
    e. Correct as written.

You may refer to the selection as you work through the remaining exercises.

D. DISTINGUISHING BETWEEN MAIN IDEAS AND SUPPORTING DETAILS

Label the following restated sentences from one paragraph in the selection as follows: MI if it represents a *main idea* and SD if it represents a *supporting detail*.

1. _____ When Frazier was young, pay phones were just there, a given.

2. _____ Pay phones were sometimes instruments of torture.

3. _____ You had to feed them lots of coins because there were no prepaid phone cards.

4. _____ There was an operator between you and the person you were calling.

5. _____ Things would often go wrong with the call, and the caller would get really angry.

6. _____ Public phone booths weren't very well maintained.

7. _____ The phone receivers were often shattered.

8. _____ There would often be chewing gum jammed into the coin slots.

E. MAKING INFERENCES

Write the answers to these inference questions in your own words.

1. From paragraph 1, what single fact suggests that the relationship between Frazier and his future wife wasn't good? _____

2. If Frazier's future wife had not picked up the ringing pay phone on that Sarasota, Florida, street, what most likely would have happened? _____

3. Read paragraph 4 and the first sentence of paragraph 5 again. What might be two likely reasons that someone would curse the phone inside a pay phone booth? _____

4. According to the details in paragraph 6, what does Frazier find particularly intriguing about pay phones? _____

5. From what Frazier writes in paragraph 10, aside from the fact that we are subjected to their conversations, why are cell phone users so annoying to be around? _____

6. Read paragraph 11 again. What is ironic about the relationship between the cell phone user and the person sitting next to her? _____

F. UNDERSTANDING VOCABULARY

Look through the paragraphs listed below and find a word that matches each definition. Refer to a dictionary if necessary. An example has been done for you.

Ex. something taken for granted or assumed
[paragraphs 3–4] _____given_____

1. lacking distinctive qualities in appearance [3–4] _____

2. a feeling of sadness or gloom, depression of the spirit [4–5] _____

3. not pleasing, unfriendly [4–5] _____

4. quality of being disreputable, sleazy [5–6] _____

5. state of impermanence, of not lasting long
   [6 and 10]   _____

6. describing a person of questionable character
   [5–6]   _____

7. ordinary, commonplace [5–6]   _____

8. appointments between lovers, trysts [5–6]   _____

9. restrictions, limits [9–10]   _____

10. experiencing sensation or feeling [11–12]   _____

11. improper, not following standards of good taste
    [11–12]   _____

12. unconnected, untethered [12–13]   _____

G. USING VOCABULARY

Write the correct inflected form of the base word (in parentheses) in each of the following sentences. Be sure to add the appropriate ending to fit the grammatical requirements of the sentence. Refer to your dictionary if necessary.

1. (*entanglement*—use a verb) Frazier writes that he has been somehow

   _____ with pay phones for most of his life, which he readily admits dates him.

2. (*muteness*—use an adverb) When you walk next to a pay phone while someone is talking on the phone, it appears as if the person is

   speaking _____ .

3. (*mobility*—use an adjective) Another word for cell phone is _____ phone, because you can use them while moving around and because the phone itself is portable.

4. (*fluid*—use a noun) Frazier expresses his sadness that pay phones are

   vanishing from the landscape; the _____ of the new world of technology is to blame.

5. (*proliferate*—use a noun) The _____ of cell phones will surely result in the extermination of pay phones at some time in the future.

H. PARAPHRASING EXERCISE

Here are some sentences from the selection. Write a paraphrase of each passage in the space provided.

1. There was always a touch of seediness and sadness to pay phones, and a sense of transience. Drug dealers made calls from them, and shady types who did not want their whereabouts known, and otherwise respectable

people planning assignations, and people too poor to have phones of their own. _____

_____

_____

_____

_____

2. It's the cell phone, of course, that's putting the pay phone out of business. The pay phone is to the cell phone as the troubled and difficult older sibling is to the cherished newborn. _____

_____

_____

I. SUMMARIZING EXERCISE

Write a summary of the last paragraph. _____

_____

_____

_____

_____

J. TOPICS FOR DISCUSSION

1. Is Frazier simply an old fuddy-duddy, as he says, who dates himself by reminiscing fondly about pay phones, or does he have a larger, deeper purpose in lamenting the decline of this public institution? If so, what is it? How would you define his real concern?
2. Is the pay phone doomed to extinction, as were the horse and carriage, the slide rule, and the typewriter? What are the advantages of the old way of doing something? Are the advantages of the new way really so much better? Debate this issue by going beyond the obvious advantages of saving time and being more efficient.
3. In his conclusion, Frazier includes the demise of the pay phone, along with the demise in public transportation and public schools, as signifying a loss of our "commonality." He does not go further into this connection, however. What do you think he means?

K. TOPICS FOR WRITING

1. Frazier offers many illustrations to suggest that pay phones, at least when Frazier was younger, were always associated with shadiness, sadness, and seediness. Find a pay phone, preferably on the street, sit quietly for a while, and observe the people who use it. Write a brief descriptive essay recording your impressions.

2. How would you define cell phone etiquette? Write a short essay in which you set forth some basic principles for using cell phones that would follow a sort of Cell Phone Golden Rule—behaviors that you wish everyone with a cell phone would follow.
3. Nearly 10 years have passed since Frazier wrote this essay, and cell phones are now even more ubiquitous than they were in 2000. What are some effects of our increasing reliance on cell phones, aside from the fact that pay phones are even scarcer?
4. Frazier remarks in at least two places in the selection that particular pay phones represented something notable in his past. In the same way, think of a public place (or phone booth) that was the location for something momentous in your life. Describe the place and describe what happened there.

Exploring Related Web Sites

There has been a great deal of discussion about the use of cell phones (including text messaging) while driving. What is the law in your state about driving while talking on a cell phone? Do some online research to find the answer.

19

LAWRENCE SHAMES
The Hunger for More

Why do Americans enjoy spending money and acquiring so much? Why are we seemingly never satisfied with what we already have? Lawrence Shames attempts to identify some reasons in his book, The Hunger for More: Searching for Values in an Age of Greed, *published in 1989. In this excerpt from the first chapter, Shames examines the American frontier and its influence on our tradition of materialism. A former writer for* Esquire *magazine on ethical issues, Shames has also written for many national publications, among them the* New York Times, Vanity Fair, *and* Playboy.

Vocabulary Preview

WORD PARTS

tri- *Tri-* is both a Greek and a Latin prefix, always indicating the numeral "three." Shames speaks of the American *trinity*—"frontier, opportunity, more"—in other words, ideas that Americans revere. (In traditional Christianity, the divine God is usually referred to as a trinity—God the father, God the Son, and God the Holy Spirit—three persons in one God.) Other words beginning with this prefix are *tricycle, triad, triplets, trio, trident,* and *trimester*.

What do these two words mean, and what is their etymology? Consult a dictionary if you are unsure.

tridentate _____

triumvirate _____

WORD FAMILIES

Speculate, speculative, speculators [paragraphs 1 and 3] Shames writes in the opening paragraph that Americans "have always been optimists, and optimists have always liked to *speculate*." This verb and its relatives, *speculative* and *speculators*, all derive from the Latin word *specere* ("to watch," "to observe"). To *speculate*, in the sense that Shames uses the word, means to buy something risky with the idea that it may make a profit in the future. The root suggests here that one cannot "see" into the future, hence the risk. The connection with "watching" or "seeing" is more apparent in these words:

spectacle — a public performance, an object of interest (in other words, something worth looking at)
spectacular — describing an impressive or elaborate display (again, describing something worth looking at)
spectator — one who attends and sees a show or an event
spectacles — eyeglasses, enabling one to see clearly

LAWRENCE SHAMES

The Hunger for More

1   Americans have always been optimists, and optimists have always liked to speculate. In Texas in the 1880s, the speculative instrument of choice was towns, and there is no tale more American than this.

2   What people would do was buy up enormous tracts of parched and vacant land, lay out a Main Street, nail together some wooden sidewalks, and start slapping up buildings. One of these buildings would be called the Grand Hotel and would have a saloon complete with swinging doors. Another might be dubbed the New Academy or the Opera House. The developers would erect a flagpole and name a church, and once the workmen had packed up and moved on, the towns would be as empty as the sky.

3   But no matter. The speculators, next, would hire people to pass out handbills in the Eastern and Midwestern cities, tracts limning the advantages of relocation to "the Athens of the South" or "the new plains Jerusalem." When persuasion failed, the builders might resort to bribery, paying people's moving costs and giving them houses, in exchange for nothing but a pledge to stay until a certain census was taken or a certain inspection made. Once the nose-count was completed, people were free to move on, and there was in fact a contingent of folks who made their living by keeping a cabin on skids, and dragging it for pay from one town to another.

4   The speculators' idea, of course, was to lure the railroad. If one could create a convincing semblance of a town, the railroad might come through it, and a real town would develop, making the speculators staggeringly rich. By these devices a man named Sanborn once owned Amarillo.

5   But railroad tracks are narrow and the state of Texas is very, very wide. For every Wichita Falls or Lubbock there were a dozen College Mounds or Belchervilles, bleached, unpeopled burgs that receded quietly into the dust, taking with them large amounts of speculators' money.

6   Still, the speculators kept right on bucking the odds and depositing empty towns in the middle of nowhere. Why did they do it? Two reasons—reasons that might be said to summarize the central fact of American economic history and that go a fair way toward explaining what is perhaps the central strand of the national character.

7   The first reason was simply that the possible returns were so enormous as to partake of the surreal, to create a climate in which ordinary logic and prudence did not seem to apply. In a boom like that of real estate when the railroad barreled through, long shots that might pay 100,000 to one seemed worth a bet.

8   The second reason, more pertinent here, is that there was a presumption that America would *keep on* booming—if not forever, then at least longer than it made sense to worry about. There would always be another gold rush, another Homestead Act, another oil strike. The next generation would always ferret out opportunities that would be still more lavish than any that had gone before. America *was* those opportunities. This was an article not just of faith, but of

strategy. You banked on the next windfall, you staked your hopes and even your self-esteem on it; and this led to a national turn of mind that might usefully be thought of as the habit of more.

9   A century, maybe two centuries, before anyone had heard the term *baby boomer,* much less *yuppie,* the habit of more had been installed as the operative truth among the economically ambitious. The habit of more seemed to suggest that there was no such thing as getting wiped out in America. A fortune lost in Texas might be recouped in Colorado. Funds frittered away on grazing land where nothing grew might flood back in as silver. There was always a second chance, or always seemed to be, in this land where growth was destiny and where expansion and purpose were the same.

10   The key was the frontier, not just as a matter of acreage, but as idea. Vast, varied, rough as rocks, America was the place where one never quite came to the end. Ben Franklin explained it to Europe even before the Revolutionary War had finished: America offered new chances to those "who, in their own Countries, where all the Lands [were] fully occupied . . . could never [emerge] from the poor Condition wherein they were born."

11   So central was this awareness of vacant space and its link to economic promise, that Frederick Jackson Turner, the historian who set the tone for much of the twentieth century's understanding of the American past, would write that it was "not the constitution, but free land . . . [that] made the democratic type of society in America." Good laws mattered; an accountable government mattered; ingenuity and hard work mattered. But those things were, so to speak, an over-lay on the natural, geographic America that was simply *there,* and whose vast and beckoning possibilities seemed to generate the ambition and the sometimes reckless liberty that would fill it. First and foremost, it was open space that pro-vided "the freedom of the individual to rise under conditions of social mobility."

12   Open space generated not just ambition, but metaphor. As early as 1835, Tocqueville was extrapolating from the fact of America's emptiness to the observation that "no natural boundary seems to be set to the efforts of man." Nor was any limit placed on what he might accomplish, since, in that heyday of the Protestant ethic, a person's rewards were taken to be quite strictly proportionate to his labors.

13   Frontier; opportunity; more. This has been the American trinity from the very start. The frontier was the backdrop and also the raw material for the streak of economic booms. The booms became the goad and also the justification for the myriad gambles and for Americans' famous optimism. The optimism, in turn, shaped the schemes and visions that were sometimes noble, sometimes appalling, always bold. The frontier, as reality and as symbol, is what has shaped the American way of doing things and the American sense of what's worth doing.

14   But there has been one further corollary to the legacy of the frontier, with its promise of ever-expanding opportunities: given that the goal—a realistic goal for most of our history—was *more,* Americans have been somewhat backward in adopting values, hopes, ambitions that have to do with things *other than* more. In America, a sense of quality has lagged far behind a sense of scale. An ideal of contentment has yet to take root in soil traditionally more hospitable to an ideal

of restless striving. The ethic of decency has been upstaged by the ethic of success. The concept of growth has been applied almost exclusively to things that can be measured, counted, weighed. And the hunger for those things that are unmeasurable but fine—the sorts of accomplishment that cannot be undone by circumstance or a shift in social fashion, the kind of serenity that cannot be shattered by tomorrow's headline—has gone largely unfulfilled, and even unacknowledged. ✳

From Lawrence Shames, *The Hunger for More: Searching for Values in an Age of Greed.* © 1989 by Lawrence Shames. Used by permission of Alfred A. Knopf, a division of Random House, Inc.

Exercises

Do not refer to the selection for Exercises A and B unless your instructor directs you to do so.

A. DETERMINING THE MAIN IDEA AND PURPOSE

Choose the best answer.

_____ 1. The main idea of the selection is that

   a. the American frontier, with its endless possibilities for opportunity and expansion, has shaped the country's national character.
   b. Americans are by nature an optimistic people who are willing to gamble and take bold risks.
   c. Americans believe in the Protestant ethic, the idea that one's rewards are proportionate to one's labors.
   d. American values are in the process of being redefined as the nation experiences diminished opportunities and declining natural resources.

_____ 2. With respect to the main idea concerning American cultural values and the American character, the writer's purpose is to

   a. criticize, even condemn, them.
   b. express regret for them.
   c. examine the historical and geographic conditions that gave rise to them.
   d. contrast them with older values and behavior patterns of earlier eras.

B. COMPREHENDING MAIN IDEAS

Choose the correct answer.

_____ 1. Shames states that American optimism and speculation began in the 1880s, specifically with the

   a. desire to escape the densely populated cities of the Midwest and the East.

    b. promise of easy money during the Gold Rush era.
    c. building of new towns in Texas.
    d. coming of the railroad to the American frontier.

_____ **2.** Ultimately, land speculators hoped to attract

    a. recent immigrants.
    b. cattle ranchers.
    c. railroads.
    d. gold prospectors.

_____ **3.** Shames writes that when speculators lost money, they did not mind too much because they presumed that

    a. the government would bail them out if they failed.
    b. they could always keep on moving west.
    c. the Homestead Act would be renewed every year.
    d. America would continue to experience booms.

_____ **4.** The crucial concept to explain the American belief in opportunity and expansion was the

    a. country's rich store of natural resources.
    b. frontier, with its unlimited space.
    c. American inclination for hard work.
    d. country's strong democratic system.

_____ **5.** Shames writes that, from the beginning, the American "trinity" has been

    a. ambition, wealth, and success.
    b. booms, gambles, and high risk.
    c. optimism, boldness, and social mobility.
    d. frontier, opportunity, and more.

_____ **6.** Shames concludes with the idea that, in America, "the concept of growth" has been applied almost exclusively to

    a. upward mobility.
    b. things that can be measured.
    c. the economy.
    d. personal accomplishments and achievements.

COMPREHENSION SCORE

Score your answers for Exercises A and B as follows:

A. No. right _____ × 2 = _____
B. No. right _____ × 1 = _____
Total points from A and B _____ × 10 = _____ percent

You may refer to the selection as you work through the remaining exercises.

C. DISTINGUISHING BETWEEN MAIN IDEAS AND SUPPORTING DETAILS

Label the following statements from the selection as follows: MI if it represents a *main idea* and SD if it represents a *supporting detail.*

1. _____ The speculators' idea, of course, was to lure the railroad.

2. _____ If one could create a convincing semblance of a town, the railroad might come through it, and a real town would develop, making the speculators staggeringly rich.

3. _____ By these devices a man named Sanborn once owned Amarillo.

4. _____ But railroad tracks are narrow and the state of Texas is very, very wide.

5. _____ For every Wichita Falls or Lubbock there were a dozen College Mounds or Belchervilles.

6. _____ These were bleached, unpeopled burgs that receded quietly into the dust, taking with them large amounts of speculators' money.

D. INTERPRETING MEANING

Where appropriate, write your answers for these questions in your own words.

1. In paragraph 2, Shames writes that the real estate speculators would "start slapping up buildings" in Texas. What does this phrase suggest about the

   quality of these buildings? _____

   _____

2. _____ Read paragraph 9 again. A good title for this paragraph is

   a. "Nineteenth-Century Baby Boomers and Yuppies."
   b. "The Habit of More."
   c. "Second Chances."
   d. "Growth and Destiny."

3. In paragraph 12, Shames discusses the concept of the frontier as metaphor.

   What exactly does he mean? _____

   _____

   _____

4. _____ Which of the following sentences from the selection *best* states the main idea of the selection as a whole?

   a. "Americans have always been optimists, and optimists have always liked to speculate."
   b. "The next generation would always ferret out opportunities that would be still more lavish than any that had gone before."
   c. "Nor was any limit placed on what he might accomplish, since, in that heyday of the Protestant ethic, a person's

rewards were taken to be quite strictly proportionate to his labors."

d. "The frontier, as reality and as symbol, is what has shaped the American way of doing things and the American sense of what's worth doing."

E. MAKING INFERENCES

For each of these statements write Y (yes) if the inference is an accurate one, N (no) if the inference is an inaccurate one, or CT (can't tell) if the writer does not give enough information to make an inference one way or another. Be sure to return to the paragraph indicated before choosing your answer. In addition, write a brief explanation in support of your answer choice.

1. _____ Developers named buildings the Grand Hotel and the New Academy and named towns "the Athens of the South" or "the new plains Jerusalem" to make them sound more impressive than they really were. [paragraphs 2 and 3]

Explanation: _____

_____

2. _____ In the 1880s, the railroad companies would put a train through a Texas town only if the population was high enough to justify it. [paragraph 4]

Explanation: _____

3. _____ The majority of real estate speculators made huge fortunes building towns in hopes of attracting the railroads. [paragraphs 6 and 7]

Explanation: _____

_____

4. _____ A prospector who lost a fortune in gold or silver or oil was almost always ruined financially. [paragraph 8]

Explanation: _____

_____

5. _____ The ambitions of today's yuppies and baby boomers can be directly traced back to the habit of more. [paragraph 9]

Explanation: _____

6. _____ If the United States were not so big geographically, it would not have developed such optimism in economic promise and expansion. [paragraphs 10–12]

Explanation: _____

_____

F. UNDERSTANDING VOCABULARY

Look through the paragraphs listed below and find a word that matches each definition. Refer to a dictionary if necessary. An example has been done for you.

Ex. very dry, arid [paragraph 2]   _____parched_____

1. representative group [3]   _____

2. outward appearance, barest trace [4]   _____

3. small towns [5]   _____

4. uncover or reveal by searching
   [8—two words]   _____

5. regained, made up for [9]   _____

6. squandered little by little, wasted [9]   _____

7. period of greatest popularity or success [12]   _____

8. stimulus, incentive [13]   _____

9. causing consternation or dismay, terrible [13]   _____

10. natural consequence or effect [14]   _____

G. USING VOCABULARY

Here are some words from the selection. Write an original sentence using each word that shows both that you know how to use the word and what it means.

1. *speculation* _____

2. *optimistic* _____

3. *prudent* _____

4. *presume* _____

5. *surreal* _____

H. PARAPHRASING EXERCISE

Here are some sentences from the selection. Write a paraphrase of each passage in the space provided.

1. In America, a sense of quality has lagged far behind a sense of scale. An ideal of contentment has yet to take root in soil traditionally more hospitable to an ideal of restless striving.

   _____

   _____

   _____

2. The concept of growth has been applied almost exclusively to things that can be measured, counted, weighed. And the hunger for those things that are unmeasurable but fine—the sorts of accomplishments that cannot be undone by circumstance or a shift in social fashion, the kind of serenity that cannot be shattered by tomorrow's headline—has gone largely unfulfilled, and even unacknowledged.

_____

_____

_____

I. LOCATING INFORMATION

Go through the article and locate any piece of information that supports this idea:

As a society, the United States is paying a price for our "hunger for more."

Identify the information by putting a star in the margin next to the sentence or by putting a bracket around the words.

J. TOPICS FOR DISCUSSION

1. Shames published the book from which this excerpt comes in 1989. How pertinent are his remarks in helping you understand these recent developments?

   • The Internet and technology boom of the late 1990s and the bursting of the technology bubble.
   • The speculative real estate bubble of the early twenty-first century, when homeowners were speculating that housing prices would continue to rise, followed by foreclosures and an economic recession.
   • The problem of rising consumer debt whereby consumers are overextended financially and unable to pay their credit card debt.

2. Shames strongly emphasizes the role of the frontier—with its symbolic and literal significance of unlimited land and unlimited opportunities. Based on your knowledge of American history and culture, what might be some other explanations that account for Americans' "hunger for more"?

K. TOPICS FOR WRITING

1. Write a paragraph or two as a personal response to this sentence from the selection: "The ethic of decency has been upstaged by the ethic of success."
2. To what extent do you accept Shames's thesis? What motivates you? Are you more committed to the typical "ideal of restless striving," as Shames calls it in his conclusion, or are you perhaps more committed to striving for an "ideal of contentment"? Ponder these two concepts and write an essay setting forth and examining your life as you are leading it now.
3. Do you use a credit card? Write an essay in which examine your use of credit, your motivations, your buying behavior, your management of credit card debt, along with your reasons and any other information that seems pertinent to the discussion.

Exploring Related Web Sites

Shames mentions in paragraph 12 the contribution of Frederick Jackson Turner to our understanding of the American past. Turner specifically espoused the frontier theory, which declared that the vast American frontier was the single element that explained America's distinctive history. Turner's "frontier thesis" is explained well on several Web sites. You can begin with this one:

www.pbs.org/weta/thewest/people/s_z/turner.htm

20

BILL BRYSON

Lonely Planet

Bill Bryson is the best-selling author of several nonfiction books on a wide variety of subjects—the English language, travel books, the universe—that are graced with a clear writing style and sense of humor. His best known travel memoirs are A Walk in the Woods *(1998), about a long trek along the Appalachian Trail, and* In a Sunburned Country *(2000), about Australia. Bryson was born in Des Moines, Iowa; he chronicles his Midwestern childhood in a recent book,* The Life and Times of the Thunderbolt Kid: A Memoir *(2006). This selection represents a portion of a chapter titled "Lonely Planet" from his 2003 book,* A Short History of Nearly Everything.

Vocabulary Preview

WORD PARTS

nano- [paragraph 4] The Greek prefix *nano-* means extremely small and has an interesting derivation. The Greek noun *nannos* means, literally, "little old man" or "dwarf." *Nanosecond*, then, refers to a very short time, or to be more specific, one billionth of a second. *Nanotechnology* refers to a new way of building electronic circuits using single atoms and molecules.

WORD FAMILIES

terra, terrestrial [paragraph 4] The Latin root noun *terra* means "earth"; *terrestrial*, the adjective derived from this root, describes things relating to the Earth and to its inhabitants. The reference to earth can be seen in several words composing this family, among them *terrain, terrarium, terrace,* and *territory.*

Sometimes people say, when they land after a particularly bumpy airplane ride,

that they are glad to be on *terra firma*. What do they mean? _____

And flower pots are frequently made of *terra cotta*, a dark red earthy color.

What language does this come from, and what does it literally mean? _____

_____

BILL BRYSON

Lonely Planet

1   It isn't easy being an organism. In the whole universe, as far as we yet know, there is only one place, an inconspicuous outpost of the Milky Way called Earth, that will sustain you, and even it can be pretty grudging.

2   From the bottom of the deepest ocean trench to the top of the highest mountain, the zone that covers nearly the whole of known life, is only something over a dozen miles–not much when set against the roominess of the cosmos at large.

3   For humans it is even worse because we happen to belong to the portion of living things that took the rash but venturesome decision 400 million years ago to crawl out of the seas and become land based and oxygen breathing. In consequence, no less than 99.5 percent of the world's habitable space by volume, according to one estimate, is fundamentally—in practical terms completely—off-limits to us.

4   It isn't simply that we can't breathe in water, but that we couldn't bear the pressures. Because water is about 1,300 times heavier than air, pressures rise swiftly as you descend—by the equivalent of one atmosphere for every ten meters (thirty-three feet) of depth. On land, if you rose to the top of a five-hundred-foot eminence—Cologne Cathedral or the Washington Monument, say—the change in pressure would be so slight as to be indiscernible. At the same depth underwater, however, your veins would collapse and your lungs would compress to the approximate dimensions of a Coke can. Amazingly, people do voluntarily dive to such depths, without breathing apparatus, for the fun of it in a sport known as free diving. Apparently the experience of having your internal organs rudely deformed is thought exhilarating (though not presumably as exhilarating as having them return to their former dimensions upon resurfacing). To reach such depths, however, divers must be dragged down, and quite briskly, by weights. Without assistance, the deepest anyone has gone and lived to talk about it afterward was an Italian named Umberto Pelizzari, who in 1992 dove to a depth of 236 feet, lingered for a nanosecond, and then shot back to the surface. In terrestrial terms, 236 feet is just slightly over the length of one New York City block. So even in our most exuberant stunts we can hardly claim to be masters of the abyss.

5   Other organisms do of course manage to deal with the pressures at depth, though quite how some of them do so is a mystery. The deepest point in the ocean is the Mariana Trench in the Pacific. There, some seven miles down, the pressures rise to over sixteen thousand pounds per square inch. We have managed once, briefly, to send humans to that depth in a sturdy diving vessel, yet it is home to colonies of amphipods, a type of crustacean similar to shrimp but transparent, which survive without any protection at all. Most oceans are of course much shallower, but even at the average ocean depth of two and a half miles the pressure is equivalent to being squashed beneath a stack of fourteen loaded cement trucks.

6   Nearly everyone, including the authors of some popular books on oceanography, assumes that the human body would crumple under the immense pressures

of the deep ocean. In fact, this appears not to be the case. Because we are made largely of water ourselves, and water is "virtually incompressible," in the words of Frances Ashcroft of Oxford University, "the body remains at the same pressure as the surrounding water, and is not crushed at depth." It is the gases inside your body, particularly in the lungs, that cause the trouble. These do compress, though at what point the compression becomes fatal is not known. Until quite recently it was thought that anyone diving to one hundred meters or so would die painfully as his or her lungs imploded or chest wall collapsed, but the free divers have repeatedly proved otherwise. It appears, according to Ashcroft, that "humans may be more like whales and dolphins than had been expected."

7   Plenty else can go wrong, however. In the days of diving suits—the sort that were connected to the surface by long hoses–divers sometimes experienced a dreaded phenomenon known as "the squeeze." This occurred when the surface pumps failed, leading to a catastrophic loss of pressure in the suit. The air would leave the suit with such violence that the hapless diver would be, all too literally, sucked up into the helmet and hosepipe. When hauled to the surface, "all that is left in the suit are his bones and some rags of flesh," the biologist J. B. S. Haldane wrote in 1947, adding for the benefit of doubters, "This has happened."

8   (Incidentally, the original diving helmet, designed in 1823 by an Englishman named Charles Deane, was intended not for diving but for firefighting. It was called a "smoke helmet," but being made of metal it was hot and cumbersome and, as Deane soon discovered, firefighters had no particular eagerness to enter burning structures in any form of attire, but most especially not in something that heated up like a kettle and made them clumsy into the bargain. In an attempt to save his investment, Deane tried it underwater and found it was ideal for salvage work.)

9   The real terror of the deep, however, is the bends—not so much because they are unpleasant, though of course they are, as because they are so much more likely. The air we breathe is 80 percent nitrogen. Put the human body under pressure, and that nitrogen is transformed into tiny bubbles that migrate into the blood and tissues. If the pressure is changed too rapidly—as with a too-quick ascent by a diver—the bubbles trapped within the body will begin to fizz in exactly the manner of a freshly opened bottle of champagne, clogging tiny blood vessels, depriving cells of oxygen, and causing pain so excruciating that sufferers are prone to bend double in agony—hence "the bends."

10   The bends have been an occupational hazard for sponge and pearl divers since time immemorial but didn't attract much attention in the Western world until the nineteenth century, and then it was among people who didn't get wet at all (or at least not very wet and not generally much above the ankles). They were caisson workers. Caissons were enclosed dry chambers built on riverbeds to facilitate the construction of bridge piers. They were filled with compressed air, and often when the workers emerged after an extended period of working under this artificial pressure they experienced mild symptoms like tingling or itchy skin. But an unpredictable few felt more insistent pain in the joints and occasionally collapsed in agony, sometimes never to get up again.

11   It was all most puzzling. Sometimes workers would go to bed feeling fine, but wake up paralyzed. Sometimes they wouldn't wake up at all. Ashcroft

relates a story concerning the directors of a new tunnel under the Thames who held a celebratory banquet as the tunnel neared completion. To their consternation their champagne failed to fizz when uncorked in the compressed air of the tunnel. However, when at length they emerged into the fresh air of a London evening, the bubbles sprang instantly to fizziness, memorably enlivening the digestive process.

12　　Apart from avoiding high-pressure environments altogether, only two strategies are reliably successful against the bends. The first is to suffer only a very short exposure to the changes in pressure. That is why the free divers I mentioned earlier can descend to depths of five hundred feet without ill effect. They don't stay under long enough for the nitrogen in their system to dissolve into their tissues. The other solution is to ascend by careful stages. This allows the little bubbles of nitrogen to dissipate harmlessly.

13　　A great deal of what we know about surviving at extremes is owed to the extraordinary father-and-son team of John Scott and J. B. S. Haldane. Even by the demanding standards of British intellectuals, the Haldanes were outstandingly eccentric. The senior Haldane was born in 1860 to an aristocratic Scottish family (his brother was Viscount Haldane) but spent most of his career in comparative modesty as a professor of physiology at Oxford. He was famously absent-minded. Once after his wife had sent him upstairs to change for a dinner party he failed to return and was discovered asleep in bed in his pajamas. When roused, Haldane explained that he had found himself disrobing and assumed it was bedtime. His idea of a vacation was to travel to Cornwall to study hookworm in miners. Aldous Huxley, the novelist grandson of T. H. Huxley, who lived with the Haldanes for a time, parodied him, a touch mercilessly, as the scientist Edward Tantamount in the novel *Point Counter Point*.

14　　Haldane's gift to diving was to work out the rest intervals necessary to manage an ascent from the depths without getting the bends, but his interests ranged across the whole of physiology, from studying altitude sickness in climbers to the problems of heatstroke in desert regions. He had a particular interest in the effects of toxic gases on the human body. To understand more exactly how carbon monoxide leaks killed miners, he methodically poisoned himself, carefully taking and measuring his own blood samples the while. He quit only when he was on the verge of losing all muscle control and his blood saturation level had reached 56 percent—a level, as Trevor Norton notes in his entertaining history of diving, *Stars Beneath the Sea*, only fractionally removed from nearly certain lethality.

15　　Haldane's son Jack, known to posterity as J. B. S., was a remarkable prodigy who took an interest in his father's work almost from infancy. At the age of three he was overheard demanding peevishly of his father, "But is it oxyhaemoglobin or carboxyhaemoglobin?" Throughout his youth, the young Haldane helped his father with experiments. By the time he was a teenager, the two often tested gases and gas masks together, taking turns to see how long it took them to pass out.

16　　Though J. B. S. Haldane never took a degree in science (he studied classics at Oxford), he became a brilliant scientist in his own right, mostly in Cambridge. The biologist Peter Medawar, who spent his life around mental Olympians, called him "the cleverest man I ever knew." Huxley likewise parodied the younger Haldane in his novel *Antic Hay,* but also used his ideas on genetic manipulation of humans as the basis for the plot of *Brave New World.* Among many other achievements, Haldane played a central role in marrying Darwinian principles of evolution to the genetic work of Gregor Mendel to produce what is known to geneticists as the Modern Synthesis.

17   Perhaps uniquely among human beings, the younger Haldane found World War I "a very enjoyable experience" and freely admitted that he "enjoyed the opportunity of killing people." He was himself wounded twice. After the war he became a successful popularizer of science and wrote twenty-three books (as well as over four hundred scientific papers). His books are still thoroughly readable and instructive, though not always easy to find. He also became an enthusiastic Marxist. It has been suggested, not altogether cynically, that this was out of a purely contrarian instinct, and that if he had been born in the Soviet Union he would have been a passionate monarchist. At all events, most of his articles first appeared in the Communist *Daily Worker.*

18   Whereas his father's principal interests concerned miners and poisoning, the younger Haldane became obsessed with saving submariners and divers from the unpleasant consequences of their work. With Admiralty funding he acquired a decompression chamber that he called the "pressure pot." This was a metal cylinder into which three people at a time could be sealed and subjected to tests of various types, all painful and nearly all dangerous. Volunteers might be required to sit in ice water while breathing "aberrant atmosphere" or subjected to rapid changes of pressurization. In one experiment, Haldane simulated a dangerously hasty ascent to see what would happen. What happened was that the dental fillings in his teeth exploded. "Almost every experiment," Norton writes, "ended with someone having a seizure, bleeding, or vomiting." The chamber was virtually soundproof, so the only way for occupants to signal unhappiness or distress was to tap insistently on the chamber wall or to hold up notes to a small window.

19   On another occasion, while poisoning himself with elevated levels of oxygen, Haldane had a fit so severe that he crushed several vertebrae. Collapsed lungs were a routine hazard. Perforated eardrums were quite common, but, as Haldane reassuringly noted in one of his essays, "the drum generally heals up; and if a hole remains in it, although one is somewhat deaf, one can blow tobacco smoke out of the ear in question, which is a social accomplishment."

20   What was extraordinary about this was not that Haldane was willing to subject himself to such risk and discomfort in the pursuit of science, but that he had no trouble talking colleagues and loved ones into climbing into the chamber, too. Sent on a simulated descent, his wife once had a fit that lasted thirteen minutes. When at last she stopped bouncing across the floor, she was helped to her feet and sent home to cook dinner. Haldane happily employed whoever happened to be around, including on one memorable occasion a former prime minister of Spain, Juan Negrín. Dr. Negrín complained afterward of minor tingling and "a curious velvety sensation on the lips" but otherwise seems to have escaped unharmed. He may have considered himself very lucky. A similar experiment

with oxygen deprivation left Haldane without feeling in his buttocks and lower spine for six years.

21   Among Haldane's many specific preoccupations was nitrogen intoxication. For reasons that are still poorly understood, beneath depths of about a hundred feet nitrogen becomes a powerful intoxicant. Under its influence divers had been known to offer their air hoses to passing fish or decide to try to have a smoke break. It also produced wild mood swings. In one test, Haldane noted, the subject "alternated between depression and elation, at one moment begging to be decompressed because he felt 'bloody awful' and the next minute laughing and attempting to interfere with his colleague's dexterity test." In order to measure the rate of deterioration in the subject, a scientist had to go into the chamber with the volunteer to conduct simple mathematical tests. But after a few minutes, as Haldane later recalled, "the tester was usually as intoxicated as the testee, and often forgot to press the spindle of his stopwatch, or to take proper notes." The cause of the inebriation is even now a mystery. It is thought that it may be the same thing that causes alcohol intoxication, but as no one knows for certain what causes *that* we are none the wiser. At all events, without the greatest care, it is easy to get in trouble once you leave the surface world.

22   Which brings us back (well, nearly) to our earlier observation that Earth is not the easiest place to be an organism, even if it is the only place. Of the small portion of the planet's surface that is dry enough to stand on, a surprisingly large amount is too hot or cold or dry or steep or lofty to be of much use to us. Partly, it must be conceded, this is our fault. In terms of adaptability, humans are pretty amazingly useless. Like most animals, we don't much like really hot places, but because we sweat so freely and easily stroke, we are especially vulnerable. In the worst circumstances—on foot without water in a hot desert—most people will grow delirious and keel over, possibly never to rise again, in no more than six or seven hours. We are no less helpless in the face of cold. Like all mammals, humans are good at generating heat but—because we are so nearly hairless—not good at keeping it. Even in quite mild weather half the calories you burn go to keep your body warm. Of course, we can counter these frailties to a large extent by employing clothing and shelter, but even so the portions of Earth on which we are prepared or able to live are modest indeed: just 12 percent of the total land area, and only 4 percent of the whole surface if you include the seas.

23   Yet when you consider conditions elsewhere in the known universe, the wonder is not that we use so little of our planet but that we have managed to find a planet that we can use even a bit of. You have only to look at our own solar system—or, come to that, Earth at certain periods in its own history—to appreciate that most places are much harsher and much less amenable to life than our mild, blue watery globe. ✳

Exercises

Do not refer to the selection for Exercises A–C unless your instructor directs you to do so.

A. DETERMINING THE MAIN IDEA AND PURPOSE

Choose the best answer.

_____ 1. The main idea of the selection is that

    a. because so much of the planet's environment is not available or not usable to human beings, it's remarkable that there is at least a small part of the Earth where we can live.

    b. Unlike human beings, most other organisms are able to inhabit various regions on Earth because their organs have adapted to the atmosphere's requirements.

    c. human beings occupy only 12 percent of Earth's total land mass.

    d. it is only because of clothing and shelter that we have been able to adapt to the Earth's varied environments.

_____ 2. The writer's purpose is to

    a. explain how evolution allowed living things to survive on earth after emerging from the ocean.

    b. explain the many problems deep sea divers face when diving to great depths.

    c. examine the and obstacles that human beings face in trying to use the Earth's environment, in particular the sea.

    d. trace some unique experiments done to determine survival rates in the ocean.

B. COMPREHENDING MAIN IDEAS

Choose the correct answer.

_____ 1. When compared to the cosmos, or universe, as a whole, the total zone where organisms can live, from the bottom of the ocean to the top of the tallest mountain, is

    a. as big as the cosmos itself.

    b. very small, only about a dozen miles.

    c. very large, more than 100 miles.

    d. incalculable, as there is no way to measure the space scientifically.

_____ 2. The primary difficulty for divers who descend to great depths in the ocean is

    a. finding suitable diving equipment that allows them to breathe.

    b. the intense cold, which is difficult to withstand for very long.

    c. the presence of dangerous organisms, particularly sharks and giant squid.

    d. the pressure water creates.

_____ **3.** The most dangerous and painful condition modern deep sea divers face is

    a. the bends.
    b. the squeeze.
    c. tingling or itchy skin.
    d. the blood's getting cold and fizzing like champagne bubbles.

_____ **4.** In order to test the effects of toxic gases, in particular carbon monoxide, on the human body, the Scottish scientist John Scott Haldane

    a. used his son J. B. S. as a sort of human guinea pig.
    b. became a deep sea diver.
    c. poisoned himself and studied his own blood samples.
    d. studied altitude sickness in mountain climbers.

_____ **5.** Little of the Earth's surface is habitable for human beings primarily because

    a. the planet's surface has too many extremes—it's too hot, too cold, or too dry, and so forth.
    b. most people want to congregate near the coasts, where the temperatures are mild.
    c. we haven't yet figured out how to adapt our bodies to harsh climates.
    d. the soil isn't suitable for agriculture, making human life impossible to sustain.

_____ **6.** Bryson concludes that most humans are actually pretty useless when it comes to adaptability, primarily because we

    a. a lack the ability to live in the ocean or at high elevations.
    b. are vulnerable to extremes in both high and low temperatures.
    c. find it difficult to migrate, unlike other organisms.
    d. have not yet found a way to adapt to life outside our own solar system.

COMPREHENSION SCORE

Score your answers for Exercises A and B as follows:

A. No. right _____ × 2 = _____
B. No. right _____ × 1 = _____
Total points from A and B _____ × 10 = _____ percent

C. SEQUENCING

These sentences from one paragraph in the selection have been scrambled. Read the sentences and choose the sequence that puts them back into logical order. Do not refer to the original selection.

   1 The first is to suffer only a very short exposure to the changes in pressure.
   2 They don't stay under long enough for the nitrogen in their system to

dissolve into their tissues. **3** Apart from avoiding high-pressure environments altogether, only two strategies are reliably successful against the bends. **4** That is why the free divers I mentioned earlier can descend to depths of five hundred feet without ill effect. **5** This allows the little bubbles of nitrogen to dissipate harmlessly. **6** The other solution is to ascend by careful stages.

_____ Which of the following represents the correct sequence for these sentences?

a. 3, 1, 4, 2, 6, 5
b. 1, 4, 5, 3, 6, 2
c. 3, 1, 5, 6, 2, 5
d. 4, 2, 1, 3, 5, 6
e. Correct as written.

You may refer to the selection as you work through the remaining exercises.

D. LOCATING INFORMATION

Why was the father-son team of scientists, John Scott and J. B. S. Haldane, so helpful to science in general and to future generations of deep sea divers in particular? Look through the selection from paragraphs 13–21 and list four or five details that provide evidence about their accomplishments.

_____

_____

_____

_____

_____

E. DISTINGUISHING BETWEEN MAIN IDEAS AND SUPPORTING DETAILS

Label the following sentences rewritten from paragraph 9 in the selection as follows: MI if it represents a *main idea* and SD if it represents a *supporting detail*.

1. _____ The real terror of the deep is the bends, which are not only unpleasant but also likely.

2. _____ The air we breathe is 80 percent nitrogen.

3. _____ When the human body is put under pressure, the nitrogen is transformed into tiny bubbles that migrate into the blood and tissues.

4. _____ If the pressure is changed too rapidly—as, for example, when a diver ascends too quickly—the bubbles trapped in the body begin to fizz just as do the bubbles in champagne.

5. _____ The bubbles clog the tiny blood vessels and deprive the cells of oxygen.

6. _____ The pain is so excruciating that sufferers are prone to double over in agony, hence, "the bends."

F. MAKING INFERENCES

Each of these inference questions pertains to information in paragraph 21. For each of these statements write Y (yes) if the inference is an accurate one, N (no) if the inference is an inaccurate one, or CT (can't tell) if the writer does not give enough information to make an inference one way or another.

1. _____ Scientists have studied the effects of nitrogen on divers but have not reached any definite conclusions.

2. _____ When divers go to depths over 100 feet, nitrogen acts like an intoxicant so that they begin to exhibit very bizarre behavior under water.

3. _____ J. B. S. Haldane was the first scientist to study nitrogen intoxication.

4. _____ Doing experiments at great depths to study the effects of nitrogen was just as dangerous for the experimenters as it was for the subjects.

5. _____ Scientists now understand that intoxication from nitrogen is exactly the same as intoxication from consuming too much alcohol.

G. UNDERSTANDING VOCABULARY

Look through the paragraphs listed below and find a word that matches each definition. Refer to a dictionary if necessary. An example has been done for you.

Ex. not noticeable or obvious
[paragraphs 1–2]   ____inconspicuous____

1. done with boldness or haste [2–3]   _____

2. invigorating, stimulating, exciting [4]   _____

3. difficult to perceive [4]   _____

4. a place of great depth; here, the ocean [4]   _____

5. collapsed from the outside in [6]   _____

6. to disperse, to go away until almost
   disappeared [11–12]   _____

7. made fun of, imitated in a humorous
   manner [15–16]   _____

8. future generations [15–16]   _____

9. negatively, skeptically, pessimistically
   [17–18]   _____

10. deviating from the proper or normal course
    [18–19]   _____

H. USING VOCABULARY

From the following list of vocabulary words, choose a word that fits in each blank according to both the grammatical structure of the sentence and the context. Use each word in the list only once. Do not change the form of the word. (Note that there are more words than blanks.)

cumbersome	dissipate	verge	toxic
exhilarating	abyss	catastrophic	dexterity
posterity	excruciating	lethal	prone

1. Even when divers wear _____ diving equipment, they experience an _____ sensation when they dive deep into the ocean, which is sometimes called a watery _____.

2. Before diving suits were improved, divers had to be really careful because they could experience a _____ loss of pressure, making them _____ to suffer _____ pain from a dangerous condition called "the squeeze."

3. John Scott Haldane, a Scottish scientist, conducted experiments to determine the effect of _____ gases on the human body, but during one experiment, he was on the _____ of losing all control of his muscles after he took a nearly _____ dose.

I. PARAPHRASING EXERCISE

Here are some sentences from the selection. Write a paraphrase of each passage in the space provided.

1. From the bottom of the deepest ocean trench to the top of the highest mountain, the zone that covers nearly the whole of known life, is only something over a dozen miles—not much when set against the roominess of the cosmos at large.

   _____

   _____

   _____

2. You have only to look at our own solar system—or, come to that, Earth at certain periods in its own history—to appreciate that most places are much harsher and much less amenable to life than our mild, blue watery globe.

   _____

   _____

   _____

J. SUMMARIZING EXERCISE

Bryson spends a significant amount of space in paragraphs 9–12 discussing the bends. Write a summary of this section of the essay. The original is approximately 425 words, so your summary should be between 75 and 100 words.

_____

_____

_____

_____

_____

K. TOPICS FOR DISCUSSION

1. What seems to be Bryson's main purpose in this selection, apart from conveying information about the suitability of the Earth as a dwelling place for human beings?
2. What assumptions does he make about his audience? Does one need to have a strong scientific background to understand what Bryson is talking about?
3. Given the scope of his discussion, does Bryson spend too much time talking about the Haldanes and about the problems deep sea divers face when they descend to great depths, or do these parts somehow serve his larger purpose? Explain your thinking.

L. TOPICS FOR WRITING

1. In paragraph 9 Bryson describes the effects of the bends on deep sea divers. Taking any ailment—for example, the common cold, flu, measles, poison ivy rash, or something similar—write two paragraphs in which you explain the symptoms and physical effects this particular ailment has on the human body.
2. Bryson is concerned throughout the selection with the problem of adaptability to climate. Take the particular climate or environment that you live in, and in two or three paragraphs, explain its characteristics and its suitability for human settlement and for agriculture, including both positive and negative features. For example, where I live, on the California coast near Half Moon Bay south of San Francisco, the climate is temperate and mild. The morning fog cools the temperature, making the climate perfect for growing artichokes, peas, and pumpkins. Yet the fog can also pose treacherous conditions for fishermen.

Exploring Related Web Sites

- Look at photos of the Mariana Trench, the deepest part of the Pacific Ocean (see paragraph 5). Go to Google or your favorite search engine and type "Mariana Trench" in the search box.

- A great deal of information is available online about the bends, otherwise known as decompression syndrome. The following online article from *New Scientist* explains that ancient fossils suggest that whales showed signs of suffering this condition.

    www.newscientist.com/channel/life/dn13862-early-whales-got-the-bends.html?feedId=online-news_rss20

- You will recall from the Vocabulary Preview that the prefix *nano-* refers to something very small. Now the Indian automobile maker Tata has released a new car called the Nano, the world's smallest car. It costs $2,500. In the search box of your favorite search engine, type in "nano, car from India," and you will find several articles and photographs. Here is one:

    http://jalopnik.com/343003/the-2500-tata-nano-unveiled-in-india

PART FOUR

Mastering Reading about Complex Ideas

In order to comprehend nonfiction (including textbooks), you'll need the ability to recognize two important features of this kind of writing: patterns of development and transitional elements.

Patterns of Development

The patterns of development and their functions are listed here:

PATTERNS OF DEVELOPMENT				
List of Facts or Details	**Examples**	**Reason—Cause and Effect**	**Description of a Process**	**Contrast**
Includes factual details to support the main idea.	Uses specific instances of something more general to support the main idea.	Offers reasons (shows causes and effects) that explain why as support for the main idea.	Explains the steps one needs to follow to support the main idea.	Sets two subjects side by side and examines their differences to support the main idea.

Let's say that you are wrestling with a big decision that you must make about your future. You know that you are interested in helping people, and you come up with a list of careers where such an interest would be required for someone to succeed and be happy. On a sheet of paper you note the following: nurse, doctor, teacher, charity worker, mental health worker, social worker. What you have done is provide *examples,* specific instances of careers that involve helping others.

Now you have another decision: Should you apply to the four-year state university 50 miles away or should you study for the first two years at your local community college and then transfer? Again, you write down the good and bad aspects of both institutions and analyze their differences. Now you're *contrasting.* And when a friend asks you why you want to become, say, a social worker, you come up with some *reasons* that the field of social work appeals to you.

These logical processes, which we do all the time in our daily lives, are also present in writing. Called *patterns of development*, they refer to the internal logic of a passage, the way the writer gets his or her ideas across, the pattern that the writer imposes on his or her material. The choice of the appropriate pattern of development depends on the subject. But your starting point, as the reader, is to recognize that these patterns of development pertain to our thought processes. When looked at this way, you can see that you are already familiar with them. In this introduction we will examine each briefly and illustrate them with some short passages. Studying these patterns will help you keep on track as you read and allow you to follow the writer's thinking process.

LIST OF FACTS OR DETAILS

The pattern of *listing facts* or *listing details* is perhaps the simplest one to recognize. Following the main idea, each supporting sentence presents factual evidence to support the main assertion. Consider this passage from Selection 12 by Virginia Morell. You may recall the discussion of Betsy, the border collie, who has an amazing grasp of language. In a sidebar to the article (not reprinted in the selection), Morell supports the main idea that Betsy has an unusually large vocabulary.

How much thought goes on behind those eyes? A lot, in this case. Six-year-old "Betsy" can put names to objects faster than a great ape, and her vocabulary is at 340 words and counting. Her smarts showed up early: At ten weeks she would sit on command and was soon picking up on names of items and rushing to retrieve them—ball, rope, paper, box, keys, and dozens more. She now knows at least 15 people by name, and in scientific tests she's proved skilled at linking photographs with the objects they represent. Says her owner, "She's a dog in a human [pack]. We're learning her language, and she's learning ours."

—Virginia Morell, "Minds of Their Own," *National Geographic*

EXAMPLES

An *example* is a specific instance of something more general. As you saw earlier, nursing and social work are examples of fields involving helping people. Consider this paragraph about the Ohlone Indians, who inhabited parts of Northern

California hundreds of years ago. Malcolm Margolin begins with the statement that, in comparison to Europeans, Ohlones seemed lazy. (You can tell that the writer is challenging this observation because he puts the word *laziness* in quotation marks.) The examples have been briefly annotated for you in the margin. Note that the first example is preceded with the helpful transitional phrase, "for example," and the next three little examples follow logically from that connector.

Main idea: Episodic harvesting explains "laziness"

Examples: deer hunting—arduous

Acorn, seed, and salmon harvests—hard work but for short periods

No crops to cultivate, animals to tend, ditches to dig

The episodic character of the harvesting also helps explain another much noted Ohlone characteristic: their so-called "laziness." For them hard work came only in spurts. Deer hunting, for example, was an arduous pursuit that demanded fasting, abstinence, great physical strength, and single-mindedness of purpose. The acorn harvest, the seed harvest, and the salmon harvest also involved considerable work for short periods of time. But when the work was over, there was little else to do. Unlike agricultural people, the Ohlones had no fields to plow, seeds to plant, crops to cultivate, weeds to pull, domestic animals to care for, or irrigation ditches to dig or maintain. So at the end of a harvest they often gave themselves over to "entire indolence," as one visitor described it—a habit that infuriated the Europeans who assumed that laziness was sinful and that hard work was not just a virtue for a God-given condition of human life.

—Malcolm Margolin, *The Ohlone Way*

REASONS—CAUSE AND EFFECT

The cause–effect relationship means that an *effect*—a situation, a problem, a trend—has *reasons* for its existence. In writing, this pattern answers the question "why?" Every effect (every situation, every problem, every trend) has at least one cause or reason to explain it—and often multiple reasons.

If you write, for example, "Vinh passed his English class because he studied hard every day and got help from a tutor," the *effect* is that Vinh passed his class, and the *reasons* or the *causes* are that he studied hard and had a tutor.

Students often find it difficult to separate the cause and the effect in their reading, so let's practice with a few examples. In this excerpt from Judith Lewis's article, "Walk on the Wilshire Side," examine the *second* sentence. In the spaces below, write the part of the sentence that expresses the *cause* and the part that expresses the *effect*.

Walking it [Wilshire Boulevard] is a proclamation of freedom for kids from the neighborhoods that surround Crenshaw. Because of the strife and stray bullets of warring gangs, few venture far from their home turf, and fewer still do so on foot.

Cause: _____

Effect: _____

Now analyze this sentence to identify its cause–effect relationship. It's from Tim Guest's selection, "Linden Lab's Second Life: Dreamers of the Dream."

What made Second Life different from most virtual worlds was that Linden Lab sculpted only the landscape.

Cause: _____

Effect: _____

Now do the same thing with this sentence from Frances Moore Lappé and Jeffrey Perkins's article, "The Two Sides of Fear." Which is the cause and which is the effect?

Living in fear robs us of life.

Cause: _____

Effect: _____

Notice that the words "because" or "since" do not have to be present in a cause-effect relationship. Often, you will have to infer the pattern. For example, study this final passage from Cornelia Bailey's selection, "Still Gullah." In the left margin, write *cause* next to the situation. Then number each of the effects as she lists them.

> Bit by bit our communities dispersed, so that now there is only one main settlement here—Hog's Hummock in the south. Our churches have only a handful of worshipers left, and our organizations such as the Farmers Alliance are gone. We grow few crops and hardly hunt game on the island any more. Instead we catch the ferry to the mainland to do our supermarket and other shopping. There are no more weeknight meetings in local prayer houses, no more hot-supper evenings at which young people meet. . . .

So the passage consists of one cause followed by seven specific effects. Notice, too, that the passage actually combines two patterns: a list of details that are also effects of the community's loss of population.

In this excerpt from Selection 7, "The Life and Death of a Western Gladiator," Charles Finney discusses the situation faced by a newborn diamondback rattlesnake.

> The direct rays of the sun could, in a short time, kill him. If the temperature dropped too low he would freeze. Without food he would starve. Without moisture he would die of dehydration. If a man or a horse stepped on him he would be crushed.

Here is the passage printed again, with the cause–effect relationships marked for you. The causes are set in colored blocks and the effects are underlined. The arrows show the relationship between the two.

> The direct rays of the sun could, in a short time, kill him. If the temperature dropped too low he would freeze. Without food he would starve. Without moisture he would die of dehydration. If a man or horse stepped on him he would be crushed.

Here is another example of a paragraph using the cause and effect pattern; however, unlike the one about the causes of death for a baby rattlesnake, this one begins with a single *cause* or *reason*, followed by a series of *effects*. Follow the annotations as you read.

Cause: Civil rights movement

Effects: gave us Dr. King; each other; material things; knowledge; pride; gave men a purpose; broke black servitude; heroes & leaders; hope; gave us history; a call to life

What good was the civil rights movement? If it had just given this country Dr. King, a leader of conscience for once in our lifetime, it would have been enough. . . . If the civil rights movement is "dead," and if it gave us nothing else, it gave us each other forever. It gave some of us bread, some of us shelter, some of us knowledge and pride, all of us comfort. It gave us our children, our husbands, our brothers, our fathers, as men reborn and with a purpose for living. It broke the pattern of black servitude in this country. . . . It gave us history and men far greater than Presidents. It gave us heroes, selfless men of courage and strength, for our little boys to follow. It gave us hope for tomorrow. It called us to life.

Because we live, it can never die.

—Alice Walker, "The Civil Rights Movement: What Good Was It?" *American Scholar*

DESCRIPTION OF A PROCESS

If you want to make an omelet for your Sunday morning breakfast, you could follow a cookbook recipe or you could follow your instincts. Either way, you would go through a *process*, a series of steps that, if followed in order, would produce something edible. First you would crack three eggs into a bowl and beat them. Then you would heat a little butter in your pan. Next, you would grate some cheese and chop some onions, add the eggs to the pan, and so forth. Writers use the process pattern for two primary purposes: (1) to show how to do something, for example, how to make an omelet, how to change a flat tire, or how to burn CDs; or (2) to show how something occurred, for example, how glaciers formed during the Ice Age or how a surfer tackles a big wave.

In this illustrative paragraph, Sophie Petit-Zerman discusses the phenomenon of laughter and answers this question: "Is it true that laughing can make us healthier?" Each step in the process is numbered to help you follow the discussion:

[Laughter is] undoubtedly the best medicine. For one thing it's exercise. [1] It activates the cardiovascular system, so heart rate and blood pressure increase, [2] then the arteries dilate, causing blood pressure to fall again. [3] Repeated short, strong contractions of the chest muscles, diaphragm, and abdomen increase blood flow into our internal organs, and forced respiration—the *ha! ha!*—makes sure that this blood is well oxygenated. [4] Muscle tension decreases, and indeed [5] we may temporarily lose control of our limbs, as in the expression "weak with laughter."

—Sophie Petit-Zerman, "No Laughing Matter," *Discover*

CONTRAST

How does a Honda differ from a Toyota? How are high school English classes different from college English courses? What are the major differences between the two sports Web sites espn.com and sportsline.com? When a writer sets two subjects side by side and examines their differences, he or she is using the *contrast* pattern. In this example, Bruno Bettelheim explores the main idea stated in the first sentence by contrasting fairy tales and dreams. Again, study the annotations:

Differences between fairy tales & dreams

Open vs. disguised wish fulfillment

Relief of pressure and happy ending vs. lack of solution for inner pressures

> There are, of course, very significant differences between fairy tales and dreams. For example, in dreams more often than not the wish fulfillment is disguised, while in fairy tales much of it is openly expressed. To a considerable degree, dreams are the result of inner pressures which have found no relief, of problems which beset a person to which he knows no solution and to which the dream finds none. The fairy tale does the opposite: it projects the relief of all pressures and not only offers ways to solve problems but promises that a "happy" solution will be found.
>
> —Bruno Bettelheim, *The Uses of Enchantment: The Meaning and Importance of Fairy Tales*

Transitional Elements

TYPES OF TRANSITIONS

- Additional Information
- Examples or Illustrations
- Cause–Effect Connections
- Chronology
- Contrasts

Transitions or *transitional elements* make the logical relationships between ideas clear. They are sometimes called *markers*, because they "mark" the place where a writer shifts ideas or indicates a particular logical connection. In this way, they serve as a bridge between ideas, helping us follow the writer's thinking, keeping us on track, and showing us where a shift—sometimes a very subtle shift—in thought begins. As you will see, transitions can be either single words or phrases. And sometimes an entire paragraph may be used in this way, pointing back to the preceding paragraph and at the same time pointing ahead to the next idea in the chain of ideas.

Some writers use lots of transitions; others use none at all. But when they are present, they are useful. Contrary to what some students have been taught, transitions do not necessarily come at the beginning of sentences. They can appear in the middle of sentences or even at the end. By studying a number of examples, you will quickly become proficient at locating transitions. The most common types of transitional elements follow. Each is illustrated by a passage from a reading in Parts One through Three that you may have already read.

TRANSITIONS THAT INDICATE ADDITIONAL INFORMATION IS COMING

These transitions are most commonly used in the first two patterns: listing facts and details and offering examples. Here are some examples:

and
next
first, second . . .
besides
in the same way
in addition
further
furthermore
moreover
also

EXAMPLES FROM THE READINGS

- The only effect on my writing I have noticed is that the darkness lifted. I can still channel anger, humor, and irony, the three speeds I need on my editorial stick shift. *And* I'm not the only one who senses the change. Everyone sees the difference, even readers.

  —Chris Rose, "Hell and Back"

- Markman has shown that instead of testing endless hypotheses about each word's meaning, kids start from three basic assumptions. *First*, they figure that labels refer to whole objects, not parts or qualities. *Second*, they expect labels to denote classes of things . . . rather than individual items. *Third*, they assume that anything with a name can have only one.

  —Geoffrey Cowley, "The Language Explosion"

TRANSITIONS THAT INTRODUCE EXAMPLES OR ILLUSTRATIONS

These transitions signal that a writer is going to give an example or illustration to reinforce a more general idea. Here are some examples:

for example
for instance
to illustrate
such as
as a case in point
consider the following
namely

EXAMPLES FROM THE READINGS

- A 1993 U.S. Department of Education report on illiteracy says 21–23 percent of U.S. adults—about 40 million—read minimally, enough to decipher an uncomplicated meeting announcement. Another 25–28 percent read and write only slightly better. *For instance*, they can fill out a simple form.

  —Richard Wolkomir, "Making Up for Lost Time: The Rewards of Reading at Last"

- Dolphins often synchronize their movements in the wild, *such as* leaping and diving side by side, but scientists don't know what signal they use to stay so tightly coordinated.

  —Virginia Morell, "Minds of Their Own"

TRANSITIONS THAT SHOW CAUSE–EFFECT CONNECTIONS

Although not as common, a few transitional elements signal a cause–effect relationship. Interestingly, there are few transitional or connector words that indicate *cause*. The writer can show cause only by using words like *because* or *since* or *given* or *for* (in the sense of "because") or by writing a phrase like *that being the case* or *one reason for*, or something similar. There are, however, a few transitions that indicate *effect* or *result*:

> as a result
> consequently
> therefore
> thus
> then
> hence

EXAMPLES FROM THE READINGS

- New Caledonian crows are among the most skilled of tool-making and tool-using birds, forming probes and hooks from sticks and leaf stems to poke into the crowns of the palm trees, where fat grubs hide. *Since* these birds, like chimpanzees, make and use tools, researchers can look for similarities in the evolutionary processes that shaped their brains.

  —Virginia Morell, "Minds of Their Own"

- I wanted to meet nonreaders *because* I could not imagine being unable to decipher a street signs, or words printed on supermarket jars, or stories in a book.

  —Richard Wolkomir, "Making Up for Lost Time: The Rewards of Reading at Last"

TRANSITIONS THAT SHOW CHRONOLOGICAL ORDER OR TIME PROGRESSION

This group of transitions is most evident in the process pattern or in narrative writing. Writers use them to ensure a logical progression of steps or a sequence of events. Study these examples:

then
meanwhile
later
eventually
after a few days
next
in 2009

TRANSITIONS THAT SHOW CONTRAST

This last group of transitions helps keep the reader on track when the writer is moving back and forth between two subjects to show the differences between them. Consider these examples:

but
yet
still
however
nevertheless
nonetheless
on the other hand
in contrast
instead
whereas

EXAMPLES FROM THE READINGS

- Then he takes her home, and she lies on her bed, a conflicted, tortured soul, and weeps until dawn, *whereas* when Roger gets back to his place, he opens a bag of Doritos. . . .

  —Dave Barry, "Tips for Women: How to Have a Relationship with a Guy"

- At school things were no better. The teacher's instructions would wash over me like a wave; I heard the sounds *but* didn't understand their purpose. *But* eventually, slowly and unexpectedly the English language revealed itself to me.

  —Rose Guilbault, "School Days"

- He could see things well enough within his limited range, but a five-inch-long snake can command no great field of vision. . . . *On the other hand*, he had a pit, a deep pock mark between eye and nostril. Unique, this organ was sensitive to animal heat.

  —Charles Finney, "The Life and Death of a Western Gladiator"

Some Final Considerations

As mentioned earlier, a writer is under no obligation to use transitional elements to make the your reading easier. When a writer doesn't use transitions, how can you maintain focus, keep on track, and follow along with the writer's words? As stated frequently in this text, reading with a pencil in your hand—actively annotating—can help. Also actively thinking about the connections between ideas can help. To illustrate, consider this short excerpt by Tim Guest from his discussion of the online virtual world, Second Life. It has only four transitions, which are underlined. However, there are numerous logical patterns embedded in the sentences. I have noted them in the left margin.

chronological— establishes time

contrast

detail

time (next step in the narrative)

more details

time progression

contrast

cause–effect

example

another example

cause–effect

<u>By June 1999</u>—after putting himself through college with the profits from his own software company—Philip decided that what he wanted wasn't the ability to change the real world, <u>but</u> to conquer it and replace it with something better: a virtual world with no barrier between thought and action. He left his position as chief technology officer of RealNetworks, which had bought out his video streaming software, and joined forces with an old colleague to form Linden Lab. Their vision was a renovation of Philip's childhood dream: a world where people could build whatever they liked, and become whoever they wanted.

Right from the beginning of online worlds, the players were quicker than the developers to recognize the possibilities in their new virtual lives. The designers of EverQuest were stunned when they discovered players were getting married online. In The Sims Online, you can combine objects, but not create new ones, and the residents worked hard to overcome this limitation. <u>In one case</u>, a group of Sims residents decided they wanted a piano, <u>so</u> they built one out of a desk and chairs, with cigars for piano keys.

Of course, people don't really read this way; that is, it seems a bit tedious to label ideas like this. Still, it *does* show the process, and with practice, that process of seeing the logical connections between thoughts becomes so automatic that you no longer have to think about them as you read. With practice and experience, you will get better at seeing these connections, and your reading comprehension will be much the better for it.

Finally, pay attention to repeated words and phrases in what you read. For example, read this opening paragraph from "Long Walk to Freedom" by Nelson Mandela, one of the selections that you will read in Part Four. Study the highlighted words and phrases:

> When I was sixteen, the regent decided that it was time that I became a man. In Xhosa tradition, this is achieved through one means only: circumcision. In my tradition, an uncircumcised male cannot be heir to his father's wealth, cannot marry or officiate in tribal rituals. An uncircumcised Xhosa man is a contradiction in terms, for he is not considered a man at all, but a boy. For the Xhosa people, circumcision represents the formal incorporation of males into society. It is not just a surgical procedure, but a lengthy and elaborate ritual in preparation for manhood. As a Xhosa, I count my years as a man from the date of my circumcision.

The highlighted words and phrases are not there by accident. Mandela is a careful writer, and the repetition of the key words *Xhosa, circumcision, tradition,* and the synonyms *man* and *male* is deliberate. Paying attention to these repetitions makes this paragraph quite readable, even if the concepts are foreign.

21

DEBRA J. DICKERSON

Raising Cain

From college dropout, to Korean linguist serving in the United States Air Force, to intelligence officer, to Harvard law student, and now to nationally recognized writer, Debra J. Dickerson has had a remarkably versatile career. She began writing while she was in law school and soon discovered that she had both talent and the fortitude for writing as a career. Her 1996 essay "Who Shot Johnny?" published in the New Republic, *was later included in* Best American Essays of 1997. *Dickerson is now a freelance writer for various publications, among them the* New York Times Magazine, Good Housekeeping, Mother Jones, *and the online site Salon.com, where "Raising Cain" was first published. In it, she talks about her feelings of ambivalence when she learned that she was pregnant with a boy. As an African-American feminist concerned about the real problems that American black males face in the United States, she worried about how she could raise her son to be a caring, compassionate person without being, as she says, "a hypocrite or a castrator."*

Vocabulary Preview

androgynous [paragraph 9] The noun form of *androgynous* is *androgyny*. These words combine two Greek roots: *andro-* ("man") and *gyn-* ("woman"). Thus, if someone is described as *androgynous*, he or she has both male and female characteristics; an androgynous person might dress in gender-neutral clothing. You can see these two roots in the following English words:

polyandry	the practice of having more than one husband at a time
polygyny	the practice of having more than one wife at a time

(Note: The more general term for multiple spouses is *polygamy*, from *poly* ["many"] + *gamy* ["marriage"])

android	a creature that possesses human features
gynecologist	a medical doctor specializing in women's health

What is a misogynist? _____

WORD FAMILIES

phobia [paragraph 7] A *phobia* is an irrational fear of something. Derived from the Greek word part meaning "fear," *phobia* is a noun that can stand by itself. As a suffix it is attached to many words in English to describe various persistent or abnormal psychological conditions. For example, *homophobia* is fear of homosexuality. *Claustrophobia* is a fear of confined spaces, from *claustrum* ("enclosed place") + *phobia*. What do these common "phobia" words mean? Check a dictionary if you are unsure.

hydrophobia   _____

agoraphobia   _____

xenophobia   _____

DEBRA J. DICKERSON

Raising Cain

1   Dec. 11, 2006   When I was pregnant with my first child, who is now 5, I was ecstatic to learn he was a boy. This was odd, since I did not much like those of the male gender. Little boys even less, because I'd seen the center-of-the-universe process by which they become men.

2   I might have been equally happy to learn he was a girl (as I was with my second, who is 3). I was just plain happy to know more, anything, about this mysterious new presence that was dismantling my carefully constructed life. Yet, from the beginning, I wondered how I would reconcile my feminism with raising a son. How could I do it without becoming either a castrating mother straight out of O'Neill[1] or an ovo-hypocrite[2] who talks woman power but raises her own precious boy to be no more enlightened, and no less entitled, than any Promise Keeper?[3]

3   Black people always demand that I focus only on the holy calling of raising a black man, period. But it seems to me that if I get the manhood part right, the black part will take care of itself. If he earns my respect by becoming a moral, hardworking, courageous humanist who shoulders his responsibilities, he can be as "incognegro" as Wayne Brady.[4] Race schmace:[5] His blackness is his to define.

---

[1]Eugene O'Neill (1888–1953) was an American playwright best known for *Mourning Becomes Electra* and *Long Day's Journey into Night*. He won the Nobel Prize for literature in 1936.

[2]*Ovo-* is the Latin root for "egg." (Ed.)

[3]A Christian organization based in Denver, Colorado, that seeks to help men take responsibility for their families by fulfilling seven promises. (See the Web site at the end of the Exercises.) In 1997 the Promise Keepers held a march in Washington, DC, at which it was estimated that one million men, many of them African-American men, attended. (Ed.)

[4]*Incognegro* is a blend of *incognito* ("unknown") + the Spanish word for black. Wayne Brady is a television talk-show host, actor, and comedian. Dickerson means that Wayne Brady is not culturally black, in other words, he is post-racial, like Barack Obama. (Ed.)

[5]"Race schmace" is an example of a Yiddish expression in which one says a word and then repeats it, but this time changing the first consonant to "sch." The phrase thus dismisses the idea. See footnote 4 in Selection 8 on page 128. (Ed.)

My dilemma is raising a man when he's the only one of his gender to whom I give the benefit of the doubt.

4   I should explain: When I say I don't like little boys, I mean that, before I had kids, all children annoyed me, albeit boys in particular because of their penchant for a mayhem that left obedient little girls ignored. When I was growing up in the inner city, children were the A-No. 1 way to ruin your life and guarantee that you'd be broke and tied to one loser or the other for the rest of your life. Once I was grown, and single till 40, children became the whining pests who kept my friends from being able to carry on a conversation for more than five minutes or who kept insisting that I exclaim over their crayon scrawls and stuttered nonsense.

5   While my own childhood was wonderful in some ways, it was so much grimmer than that of the privileged children I've encountered as an adult that I found myself resenting them both their freedom to be children and the unceasing stream of nurturing adult attention they received. Poor kids have to fend more for themselves emotionally; it makes us strong but it also makes us sad.

6   Putting the mourning of my own childhood aside, I just mean to say that children primarily meant to me that I'd always be taking care of someone, a fate too many women accept as given. When you grow up a poor black girl in a huge family you spend your life caring for the whole world. Children, I knew, meant that I'd be a human mop and short-order cook forever (see Katherine Newman's "A Different Shade of Gray" for an excellent, if depressing, look at how most inner-city grandmothers never get to retire, since they have to pick up everybody's slack). I wasn't always sure I'd escape poverty but I was damn sure I could escape parenthood.

7   So having children, while always a leap of faith, was especially hard for me because I knew there was a strong chance that the same fear of losing control that led me out of poverty might well keep me from surrendering myself to those walking little need-bags. Here's what I mean: for decades, I was the living embodiment of delayed gratification. I had something like a phobia of indulging myself, as people from my background understandably did with sloth, crime or drugs. The first time it ever occurred to me to lie down with a nasty cold was my first year of law school. I actually stared, appalled at what I was thinking, at the bed in my dorm room like a thief looking at an open bank teller's drawer. I was 33. That was also the year I took my first aspirin. I was afraid that if I weakened for even one moment the downhill slide might never stop.

8   The poor have no backup system, and I worried where such self-indulgence might lead. And what are children but the ultimate self-indulgence, the perfect monkey wrench thrown into even the most together woman's life? I knew women who kept their children at arm's length and it broke even *my* heart. At 41, I was less afraid of miscarriage or birth defects than of being a cold, distant mom too neurotic to surrender to her own babies. But when I found myself constantly stroking the same spot on the right side of my belly as my son grew, exulting in every blurry ultrasound of his huge head and tiny little spine, I was pitifully grateful. Thank God, my fears about not being able to love him were easily squashed.

9   Two kids later, I know my fears about kids being the perfect trap were justi-fied because I have completely "mommed out." Though even before I conceived I told anyone who would listen that I was going to hire a nanny and get right back to my work and travel, now I get teary because my daughter insists on dressing herself and my son no longer accepts being called Boo Boo. ("That's not my name, Mom.") Now that he's past the androgynous baby stage my dilemma is how to be true to my feminist principles and true to my son's needs. In my community, it is often noted that black mothers raise their daughters but merely love their sons. How do I raise them both?

10   My unapologetic, "bite me" feminism was formed as I grew up in the funda-mentalist Christian black working class, where I was supposed to be seen working and not heard questioning. I'm still pissed off about it. However much racism a black man encountered in the outside world, he always had his women folk to come home to and lord over, however benignly he might choose to do so. When my handyman, truck-driving father returned from a grueling day's work, he filled his time as he chose. I have few memories of my mother when she wasn't still in her pink waitress uniform cooking, cleaning, doing laundry or tending to one of her six kids until long past my bedtime. As soon as each girl was old enough to reach the stove, we joined her on the bucket brigade while my brother idled. I was raised to be such a rough-knuckled chambermaid, I thought the hospital corners and tongue lashings of Basic Training and Officer Training School were a respite.

11   When I was 16 and he was 12, my brother and I had the same curfew. My father actually punished him the few times he helped us girls, so we didn't have the heart to keep making him help. When we feminists go on about institution-alized sexism, this is what we mean; thanks, Dad, for making me complicit in my own subjugation. There's nothing lower than a black woman who keeps a dirty house or neglects her kids (except a lesbian), but a happily unemployed black man shuffling between his mama's, his big mama's and his latest girl-friend's house? It's hard out there for a brother. Spending 12 years in the mili-tary, where the black men worked just as hard to keep the women in their place as did Mr. Charlie, sealed the feminist deal.

12   So what to do with this son of mine? How to love him? How to *raise* him? How to mold him into a manly man but not a bruiser? And most of all, how not to interpret his every troubling move (e.g., refusing to wait to be called on, hit-ting a classmate who was uninterested in being his girlfriend, torturing his little sister) as a harbinger of a male chauvinist pig in the making?

13   But, adding another princess costume to my daughter's cache the other day, it occurred to me that I *was* a hypocrite, just not the kind I had so feared. I have no doubt that indulging (OK, creating) my daughter's Cinderella fascination is but one, far from definitive layer in her development as a woman. With something like evil satisfaction this summer, I feigned deafness when her princess regalia repeatedly got caught in her trike's wheels. When I finally came to help, I told her, "Princesses sit on thrones, honey. They can't ride bikes. So I think you'll have to choose either the ball gown or the bike." She chose the ball gown and we sat on the porch together while her brother NASCAR'd up and down on his bike. I wasn't the least bit concerned. "We got nothing but time," I thought happily as I watched her watch her brother's freedom.

14   So why no patience with, or confidence in, my son?

15   I see now that it's my anger, however justified, and not my feminism, that clouds this particular issue. There's no inherent difference between either my daughter or my son's interrupting class, hitting classmates, abusing the weak. The problem is my having read gender in, making it worse for a boy, my boy, any boy, to do those things. If I stay focused in the now and in transcendent principles—pacifism except in self-defense or in protection of others, good citizenship, empathy, tolerance, fairness, responsibility—I can stay focused on my kids' actual needs and not their amorphous future potential to be either victim or victimizer. My goal is to raise two feminists too smart and too honest to either accept or perpetuate gender-based unfairness. Now I have a story to tell them about how easy it is to fall into those traps. ✳

Debra Dickerson, "Raising Cain" from Salon.com (December 11, 2006). Reprinted with the permission of Salon.

Exercises

Do not refer to the selection for Exercises A and B unless your instructor directs you to do so.

A. DETERMINING THE MAIN IDEA AND PURPOSE

Choose the best answer.

_____ 1. The main idea of the selection is that the writer

   a. experienced a very different childhood growing up in the inner city than the more privileged children she has observed.
   b. wrestled with the problems of how to raise her son in such a way that he would become a good man without being a chauvinist brute.
   c. experienced a conflict about how to raise her son and daughter because she had different expectations for their futures.
   d. enthusiastically accepted the role of mother even though it disrupted her career.

_____ 2. The writer's purpose is to

   a. recommend strategies for coping with the various problems all mothers face.
   b. argue for a gender-free course of action when raising children of both sexes.
   c. examine the conflicts and ambivalent feelings she had about how to raise a black boy to become a man.
   d. challenge others in the African-American community to change their lax child-rearing practices with regard to raising boys.

B. COMPREHENDING MAIN IDEAS

Choose the correct answer.

_____ 1. Dickerson faced a conflict in dealing with her son, namely, the conflict between her desire to raise her son to be a moral and hardworking black man and

    a. her family's expectations for him.
    b. his own desires and personality traits.
    c. the pressures of his peers who might not share her values.
    d. her feminist ideals.

_____ 2. The writer states that before she had children she generally didn't like children. Which of the following does she _not_ mention as a reason for this feeling?

    a. Children require an unlimited supply of energy, and the writer doubted that she was up to the task.
    b. Little girls are taught to be obedient and are generally ignored while little boys are allowed to get away with creating turmoil or with being idle.
    c. Children disrupt one's career plans.
    d. Other people's children are whining pests whose every word and every drawing is a work of art.
    e. Children require constant attention from their mothers, thus assuring women a life of constant drudgery.

_____ 3. Dickerson describes several aspects of her own childhood and concludes that children who grow up in a large family in a poor community

    a. are better off than more privileged children because they're not so spoiled.
    b. are stronger for the experience but are often left on their own emotionally.
    c. are doomed to take care of others for the rest of their lives.
    d. become self-indulgent and irresponsible because their mothers do everything for them.

_____ 4. The writer cites an often-repeated concept about raising children in the black community, namely that black mothers

    a. merely love their daughters but raise their sons.
    b. raise their sons but merely love their daughters.
    c. raise their daughters but merely love their sons.
    d. raise their sons and daughters with equal expectations.

_____ 5. Dickerson says that in the working-class family she grew up in,

    a. her brother worked just as hard around the house as his sisters.
    b. her younger brother was treated very differently from her and her sisters, in particular because he was not expected to help.

    c. everybody pitched in to do household chores according to a posted chart.

    d. both parents indulged all the children and asked them to do only minor chores.

_____ **6.** In her conclusion, Dickerson realizes that, despite all her worrying, what she really needs to stay focused on is

    a. her career.

    b. following traditional gender roles for each child.

    c. raising her children in such a way that their values and needs transcend gender.

    d. being stricter with her son than with her daughter, since boys are more likely to act out and to cause harm to others.

COMPREHENSION SCORE

Score your answers for Exercises A and B as follows:

A. No. right _____ × 2 = _____

B. No. right _____ × 1 = _____

Total points from A and B _____ × 10 = _____ percent

You may refer to the selection as you work through the remaining exercises.

C. LOCATING INFORMATION

Locate the specific information that reinforces each idea from the selection. Paragraph numbers are provided for you.

1. What is Dickerson's specific complaint about the way black boys are raised in the African-American community? [paragraphs 1–2] _____

_____

2. Why didn't Dickerson indulge herself, even going so far as never to take an aspirin for a headache before she was in law school? [paragraph 7] _____

_____

_____

3. According to Dickerson, who in the family is responsible for subjugating women, for institutionalized sexism? [paragraphs 10–11] _____

_____

4. In what way was basic training and officer training school different from the discipline Dickerson underwent at home? [paragraphs 10–11] _____

_____

D. UNDERSTANDING STRUCTURE

Choose the best answer.

_____ 1. Read paragraph 2 again and locate the single transitional word. Then decide which pattern of development the paragraph represents.

    a. list of facts or details
    b. examples
    c. steps in a process
    d. contrast

_____ 2. Paragraph 4 is developed primarily by

    a. lists of facts or details.
    b. reasons.
    c. steps in a process.
    d. contrast.

_____ 3. The discussion in paragraph 5 implies which of these logical relationships?

    a. contrast—showing the difference between two things
    b. reasons—showing why something exists
    c. process—showing the steps in chronological order
    d. examples—showing specific illustrations of something

_____ 4. The pattern of development in both paragraphs 7 and 10 is primarily

    a. lists of facts or details.
    b. examples.
    c. reasons.
    d. steps in a process.
    e. contrast.

E. UNDERSTANDING VOCABULARY

Look through the paragraphs listed below and find a word that matches each definition. Refer to a dictionary if necessary. An example has been done for you.

Ex. emasculating, depriving of masculinity
[paragraphs 2–3]   _____ castrating _____

1. although, even though [3–4]   _____

2. state of disorder, causing chaos or destruction [3–4]   _____

3. inclination, liking for [3–4]   _____

4. attempt or manage without help [5–6]   _____

5. short interval of rest or relief [10]   _____

6. physically demanding, exhausting [10]   _____

7. gently, kindly [10]   _____

8. something that indicates or foreshadows what is to come [11–12]   _____

9. associated with wrongdoing, participating in a bad tradition [11–12]   _____

10. pretended [13]   _____

11. cause to continue, prolong the existence of [15]   _____

12. having no definite form, shapeless [15]   _____

F. USING VOCABULARY

Write the correct inflected form of the base word (in parentheses) in each of the following sentences. Be sure to add the appropriate ending to fit the grammatical requirements of the sentence. Refer to your dictionary if necessary.

1. (*ecstatic*—use a noun) When Dickerson discovered that she was pregnant with a boy, she experienced the same _____ that most women feel.

2. (*reconciliation*—use a verb) For Dickerson, the hardest part about raising a boy is the need for _____ the dilemma between adhering to her feminist ideals and raising a boy.

3. (*hypocrite*—use an adjective) Women who raise boys, especially if they are feminists, often feel _____ because they are torn between sticking to their feminist ideals and spoiling their sons.

4. (*sloth*—use an adjective) The writer claims that for many African-Americans who were raised in poverty, self-indulgence means living a _____ life or getting involved with crime or drugs.

5. *subjugation*—use a verb) Dickerson blames her father who, like many black men, _____ their women by not making the same demands on their sons as they do on their daughters.

6. (*transcendent*—use a verb) Dickerson concludes that certain principles— pacifism, responsibility, and fairness— _____ all gender issues.

G. LANGUAGE ANALYSIS—UNDERSTANDING SLANG

Dickerson uses several informal and slang words and phrases. Consider these examples in their context and then write the meaning of each in the space provided. The paragraph number where each occurs is included. If you are unsure, ask your instructor or other classmates for help.

1. children were the *A-No. 1 way* to ruin your life [paragraph 4] _____

_____

2. Children, I knew, meant that I'd be a *human mop and short-order cook* [6] _____

_____

3. keep me from surrendering myself to those walking little *need-bags* [7] _____

_____

4. Children [are] . . . the perfect *monkey wrench* thrown into even the most together

woman's life [8] _____

5. I have completely *"mommed out"* [9] _____

6. My unapologetic, *"bite me"* feminism [10] _____

_____

7. we joined her on *the bucket brigade* [10] _____

_____

8. *tongue lashings* of Basic Training [10] _____

_____

9. a harbinger of a *male chauvinist pig* in the making [12] _____

_____

10. while her brother *NASCAR'd* up and down on his bike [13] _____

_____

H. TOPICS FOR DISCUSSION

1. Think about Dickerson's attitude (point of view) in this essay. Does she seem angry, realistic, hostile, clear-thinking, or something altogether different?
2. Are Dickerson's concerns about how to raise her son (as opposed to how to raise her daughter) a result of her feminism, of the specific characteristics of the African-American community, or of the concerns of all parents who wrestle with expectations for their children?
3. Dickerson's assessment and explanation of the divergence in the way black boys and black girls are raised is rather harsh. As she writes, "It's hard out there for a brother." Yet there might be other reasons—besides parental indulgence—to explain why "sloth, crime or drugs" have exercised so much of a pull in poor communities. Discuss other points of view that are contrary to her thinking.
4. What are the origins of Dickerson's feminism as they are revealed throughout the selection? Has having two children changed her thinking? If so, how?

I. TOPICS FOR WRITING

1. Write a rebuttal to Dickerson's essay, in which you offer different explanations and counterarguments for her ideas.

2. Dickerson emphasizes the hard work African-American women do, especially in poor households, a tradition that starts in childhood. As she says, "When you grow up a poor black girl in a huge family you spend your life caring for the whole world." How different is the situation for girls from another ethnic or economic group that you are familiar with? Write a short essay in which you address the role of a young girl in a family you are familiar with.

3. If you have a sibling or siblings of the opposite sex, were you raised differently from them? If so, how? What were your parents' expectations? disciplinary measures? curfew rules? requirements for performing household chores? Write an essay in which you examine these areas with respect to your upbringing and that of your siblings.

Exploring Related Web Sites

- Debra Dickerson's Web site offers a more detailed—and very interesting— biographical sketch and complete access to her articles. In particular, you might want to read "Who Shot Johnny?" which has become a contemporary classic.

  www.debradickerson.com

- Find out what the Promise Keepers, mentioned in paragraph 2, are all about on the homepage of their Web site:

  www.promisekeepers.org/about

Long Walk to Freedom

*Nelson Mandela, former president and now elder statesman of South Africa, was impris-
oned for 26 years for his outspoken stand on apartheid—the policy of "separateness"
established early in the century by South Africa's white-minority government. After his
release in 1990, he continued to speak out against apartheid from his position as leader of
the African National Congress (ANC). In 1994 South Africa held its first all-races election, and Mandela was elected president, ending white-minority rule in that long-troubled
country.* Long Walk to Freedom *(1994) is Nelson Mandela's autobiography. In this
selection, he explains the Xhosa tradition of circumcision, the ceremony whereby Xhosa
boys become men.*

Vocabulary Preview

WORD PARTS

bene- [paragraph 17] Although you have already been introduced to the prefix
bene- (Selection 2), a little review never hurts. A *benefactor* is a person who gives
help or aid to another. The Latin prefix *bene-* means "well," and it begins many
so-called loan words from Latin, among them *benefit*, *beneficial*, *benevolence*
("wishing [someone] well"), *benediction* ("good saying"), and *benign*.

What is a *beneficiary* of a life insurance policy? _____

WORD FAMILIES

initiates [paragraph 12] Mandela's subject is the circumcision ceremony, after which
young Xhosa boys become *abakhwetha*, "*initiates* into the world of manhood." As a
verb, *initiate* comes from the Latin word *initiare*, meaning "to begin." As a noun,
initiate refers to a new member who has been introduced into a group, either
by means of a ceremony or of a test. Two other relatives in this word family are
initiation (the ceremony, ritual, or test by which a person is admitted) and *initial*
(the first letter of a name or something that occurs at the beginning, like an *initial*
step).

What does the word *initiative* mean? _____

NELSON MANDELA

Long Walk to Freedom

1   When I was sixteen, the regent[1] decided that it was time that I became a man. In Xhosa tradition, this is achieved through one means only: circumcision. In my tradition, an uncircumcised male cannot be heir to his father's wealth, cannot marry or officiate in tribal rituals. An uncircumcised Xhosa man is a contradiction in terms, for he is not considered a man at all, but a boy. For the Xhosa people, circumcision represents the formal incorporation of males into society. It is not just a surgical procedure, but a lengthy and elaborate ritual in preparation for manhood. As a Xhosa, I count my years as a man from the date of my circumcision.

2   The traditional ceremony of the circumcision school was arranged principally for Justice—the rest of us, twenty-six in all—were there mainly to keep him company. Early in the new year, we journeyed to two grass huts in a secluded valley on the banks of the Mbashe River, known as Tyhalarha, the traditional place of circumcision for Thembu kings. The huts were seclusion lodges, where we were to live isolated from society. It was a sacred time; I felt happy and fulfilled taking part in my people's customs and ready to make the transition from boyhood to manhood.

3   We had moved to Tyhalarha by the river a few days before the actual circumcision ceremony. These last few days of boyhood were spent with the other initiates, and I found the camaraderie enjoyable. The lodge was near the home of Banabakhe Blayi, the wealthiest and most popular boy at the circumcision school. He was an engaging fellow, a champion stickfighter and a glamour boy, whose many girlfriends kept us all supplied with delicacies. Although he could neither read nor write, he was one of the most intelligent among us. He regaled us with stories of his trips to Johannesburg, a place none of us had ever been before. He so thrilled us with tales of the mines that he almost persuaded me that to be a miner was more alluring than to be a monarch. Miners had a mystique; to be a miner meant to be strong and daring, the ideal of manhood. Much later, I realized that it was the exaggerated tales of boys like Banabakhe that caused so many young men to run away to work in the mines of Johannesburg, where they often lost their health and their lives. In those days, working in the mines was almost as much of a rite of passage as circumcision school, a myth that helped the mine-owners more than it helped my people.

4   A custom of circumcision school is that one must perform a daring exploit before the ceremony. In days of old, this might have involved a cattle raid or even a battle, but in our time the deeds were more mischievous than martial. Two nights before we moved to Tyhalarha, we decided to steal a pig. In Mqhekezweni there was a tribesman with an ornery old pig. To avoid making noise and alarming him, we arranged for the pig to do our work for us. We took handfuls of sediment from homemade African beer, which has a strong scent

[1]A ruler or governor. (Ed.)

much favored by pigs, and placed it upwind of the pig. The pig was so aroused by the scent that he came out of the kraal,[2] following a trail we had laid, gradually made his way to us, wheezing and snorting and eating the sediment. When he got near us, we captured the poor pig, slaughtered it, and then built a fire and ate roast pork underneath the stars. No piece of pork has ever tasted as good before or since.

5   The night before the circumcision, there was a ceremony near our huts with singing and dancing. Women came from the nearby villages, and we danced to their singing and clapping. As the music became faster and louder, our dance turned more frenzied and we forgot for a moment what lay ahead.

6   At dawn, when the stars were still in the sky, we began our preparations. We were escorted to the river to bathe in its cold waters, a ritual that signified our purification before the ceremony. The ceremony was at midday, and we were commanded to stand in a row in a clearing some distance from the river where a crowd of parents and relatives, including the regent, as well as a handful of chiefs and counselors, had gathered. We were clad only in our blankets, and as the ceremony began, with drums pounding, we were ordered to sit on a blanket on the ground with our legs spread out in front of us. I was tense and anxious, uncertain of how I would react when the critical moment came. Flinching or

[2]A South African word denoting either a rural village or an enclosure for livestock. Mandela probably uses the word in the second sense. (Ed.)

crying out was a sign of weakness and stigmatized one's manhood. I was determined not to disgrace myself, the group, or my guardian. Circumcision is a trial of bravery and stoicism; no anesthetic is used; a man must suffer in silence.

7   To the right, out of the corner of my eye, I could see a thin, elderly man emerge from a tent and kneel in front of the first boy. There was excitement in the crowd, and I shuddered slightly knowing that the ritual was about to begin. The old man was a famous *ingcibi,* a circumcision expert, from Gcalekaland, who would use his assegai[3] to change us from boys to men with a single blow.

8   Suddenly, I heard the first boy cry out, *"Ndiyindoda!"* (I am a man!), which we were trained to say in the moment of circumcision. Seconds later, I heard Justice's strangled voice pronounce the same phrase. There were now two boys before the *ingcibi* reached me, and my mind must have gone blank because before I knew it, the old man was kneeling in front of me. I looked directly into his eyes. He was pale, and though the day was cold, his face was shining with perspiration. His hands moved so fast they seemed to be controlled by an other-worldly force. Without a word, he took my foreskin, pulled it forward, and then, in a single morion, brought down his assegai. I felt as if fire was shooting through my veins; the pain was so intense that I buried my chin into my chest. Many seconds seemed to pass before I remembered the cry, and then I recovered and called out, *"Ndiyindoda!"*

9   I looked down and saw a perfect cut, clean and round like a ring. But I felt ashamed because the other boys seemed much stronger and braver than I had been; they had called out more promptly than I had. I was distressed that I had been disabled, however briefly, by the pain, and I did my best to hide my agony. A boy may cry; a man conceals his pain.

10   I had now taken the essential step in the life of every Xhosa man. Now, I might marry, set up my own home, and plow my own field. I could now be admitted to the councils of the community; my words would be taken seriously. At the ceremony, I was given my circumcision name, Dalibunga, meaning "Founder of the Bungha," the traditional ruling body of the Transkei.[4] To Xhosa traditionalists, this name is more acceptable than either of my two previous given names, Rolihlahla or Nelson, and I was proud to hear my new name pronounced: Dalibunga.

11   Immediately after the blow had been delivered, an assistant who follows the circumcision master takes the foreskin that is on the ground and ties it to a corner of your blanket. Our wounds were then dressed with a healing plant, the leaves of which were thorny on the outside but smooth on the inside, which absorbed the blood and other secretions.

12   At the conclusion of the ceremony, we returned to our huts, where a fire was burning with wet wood that cast off clouds of smoke, which was thought to

---

[3]A spear or lance used by South African tribesmen. (Ed.)
[4]Now a semi-independent area in southeast South Africa on the Indian Ocean, at the time Mandela was writing, it was a Black African Homeland. It received nominal independence in 1976. (Ed.)

promote healing. We were ordered to lie on our backs in the smoky huts, with one leg flat, and one leg bent. We were now *abakhwetha,* initiates into the world of manhood. We were looked after by an *amakhankatha,* or guardian, who explained the rules we must follow if we were to enter manhood properly. The first chore of the *amakhankatha* was to paint our naked and shaved bodies from head to foot in white ocher, turning us into ghosts. The white chalk symbolized our purity, and I still recall how stiff the dried clay felt on my body.

13   That first night, at midnight, an attendant, or *ikhankatha,* crept around the hut, gently waking each of us. We were then instructed to leave the hut and go tramping through the night to bury our foreskins. The traditional reason for this practice was so that our foreskins would be hidden before wizards could use them for evil purposes, but, symbolically, we were also burying our youth. I did not want to leave the warm hut and wander through the bush in the darkness, but I walked into the trees and after a few minutes, untied my foreskin and buried it in the earth. I felt as though I had now discarded the last remnant of my childhood.

14   We lived in our two huts—thirteen in each—while our wounds healed. When outside the huts, we were covered in blankets, for we were not allowed to be seen by women. It was a period of quietude, a kind of spiritual preparation for the trials of manhood that lay ahead. On the day of our reemergence, we went down to the river early in the morning to wash away the white ocher in the waters of the Mbashe. Once we were clean and dry, we were coated in red ocher. The tradition was that one should sleep with a woman, who later may become one's wife, and she rubs off the pigment with her body. In my case, however, the ocher was removed with a mixture of fat and lard.

15   At the end of our seclusion, the lodges and all their contents were burned, destroying our last links to childhood, and a great ceremony was held to welcome us as men to society. Our families, friends, and local chiefs gathered for speeches, songs, and gift-giving. I was given two heifers and four sheep, and felt far richer than I ever had before. I who had never owned anything suddenly possessed property. It was a heady feeling, even though my gifts were paltry next to those of Justice, who inherited an entire herd. I was not jealous of Justice's gifts. He was the son of a king; I was merely destined to be a counselor to a king. I felt strong and proud that day. I remember walking differently on that day, straighter, taller, firmer. I was hopeful, and thinking that I might someday have wealth, property, and status.

16   The main speaker of the day was Chief Meligqili, the son of Dalindyebo, and after listening to him, my gaily colored dreams suddenly darkened. He began conventionally, remarking on how fine it was that we were continuing a tradition that had been going on for as long as anyone could remember. Then he turned to us and his tone suddenly changed. "There sit our sons," he said, "young, healthy, and handsome, the flower of the Xhosa tribe, the pride of our nation. We have just circumcised them in a ritual that promises them manhood, but I am here to tell you that it is an empty, illusory promise, a promise that can never be fulfilled. For we Xhosas, and all black South Africans, are a conquered

people. We are slaves in our own country. We are tenants on our own soil. We have no strength, no power, no control over our own destiny in the land of our birth. They will go to cities where they will live in shacks and drink cheap alcohol all because we have no land to give them where they could prosper and multiply. They will cough their lungs out deep in the bowels of the white man's mines, destroying their health, never seeing the sun, so that the white man can live a life of unequaled prosperity. Among these young men are chiefs who will never rule because we have no power to govern ourselves; soldiers who will never fight for we have no weapons to fight with; scholars who will never teach because we have no place for them to study. The abilities, the intelligence, the promise of these young men will be squandered in their attempt to eke out a living doing the simplest, most mindless chores for the white man. These gifts today are naught, for we cannot give them the greatest gift of all, which is freedom and independence. I well know that Qamata is all-seeing and never sleeps, but I have a suspicion that Qamata may in fact be dozing. If this is the case, the sooner I die the better because then I can meet him and shake him awake and tell him that the children of Ngubengcuka, the flower of the Xhosa nation, are dying."

17   The audience had become more and more quiet as Chief Meligqili spoke and, I think, more and more angry. No one wanted to hear the words that he spoke that day. I know that I myself did not want to hear them. I was cross rather than aroused by the chief's remarks, dismissing his words as the abusive comments of an ignorant man who was unable to appreciate the value of the education and benefits that the white man had brought to our country. At the time, I looked on the white man not as an oppressor but as a benefactor, and I thought the chief was enormously ungrateful. This upstart chief was ruining my day, spoiling the proud feeling with wrongheaded remarks.

18   But without exactly understanding why, his words soon began to work in me. He had planted a seed, and though I let that seed lie dormant for a long season, it eventually began to grow. Later, I realized that the ignorant man that day was not the chief but myself.

19   After the ceremony, I walked back to the river and watched it meander on its way to where, many miles distant, it emptied into the Indian Ocean. I had never crossed that river, and I knew little or nothing of the world beyond it, a world that beckoned me that day. It was almost sunset and I hurried on to where our seclusion lodges had been. Though it was forbidden to look back while the lodges were burning, I could not resist. When I reached the area, all that remained were two pyramids of ashes by a large mimosa tree. In these ash heaps lay a lost and delightful world, the world of my childhood, the world of sweet and irresponsible days at Qunu and Mqhekezweni. Now I was a man, and I would never again play *thinti,* or steal maize, or drink milk from a cow's udder. I was already in mourning for my own youth. Looking back, I know that I was not a man that day and would not truly become one for many years. ✱

Exercises

Do not refer to the selection for Exercises A–C unless your instructor directs you to do so.

A. DETERMINING THE MAIN IDEA AND PURPOSE

Choose the best answer.

_____ 1. The main idea of the selection is that

    a. all cultures conduct rituals to initiate boys into manhood.

    b. the circumcision ceremony is performed on teenaged Xhosa boys, the only way to become a man in that culture.

    c. uncircumcised Xhosa males are not eligible to become leaders.

    d. a boy must perform a daring exploit before the circumcision ritual.

_____ 2. The writer's purpose is to

    a. describe the actual circumcision he underwent.

    b. describe his emotional state before, during, and after the ceremony.

    c. honor the role this initiation ceremony plays in his culture.

    d. explain the tradition associated with the circumcision ceremony and his experience undergoing it.

B. COMPREHENDING MAIN IDEAS

Choose the correct answer.

_____ 1. In the Xhosa tradition, an uncircumcised male

    a. is allowed to remain intact only in certain extreme cases, for reasons of health.

    b. has no rights to inherit, to marry, or to take part in tribal rituals.

    c. is an object of ridicule and jokes among the tribespeople.

    d. is allowed to remain intact if his family rejects the tradition.

_____ 2. The daring exploit that Mandela and his comrades performed before the ceremony was

    a. climbing the tallest tree in the vicinity.

    b. killing a leopard.

    c. stealing a pig.

    d. drinking homemade beer.

_____ 3. Bathing in the cold river waters before the ceremony was intended to

    a. test their endurance.

    b. purify them.

    c. baptize them.

    d. symbolically wash away their boyhood.

_____ **4.** Flinching or crying out during the circumcision ceremony was considered disgraceful behavior because it

   a. ruined the ceremony for the other participants.
   b. showed disrespect for the elders and the circumcision expert.
   c. made the participants' relatives anxious and tense.
   d. stigmatized one's manhood.

_____ **5.** To symbolize the destruction of the young men's last links to childhood, the final step in the ritual was to

   a. burn the seclusion lodges and everything in them.
   b. bathe again in the river.
   c. paint their bodies with white chalk.
   d. chant traditional tribal songs.

_____ **6.** Chief Meligqili, the main speaker of the day, warned the initiates that the promise of manhood was an illusory one that could never be fulfilled because black South Africans were

   a. not well enough educated to get good jobs.
   b. a conquered people with no control over their own destiny.
   c. too content to work for low wages and not fight for a higher standard of living.
   d. too timid to fight their oppressors.

COMPREHENSION SCORE

Score your answers for Exercises A and B as follows:

A. No. right _____ × 2 = _____
B. No. right _____ × 1 = _____
Total points from A and B _____ × 10 = _____ percent

C. SEQUENCING

These sentences from one paragraph in the selection have been scrambled. Read the sentences and choose the sequence that puts them back into logical order. Do not refer to the original selection.

   1 Later, I realized that the ignorant man that day was not the chief but myself.
   2 He had planted a seed, and though I let that seed lie dormant for a long season, it eventually began to grow. **3** But without exactly understanding why, his words soon began to work in me.

_____ Which of the following represents the correct sequence for these sentences?

   a. 3, 2, 1
   b. 2, 3, 1
   c. 1, 3, 2
   d. Correct as written.

You may refer to the selection as you work through the remaining exercises.

D. IDENTIFYING SUPPORTING DETAILS

For each main idea stated here, find and write down two supporting details.

1. In Xhosa culture, the circumcision ceremony marks a significant step in a young boy's life. [paragraph 1]

   a. _____

   b. _____

   _____

2. Initially, Mandela was irritated by Chief Meligqili's remarks after the ceremony. [paragraph 17]

   a. _____

   _____

   b. _____

E. MAKING INFERENCES

For each of these statements write Y (Yes) if the inference is an accurate one, N (No) if the inference is an inaccurate one, or CT (Can't Tell) if the writer does not give you enough information to make an inference one way or another.

1. _____ Not all males in Xhosa culture are circumcised. [paragraph 1]

2. _____ The circumcision ceremony that Mandela describes has more symbolic than actual practical value in terms of a man's worth to the community. [paragraph 1]

3. _____ The circumcision ceremony was arranged principally for Justice because he was the son of a king. [paragraphs 2 and 15]

4. _____ The young black South Africans who ran away to work in the mines were well informed about the working conditions before they began their jobs. [paragraph 3]

5. _____ Some of the boys who were circumcised with Mandela went on to become great chiefs and advisers to kings. [essay as a whole]

6. _____ Although only 16 at the time he was initiated, Mandela was well educated and well informed about South Africa's political situation, and he understood clearly the white role in black oppression. [paragraph 18]

F. INTERPRETING MEANING

Where appropriate, write your answers for these questions in your own words.

1. _____ Which of the following sentences from the selection best states the thesis?

   a. "When I was sixteen, the regent decided that it was time that I became a man."

    b. "For the Xhosa people, circumcision represents the formal incorporation of males into society."

    c. "As a Xhosa, I count my years as a man from the date of my circumcision."

    d. "At the end of our seclusion, the lodges and all their contents were burned, destroying our last links to childhood, and a great ceremony was held to welcome us as men to society."

2. Explain the fundamental irony that underlies paragraphs 3 and 16, concerning black South Africans working in the mines. _____

_____

3. Write the sentence that represents the main idea of paragraph 9. _____

_____

4. _____ Look again at paragraph 12. A good title for this paragraph is
    a. "Concluding the Ceremony."
    b. "Becoming *Abakhwetha*."
    c. "Symbols of Purity."
    d. "How We Were Initiated."

5. Locate the metaphor, or imaginative comparison, in paragraph 18 and explain its meaning. _____

_____

6. In your own words, explain the main idea of paragraph 19. _____

_____

_____

G. UNDERSTANDING VOCABULARY

Choose the best definition according to an analysis of word parts or to the context.

_____ **1.** I found the *camaraderie* enjoyable [paragraph 3]
    a. isolation from adults
    b. good fellowship among friends
    c. conversation, lighthearted talk
    d. anticipation of the future

_____ **2.** more mischievous than *martial* [4]
    a. ridiculous, absurd
    b. far-fetched, incredible
    c. harmless, mild
    d. military, warlike

_____ 3. *clad* only in blankets [6]

    a. wrapped tightly
    b. clothed
    c. hidden
    d. identified

_____ 4. *Flinching* or crying out [6]

    a. screaming in terror
    b. becoming visibly nervous
    c. letting tears flow
    d. shrinking back in fear

_____ 5. a trial of bravery and *stoicism* [6]

    a. indifference to pain
    b. physical strength and endurance
    c. manliness
    d. heroism

_____ 6. the last *remnant* [13]

    a. scrap, small piece
    b. vestige, remainder
    c. example, illustration
    d. memory, reminiscence

_____ 7. a *heady* feeling [15]

    a. relieved
    b. anxious
    c. desirable
    d. exhilarating

_____ 8. my gifts were *paltry* [15]

    a. meager
    b. unwanted
    c. cherished
    d. generous

_____ 9. These gifts today are *naught* [16]

    a. treasured
    b. undeserved
    c. nothing, of no value
    d. taken for granted

_____ 10. I let that seed lie *dormant* [18]

    a. inactive, but capable of coming alive
    b. undisturbed by any negative thoughts
    c. inflexible, unmoving
    d. unquestioned, unchallenged

H. USING VOCABULARY

In parentheses before each sentence are some inflected forms of words from the selection. Study the context and the sentence. Then write the correct form in the space provided.

1. (*allure, alluring*) The stories that Banabakhe told about working in the mines

   held great _____ for the other boys.

2. (*purify, purified, purification, pure*) Mandela and the other boys _____
   themselves by bathing in the cold waters of the river.

3. (*stoic, stoicism, stoically*) Above all, the boys had to withstand the pain of the

   circumcision ceremony, _____ refusing to flinch or cry.

4. (*illusion, illusory, illusionary*) The main speaker warned the initiates that the

   promise of manhood was at best an _____ that would never be
   fulfilled.

5. (*prosperity, prosper, prospered, prosperous*) White South Africans were

   _____ because black South Africans worked hard to maintain the
   whites' levels of wealth.

6. (*abuse, abused, abusiveness, abusive, abusively*) At the time, Mandela believed that

   the chief spoke wrongly about the way whites supposedly _____ black
   workers.

I. ANNOTATING EXERCISE

Go through the article and locate any piece of information that supports this idea: The circumcision ceremony is an **important ritual in Xhosa society.**

To identify it, put a star in the margin next to the sentence or bracket the words.

J. TOPICS FOR DISCUSSION

1. How would you describe Nelson Mandela as his character emerges from this autobiographical account?
2. What are the advantages of a formalized ritual such as the Xhosa have devised to initiate young boys to take part in the larger community? What are the disadvantages?

K. TOPICS FOR WRITING

1. How are young American boys initiated into manhood? Write a short paper in which you contrast the Xhosa circumcision ceremony Mandela describes with American traditions.
2. Although modern parents try hard to treat their children equally, inequalities and differing expectations according to gender are nearly impossible to avoid.

In what ways have gender expectations demonstrated by your family, friends, and teachers made you the person you are today? Identify these expectations and assess their impact on your personality, your values, your interests, and anything else that seems pertinent to you.

3. If you read Debra J. Dickerson's article, "Raising Cain" (Selection 21), write a short essay contrasting the expectations for young boys as she describes them in her article with those suggested in Mandela's selection.

Exploring Related Web Sites

- Photos of South Africa are available at this site:

  www.africaguide.com/country/safrica/photolib.htm

- These sites are devoted to Xhosa culture. The second one contains more information about the initiation of boys into Xhosa life.

  www.questconnect.org/africa_xhosa.htm

  www.southafricalogue.com/features/the-xhosa-circumcision-ritual.html

- A good introduction to the life and times of Nelson Mandela is available at The Mandela Page:

  www.anc.org.za/people/mandela

23

LYNNE DUKE
The Picture of Conformity

Lynne Duke covered national and international news for the Washington Post *for 20 years. In the mid-1990s, she served as the newspaper's Johannesburg, South Africa, bureau chief, where she was responsible for news happening in central and southern Africa. She wrote often about South Africa's first democratically elected government under Nelson Mandela. She also traveled widely through the region and wrote about events unfolding in postgenocide Rwanda, in Congo-Zaire as well as Angola, Zimbabwe, Mozambique, Namibia, and elsewhere. Duke also covered the aftermath of the September 11, 2001, terror attacks and issues related to the war in Iraq and security. Duke studied political science at Columbia and received her master's degree from Columbia's Graduate School of Journalism.*

Although surveillance cameras were used before the terrorist attacks of September 11, 2001, they have become even more widespread in the intervening years. Cameras are not only used in retail stores, banks, gas stations, supermarkets, and convenience stores; they are also increasingly used in public spaces. In many American cities, surveillance cameras are mounted at street intersections to monitor motorists' driving habits. In this article, Duke describes some of the ramifications of our increasingly Big Brother society. "Big Brother" is a reference to the system of surveillance used by the totalitarian government in George Orwell's 1949 novel 1984.

Vocabulary Preview

WORD PARTS

a-, an- [paragraphs 15, 25, 34] The Greek prefix *a-* (occasionally spelled *an-*) is attached to several English roots to indicate an absence or a complete lack of. In the selection, the word *amorphous* in paragraph 15 means having no shape, from *a-* ("without") + *morph* ("shape"); and in paragraphs 25 and 34 respectively, *anomalous* and *anomalies* means "deviating from the common order, norm, or form" (from *a-* + *homos* ["same"]). Other words beginning with this prefix are *apolitical* (having no interest in politics), *amoral* (having no sense of morality), *apathy* (having no feeling, indifferent), and *agnostic* (one who does not know if God exists).

What does the word *anarchy* mean? What is its derivation? Check a dictionary if necessary.

_____

WORD FAMILIES

trans- [paragraphs 2 and 6] The Latin word part *trans-* can be both a prefix and a word root, and it is the basis of a large number of words in English. As a prefix, *trans-* means "across," as in *transatlantic* or *transport* (*trans-* + *port* ["to carry"]). As a word root, it has the same meaning. You have already seen this usage in the discussion of *transitions* at the beginning of Part Four—words and phrases that indicate a passage from one thought to another. This selection contains three words beginning with *trans: Transponder*, mentioned in paragraph 2, refers to an electronic device used to transmit signals. For example, many people mount transponders on their car windshields to pay bridge or highway tolls electronically. *Transit* (paragraph 6) means, literally, the act of passing across or through. And finally, *traverse* (paragraph 2) means to move or travel across an area. Here are some other common words in this word family:

transcontinental	crossing a continent
transmit	to send from one place to another (*trans-* + *mittere* ["to send"])
transcribe	to write a copy of; to transfer information (*trans-* + *scribere* ["to write"])
transitory	lasting only a short time

What do these two words mean, and what is the meaning of the roots to which the prefix is attached?

transgression   _____

transpire   _____

LYNNE DUKE

The Picture of Conformity

1   Don't look now. Somebody's watching.

2   But you knew that, didn't you? How could you not? It's been apparent for years that we're being watched and monitored as we traverse airports and train stations, as we drive, train, fly, surf the Web, e-mail, talk on the phone, get the morning coffee, visit the doctor, go to the bank, go to work, shop for groceries, shop for shoes, buy a TV, walk down the street. Cameras, electronic card readers and transponders are ubiquitous. And in that parallel virtual universe, data miners are busily and constantly culling our cyber selves.

3   Is anywhere safe from the watchers, the trackers? Is it impossible to just be let alone?

4   There, in that quintessentially public space, the National Mall in Washington, came Michael Thrasher, 43, an ordinary guy, just strolling on a lovely recent day. We found him near an entrance to the Franklin Delano Roosevelt Memorial, where a tower-high surveillance camera loomed overhead.

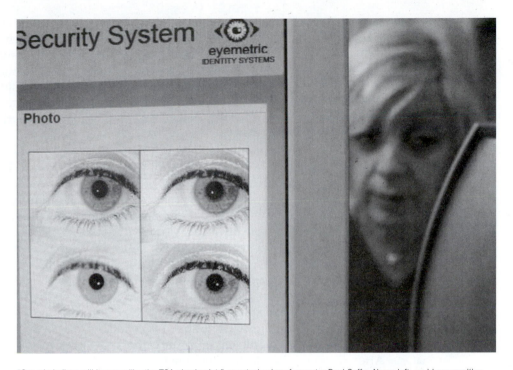

"Our whole lives will become like the TSA checkpoint," says technology forecaster Paul Saffo. Above left, an iris recognition system in a New Jersey elementary school. (By William Thomas Cain—Getty Images)

5   Thrasher didn't immediately see it. But when asked his feelings about privacy and surveillance, he said, "You just feel like there's always someone looking at you."

6   He's a baggage handler at Reagan National Airport, so he knows that he's watched at the workplace. Since Sept. 11, 2001, transit hubs have been laden with layer upon layer of surveillance: cameras, biometrics, sensors, even a new thing called the "behavior detection officer."

7   And it's good, Thrasher says, that someone's watching out for the bad guys. "Look what kind of world we're in now."

8   But Thrasher doesn't like the way his private space is shrinking. Like surfing the Web and knowing his data trail can easily be mined: "If I'm not doing anything illegal, why is it any of their business?"

9   Like being on the telephone and believing it could be tapped: "In the back of my mind, I'm thinking anybody could be listening to whatever I say."

10   And just going about one's daily business, walking down the street, going to the market?

11   "It just feels like there's no privacy now at all when you're doing public stuff."

12   Suddenly, he sees the camera, his exclamation point, and throws his hands in the air.

13   All this surveillance, monitoring and eavesdropping is changing our culture, affecting people's behavior, altering their sense of freedom, of autonomy. That's

what the experts say: that surveillance robs people of their public anonymity. And they go even further, saying that pressure for conformity is endemic in a surveillance culture; that creativity and uniqueness become its casualties.

14   While there are benefits to surveillance—the sense of security, the ability to view crime scenes—the loss of autonomy represents the downside of our surveillance-heavy culture, says Jeffrey Rosen, a George Washington University law professor and author of "The Naked Crowd: Reclaiming Security and Freedom in an Anxious Age."

15   "You need a sphere of immunity from surveillance to be yourself and do things that people in a free society take for granted," says Rosen. Things like going to the park or to the market. The loss of such autonomy is one of the "amorphous costs of having a world where there's no immunity from surveillance.

16   "This will transform the nature of public spaces in ways we could hardly imagine," he says. "People obviously behave differently when they're unsure about whether they're being observed. We know this from personal experience.

17   "I'm not at all suggesting that Orwell's '1984' is around the corner," he continues. "But things will change, and some of the changes will be good and others will be bad.

18   Christopher Slobogin, a University of Florida law professor, writes in his upcoming book, "Privacy at Risk":

19   "Anonymity in public promotes freedom of action and an open society. Lack of public anonymity promotes conformity and an oppressive society."

20   After all, who is Big Brother looking for in all this surveillance? People who are different, who do not fit a preconceived norm.

21   In their insistent way, those public digital message boards that urge us to "Report Suspicious Activity" are pushing a sense of that norm. In effect, they call upon ordinary people with no training or expertise to become surveillants and enforce a code of conduct, an expected norm, based on what might seem, to them, suspicious, or just different.

22   We watch what we say on the phone. Where once it was just a joke, now it is real: You never know if you might be tapped. We don't joke about bombs or hijacking, especially not in public. Not that we'd want to, mind you, but who remembers the days when it was just a joke? In mixed company, we don't say anything about al-Qaeda that isn't flat out condemnatory. And we are aware, alas, that our library book selections could be added to our possible dossiers, as per the USA Patriot Act.

23   How far can it go? We have only to recall the 2006 film "The Lives of Others," which portrays how the Stasi of Communist East Germany deployed hundreds of thousands of ordinary people to spy on their fellow citizens and turn them in.

24   The work of the new "behavior detection officers" watching us at airports is all about enforcing a norm. Part of the Transportation Security Administration, the officers are trained to detect extremely nervous, deceitful or unusual travelers by observing travelers' facial expressions and their behavior.

25   In training the BDOs, "we teach that everybody's been in an airport long enough to know what the norm is," says Carl Maccario, a program analyst for what the TSA calls SPOT, or Screening Passengers by Observation Techniques. "There's an expected norm or an expected baseline environment. . . . We teach the BDOs, in a simplified form, to look for anomalous behavior in that environment."

26   Being different? A big problem.

27   If we know we're being watched and know there is an expected mode of behavior, how does that change our actions?

28   Call it "anticipatory conformity." Shoshana Zuboff, a Harvard social psychologist who has studied information technology for decades, coined the phrase in 1988.

29   Applying that concept to the post-9/11 era, Zuboff says she sees anticipatory conformity all around and expects it to grow even more intense.

30   "I think the first level of that is we anticipate surveillance and we conform, and we do that with awareness," she says. "We know, for example, when we're going through the security line at the airport not to make jokes about terrorists or we'll get nailed, and nobody wants to get nailed for cracking a joke. It's within our awareness to self-censor. And that self-censorship represents a diminution of our freedom."

31   We self-censor, she says, not only to follow the rules, but also to avoid the shame of being publicly singled out.

32   Once anticipatory conformity becomes second nature, it becomes progressively easier for people to adapt to new impositions on their privacy, their freedoms. The habit has been set. People have "internalized the surveillance architecture" within their own subconscious.

33   We have yet to reach the level of surveillance of, say, the ubiquitous retina-scanning in the movie "Minority Report." But the technology is changing quickly.

34   "The next thing is they'll just have cameras everywhere," Zuboff says. "They'll have software programmed with algorithms, and the algorithms will be able to detect these so-called anomalies. And so you may be distraught because you're flying home to your grandmother's funeral, but the algorithm has detected an anomalous behavior, and the next thing you're being strip-searched by a couple of FBI agents."

35   And the technology advances so insidiously, so imperceptibly, that only later will we notice how deep the changes in our lives have been.

36   "It's a little bit like locked doors," says Paul Saffo, a technology forecaster and Stanford University instructor. "Today nobody has any concept of what it's like to have a house without a locked door or a security system.

37   "As the memory of a world without surveillance disappears, society will just create a new normal, and then you'll see worse horrors," he says. "Our whole lives will become like the TSA checkpoint. You walk in there, you don't look mad, don't look upset, don't look distracted. Do nothing to stand out."

38   Recalling an old Japanese saying that "the pheasant who flies gets shot," Saffo says the mindset of the future may be: "Practice being invisible."

39   Surveys reflect a mixed national mood on Big Brother. In a Washington Post-Kaiser Family Foundation-Harvard University poll conducted earlier this year respondents were split, 48 to 48 percent, on whether the government is doing enough to protect civil liberties as it fights terrorism.

40   More than a year earlier, in a Post-ABC News poll, 62 percent said the FBI should continue to have extra authority for wiretapping, obtaining records and surveillance in terror investigations.

41   In a different kind of opinion sample, Slobogin, the law professor, randomly selected 70 people from Florida jury pools and asked them to rank the level of intrusiveness of 25 law enforcement tactics, including several surveillance techniques.

42   In that 2006 study, the respondents ranked bedroom searches as the highest level of intrusiveness, followed by searches of e-mails, records from banks, pharmacies and credit cards, and the use of snoopware. The police pat-down—that classic of perceived intrusiveness—didn't rank as high.

43   In an earlier study, in 2002, 190 respondents also said bedroom searches were most intrusive, followed by body cavity searches at the border. But the monitoring of street surveillance cameras was a close third, deemed more intrusive than even a helicopter hovering over one's back yard.

44   People "don't expect to be stalked either by a person or by a camera—at least they don't like it," says Slobogin. "They expect to get lost in the crowd, or at least not to be monitored continuously."

45   And the "surveillance industrial complex," as some call it, is churning out ever more sophisticated methods for watching us, tracking us. Think: radio frequency identification chips. Think: iris recognition.

46   The surveillance camera? It is "no longer simply the fixed camera that looks like it's sitting inside a white shoe box pointing at the register of a 7-Eleven," says Marc Rotenberg, executive director of the Electronic Privacy Information Center.

47   "Now we have cameras that sit in black globes that zoom and pan at 360 degrees, have telescopic lenses and are beginning to interface with databases of facial images to try to do real-time matching of people in public places."

48   And cyberspace is littered with our spoor, our data trails, just lying there ready for the data miners to probe and find out what we buy, read, eat, how we spend, where we travel.

49   Just because you're paranoid doesn't mean no one's watching.

50   In fact, we can be watched and tracked from so many different angles in so many different ways that hints of the Panopticon are hard to ignore. That was the invention of the 18th century British economist Jeremy Bentham, who conceived of the Panopticon as a circular prison in which wardens could see prisoners at all times.

51   The Panopticon would create in the inmate a sense of "conscious and permanent visibility," and yet he "must never know whether he is being looked at at any one moment; but he must be sure that he may always be so," wrote philosopher Michel Foucault in his 1975 book, "Discipline & Punish: The Birth of the Prison."

52   Today, says Zuboff, we operate within an "information Panopticon."

53   "In our modern dematerialized world, you don't have to build a building to have permanent surveillance over individuals and their behavior," she says. "You can do it with an information system."

54   There is, admittedly, something creepy about all this: creepy, serious and very real, so much so that ordinary people are aware of the extent to which they are being watched and monitored. All that Doug Gooch asks is that data miners be honest about what they're doing.

55   "If they're going to monitor my use of the Internet, I should know up front," Gooch says. "Everything, to me, should be disclosed."

56   Gooch, 51, an engineer on vacation from Michigan, strolled the Mall last month with his wife and law-student son as the family took a few moments to mull the weighty questions of surveillance and a free society. They spoke with a hint of resignation.

57   "Maybe the free market will sort it out," said Kyle Gooch, 23. He was talking about data mining and the push by government agencies to get the records of some search engines. Maybe people will simply stop using certain sites, he offered.

58   "There needs to be a balance," said his mother, Shirlene Gooch, 49. While she wants law enforcement to be able to search for terrorists through cyberspace, she worries it could go too far. She worries, too, that worrying may be futile; that the proverbial train is well down the tracks, and it may be too late to intervene in technology's uses.

59   "It's hard to know when to stop," she said of law enforcement, adding, "There's no way to stop technology."

60   The Gooches strolled onward, under the surveillance camera's watchful eye. ✳

Exercises

Do not refer to the selection for Exercises A and B unless your instructor directs you to do so.

A. DETERMINING THE MAIN IDEA AND PURPOSE

Choose the best answer.

_____ 1. The main idea of the selection is that the increase in surveillance systems
  a. keeps the public safe, especially from terrorist attacks.
  b. is changing our culture, altering our behavior, and taking away our autonomy.
  c. promotes freedom of action since only wrongdoers have anything to worry about.
  d. has resulted in every aspect of our private lives being recorded in data files.

_____ 2. The writer's purpose is to
  a. debate the advantages and disadvantages of surveillance systems.
  b. examine her own experiences with being watched by cameras.
  c. explain the reasons that surveillance systems have become so prevalent.
  d. examine some psychological and social effects of surveillance systems.

B. COMPREHENDING MAIN IDEAS

Choose the correct answer.

_____ 1. At the beginning of the article, Duke cites a tower-high surveillance camera in Washington, DC, in a public area, specifically

   a. at the National Mall.
   b. in front of the White House.
   c. at Ronald Reagan National Airport.
   d. on Capitol Hill.

_____ 2. The writer cites several major effects of surveillance systems on the public. Which one was *not* mentioned?

   a. We experience a lack of public anonymity.
   b. We feel pressure to conform.
   c. Uniqueness and creativity become suspicious.
   d. We become increasingly anxious and suspicious of those around us.

_____ 3. Christopher Slobogin, a law professor at the University of Florida, has written that lack of public anonymity will result in

   a. more deviant behavior as people rebel against being constantly watched.
   b. surveillance systems being installed in our homes, just like Big Brother in *1984*.
   c. an increasingly oppressive society.
   d. a decrease in all types of crime.

_____ 4. Airports are now staffed with BDOs, "behavior detection officers," whose job it is to

   a. search baggage for bombs or other weapons.
   b. observe travelers' facial expressions and look for anomalous behavior.
   c. spy on fellow citizens to uncover any evidence of links to terrorists.
   d. strip-search passengers who behave in suspicious ways.

_____ 5. Paul Saffo, a professor at Stanford University, warns that, as the memory of a world without surveillance systems fades, a new normal will take over, resulting in

   a. every aspect of our lives being like airport security systems, and we will learn to act invisible.
   b. increased sales for biometric, security, and other surveillance equipment.
   c. increased fear and anxiety and public demand for even more surveillance equipment to keep us safe.
   d. increasingly secure houses that resemble residential forts.

_____ **6.** The Panopticon was invented by the eighteenth-century British economist Jeremy Bentham. Its purpose was to

    a. monitor people's behavior in public places.

    b. record people going about their daily business in public places.

    c. allow prison wardens to observe prisoners at all times.

    d. help sort through information compiled about people suspected of illegal activity.

COMPREHENSION SCORE

Score your answers for Exercises A and B as follows:

A. No. right _____ × 2 = _____

B. No. right _____ × 1 = _____

Total points from A and B _____ × 10 = _____ percent

You may refer to the selection as you work through the remaining exercises.

C. DISTINGUISHING BETWEEN MAIN IDEAS AND SUPPORTING DETAILS

Label the following ideas from the selection as follows: MI if it represents a _main idea_ and SD if it represents a _supporting detail_.

1. _____ According to Christopher Slobogin of the University of Florida, "Anonymity in public promotes freedom of action and an open society. Lack of public anonymity promotes conformity and an oppressive society."

2. _____ The Big Brother in all this surveillance is looking for people who are different, who do not fit a preconceived norm.

3. _____ Digital message boards that urge us to "Report Suspicious Activity" are an example of pushing this norm.

4. _____ Ordinary citizens with no training or expertise become surveillants and enforce a code of conduct based on what might seem suspicious or even just different.

5. _____ We watch what we say on the phone because we never know when the phone might be tapped.

6. _____ We no longer joke about hijackings or bombs in public, and our library book selections can be monitored under a certain provision of the Patriot Act.

D. DISTINGUISHING BETWEEN FACT AND OPINION

For each of the following ideas from the selection, write F if the statement represents a factual statement that can be verified or O if the statement represents the writer's or someone else's subjective interpretation. The first one is done for you.

1. _____ Surveillance robs people of their public anonymity.

2. _____ The pressure for conformity is endemic in a surveillance culture; creativity and uniqueness become its casualties.

3. _____ The loss of autonomy represents the downside of our surveillance-heavy culture.

4. _____ Our library book selections could be added to our possible dossiers, as per the USA Patriot Act.

5. _____ Officers for TSA, the Transportation Security Administration, are trained to detect extremely nervous, deceitful or unusual travelers by observing travelers' facial expressions and their behavior.

6. _____ Shoshana Zuboff, a Harvard social psychologist, calls the change in our behavior when we know we're being watched "anticipatory conformity."

7. _____ Once anticipatory conformity becomes second nature, it becomes progressively easier for people to adapt to new impositions on their privacy, their freedoms.

8. _____ In a *Washington Post*-Kaiser Family Foundation-Harvard University poll conducted in 2008 respondents were split, 48 to 48 percent, on whether the government is doing enough to protect civil liberties as it fights terrorism.

E. IDENTIFYING PATTERNS OF DEVELOPMENT

Read again the paragraphs listed below. Then write the pattern of development each passage uses. Here are your answer choices:

> list of facts or details
> examples
> cause and effect (reasons or results)
> process
> contrast

1. paragraph 2   _____

2. paragraphs 13 and 15   _____

3. paragraph 14   _____

4. paragraph 22   _____

5. paragraph 32 and 34   _____

6. paragraphs 41–43   _____

F. UNDERSTANDING VOCABULARY

Look through the paragraphs listed below and find a word that matches each definition. Refer to a dictionary if necessary. An example has been done for you.

Ex. seeming to exist everyone at once [paragraphs 2–4]   _____ubiquitous_____

1. gathering, collecting, picking out [2–4]   _____

2. most typically, describing the most characteristic [2–4]   _____

3. weighed down with, burdened with [5–7]   _____

4. lacking definite form or shape [13–15]   _____

5. independence, self-determination [13–15]   _____

6. standard model or pattern regarded as typical [used six times, 20–25]   _____

7. papers or folders containing information about people [20–23]   _____

8. put into use, brought into action [20–23]   _____

9. the process of reducing, diminishing, or decreasing [29–32]   _____

10. deeply agitated, emotionally upset [34–37]   _____

11. spreading harmfully in a subtle or stealthy manner [34–37]   _____

12. track or trail (in this usage); usually a track left by an animal [46–49]   _____

13. come between two things to prevent further use [55–60]   _____

14. think about extensively, ponder [55–60]   _____

G. USING VOCABULARY

In parentheses before each sentence are some inflected forms of words from the selection. Study the context and the sentence. Then write the correct form in the space provided.

1. (*oppress, oppression, oppressive, oppressively*) Law professor Christopher Slobogin worries that increased surveillance will lead to political

   _____ in our society.

2. (*condemn, condemnation, condemnatory*) If we don't flat out _____ terrorist groups like al-Qaeda, we could find ourselves in trouble if someone overhears us.

3. (*anticipate, anticipation, anticipatory*) Shoshana Zuboff calls our new behavior "_____ conformity," because we know we're being watched and we act accordingly.

4. (*randomize, random, randomly; intrude, intrusion, intrusive, intrusively*) When Slobogin asked 70 _____ people their views on surveillance techniques and asked them to rank which _____ most in their lives, bedroom searches were ranked first.

5. (*visibility, visible, visibly*) The Panopticon is a device used to give prison inmates the feeling of constant _____ .

H. PARAPHRASING EXERCISE

Here are some passages from the selection. Write a paraphrase of each passage in the space provided.

1. That's what the experts say: that surveillance robs people of their public anonymity. And they go even further, saying that pressure for conformity is endemic in a surveillance culture; that creativity and uniqueness become its casualties.

   _____

   _____

   _____

2. Once anticipatory conformity becomes second nature, it becomes progressively easier for people to adapt to new impositions on their privacy, their freedoms. The habit has been set. People have "internalized the surveillance architecture" within their own subconscious.

   _____

   _____

   _____

4. Recalling an old Japanese saying that "the pheasant who flies gets shot," [Paul] Saffo says the mindset of the future may be: "Practice being invisible." [Note: Do not paraphrase the Japanese saying but do explain its meaning in your paraphrase.]

   _____

   _____

   _____

I. ANNOTATING EXERCISE

For this exercise, assume that you are preparing to write an essay on the negative long-term effects of surveillance on our behavior. Go through Duke's article and locate any piece of information that supports this idea. To identify it, put a star in the margin next to the sentence or bracket the words.

J. TOPICS FOR DISCUSSION

1. How does the writer bolster her claim that increased surveillance is altering our behavior and producing what one expert calls "anticipatory conformity"? Is there sufficient evidence throughout the selection to support the claim?
2. Is the situation as serious as the writer suggests? That is, have you noticed your behavior in public changing as a result of security cameras or surveillance equipment? To what extent are monitoring devices (cameras and other forms of surveillance) used in your community? Do these devices make you feel safer, or do you consider them intrusive and threatening to your civil liberties?

K. TOPICS FOR WRITING

1. Write an essay in which you address this question: What limits, if any, should be placed on government surveillance in public places?
2. One of the most contested provisions of the USA Patriot Act, enacted by Congress in response to the 2001 terrorist attacks, was the right of the government to monitor the books one borrows from a public library. Write an essay in which you present arguments for one side or the other. Defend or attack the idea that the federal government has the right to subpoena and review books one borrows from a public library.
3. Write a short essay countering the evidence presented by the writer and the authorities she cites in the article. What are the positive aspects of increased surveillance both for individuals and for the society as a whole?

Exploring Related Web Sites

- Liberals and conservatives alike are united in opposition to the increase in surveillance of the American public. The American Civil Liberties Union, or ACLU, is liberal-leaning organization dedicated to protecting civil liberties from government intrusion. It has published an online document criticizing the government surveillance systems described in the article. Read the material titled "What's Wrong with Public Video Surveillance?" and evaluate it in light of the evidence Duke presents in the article.

   www.aclu.org/privacy/spying/14863res20020225.html

- Duke mentions the work of "behavior detection officers," who work for the TSA and who monitor passengers' behavior. The article, "Searching Passengers' Faces for Subtle Cues to Terror" by Del Quentin Wilber and Ellen Nakashima, also published in the *Washington Post* (September 19, 2007), explains what these BDOs look for:

  www.washingtonpost.com/wp-dyn/content/article/2007/09/18/AR2007091801891.html

24 DAVID FERRELL
Badwater: The Ultra-Marathon

David Ferrell is a journalism graduate of California State University, Fullerton. He wrote stories for the Los Angeles Times *for over 20 years, and he has also published a novel,* Screwball *(2003). In 1997, the* Times *published Ferrell's series of feature articles on extreme sports, which was nominated for a Pulitzer Prize in feature writing in 1998. Other articles in the series described the extreme sports of ice climbing, monster truck races, Ultimate Fighting, extreme kayaking, and BASE jumping, an illegal and extremely dangerous form of parachuting that jumpers do from land-based objects. (BASE is an acronym for buildings, antennas, spans [bridges], and earth [cliffs].)*

This article describes an annual ultra-race called Badwater—a punishing 135-mile race from Badwater in California's Death Valley to Mt. Whitney. The heat during the race can reach 118 degrees. Badwater is actually a salty pool with many dried salt beds. The area is distinguished because it is the lowest point in the Western Hemisphere, 282 feet below sea level. Temperatures there during the summer months have been recorded at 130 degrees Fahrenheit.

Vocabulary Preview

WORD PARTS

eu- [paragraph 22] Many long-distance runners commonly experience *euphoria*, a feeling of intense well-being and pleasure. As Ferrell writes, "For superbly fit athletes, who train by doing 10 or 20 miles a day, the early stages of a long race often produce the *euphoric* sensation that they could go on forever." The Greek prefix *eu-* means "well." (Be careful, however, not to confuse *eu-* with *eur-*, a prefix that generally denotes Europe.) Other words beginning with *eu-* are *euphony* (agreeable sound); *euphemism* (the substitution of an inoffensive term for one considered offensive or too explicit); and *eulogy* (a speech of praise of a person, usually of someone who has recently died). Consult your dictionary, if necessary, and define these words:

eugenics _____

euthanasia _____

Why did a popular new wave rock band of the 1980s call themselves the Eurhythmics? _____

_____

WORD FAMILIES

ignominious [paragraph 63] According to Ferrell, a runner who does not finish the Badwater race is called a "DNF," standing for "Did Not Finish," which Ferrell calls an *ignominious* epitaph, the worst thing a runner can be called. The difficult word *ignominious* has its origin in the Latin root *nomen*. Meaning "dishonor" or "disgrace," this word has a strongly negative connotation. The noun form can be broken down like this: *in-* ("not") + *nomen* ("name" or "reputation"). Other words containing the root *nomen* are *anonymity* (having no name); *nominal* (existing in name only); and oddly, the word *noun* itself, literally, the name of something.

DAVID FERRELL

Badwater: The Ultra-Marathon

1   Badwater is a madman's march, a footrace through the summer heat of the hottest spot in America. It extends 135 miles from a stinking water hole on the floor of Death Valley to a piney oasis 8,300 feet up the side of Mt. Whitney. The course is nothing but asphalt and road gravel. Feet and knees and shins ache like they are being whacked with tire irons. Faces turn into shrink-wrap.

2   Lisa Smith is 102 miles into it. She has been running, and now walking, for almost 27 hours, through yesterday's 118-degree heat, up 6,000 feet of mountain passes into a 40 mph head wind. The night brought her 40 minutes of sleep, if that—two catnaps.

3   Her feet are blistered and taped up, and she is wearing shoes with the toes cut out to relieve the pressure. Her right ankle, sprained twice since February, is so swollen she can no longer wear the air cast that was supporting it. She is also cramping with diarrhea.

4   "It's bad," she says, gasping. "My stomach is killing me."

5   Grimacing, spitting, bending over at times to fight the nausea, she trudges on, pushing down the undulating highway toward Keeler, a ramshackle mining outpost. Visible ahead is the serrated peak of Whitney, as distant as Oz. If she can hang on, it will take most of the day—and a 4,000 foot ascent over the final 13 miles— to get there.

6   Every year, two or three dozen elite ultra-marathoners come to Badwater, and every year Badwater beats them down. About a third fail to finish; after 50 miles or 70 miles or 110 miles, the torture exceeds their desire to go on, and they end up rolling away in their cars and minivans, faces covered with wet towels, their bodies stretched out like corpses.

7   For a thin slice of society—zealots who live to train, who measure themselves by their mental toughness—the ultra-marathon is the consummate test of human character. No other event in sport, except possibly a prizefight, is as punishing, as demanding of the mind and body. No other athlete is more

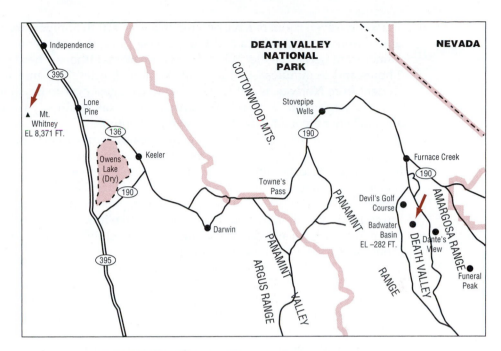

The course of the ultra-marathon starts at Badwater (right arrow) and ends at Mt. Whitney (left arrow).

revered than the distance runner. Indefatigable, heroic, celebrated in poetry and myth, the Greek soldier, Pheidippides, ran 26 miles from Marathon to Athens to herald victory over the Persians in 490 B.C., then collapsed and died. It was the first marathon. To fill the unforgiving minute, to persevere, is one of the highest ideals of man—who, after all, was born to hardship, cast from Eden.

8   The explosion of extreme sports in recent years has produced an unprecedented number of ultra-endurance races. Several thousand men and women travel the country—and abroad—competing in events from 30 miles to more than 300 miles. There are weeklong "adventure races" by foot, bike and kayak across Patagonia, South Africa, and Australia.

9   In Morocco, there is the Marathon des Sables—"the Marathon of the Sands"— a six-day trek, in stages, across 150 miles of the Sahara. Colorado has the Hardrock 100, snaking 100 miles through the 11,000-foot peaks of the San Juan Mountains. In Alaska it's the Coldfoot, a 100-miler in October with the wind roaring and the temperatures plunging to 40 below.

10   Death Valley has Badwater: "probably the most physically taxing competitive event in the world," according to the runners' handbook, which warns that you could die out here—though no one yet has. "Heat illness or heat stroke . . . can cause death, kidney failure and brain damage. It is important that runners and crews be aware of the symptoms . . . vomiting, headache, dizziness, faintness, irritability, lassitude, weakness and rapid heart rate. . . . Heat stroke may progress from minimal symptoms to complete collapse in a very short period of time."

11   Twenty-seven runners have entered this year's 10th anniversary race, a field drawn from North America and Europe. Lisa, 36, is the only woman, a fitness trainer from Bernardsville, N.J., who has run 60 marathons—her fastest in 2 hours and 48 minutes—and four ultras. Bjarte Furnes, 23, a molecular biology student from Norway, is out to become the youngest ever to finish. Beacham Toler, 69, a retired boilermaker from Amarillo, Texas, is already the oldest; he aims to better a personal best by breaking 50 hours.

12   The course record, set five years ago, is 26 hours and 18 minutes, but few concern themselves with that or the first place prize money—$500. The main goal is to go the distance, because Badwater, like every extreme race, is less a competition among runners—whose training and talents vary widely—than it is a struggle between each runner and the miles. To conquer the course, you must get through it in less than 60 hours. Those who make it in under 48—two days and two nights—are awarded a special memento, a belt buckle, a modest hunk of bronze featuring a bas relief of the desert.

13   "If I don't make it, I'll be back every year until I do," vows U.S. Marine Corps Major W. C. Maples, 33, a second-time entrant from Camp Pendleton who stands now at the starting line, shortly before dawn. Three years back, during Utah's Wasatch 100, he got off the floor of an aid station despite hypothermia and winced through the last 50 miles with a stress fracture in his right leg.

14   But Badwater got him a year ago. The Major, as other runners call him, quit after vomiting up a bunch of pink, fleshy tissue that turned out to be part of his stomach lining. It was the only endurance race he failed to complete.

15   "I have fumed over that," he says. "One way I define a challenge is something that does not have a guaranteed outcome. I know that on my worst day I can strap on a pair of shoes and run 26 miles. But here, no matter what kind of shape you're in, there's no guarantee you're going to finish. I can relate to that. I train for combat. Combat does not have a guaranteed outcome."

THE BODY IS UNDER ENORMOUS ASSAULT

16   The race begins in the dawn glow of a clear, breezy morning, below a craggy cliff of the Amargosa Mountains on the valley's east rim. From a casino-hotel on the Nevada-California border, where the runners spent the night, it has taken more than 40 minutes to reach Badwater, so named for an acrid, amoeba-shaped pool of salt and brimstone just off the road. Its brittle white edges look like crusts of ice, but that is a desert illusion because the temperature at 5:30 A.M. is 92 degrees.

17   A weather-chipped placard notes that the earth here sinks to the lowest point in the Western Hemisphere: 282 feet below sea level. Minivans and cars fill a narrow parking lot. The support crews tend to number one to four people—wives, coaches, in-laws, friends, gurus, anyone willing to dispense water, food and exhortations. The vans are packed high with provisions—gallons of water, sandwiches, fruit, candy bars, protein bars, Gatorade, pretzels, crackers, salt tablets, sea salt, socks, shorts, blister pads, tape, towels, ankle braces, sunglasses, sunscreen, five or six pairs of shoes, and a bathroom scale.

18   Sahara hats are popular—white, Lawrence of Arabia headgear that shades the neck and cheeks. A few runners, like the Norwegian, wear them tailored to hold

clumps of crushed ice, a cold skullcap. Dr. Dale Sutton, 57, a San Diego dentist, carries ice atop his head and in hanging pouches near his cheeks as well as in the pockets of his running togs: pinstriped blue pajamas sliced with ventilation holes. He is known as the Pajama Man.

19   Runners stretch, mingle and pose for pictures—all in eerie quiet, because it is so early, or because they are about to wage combat, or because the open desert sky swallows up most of the sound. At 6 A.M., they assemble on the road. No speeches, no fanfare. They are told to go. They take off to the whoops and claps of the support crews.

20   In all the miles to follow, these will be the only spectators; no one else will appreciate their toil, except perhaps the whizzing motorists and the occasional bystanders who have stopped for a Coke or radiator coolant in towns hardly larger than a gas station.

21   At first the road climbs gradually north along the valley floor, away from hills and escarpments named Funeral Peak, Coffin Canyon and Dante's View. The ruddy desert loam tilts toward ridges to the east and falls to the yellow-white valley bowl to the west. For long stretches there is almost no vegetation, just rocky fields divided by the winding asphalt.

22   They move at a fast, easy gait. For superbly fit athletes, who train by doing 10 or 20 miles a day, the early stages of a long race often produce the euphoric sensation that they could go forever. Runners like to savor it, aware of their own breathing, the length and balance of their strides.

23   "I focus on what I'm doing, how I'm feeling," says the man who takes the early lead, Eric Clifton, one of America's great ultra-marathoners. "I'm constantly monitoring myself, keeping my legs relaxed, running smoothly, keeping my arm relaxed. Is my face tensed up? I'm trying to be as efficient as possible."

24   The 39-year-old movie buff, a theater projectionist from Crownsville, Md., has won more than half of the 68 ultra-marathons he has completed; he set an unofficial record last year by running a 100-miler in 13 hours and 16 minutes. Like most who venture into such extreme races, Eric began more modestly, running the two-mile in high school, later dabbling in 5- and 10-kilometer road races. Once he realized his own exceptional stamina, he advanced to marathons and triathlons, then ultra-marathon cycling races.

25   With his long, pendular strides and short, pink socks, Eric moves well in front, followed by a pack that includes Lisa and the Major, steady at 9 minutes per mile.

26   At 7 A.M., the sun emerges above the Amargosas; it is 105 degrees—in the shade. At 7:15, it is 108. At 7:25, it is 110. A hot, dry wind pushes the competitors along. Dragonflies blow around in it. Tinder-dry weeds quiver in the canyon washes. At Furnace Creek, 17 miles out, the runners veer northwest on California 190, passing a borax museum and descending again into the yawning desolation of a dry lake bed where the thermometer reads 114. The asphalt is at least 20 degrees hotter.

27   Faces and shirts are sweat-soaked. Support vans play leapfrog with the runners, moving ahead a mile or so at a time. Runners stop briefly to drink, many alternating water and electrolyte supplements. How much they drink, eat, weigh, how hot they are, how fast they are going—every detail is logged by

crew members, who take on the mien of anxious scientists, recording the vitals of subjects in some grotesque lab experiment.

28   The body is already under enormous assault; the success of the hours ahead will hinge largely on the fickle alchemy of supplying it proper nutrition. Sweat loss alone in this heat can exceed a gallon an hour. Dehydration is a constant danger. Usually, it is accompanied by the depletion of blood sugar and electrolytes—sodium, potassium and other ions that are vital to cells and muscles.

29   Cells die; muscles cramp. In extreme cases, the heart may go into fibrillation, which can be fatal. More often, the body channels extra blood to the heart and brain, robbing it from other places—the skin, kidneys and bowels. A runner gets the chills. Kidneys clog with protein from damaged muscles, damming up toxins in the blood. The walls of the empty bladder sometimes rub at the pubic bone, causing internal bleeding and producing an intense urge to urinate. Pieces of the bowel or stomach wall may slough off in diarrhea.

30   Rarely, the body temperature climbs high enough, 104 degrees, to affect the brain; the runner may slip into convulsions or a coma.

31   Drinking is a safeguard, but huge amounts of water may overwhelm the gastrointestinal tract, causing cramps, bloating, nausea. Even sports drinks may not contain enough electrolytes—or the body may not absorb them well enough—to prevent problems. It is often a matter of luck, experience or genetics that enables one runner to endure while the man behind him folds up like a scarecrow.

DISTANCE RUNNER'S RITE OF PASSAGE

32   Badwater delivers its earliest savagery to those from cooler climes. A Swiss runner with stomach cramps is the first to drop out. Bjarte, the Norwegian, vomits after 18 miles—the beginnings of an agonizing downward spiral that would end with his surrender, 10 hours later, at Mile 53, by which point he had thrown up, in the estimation of one crew member, at least 40 more times.

33   A 33-year-old Canadian, Paul Braden, once ran a Colorado 100-miler in which his blisters got so bad he had to cut off his shoes with scissors, drain the wounds and go the last 15 miles with sandals taped to his feet. But that was not as agonizing as the cramps and nausea he now suffers as he nears Devil's Cornfield, a grove of clumpy arrow weed bushes 36 miles out.

34   With the wind raking across the road, with the temperature reaching 118 degrees, Paul drops a red flag—a legal means of temporarily leaving the course—and accepts a car ride to Stovepipe Wells, a burg at 41 miles consisting of a motel, a saloon and a convenience store. There, officials from Hi-Tec, the athletic gear company that sponsors the race, help him into the back of a refrigerated bottled-water truck. His legs keep cramping and he is screaming so loud that a few tourists wander over, trying to see what is going on.

35   A white-haired race official administers a carbonated electrolyte beverage whose effect is immediate: Paul vomits all over the truck bed. The theory is that his balky digestion—gummed up by too much fruit—will now return to normal. Looking queasy, Paul is driven back to his flag. He resumes, suffers more cramps, ends up resting, falling asleep and finally dragging himself back onto the road in the evening, when the worst of the heat is over.

36   Finishing the race is the rite of passage of the distance runner. The sport culls out the weak and rewards the dogged. The runner learns that pain is temporary, but the gulf between those who drop out and those who finish is vast and enduring. With every step, an investment is made. It is either lost on the roadside or it becomes a jackpot that you reap at the end.

37   Having completed Badwater three times, Barbara Warren, a San Diego sports psychologist, has found that "the deep satisfaction in life comes from this enormous achievement. You feel like a giant."

38   Often, athletes spend months training and planning for Badwater, which raises the emotional stake in how it turns out. Paul tried to prepare himself for Death Valley by traveling to Amarillo, Texas, a month beforehand, running 10 to 15 miles a day in 100-degree heat.

39   The Major began training for Badwater in January, expanding his regimen to include twice-monthly workouts in the desert near Borrego Springs. Every trip he ran 25 to 30 miles, alone, bored, baking in the sun. "By the end of June, I had put in almost 1,600 miles just for this one race," he says. There are other forces: All the Marines at Camp Pendleton who know he is representing the Corps—what will they think if he quits? The lessons he learned from his mother, who has spent 27 years battling a degenerative stomach disorder, and his grandfather, who survived the same malady until he was 87, still mowing his lawn at 86.

40   If you get through a thing like Badwater, a lot of life's other problems seem far more manageable, the Major says. But the moment you let yourself quit, you step onto a slippery slope. One day you quit at 90 miles and the next you quit at 60. Before long you are getting by with the minimum, rationalizing mediocrity.

41   "Quitting is a disease," he says. "I can't bear the idea of looking in a mirror and seeing a quitter."

42   The Major is now bearing down on the 50-mile mark, nine miles beyond Stovepipe. It is well into afternoon. The road climbs; it will reach 6,000 feet at the end of the 18-mile stretch to Towne's Pass in the Panamint Mountains. The wind is coming downhill, and it is directly in the runners' faces—a steady blast that seems to come from some humongous hair dryer. No one runs; they walk tilting into the wind at comical angles, like a bunch of Charlie Chaplins.

43   The Marine Corps flag snaps wildly from the rear of the Major's support van. His face, faintly freckled, is rigid, his eyes fixed on the road. All of his elaborate philosophy has been bludgeoned down into a tight-lipped, 10-word mantra: "Mind over matter: If you don't mind, it doesn't matter."

44   Much of the first half of the field is scattered along the 18-mile climb. Eric is still well in front—he's already through the pass—trailed by a runner from Tennessee and then Lisa, in third place, but well back and struggling. Her 10- and 12-minute miles have disintegrated to this: a mile logged at a woeful 25 minutes.

45   Nauseated, weakened by diarrhea that began the night before the race—a result of nerves, her crew thinks—she is limping too, with an air cast supporting her bad right ankle. It is still hot—107 at 4:30 P.M.—and she has at least 24 hours to go.

46   She tries not to think about the punishment ahead. Long-haired and purposeful, a former springboard diver at the University of Wisconsin, she is a staunch believer in mental strength, spiritualism, holistic healing. Like the Major, she is inspired by the courage of others: her younger sister, Julie, a member of her support crew, who overcame life-threatening surgery to repair three small holes in her heart; her cousin Joe, who was Lisa's age when he died last year of AIDS.

47   "He got a tattoo in New Orleans," she says. "Seven guys all used the same needle. All seven of them are dead."

48   Music from a movie they enjoyed together, "The Last of the Mohicans," plays on her headphones.

49   All the runners are adrift out here, sorting through their thoughts, weighing the reasons to push on. A few miles behind Lisa is the 69-year-old Texan, Beacham, who slumps into a folding chair to gulp water from a plastic bottle.

50   "This right here is pretty agonizing," he says, but nothing of the ordeal shows on his face, thin as a hawk's. Beacham looks as if everything soft in him has boiled away on the hard roads—and maybe it has. He runs 3,000 miles a year, seven or eight ultra-marathons.

51   Despite a poor spell at 38 miles, where he had to lie down and take some chicken noodle soup, he is keeping up at a formidable pace. The drive seems to come from a fear of growing old, says crew member Jim Davis, who is 58. Ultras are especially important to Beacham because without them, without all the training, he would figure to start withering away.

52   "I think he wants to get in as many of them as he can," Jim says, "before he gets to where he can't."

HALLUCINATIONS NOT UNCOMMON

53   Evening is falling. The corrugated mountains near Towne's Pass glow warm orange and black, painted by slanting sunlight and shadows. Bruised clouds blow over the ridges. At 7:30, the sun sinks into the clouds rimming 6,585-foot Panamint Butte, gone until morning, and a soft violet haze settles over Death Valley. The plum-colored Amargosas, where the day began, are a ruffled curtain across the other side of the world.

54   The heat subsides—it is 86 degrees at 8:10, when the first automobile headlights fill the shadows. Eric, the race leader, descends into the Panamint Valley, where indolent followers of Charles Manson are still said to inhabit the brushy foothills near the Barker Ranch.

55   Eric is now feeling it. Downhills are murder on the thighs; after the intense early pace, his are aching like "somebody was beating them with baseball bats." At Mile 68, near a motel stop called Panamint Springs, he is passed by a 45-year-old investor named David Jones, who has yet to take a rest. Even when he had to vomit, up at the pass, he turned his head, retched and pressed on.

56   David opens a substantial lead. With the light fading in a landscape of rolling hills and ridges, Eric and Lisa contend for second place. A quick glance up to a stream of purple-orange clouds and Lisa sees a face—her cousin Joe's face, a vision that lasts an instant and is gone. It inspires her, but also saddens her. She cries. She tells her crew about it. Soon, the sky deepens, and even those tangled clouds disappear, leaving her there on the road toiling.

57   The darkness takes over. She sees a shooting star and is heartened by whatever hope it might portend, but before long she is crying again.

58   Night is hard. Night is for demons. Night is when rationality shrinks away, slipping down a rabbit hole, and nothing remains but the black asphalt and black sky and the questions that flicker through shorting mental circuits, like: Where is the horizon, what creatures are out here, why does it matter, really, to keep on going?

59   Hallucinations are not uncommon. Two years ago, when she got through Badwater in less than 42 hours, her first ultra-marathon, Lisa had a conversation with her dead grandmother. She heard babies crying, Indians chanting. "I saw things flying through the air," she remembers. "All the trees on Whitney, I thought they were people climbing."

60   Others have seen dogs, herds of cows, miniature people pushing tiny sleds, women showering, cactuses magically transformed into rocket launchers, highway skid marks shooting away like harpoons, flying off to infinity. One runner remembers an elaborate bridge under construction, spanning the highway, with an office building next door. Only the next day, when he was driving back over the course and looking for it, did he learn from his crew that all of it was pixie dust.

61   The runners are illuminated for periods of time by headlights, until the support vans pull ahead, leaving them to catch up again. At the west rim of Panamint Valley is another climb, through a 4,000-foot pass called Father Crowley's. It is cool enough there for long sleeves and sweatpants; the runners change during the stops. Here and there, they nap—half an hour, an hour, rarely longer.

62   Two more drop out, one because of a long, purple thigh bruise, the result of a pinched nerve and tendinitis. Eric goes lame on the downside of Crowley's; he dawdles through 10 miles in six hours and quits at dawn at Mile 94. Having won so many times, he places no stigma on stepping away, regrouping, aiming for another race. That is not the case for the less accomplished. For most who quit, the failure is a trauma almost equal to the pounding of the miles.

63   A runner who stops ceases to be a runner. It is a death of that identity, marked by an ignominious epitaph: "Did not finish." The phrase is abbreviated on the printouts that list the winners, and the slang verb, "DNF-ing," has an obscene sound, foul with shame. The runner who succumbs often goes to extraordinary lengths for resurrection, training for months and traveling back to the same race, the same course, a year or two later, to try again.

64   Twenty-four hours have gone by. Fatigue seeps like ice water into bones and joints. Walking is the rule now. Rest stops lengthen. Closing their eyes, they get leg massages. They take time to patch blisters, tape their feet, change shoes. They go up half a size when the swelling is bad. They drink hot soup and get up with the painful slowness of old men.

65   Gossip travels up and down the course in irregular pulses, moving from race officials to support crews, then to the runners. They crave information about the whereabouts of others, how they are doing. Eric's withdrawal is surprising news. It is rare now that one runner sees another, except on arduous grades or during long stops when someone is passed.

66   Lisa slips into third place. Beacham drops back into 10th, an hour ahead of the Major. Only twice during the night has Beacham slept, once for 15 minutes, another time for 20. He maintains a steady pace through Crowley's despite a blister on the ball of each foot, wounds that have been growing for almost 60 miles.

67   "It was pretty painful until I got them lanced," he says, his breath as sharp as piston stokes. "They hurt now, but I can stand it."

68   Beyond the pass, the road levels out near 4,000 feet, angling northwest along the Saline Valley and the dry Owens Lake bed: contoured terrain that grows nothing but rust-colored scrub. A wall of white mountains fills the far horizon. This is another of Badwater's psychological slams. One of those distant, chiseled peaks is Whitney.

69   "You can see the finish," says a runner, "but it's 51 miles away."

70   The sun climbs into the blue vastness of space and they pass one by one down the long, rippled road, a line of asphalt that runs forever.

71   "The sun's coming up, and pretty soon the sun will go down, and that's what you have to think about," says Dale, the Pajama Man, who at 7 A.M. is distracting himself, playing mental word games, his gangly limbs swinging as if they are loose in their sockets. "You have to disassociate your body from the pain."

72   At a drink stop, he sips slowly, to avoid spitting it up, and tries to gauge his progress.

73   "I have, what? Thirty-five miles to go?"

74   "No," a crew member tells him. "Forty-seven."

"IT'S BEYOND EXHILARATION"

75   In spite of the distance remaining, race officials are able to make a reasonably accurate projection of the finishers. They can see who is going well, the ones who will probably hang on.

76   David Jones, victorious only once in 57 prior marathons and ultra-marathons, is far ahead in first, already nearing Lone Pine, the tree-lined town at the base of Whitney. He is on his way to clocking 29 hours and 10 minutes, more than five hours ahead of the man in second.

77   Most of the top 10 runners will earn a buckle. Beacham's blisters will continue to plague him, but he is on his way to finishing in 43 hours and 53 minutes, well under his goal of 50 hours. The Major limps on a swollen right knee and is chafing so badly in the crotch that a streak of blood runs to the knee of his white sweatpants. His crew has dubbed him "Mad Mood Maples"; he is headed for a time of 45:15.

78   At least 18 others are also on the way to finishing. Seven have quit. That number might reach eight. Lisa is the one in doubt—the only remaining runner in serious trouble who has not yet withdrawn.

79   At 102 miles, she clings to third, reeling from her bad ankle and diarrhea and sleep loss. To go the next six miles to Keeler takes her four hours. Lone Pine is 16 miles beyond Keeler. Morning turns to afternoon. The sun beats down; temperatures soar into the 90s. The highway veers right into Long Pine, past an airport, motels, diners, then left at a traffic light onto the two-lane road up Whitney.

80   This final stretch, a 4,000 foot ascent over 13 winding miles, is by far the most daunting. It begins gradually—the road flanked by sagebrush and boulders and tall rock formations that look like brown crispy cereal all glued together. Soon it rises to impossible steepness.

81   Lisa is still on the lower slopes at 3 o'clock, taking ice treatments on her ankles. They are both so badly swollen they barely move. Coming out of the motor home, she is staggering. Turning uphill, her mirrored glasses catching the hot sun, she looks ready to cry. Two crew members walk alongside, ready in case she should collapse.

82   "Never, Never Quit," says a spray-painted slogan across the back of the motor home, but sometimes such lofty ideals must give way to reason. Her crew huddles in the road, discussing whether to make her stop. Her mother, Dot, squints up the mountain.

83   "It's scary," she says. "She doesn't want to give up. I think we're trying to make the decision for her. My theory is, live to race another day."

84   Arguing for surrender is that in two weeks she is scheduled to compete in a 300-mile adventure race, a team event for which she and her friends have paid hefty entrance fees. It is unthinkable to miss it, but the recovery from an ultra-marathon can take weeks. Most runners are fortunate to begin training again in six or seven days; stamina may not return for a month or two.

85   Lisa, though, doesn't always make the rational decision. Crew member Tony Di Zinno remembers an earlier adventure race, when she suffered a sprained ankle and a hairline fracture of her right leg on the second day out. She strapped on an air cast and kept going, six more days, 250 more miles.

86   Her hope had been to break the women's record for Badwater—36 hours and 19 minutes, set during a race that began at night. That goal is now out of reach. With eight miles to go, Lisa disappears into the motor home. Sister Julie stands outside, helpless, wondering if this is where Lisa will yield.

87   "She says she's never felt this bad," Julie says. "She can't bend her ankles, they're so swollen. There's no blood in her urine yet, but she thinks she lost her stomach lining."

88   For almost half an hour, there is only this still-life picture: the motor home under a cloudless sky, the rugged mountainside rising above it. Now and then a breeze stirs, but all the air seems to move at once, muffling sounds, preserving a strange hush. Insects clicking softly in the sagebrush. Inside, Lisa lies on her ravaged stomach. She will explain later that it is unwise at this point to sleep: The body begins to shut down. Instead, she meditates. In her mind she makes a list of all those reasons she should quit, the complaints of 127 horrific miles, every negative thought. When the list is as long as she can make it, she lights a tiny imaginary fire—and she burns it.

89   The door opens. She is helped down to the pavement, and she turns to confront the mountain.

90   "I'm going to get to the top."

91   Upward, then, with the road growing steeper. Her ankles cannot handle the slope, and so she turns around, walking backward, tiny three-inch steps. Up, up, up, staring into the sky, Whitney rising behind her. At 5:45, she is well up the mountain, the road at last curving into the afternoon shadows.

92   Pine trees begin to appear. Her legs look puffed up, rubbery, but they keep moving. Where the road levels out she turns around, walking forward until it rises again. At 6 o'clock, she has less than four miles to go. Every step is precarious, but her mood soars—"it's beyond exhilarating"—and she talks in strained breaths about a book, "The Power Within," by Chuck Norris, and how its lessons helped her through the hard moments.

93   Less than a mile to go and the road rounds a steep turn. Lisa goes through it backward, her arms out, as if dizzy. Immediately, four Marines—the advance guard from the Major's group—jump out of a van and join her, like jet fighters forming an escort, but they drop away after the final curve, letting Lisa take the last hill alone.

94   Whitney Portals, where the race ends, is tucked within a nook of chalky granite: a clear pool fed by a plunging waterfall, hillsides thick with tall evergreens. A yellow tape is stretched across the road and Lisa hits it, finishing in 37 hours and 1 minute. It is not the record she wanted, but it is the fastest a woman has gone from a daytime start, when the racers cross the floor of Death Valley in the heat.

95   Officials, crew members and five or six bystanders surround her, applauding. She is weeping, relieved, overjoyed, falling into the embrace of her sister, her mom, her friends. She looks up at the sky and says thank you. A huge bouquet of red roses is placed in her arms, spilling over them in a glorious scene of triumph—a portrait somehow perfect, but also fleeting, because Lisa quickly hands the roses away.

96   "Can't hold them," she whispers. "They're too heavy." ✳

From David Ferrell, "Far Beyond a Mere Marathon," *Los Angeles Times,* August 23, 1997. © 1997 Los Angeles Times. Reprinted by permission of *Los Angeles Times* Syndication.

Postscript: In July 2002, Pam Reed of Tucson, Arizona, became the first woman to win the Badwater Marathon, running the course in 27 hours and 56 minutes, which shattered the women's record. Lisa Smith also ran in the 2002 race. Of the 79 who entered, 24 runners had "DNF" next to their names on the leader board. The 30th anniversary of the Badwater race was held in July 2007. See Exploring Related Web sites for more information.

Exercises

Do not refer to the selection for Exercises A and B unless your instructor directs you to do so.

A. DETERMINING THE MAIN IDEA AND PURPOSE

Choose the best answer.

_____ **1.** The main idea of the selection is that

    a. ultra-races like Badwater should be abolished or at least regulated by the government.

    b. ultra-marathoners like those who enter the Badwater race are the elite of the running world.

    c. for running zealots, an ultra-marathon like Badwater is the supreme test of human character and the ability to endure.

    d. the climate in Death Valley is not suitable for ultra-marathon races like the annual Badwater race.

_____ **2.** The writer's purpose is to

    a. convince the reader that reform of ultra-races like Badwater is necessary.

    b. explain how the Badwater ultra-race works and why runners enter such races.

    c. discuss the physiological changes and long-term physical damage caused by participating in ultra-marathon races.

    d. trace the history of ultra-marathon races.

B. COMPREHENDING MAIN IDEAS

Choose the correct answer.

_____ **1.** Every year around a third of the runners who attempt the Badwater race fail to finish because

    a. their physicians and trainers make them stop to avoid permanent damage.

    b. the torture they experience is greater than their desire to go on.

    c. they realize that their training was not sufficient to complete the race.

    d. they collapse, unable to continue.

_____ **2.** Because of the extreme heat, the *primary* physical danger to runners in the Badwater race is

    a. dehydration.

    b. kidney failure.

    c. loss of memory.

    d. heat stroke.

_____ **3.** The beginning point of the race is at Badwater, known specifically as the Western Hemisphere's

    a. highest point.

    b. hottest point.

    c. lowest point.

    d. only salt-and-brimstone pool.

_____ **4.** For runners who participate in the Badwater race, the most serious offense, one that assumes enormous significance for everyone concerned, is

    a. not having a reliable crew along the course.

    b. attempting the race without preparing for it adequately.

      c. quitting before reaching the end.
      d. letting down their sponsors.

_____ 5. Ferrell writes that those runners who do not finish the course (those who have "Did not finish" written next to their names on the list of entrants) generally

      a. decide to give up running permanently.
      b. suffer such physical damage that they can no longer compete in ultra-races.
      c. are scorned and ridiculed by their fellow runners.
      d. train even harder for the race the next year.

_____ 6. Lisa Smith, the only woman to enter this particular year's race (in 1997), eventually made it to the finish line on Mt. Whitney by

      a. crawling on her hands and knees.
      b. walking backward.
      c. experiencing a last-minute burst of energy.
      d. becoming revitalized from her family's support.

COMPREHENSION SCORE

Score your answers for Exercises A and B as follows:

A. No. right _____ × 2 = _____
B. No. right _____ × 1 = _____
Total points from A and B _____ × 10 = _____ percent

You may refer to the selection as you work through the remaining exercises.

C. DISTINGUISHING BETWEEN FACT AND OPINION

For each of the following statements from the selection, write F if the statement represents a factual statement that can be verified or O if the statement represents the writer's or someone else's subjective interpretation. The first one is done for you.

1. ___F___ Every year, two or three dozen elite ultra-marathoners come to Badwater, and every year Badwater beats them down.

2. _____ For a thin slice of society—zealots who live to train, who measure themselves by their mental toughness—the ultra-marathon is the consummate test of human character.

3. _____ About a third fail to finish; after 50 miles or 70 miles or 110 miles, the torture exceeds their desire to go on, and they end up rolling away in their cars or minivans, faces covered with wet towels, their bodies stretched out like corpses.

4. _____ No other event in sport, except possibly a prizefight, is as punishing, as demanding of the mind and body.

5. _____ No other athlete is more revered than the distance runner.

6. _____ To fill the unforgiving minute, to persevere, is one of the highest ideals of man—who, after all, was born to hardship, cast from Eden.

7. _____ The explosion of extreme sports in recent years has produced an unprecedented number of ultra-endurance races.

8. _____ Several thousand men and women travel the country—and abroad—competing in events from 30 miles to more than 300 miles.

D. MAKING INFERENCES

For each of these statements write Y (Yes) if the inference is an accurate one, N (No) if the inference is an inaccurate one, or CT (Can't Tell) if the writer does not give you enough information to make an inference one way or another.

1. _____ Badwater is an unusual kind of ultra-marathon because the outcome is not guaranteed. [paragraph 15]

2. _____ For the runners who enter the Death Valley race, competition between them is keen, and their desire to place first is their main motivation. [selection as a whole]

3. _____ During the race, participants must run at all times; walking is not permitted. [selection as a whole]

4. _____ If Lisa Smith had started the Badwater race at night, rather than during the day, her finish time would probably have been better. [selection as a whole]

5. _____ Runners from cool climates, for example, Switzerland or Norway, are at a disadvantage because they do not train in the hot-weather conditions that they will encounter in the real race. [paragraph 32]

6. _____ Ferrell is a marathon runner. [selection as a whole]

E. INTERPRETING MEANING

Where appropriate, write your answers for these questions in your own words.

1. _____ Which sentence *best* represents the thesis of the article as a whole?
   a. "Badwater is a madman's march, a footrace through the summer heat of the hottest spot in America."
   b. "Every year, two or three dozen elite ultra-marathoners come to Badwater, and every year Badwater beats them down."
   c. "For a thin slice of society—zealots who live to train, who measure themselves by their mental toughness—the ultra-marathon is the consummate test of human character."
   d. "The explosion of extreme sports in recent years has produced an unprecedented number of ultra-endurance races."

   Explain the reason for your answer. _____

   _____

2. What are some characteristics of long-distance runners who enter ultra-marathons like the one Ferrell describes? List two or three qualities that the writer emphasizes. _____

_____

3. Identify three metaphors or similes—imaginative comparisons—in paragraph 1. _____

_____

4. An *allusion* is a reference to something outside a particular piece of writing. Allusions can refer to literature, to religion, to historical events, and so forth. In paragraph 5, Ferrell writes that the peak of Mt. Whitney is as distant as Oz, and at the end of paragraph 7, he writes, "To fill the unforgiving minute, to persevere, is one of the highest ideals of man—who, after all, was born to hardship, cast from Eden." Consult a dictionary if necessary, and explain these two allusions in your own words.

Oz _____

_____

Eden _____

_____

5. Look again at paragraphs 95 and 96 and then explain the irony in Lisa Smith's handing the bouquet of red roses away. _____

_____

F. UNDERSTANDING VOCABULARY

Choose the best definition according to an analysis of word parts or the context.

_____ 1. the *undulating* highway [paragraph 5]
   a. having a wavy appearance
   b. tortuous, twisting and turning
   c. poorly maintained
   d. radiating heat

_____ 2. the *consummate* test [7]
   a. well publicized
   b. requiring energy
   c. impossible to complete
   d. supreme, perfect

_____ 3. *indefatigable*, heroic [7]
   a. athletic in appearance
   b. difficult to comprehend

    c. tireless

    d. handsome, attractive

_____ **4.** an *unprecedented* number [8]

    a. infinite, uncountable

    b. having no previous example

    c. small, tiny

    d. having no equal, unsurpassed

_____ **5.** willing to dispense . . . *exhortations* [17]

    a. words of encouragement

    b. words to discourage

    c. complaints

    d. good fortunes

_____ **6.** the *mien* of anxious scientists [27]

    a. interest, curiosity

    b. appearance, manner

    c. field of specialization

    d. politeness, courtesy

_____ **7.** The sport *culls* out the weak [36]

    a. removes

    b. determines

    c. strengthens

    d. makes allowances for

_____ **8.** the same *malady* [39]

    a. tension

    b. heredity

    c. illness

    d. adventure

_____ **9.** a *staunch* believer [46]

    a. firm

    b. without much conviction

    c. enthusiastic

    d. unwilling

_____ **10.** The heat *subsides* [54]

    a. grows worse

    b. remains the same

    c. lessens in intensity

    d. disappears

_____ **11.** the most *daunting* [80]

    a. visible

    b. discouraging

    c. easy to accomplish

    d. irritating

_____ **12.** Every step is *precarious* [92]
   a. easy to complete
   b. close to the goal
   c. uncertain, unstable
   d. exhausting, fatiguing

G. USING VOCABULARY

Write the correct inflected form of the base word (in parentheses) in each of the following sentences. Be sure to add the appropriate ending to fit the grammatical requirements of the sentence. Refer to your dictionary if necessary.

1. (*zealot*—use an adjective) Ferrell describes the Badwater marathon runners as _____ athletes who push themselves often beyond what is physically safe.

2. (*eeriness*—use an adverb) The morning that the race begins is _____ quiet.

3. (*euphoric*—use a noun) Superbly fit athletes often feel a sense of _____, feeling as if they could run forever.

4. (*indolence*—use an adverb) One cannot say that ultra-marathon runners pass their time _____.

5. (*portend*—use a noun) A runner might look upon a shooting star as a _____ of what is to come the next day.

6. (*ignominy*—use an adjective) Quitting before the end is considered an _____ defeat, marked by the insulting acronym "DNF."

H. SUMMARIZING EXERCISE

Read paragraph 7 again in the left column. On the right is a summary of the information in it.

Original Passage

For a thin slice of society—zealots who live to train, who measure themselves by their mental toughness—the ultra-marathon is the consummate test of human character. No other event in sport, except possibly a prizefight, is as punishing, as demanding of the mind and body. No other athlete is more revered than

Summary

A small group of zealots devote their lives to training for ultra-marathons and developing the mental toughness the races demand. Marathon running is a very difficult sport because it punishes both the mind and the body. Since the first marathon was run in ancient Greece, marathon races seem to fulfill a need in humans—the need to persevere, despite the hardships.

the distance runner. Indefatigable, heroic, cele- _____

brated in poetry and myth, the Greek soldier, _____

Pheidippides, ran 26 miles from Marathon to _____

Athens to herald victory over the Persians in _____

490 B.C., then collapsed and died. It was the _____

first marathon. To fill the unforgiving minute, _____

to persevere, is one of the highest ideals of _____

man—who, after all, was born to hardship, _____

cast from Eden. _____

Study the above summary. Then write a summary of paragraph 63 below.

Original Passage   **Summary**

A runner who stops ceases to be a runner. It is _____

a death of that identity, marked by an igno- _____

minious epitaph: "Did not finish." The phrase _____

is abbreviated on the printouts that list the _____

winners, and the slang verb, "DNF-ing," has _____

an obscene sound, foul with shame. The run- _____

ner who succumbs often goes to extraordinary _____

lengths for resurrection, training for months _____

and traveling back to the same race, the same _____

course, a year or two later, to try again. _____

I. TOPICS FOR DISCUSSION

1. In what ways are the runners who subject themselves to the punishing demands of the Badwater marathon different from athletes who participate in regular athletic competition (non-extreme sports contests)?
2. What might be some reasons to account for the "explosion of extreme sports in recent years" that Ferrell notes in the article?

J. TOPICS FOR WRITING

1. Write a paragraph in which you analyze some of the devices that Ferrell uses to make these runners' experiences so vivid.
2. Ferrell's purpose in writing is to describe how one athletic contest is conducted. Choose a sport or game that you are familiar with and write an essay

of four or five paragraphs explaining it to someone who is unfamiliar with it. Include in your discussion the rules, the way the game or sport is conducted, the requirements or special equipment, if necessary, and the physical requirements of its players.

Exploring Related Web Sites

- There is a great deal of information available about the annual Badwater race. If you type "Badwater race" in a search engine, you will get several sites to explore. The site below includes photos and personal narratives of the 2007 race:

  http://adventurecorps.com/downloads/bw/2007racemag.pdf

- Information and photographs about Death Valley are available at these two sites:

  www.americansouthwest.net/california/death_valley/national_park.html

  http://ngm.nationalgeographic.com/2007/11/death-valley/death-valley-map-interactive (Click on "interactive map.")

25

CARLIN FLORA

Hello, My Name Is Unique

Does one's name alter one's self-perception? This is the question Carlin Flora takes up in this article. Parents are increasingly giving their children distinctive names with the idea that such names can influence a child's destiny. The original article included a sidebar with dozens of names in alphabetical order from the Class of 2022 (that is, children born in 2004). Among them are Atom, Chianti, Desperate, Gator, Jaguar, Maverick, Poppy, Reality, Skyy, Sy'rai, Tookie, Unique, and Xerox, to cite a few from the list. Carlin Flora is senior editor at Psychology Today *magazine, where this article was first published.*

Vocabulary Preview

WORD PARTS

homogeneous [paragraph 4] The adjective *homogeneous* is formed from the Greek prefix *homo-* ("same") and *genos* ("kind"). The adjective thus describes people who are alike in their characteristics, whether by virtue of their age, interests, gender, political preferences, or some other characteristic. Other words beginning with this prefix are *homonym*, words that have the same sound but different meanings (like *cash* and *cache*, or *sew, sow*, and *so*) and *homosexuality*, a sexual preference for a person of the same sex. But be careful not to confuse the Greek prefix with the Latin one, which, unfortunately, is spelled the same. In Latin *homo* means "man," as in *homicide* or *homo sapiens*.

In your dictionary, look up the word *homophonic*. What does it mean? What are the word parts? Does the prefix *homo-* come from Latin or Greek?

homophonic _____

WORD FAMILIES

idiosyncratic [paragraph 3] The adjective *idiosyncratic* and the noun *idiosyncrasy* also derive from Greek word parts, and though there are only a few words in English beginning with *idio-*, they form an interesting group. The prefix *idio-* means "own" or "private." An *idiosyncrasy* is a characteristic that is peculiar to a particular person or group. For example, Pierre, the husband of my friend Therese, will not allow onions in their house. The eighteenth-century German writer Friedrich Schiller kept a bag of rotting green apples in his desk drawer because he thought that the smell inspired him to write. These are idiosyncrasies. Three other words in this family are these:

idiom   an expression peculiar to a particular language
idiot   a foolish or stupid person, now offensive, from Greek *idiotes* ("a private person")
idiopathic describing a disease with no particular cause, in other words, a disease peculiar to a particular individual

CARLIN FLORA

Hello, My Name Is Unique

1   Proper names are poetry in the raw, said the bard W. H. Auden. "Like all poetry, they are untranslatable." Mapping your name onto yourself is a tricky procedure indeed. We exist wholly independently of our names, yet they alone represent us on our birth certificates and gravestones.

2   Would a Rose by any other name be just as sweet-tempered? Does Orion feel cosmically special? Psychologists, parents and the world's Oceans, Zanes and Timothys are divided on the extent to which first names actually matter.

YOU NAMED HIM *WHAT*?

3   Today's parents seem to believe they can alter their child's destiny by picking the perfect—preferably idiosyncratic—name. (Destiny, incidentally, was the ninth most popular name for girls in New York City last year.) The current crop of preschoolers includes a few Uniques, with uncommonly named playmates like Kyston, Payton and Sawyer. From Dakota to Heaven, Integrity to Serenity, more babies are being named after places and states of mind. Names with alternative spellings are on the upswing, like Jaxon, Kassidy, Mikayla, Jazmine and Nevaeh (Heaven spelled backward), as are mix-and-match names such as Ashlynn and Rylan.

4   "For the first time in history, the top 50 names account for less than 50 percent of boys born each year, and for less than 40 percent of girls," says Cleveland Kent Evans, professor of psychology at Bellevue University in Nebraska and author of *Unusual & Most Popular Baby Names.* Evans believes that our homogeneous strip-mall culture fosters the desire to nominally distinguish our children. He cites a boom in unique names dating to the late 1980s but says the taste for obscure monikers developed in the 1960s, when parents felt less obligated to keep certain names in the family.

5   "It's really hard to name a kid," says Jill Bass, 35, who is expecting her second child. "It reflects what kind of person you are." She and her husband, Carl Vogel, 37, are struggling to find a name that is unique but not too trendy. "We don't want to go the Jake, Zak and Tyler route," says Bass. "It will sound like one of those year-2000 names. We don't want to sound as though we were trying so hard."

6　　Distinguishing a child in just the right way is the first task parents feel charged with. Accordingly, parents-to-be increasingly track the popularity of names on the Social Security Administration's Web site and canvas the cottage industry of baby-name books. About 50 such books were published between 1990 and 1996. Since 1997, more than 100 new books have been published.

7　　New parents rattle off diminutives and acronyms as if reciting scales. "I wanted a truly awesome, convertible name that could collapse into a normal name. Something like Charles Henry Underhill Grisham Sernovitz, because CHUGS would be a great college nickname," says Andy Sernovitz, 33, whose son Charles Darwin Grisham Sernovitz was born last November. Darwin was a nod to mom Julie Grisham's science-writing vocation.

8　　Today, children are christened in honor of sports teams, political parties, vacation spots and food cravings. Adam Orr, a die-hard Cubs fan, wanted to name his first child Clark Addison or Addison Clark, the names of the streets that form the intersection at Chicago's Wrigley Field. Alas, he and his wife, Annisa, are expecting a daughter this spring. Records of kids named Espn tell of parents with a more general love of sports. Christie Brinkley reportedly named her youngest child Sailor as a tribute to a favorite pastime. Jamie Oliver, the British culinary star, christened his child Poppy Honey, not nearly so unfortunate a name as that of a poor soul dubbed Gouda.

9　　Increasingly, children are also named for prized possessions. In 2000, birth certificates revealed that there were 298 Armanis, 269 Chanels, 49 Canons, 6 Timberlands, 5 Jaguars and 353 girls named Lexus in the U.S. The trend is not surprising: In an era in which children are viewed as accessories, such names telegraph our desire for creative, social or material success. It would be ironic if young Jaguar or Lexus grew up to drive a Honda Accord.

10　　While a name may be a palimpsest for parental aspirations (hence the concerns of savvy parents that they not appear to be striving too hard), a name also reflects high hopes for the child himself. Choosing an uncommon name is perceived as an opportunity to give your child a leg up in life, signaling to the world that he or she is different. In *Snobbery,* cultural critic Joseph Epstein argues that a child named Luc or Catesby seems poised for greater achievements than selling car insurance.

AM I REALLY A JORDAN?

11　　The announcements are in the mail; a religious ceremony may seal the decision. The name is chosen, and it is a word that will become so familiar that the child's brain will pull it out of white noise. It is the first word she will learn to write. But what are the consequences of a particular name for self-image?

12　　They're not earth-shattering, according to a study by psychologist Martin Ford, an assistant dean at George Mason University in Virginia. Ford found no correlation between the popularity or social desirability of a given name and academic or social achievement. "This doesn't mean that a name would never have any effect on a child's development," he explains. "But it does suggest that the probability of a positive effect is as large as that of a negative effect. It also suggests that a name is unlikely to be a significant factor in most children's development."

13   Children and teens either struggle to stand apart or try desperately to fit in. A singular name eases the former pursuit but thwarts the latter. If parents give a child an offbeat name, speculates Lewis Lipsitt, professor emeritus of psychology at Brown University, "they are probably outliers willing to buck convention, and that [parental trait] will have a greater effect on their child than does the name."

14   A name may occasionally trigger expectations that are difficult to meet because a child lacks the appropriate talent or temperament. "If your parents are great musicians, and they name you Yehudi, there could be a sense that you cannot live up to your name," Lipsitt says. Likewise, a naturally shy child may cringe when he is introduced as Attila.

15   No one can predict whether a name will be consistent with a child's or a teen's view of herself. The name could be ethnic, unique or white-bread, but if it doesn't reinforce her sense of self, she will probably be unhappy with it and may even feel alienated from parents or peers because of it. An Annika with iconoclastic taste will be happy with her name, but a Tallullah who longs for a seat at the cheerleaders' table may feel that her name is too weird.

16   A child's attitude toward his name is a gauge of self-esteem, says psychologist Ron Taffel, author of *Nurturing Good Children Now.* "If self-esteem is low, even a David or Jenny could hate their name—as a reflection of how they feel about themselves."

17   By the time most people reach adulthood, they have made peace with their name or changed it. And, as parents of Dax and Skyy will be gratified to learn, young adults today report that they feel buoyed by an unorthodox appellation.

18   "It's interesting knowing that very few people have your name," says Cabot Norton, 35. "It's a point of pride to say, 'I've never met another Cabot.'"

19   Says Maren Connary, 29, "I had a rebellious nature that I felt was justified by my name. If I'd been named Mary, I think I'd be more conformist."

20   "I hated my name when I was a kid," Wven (pronounced *you-vin*) Villegas, 29, says. "I stood out for all the wrong reasons. But I decided that if my name wasn't the same as everyone else's, then I wouldn't be the same, either. Now I love my name so much that I had it tattooed on my right arm."

21   Parents may be further empowered to christen their children idiosyncratically given that names aren't the rich source for taunts they once were. "Kids today are used to a variety of names, so it is almost too simple for them to make fun of each other for that," says Taffel. "Cruelty is more sophisticated now."

22   The experiences of children of mixed ethnic and racial backgrounds shed light on the power of names to determine identity. If such children are insecure or confused about their origins, the role of their name becomes more important. Donna Jackson Nakazawa, author of *Does Anybody Else Look Like Me?*, advises parents of biracial or multi-ethnic children to choose a name that represents both branches of the family tree, or at least a nickname that does so. Nakazawa's nine-year-old son is Christian Jackson Nakazawa; his nickname is Chrischan, which means "dear beloved child" in Japanese.

23   Nakazawa cites the cautionary tale of a young woman who was adopted from China by a white American couple who gave her a Chinese-sounding name. As a teenager, the girl began researching her heritage and discovered her name was not, in fact, Chinese. She was devastated.

24   Cleveland Evans believes the personal story behind a name can serve as an anchor. In most cases, Evans says, people are only at a disadvantage if there is no story attached to their name. "It doesn't matter what the story is, as long as it is more complex than, 'We just liked the name.'" A name connected to previous generations can feel like your ancestors' arms wrapped warmly around you.

25   Not everyone agrees that the rationale behind a name is crucial. Misia Landau, a narratologist and science writer at Harvard Medical School, argues that the "story" of a name doesn't necessarily drive personal narratives, because of the myriad factors at play. "Providing a child with a name is incredibly variable," says Landau. "And I don't think people today say, 'Your namesake would never have acted that way.'"

BUT YOU DON'T LOOK LIKE A MARTHA!

26   There are names you probably don't think about at all—the equivalent of a black suit. And there are busy purple scarves of names, names that cannot be ignored, that must be reckoned with. "People are always going to ask me why I am named Cabot," Norton says. "And they are probably going to assume I am an East Coast WASP,[1] whereas I'm actually a North Florida atheist."

27   Names produce piquant impressions: Olaf sounds oafish to non-Scandinavians. Shirley is perky. A ballerina named Bertha doesn't sound as compelling as one named Anastasia. But are certain names better suited to some people than to others, and can a name change overhaul one's self-image?

28   Michael Mercer, an industrial psychologist and co-author of *Spontaneous Optimism*, recalls a former co-worker who had interpersonal and legal problems: "She changed her name to Honore, and it was her way of mutating from someone who goofed things up to someone who is honorable."

29   Norma Sofía Marsano, 28, had always been a Norma but decided to go by her middle name when she left Kentucky to attend college in Michigan. "I felt that Norma held me back. Sofía sounds fun and cute, whereas Norma sounds like an ugly-girl's name. I liked myself more when I started going by Sofía."

30   A name change may influence how we perceive ourselves and others because of racial, class or geographical stereotypes. Our "Anastasia" file may include adjectives like *attractive, graceful* and *vaguely Slavic*—descriptors that fit our conception of a ballerina but not a Bertha.

31   Author Bruce Lansky has capitalized on these implicit associations with *The Baby Name Survey Book: What People Think About Your Baby's Name*. Lansky compiled 100,000 impressions of 1,700 names, promising to help parents pick a name with positive connotations. Readers learn that Vanna is considered dumb, Jacqueline is elegant and Jacob, the number-one baby name for boys, is "a highly religious man who is old-fashioned and quiet."

32   Lansky's "namesakes" (Vanna White, Jackie O., Jacob in the Old Testament) are achingly transparent. And such associations hold only until we meet another Vanna, according to psychologist Kenneth Steele, who found that a name attached to a "real" person, or even a photograph, will transcend stereotypes. Steele exposed a group of subjects to a set of names previously judged to be

[1]An acronym for white Anglo-Saxon Protestant (Ed.)

socially desirable (Jon, Joshua, Gregory) or undesirable (Oswald, Myron, Reginald). A second group of subjects viewed these names accompanied by photographs. The addition of the photos erased the good or bad impression left by the name alone.

33   To what degree, then, does a name elicit racial or ethnic bias? Marianne Bertrand, a professor of economics at the University of Chicago, created résumés with names that are considered conspicuously white (such as Brendan) or black (such as Jamal) and found that regardless of credentials, résumés with white-sounding names generated twice as many callbacks. But this doesn't mean that conspicuously "black" names, like Lashonda or Tremayne, are themselves liabilities: The employers in Bertrand's study might have discriminated against a black applicant regardless of his name. Roland Fryer, a professor of economics at Harvard University found that a black Molly and a black Lakeisha with similar socioeconomic backgrounds fared equally well.

34   Whether people swoon over—or even disdain—our name is beyond our control. Ultimately, self-esteem and the esteem of the world dictate the degree to which we hold our name dear. Like our vocation or hometown, we tout our name as a distinguishing mark if it "fits." If it doesn't, we might say that, like an inaccurate horoscope, we don't believe in that stuff anyway. We'll change our name, disregard it or consider it just a synonym for *me*. ✳

Carlin Flora, "Hello, My Name Is Unique" from *Psychology Today* (March–April 2004). Copyright © 2004 by Sussex Publishers, LLC. Reprinted with the permission from Psychology Today Magazine.

Exercises

Do not refer to the selection for Exercises A–C unless your instructor directs you to do so.

A. DETERMINING THE MAIN IDEA AND PURPOSE

Choose the best answer.

_____ 1. The main idea of the selection is that

    a. many parents today believe that choosing an idiosyncratic or unusual name for their child can change his or her destiny.

    b. psychologists have determined that one's name influences a person's self-image and the kind of person he or she becomes.

    c. parents should be careful when naming their child, since weird names can follow a child for life and cause embarrassment and teasing from others.

    d. since the 1960s parents have sought to rebel against tradition by abandoning the long-time practice of conferring family names on their children.

_____ 2. The writer's purpose is to

    a. list some unusual names and explain what they reveal about people.

    b. warn parents not to give their children unusual names that will haunt them for the rest of their lives.

    c. trace the history of naming practices in the United States.

    d. examine some theories about the effects of giving children unusual or idiosyncratic names.

B. COMPREHENDING MAIN IDEAS

Choose the correct answer.

_____ **1.** Flora mentions several categories of contemporary names and naming practices. Which of the following was *not* mentioned?

    a. Names for places and states of mind, like Dakota, Serenity, or Ocean.

    b. Reversing names traditionally associated with the opposite gender, for example, naming a girl Stephen or a boy Louise.

    c. Names with alternative spellings, like Jazmine, Kassidy, or Nevaeh (Heaven spelled backward).

    d. Names associated with sports teams or food, like Sailor, Poppy Honey, or Gouda.

    e. Names associated with prized possessions, like Jaguar, Timberland, or Armani.

_____ **2.** According to a theory espoused by psychology professor Cleveland Kent Evans, giving children unusual names may be the result of

    a. the need to outdo other parents by choosing ever more distinctive names.

    b. the acknowledgement that a name really does affect a child's destiny.

    c. a reaction against our homogeneous "strip-mall" culture.

    d. the lack of tradition in American culture.

_____ **3.** Naming a child Armani, Chanel, Lexus, or Canon, according the writer, reflects the current era where children are regarded as

    a. accessories.

    b. luxury items.

    c. possessions.

    d. material symbols of wealth.

_____ **4.** Psychologist Martin Ford, who has studied the correlation between names and academic and social achievement, concluded that

    a. a name positively affects a child's self-esteem and achievement.

    b. more study is needed before a clear pattern of effects becomes evident.

    c. a name is unlikely to be a significant factor in a child's development.

    d. the current generation of children has been seriously damaged by having such singular names.

_____ **5.** Parents of biracial or multiethnic children are advised to choose
   a. a "white-bread" or plain name that minimizes the child's mixed heritage.
   b. a name or nickname that represents the child's various heritages.
   c. a name that combines both family names to emphasize the child's ancestry.
   d. a name that they personally like whether it matches the child's heritage or not.

_____ **6.** Certain names may influence how we perceive ourselves and others because they reflect
   a. our unconscious feelings about real people who share those names.
   b. impressions created by the media.
   c. our unfulfilled desires and ambitions.
   d. racial, class, or geographical stereotypes.

COMPREHENSION SCORE

Score your answers for Exercises A and B as follows:

A. No. right _____ × 2 = _____

B. No. right _____ × 1 = _____

Total points from A and B _____ × 10 = _____ percent

C. SEQUENCING

These sentences from one paragraph in the selection have been scrambled. Read the sentences and choose the sequence that puts them back into logical order. Do not refer to the original selection.

1 About 50 such books were published between 1990 and 1996. **2** Accordingly, parents-to-be increasingly track the popularity of names on the Social Security Administration's Web site and canvas the cottage industry of baby-name books. **3** Distinguishing a child in just the right way is the first task parents feel charged with. **4** Since 1997, more than 100 new books have been published.

_____ Which of the following represents the correct sequence for these sentences?
   a. 3, 2, 1, 4
   b. 1, 2, 4, 3
   c. 3, 1, 4, 2
   d. Correct as written.

You may refer to the selection as you work through the remaining exercises.

D. DISTINGUISHING BETWEEN MAIN IDEAS AND SUPPORTING DETAILS

Label the following sentences from two paragraphs in the selection as follows: MI if it represents a *main idea* and SD if it represents a *supporting detail*.

1. _____ Children and teens either struggle to stand apart or try desperately to fit in.

2. _____ A singular name eases the former pursuit but thwarts the latter.

3. _____ If parents give a child an offbeat name, speculates Lewis Lipsitt, professor emeritus of psychology at Brown University, "they are probably outliers willing to buck convention, and that [parental trait] will have a greater effect on their child than does the name."

4. _____ A name may occasionally trigger expectations that are difficult to meet because a child lacks the appropriate talent or temperament.

5. _____ "If your parents are great musicians, and they name you Yehudi, there could be a sense that you cannot live up to your name," Lipsitt says.

6. _____ Likewise, a naturally shy child may cringe when he is introduced as Attila.

E. IDENTIFYING PATTERNS OF DEVELOPMENT

Read again the paragraphs listed below. Then write the pattern of development each passage uses. Here are your answer choices:

list of facts or details
examples
cause and effect (reasons or results)
process
contrast

1. paragraph 3 _____

2. paragraph 4 _____

3. paragraph 14 _____

4. paragraph 15 _____

5. paragraph 28 _____

F. UNDERSTANDING VOCABULARY

Look through the paragraphs listed below and find a word that matches each definition. Refer to a dictionary if necessary. An example has been done for you.

Ex. traditional word for a poet [paragraphs 1–2] _____ bard _____

1. slang word meaning personal names [3–4] _____

2. characteristic of a particular person [3–4] _____

3. words made from the initial letters of a name [7–8] _____

4. short, often endearing forms of names [7–8] _____

5. given the name of, often facetiously [7–8] _____

6. well-informed, perceptive, shrewd [9–10] _____

7. describing a person who likes to overthrow established traditions [14–15] _____

8. breaking with convention or tradition [16–20] _____

9. innumerable, a large indefinite number [24–26] _____

10. fundamental reasons or basis for an action [24–26] _____

11. describing a stupid, clumsy person [27–29] _____

12. changing from one form to another [27–29] _____

13. call forth, draw out [32–33] _____

14. go beyond, rise above [32–33] _____

G. USING VOCABULARY

From the following list of vocabulary words, choose a word that fits in each blank according to both the grammatical structure of the sentence and the context. Use each word in the list only once. Do not change the form of the word. (Note that there are more words than blanks.)

cosmically	oafish	obscure	devastated
homogeneous	ironic	correlation	sophisticated
singular	crucial	taunts	stereotype

1. Flora writes that parents are choosing _____ names as a way of rebelling against what she calls our _____ strip-mall culture.

2. In the past children with unusual names might suffer _____ from other children on the playground, but she says that today's children are cruel in more _____ ways.

3. Kent Evans, a professor of psychology, says that the urge to give children unusual or _____ names actually started in the 1960s when it became less _____ to give children traditional family names.

4. Although Olaf is a common Scandinavian name, to non–Scandinavians it sounds _____, nor does the name Bertha fit the _____ of a classical ballerina.

H. ANNOTATING EXERCISE

For this exercise, assume that you are preparing to write an essay on the question of whether one's name affects—whether positively or negatively—one's self-image or self-esteem. Go through the article and locate any piece of information that supports this idea. To identify it, put a star in the margin next to the sentence or bracket the words.

I. TOPICS FOR DISCUSSION

1. Why is it so hard for parents to name their children? What does the writer say about this problem? What are some other reasons that it exists?
2. In *Romeo and Juliet,* Shakespeare asked, "What's in a name? That which we call a rose by any other name would smell as sweet." The writer alludes to this quotation in paragraph 2. If the flower we know as a rose were called, say, a skunk cabbage flower, would it alter our perception of its essence? This is the central question Flora poses in her article: To what extent do our names affect our concept of ourselves and others' perception of us?
3. What are some truly awful names of people you know or have heard of?

J. TOPICS FOR WRITING

1. Do some research on your first name. You can consult your parents or other family members or use one of the online sites listed below. Then write an essay in which you explain the origin of your name, its meaning, why the name was given to you, and finally, your feelings about it.
2. If friends told you that they were going to name their child something you consider outlandish, how would you respond? Write a paragraph or two in which you address this question. Your focus should be on warning them against choosing such a name.

Exploring Related Web Sites

- Information about baby's names, their origin, meaning, rankings, and popularity can be found at these two sites. Both are easy to navigate.

  www.babynamesworld.com
  www.thinkbabynames.com

- The Social Security Administration maintains a Web site (mentioned in paragraph 6) that tracks the popularity of names each year. In 2007, Emily was the most popular name for a girl for the twelfth straight year, followed by Isabella, Emma, Ava, Madison, Sophia, Olivia, Abigail, Hannah, and Elizabeth. Jacob was the most popular name for a boy for the ninth year in a row, followed by Ethan, Daniel, Christopher, Anthony, William, and Andrew. But more unusual names were gaining ground, for example, Nevaeh ("Heaven" backward) was number 31, Destiny was number 41, Trinity was number 72, and Miracle was number 461. Here is the Web site:

  www.ssa.gov/OACT/babynames

26

JARED DIAMOND
Easter's End

"Easter's End," first published in Discover *(a magazine devoted to the world of science) is a thought-provoking look at the civilization that flourished on Easter Island in Polynesia. In it, Diamond describes what the civilization was like when it reached its peak between 1200 and 1500, marked in particular by the hundreds of mysterious and huge stone statues, called* moai, *along the coast. But the civilization—including both human and plant life—eventually declined. Diamond offers some hypotheses to explain why, and in telling Easter Island's story, he finds a grim parallel for modern human civilization. An expanded version of this material is included in Diamond's book* Collapse: How Societies Choose to Fail or Succeed *(2005).*

Jared Diamond is currently a professor of physiology at the UCLA School of Medicine and a contributing editor of Discover. *He has made several expeditions to New Guinea and the Solomon Islands. Some of his* Discover *columns were collected in* The Third Chimpanzee: The Evolution and Future of the Human Animal *(1992). His book* Guns, Germs, and Steel: The Fates of Human Societies *(1997) investigates the effects of geography on human societies and their evolution. It was awarded the Pulitzer Prize in 1998 in the category of general nonfiction.*

Vocabulary Analysis

WORD PARTS

extra- [paragraph 13] In English, many compound words are formed with the prefix *extra-*, meaning "outside" or "beyond." The word *extraterrestrial* describes an inhabitant of another world, a combination of the prefix and *terra*, the Latin root for "earth." Other words beginning with this prefix are *extraordinary*, *extramarital*, *extracurricular*, and *extrasensory*.

WORD FAMILIES

revive [paragraph 4] In Selection 5 by Cornelia Bailey, you were introduced to the word *vivid*, from the Latin verb *vivere* ("to live"). *Revive* is a member of the family derived from this root, meaning "to bring back to life," from *re-* ("again") + *vivere*. This verb and the noun *vita* ("life") have given rise to other words in this linguistic family, among them: *vital* (essential for life), *vitamin* (an essential food element), *revitalize* (to give new life to), and *vivacious* (full of life and spirit).

JARED DIAMOND

Easter's End

1   Among the most riveting mysteries of human history are those posed by vanished civilizations. Everyone who has seen the abandoned buildings of the Khmer, the Maya, or the Anasazi is immediately moved to ask the same question: Why did the societies that erected those structures disappear?

2   Their vanishing touches us as the disappearance of other animals, even the dinosaurs, never can. No matter how exotic those lost civilizations seem, their framers were humans like us. Who is to say we won't succumb to the same fate? Perhaps someday New York's skyscrapers will stand derelict and overgrown with vegetation, like the temples at Angkor Wat and Tikal.

3   Among all such vanished civilizations, that of the former Polynesian society on Easter Island remains unsurpassed in mystery and isolation. The mystery stems especially from the island's gigantic stone statues and its impoverished landscape, but it is enhanced by our associations with the specific people involved: Polynesians represent for us the ultimate in exotic romance, the background for many a child's and an adult's vision of paradise. My own interest in Easter was kindled over 30 years ago when I read Thor Heyerdahl's fabulous accounts of his *Kon-Tiki* voyage.

Mysterious statues, called *moai*, on Easter Island.

4   But my interest has been revived recently by a much more exciting account, one not of heroic voyages but of painstaking research and analysis. My friend David Steadman, a paleontologist, has been working with a number of other researchers who are carrying out the first systematic excavations on Easter intended to identify the animals and plants that once lived there. Their work is contributing to a new interpretation of the island's history that makes it a tale not only of wonder but of warning as well.

5   Easter Island, with an area of only 64 square miles, is the world's most isolated scrap of habitable land. It lies in the Pacific Ocean more than 2,000 miles west of the nearest continent (South America), 1,400 miles from even the nearest habitable island (Pitcairn). Its subtropical location and latitude—at 27 degrees south, it is approximately as far below the equator as Houston is north of it— help give it a rather mild climate, while its volcanic origins make its soil fertile. In theory, this combination of blessings should have made Easter a miniature paradise, remote from problems that beset the rest of the world.

6   The island derives its name from its "discovery" by the Dutch explorer Jacob Roggeveen, on Easter (April 5) in 1722. Roggeveen's first impression was not of a paradise but of a wasteland: "We originally, from a further distance, have considered the said Easter Island as sandy; the reason for that is this, that we counted as sand the withered grass, hay, or other scorched and burnt vegetation, because its wasted appearance could give no other impression than of a singular poverty and barrenness."

7   The island Roggeveen saw was a grassland without a single tree or bush over ten feet high. Modern botanists have identified only 47 species of higher plants native to Easter, most of them grasses, sedges, and ferns. The list includes just two species of small trees and two of woody shrubs. With such flora,[1] the islanders Roggeveen encountered had no source of real firewood to warm themselves during Easter's cool, wet, windy winters. Their native animals included nothing larger than insects, not even a single species of native bat, land bird, land snail, or lizard. For domestic animals, they had only chickens.

8   European visitors throughout the eighteenth and early nineteenth centuries estimated Easter's human population at about 2,000, a modest number considering the island's fertility. As Captain James Cook recognized during his brief visit in 1774, the islanders were Polynesians (a Tahitian man accompanying Cook was able to converse with them). Yet despite the Polynesians' well-deserved fame as a great seafaring people, the Easter Islanders who came out to Roggeveen's and Cook's ships did so by swimming or paddling canoes that Roggeveen described as "bad and frail." Their craft, he wrote, were "put together with manifold small planks and light inner timbers, which they cleverly stitched together with very fine twisted threads. . . . But as they lack the knowledge and particularly the materials for caulking and making tight the great number of seams of the canoes, these are accordingly very leaky, for which reason they are compelled to spend half the time in bailing." The canoes, only ten feet long, held at most two people, and only three or four canoes were observed on the entire island.

---

[1]Plants as a group; often used with *fauna,* or animals as a group. (Ed.)

9   With such flimsy craft, Polynesians could never have colonized Easter from even the nearest island, nor could they have traveled far offshore to fish. The islanders Roggeveen met were totally isolated, unaware that other people existed. Investigators in all the years since his visit have discovered no trace of the islanders' having any outside contacts: not a single Easter Island rock or product has turned up elsewhere, nor has anything been found on the island that could have been brought by anyone other than the original settlers or the Europeans. Yet the people living on Easter claimed memories of visiting the uninhabited Sala y Gomez reef 260 miles away, far beyond the range of the leaky canoes seen by Roggeveen. How did the islanders' ancestors reach that reef from Easter, or reach Easter from anywhere else?

10   Easter Island's most famous feature is its huge stone statues, more than 200 of which once stood on massive stone platforms lining the coast. At least 700 more, in all stages of completion, were abandoned in quarries or on ancient roads between the quarries and the coast, as if the carvers and moving crews had thrown down their tools and walked off the job. Most of the erected statues were carved in a single quarry and then somehow transported as far as six miles—despite heights as great as 33 feet and weights up to 82 tons. The abandoned statues, meanwhile, were as much as 65 feet tall and weighed up to 270 tons. The stone platforms were equally gigantic: up to 500 feet long and 10 feet high, with facing slabs weighing up to 10 tons.

11   Roggeveen himself quickly recognized the problem the statues posed: "The stone images at first caused us to be struck with astonishment," he wrote, "because we could not comprehend how it was possible that these people, who are devoid of heavy thick timber for making any machines, as well as strong ropes, nevertheless had been able to erect such images." Roggeveen might have added that the islanders had no wheels, no draft animals, and no source of power except their own muscles. How did they transport the giant statues for miles, even before erecting them? To deepen the mystery, the statues were still standing in 1770, but by 1864 all of them had been pulled down, by the islanders themselves. Why then did they carve them in the first place? And why did they stop?

12   The statues imply a society very different from the one Roggeveen saw in 1722. Their sheer number and size suggest a population much larger than 2,000 people. What became of everyone? Furthermore, that society must have been highly organized. Easter's resources were scattered across the island: the best stone for the statues was quarried at Rano Raraku near Easter's northeast end; red stone, used for large crowns adorning some of the statues, was quarried at Puna Pau, inland in the southwest; stone carving tools came mostly from Aroi in the northwest. Meanwhile, the best farmland lay in the south and east, and the best fishing grounds on the north and west coasts. Extracting and redistributing all those goods required complex political organization. What happened to that organization, and how could it ever have arisen in such a barren landscape?

13   Easter Island's mysteries have spawned volumes of speculation for more than two and a half centuries. Many Europeans were incredulous that Polynesians—commonly characterized as "mere savages"—could have created the statues or the beautifully constructed stone platforms. In the 1950s, Heyerdahl argued that Polynesia must have been settled by advanced societies of American Indians, who

in turn must have received civilization across the Atlantic from more advanced societies of the Old World. Heyerdahl's raft voyages aimed to prove the feasibility of such prehistoric transoceanic contacts. In the 1960s the Swiss writer Erich von Däniken, an ardent believer in Earth visits by extraterrestrial astronauts, went further, claiming that Easter's statues were the work of intelligent beings who owned ultramodern tools, became stranded on Easter, and were finally rescued.

14   Heyerdahl and Von Däniken both brushed aside overwhelming evidence that the Easter Islanders were typical Polynesians derived from Asia rather than from the Americas and that their culture (including their statues) grew out of Polynesian culture. Their language was Polynesian, as Cook had already concluded. Specifically, they spoke an eastern Polynesian dialect related to Hawaiian and Marquesan, a dialect isolated since about A.D. 400, as estimated from slight differences in vocabulary. Their fishhooks and stone adzes resembled early Marquesan models. Last year DNA extracted from 12 Easter Island skeletons was also shown to be Polynesian. The islanders grew bananas, taro, sweet potatoes, sugarcane, and paper mulberry—typical Polynesian crops, mostly of Southeast Asian origin. Their sole domestic animal, the chicken, was also typically Polynesian and ultimately Asian, as were the rats that arrived as stowaways in the canoes of the first settlers.

15   What happened to those settlers? The fanciful theories of the past must give way to evidence gathered by hardworking practitioners in three fields: archeology, pollen analysis, and paleontology.

16   Modern archeological excavations on Easter have continued since Heyerdahl's 1955 expedition. The earliest radiocarbon dates associated with human activities are around A.D. 400 to 700, in reasonable agreement with the approximate settlement date of 400 estimated by linguists. The period of statue construction peaked around 1200 to 1500, with few if any statues erected thereafter. Densities of archeological sites suggest a large population; an estimate of 7,000 people is widely quoted by archeologists, but other estimates range up to 20,000, which does not seem implausible for an island of Easter's area and fertility.

17   Archeologists have also enlisted surviving islanders in experiments aimed at figuring out how the statues might have been carved and erected. Twenty people, using only stone chisels, could have carved even the largest completed statue within a year. Given enough timber and fiber for making ropes, teams of at most a few hundred people could have loaded the statues onto wooden sleds, dragged them over lubricated wooden tracks or rollers, and used logs as levers to maneuver them into a standing position. Rope could have been made from the fiber of a small native tree, related to the linden, called the hauhau. However, that tree is now extremely scarce on Easter, and hauling one statue would have required hundreds of yards of rope. Did Easter's now barren landscape once support the necessary trees?

18   That question can be answered by the technique of pollen analysis, which involves boring out a column of sediment from a swamp or pond, with the most recent deposits at the top and relatively more ancient deposits at the bottom. The absolute age of each layer can be dated by radiocarbon methods. Then begins the hard work: examining tens of thousands of pollen grains under a

microscope, counting them, and identifying the plant species that produced each one by comparing the grains with modern pollen from known plant species. For Easter Island, the bleary-eyed scientists who performed that task were John Flenley, now at Massey University in New Zealand, and Sarah King of the University of Hull in England.

19   Flenley and King's heroic efforts were rewarded by the striking new picture that emerged of Easter's prehistoric landscape. For at least 30,000 years before human arrival and during the early years of Polynesian settlement, Easter was not a wasteland at all. Instead, a subtropical forest of trees and woody bushes towered over a ground layer of shrubs, herbs, ferns, and grasses. In the forest grew tree daisies, the rope-yielding hauhau tree, and the toromiro tree, which furnishes a dense, mesquite-like firewood. The most common tree in the forest was a species of palm now absent on Easter but formerly so abundant that the bottom strata of the sediment column were packed with its pollen. The Easter Island palm was closely related to the still-surviving Chilean wine palm, which grows up to 82 feet tall and 6 feet in diameter. The tall, unbranched trunks of the Easter Island palm would have been ideal for transporting and erecting statues and constructing large canoes. The palm would also have been a valuable food source, since its Chilean relative yields edible nuts as well as sap from which Chileans make sugar, syrup, honey, and wine.

20   What did the first settlers of Easter Island eat when they were not glutting themselves on the local equivalent of maple syrup? Recent excavations by David Steadman, of the New York State Museum at Albany, have yielded a picture of Easter's original animal world as surprising as Flenley and King's picture of its plant world. Steadman's expectations for Easter were conditioned by his experiences elsewhere in Polynesia, where fish are overwhelmingly the main food at archeological sites, typically accounting for more than 90 percent of the bones in ancient Polynesian garbage heaps. Easter, though, is too cool for the coral reefs beloved by fish, and its cliff-girded coastline permits shallow-water fishing in only a few places. Less than a quarter of the bones in its early garbage heaps (from the period 900 to 1300) belonged to fish; instead, nearly one-third of all bones came from porpoises.

21   Nowhere else in Polynesia do porpoises account for even 1 percent of discarded food bones. But most other Polynesian islands offered animal food in the form of birds and mammals, such as New Zealand's now extinct giant moas and Hawaii's now extinct flightless geese. Most other islanders also had domestic pigs and dogs. On Easter, porpoises would have been the largest animal available—other than humans. The porpoise species identified at Easter, the common dolphin, weighs up to 165 pounds. It generally lives out at sea, so it could not have been hunted by line fishing or spearfishing from shore. Instead, it must have been harpooned far offshore, in big seaworthy canoes built from the extinct palm tree.

22   In addition to porpoise meat, Steadman found, the early Polynesian settlers were feasting on seabirds. For those birds, Easter's remoteness and lack of predators made it an ideal haven as a breeding site, at least until humans arrived. Among the prodigious numbers of seabirds that bred on Easter were albatross, boobies, frigate birds, fulmars, petrels, prions, shearwaters, storm petrels, terns, and tropic birds. With at least 25 nesting species, Easter was the richest seabird breeding site in Polynesia and probably in the whole Pacific.

23   Land birds as well went into early Easter Island cooking pots. Steadman identified bones of at least six species, including barn owls, herons, parrots, and rail.
Bird stew would have been seasoned with meat from large numbers of rats,
which the Polynesian colonists inadvertently brought with them; Easter Island is
the sole known Polynesian island where rat bones outnumber fish bones at
archeological sites. (In case you're squeamish and consider rats inedible, I still
recall recipes for creamed laboratory rat that my British biologist friends used to
supplement their diet during their years of wartime food rationing.)

24   Porpoises, seabirds, land birds, and rats did not complete the list of meat
sources formerly available on Easter. A few bones hint at the possibility of breeding seal colonies as well. All these delicacies were cooked in ovens fired by
wood from the island's forests.

25   Such evidence lets us imagine the island onto which Easter's first Polynesian
colonists stepped ashore some 1,600 years ago, after a long canoe voyage from
eastern Polynesia. They found themselves in a pristine paradise. What then happened to it? The pollen grains and the bones yield a grim answer.

26   Pollen records show that destruction of Easter's forests was well under way
by the year 800, just a few centuries after the start of human settlement. Then
charcoal from wood fires came to fill the sediment cores, while pollen of palms
and other trees and woody shrubs decreased or disappeared, and pollen of the
grasses that replaced the forest became more abundant. Not long after 1400 the
palm finally became extinct, not only as a result of being chopped down but also
because the now ubiquitous rats prevented its regeneration: of the dozens of
preserved palm nuts discovered in caves on Easter, all had been chewed by rats
and could no longer germinate. While the hauhau tree did not become extinct in
Polynesian times, its numbers declined drastically until there weren't enough
left to make ropes from. By the time Heyerdahl visited Easter, only a single,
nearly dead toromiro tree remained on the island, and even that lone survivor
has now disappeared. (Fortunately, the toromiro still grows in botanical gardens
elsewhere.)

27   The fifteenth century marked the end not only for Easter's palm but for the
forest itself. Its doom had been approaching as people cleared land to plant gardens; as they felled trees to build canoes, to transport and erect statues, and to
burn; as rats devoured seeds; and probably as the native birds died out that had
pollinated the trees' flowers and dispersed their fruit. The overall picture is
among the most extreme examples of forest destruction anywhere in the world:
the whole forest gone, and most of its tree species extinct.

28   The destruction of the island's animals was as extreme as that of the forest:
without exception, every species of native land bird became extinct. Even shellfish
were overexploited, until people had to settle for small sea snails instead of larger
cowries. Porpoise bones disappeared abruptly from garbage heaps around 1500;
no one could harpoon porpoises anymore, since the trees used for constructing the
big seagoing canoes no longer existed. The colonies of more than half of the
seabird species breeding on Easter or on its offshore islets were wiped out.

29   In place of these meat supplies, the Easter Islanders intensified their production of chickens, which had been only an occasional food item. They also turned

to the largest remaining meat source available: humans, whose bones became common in late Easter Island garbage heaps. Oral traditions of the islanders are rife with cannibalism; the most inflammatory taunt that could be snarled at an enemy was "The flesh of your mother sticks between my teeth." With no wood available to cook these new goodies, the islanders resorted to sugarcane scraps, grass, and sedges to fuel their fires.

30   All these strands of evidence can be wound into a coherent narrative of a society's decline and fall. The first Polynesian colonists found themselves on an island with fertile soil, abundant food, bountiful building materials, ample lebensraum,[2] and all the prerequisites for comfortable living. They prospered and multiplied.

31   After a few centuries, they began erecting stone statues on platforms, like the ones their Polynesian forebears had carved. With passing years, the statues and platforms became larger and larger, and the statues began sporting ten-ton red crowns—probably in an escalating spiral of one-upmanship, as rival clans tried to surpass each other with shows of wealth and power. (In the same way, successive Egyptian pharaohs built ever-larger pyramids. Today Hollywood movie moguls near my home in Los Angeles are displaying their wealth and power by building ever more ostentatious mansions. Tycoon Marvin Davis topped previous moguls with plans for a 50,000-square-foot house, so now Aaron Spelling has topped Davis with a 56,000-square-foot house. All that those buildings lack to make the message explicit are ten-ton red crowns.) On Easter, as in modern America, society was held together by a complex political system to redistribute locally available resources and to integrate the economies of different areas.

32   Eventually Easter's growing population was cutting the forest more rapidly than the forest was regenerating. The people used the land for gardens and the wood for fuel, canoes, and houses—and, of course, for lugging statues. As forest disappeared, the islanders ran out of timber and rope to transport and erect their statues. Life became more uncomfortable—springs and streams dried up, and wood was no longer available for fires.

33   People also found it harder to fill their stomachs, as land birds, large sea snails, and many seabirds disappeared. Because timber for building seagoing canoes vanished, fish catches declined and porpoises disappeared from the table. Crop yields also declined, since deforestation allowed the soil to be eroded by rain and wind, dried by the sun, and its nutrients to be leeched from it. Intensified chicken production and cannibalism replaced only part of all those lost foods. Preserved statuettes with sunken cheeks and visible ribs suggest that people were starving.

34   With the disappearance of food surpluses, Easter Island could no longer feed the chiefs, bureaucrats, and priests who had kept a complex society running. Surviving islanders described to early European visitors how local chaos replaced centralized government and a warrior class took over from the hereditary chiefs. The stone points of spears and daggers, made by the warriors during their heyday in the 1600s and 1700s, still litter the ground of Easter today. By around 1700, the population began to crash toward between one-quarter and one-tenth of

[2]German word meaning "living space." (Ed.)

its former number. People took to living in caves for protection against their enemies. Around 1770 rival clans started to topple each other's statues, breaking the heads off. By 1864 the last statue had been thrown down and desecrated.

35   As we try to imagine the decline of Easter's civilization, we ask ourselves, "Why didn't they look around, realize what they were doing, and stop before it was too late? What were they thinking when they cut down the last palm tree?"

36   I suspect, though, that the disaster happened not with a bang but with a whimper. After all, there are those hundreds of abandoned statues to consider. The forest the islanders depended on for rollers and rope didn't simply disappear one day—it vanished slowly, over decades. Perhaps war interrupted the moving teams; perhaps by the time the carvers had finished their work, the last rope snapped. In the meantime, any islander who tried to warn about the dangers of progressive deforestation would have been overridden by vested interests of carvers, bureaucrats, and chiefs, whose jobs depended on continued deforestation. Our Pacific Northwest loggers are only the latest in a long line of loggers to cry, "Jobs over trees!" The changes in forest cover from year to year would have been hard to detect: yes, this year we cleared those woods over there, but trees are starting to grow back again on this abandoned garden site here. Only older people, recollecting their childhoods decades earlier, could have recognized a difference. Their children could no more have comprehended their parents' tales than my eight-year-old sons today can comprehend my wife's and my tales of what Los Angeles was like 30 years ago.

37   Gradually trees became fewer, smaller, and less important. By the time the last fruit-bearing adult palm tree was cut, palms had long since ceased to be of economic significance. That left only smaller and smaller palm saplings to clear each year, along with other bushes and treelets. No one would have noticed the felling of the last small palm.

38   By now the meaning of Easter Island for us should be chillingly obvious. Easter Island is Earth writ small. Today, again, a rising population confronts shrinking resources. We too have no emigration valve, because all human societies are linked by international transport, and we can no more escape into space than the Easter Islanders could flee into the ocean. If we continue to follow our present course, we shall have exhausted the world's major fisheries, tropical rain forests, fossil fuels, and much of our soil by the time my sons reach my current age.

39   Every day newspapers report details of famished countries—Afghanistan, Liberia, Rwanda, Sierra Leone, Somalia, the former Yugoslavia, Zaire—where soldiers have appropriated the wealth or where central government is yielding to local gangs of thugs. With the risk of nuclear war receding, the threat of our ending with a bang no longer has a chance of galvanizing us to halt our course. Our risk now is of winding down, slowly, in a whimper. Corrective action is blocked by vested interests, by well-intentioned political and business leaders, and by their electorates, all of whom are perfectly correct in not noticing big changes from year to year. Instead, each year there are just somewhat more people, and somewhat fewer resources, on Earth.

40   It would be easy to close our eyes or to give up in despair. If mere thousands of Easter Islanders with only stone tools and their own muscle power sufficed to

destroy their society, how can billions of people with metal tools and machine power fail to do worse? But there is one crucial difference. The Easter Islanders had no books and no histories of other doomed societies. Unlike the Easter Islanders, we have histories of the past—information that can save us. My main hope for my sons' generation is that we may now choose to learn from the fates of societies like Easter's. ✳

From Jared Diamond, "Easter's End," *Discover,* August 1995. Copyright © 1995 Jared Diamond. Reprinted with permission of the author.

Exercises

Do not refer to the selection for Exercises A and B unless your instructor directs you to do so.

A. DETERMINING THE MAIN IDEA AND WRITER'S PURPOSE

Choose the best answer.

_____ 1. The main idea of the selection is that, among all vanished civilizations, the former Polynesian society on Easter Island remains unsurpassed in mystery and isolation, *and* it

    a. sparks our imagination and interest in other remote and vanished civilizations.

    b. offers paleontologists a place to conduct research to identify the plants and animals that once flourished there.

    c. is the world's most isolated scrap of habitable land.

    d. recently offered us a new interpretation of the island's history that parallels the dangers confronting modern civilization.

_____ 2. The author's purpose is to

    a. warn us that the disaster and chaos that befell Easter Island could happen to us.

    b. trace the history of human civilization on Easter Island.

    c. describe the statues on Easter Island and explain how they were built and erected.

    d. show the painstaking work and important scientific contribution that paleontologists add to the world's store of knowledge.

B. COMPREHENDING MAIN IDEAS

Choose the correct answer.

_____ 1. Which geographical characteristics of Easter Island's should have made it a "miniature paradise, remote from problems that beset the rest of the world"?

    a. Its fertile soil and ample water supply

    b. Its remoteness, fertile soil, and mild climate

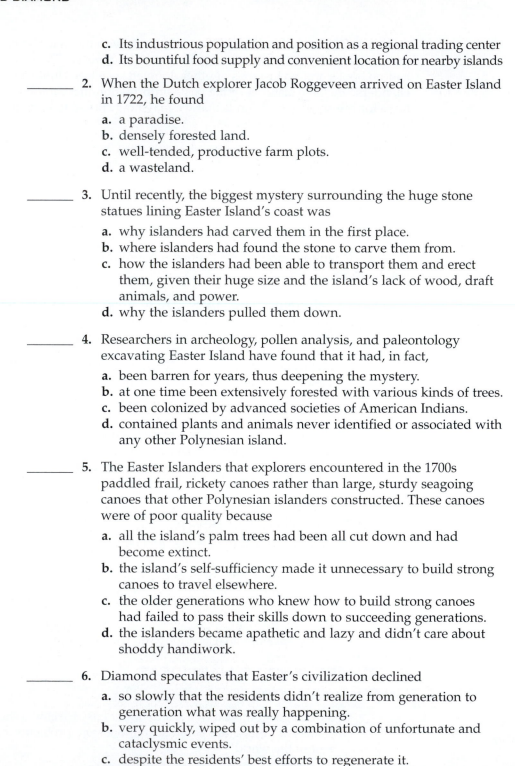

     c. Its industrious population and position as a regional trading center

     d. Its bountiful food supply and convenient location for nearby islands

_____ **2.** When the Dutch explorer Jacob Roggeveen arrived on Easter Island in 1722, he found

     a. a paradise.

     b. densely forested land.

     c. well-tended, productive farm plots.

     d. a wasteland.

_____ **3.** Until recently, the biggest mystery surrounding the huge stone statues lining Easter Island's coast was

     a. why islanders had carved them in the first place.

     b. where islanders had found the stone to carve them from.

     c. how the islanders had been able to transport them and erect them, given their huge size and the island's lack of wood, draft animals, and power.

     d. why the islanders pulled them down.

_____ **4.** Researchers in archeology, pollen analysis, and paleontology excavating Easter Island have found that it had, in fact,

     a. been barren for years, thus deepening the mystery.

     b. at one time been extensively forested with various kinds of trees.

     c. been colonized by advanced societies of American Indians.

     d. contained plants and animals never identified or associated with any other Polynesian island.

_____ **5.** The Easter Islanders that explorers encountered in the 1700s paddled frail, rickety canoes rather than large, sturdy seagoing canoes that other Polynesian islanders constructed. These canoes were of poor quality because

     a. all the island's palm trees had been all cut down and had become extinct.

     b. the island's self-sufficiency made it unnecessary to build strong canoes to travel elsewhere.

     c. the older generations who knew how to build strong canoes had failed to pass their skills down to succeeding generations.

     d. the islanders became apathetic and lazy and didn't care about shoddy handiwork.

_____ **6.** Diamond speculates that Easter's civilization declined

     a. so slowly that the residents didn't realize from generation to generation what was really happening.

     b. very quickly, wiped out by a combination of unfortunate and cataclysmic events.

     c. despite the residents' best efforts to regenerate it.

     d. in the same fashion and for the same reasons that all the other civilizations in Polynesia declined.

COMPREHENSION SCORE

Score your answers for Exercises A and B as follows:

A. No. right _____ × 2 = _____

B. No. right _____ × 1 = _____

Total points from A and B _____ × 10 = _____ percent

You may refer to the selection as you work through the remaining exercises.

C. DISTINGUISHING BETWEEN MAIN IDEAS AND SUPPORTING DETAILS

The following sentences come from paragraphs 27 and 28. Label them as follows: MI if the sentence represents a *main idea* and SD if the sentence represents a *supporting detail*.

1. _____ The fifteenth century marked the end not only for Easter's palm but for the forest itself.

2. _____ Its doom had been approaching as people cleared land to plant gardens; as they felled trees to build canoes, to transport and erect statues, and to burn; as rats devoured seeds; and probably as the native birds died out that had pollinated the trees' flowers and dispersed their fruit.

3. _____ The overall picture is among the most extreme examples of forest destruction anywhere in the world: the whole forest gone, and most of its tree species extinct.

4. _____ The destruction of the island's animals was as extreme as that of the forest: without exception, every species of native land bird became extinct.

5. _____ Even shellfish were overexploited, until people had to settle for small sea snails instead of larger cowries.

6. _____ Porpoise bones disappeared abruptly from garbage heaps around 1500; no one could harpoon porpoises anymore, since the trees used for constructing the big seagoing canoes no longer existed.

D. DRAWING CONCLUSIONS

Place an X beside each statement that represents a reasonable conclusion you can draw from this selection.

1. _____ The most serious threat to our survival lies in overpopulation.

2. _____ Reconstructing the civilization on Easter Island and the reasons for its decline would not have been possible without the research done by paleontologists and biologists.

3. _____ Those Easter Islanders who tried to warn the younger generation about their harmful practices were dismissed as eccentrics or doomsayers.

4._____   The people who inhabit Easter Island today are making every attempt to recapture its past glory.

5._____   It is not within our power to change the course of civilization; cultures are born, flourish, and die, just as all life on earth does, and human intervention in a society's evolution is futile.

6._____   Written records—the mark of literate societies—are a better way of preserving descriptions of an area's landscape than are oral tales handed down from generation to generation.

7._____   Despite the technological advancements that our civilization has produced, it is likely that Earth in the future—with its billions of people and dwindling resources—could succumb to the same fate that befell the Easter Islanders.

E. INTERPRETING MEANING

Where appropriate, write your answers for these questions in your own words.

1. _____   Which of the following would be a good title for paragraph 3?
   a. "Mysterious Stone Statues"
   b. "Easter Island: A Place of Exotic Romance"
   c. "Easter Island: A Vanished Civilization of Mystery and Isolation"
   d. "Polynesian Paradise"

2. Describe the kinds of evidence that Diamond uses to reinforce his theory that Easter Island, at one time, was a fertile, productive island, capable of sustaining life._____

3. In paragraph 36, what words and phrases show us that Diamond's ideas are hypothetical and not factual?_____

4. Find the quotation and identify the number of the paragraph that represents the *single* most important reason Diamond cites to explain Easter Island's demise? _____

5. Look again at almost any of the paragraphs throughout the body of the article and determine what they have in common structurally. _____

6. _____   Which of the following best describes Diamond's *tone*, or emotional attitude, toward his subject in this piece?
   a. neutral, informative, objective
   b. somber, concerned, and admonishing
   c. philosophical, reflective, and pensive
   d. provocative, shrill, inflammatory

F. UNDERSTANDING VOCABULARY

Look through the paragraphs listed below and find a word that matches each definition. Refer to a dictionary if necessary. An example has been done for you.

Ex. suitable for living [paragraphs 4–5]   _____habitable_____

1. many and varied [8–9]   _____

2. completely lacking, without [10–11—phrase]   _____

3. skeptical, disbelieving [12–13]   _____

4. practicability, likelihood [12–13]   _____

5. passionate, enthusiastic [12–13]   _____

6. horizontal layers, bands, or beds [18–19]   _____

7. easily sickened or disgusted [22–23]   _____

8. immense, huge [22–23]   _____

9. untouched, unspoiled [25–26]   _____

10. insult, verbal abuse [28–29]   _____

11. grandiose, pretentiously showy [30–31]   _____

12. was capable of, or equal to, a specified task [39–40]   _____

G. USING VOCABULARY

Here are some words from the selection. Write an original sentence using each word that shows both that you know how to use the word and what it means.

1. *succumb* [paragraph 2]_____

_____

2. *barrenness* [6]   _____

_____

3. *implausible* [16] _____

_____

4. *haven* [22] _____

_____

5. *ubiquitous* [26] _____

_____

6. *moguls* [31] _____

_____

H. PARAPHRASING AND SUMMARIZING EXERCISE

1. Paraphrase these sentences from paragraph 38.

Original Passage	**Paraphrase**
By now the meaning of Easter Island for us should be chillingly obvious. Easter Island is Earth writ small. Today, again, a rising population confronts shrinking resources.	_____ _____ _____ _____

2. Paragraph 36 is one of the most moving passages in the article. Summarize it in 25 to 30 words. _____

_____

_____

I. TOPICS FOR DISCUSSION

1. What evidence in the article makes Diamond's hypothesis irrefutable?
2. Look through the essay again, and in particular reread the section from paragraphs 31–36 and find two parallels Diamond draws between the Easter Islanders and issues and/or behavior in our civilization today.
3. In the last two paragraphs, what is the fundamental irony that Diamond implies?
4. As citizens concerned about the fate of our universe and of the human race, what practical measures can we take to avoid the fate of the Easter Islanders?

J. TOPICS FOR WRITING

1. Search in the library or on the World Wide Web for information that offers a different theory to explain the decline of Easter Island's civilization. Write a short report summarizing your findings.
2. What environmental change—especially one that has been a long time in the making—have you observed in a neighborhood, town, city, or even a place in nature that you are well acquainted with? Write an essay in which you discuss the change, the reasons for the change, and its impact on the environment.
3. Using both print sources in the library and Web sites, do some research and report on what the environment and culture of Easter Island are like now.

Exploring Related Web Sites

Information about Easter Island is available at these two sites. The first is Easter Island's home page, which includes several links. The second lists four topics for further exploration of the subject—The Story, Island Tour, Controversies, and Resources.

www.netaxs.com/trance/linklist.html

www.mysteriousplaces.com/Easter_Island/index.html

PART FIVE

Reading about Issues

Persuasive Writing and Opinion Pieces

In this introductory section, you will learn about these topics:

- The principles of persuasive writing
- The aims of persuasive writing
- How to read persuasive writing
- Types of claims
- Kinds of evidence
- The refutation
- The structure of an argument
- Bias

The Principles of Persuasive Writing

As you will recall from the introduction to Part One, to *persuade* is one of the primary purposes of nonfiction prose. The art of persuasion is a worthwhile skill to develop. Consider its usefulness in practical terms. Let's say that you have been working at your current part-time job for a year, you think you have done a good job, you take on new responsibilities willingly and without complaint, you arrive on time, and you don't fool around on the job. But your boss has never given you a raise. How would you approach your boss to ask for a higher salary? And what reasons would you give to support your request?

You would certainly wait to make sure that he or she was in a good mood and not stressed out about meeting deadlines or dealing with grumpy customers. You might point to your fine qualities listed above. You would mention your loyalty, your dedication to the job, and other stellar traits. And if you were lucky, you might succeed in getting that raise. This real-life example shows that understanding the tactics of persuasion can yield tangible rewards.

Learning to read persuasive prose with understanding and a critical eye also yields rewards. It is the basis on which our democratic society is built. A significant part of being a good citizen is learning about the issues of the day, weighing the arguments for and against proposed policies, and coming to a decision on your own, not one imposed by someone else. The right to make an informed decision on one's own is one of many rewards of living in a democratic country with a free press and the freedom to express oneself without fear of punishment, retaliation, or censorship, as occurs in repressive societies or in dictatorships. In sum, learning to see issues from a variety of perspectives, not merely from one person's (or our own) point of view is an important part of becoming an educated citizen.

The Aims of Persuasive Writing

Persuasive writing essentially aims to convince you in various ways of something. A person may try to convince you to accept his or her point of view. Politicians do this all the time, when they try to persuade us that they are the best candidate for public office. Someone may try to persuade us to change our behavior—for example, to get us to exercise more, to stop smoking, to get better grades, to protest against the war in Iraq, to volunteer to work in a soup kitchen—or simply to consider that another point of view has merit. All of these are common aims of persuasion and of persuasive writing as well.

AIMS OF PERSUASIVE WRITING

- To convince you to accept a particular point of view
- To convince you to change your thinking
- To convince you to take action
- To convince you to at least consider that another point of view has merit

---

What follows is a brief discussion of the component parts of opinion pieces, typically found on the op-ed pages of newspapers, in magazines, on Web sites, or in blogs. This discussion is followed by a practice editorial that I have annotated in the margin to show you how an experienced reader might read and analyze an opinion piece. Part Five concludes with seven pieces of persuasive writing from several print and online sources: three major newspapers (the *New York Times*, the *Washington Post*, and the *San Francisco Chronicle*), one magazine (*In These Times*), and two Web sites (*www.realclearpolitics.com* and *www.alternet.org*).

The pieces take up some issues that I hope you will find interesting and provocative. All of them relate to the future of our society and our way of life: one solution for the problem of unrecycled plastic bottles, global warming and climate change, the fading American dream, racial profiling, and the fence being built on the U.S.–Mexico border to prevent illegal immigrants from sneaking into the country. For this last issue, three selections are provided: one background article and two opinion pieces, one for and the other against the border fence. The section ends with paired Web sites that provide conflicting information about global warming, one sponsored by the Union of Concerned Scientists and the other by the Heartland Institute. Reading these selections and working through the exercises—which differ markedly from those in the rest of the text—will help you learn to read prose expressing an opinion.

How to Read Persuasive Writing

When you read the opinion pieces in this text and in other sources like your daily newspaper, first you decide on the aim of the article or opinion piece. By definition, persuasive writing presents a controversial issue that is open to discussion. Also by definition, a persuasive piece presents the writer's subjective opinions. But there is wide latitude in what persuasive writers do: Some writers present two or even three points of view and leave you to make up your own mind about where you stand. Other writers present only one side, an obvious attempt to change your mind or to get you to adopt their position. Still other writers may resort to bias, slanted language, emotional appeals, and other manipulative devices.

Whichever technique the opinion writer uses, the most important step—and your starting point—is to determine his or her central *argument*, also called the *claim*—the proposition or idea to be backed up and defended—that lies at the heart of the piece. Like the thesis statement in an informative or expository essay (discussed in Part One), the claim or argument in a persuasive piece may be *stated* directly or implied. Those who study argumentation classify claims into three types: *claims of fact*, *claims of value*, and *claims of policy*. Study the explanations and examples that follow.

Types of Claims

Claims of fact can be verified, measured, tested, and proved by citing factual evidence, the results of scientific research, or in the case of predictions, by the passage of time. *Claims of value* involve matters of taste, morality, opinion, and ideas about right and wrong, and because of this, they are harder to prove than are claims of fact. The support for a claim of value is usually in the form of reasons, examples, reference to a book of rules or other work (such as the Bible, the Koran, or the Constitution), and personal experience. *Claims of policy* argue for a recommended course of action, propose a change or a new policy, or identify a problem that needs a solution. Note that claims of policy may include a word like "should," "must," or "ought to." They are typically supported by good reasons, facts and statistics, examples, or the testimony of authorities or experts. Study the examples in these three charts so that you can practice distinguishing among them.

CLAIMS OF FACT
• Smoking causes numerous health problems for long-term smokers.
• Genetically modified crops will help feed Third World nations.
• The Boston Patriots will win the Super Bowl again.

CLAIMS OF VALUE
• Community colleges offer students a good education at relatively little cost.
• Broccoli tastes better than spinach.
• *Juno* is an intriguing, engaging movie about a serious subject—a teenage girl's unwanted pregnancy and the decision she makes.

CLAIMS OF POLICY

- Because of overcrowded classes, Centerville Community College should raise its tuition so that more teachers can be hired.
- Elementary schools must do their part to discourage obesity in the nation's children by removing candy and soft drink machines from campuses.
- High schools ought to require students to complete a course in consumer economics as a requirement for graduation.

A little later in this section, you will read an editorial about one way to help solve the problem of plastic water bottles in the nation's landfills. The exercise that follows presents several claims relating to this issue of proliferating water bottles. Study them and then in the space provided write whether it represents a claim of fact, a claim of value, or a claim of policy.

1. _____ Bisphenol A (BPA), a compound in hard, clear plastics, should be banned from containers such as baby bottles and water bottles.

2. _____ The drinking water in metropolitan areas like New York City and the San Francisco Bay Area tastes just as good as, if not better than, the water you buy in plastic bottles like Evian, Calistoga, Dasani, or Crystal Geyser.

3. _____ BPA is a potentially harmful chemical found in hard, clear plastic water bottles that has been associated with some types of cancer and with early onset of puberty.[1]

4. _____ Discarded plastic water bottles pose a serious problem because they clog our nation's landfills.

5. _____ Municipalities should encourage people to give up drinking water from plastic bottles by installing public drinking fountains on city sidewalks.

6. _____ Portland, Oregon, is one city that has installed drinking fountains on city sidewalks, and because many of them were designed by artists, they are not only useful but also esthetically pleasing.

Kinds of Evidence

After you have located the writer's argument or claim in an opinion piece, then you can identify and evaluate the *evidence* used to support it. Writers of opinion pieces may use a single kind of evidence, or they may combine various kinds. Here are the most common: facts and statistics, which may derive from scientific

[1]For more information on bisphenol A, visit these two Web sites: *www.commondreams.org/archive/2008/04/23/8479*; *http://health.usnews.com/articles/health/living-well-usn/2008/04/16/study-of-chemical-in-plastic-bottles-raises-alarm.html.*

studies, research reports, government-sponsored investigations or surveys, census reports, clinical tests, and so forth; examples and observations from the writer's experience or from reading; rational, plausible explanations (good reasons) that answer the question "why?"; and finally, quotation or testimony from authorities and experts in a particular field. This chart summarizes each kind:

KINDS OF EVIDENCE USED IN PERSUASIVE WRITING

- **Facts and statistics:** From scientific studies and research reports
- **Examples and observations:** From the writer's experience and/or reading
- **Good reasons:** Rational explanations that answer the question "why?"
- **Quotation or testimony:** The opinion of experts

The first step in reading opinion pieces is to locate the *claim* and then identify the *supporting evidence*. Try to separate the two, because some writers mix the claim and the evidence in the same sentence, for example:

> Because obesity has become such a serious health risk for our nation's children (the government estimates that 11 percent of American children are obese), our public schools should encourage children to walk or ride their bikes to school and should eliminate candy and snack food machines from school grounds.

Which part of the sentence represents the claim and which part represents the evidence? Write the claim in the first space.

Claim: _____

_____

Evidence: _____

_____

The Refutation

The final step in reading persuasive pieces is to look for a *refutation*, wherein the writer deals with the opposing side. Note that many editorial writers do not include a refutation, but if there is one, it might look like this: First the writer *concedes* that there is some merit to the opposing side. (After all, every question has two sides, and often more.) The writer then takes one or two of the opposition's major arguments and *refutes* them, offering counterarguments against them.

An example from real life will help you understand this process better. Let's say that there is a dangerous intersection near campus where some students have been injured while they were trying to cross the street. You get some concerned students and citizens to request a meeting of the municipal transportation and safety board. At the meeting your group explains the problem, gives evidence that the problem is serious, and offers a solution—that is, you present your claim of policy: The intersection needs a stoplight, so someone doesn't get killed.

The safety director counters your proposal by saying that the city's budget is tight, that a new light will cost $100,000, and that the community has more pressing needs to meet. For example, the city has just committed the same amount of money to an after-school program for disadvantaged boys and girls. Hard to argue against that!

Still, you and your fellow students are convinced that your position is right. You prepare your refutation and come up with the following counterarguments:

1. An after-school program for disadvantaged youth is surely a worthy cause (your concession), but the board needs to reexamine its priorities. Saving the lives of students who attend the local college is more important. Also, a stoplight is the city's responsibility; an after-school club is not. It would be more appropriate to seek funding for a club from private grants and charitable foundations. (This is your first counterargument.)
2. Your second counterargument appeals to the board's conscience: If a stoplight isn't installed, more injuries will occur, and someone might die. Although $100,000 might seem like a lot of money for a simple stoplight, it will be money well spent. A human life is more precious than the $100,000 saved by not installing one. How many people must die or be seriously injured before the board decides that a light is necessary?
3. Your third counterargument appeals to the emotions: It's unconscionable that the board is willfully ignoring traffic hazards.
4. Finally, you offer some hard evidence refuting the board's contention that the town doesn't have enough money in its budget for the project: Recently, the local newspaper ran a series of articles criticizing frivolous expenditures at city hall. For example, the mayor redecorated her office at taxpayer expense, buying leather couches, matching chairs, an expensive Persian rug, and installing a bar; she also requisitioned a new limousine. Surely pedestrians' lives are more important than an elegant mayor's office and a fancy car.

Your refutation might work, or it might not, but at least you have dealt with your opponent's primary objections to spending this money.

The refutation or counterargument can take many forms. The writer may agree that there is some merit to the opposition but that the issue is more serious or complicated than the opponent realizes. The writer may argue that the opposing argument is somehow flawed. Finally, and probably most effective, the writer may admonish the opponent by warning of the consequences of not acting. Or the reverse might be appropriate. For example, when George W. Bush and many Republican supporters argued for going to war to remove the Iraqi leader, Saddam Hussein, many writers, scholars, and government officials argued for *not* acting because attacking Iraq would have severe political and economic consequences. This is a good example of a claim of fact that proved to be true by virtue of the passage of time.

When you read persuasive pieces, look for a refutation. The best opinion writers anticipate their opponents' objections and offer a rebuttal.

The Structure of an Argument

An argumentative piece must be clearly organized if the writer is to get the point across effectively and to convince the audience to adopt the particular claim. Most good opinion pieces contain the elements you have examined above—a claim, evidence, and a refutation. How these elements are arranged depends on convention and to some extent the writer's personal preference. Practicing locating the component parts in opinion pieces is an excellent way to sharpen your thinking skills, and at the same time, to make you more aware of the problems that abound in today's world.

A conventional opinion piece might follow this organizational scheme: The introduction provides background, introduces the subject, and perhaps engages the reader's attention with a meaningful anecdote. The introduction *may* also contain the claim. The body of the opinion piece contains evidence to support or to prove the claim along with a *refutation*, a section (usually quite short) in which the writer considers *opposing views* and offers a counterargument against them. (Note, however, that many writers do not include refutations.) Finally, the conclusion, which also may contain the claim, recommends future action, gives a warning about what will happen if the claim is not accepted, or states the seriousness of the problem. Here, again in chart form, is a summary of the arrangement of elements in opinion pieces.

- **Introduction:** Provides background for the subject and *may* contain the argument or claim
- **Body:** Contains the evidence—various kinds of material to support or prove the claim
- **Refutation:** Contains opposing views or a counterargument against the claim
- **Conclusion:** May contain the claim; also may recommend future action or give a warning

Not every argument you read will be arranged like this, since some writers prefer to begin with the evidence and end with the claim. Still, these are the elements to look for when you read opinion pieces.

Bias

Last, when you read opinion pieces, look for evidence of *bias*—prejudice or unfair preconceived ideas. Obviously, complete objectivity is humanly impossible, since we are all the products of our environment, ethnic and religious heritage, social class, and the like. Yet a writer should not come across as having an axe to grind— a particular point of view that he or she bludgeons the reader with. Nor should the writer stand to gain (or lose) economically if the reader accepts the argument. For example, if Elizabeth Royte were an artist who designed public water fountains, you might consider her bias when reading her editorial. Since she is not, and since she has written two books on environmental matters pertaining to garbage, you can safely assume that her opinion piece is motivated by environmental concerns, not by her desire to profit personally.

Therefore, you can ask yourself if the writer treats the issue fairly, whether there is sufficient evidence to support the argument, and whether the writer appeals to your sense of reason or to your emotions (or perhaps to both). There is nothing wrong with a writer's appealing to the emotions, as long as you are aware that it is going on.

A Practice Editorial

ELIZABETH ROYTE

A Fountain on Every Corner

Let us consider the issue of plastic water bottles. We see people carrying them everywhere, and though the single water bottle you carry with you to class or to the gym might not seem to constitute a serious problem like war, hunger, the price of gasoline, AIDS, or the melting of the Arctic ice cap and its effects on the polar bear population, the issue is in fact serious. It is aptly illustrated in this photograph:

The photo accompanied an online article titled "Bottled Water: Environmental, Social Burdens and What Seattle is Doing About It."[2] Since estimates about the percentage of water bottles recycled ranges from 12 to 23 percent, the remaining number of bottles accumulate in landfills, creating a serious problem.[3]

This practice editorial gives you the opportunity to study the structure of a typical opinion piece. It was written by Elizabeth Royte and published on the New York Times *editorial page. Royte is the author of* Garbage Land: On the Secret Trail of Trash *and* Bottlemania: How Water Went on Sale and Why We Bought It *(2005). This information suggests that she is an authority on the subject. I have annotated the piece for you, paragraph by paragraph, pointing out the significant elements.*

1 Establishes background & states claim of policy.

1 Water fountain season is here. New York City workers have turned on bubblers in the parks, and the Icelandic artist Olafur Eliasson has begun to erect four enormous waterfalls in the harbor, each 90 to 120 feet high, that are scheduled to flow from July to October. The shimmering cascades will cost the city nothing (the $15 million cost is being paid by private donations to the Public Art Fund), but here's a better idea for a civic-minded organization or person interested in celebrating water: sidewalk fountains in places outside the parks.

2 A concession—water bottles are convenient. Evidence—the 50 billion bottles have a big economic and environmental impact. Most important reason—tap water tastes good and is free.

2 Convenience is said to be one of bottled water's greatest allures: we're a grab-and-go society, consuming roughly 50 billion bottles of water a year. But as awareness of the product's economic and environmental impact has escalated, mayors across the nation (although not Michael Bloomberg of New York) have canceled city contracts with bottled water purveyors, citing the expense of hauling away empties (less than 20 percent make it into recycling systems); the vast amounts of oil used in producing, transporting and refrigerating the bottles; and the hypocrisy of spending taxpayer dollars on private water while touting the virtues of public supplies. Last summer, New York City spent $700,000 on a campaign reminding New Yorkers that their tap water is tasty and affordable.

3 Advantages of tap water and one concession.

3 Delivered by gravity, tap water generates virtually no waste. All that, and it contains no calories, caffeine or colorants either. (Yes, New York's water—like that of other cities—contains trace amounts of drugs, but we lack proof, so far, that exposure at these low levels is a human health risk.)

4 A second concession.

4 Bottled water's main virtue, it seems, is convenience, especially for people at large in the city. As the editor of Beverage Digest told The Times, "It's not so easy, walking down Third Avenue on a hot day, to get a glass of tap water."

5–6 Precedents exist in other cities.

5 But it needn't be so. Paris has its ornate cast-iron Wallace fountains (donated in the late 19th century by a wealthy philanthropist hoping to steer the homeless from alcohol toward a healthier beverage); Rome its ever-running street spigots; Portland, Ore., its delightful four-bowl Benson Bubblers.

6 In the 1880s, several American cities had "temperance fountains," paid for by the philanthropist (and dentist) Henry D. Cogswell of San Francisco. New

[2]http://frommyeyestoyours.wordpress.com/2008/03/23/bottled-water-environmental-social-burdens-and-what-seattle-is-doing-about-it

[3]http://earth911.org/recycling/plastic-bottle-recycling/plastic-bottle-recycling-facts

York City had six of these, placed at busy corners: "In the brief space of 10 minutes one morning 40 persons were recently observed to stop for a refreshing drink," observed an officer of the New York Association for Improving the Condition of the Poor, which helped place the fountains.

7 Facts—no fountains in Midtown.

7   Such fountains have largely disappeared (although the temperance fountain in Tompkins Square Park still stands). Today, we've got plenty of bubblers in parks, but Midtown is a Sahara for parched pedestrians, who don't even think of looking for public sources of tap water.

8 Time to change our thinking. A claim of value.

8   An entire generation of Americans has grown up thinking public faucets equal filth, and the only water fit to drink comes in plastic, factory sealed. It's time to change that perception with public fountains in the city's busiest quadrants, pristine bubblers that celebrate the virtues of our public water supply, remind us of our connection to upstate watersheds and reinforce our commitment to clean water for all.

9 Practical advice.

9   On a more practical note: let's make them easy to maintain, with water pressure adequate to fill our reusable bottles. And germophobes, relax: city water is chlorinated, and experts report that pathogens impolitely left on spigots by the lips of preceding drinkers don't creep down into pipes. In other words, the bubbling water is clean, so get over it.

10 More examples to bolster & repeat claim of policy. Repeats good reasons.

10   Minneapolis recently committed to spending $500,000 on 10 artist-designed fountains that will be placed in areas of high foot and bike traffic. Mayor Gavin Newsom of San Francisco, archenemy of bottled water, is pursuing a similar plan. New York and other cities should swiftly follow suit, if not with fancy fountains then with several dozen off-the-shelf models. Wheelchair-accessible, and vandal- and frost-resistant, they can be had for less than $2,000 apiece (plumbing not included). It's a small price to pay to quench thirst, reduce bottle litter, slash our collective carbon footprint and reaffirm our connection with the city's most valuable resource: its public water supply. ✻

First, read the annotations in the margin alongside the editorial. Be sure that you know the meanings of any unfamiliar words in them. Then in your own words, state the primary *claim* in this editorial. Then identify the type of claim—fact, value, or policy. (Note that there may be a primary claim and a secondary one, as well.) Be sure not to include any supporting evidence in this section.

Claim: _____

_____

_____

Now list four pieces of supporting evidence. Use the annotations to help you. After you write each one, identify the type of evidence according to this list: facts and statistics; examples and observations; good reasons; or quotation or testimony.

Evidence

_____

_____

_____

_____

_____

_____

_____

_____

_____

Finally, look through the editorial again, this time locating three ideas Royte uses as a concession or a refutation—that is, objections those opposed to her proposal might raise and her counterarguments against them.

Refutation

_____

_____

_____

_____

FORMING YOUR OWN OPINIONS

A final suggestion: You are not being wishy-washy if you read an opinion piece and are unable to come to a conclusion about which side you favor. Complex issues require complex analysis. And complex issues often produce plenty of argument and discussion but few workable solutions. Good readers do not necessarily become immediate converts to one side or the other. Before taking a decisive stance that agrees with your general outlook and perspective, you can read more material expressing other points of view. Reading the op-ed pages of the daily newspaper and reading Web sites and blogs devoted to the issues of the day are important ways of getting more information.

In sum, if you know what to look for when you tackle persuasive prose, your reading will be at once more critical and more intelligent; and this awareness will serve you well for the rest of your life.

27

CHARLES M. BLOW
Farewell, Fair Weather

The subject of climate change has many components—the melting of the polar ice cap in the Arctic, rising sea levels, drought, and extreme weather, to name just a few. In this short editorial from the New York Times, *columnist Charles M. Blow describes the Age of Extreme Weather. The opinion piece was published the day before the official start of the 2008 hurricane season. A graduate of Grambling State University in Louisiana, Blow also worked as a graphic artist at the* Detroit News *and as the art director for* National Geographic *before becoming the* Times' *visual op-ed columnist.*

Vocabulary Preview

WORD PARTS

co-, [paragraph 12], con- [paragraph 5] The words *contributed* (paragraph 5) and *coordinated* (paragraph 12) begin with the Latin prefix *co-*, meaning "together." You can see this prefix in the common words *cooperate, co-worker, coauthor,* and *codefendant.* The prefix is spelled *cor-* when the root begins with the letter "r," as in *correspond.* Sometimes it is spelled *com-*, as in the word *combination.*

If a college is coeducational, what does that mean? _____

WORD FAMILIES

demos, epidemiology [paragraph 2] The word *epidemiology* refers to a branch of medicine that studies the causes and control of disease in human populations. This word combines three Greek word parts—*epi-* ("among") + *demos* ("people") + *-ology* ("study of"). A related word is *epidemic,* a disease that spreads throughout a population. Some other words containing the Greek root *demos* are these three:

democracy	government by the people (*demos* + *-cracy* ["rule"])
demography	the study of human populations (*demos* + *graphein* ["to write"])
demagogue	a leader who appeals to the people's prejudices and emotions (*demos* + *agogos* ["leader"])

CHARLES M. BLOW

Farewell, Fair Weather

1   We are now firmly ensconced in the Age of Extreme Weather.

2   According to the Center for Research on the Epidemiology of Disasters, there have been more than four times as many weather-related disasters in the last 30 years than in the previous 75 years. The United States has experienced more of those disasters than any other country.

3   Just this month, a swarm of tornadoes shredded the central states. California and Florida have been scorched by wildfires, and a crippling drought in the Southeast has forced Georgia to authorize plans for new reservoirs.

4   Who do we have to thank for all this? Probably ourselves.

5   Last year, the Intergovernmental Panel on Climate Change issued reports concluding that "human influences" (read greenhouse-gas emissions) have "more likely than not" contributed to this increase. The United States is one of the biggest producers of greenhouse-gas emissions.

6   Furthermore, a White House report about the effect of global climate change on the United States issued Thursday (years late and under court order) reaffirmed that the situation will probably get worse: In addition to temperature extremes, "precipitation is likely to be less frequent but more intense. It is also likely that future hurricanes will become more intense, with higher peak speeds and more heavy precipitation. . . ."

7   This increase is deadly and disruptive—and could become economically unbearable.

8   According to the National Hurricane Center, 10 of the 30 costliest American hurricanes have struck since 2000, even after adjusting the figures for inflation and the cost of construction.

9   In 2005, the year of Hurricane Katrina, the estimated damage from storms in the United States was $121 billion. That is $39 billion more than the 2005 supplemental spending bill to fight the wars in Afghanistan and Iraq.

10 About $3 billion has been allocated to assist farmers who suffer losses because of droughts, floods and tornadoes among other things.

11 And, a recent report in The Denver Post said the Forest Service plans to spend 45 percent, or $1.9 billion, of its budget this year fighting forest fires.

12 This surge in disasters and attendant costs is yet another reason we need to declare a coordinated war on climate change akin to the wars on drugs and terror. It's a matter of national security.

13 By the way, hurricane season begins Sunday. ✳

Exercises

You may refer to the selection as you complete these exercises. Write your answers to these questions in the spaces provided.

A. IDENTIFYING THE CLAIM

1. Using your own words as much as possible, write Blow's central claim or proposition. Also indicate the number of the paragraph where it is

   located. _____

   _____

2. Then decide if the claim is a claim of fact, a claim of value, or a claim of policy. Remember that an argument may have a secondary claim as well.

   _____

B. LOCATING EVIDENCE AND THE REFUTATION

1. One piece of evidence is listed for you. List two or three other major pieces of evidence that the writer uses to support the claim. Also characterize each piece of evidence according to whether it represents facts and statistics; examples and observations; good reasons; or quotation or testimony.

   a. The Center for Research on the Epidemiology of Disasters reports that we have experienced four times the number of weather disasters in the last 30 years as we have in the last 75 years. These include tornadoes, wildfires, and drought. (facts)

   b. _____

   c. _____

   d. _____

   _____

2. Finally, if there is a refutation, list that as well. _____

C. IDENTIFYING SOLUTIONS

1. Does the writer provide a solution to the problem he discusses? If so, write it in the space provided. Be sure to use your own words. _____

   _____

   _____

2. What is your proposal to help solve this problem? _____

D. USING VOCABULARY

Here are some words from the selection. Write an original sentence using each word that shows both that you know how to use the word and what it means.

1. *ensconced* [paragraph 1] _____

   _____

2. *emissions* [5] _____

   _____

3. *supplemental* [9] _____

   _____

4. *allocated* [10] _____

   _____

5. *akin (to)* [12] _____

   _____

E. TOPICS FOR DISCUSSION

1. What evidence does Blow present that global warming and increased emissions in greenhouse gases are to blame for the extreme weather that the United States is experiencing? How would you characterize the evidence? Does he rely more on fact, on opinion, or on a combination of both? What kinds of information would have strengthened his argument?
2. At the end of the editorial, Blow argues that we need to "declare a coordinated war on climate change akin to the wars on drugs and terror." Comment on the effectiveness of this comparison.
3. Consider again the last sentence of the editorial. Why does the writer end the piece in this way? What effect on the reader does he intend?

F. TOPICS FOR WRITING

1. The consensus in the past few years is that the weather in the United States has been unusually extreme. Various parts of the country have experienced wildfires, drought, deadly tornadoes, and destructive hurricanes like Katrina, Rita, and Ike. Do some research on an unusual weather condition in your area and write a brief report explaining why it was so unusual.
2. Blow does not offer any practical suggestions for reducing greenhouse emissions. Correct this omission by writing a paper in which you present three suggestions that every American could implement to combat climate change. Use one or both of the Web sites listed below or others that offer similar information.

Exploring Related Web Sites

The two agencies mentioned in the editorial both have extensive Web sites—the Center for Research on the Epidemiology of Disasters and the Intergovernmental Panel on Climate Change. Their home pages can be accessed at these addresses:

www.cred.be   *www.ipcc.ch*

28

BILL McKIBBEN

The Environmental Issue from Hell

In this opinion piece, Bill McKibben writes about global warming, a problem he characterizes as "the great moral crisis of our time." Although fewer Americans are buying SUVs and light trucks, given the soaring price of fuel, still we buy much larger cars than people drive in other parts of the world, thus contributing to climate change in numbers disproportionate to our population. McKibben is the author of The End of Nature *(1997) and* Fight Global Warming Now: The Handbook for Taking Action in Your Community *(2007). This piece was originally published in the progressive news magazine* In These Times.

Vocabulary Preview

WORD PARTS

equivalent [paragraph 3] McKibben writes that driving a big SUV for one year "is the *equivalent* of opening your refrigerator door and then forgetting to close it for six years" in terms of the amount of carbon dioxide produced. The prefix *equi-* indicates "equality." *Equivalent* therefore means "equal in value or measure." Here are some other words with this prefix:

equilibrium	state of balance due to the equal action of opposing forces (*equi-* + *libra* ["balance"])
equinox	the two times of the year when the length of the day and the length of the night are approximately equal (*equi-* + *nox* or *noct-* ["night"])
equidistant	equally distant from one another

What does this word mean? Check a dictionary if you are unsure.

equivocal _____

WORD FAMILIES

magnitude [paragraph 2] A microscope *magnifies* things or provides *magnification*. *Magnitude* means "great size or amount." All three words come from the root *magnus*, meaning "large" or "great." You can also see the same root in these two words:

magnificent	great in splendor, lavish
magnanimous	generous in giving or in forgiving an insult (*magnus* + *animus* ["spirit"])

If a student graduates from college *magna cum laude*, what does that mean? _____

What is a real estate magnate? _____

The Environmental Issue from Hell

1   When global warming first emerged as a potential crisis in the late 1980s, one academic analyst called it "the public policy problem from hell." The years since have only proven him more astute: Fifteen years into our understanding of climate change, we have yet to figure out how we're going to tackle it. And environmentalists are just as clueless as anyone else: Do we need to work on lifestyle or on lobbying, on photovoltaics or on politics? And is there a difference? How well we handle global warming will determine what kind of century we inhabit—and indeed what kind of planet we leave behind. The issue cuts close to home and also floats off easily into the abstract. So far it has been the ultimate "can't get there from here" problem, but the time has come to draw a road map—one that may help us deal with the handful of other issues on the list of real, world-shattering problems.

2   Typically, when you're mounting a campaign, you look for self-interest, you scare people by saying what will happen to us if we don't do something: All the birds will die, the canyon will disappear beneath a reservoir, we will choke to death on smog. But in the case of global warming, that doesn't exactly do the trick, at least in the time frame we're discussing. In temperate latitudes, climate change will creep up on us. Severe storms already have grown more frequent and more damaging. The progression of seasons is less steady. Some agriculture is less reliable. But face it: Our economy is so enormous that it takes those changes in stride. Economists who work on this stuff talk about how it will shave a percentage or two off the GNP over the next few decades. And most of us live lives so divorced from the natural world that we hardly notice the changes anyway. Hotter? Turn up the air-conditioning. Stormier? Well, an enormous percentage of Americans commute from remote-controlled garage to office parking garage—it may have been some time since they got good and wet in a rainstorm. By the time the magnitude of the change is truly in our faces, it will be too late to do much about it: There's such a lag time to increased levels of carbon dioxide in the atmosphere that we need to be making the switch to solar and wind and hydrogen power right now to prevent disaster decades away. Yesterday, in fact.

3   So maybe we should think of global warming in a different way—as the great moral crisis of our time, the equivalent of the civil rights movement of the 1960s.

4   Why a moral question? In the first place, no one's ever figured out a more effective way to screw the marginalized and poor of this planet than climate change. Having taken their dignity, their resources, and their freedom under

a variety of other schemes, we now are taking the very physical stability on which their already difficult lives depend.

5   Our economy can absorb these changes for a while, but consider Bangladesh for a moment. In 1998 the sea level in the Bay of Bengal was higher than normal, just the sort of thing we can expect to become more frequent and severe. The waters sweeping down the Ganges and the Brahmaputra rivers from the Himalayas could not drain easily into the ocean—they backed up across the country, forcing most of its inhabitants to spend three months in thigh-deep water. The fall rice crop didn't get planted. We've seen this same kind of disaster over the past few years in Mozambique and Honduras and Venezuela and other places.

6   And global warming is a moral crisis, too, if you place any value on the rest of creation. Coral reef researchers indicate that these spectacularly intricate ecosystems are also spectacularly vulnerable. Rising water temperatures are likely to bleach them to extinction by mid-century. In the Arctic, polar bears are 20 percent scrawnier than they were a decade ago: As pack ice melts, so does the opportunity for hunting seals. All in all, the 21st century seems poised to see extinctions at a rate not observed since the last big asteroid slammed into the planet. But this time the asteroid is us.

7   It's a moral question, finally, if you think we owe any debt to the future. No one ever has figured out a more thoroughgoing way to strip-mine the present and degrade what comes after—all the people who will ever be related to you. Ever. No generation yet to come will ever forget us—we are the ones present at the moment when the temperature starts to spike, and so far we have not reacted. If it had been done to us, we would loathe the generation that did it, precisely as we will one day be loathed.

8   But trying to launch a moral campaign is no easy task. In most moral crises, there is a villain—some person or class or institution that must be overcome. Once the villain is identified, the battle can commence. But you can't really get angry at carbon dioxide, and the people responsible for its production are, well, us. So perhaps we need some symbols to get us started, some places to sharpen the debate and rally ourselves to action. There are plenty to choose from: our taste for ever bigger houses and the heating and cooling bills that come with them, our penchant for jumping on airplanes at the drop of a hat. But if you wanted one glaring example of our lack of balance, you could do worse than point the finger at sport utility vehicles.

9   SUVs are more than mere symbols. They are a major part of the problem—we emit so much more carbon dioxide now than we did a decade ago in part because our fleet of cars and trucks actually has gotten steadily less fuel efficient for the past 10 years. If you switched today from the average American car to a big SUV, and drove it for just one year, the difference in carbon dioxide that you produced would be the equivalent of opening your refrigerator door and then forgetting to close it for six years. SUVs essentially are machines for burning fossil fuel that just happen to also move you and your stuff around.

10   But what makes them such a perfect symbol is the brute fact that they are simply unnecessary. Go to the parking lot of the nearest suburban supermarket and look around: The only conclusion you can draw is that to reach the grocery,

people must drive through three or four raging rivers and up the side of a canyon. These are semi-military machines, armored trucks on a slight diet. While they do not keep their occupants appreciably safer, they do wreck whatever they plow into, making them the perfect metaphor for a heedless, super-sized society.

11   That's why we need a much broader politics than the Washington lobbying that's occupied the big environmental groups for the past decade. We need to take all the brilliant and energetic strategies of local grassroots groups fighting dumps and cleaning up rivers and apply those tactics in the national and international arenas. That's why some pastors are starting to talk with their congregations about what cars to buy, and why some college seniors are passing around petitions pledging to stay away from the Ford Explorers and Excursions, and why some auto dealers have begun to notice informational picketers outside their showrooms on Saturday mornings urging customers to think about gas mileage when they look at cars.

12   The point is not that such actions by themselves—any individual actions—will make any real dent in the levels of carbon dioxide pouring into our atmosphere. Even if you got 10 percent of Americans really committed to changing their energy use, their solar homes wouldn't make much of a difference in our national totals. But 10 percent would be enough to change the politics around the issue, enough to pressure politicians to pass laws that would cause us all to shift our habits. And so we need to begin to take an issue that is now the province of technicians and turn it into a political issue, just as bus boycotts began to make public the issue of race, forcing the system to respond. That response is likely to be ugly—there are huge companies with a lot to lose, and many people so tied in to their current ways of life that advocating change smacks of subversion. But this has to become a political issue—and fast. The only way that may happen, short of a hideous drought or monster flood, is if it becomes a personal issue first. ✳

From Bill McKibben, "The Environmental Issue from Hell," From *In These Times*, April 30, 2001. Reprinted with the permission of the author.

Exercises

You may refer to the selection as you complete these exercises. Write your answers to these questions in the spaces provided.

A. IDENTIFYING THE CLAIM

1. Using your own words as much as possible, write McKibben's central claim or proposition. Also indicate the number of the paragraph where it is located. Remember that an argument may have a secondary claim as well.

   _____

   _____

2. Then decide if the claim is a claim of fact, a claim of value, or a claim of policy.

   _____

B. LOCATING EVIDENCE AND THE REFUTATION

1. One piece of evidence is listed for you. List two other major pieces of evidence that the writer uses to support the claim. Also characterize each piece of evidence according to whether it represents facts and statistics; examples and observations; good reasons; or quotation or testimony.

a. Although we may not see the damage done because the changes in the atmosphere occur so slowly, there is already evidence of climate and seasonal changes. (observations)

b. _____

_____

c. _____

_____

_____

2. Finally, if there is a refutation, list that as well. _____

_____

C. IDENTIFYING SOLUTIONS

1. Does McKibben provide a solution to the problem he discusses? If so, write it

in the space provided. Be sure to use your own words. _____

_____

_____

2. What is your proposal to help solve this problem? _____

D. USING VOCABULARY

Here are some words from the selection. Write an original sentence using each word that shows both that you know how to use the word and what it means.

1. *astute* [paragraph 1] _____

_____

2. *penchant* [8] _____

_____

3. *heedless* [10] _____

_____

4. *advocating* [12] _____

_____

5. *subversion* [12] _____

_____

E. LOCATING EVIDENCE

Go through the editorial and locate the evidence that supports this idea: Consumers who care about solving the problem of global warming should not buy SUVs. To identify it, put a star in the margin next to each piece of evidence or bracket the words.

F. TOPICS FOR DISCUSSION

1. How would you characterize the evidence McKibben uses to support his claim? Does he rely more on fact, on opinion, or on a combination of both? What kinds of information would have strengthened his argument?
2. Despite the increase in the price of gas over the past two years or so, SUVs remain popular in America. Why? And despite the expense of filling their gas tanks and the environmental problems associated with them, what does their popularity say about our society?
3. What are some practical measures that you have taken to reduce global warming and your carbon footprint? Are you willing to sacrifice some material comfort to save the planet? If so, what sacrifices seem reasonable to make? Which seem unreasonable?

G. TOPICS FOR WRITING

1. Imagine that a good friend has decided to buy an SUV. Write a letter in which you try to convince the person to change his or her mind.
2. Write a refutation of your own to McKibben's opinion piece. Can you come up with two or three reasons in favor of buying an SUV?

Exploring Related Web Sites

- National Climatic Data Center
  http://lwf.ncdc.noaa.gov/oa/climate/globalwarming.html
- U.S. Environmental Protection Agency
  www.epa.gov/climatechange/index.html
- Finally, go to the home pages of these environmental organizations and see what information they offer about global warming:

  Audubon Society (*www.audubonsociety.org*)

  World Wildlife Fund (*www.worldwildlife.org*)

  Sierra Club (*www.sierraclub.org*)

Two other Web sites dealing with the problem of global warming are listed in Reading 35 (page 446).

29

COURTNEY E. MARTIN

Is the American Dream a Delusion?

This opinion piece was published on AlterNet, a Web site and online community devoted to publishing original journalism from a variety of independent media sources. Its mission is to challenge individuals to action on a variety of issues, among them, the environment, civil liberties, social justice, and the like, and to challenge what AlterNet calls the "vitriol and disinformation of right-wing media" (www.alternet.org/about). Courtney Martin teaches gender studies at Hunter College in New York and is the author of Perfect Girls, Starving Daughters: The Frightening New Normalcy of Hating Your Body *(2007).*

Vocabulary Preview

WORD PARTS

-ist [paragraph 12] An *elitist* is a person associated with the elite, people who enjoy superior intellectual, economic, or social status. The suffix *-ist* refers broadly to one who "supports or follows." Feminists, for example, believe in and follow women's causes. A realist believes in looking at things realistically rather than idealistically. This prefix also can describe one who is skilled, or trained, or employed in a particular field. For example, an *orthopedist* specializes in injuries to and disorders of the skeletal system. An *anatomist* specializes in anatomy, and so on.

WORD FAMILIES

mobility [paragraph 3] From the Latin verb *movere* meaning "to move," this word has a number of related words in the English language. *Mobility* refers to the ability to move. *Mobile*, the adjective form, can apply to a person who is capable of moving on his or her own, to a type of house, or, as a noun, to an art form—a type of sculpture with movable elements, often used in a baby's crib. The opposite of *mobile* is *immobile*. The verb *mobilize* means to assemble or to prepare, usually for war.

What is the derivation of the word *automobile*? _____

COURTNEY E. MARTIN

Is the American Dream a Delusion?

1   "My uncle came to this country with nothing. Nothing. And now he has a lucrative carpet business and season tickets to the Mets," says one of my students, a wide-eyed, 18-year-old Pakistani immigrant, on a Monday evening in room 605, the light just disappearing behind the Manhattan skyscrapers through the windows.

2   As a gender studies professor at Hunter College—one of the most ethnically diverse schools in the nation—I am used to provoking passionate and often personal reactions in my students. We drift onto some fairly dangerous ground—abortion, rape, love, war—but after two and half years of teaching this material I have realized that I am never so uncomfortable as when class discussion turns to the American Dream.

3   You know the story: Once upon a time there was a hardworking, courageous young man, born in a poor family, who came to America, put in blood, sweat and tears, and eventually found riches and respect. But knowing the statistics on social mobility and the ever-widening gap between rich and poor, I just can't stomach this "happily ever after" scenario. It is too clean. Real life is full of messy things like racism and the wage gap and child care and nepotism.

4   The working-class students in my class are often struggling, and sometimes failing, with full-time jobs and full-time academic loads. You might predict that they would welcome the idea that if you're born poor, no matter how hard you work, sometimes success is still outside your grasp.

5   But semester after semester, student after student, when I suggest that the American Dream might be more fairy tale and less true story, I encounter the opposite reaction. As if by gut survival instinct, students hold up their favorite uncle or a distant cousin, or my personal favorite, Arnold Schwarzenegger, as evidence that the American Dream is alive and well.

6   Part of me wants to cringe, lecture them about how one success story is dangled in front of a struggling public so they won't get angry enough to revolt against an unfair system. How oppression can so easily be mistaken for personal failure. How many employers won't even look at their resumes if they don't see an Ivy League college at the top. But another part of me wants to keep my white, upper-middle-class mouth shut.

7   Many of these students' parents—some of whom have left behind mothers, friends, respect and status in their countries of origin—have sacrificed their lives on the altar of the American Dream. Some of my students are recent immigrants themselves, so relieved to have made it out of violent and poverty-stricken places like Haiti and Colombia that they aren't ready to criticize the country that is their haven. Others, American as apple pie, are the first to go to college in their families and believe ardently that this guarantees a better life. At what cost do I ask them to question their

beliefs? What right do I have to deconstruct one of the foundations they stand on?

8   Discomfort produces learning; Piaget taught me that. When I ask my students to read about intersexuality, I know that they will be surprised and "weirded out," as they often put it, that sex may be more accurately thought of as a spectrum rather than a binary. This, of course, shatters their previous understanding of male and female, blue and pink, penis and vagina, but I find that they can usually process this exploration with a bit of distanced wonder. It doesn't appear to threaten their sense of self, as much as expand it.

9   But when it comes to exploring the validity of the American Dream, I find myself—perhaps too sensitively—afraid of breaking them. I can see that their feverish daily schedules from home to daycare to work to school to daycare to home, repeat, are running not on caffeine or a love of learning, but on potent "someday" dreams. They have landed in my class not by accident, but as one more small step in their destiny to make it big, they believe.

10   And maybe this is the crux of it after all. "Making it big," for my wide-eyed, 18-year-old Pakistani student, is not Bill Gates or Bill Clinton or even Bill Cosby. It is getting to see the Mets whenever he wants. For him, the American Dream is not so damaging because he has revisioned its scope.

11   But at the risk of falling into the same trap that my students sometimes do, I have to attest that he is not the rule. Many have dreams of Hummers and fame and multiple vacation homes. I don't want to be the pinprick that lets the air out of the swollen balloon of hope, but at the same time I desperately want them to see that their wholehearted belief in the American Dream is actually doing more to benefit people far richer and whiter than they are.

12   As long as they are distracted by their own dedication, they won't stop to question why the richest people in this country pay far less in taxes, proportionally, than the middle class. They won't have the time to organize against elitist candidates because they will be too busy working dead-end jobs. As a friend once explained to me, "The proletariat didn't rise up like Marx predicted because he was too tired after work. All he wanted to do was watch TV and have a beer."

13   I want to give my students an intellectual tool that can serve as an emotional cushion, convincing them that it isn't "all their fault" if things don't work out exactly as planned. I want them to imagine living in a genuinely more equal society, not just one that pays lip service to it. What could they accomplish if it didn't take a million-dollar budget to run for political office, and if people didn't hire their friends' kids, and if college was free?

14   So I push. I push beyond my own comfort zone. I certainly push beyond theirs. In fact, I put faith in my own version of the American Dream—that dialogue makes people smarter, kinder, happier—and hope that my students don't prove it a myth. ✳

Exercises

You may refer to the selection as you complete these exercises. Write your answers to these questions in the spaces provided.

A. IDENTIFYING THE CLAIM

1. Using your own words as much as possible, write Martin's central claim or proposition. Also indicate the number of the paragraph where it is located.

   _____

   _____

   _____

   _____

2. Then decide if the claim is a claim of fact, a claim of value, or a claim of policy. Remember that an argument may have a secondary claim as well.

   _____

B. LOCATING EVIDENCE AND THE REFUTATION

1. One piece of evidence is listed for you. List two other major pieces of evidence that the writer uses to support the claim. Also characterize each piece of evidence according to whether it represents facts and statistics; examples and observations; good reasons; or quotation or testimony.

   a. Martin is always uncomfortable when the subject of the American dream comes up in class because she understands that, despite the fact that it motivates her students, at the same time she also knows that it's more a myth than a reality. (observation)

   b. _____

      _____

      _____

   c. _____

      _____

      _____

2. Finally, if there is a refutation, list that as well. _____

   _____

   _____

   _____

   _____

C. IDENTIFYING SOLUTIONS

1. Does Martin provide a solution to the problem she discusses? If so, write it in the space provided. Be sure to use your own words. _____

_____

_____

_____

2. What is your proposal to help solve this problem? _____

D. USING VOCABULARY

Here are some words from the selection. Write an original sentence using each word that shows both that you know how to use the word and what it means.

1. *lucrative* [paragraph 1]   _____

_____

2. *mobility* [3]   _____

_____

3. *scenario* [3]   _____

_____

4. *nepotism* [3]   _____

_____

5. *ardently* [7]   _____

_____

6. *potent* [9]   _____

_____

E. TOPICS FOR DISCUSSION

1. Is Martin overstating the situation? Do you accept her characterization—that working-class people don't recognize oppression, which allows the ruling elite to keep people in their place and to blame their problems on personal failure?
2. Martin is obviously biased. Characterize her bias. Is it fair or unfair? That is, is her bias rooted in a desire to do good or to achieve personal gain? What measures does she take to mitigate, or to soften, this bias?

F. TOPICS FOR WRITING

1. Write a rebuttal to Martin's editorial, in particular focusing on her claims that for working-class people the American dream is a delusion.
2. Choose a relative, friend, co-worker, or acquaintance who immigrated to this country and who achieved the American dream. Write a short essay in which

you examine the person's experience in this country—including his or her motivations for coming here and to what extent the person bears out Martin's observations about the lure of the myth of the American dream. Be sure to define the dream as you interpret it.

Exploring Related Web Sites

- The Web site where this editorial was published offers a compendium of articles and editorials from a liberal perspective on a variety of topics—hunger, immigration, drug laws, politics, health, and the environment, just to name a few.

  www.AlterNet.org

- Courtney Martin's complete biography is available on her Web site:

  www.courtneyemartin.com/biography.php

- Coincidentally, the day I was preparing the exercises for this piece, the *San Francisco Chronicle* ran this story about Leopoldine Matialeu, a native of Cameroon, who was selected to be the valedictorian of her class at Cañada College in Redwood City, California. It is, of course, only one example of an immigrant success story, but it does serve as one rebuttal to Martin's claim. Here are the first two paragraphs from the story. The remainder of Matialeu's story can be read at the Web site below.

  Leopoldine Matialeu always assumed she would get a college education. But when she arrived in Redwood City three years ago from her native Cameroon, her English was shaky and her family's finances were so tough that she and her mother and little sister spent a year living in homeless shelters.

  That didn't deter Matialeu. Today, the 21-year-old will graduate from Cañada College with a perfect 4.0 grade point average. She is the valedictorian of her class. And she's heading off to UC Davis in the fall with a highly competitive Regents Scholarship.

  www.sfgate.com/cgi-bin/article.cgi?f=/c/a/2008/05/30/BA3E10U9D2.DTL

30

RUBEN NAVARRETTE

Racial Profiling Is Un-American

Ruben Navarrette Jr. is an editorialist for the San Diego Union-Tribune. *His nationally syndicated columns for The Washington Post Writers Group appear in newspapers all over the country. Navarrette is a 1990 graduate of Harvard College and of Harvard's Kennedy School of Government where he earned a master's in public administration. He has written a book about his experiences at Harvard,* A Darker Shade of Crimson: Odyssey of a Harvard Chicano *(1993), and he has contributed to* Chicken Soup for the Writer's Soul *and* Chicken Soup for the Latino Soul. *This editorial was published on the Web site www.realclearpolitics.com in 2006. The piece appeared a few days after a terrorist plot was thwarted in Great Britain to destroy 10 passenger planes and five years after the terrorist attacks of September 11 that destroyed the World Trade Center in New York City and killed 3,000 people.*

Vocabulary Preview

WORD PARTS

prejudice [paragraphs 5 and 7] The prefix *pre-* meaning "before" is attached to dozens of English roots. *Prejudice*, from the Latin *pre-* + *judicium* ("judgment"), then, literally means that we judge before we examine the facts. Other words with this prefix are *prearrange*, *precede* (to come before), *predict* (to tell before), and *preeminent* (to stand out before all others).

WORD FAMILIES

psychological [paragraph 2] *Psychological* is the adjective form of *psychology*, the study of the human mind. The root of this word is Psyche, the Greek goddess who personified the soul and who fell in love with Cupid. In the Greek, *psyche* means "soul," "spirit," or "mind," from the verb *psychein*, meaning, appropriately, "to breathe." Here are some other words in this family:

psychodrama	a form of therapy where patients act out roles
psychic	describing one who has extraordinary mental powers; a medium
psychoanalysis	a form of psychological therapy devised by Sigmund Freud
psychosomatic	a type of disorder where physical symptoms originate in the mind

What do these two words mean? Consult a dictionary if you are unsure.

psychopath _____

_____

psychobabble _____

_____

RUBEN NAVARRETTE

Racial Profiling Is Un-American

1   Is this a bad time to argue we shouldn't profile Muslim Americans?

2   In light of a recent _USA Today_/Gallup poll that found that many Americans harbor anti-Muslim feelings, I had planned to make another plea that we stop blaming an entire community of people for the reprehensible acts of a few bad actors. And on the heels of a new study—presented last week at a meeting of the American Psychological Association—which found that Muslim Americans and Arab-Americans are experiencing poorer mental health than other Americans, I intended to say that we should celebrate differences and have zero tolerance for those who harass, condemn and even assault other human beings because of their religion or physical appearance.

3   Then came the chilling news that British authorities had foiled a terror plot by Islamic radicals to bring down up to 10 passenger planes set to leave the United Kingdom for the United States, a plot that—had it been successful—would have achieved what one British law enforcement official described as "mass murder on an unimaginable scale."

4   I still believe that Americans should strive to be fair and tolerant and respectful of diversity, and that we shouldn't issue blanket indictments. It's just that now, I bet, most Americans aren't in the mood to hear that message.

5   They don't want to hear about how unfair it is that Muslim Americans—even those who have no ties to terrorism—are routinely singled out for additional scrutiny and subjected to resentment and prejudice at the hands of their countrymen. They probably don't want to hear about how we mustn't sacrifice our civil liberties—or anyone else's—or paint all Muslim Americans with the same broad brush. And they certainly don't want to hear that the reason we have to avoid doing all this isn't just to protect the rights of ethnic groups and the personal safety of individuals, but also the spirit of a great country.

6   Yet it is at moments like this—when passions are running hot—that such messages really need to sink in. After all, when are we supposed to discuss the subject—when the threat level decreases and things cool down? What good would it do then? That's like holding your tongue when Japanese-Americans were placed in internment camps during World War II and speaking up only when the war was over and the camps were closed. It's like sitting out the civil rights movement, and speaking up only once the major battles were won.

7   Now the embattled group is Muslim Americans. In the *USA Today*/Gallup poll, 39 percent of Americans said they felt at least some prejudice against Muslims. The same percentage favored requiring Muslims, including those who were U.S. citizens, to carry a special ID to help prevent future terrorist attacks. And 22 percent of respondents said they wouldn't want Muslims as neighbors.

8   Eavesdropping on talk radio and conservative blogs since the terror plot was revealed, one would think we've gone back in time to the days following Sept. 11, 2001, when hate crimes were on the rise and some people called for racial profiling of Arab-Americans. That's happening again, as some Americans are once more proposing that we behave in very un-American ways.

9   During an interview on "Fox News Sunday," host Chris Wallace asked Homeland Security chief Michael Chertoff if we shouldn't engage in "security profiling" of Muslims who want to get on airplanes instead of "wasting time" screening 85-year-old grandmothers—even if such profiling isn't "politically correct." (From the way the question was phrased, Wallace presumably was talking about 85-year-old grandmothers who aren't Muslim.)

10   Chertoff could have answered the question in a variety of ways. He could have talked about how it's wrong to single out members of a particular ethnic group when—as Wallace acknowledged—"all Muslims aren't terrorists." Or he could have said that we're at war and that everyone has to make sacrifices—not just Muslims of all ages but also 85-year-old grandmothers. Instead, Chertoff fell back on pragmatism. He responded that while we have to use common sense, terrorists often use people "who do not look like our ordinary conception of terrorists precisely in order to get around our security." So if we get too locked into a profile, and exclude all other possibilities, we'll end up "dropping our guard."

11   That's not a bad answer either. But shame on those who would even ask the question. ✳

Ruben Navarette, "Racial Profiling Is Un-American" (August 16, 2006). Copyright © The San Diego Union-Tribune. Reprinted with permission.

Exercises

You may refer to the selection as you complete these exercises. Write your answers to these questions in the spaces provided.

A. IDENTIFYING THE CLAIM

1. Using your own words as much as possible, write Navarrette's central claim or proposition. Also indicate the number of the paragraph where it is located. Remember that an argument may have a secondary claim as well.

_____

_____

_____

_____

2. Then decide if the claim is a claim of fact, a claim of value, or a claim of policy.

_____

B. LOCATING EVIDENCE AND THE REFUTATION

1. One piece of evidence is listed for you. List two or three other major pieces of evidence that the writer uses to support the claim. Also characterize each piece of evidence according to whether it represents facts and statistics; examples and observations; good reasons; or quotation or testimony.

    a. The British uncovered a plot by Arab terrorists to blow up passenger planes, making this a difficult time to remind Americans that they must not indulge in racial profiling and assume that all Arab Americans are terrorists as a stereotype. (reasons)

    b. _____

    _____

    c. _____

    _____

    d. _____

    _____

2. Finally, if there is a refutation, list that as well. _____

_____

C. IDENTIFYING SOLUTIONS

1. Does Navarrette provide a solution to the problem he discusses? If so, write

    it in the space provided. Be sure to use your own words. _____

    _____

    _____

2. What is your solution to this problem? _____

D. USING VOCABULARY

Here are some words from the selection. Write an original sentence using each word that shows both that you know how to use the word and what it means.

1. _harbor_ [paragraph 2] _____

    _____

2. _foiled_ [3] _____

    _____

3. _indictments_ [4] _____

    _____

4. *scrutiny* [5] _____

_____

5. *acknowledged* [10] _____

_____

6. *pragmatism* [10] _____

_____

E. SUMMARIZING EXERCISE

Read paragraphs 5 and 6. Then write a summary in the space provided.

_____

_____

_____

_____

F. TOPICS FOR DISCUSSION

1. What is the occasion for this column? What role does that occasion play in his discussion?
2. How would you characterize the evidence Navarrette uses to support his claim? Does he rely more on fact, on opinion, or on a combination of both? What kinds of information would have strengthened his argument?
3. Why does Navarrette refer to the Japanese internment camps and to the civil rights movement? (See paragraph 6.)
4. What is Navarrette's particular criticism of Chris Wallace and his question (see paragraph 9) and Michael Chertoff's answer to it (see paragraph 10)? Why is Navarrette so disappointed in their exchange?

G. TOPICS FOR WRITING

1. Write a paragraph or two in which you relate an incident that involved racial profiling, whether the incident involved you personally or was a scene that you witnessed.
2. Should, in fact, Arab Americans or Muslims be singled out for special scrutiny before, say, boarding a flight? In other words, write a refutation to Navarrette's opinion piece. Be sure to include a debate on the inherent unfairness of this kind of treatment versus the public's right to safety.

Exploring Related Web Sites

For up-to-date information and articles on racial profiling (or "security profiling"), go to your favorite search engine and enter these words: "racial profiling, Arab Americans, Muslims."

31

JOHN POMFRET

Two Sides to the Border Fence

This article, from the Washington Post, *is intended as background reading before you read and evaluate the pair of editorials on the same issue that follow it. The issue is the federally mandated fence along the border of the United States and Mexico to stop the flow of illegal immigrants from Mexico and Central America. It is estimated that there are 12 million illegal immigrants living and working in the United States. The government has put into place several measures to stop them—requiring employers to check employees' residency, fining employers who hire illegal immigrants, implementing a guest-worker program, and so forth. But the most controversial measure has been the fence.*

A graduate of Stanford University, John Pomfret is the editor of the Washington Post's *weekend opinion section, Outlook. Prior to that, he was a foreign correspondent for 15 years, covering wars in Afghanistan, Bosnia, Congo, Sri Lanka, Iraq, Turkey, and Iran. Currently, he writes about China for the* Post. *The dateline for the article is Calexico, California, a town on the border of California and Mexico; on the Mexican side is Mexicali.*

Only an annotating exercise is provided following the article.

JOHN POMFRET

Two Sides to the Border Fence

CALEXICO, Calif.—Legislation passed by Congress mandating the fencing of 700 miles of the U.S. border with Mexico has sparked opposition from an array of land managers, businesspeople, law enforcement officials, environmentalists and U.S. Border Patrol agents as a one-size-fits-all policy response to the nettlesome task of securing the nation's borders.

Critics said the fence does not take into account the extraordinarily varied geography of the 2,000-mile-long border, which cuts through Mexican and U.S. cities separated by a sidewalk, vast scrubland and deserts, rivers, irrigation canals and miles of mountainous terrain. They also say it seems to ignore advances in border security that don't involve construction of a 15-foot-high double fence and to play down what are expected to be significant costs to maintain the new barrier.

And, they say, the estimated $2 billion price tag and the mandate that it be completed by 2008 overlook 10 years of legal and logistical difficulties the federal government has faced to finish a comparatively tiny fence of 14 miles dividing San Diego and Tijuana.

"This is the feel-good approach to immigration control," said Wayne Cornelius, an expert on immigration issues at the University of California at San Diego. "The only pain is experienced by the migrants themselves. It doesn't hurt U.S. consumers; it doesn't hurt U.S. businesses. It only hurts taxpayers if they pay attention to spending on border enforcement."

Congress has decreed that five sections of reinforced fencing—most probably a double fence with stadium lighting—will be built along a third of the border, in California, Arizona, New Mexico and Texas. The biggest section is planned from east of Calexico stretching more than 300 miles to west of Douglas, Ariz.

There also are questions of whether the fence will be more of a symbol to be used in elections than a reality along the border. For one thing, shortly before Congress adjourned, the House and Senate gave the Bush administration leeway to distribute the money allocated for the fence to other projects, including roads, technology and other infrastructure items to support the Department of Homeland Security's preferred option of building a "virtual fence."

Currently, less than 100 miles of the border is fenced, primarily in populated areas. San Diego has become a symbol for the efficacy of fences, but a closer look at the experience of that seaside city also illustrates the potential pitfalls.

In the mid-1990s, the city was awash in illegal immigrants. Hundreds would gather by a soccer field near Otay Mesa, east of San Diego, and rush into the United States on what the Border Patrol termed "banzai runs." During those years, Border Patrol agents routinely apprehended 200,000 illegal entrants a year in the sector. Rep. Duncan Hunter (R-Calif.) got funding to build a fence and thousands more Border Patrol officers were dispatched to the area. The number of crossers plummeted.

But the fence, originally estimated at $14 million, incurred huge cost overruns and logistical and legal hurdles. It took $39 million to build the first nine miles, and the fence has yet to be finished. For a decade, litigation has delayed construction of 3.5 miles of the structure because environmental groups have opposed a federal plan to lop the tops off two mesas and pour 5.5 million cubic feet of dirt into a valley, called "Smuggler's Gulch," to flatten the terrain. Environmental groups lost the case when the Department of Homeland Security invoked a law exempting it from federal and state regulations in the interest of national security. DHS recently appropriated an additional $35 million to complete the fence—for a total of $74 million, or more than $5 million a mile.

The fence in San Diego forced illegal traffic into the deserts to the east, leading thousands of migrants to their death. In response, the Border Patrol shifted thousands of agents to Arizona to deal with the flow. But many of those agents came from the San Diego and El Centro sectors. So once again, the number of crossers in San Diego and El Centro is increasing even though the two sectors are the most heavily fenced in the nation.

"Tucson now has 2,600 agents. San Diego has lost 1,000 agents. Guess where the traffic is going? Back to San Diego." said T. J. Bonner, the president of the National Border Patrol Council, the main union for Border Patrol agents. "San Diego is the most heavily fortified border in the entire country, and yet it's not stopping people from coming across."

There are concerns along the border that the congressionally mandated fence could overshadow new, cheaper technologies that show some promise. For example, 30 miles of reinforced vehicle barriers, which cost on average $1 million a mile, have reduced by 95 percent road traffic from drug and migrant smugglers into the Organ Pipe Cactus National Monument, where a park ranger was shot and killed by narcotics traffickers in 2002, said Kathy Billings, superintendent of the territory. "We used to have two to three high-speed chases a month," she said. "Now we have less than six a year."

But even the vehicle barriers, posts in the ground connected to each other by railroad ties, need year-round maintenance. The barriers at Organ Pipe have already been breached four times since they were completed this summer. A full-scale double fence in the Arizona desert, where summer rains cause flash floods that often rip up anything in their path, would be extremely costly to build, let alone maintain, Billings said.

The ecological effect of a fence would be significant, according to Roger Di Rosa, manager of the Cabeza Prieta National Wildlife Refuge in Arizona, which runs along about 50 miles of the Mexican border. Efforts to protect pronghorn sheep and encourage the jaguar to return to the United States could be seriously affected, he said. "If it doesn't fly, it's not getting across," he said. "The law is pretty straightforward but the border is very unique."

Marine Corps officers in the region also have questioned the need for a fence. Using a combination of vehicle barriers and ground-based radar, they had blocked a significant portion of smuggling traffic through their land on the Yuma Proving Ground, which runs along 30 miles of the border, Di Rosa and others said. In recent months, however, the Pentagon for unknown reasons ordered the base to install a fence. Marine Corps officers at the facility did not return a call seeking comment.

Di Rosa and others cited other potential unintended consequences of fence-building. In some regions along the border, the nearest main road can be 80 miles away. So to build the barrier, roads must be created. That could end up facilitating movement into the United States rather than blocking it. Officials along the border challenged optimistic timelines that the wall could be built in two years, citing the high probability of lawsuits from environmental agencies and land owners.

In Texas, which is to get 200 miles of fencing, opposition to the plan has come from law enforcement and city governments. The City of El Paso has officially opposed the plan, as has the Texas Border Sheriff's Association.

Maverick County Sheriff Tomas S. Herrera predicted ranchers would sue the federal government to fight the installation of a fence on their property. One reason is that ranchers want access to the Rio Grande, which snakes 1,254 miles along the border, to water their herds and for sport fishermen who pay to use the waterway.

Perhaps because of these objections, Congress, in a late-night concession just before adjournment, pledged that Native American tribes, members of Congress, governors and local leaders would get a say in "the exact placement" of any structure, and that Homeland Security Secretary Michael Chertoff has discretion to use alternatives "when fencing is ineffective or impractical."

Herrra thinks flexibility might be needed. He echoed a widespread skepticism about federal programs, hatched in Washington, designed to deal with the border problems.

"A few years ago, they installed cameras and said the cameras would solve things," he said. "Those cameras can pick up a tick on a cow's back. But when half the monitors are all busted like they are now, they don't work."

His prediction for how illegal immigrants would deal with the wall: "They will get ladders made out of mesquite and climb it." ✻

ANNOTATING EXERCISE

Assume that you are assigned to write an essay on the merits and demerits of the border fence now being constructed along the U.S.–Mexico border. Read the article again carefully. Annotate the article noting the positive and negative features of the fence that Pomfret discusses.

PAIRED EDITORIALS— THE FENCE ALONG THE U.S.–MEXICAN BORDER

32

LUIS ALBERTO URREA

$1.2 Billion Fence Adds Little or No Security

Luis Alberto Urrea is the son of an American mother and a Mexican father. A native of Tijuana, Mexico, on the California border just south of San Diego, Urrea has done relief work with immigrants. Currently, he teaches at the University of Illinois at Chicago. His two best-known books are Across the Wire: Life and Hard Times on the Mexican Border *(1993) and* The Devil's Highway *(2004). This editorial appeared in the* San Francisco Chronicle *as one of a pair of editorials published on the controversy surrounding the border fence between the United States and Mexico. It should be noted that the current controversy is not only about whether the fence should be completed, but also whether it will work to stop terrorists and illegal immigrants from crossing the border and whether it is a sound idea economically or ecologically.*

Vocabulary Preview

WORD PARTS

eco- [paragraph 13] The word *ecosystem* derives from the word *ecology*, the study of the relationship between organisms and the environments they inhabit. An *ecosystem*, therefore, is an ecological community. Other words beginning with this prefix are the following:

ecomanagement	a management system whereby scientists try to minimize the adverse effects of human activity on a particular environment
ecotourism	a type of travel where tourists visit areas of ecological importance with the idea of learning about the plant and animal life in those environments
ecoterrorism	terrorism committed in the name of environmental causes, for example by Earth First! (see *www.earthfirst.org/about.htm*)

Note that the words *economy* and *ecology* both derive from the same Greek root *oikos*, or "household."

WORD FAMILIES   acronyms—snafu [paragraph 12] An *acronym* is a word composed of the initial letters in a phrase pronounced as a word. The word *snafu* means "s(ituation) n(ormal) a(ll) f(ucked) u(p)."[1] A *WAC* is a member of the Women's Army Corps. *scuba*, equipment deep sea divers use on underwater expeditions, stands for self-contained underwater breathing apparatus. *FAQ*, standing for "frequently asked questions," is technically not an acronym because the letters are pronounced separately, not as a stand-alone word. Here are some other common acronyms. Write their meaning in the space provided. If you are unsure of their meaning, do an online search, as some of these will not be listed in a dictionary.

UNESCO _____

DARE _____

CAD/CAM _____

RADAR _____

RAM _____

LUIS ALBERTO URREA

$1.2 Billion Fence Adds Little or No Security

1   The Border Patrol agent was a 30-year veteran.

2   He walked me across a patch of desolation to the Mexican border. There was no border fence there yet. Just Arizona desert, a dusty dry creekbed, and Mexican desert beyond, indistinguishable from the United States.

3   If you want to hear philosophical reflections from an agent, you have to talk to old-timers. The hundreds of new Homeland Security–era officers who have flooded the border are extremely well trained—the Border Patrol academy is a monster among law enforcement training programs—and they are certainly

---

[1] A less offensive way to write out the words comprised in *snafu* is "s(ituation) n(ormal) a(ll) f(ouled) u(p)."

gung-ho. But the old guys will tell you the new ones don't know the territory very well. There are fine points it might take 30 years to learn.

4   "My dad was a rancher," the veteran agent said. "I'm a rancher. I come out here and you know who I chase? Ranch hands and farmers." He wiped his brow, toed some possibly Mexican dirt. "Buddy, I am chasing my own people."

5   This hotly contested stretch of sand and cinders stands to become a beneficiary of the $1.2 billion border fence that will seal off the southern American border. Well, it will seal off part of it. OK—it will seal off small areas of the border. Just east of where we stood, for example, the fence will stop. There are big scary mountains in place that will be included in the plan as natural immigration barriers. These are the same mountains over which many of the undocumented are already walking to avoid the good men and women of the U.S. Border Patrol.

6   But, the thinking goes, we have to start somewhere. On the Mexican side, among much gnashing of teeth, there is a joke that has been circulating the whole time. The gist of it is: Let them put up a fence! They'll hire us to build it! Then, when it's done, we'll run the tourist concessions and the taco stands. Then, when they get tired of it, they'll hire us to tear it down![2]

7   What are you getting for your 1 billion tax dollars? Well, you're getting a little less than 700 miles of fence. Much of it double-fencing, but substantial segments to be single-fence. That's the kind of security that has so successfully kept kids out of closed softball fields and skinny-dippers from midnight visits to neighborhood swimming pools.

8   Al Qaeda will weep with frustration when they encounter it and just go home.

9   Critics like to point out that the plan had originally called for triple-fencing, but somehow the folks who brought us Katrina relief can't manage that on a budget. Critics also seem to enjoy reminding us that the border is 2,000 miles long. Of course, that would be as the crow flies. If you ironed out the Southwest, spread its many mountains (Homeland Security Immigration Barriers) flat, then pulled the squiggles and turns of the Rio Grande straight, how long would it really be? Buddy, that's a lot of fence for them ranchers to ride.

10   What is a border? According to Webster's, it is a margin. If one were to look at the margins of the United States, 700 miles of rockin' chain-link might not seem like enough. Although it's macho—it lends the desert a sense of WWF Steel Cage Death Match—a glance at the Canadian border suggests that it's even less secure than we hope. That same Border Patrol veteran pointed out to me that the one real terrorist they caught was coming out of Canada with his trunk full of bombs. And, of course, those 9/11 bastards were "legal aliens."

11   However, if we keep staring at the map with Zen clarity, a new revelation offers itself. I'll warn you, it takes work. But we suddenly see there is another border of the United States. It's called a coastline. Talk about unprotected. Why isn't somebody fencing in Miami? They hate us for our thongs, people. Where is the fence at Malibu?

---

[2]See Walt Handelsman's cartoon at the end of the exercises (page 436) for a satirical expression of this possibility—hiring illegal aliens to build a fence to keep illegal aliens out of the country. (Ed.)

12   Of course, terrorism is only part of the paradigm—it's illegal immigration, stupid. California has long struggled with remaining a good neighbor while bringing the hammer down. It might have rankled to read the insensitive Mexican jokes about the border fence, but the Golden State Fence Company actually did hire "illegals" to build border fences in San Diego. Not only that, of course, but they seem to have used the undocumented to build fences at military bases, immigration jails and Border Patrol stations. They were fined $5 million in 2006; if you think about it, when you combine the cost-cutting involved in the illegal workforce and the hefty fine, the actual cost of the border fence might have shrunk by several percentage points. Voters and columnists might express outrage, but federal border agents are realists and ironists—they shake their heads and laugh. They know a snafu when they see it.

13   It's one thing to fence off a few miles of California or Arizona. It is quite another to try to fence off the meandering bed of the mighty Rio Grande in Texas. Somehow, much of the border has remained, for all its media and political notoriety, invisible. Nothing reveals this more than the Rio Grande. (Or, as those darned Mexicans call it, El Rio Bravo—the untamed or brave river.) One of the most interesting border books to appear in recent days is Keith Bowden's "The Tecate Journals." He somewhat maniacally canoes the entire length of the river. The book shows a major American riverine ecosystem that remains ignored and reviled—perhaps because it is also the border barrier of record. Beavers and deer—who knew?

14   Strangely, a coalition of Texas mayors came up with a proposal to strengthen the border while avoiding the fence. They suggested that the river itself be dredged and deepened and widened. The natural demarcation line between our nations, in other words, could be revived and cleaned up to do its ancient work. Fences? We don't need no stinkin' fences! A plan due to fail.

15   The problem in Texas is simple—180 miles of proposed fence must follow the river, but not get too close to the river, because the river itself is the classic illegal alien and will change course, wiggle under fences, even erode banks and topple fences and open big gaps. Obviously, Mexico will stop at nothing—if an old truck won't bust the fence, they'll send a river. So the fence must, at certain points, be built up to a mile from the banks of the river.

16   Unfortunately, landowners (ranchers and farmers again) have lived on this land for hundreds of years. Some farm plots along the river have been in the same families since 1767. Mexicans were living there eating frijoles before American revolutionaries ate baked beans at the signing of the Constitution? That's awkward.

17   Although it is true that everyone ought to be willing to suffer for the security of the nation, in Brownsville, the fence line has cut off a section of the college's soccer field and given it back to Mexico. Gen. Santa Anna is rising from his grave, rubbing his hands in glee: He's actually getting back some of the Treaty of Guadalupe Hidalgo.

18   The Chicago Tribune quoted the mayor of Brownsville on Jan. 16: "To appease people in middle America, they are going to kill our communities along the border. The rest of America has no idea how we live our lives here. We are linked by the Rio Grande, not divided by it." Linked? By a border? Not divided? What a concept.

19   If Americans want security, then they should get real security. If you really want a border fence, build a real border fence. I have some nephews in Tijuana who need work. But please, Mr. Chertoff—fence off Cannery Row while you still can. ✳

Luis Alberto Urrea, "$1.2 Billion Fence Adds Little or No Security" from *San Francisco Chronicle* (February 20, 2008). Copyright © 2008 by Luis Alberto Urrea. Reprinted with the permission of Sandra Dijkstra Literary Agency.

Exercises

You may refer to the selection as you complete these exercises. Write your answers to these questions in the spaces provided.

A. IDENTIFYING THE CLAIM

1. Using your own words as much as possible, write Urrea's central claim or proposition. Also indicate the number of the paragraph where it is located. Remember that an argument may have a secondary claim as well.

   _____

   _____

   _____

2. Then decide if the claim is a claim of fact, a claim of value, or a claim of policy.

   _____

B. LOCATING EVIDENCE AND THE REFUTATION

1. One piece of evidence is listed for you. List two or three other major pieces of evidence that the writer uses to support the claim. Also characterize each piece of evidence according to whether it represents facts and statistics; examples and observations; good reasons; or quotation or testimony.

   a. The border fence will seal off only part of the border; and the big mountains that are considered a natural barrier are already crossed by illegals. (reasons/facts)

   b. _____

      _____

   c. _____

   d. _____

      _____

2. Finally, if there is a refutation, list that as well.

   _____

   _____

   _____

C. IDENTIFYING SOLUTIONS

1. Does Urrea provide a solution to the problem he discusses? If so, write it in the space provided. Be sure to use your own words. _____

_____

_____

_____

2. What is your solution to this problem? _____

D. USING VOCABULARY

Here are some words from the selection. Write an original sentence using each word that shows both that you know how to use the word and what it means.

1. *desolation* [paragraph 2] _____

_____

2. *macho* [10] _____

_____

3. *clarity* [11] _____

_____

4. *outrage* [12] _____

_____

5. *rankled* [12] _____

_____

6. *meandering* [13] _____

_____

7. *notoriety* [13] _____

_____

8. *reviled* [13] _____

_____

9. *coalition* [14] _____

_____

10. *appease* [18] _____

_____

E. SUMMARIZING EXERCISE

Write a summary of approximately 150 to 200 words summarizing Urrea's many objections to the border fence now being constructed along the U.S.–Mexico border.

F. TOPICS FOR DISCUSSION

1. Comment on the structure of this opinion piece. Notice that Urrea does not follow the conventional pattern of stating the claim, followed by evidence. He prefers to let his argument and evidence emerge in bits and pieces throughout the editorial. Does this episodic structure make the piece difficult to comprehend or not?
2. Read paragraphs 7 and 8 again. How would you characterize his tone in this section? What point is he making here?
3. Urrea doesn't seem to think that the problem of illegal immigrants sneaking across the border is a particularly big problem. Why not? What evidence in the editorial confirms this observation?

G. TOPICS FOR WRITING

1. Write a counterargument to Urrea's opinion piece. That is, present evidence to bolster the claim that the border fence is a good idea, one that deserves a chance to prove itself as effective in deterring illegals from crossing the border.
2. Study this cartoon by *Newsday* cartoonist Walt Handelsman. Then write a paragraph analyzing it as you would any other argument by including these elements: the claim that the cartoon depicts, the cartoonist's purpose in drawing it, and the point of view toward the issue that the cartoonist is depicting. Finally, connect the point made in the cartoon with what Urrea writes in paragraphs 6 and 12.

Walt Handelsman, cartoon, Copyright © Tribune Media Services, Inc. All rights reserved. Reprinted with permission.

Exploring Related Web Sites

Luis Alberto Urrea's blog can be read at this Web site:

www://luisurrea.com/home.php

33

Building a Wall between Worlds

The second of the paired editorials on the border fence between the United States and Mexico is written by Duncan Hunter. Hunter is a Republican congressman from California's 52nd congressional district, representing the eastern and northern portions of San Diego county near the Mexican border. He is a Vietnam veteran who later attended law school on the G.I. Bill. As a member of the House Armed Services Committee, Hunter has worked to strengthen the military by increasing efficiency and by ensuring that military personnel are well-equipped. Hunter has also made border enforcement a priority by supporting the building of the border fence and by supporting legislation to authorize 5,000 additional Border Patrol agents to serve the area. The subtitle of this opinion piece is "Crucial Factor: Barrier Is Needed, but Wasn't Built to Specifications."

Vocabulary Preview

WORD PARTS

infrastructure [paragraphs 5, 7, 8, 13, 14] The word *infrastructure* is a collective noun referring to the entire system of roads, bridges, railroads, subways, fiber optics, cable, and other systems that allow an industrialized country to function. The prefix *infra-* means "below" or "beneath." In the editorial, Hunter refers to the border fence as part of the nation's infrastructure. Other words beginning with this prefix are *infrared*, *infrasound*, and *infrahuman*, all suggesting something underneath or below in quality or intensity.

WORD FAMILIES

omnibus [paragraph 12] In Great Britain, buses are called *omnibuses* because they transport many people. As the word is used in this editorial, however, *omnibus* is an adjective describing a legislative bill, meaning that the bill includes many elements. The Latin word part *omni-* means "all" or "every" and can be seen in a large number of linguistic relatives, among them *omnipresent* ("present everywhere"), *omnipotent* ("all powerful"), *omniscient* ("knowing everything"), and *omnivorous*, describing an organism that eats both meat and plants.

DUNCAN HUNTER

Building a Wall between Worlds

1   Our nation's greatest and most obvious vulnerability remains our porous and unprotected southern land border. Yet every day, unknown numbers of human and drug smugglers, criminals and potential terrorists continue to illegally enter the United States through our border with Mexico.

2   The exposure of our southern border demands that we take immediate action to implement the most effective enforcement mechanisms available. And while technology and manpower are an important part of this effort, the best and most effective method of preventing illegal foot and vehicle traffic from entering the United States is border security fencing.

3   In San Diego County, border fencing remains a critical part of our effort to prevent and deter illegal immigrants and drug smugglers from entering the local community. Since construction of the San Diego border fence began in 1996, the smuggling of people and narcotics has dropped drastically; crime rates have been reduced by half, according to FBI statistics; vehicle drug drive-throughs have been eliminated; and apprehensions have decreased as the result of fewer crossing attempts.

4   This level of success illustrates that border fencing works. In fact, the San Diego border fence is serving to benefit both sides of the border. As conditions in San Diego County have improved, communities on the Mexican side of the border are no longer at the mercy of the armed gangs and drug smugglers who once roamed and controlled the Tijuana smuggling corridor.

5   It is no surprise that when I proposed extending this infrastructure across 700 miles of our southern land border, critics immediately dismissed the idea that border fencing would serve any functional purpose. Recognizing the success of the San Diego border fence, however, the Secure Fence Act, which required the construction of double-layered fencing at strategic points along the U.S.-Mexico border, passed the House and Senate overwhelmingly and was signed into law by President Bush.

6   It has been more than a year since the enactment of the Secure Fence Act, and the smuggling corridors along our southern land border remain open. The American people want our borders secured, yet the Department of Homeland Security, even when presented with a mandate from Congress to get the job done, has done little of what is actually required to achieve an enforceable border.

7   Rather than adhering to the law, the department announced its intention to build 370 miles of fence, not the 700 miles required by the measure. Moreover, the department opted to build single-layered fencing instead of the double-layered infrastructure called for in the legislation. The reality is that single-layered fencing and vehicle barriers do little, if anything, to stop illegal immigration.

8   Even the Clinton administration, which initially opposed building the San Diego border fence, recognized its responsibility under the law and initiated its construction. And as a result, the smuggling corridor that existed between

Tijuana and San Diego was immediately closed. This success can be delivered to other border regions experiencing the adverse effects of illegal immigration, but it will require that the Department of Homeland Security acknowledge its responsibility to the American people and begin building the necessary infrastructure.

9   Illegal immigration is no longer an issue solely reserved for border states and communities. In the post-9/11 world, illegal immigration is a national security issue. And one of the easiest ways for terrorists to enter the United States is through our nation's southern border. We must anticipate that the same smugglers who carry humans and contraband across the border would not hesitate, especially for the right price, to help terrorists find their way into the United States.

10   Consider that in 2005 alone, more than 155,000 foreign citizens from countries other than Mexico were apprehended attempting to cross our southern land border. Many of these individuals originated from countries of national security concern, including Syria, Iran, Lebanon and Yemen, and probably represent only a fraction of those who successfully entered our country without the knowledge of border security officials or the consent of our government.

11   Today's security threat requires that we know who is crossing our border and what they are carrying with them. Unfortunately, under our current border control strategy, we are incapable of ascertaining either. Without a reinforced, physical impediment along our southern border, achieving these dual objectives is nearly impossible.

12   Further complicating this challenge is a recently enacted omnibus spending bill that eliminates the double-fencing requirement included in the Secure Fence Act and reduces required fence construction to 370 miles. This spending bill dismantles the only legislative advancement made in recent years toward securing our border with Mexico and further compromises the safety, security and prosperity of the American people.

13   Although the authority of the secretary of Homeland Security to build a fence along the border has not been rescinded, it has been made clear that most of the new fence will be single-layered and extend no more than 370 miles. During the past year, for instance, only 77 miles of fencing has been built, of which five miles is double-layered. This lack of progress is disconcerting, particularly when considering that the Department of Homeland Security has received more than $2 billion for border infrastructure.

14   It is for these reasons that I introduced the Reinstate the Secure Fence Act in the House of Representatives. My legislation restores the most substantive elements of the Secure Fence Act, requiring 700 miles of fencing be constructed within six months of the bill's enactment. If we truly hope to bring some sense of security to our southern border, then we must begin building the appropriate infrastructure in the timeliest manner possible.

15   It is time we get serious about border control, do what's right, and build the border fence. ✱

Duncan Hunter, "Building a Wall between Worlds. Crucial Factor: Barrier Is Needed but Wasn't Built to Specifications."

Exercises

You may refer to the selection as you complete these exercises. Write your answers to these questions in the spaces provided.

A. IDENTIFYING THE CLAIM

1. Using your own words as much as possible, write Hunter's central claim or proposition. Also indicate the number of the paragraph where it is located. Remember that an argument may have a secondary claim as well.

   _____

   _____

   _____

2. Then decide if the claim is a claim of fact, a claim of value, or a claim of policy.

   _____

B. LOCATING EVIDENCE AND THE REFUTATION

1. One piece of evidence is listed for you. List three or four other major pieces of evidence that the writer uses to support the claim. Also characterize each piece of evidence according to whether it represents facts and statistics; examples and observations; good reasons; or quotation or testimony.

   a. Since a border fence was constructed near San Diego, smuggling of people and drugs has dropped dramatically, and according to FBI statistics, the crime rate has dropped by half, vehicle drug drive-throughs have been eliminated, and apprehensions have decreased as fewer people attempt the crossing. (facts/statistics)

   b. _____

   _____

   c. _____

   _____

   d. _____

   _____

   e. _____

   _____

   _____

2. Finally, if there is a refutation, list that as well.

   _____

   _____

C. IDENTIFYING SOLUTIONS

1. Does Hunter provide a solution to the problem he discusses? If so, write it in the space provided. Be sure to use your own words. _____

_____

_____

2. What is your solution to this problem? _____

D. USING VOCABULARY

Here are some words from the selection. Write an original sentence using each word that shows both that you know how to use the word and what it means.

1. *vulnerability* [paragraph 1] _____

_____

2. *implement* [2] _____

_____

3. *deter* [3] _____

_____

4. *mandate* [6] _____

_____

5. *adhering* [7] _____

_____

6. *contraband* [9] _____

_____

7. *rescinded* [13] _____

_____

8. *disconcerting* [13] _____

_____

E. TOPICS FOR DISCUSSION

1. Now that you have read both opinion pieces and the article giving background about this issue, what is your considered evaluation of the border-fence proposal to stop the flow of illegal immigrants (and possibly drug smugglers and terrorists)?
2. How would you characterize the evidence Hunter uses to support his claim? Does he rely more on fact, on opinion, or on a combination of both? What kinds of information would have strengthened his argument?

3. Consider the title of this opinion piece—"Building a Wall between Worlds." What are the implications of this title?

4. Hunter does not offer much of a refutation, saying only that critics argued that the fence would not be particularly useful. Is this a serious flaw in the editorial or not? What are some arguments against the fence? Consider what Urrea wrote in this regard, but also come up with some other reasons to support the idea that the fence may not work to stop illegal immigrants (or terrorists) from entering the country.

5. If we construct a fence according to the original specifications of the Secure Fence Act along the U.S.–Mexico border to stop the potential influx of terrorists or drug smugglers, shouldn't we also build a similar fence along the U.S.–Canada border?

6. On balance, which writer—Urrea or Hunter—does a better job of arguing for his claim? Which piece is more convincing? Why? Base your evaluation on the strength of the editorial, not on whether it conforms to your opinion.

F. TOPICS FOR WRITING

1. Write a counterargument to Hunter's opinion piece. That is, present evidence to bolster the claim that the border fence is a bad idea. Be sure to offer evidence that challenges Hunter's assertions that the fence will stop not only the flow of illegal immigrants but also smugglers and potential terrorists from what he describes as countries of "national security concern."

2. Has your community been affected in any way by illegal immigrants? If so, write a paragraph or two explaining the situation—including information on the kind of work illegals perform in your community and the extent to which residency requirements are enforced.

3. Now that you have read both pieces, write an essay in which you summarize the issue, present the arguments of both writers, and then come to a conclusion of your own.

Exploring Related Web Sites

Two recent news articles add more information about the proposed border fence. For even more up-to-date information about this controversial proposal, go to your favorite search engine and type in "Mexico-U.S. border fence." Here are two recent articles to get you started:

Arthur H. Rotstein, "U.S. Scraps 'Virtual Fence' Prototype" (Associated Press) *www.freerepublic.com/focus/f-news/2005621/posts*

Juliet Eilperin, "Researchers Fear Southern Fence Will Endanger Species Further," the *Washington Post*, April 20, 2008: *www.washingtonpost.com/wp-dyn/content/article/2008/04/19/AR2008041900942.html*

34 The Line—Photographs from the U.S.–Mexican Border

In October 2006, Harper's Magazine *contributing editor Peter Turnley published a photo essay of images taken along the U.S.–Mexican border. Turnley is a photographer based in New York City and Paris. Reprinted here are three photographs from the essay. Your college library should be able to provide you with a physical copy of the magazine if you want to see the entire collection.*

Ubencia Sanchez, from the Chiapas region of Mexico, peers over a border fence in Tijuana, looking into the United States for the first time.

Unable to cross the border, a couple meet at the fence in San Diego.

A memorial in Tijuana for a Mexican who was killed in an incident with the Border Patrol in 2005.

Exercises

A. TOPICS FOR DISCUSSION

Study each photograph carefully, noting the composition of the photograph—that is, the dominant image the photographer captures, the background scene, the point of view reflected, and the situation or scene that the photo depicts. Then consider these questions:

1. Concerning photograph 1, what do you think the woman in the foreground is thinking as she looks at the United States for the first time? How old does she appear to be? How would you characterize the landscape around her? How would you describe the fence that borders the two countries as it is depicted here?
2. Now consider the second photograph. What does it depict? Why do you suppose this couple must meet at the border fence in this way?
3. The third photograph shows some rocks and a white cross commemorating a Mexican killed by Border Patrol agents. What is the emotional impact of this photo? One sees these roadside memorials often, where a victim's relatives and friends commemorate a loved one's death as the result of an automobile accident. How is this memorial different? Finally, comment on the appearance of the fence. Does it look intimidating and secure? Would a person of average height be able to scale it?

B. TOPICS FOR WRITING

1. Now that you have read the material on the subject of the border fence and examined some photographs, write an essay in which you set forth your ideas about the validity and effectiveness of the fence as a way to stop illegal immigrants from sneaking into the country.
2. Write a paragraph on these photographs as they attempt to demonstrate the human impact of the border fence.

35 Paired Web Sites—Two Scientific Views of Global Warming

Part Five ends with two Web sites for you to analyze. The subject is global warming and climate change.

Union of Concerned Scientists

The first Web site is sponsored by the Union of Concerned Scientists (Citizens and Scientists for Environmental Solutions), based in Cambridge, Massachusetts. The UCS Web site offers a great deal of information about the challenges global warming presents and specific ways to reduce greenhouse gas emissions. At the home page, click on "Global Warming" in the menu bar.

www.ucsusa.org

The Heartland Institute

The second Web site is sponsored by the Heartland Institute, a nonprofit organization based in Chicago, Illinois, and dedicated to finding free market solutions to a variety of social and economic problems, among them health care, parental choice in education, deregulation, and environmental protection. The Heartland Institute's Web site states that there is no consensus on the causes of global warming; furthermore, its sponsors believe that environmental concerns about global warming are a prime example of alarmism. Click on "Environment" at the top of the home page.

www.heartland.org

Spend some time perusing these two Web sites to get an idea of both their organization and content. Here are some general questions to get you started:

1. Does the home page provide a section called "About Us," "Our Mission," or some similar designation?
2. Is the information current? Can you tell how recently the information on the site was updated? (Note: You may have to scroll through the entire site to the bottom of each page to locate this information.)

3. Are the sponsors, authorities, or experts clearly identified? Are the scientists' academic or career affiliations provided?
4. Is the information presented objectively? That is, does it appear to be free of bias, slanted language, emotional appeals, and the like?
5. Would you feel comfortable using the information in the source for a research paper on global warming?

If you need further instruction in evaluating Web sites, you can refer to these suggestions compiled by the library staff at City College of San Francisco. First, go to this Web site:

www.ccsf.edu/Resources

Click on "Library." Then click on "Evaluating & Citing Sources." There you will find three information sheets to get you started:

- Evaluating Web Pages
- Evaluating Web Pages: Techniques to Apply
- Library Skills Workshop W Handout: Web Research and Evaluation

PART SIX

Reading Textbooks

In this final section, these topics will be taken up:

- Four Surefire Ways to Get Low Grades
- Four Suggestions for Making the Most of Your Study Time
- Applying the SQ3R Method to Reading Textbooks

At the end of Part Six, you will have an opportunity to read some selections from five college textbooks representing a variety of academic subjects.

Four Surefire Ways to Get Low Grades

It's time for some plain talk about why so many students flounder at the beginning of their college careers. I want to say a few words about self-sabotage—the ways that students get into trouble and get grades lower perhaps than they are accustomed to receiving.

City College of San Francisco, where my colleagues and I teach, is a large urban community college with 33,000 full-time and part-time students on the main campus. In the many years that I have taught reading and composition courses there, I have encountered hundreds of students and have listened to their stories in conferences and in the classroom. Every story is different, of course; every student has a different family situation, different motivations for attending college, different goals and interests, and to be sure, different intellectual abilities.

For every former student who has transferred to UC Berkeley or to UCLA (the two flagship campuses in the University of California system) or to a state university (like San Francisco State or Humboldt State University), there are dozens who have dropped out after a semester or two—unable to keep up, discouraged, disheartened, and often adrift. How does this happen? Here are some observations I have made over the years. Perhaps they will help you. Perhaps not. And although you have probably heard all of this before, these things are worth repeating. These are the four areas of common concern to me and to my colleagues.

1. Taking a Full Load of Classes and Working Full-Time Many students wildly underestimate the amount of time their college courses will require, and so they sign up for a full load (12 semester units or more) while trying to work 30 or more hours a week. Most colleges suggest that a student plan to spend two hours of study for each hour of class time. Of course, this formula is only a suggestion. Many courses—for example, math, science, and possibly English—may require *more* time—although you probably won't have any homework for your PE class. You also have to factor in any time spent commuting as well as time to do household and personal chores. If you live at home and your mother does your laundry and cooks for you, you are in luck, because you will have more free time to take another class or work a few more hours.

Here are sample weekly schedules for two hypothetical students:

Jane Doe		John Doe	
Number of units	15	Number of units	9
Number of hours of study	30	Number of hours of study	18
Number of hours at work	20	Number of hours at work	20
Hours commuting	5	Hours commuting	5
Laundry, cooking, shopping, personal chores	10	Laundry, cooking, shopping, personal chores	10
Grand Total:	**80 hours**	**Grand Total:**	**62 hours**

These two students have punishing schedules, but at least John Doe's is somewhat reasonable. If you consider that the average work week in the United States is 40 hours, both of these scenarios suggest a commitment of time way beyond that traditional benchmark. Jane Doe's schedule, furthermore, is *twice* the usual work week; there is no time for anything but work and study, study and work. It's hard to sustain a schedule like this for more than a semester. Granted the cost of living is high, especially in American metropolitan areas: Textbooks are expensive, college tuition keeps rising, the rent must be paid. Still, college is the one time in your life when you can indulge yourself in learning.

There is no time saved if you take too many courses and then end up having to drop one or more of them because you just can't keep up with the work and your job. Slow down. If you must work so many hours, accept the fact that you will probably have to stay in college for more than four years. After all, you want your degree to mean something besides a piece of paper that shows you put in time in some classrooms. You want to show the world (in particular, your future employers) that you actually learned something.

A Reasonable Study-Work Schedule	
Number of units	9
Number of hours of study	18
Number of hours of work	10
Hours commuting	5
Laundry, cooking, shopping, personal chores	10
Grand Total:	**52 hours**

This is a more reasonable schedule for a student who wants to take nine units of solid academic courses a semester. Of course, you might be able to shave some time off, for example, by working on campus, thereby avoiding a commute. Granted, 10 hours of work isn't much, so if you must work more hours, make the necessary adjustments in your schedule, at least during the first year or two of college. Your study habits and organizational skills will likely improve after this period. You can balance out your courses, for instance, by taking two classes that are lighter on reading and writing requirements if the third course is something like math or science or statistics that is going to require more than two hours of study per class hour.

2. Procrastinating This means putting off reading your assignments until the night before the midterm, putting off writing your English essay until the night before it is due, or cramming at the last minute. If you have gotten into the habit of procrastinating and have paid the price, make a serious effort to change. Some students think that marathon study sessions will get them through. In fact, hours and hours of study are counterproductive. One's brain can hold only so much during a single study session. It's impossible to maintain concentration for more than an hour or two. A better system is to do a reasonable amount of work every week. Keep up with the reading so you're not faced with the terrible prospect of trying to learn the material in five chapters for your psychology midterm the day before the test. Take advantage of breaks between classes and go to the library to study.

3. Overindulging Your Video Game/Television/Internet Habit I recall the sad cases of three former students who were all flunking my classes. In conferences I found out why. The young man revealed that he played video games six or seven hours a day, and more on the weekend. He was flunking every class but tennis. A young woman confessed that she was hooked on television reality shows to the tune of seven or eight hours a day. A third woman—this one an older woman who had been out of college for several years—told me that she spent hours in Internet chat rooms every day! Notice that the two sample schedules above do not include any time for fun—watching television or a movie, being online, playing video games, or just having a pizza and beer with your friends. Set a reasonable amount of time to indulge yourself—say an hour a day—and then turn off the television, computer, or video console.

4. Attending Class Irregularly, and When You Do Go, Arriving Late Studies have shown that students who attend class do better academically than those who don't. If you're not there, you miss out on not only the lecture material, but also the interesting dynamics of discussion that exist nowhere else outside the college classroom.

Being on time not only shows respect for the instructor but also is just a good habit to get into for the real world. Nothing is more frustrating to a teacher (I speak from long experience here) than hearing the classroom door open 15 or 20 minutes into the class. Everyone's head swivels to see the late entrant; everyone's attention is diverted; the teacher gets annoyed, especially if the problem is chronic. And it's rude.

Having said that, we must also accept that emergencies do happen. Sometimes the bus is late. The alarm fails to go off. The babysitter doesn't show up on time. What teachers find hard to tolerate is a *pattern* of late entrances. Being chronically late also suggests a lack of commitment to the class, which the instructor may remember when it comes time to assign a final grade. If your grade is hovering between a C and a D, when your instructor thinks of you, he or she will remember all those times you came in late. It's pretty obvious which way your grade will go.

Four Suggestions for Making the Most of Your Study Time

1. Take Advantage of Campus Resources Today's colleges offer a wide variety of resources to help students learn and succeed. Find out what learning resources are available on your campus and check them out. Some examples are tutoring sessions for individual courses, workshops on a variety of topics like grammar review or techniques for doing research on the Web, formal programs like the Writing Success Project that my college offers, or counseling sessions open to EOPS students. These services might well make the difference between your just scraping by and succeeding.

2. Form a Study Group If you find the course material difficult to understand and to retain, consider forming a study group with three or four other students in the class. Just be sure not to choose slackers. You want to study with students who are serious, who are going to show up regularly, who will do the reading and be ready to talk. One suggestion that students find useful is to anticipate questions that the instructor might ask on a test—including both material for multiple-choice items and for essay responses.

3. Find a Quiet Place to Study It's impossible to study with a lot going on around you. The local Starbucks may be fine for reading a magazine, but for studying your biology textbook, a quiet corner of the library or a quiet room away from everyone else at home is a better choice. Carve a time during the day when you are alert and can absorb what you study.

4. Put Only One Textbook or Study Material on the Desk at a Time Some students are organized and stack all the books that they need to read in a nice neat pile. I think this is a big mistake, because the whole time that you're studying the first book, your eyes wander over to the others in the stack. You begin to worry while studying psychology, for example, that you also have an English essay to write, math homework to complete, and a quiz in art history. Thus, your concentration is impaired with all these competing assignments. Focus on one at a time. Put the other books somewhere else.

Applying the SQ3R Study Method to Reading Textbooks

The best way to take advantage of your study time is to combine reading and studying in your study sessions. Many students read the material first, and then several days or weeks later they get around actually to learning it. This is not efficient. The SQ3R study skills method is a formula that covers all aspects of the study process. SQ3R stands for

S   Survey
Q   Question
R   Read
R   Recite
R   Review

Here is a step-by-step explanation of the SQ3R method. The first step is to *survey*. Before you begin to read a textbook chapter, survey its contents by quickly going through the chapter and doing the following:

- Read and think about the chapter title.
- Read the outline, preview, or introduction.
- Look at the main heads and subheads and become familiar with the size and appearance of primary headings and subheadings.
- Note any key terms or vocabulary defined in the margins.
- Read the chapter summary.
- Read through review questions or questions for discussion.

The survey step, which should take only 5 to 10 minutes, provides you with a framework, an overview of the chapter's contents before you actually read it. In this way, you will have a focus for your reading, and you can fit the various parts of the chapter into a coherent whole.

The next steps are *question* and *read*, which you do at the same time. Section by section, begin reading the text. *Question* by turning each major heading and subheading into a question that you will answer as you read. Let's illustrate this with the first textbook selection you will read. It's from a textbook called *AM GOV—Making Citizenship Meaningful* (*AM GOV* is short for American Government). The passage reprinted here, from Chapter 6, "Public Opinion—Listening to Citizens," is called "Measuring Public Opinion." The passage explains how opinion polls are conducted. Here are the headings (major divisions) you will encounter:

> **Public Opinion—Listening to Citizens** (chapter title)
> > **Measuring Public Opinion** (first-level heading)
> > > **Dimensions of Public Opinion** (second-level heading)
> > > **Types of Polls** (second-level heading)
> > **Polling Techniques** (first-level heading)
> > > **Who Is Asked? Selecting the Sample** (second-level heading)
> > > and so on

To do the *question* step, turn each major heading and subheading into a question that you will answer as you read. For example, for the first first-level heading, ask, "How is public opinion measured?" For the first second-level heading, ask, "What are the dimensions of public opinion?" For the second second-level heading ask, "What are the various types of polls?" And for the next first-level heading, you would ask, "What are some common polling techniques?" This may all seem either tedious or obvious. But the advantage is that while you do the next step—*reading*—you *focus* on finding the answers to your question. In this way, the content is cemented in your brain. You learn the material as you go along, not the night before a major test. The reading step will take up the bulk of your study session with each chapter, but you can go through it efficiently once you have laid the groundwork with the survey and question steps.

The next step is to *recite* the important points, using your own words as much as possible. If you prefer, you can "recite" by taking brief notes, either in the margin of the text or on separate paper. Whichever way you prefer to "recite," this step ensures that you truly understand the material and are not just parroting it back. Be sure to study any accompanying graphs and charts as an aid to comprehending the concepts. Continue in this way through the chapter.

The most crucial element in the SQ3R method is the final step, *review*. Do not give in to the temptation to review later. Immediate review helps fix the concepts in your mind and retain them better. To review, go through the chapter again, noting the main points in each section and studying again any terminology that is either boldfaced or printed in the margins. Also complete any self-quizzes and try to answer the questions for review or for discussion at the end of the chapter (and on the Web site).

To put these theoretical suggestions into practice, reprinted here are excerpts from five representative college textbooks arranged in order of difficulty:

- "Measuring Public Opinion," from Chapter 6, "Public Opinion—Listening to Citizens," *AM GOV—Making Citizenship Meaningful*
- "The Ratings Process," from Chapter 12, "Ratings and Audience Feedback," *Broadcasting, Cable, the Internet, and Beyond*
- "Sleep and Dreams: Conscious while Asleep," from Chapter 5, "States of Consciousness," *Psychology: An Introduction*
- "Race," from Chapter 14, "Ethnicity and Race," *Anthropology: The Exploration of Human Diversity*
- "Seed Plants, Gymnosperms, and Angiosperms," from Chapter 24, "Evolution and Diversity of Plants," *Biology*

Note that each textbook selection is followed by one or more of the following: summary material, discussion questions, and/or self-quizzes that accompany each chapter, thereby duplicating the actual study experience. You should *review* these items after working through the selection, since they contain the important points that an instructor might use for test questions.

JOSEPH LOSCO AND RALPH BAKER

36 Measuring Public Opinion

This selection from an introductory text takes up the subject of public opinion, including the structure and methods used in public opinion polls. This book is a jazzy, souped-up text designed to get students interested and involved in political activism.

MEASURING PUBLIC OPINION

Making meaningful assessments about public opinion requires an understanding of the dimensions around which opinions form as well as accurate ways of measuring them. Simply knowing that an individual prefers one candidate over another tells us little about the individual's likely behavior in an upcoming election or the person's reasons for holding that view. Only when pollsters apply systematic methods to measure and sample opinions can the results of a poll provide some measure of confidence about what the public is thinking.

Dimensions of Public Opinion

When legitimate pollsters ask for our views, they usually attempt to pry beneath the surface of our opinions. They seek to know not only what we believe but how strongly we believe it, how long we have held that view, the grounds on which we base that belief, how important that belief is to us, and what we might be prepared to do about it. Together, these elements make up the various dimensions of public opinion.

Direction refers to an individual's preference with respect to a particular issue. Does the respondent favor the Democrat or the Republican for president? Does he favor or oppose gay marriage? This is the dimension of an opinion that the sponsor of the poll reports most often. **Salience** refers to the importance we attach to an issue or topic about which we are asked. Conservation may be an issue we are prepared actively to lobby and work to promote, or we may think about the matter only when a pollster asks about it. **Intensity** refers to how strongly an individual holds a particular preference on an issue. This dimension is important because people are more likely to act on opinions held intensely.

Stability refers to how consistently an individual maintains a particular preference over time. Americans have had stable views about the death penalty

stability The attribute of an individual's opinion that measures how consistently it is held.

informational support The attribute of an individual's opinion that measures the amount of one's knowledge concerning the issue.

benchmark survey A campaign poll that measures a candidate's strength at the time of entrance into the electoral race.

trial heat survey A campaign poll that measures the popularity of competing candidates in a particular electoral race.

tracking polls Campaign polls that measure candidates' relative strength on a daily basis.

push poll Campaign tactic that attacks an opponent while pretending to be a poll.

exit poll Interviews of voters as they leave the polling place.

scientific polls Any poll using proper sampling designs.

but unstable opinions about foreign policy issues. This is understandable because beliefs about crime and punishment change slowly; our views about foreign policy are tied to changing world events. The dimension of **informational support** tells us how well informed the respondent is regarding an opinion. When a person responds to a multiple-choice question, we have no way of knowing whether he or she is reacting to the question from a basis of knowledge or ignorance. For example, many individuals incorrectly believe that it is a crime to burn the American flag. A person who has little or no information about a subject may readily change his or her opinion when supplied with accurate information.

Types of Polls

Political campaigns employ a wide variety of polls and surveys. Campaigns often conduct **benchmark surveys** at the time a candidate enters a political race. These surveys measure the public's knowledge and assessment of the candidate at that point in time. **Trial heat surveys** pair competing candidates and ask citizens whom they would vote for in such a contest. **Tracking polls** supply the most current information on a race by polling on a daily basis. These polls allow campaigns to change their strategies on a moment's notice to respond to the latest changes in public sentiment. Such polls often interview one hundred people a day for four days and then report the totals. On the fifth day, pollsters interview an additional one hundred people whose responses become part of the total, while the one hundred responses from the first day are dropped. Respondents are subsequently added and dropped on a rotating basis for the length of the poll. *USA Today* reports tracking poll results in the presidential contest for several months before the election.

A **push poll**, the most notorious of campaign polls, is really a campaign tactic disguised as a poll. Campaign workers contact voters to provide them with negative information about their opponent, then ask the voters questions about that candidate. The goal is not to secure accurate information but to influence attitudes. Finally, **exit polls** survey voters as they leave polling places. These polls help campaign professionals analyze demographic factors that influence election outcomes. These types of polls generally are accurate but do experience occasional problems. In the 2000 presidential election, for example, the major media networks initially cited erroneous exit poll results that awarded the state of Florida to Al Gore.

POLLING TECHNIQUES

To be informed consumers of polls, we need to understand what makes a poll scientific and which techniques differentiate good polls from bad. What makes a poll reliable? What are some of the most common flaws and how can we spot them? What information should we be looking for in order to evaluate poll results? To avoid being misled, we need to know how the poll was conducted, who was surveyed, and what questions respondents were asked.

Who Is Asked? Selecting the Sample

Scientific polls use the mathematical laws of probability to ensure accuracy. These laws specify that we don't need to count every member of a population as

sample The individuals whose opinions are actually measured.

population The people whose opinions are being estimated through interviews with samples of group members.

probability sampling A sample design showing that each individual in the population has a known probability for being included in the sample.

simple random sampling Technique of drawing a sample for interview in which all members of the targeted population have the same probability of being selected for interview.

systematic sampling A sample design providing that each individual in the population has an equal chance of being chosen after the first name or number is chosen at random.

long as we count a representative group within that population in a manner that isn't biased. For example, we don't need to count every green and red marble in a large container to know their relative proportion. So long as we select marbles in a random manner, a small sample can yield a very close approximation of the proportions in the entire container.

The individuals whose opinions pollsters measure constitute the **sample**. In a national presidential preference poll, the sample is likely to include between one thousand and twelve hundred respondents. The **population** consists of the larger group of people whose opinions the poll attempts to estimate by interviewing the selected sample. In the case of a presidential preference poll, for example, the population might all be voting age citizens or likely voters throughout the United States.

In measuring our opinions, pollsters try to select samples that accurately represent the broader population from which they are drawn. All good sampling designs use **probability sampling** in which each individual in the population has a known probability for being selected. One type of probability sampling, **simple random sampling**, gives everyone in a population an equal chance of being interviewed. A pure random sample of Americans would mean that each person interviewed has roughly one chance out of three hundred million of being selected. Probability sampling avoids the kind of selection bias that affected the 1936 *Literary Digest* presidential poll. The sample for that poll included only people with automobiles or telephones at a time when a large percentage of potential voters possessed neither of these conveniences. Without using probability sampling, it is impossible for the pollster to know how closely the sample mirrors the overall population.

Simple random sampling, however, is not feasible in a country as vast as the United States. Even census data does not contain a complete and current list of all Americans. As a result, national pollsters use **systematic sampling** as a means of approximating the ideal. They begin with a universe of known telephone numbers, names, or locations. After picking the first number or name at random, they might make additional picks in a predetermined sequence. Some polls randomly select portions of the telephone number and append randomly selected digits to complete the number. As in pure random sampling, the goal is to approximate an equal chance of selection for every individual in the population.

Sampling error refers to a poll's degree of accuracy, usually expressed as a percentage. For example, in a population where every individual has the same chance of being selected, a poll of between one thousand and twelve hundred respondents yields a sampling error of only $+/-$ 3 percent. That is, the results will deviate no more than three percentage points in either direction from results that would be obtained if every person in the entire population were surveyed. Suppose, for example, that a poll of one thousand people shows Candidate A leading Candidate B by a margin of 42 percent to 46 percent. This means that Candidate A's margin among the entire voting population is anywhere from 43 percent to 49 percent, and Candidate B's is anywhere from 39 percent to 45 percent. From that information, the pollster would be wise to conclude that the race is too close to call. Polls that survey fewer individuals have a higher sampling error rate. Polls of just a few hundred are sometimes used when the

sampling error
The measure of the degree of accuracy of a poll based on the size of the sample.

sponsor lacks the money or time to conduct a larger survey, or when there is an interest in the gross dimensions of opinion and the poll sponsor is willing to accept greater uncertainty about the results.

Until now, pollsters have usually conducted polls in person or on the telephone, but both of these methods are extremely expensive. As a result, polling has been the preserve of individuals and groups with significant resources. This could change with the advent of Internet polling, which is extremely inexpensive and could be conducted by virtually anyone with access to the Web and some simple software. These polls, however, pose significant risks regarding accuracy. Many Internet surveys are **pseudo polls** that use selective or skewed samples and often serve a partisan or public relations function. For example, an interest group may report support for its position by polling only loyal supporters who frequently visit its website. In addition, online polls reflect the views of a highly selective portion of the population, since respondents must choose to log on to a particular site to participate. Nevertheless, the potential exists for making polling more accessible and cost effective for organizations with limited resources.

Perhaps a more daunting challenge confronting pollsters is rapidly changing communication technology that makes it more difficult to reach potential respondents. A growing number of people—especially young people—no longer have land lines and do not list their cell phone numbers. Call screening technology also helps individuals avoid the sometimes prying questions of pollsters. Pollsters are currently testing new techniques to avoid systematically excluding the views of these individuals by, for example, adjusting the sample to reflect the known proportion of various groups in the general population before analyzing the results. The samples are "weighted" by region, party, age, race, religion, and gender. In other words, pollsters know the number of men and women in the population, for example, and use that information to adjust the sample if too many or too few women are in the sample. . . .

FOR REVIEW

How is opinion best measured and how do we know these measures are reliable?

> Opinion is best measured by scientific surveys using random samples in which every member of the population has a relatively equal probability of being selected for interview. The reliability of surveys depends on how well the sample is drawn and the quality of the questions. ✱

Joseph Losco and Ralph Baker, from "Measuring Public Opinion" *American Government: Making Citizenship Meaningful.* Copyright © 2009. Reprinted with the permission of The McGraw-Hill Companies, Inc.

37

JOSEPH R. DOMINICK, FRITZ MESSERE, AND BARRY L. SHERMAN

The Ratings Process

This excerpt is from a mass communications textbook, Broadcasting, Cable, the Internet, and Beyond, *and takes up how television and radio ratings are measured, their importance, and their uses. Following the selection are summary points of the material covered.*

THE RATINGS PROCESS

Measuring TV Viewing

Nielsen Media Research draws two different types of samples to measure TV viewing. The national sample used for the NTI[1] is designed to be representative of the entire U.S. population. To draw this sample, Neilsen first selects at random more than 6,000 small geographic areas, usually blocks in urban areas or their equivalent in rural areas, and lists all households in these areas. Next, a sample of 5,100 households is drawn at random. Each household is then contacted, and, if it agrees to participate in the survey, a Nielsen representative installs a People Meter and trains household members how to use it.

For the local market NSI[2] reports, Nielsen first divides the country into more than 200 markets. Within each market, a sample is drawn from phone books and supplemented by random digit dialing in order to obtain unlisted numbers. Sample sizes vary by market but are usually in the range of 1,000 to 2,000 households. Nielsen measures local station TV viewing using two different techniques. In 54 of the largest markets, SIAs[3] are attached to each television in the household and viewing data are gathered about "set tuning" behavior. This information is supplemented with demographic data collected by means of a diary that is sent to participating households. Each member of the household is supposed to record what program he or she is watching and send the diary back to Nielsen at the end of a week. Four times a year (February, May, July, and November), diary measurement is used to collect information from all

[1]Nielsen Television Index
[2]Neilsen Station Index
[3]Storage instantaneous audimeters

460

210 TV markets in the United States. These measurement periods are called "sweeps," and the information from the diaries is used by local stations to determine advertising rates.

In 2002, Nielsen started to move away from its SIA plus diary data gathering method in large markets and began to replace them with the **Local People Meter (LPM)**. The change caused controversy . . . because the LPM results were often at odds with the data gathered by the older diary method. In addition, many people protested that the new technique significantly underestimated the viewing of minority groups. In response, Nielsen made several changes to its sampling and recruiting procedures. These changes helped quiet the dispute, and as of 2006, LPMs were operating in Boston, New York, Chicago, Washington, D.C., San Francisco, and Philadelphia. Nielsen plans to have all the top 10 markets changed over to LPMs by 2007 or 2008.

The first data collected by the LPMs brought good news to cable networks and bad news to broadcast stations. In all markets, ratings of cable networks jumped anywhere from 40 to 80 percent, while broadcast ratings slipped by about 1 to 12 percent. Moreover, in the past, networks used to present some of their strongest programs during sweeps weeks to maximize the advertising rates their local affiliates would charge for the next 3 months. With the LPMs, however, audience demographic data are gathered continuously, and stations no longer have to wait 3 months for the results. It is unclear what impact this change may have on sweeps programming.

In mid-2006 Nielsen announced an ambitious plan that would ultimately lead to the phasing out of all diaries by 2011. In addition, Nielsen planned to measure out-of-home viewing on the Internet and handheld devices such as cell phones and PDAs.

Finally, in a move that might revamp the way advertising is bought, the company revealed that it will start providing ratings for commercials that air during a program. In the past Nielsen had supplied average ratings for the program, and advertisers had based their purchases on those numbers. Under the new system, advertisers will be able to determine how many viewers there were during the commercial breaks.

Processing the Data

Data from the People Meter and the SIA samples are stored in the home devices until they are automatically retrieved by Nielsen's computers. In addition, program schedules and local system cable information are also checked to make sure the viewing data match up with the correct programs. All of this information is processed overnight and made available for customer access the next day. Diary information takes longer to process. The diaries are first mailed back to Nielsen where they are checked for legibility and consistency. The data are then entered into Nielsen computers and tabulated. It usually takes several weeks before these reports are available.

The Ratings Books

The NTI contains data on the estimated audience—divided into relevant demographic categories—for each network program broadcast during the measurement period. The report also features a day-by-day comparison of the audience for each of the major networks as well as an estimate of audience watching cable channels, independent broadcast stations, public TV, and premium channels. Nielsen has recently started reporting same-day DVR playback as well.

The NSI is a little more complicated. Each local market ratings book contains a map that divides the market into three areas: (1) the metro area, where most of the population in the market lives; (2) the designated market area (DMA), where the stations in that market get most of their viewers; and (3) the NSI area, that portion of the market that surrounds the DMA and accounts for 95 percent of the total viewing audience in that market. NSI areas may overlap, but DMAs do not.

The next section of the NSI contains special information, including the number of homes actually in the sample and demographic characteristics of the market. There are also notes about technical problems the stations may have had during the ratings period, such as being knocked off the air by a thunderstorm or power failure.

Audience estimates appear next. These numbers are broken down by time periods and by programs. Thus, a station manager can see how a specific program is doing against its competition and how well it maintains the audience from the program that preceded it.

Nielsen also prepares several specialized reports: The Nielsen Homevideo Index provides measurement of cable viewing, pay cable, VCRs, satellite channels, and other video services; the Nielsen Syndication Service reports viewing levels of syndicated programs; and the Nielsen Sports Marketing Service tracks the viewing of particular sports teams. Nielsen also offers a special service that measures the Hispanic television audience.

Terms and Concepts in TV Ratings

There are three important terms in TV ratings. **Households using television (HUT)** represents the number or the percentage of households that have a TV set on during a specific time period.

The second term is **rating**. Specifically, a rating is the percentage or proportion of all households with a TV set watching a particular program at a particular time. A rating of 10 means that 10 percent of all the homes in the market were watching a specific program. Ratings consider all households in the market, not just those with TV sets in use.

The third term is *share of the audience* or **share**. The share is the total number of households watching a particular program at a specific time divided by the total number of households using TV. Thus, the share is based only on those households that actually have their TV sets turned on.

Some programs can have the same share but have different ratings. For example, let's pretend there are 1,000 households in our market. At 6 A.M., 100 of those 1,000 households have their TV sets on. Of those 100 households, 20 are watching *The Sunrise Home Shopping Show*. The rating for this program would be 20 divided by 1,000, or 2 percent. The share would be 20 divided by 100, or 20 percent. Later that night, let's say at 9 P.M., 600 households are watching TV, and of those 600, 120 are watching *Lost.* The rating for *Lost* would be 120 divided by 1,000, or 12 percent. The show's share of the audience would be 120 divided by 600, or 20 percent, exactly the same as that of *The Sunrise Home Shopping Show.*

Here are the formulas for calculating ratings and shares:

$$\text{Ratings} = \frac{\text{Number of households watching a program}}{\text{Total number of households in market}}$$

$$\text{Share} = \frac{\text{Number of households watching a program}}{\text{Total number of HUT}}$$

. . .

Measuring Radio Listening

Arbitron is the leading company that provides ratings of local radio stations and network radio listening. Arbitron uses the diary method, and many of its procedures are similar to those used by Nielsen Media Research to measure TV viewing.

Arbitron draws its sample by randomly sampling phone numbers from a list compiled by a market research company. Numbers are also randomly generated to account for unlisted phones. The number of households drawn for the sample varies based on a statistical formula that takes into account the total number of households in the market. Sample sizes may range from 750 to 4,500 for local market surveys, with medium-sized markets having a sample size of about 1,000 diaries.

Those households that are selected by Arbitron are called and asked if they would like to participate in the survey. Arbitron mails a brightly colored package to each household that agrees. Inside the package are envelopes (for each member of the household over 11 years of age) that contain a diary, instructions, a letter of thanks, and about a dollar or so.

Diaries cover a 1-week period beginning on a Wednesday. There is one page per day with a column for indicating when a person started listening to a station and when the person stopped. Another column asks the person to write down the frequency or call letters of the station while another records where the listening took place (in a car, at the office, at home, etc.).

Some simple demographic questions are included at the end of the diary. When the diary is completed, the respondent mails it back to Arbitron, where the next phase begins.

Processing the Data

Once received by Arbitron, the diaries are subject to several review procedures. The first review removes diaries that Arbitron considers unusable: those that come in late, those that are illegible, those missing demographic information, and so forth. Other reviews look for inconsistent information (e.g., reporting listening to a station that doesn't exist) and other minor errors (e.g., transposing the call letters of a station). The data are then entered into the computer for analysis.

The Radio Ratings Book

A local market radio ratings report is similar in format to its TV counterpart. The first page contains a map that divides the market into metro, DMA, and total survey areas, much like the NSI. This is followed by general market statistics—number of automobiles, housing values, retail sales data, and the like. Another section reports whether any radio stations conducted unusual promotions designed to artificially increase their audiences during the ratings period. The next section of the book presents demographic data about listeners categorized by dayparts. A station, for example, can easily find its rating among men 12 to 24 during the Monday to Friday 6 A.M. to 10 A.M. daypart. Other sections of the book summarize total time spent listening to the station, where the listening occurred, and the average audience size per station by quarter-hour estimates.

Arbitron issues its Radio Market Reports for more than 280 local markets. Ratings reports are issued four times a year for larger markets. Smaller market reports are issued less frequently.

Arbitron also provides a service called RADAR that measures network radio listening. Network ratings are computed from a nationwide sample of 50,000 radio listening diaries.

Terms and Concepts in Radio Ratings

The basic unit of measurement is different for radio and television ratings. The basic unit for most television ratings is the household. For radio, the basic unit is the person. The formulas for ratings and shares for radio listening reflect this difference. Specifically, in radio

$$\text{Ratings} = \frac{\text{Number of persons listening to a station}}{\text{Total number of persons in market}},$$

and

$$\text{Share} = \frac{\text{Number of persons listening to a station}}{\text{Total number of persons using radio}}.$$

There are two other ratings terms that are more commonly associated with radio ratings. The cumulative audience (or **cume**) is an estimate of the total number of different listeners who listen to a given station at least once during the time part under consideration. In other words, cume is a measure of how many different people listen at least once during the week during the given day part.

Average quarter-hour persons estimates the average number of persons who are listening to a station within a 15-minute period. It is calculated by dividing the estimated number of listeners in a given time period by the number of quarter hours (four per hour) in that time period.

ACCURACY OF THE RATINGS

There are more than 110 million television households in the United States. The Nielsen People Meter sample size is only 5,100, about .00005 of the total. Is it possible for a sample this small to mirror accurately the viewing behaviors of the entire population? The answer to this question is yes, within limits. A sample doesn't have to be large to represent the whole population, as long as it is *representative* of the whole population. To illustrate, when you go to the doctor for a blood test, the doctor does not draw a couple of quarts of blood from your body. A blood test uses only a few milliliters. From this small sample, the doctor can estimate your red cell count, your cholesterol, your hematocrit, and a number of other variables.

Imagine a huge container filled with thousands of coins—pennies, nickels, dimes, and quarters. Let's suppose that 50 percent of the coins are pennies but that this fact is unknown to you. The only way you could be absolutely *sure* what percentage of the coins were pennies would be to count every coin in the huge container, an arduous and time-consuming job. Suppose instead you took a random sample of 100 coins. If sampling were a perfect process, you would find that pennies accounted for 50 percent of your sample. Sometimes this happens, but more often you'll wind up with a little more or a little less than 50 percent pennies. It is also possible, but exceedingly unlikely, that you could draw a sample of 100 percent pennies or another of 0 percent pennies. The bigger the size of your sample, the more likely it is that your results will tend to cluster around the 50 percent mark.

Statisticians have studied the process of sampling and have calculated the accuracy ranges of samples of various sizes. One way of expressing accuracy is to use a concept known as the 95 percent **confidence interval**. This is an interval calculated from sample data that has a 95 percent chance of actually including the population value. For example, let's say the Nielsen People Meter sample of 5,100 homes finds that 20 percent of households watched *American Idol*. Similar to our coin example, we probably wouldn't expect that exactly 20 percent of the 110 million TV households in the United States were also watching. By using statistical formulas, however, we can estimate the 95 percent confidence interval, which in this case, ranges roughly from 19 percent to 21 percent. This means that we are 95 percent sure that, in the entire population of 110 million homes, somewhere between 19 percent and 21 percent are watching *Idol*.

To sum up this statistical discussion, Nielsen ratings are not exact estimates. They are subject to sampling error. However, when their margin of error is taken into account, Nielsen ratings (and other ratings based on a random sample) provide rather accurate estimations of audience viewing behavior.

Incidentally, there is an organization that strives to ensure reasonable accuracy in the realm of ratings: the **Media Rating Council (MRC)**. . . . This council periodically audits Nielsen, Arbitron, and other ratings services to check on their methods and reports. The MRC is an independent body whose fees are paid by the ratings companies.

It should also be noted here that factors other than sampling error also have an impact on accuracy. Note that the above discussion was based on the assumption that the ratings were drawn from a random sample of the population. Although both Nielsen and Arbitron go to great lengths to gather data from a truly random sample, that goal is seldom attained: When contacted, many households in the original sample may refuse to cooperate; individuals in the People Meter sample may get tired of pressing buttons and stop using it; people in the sample who agree to fill out a diary may get bored after a day or so and not return it; other diaries may be filled out illegibly; and People Meters and SIAs are subject to mechanical errors. All of these factors contribute to a **nonresponse bias**. Nonresponse is a more serious concern for diary samples. In many markets, Arbitron may be able to use 50 percent or less of all the radio diaries it sends out.

Additionally, some people may not tell the truth. During a telephone coincidental survey, one of the authors heard the audio from the TV set in the background that was tuned to a wrestling match. When asked what program he was watching, the respondent replied, "The local newscast." Individuals with SIAs might tune their sets to PBS whenever they leave the house. Diary keepers might fill in many educational programs that they did not watch. These are examples of the **social desirability bias**, or providing answers that the respondent thinks will make him or her look more refined or more educated.

Both of these factors reinforce the fact that ratings are estimates of viewing and listening behavior. They are not exact. Nonetheless, they are the best available means for the industry to determine who is watching or listening to what or which programs.

USES FOR RATINGS

Local stations and networks use the ratings to see how they are doing in terms of their total audience. Typically, the bigger the audience, the more money stations and networks can charge for advertising. This is why *American Idol*, which has a weekly audience of about 19 million households, can charge about $500,000 for a 30-second commercial, while *Cops*, which has a weekly audience of 4 to 5 million homes, charges only $65,000.

In addition, ratings can be used to determine what types of people are watching. Advertisers are interested not only in audience size but also in audience type. A show like MTV's *Laguna Beach*, for example, can charge higher rates, not because its total audience is particularly large, but because the show attracts 18- to 34-year-olds—an audience that many advertisers want to reach.

The sales staff at a station uses ratings to persuade potential advertisers that their stations attract the type of audience most likely to buy the advertiser's product. The salespeople at a radio station with a sports-talk format, for example, can show the owner of a cigar bar that an ad on their station would reach a predominantly male audience, a prime target for a cigar merchant.

The station's news department can use the ratings to see how much viewing occurs in neighboring communities. If the ratings show substantial viewing, the station might want to increase coverage of those areas to encourage continued viewing and better ratings.

These are just a few of the uses for ratings data. Keep in mind, however, that while the ratings are a handy tool, they are only one of several considerations that are used by broadcasters and cablecasters to make decisions. They are helpful, but as we have seen, they are not perfect.

SUMMARY

- Early ratings companies, such as the Cooperative Analysis of Broadcasting and the C.E. Hooper Company used telephone surveys to measure radio listening. The A.C. Nielsen Company (now Nielsen Media Research) used a mechanical device attached to a radio or TV set to generate its estimates of the audience.
- Currently, the Arbitron Company uses diaries to measure radio listening, while Nielsen uses a handheld device, called a *People Meter*, along with set-top meters and diaries to measure TV viewing. Media Metrix and Nielsen/NetRatings use a panel of computer users to track data on Web site visits.
- Ratings companies calculate ratings, share of the audience, households using TV, people using radio, and cumulative audience figures and publish their results online and in ratings books. The reports contain maps, demographic information, daypart results, and reports concerning specific programs. This information is used by networks, syndication companies, local stations, and advertisers.
- In addition to ratings research, radio stations use call-out research and auditorium testing to fine-tune their playlists. ✱

38

BENJAMIN B. LAHEY
Sleep and Dreams: Conscious while Asleep

This excerpt, which presents information about sleeping and dreams, is from the chapter "States of Consciousness," from an introduction to psychology textbook.

SLEEP AND DREAMS: CONSCIOUS WHILE ASLEEP

Most nights, we slip gently from wakefulness into sleep, only to return from our nocturnal vacation the next morning. Is this all there is to sleeping? Is it a mere gap in awareness that consumes one-third of our lives? Sleep is not a single state; instead, it's a complex combination of states, some involving conscious awareness. We do not leave consciousness behind for the entire night when we sleep. Rather, we enter worlds of awareness with properties that are very different from those of the wide-awake world.

Stages of Sleep

Several states of conscious awareness are part of the sleep process. As we fall asleep, we pass from waking consciousness into a semiwakeful state, into four states of progressively deeper sleep (all of which contain little or no conscious awareness). Intermittently, we shift from the four stages of sleep into dream sleep, which brings a kind of conscious awareness with a reality all its own. We need to look carefully at each of these parts of the sleep cycle.

Hypnagogic State We do not always go directly from wakefulness to sleep. Often, we daydream for a while, then pass into a "twilight" state that is neither daydreaming nor dreaming. This is the **hypnagogic state** (Vaitl & others, 2005).[1] We begin to lose voluntary control over our body movements; our sensitivity to outside stimuli diminishes; and our thoughts become more fanciful, less bound by reality. For most people, it's a highly relaxed, enjoyable state. On some occasions, however, we are rudely snapped out of the peaceful hypnagogic state. We suddenly feel as if we are falling and our bodies experience a sudden jerk called a **myoclonia.** These jerks are caused by brief (and completely normal) seizure-like states of the brain as sleep commences.

hypnagogic state (hip"nah-goj'ik) A relaxed state of dreamlike awareness between wakefulness and sleep.

myoclonia (mi"o-klō'nē-ah) An abrupt movement that sometimes occurs during the hypnagogic state in which the sleeper often experiences a sense of falling.

[1]You will find similar in-line citations to sources the author researched in many college textbooks. The full References section where these would be listed is not, of course, included here. (Ed.)

Stages of Light and Deep Sleep After making the transition from the hypnagogic state to sleep, we pass through four stages of progressively deeper sleep. Most sleep researchers distinguish among four levels of sleep defined on the basis of **electroencephalogram (EEG)** measures of electrical brain activity (Webb, 1968). The depth of sleep alternates upward and downward many times during the night. Indeed, young adults show an average of 34 shifts in the depth of sleep during the first 6 hours (Webb, 1968). Sleep, then, is not a single, continuous state; it is an almost constantly changing one. . . .

electroencephalo-gram (EEG)
(e-lek"trō-en-sef'ah-lo-gram)
A measure of electrical brain activity.

REM Sleep and Dreams

The year was 1952. University of Chicago graduate student Eugene Aserinsky was spending a sleepless night watching a child sleep in Dr. Nathaniel Kleitman's laboratory. Kleitman, Aserinsky's professor, was interested in the slow, rolling eye movements that occur during sleep in infants. The child was connected to a complicated network of wires that led from instruments to monitor many aspects of the body's functioning (such as brain waves, heartbeat, breathing) and an instrument to measure eye movements.

As Aserinsky dutifully watched the instruments, he was startled to see an unexpected pattern of rapid eye movements. Half a dozen times during the night, the child's eyes darted back and forth rapidly and irregularly under his closed eyelids. At first Aserinsky thought his instruments were not working properly, but he could easily see the child's eye movements. When Aserinsky looked again at his electroencephalograph (EEG), he saw something even more startling: The subject's brain activity looked more like he was awake than asleep. Each time the rapid eye movements returned, the same brain pattern resembling wakefulness returned.

dreaming
Conscious awareness during sleep that primarily occurs during rapid-eye-movement (REM) sleep.

When Aserinsky showed his professor the unexpected findings, the hypothesis was almost inescapable: Was the child **dreaming**? During the next several years, Aserinsky and Kleitman awakened many sleeping adult and child participants when they entered this peculiar stage of sleep characterized by rapid eye movements. When awakened during rapid-eye-movement sleep and asked if they were dreaming, more than 80 percent said yes.

The era of the scientific study of this elusive state of consciousness began with Aserinsky and Kleitman's surprising discovery of the relationship between dreaming and movements of the eyeballs (Kleitman, 1960). Their discovery that dreams are very common during a period of sleep marked by rapid eye movements and brain-wave activity that suggests the presence of conscious awareness. This provided a convenient way for scientists to know when dreams were occurring so that they could study them. Because of the characteristic eye movements, this phase of sleep is referred to as *rapid-eye-movement sleep*, or **REM sleep**.

REM sleep
Rapid-eye-movement sleep, characterized by movement of the eyes under the lids; often accompanies dreams.

Autonomic Storms Five decades of study have revealed the eyeballs are not the only parts of the body that are busy during REM dreams. Sleep researcher Wilse Webb (1968) has likened dream sleep to an "autonomic storm." The autonomic nervous system and other parts of the peripheral nervous system . . . are very active during dreams, causing noticeable changes in many parts of the body: Blood flow to the brain increases; the heartbeat becomes irregular; the muscles of the face and fingers twitch; and breathing becomes irregular. Interestingly, voluntary control of the large body muscles is largely lost during REM sleep, perhaps to keep us from acting out our dreams. Anyone who has watched a sleeping beagle twitch, make miniature running movements, and rasp muffled barks (at dream rabbits?) knows about these autonomic storms and knows that REM sleep is not limited to humans. This fact has been confirmed in many laboratory studies of sleeping mammals.

In addition, females experience vaginal lubrication and erection of the clitoris and males have erection of the penis during REM sleep. Because of erections that begin during REM sleep, the penis of an adult male is erect during one-fourth to one-half of an average night's sleep. This fact has led to advances in the diagnosis of conditions in which some males are unable to have an erection (known as *erectile dysfunction*). By having the patient spend a night in a sleep laboratory to see if he has erections during REM sleep, it is possible to determine if the cause of the problem is psychological (he would have erections during REM sleep) or physical (he would not have REM erections).

Time Spent Dreaming How often do you dream? In a survey of college-aged adults, about 15 percent said that they dream every night, and another 25 percent said that they dream on most nights. On the other hand, almost a third of young adults said that they rarely or never dream (Strauch & Meier, 1996). How often do you dream? Even if you recall a dream every night, you probably greatly underestimate the frequency of your dreams. We spend much more time in the world of dream consciousness than most of us realize.

Studies of dreaming conducted during the past 30 years show that the average college student spends about 2 hours a night in REM sleep, divided into about four to six separate episodes. Based on the reports of sleepers who were awakened during REM sleep, it is clear that we dream during at least 80 percent of these episodes of REM sleep (Strauch & Meier, 1996). The length of our REM dreams vary, but the longest REM dream, generally about an hour in duration, usually occurs during the last part of the sleep cycle (Hobson, 1989; Webb, 1982).

Therefore, young adults have 30 to 40 REM dreams per week. We do not remember dreaming nearly this often when we are awake because we forget dreams quickly unless we awaken during or soon after the dream. But we spend about 2 hours each night in the conscious state of REM dreams. There is much more to the story of consciousness while sleeping, however; REM sleep is not the only part of the sleep cycle that contains dreams.

Non-REM Sleep and Dreams

Initially, sleep researchers believed that dreams were uncommon during the non-REM parts of the sleep cycle (Kleitman, 1960). Subsequent studies showed, however, that the number of dreams that occur during non-REM sleep is much higher than suspected (Foulkes, 1962). Many studies have consistently shown that when participants are awakened during non-REM phases of sleep, they report dreaming about half of the time (Strauch & Meier, 1996; Vaitl & others, 2005). On the average, non-REM dreams are less bizarre and filled with less negative emotion than REM dreams (McNamara & others, 2005), but in most ways, recent research suggests that dreams that occur during REM and non-REM stages of sleep are more similar than different (Vaitl & others, 2005).

When both REM and non-REM dreams are considered, we spend a surprising amount of time in states of consciousness during sleep. In addition to the 2 hours of REM dreaming per night, non-REM dream activity is occurring during half of the other 4 to 6 hours that we sleep each night. Unlike waking consciousness, most of the hours that we are conscious during sleep do not become part of the permanent records of our lives by being stored in memory, but modern sleep research has revealed that we are consciously aware during sleep much more than we would have ever suspected.

Circadian Rhythms

When is it time to go to sleep? For some of us, drowsiness takes over not long after sundown. Others are night owls who find that they are wide awake until the wee hours of the morning. But all of us—even those who do not sleep well—are on a biological cycle of approximately 24 hours that regulates our pattern of sleep, called the **circadian rhythm** (*circa* = about; *dia* = day). Much remains to be learned about the biological basis of circadian rhythms. One part of the hypothalamus has been implicated as a part of the body's internal "clock." Its activity increases and decreases in a regular pattern that lasts about 24 hours. In addition, variations in the hormone *melatonin* that fluctuate on a 24-hour pattern appear to be a key factor in regulating sleepiness (Gilbertini, Graham, & Cook, 1999).

The body has many other circadian rhythms, most of which roughly follow the pattern of the sleep-wake cycle. For example, an important hormone of the pituitary that plays a key role in body growth and repair, *growth hormone*, is secreted mostly during the first 2 hours of sleep, with little secreted during the waking hours of the day. Apparently, this reflects the role that sleep plays in normal growth and the maintenance of health.

Body temperature also follows a circadian rhythm linked to the sleep cycle. As you can see in figure 5.3, body temperature falls just as you are beginning to feel sleepy and continues to fall until the middle of the sleep period. This is why you sometimes want to pull on more covers in the middle of the night, even when the temperature in your room is controlled by a thermostat.

Figure 5.3 also shows that the adrenal stress hormone *cortisol* follows a circadian rhythm that is tied to the sleep period in yet another pattern. Cortisol secretion begins to rise shortly after you fall asleep and continues to rise through the night. This is another indication that REM sleep is not a calm period for the body. The peak of cortisol secretion is just before awakening, the time of the longest period of REM sleep. The autonomic storm (p. 469) that takes place during REM dreams results in the same activation of the adrenal glands that occurs during physical or emotional stress. Ironically, a good night's sleep may be good for you, but not all of it is a "restful" time for the body.

The circadian sleep-wake cycle is obviously influenced to some extent by differences in illumination during the day and night. Although many cultures take "siestas" during the day and cultures living near the North and South poles have long periods without days and nights as we know them, people throughout the world generally are awake when it is light and asleep when it is dark. Some

circadian rhythm (sur-kā'-dē-un) Internally generated cycles lasting about 24 hours a day that regulate sleepiness and wakefulness, body temperature, and the secretion of some hormones.

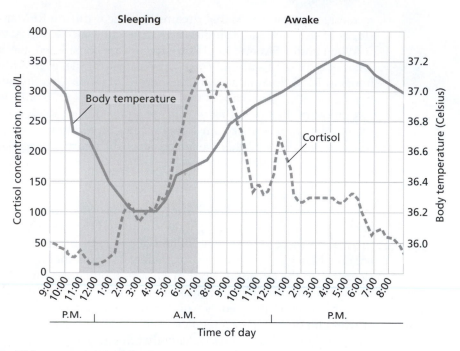

Figure 5.3 The concentration of the adrenal hormone cortisol in the blood follows a circadian rhythm, reaching its peak just before a person wakes from sleep, whereas the circadian rhythm for body temperature follows a different pattern. Source: Data based in part on J. Puig-Antich, et al., "Cortisol Secretion in Prepubertal Children with Major Depressive Disorder," *Archives of General Psychiatry,* 46:801–812, 1989.

clever experiments have shown that the circadian sleep rhythm continues even when individuals are isolated in chambers that are always kept lighted, but surprisingly, the rhythm quickly changes to a *25-hour cycle* (Aschoff, 1981; Horne, 1988). Apparently, the body's clock runs on a schedule that is a little longer than 24 hours, but is reset each day by daylight.

The most dramatic way that most of us will become aware of circadian rhythms is by disrupting them with long airline flights. If you fly west from Atlanta to Hawaii, for example, you will experience a much longer period of daylight and will generally stay awake longer than usual on the first day. If you fly to Paris, however, you will have a very short first night. Both trips will disrupt your circadian rhythms and make you inefficient and out-of-sorts—a phenomenon known as "jet lag." People differ in how much they are affected by jet lag, but interestingly, the time required to readjust to local time is generally longer when traveling from west to east (Moore-Ede, Sulzman, & Fuller, 1982; see fig. 5.4). Unfortunately, taking melatonin does nothing to minimize jet lag (Spitzer & others, 1999). Thus, you shouldn't expect to tour the entire Louvre museum the morning after arriving in Paris. You'll be lucky to have the energy to break your French bread.

The same phenomenon occurs when workers rotate the times of their work shifts (Wilkinson, Allison, Feeney, & Kaminska, 1989). It is less disruptive to rotate from the night shift (midnight to 8 A.M.) to the day shift (8 A.M. to 4 P.M.) or

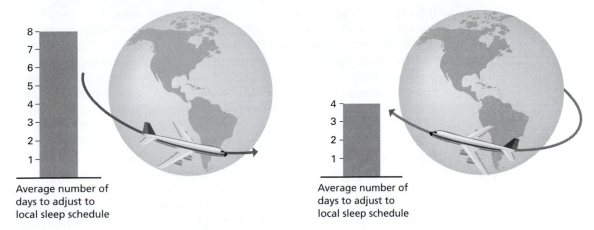

Figure 5.4 It generally takes longer to adjust to local sleep schedules and get over jet lag when traveling west to east.
Source: Data from M. C. Moore-Ede, F. M. Sulzman, and C. A. Fuller, *The Clocks That Time Us.* Harvard University Press, Cambridge: 1982.

from the day shift to the swing shift (4 P.M. to midnight) than to rotate in the opposite direction. This is because you stay awake longer on the first day of each rotation. It is apparently better to move from night to day shift and to travel from east to west because these changes are consistent with our natural tendency to lengthen our circadian rhythms (Moore-Ede & others, 1982). Jet lag and work-shift rotations have been the subject of considerable study, because of their effect on the scheduling of airline pilots, nurses, and other key employees as well as the timing of travel for diplomatic, business, and military purposes.

Sleep Deprivation and the Need for Sleep

It has long been clear that we create a "sleep debt" if we miss sleep. Students at the University of Florida participated in a sleep experiment limiting their sleep to 2 hours for one night. The next day they were irritable, fatigued, inattentive, and inefficient; the next night they fell asleep more quickly and slept longer than usual (Webb & Bonnet, 1979). In the early days of sleep research it was not at all clear that we need much sleep to maintain good health. For example, sleep researchers made much of the fact that teenager Randy Gardner set a world record by staying awake for 264 hours as a science project. Although he felt fatigue, sleepiness, and irritability, he suffered no obvious ill effects. Similarly, when a group of volunteer college students gradually reduced their sleep from 8 to 4 hours a night for a period of 2 months, there were no detectable immediate effects (Webb & Bonnet, 1979). Such observations prompted noted sleep researcher Wilse Webb (1975) to hypothesize that sleep serves a protective role rather than maintaining the health of the body. Because the eyes of animals that sleep at night are not very efficient in low light, Webb hypothesized that we fall asleep simply to keep us from moving around in the dark of night. In his view, sleep keeps us from wasting energy, falling off cliffs, and being eaten by animals that hunt at night and have better night vision.

Now it is clear that sufficient sleep is essential to maintaining good health. For example, when male college students were limited to 4 hours of sleep per night for a week, important changes in bodily functions were found that had not been detected in early sleep studies. The sleep-deprived students had increased activity of their sympathetic nervous systems and their normal patterns of hormone secretion by the adrenal glands and thyroid were altered. Perhaps most importantly, their metabolism of sugar was less efficient after sleep deprivation (Spiegel & others, 1999). In addition, short-term sleep deprivation slows down the body's immune system (Spiegel & others, 2002). Such findings raise the possibility—but do not prove by itself—that long-term sleep deprivation could be a factor in diabetes, the obesity epidemic, and other life-threatening medical conditions.

The average amount of sleep has declined from 9 hours per night in 1960 in the United States. A survey of more than 1 million adults (ages 30 to 102 years) found that most of us now sleep 7 or 8 hours per night (Kripke & others, 2002). It is striking that death rates (controlling for age and other factors) increase slightly as the number of hours of sleep increase or decrease from 7 hours per night. Only extreme deviations from the norms are associated with large differences in death rates, however. For example, sleeping less than 4.5 hours per night for men and less than 3.5 hours per night for women is associated with a 15 percent higher death rate.

One possible cause of death related to sleep deprivation is accidental death. Even small amounts of sleep deprivation can decrease alertness and increase the risk of accidents. For example, each spring when we lose an hour of sleep because of daylight savings time, there is a temporary increase in the rate of deaths due to injury in the United States, but there is not a significant change in death rates when we get an extra hour of sleep when times shift back in the fall (Coren, 1996; 2004).

Regardless of why we sleep, we appear to "need" to dream as part of that sleep process. In a number of experiments, sleeping individuals were awakened whenever they entered REM sleep. They were otherwise allowed to get a normal amount of sleep each night. Depriving participants of approximately 2 hours of REM sleep each night had the same effects as much longer deprivations of sleep in general. The participants were irritable, inefficient, and fatigued. On subsequent nights, they showed an increase in the amount of REM sleep, suggesting that they had a need to catch up on REM sleep—and perhaps on their vivid dreaming. Other studies also have shown that deprivation of the deepest part of non-REM sleep has much the same effect (Hobson, 1989; Webb & Bonnet, 1979).

In addition, there is evidence that REM sleep plays an essential role in the consolidation of newly learned information from the day before (Ribeiro, Goyal, Mello, & Pavlides, 1999; Stickgold, Hobson, Fosse, & Fosse, 2001). REM plays this important role by activating the expression of a gene that controls the modification of connections between neurons. So study hard, but leave time to get a good night's sleep (and plenty of REM) before the exam. We all need adequate sleep to be healthy, and you need to sleep to consolidate your memory of what you learned. This is one reason studying all night before a test is very inefficient.

Content of Dreams

Dreams are one of the most fascinating aspects of human consciousness. At least since the time of the Egyptian pharaohs, people have attempted to decipher the meaning of dreams—and some psychologists are still trying. Let's begin our discussion of dreams by looking at psychological studies of what people dream about. Because dreams are private, it is interesting to compare our own dreams with those of others.

The first systematic study of dreams was conducted by Mary Whiton Calkins, . . . a founder of psychology. Calkins was a pioneer in the study of memory, but she was also the founder of scientific dream research. Over a hundred years ago, Calkins and her partner wrote down a verbatim description of every dream they recalled over several months—often writing by candlelight in the middle of the night (Calkins, 1893). Since the time of Calkins, many researchers have studied thousands of dreams, both spontaneously recalled dreams and dreams that are recalled when research participants are awakened in sleep labs. Therefore, we can now confidently describe the content of human dreams.

Images and Characters in Dreams Most of the conscious experience in dreams is visual. If you dream about washing dishes, you almost always experience a visual image of dishwashing but are less likely to hear the clatter of the dishes or to feel the hot, wet dishwater. Only about one-fourth of dream images include auditory sensations, and about 20 percent include body sensations. About half of the dreams that involve body sensations are sexual—10 percent of all dreams. Less than 1 percent of dreams include tastes or smells (Hall, 1951; Strauch & Meier, 1996).

Do you dream in black-and-white or color? Most people dream in something that is in between. The visual images in dreams are usually as bright and clear as waking images, but they are drab in color. Dreams usually include few intense colors, and most have blurry backgrounds (Rechtschaffen & Buchignami, 1983). Who are the characters in your dreams—your friends and family? Are there strangers in your dreams? Are you a character in your own dreams? Because you are always the "author" of your dreams, it is not surprising that you often play a leading role. The dreamer has an active role in nearly three-fourths of dreams, and you are absent from your own dreams only 10 percent of the time (Strauch & Meier, 1996). About half of the other characters in your dreams are friends, acquaintances, or family members, but the other half are people you do not know or cannot recognize—or are animals 4 percent of the time. The characters in dreams are about an even mixture of men and women, with men being slightly more likely to dream about men than women are (Hall, 1951; Strauch & Meier, 1996).

Sweet Dreams: The Emotional Content of Dreams Are your dreams mostly happy or sad or scary? Most dreams contain positive emotions (Fosse, Stickgold, & Hobson, 2001), but mother nature plays a little trick on us. When people are asked about the emotional content of their dreams as soon as they spontaneously wake up, about 60 percent of their emotional dreams contain negative emotions (Strauch & Meier, 1996). When researchers wake up people during REM sleep, however, most of the emotional dreams they report are positive (Fosse & others, 2001). What is happening here? Why don't we remember all of our sweet dreams in the morning? Although we dream mostly of positive things, negative dreams late in the sleep cycle are more likely to wake us up. We forget many of our positive dreams (because they don't wake us up) and are more likely to be aware of the negatively charged dreams that awaken us. It's totally unfair, but reassuring to know that usually we are happy in our dreams.

There are gender differences in the emotional qualities of the dreams that we recall when we spontaneously awake. Overall, men are a little more likely to recall positive dreams than are women. Similarly, the actions of the characters in men's dreams are somewhat more socially restrained than the characters in women's dreams. The people in men's dreams are both less likely to act in friendly ways and less likely to act aggressively toward other dream players. When verbal or physical aggression occurs in dreams, both men and women are more likely to dream that they are the victims rather than the perpetrators. This tendency is somewhat stronger for women than men (Strauch & Meier, 1996).

Creative and Bizarre Aspects of Dreams Dreams fascinate us largely because they can be amazingly creative and bizarre. Most of our dreams are not particularly bizarre, but even our more realistic dreams often contain creative and unusual elements. About three-fourths of our dreams contain at least one bizarre and unrealistic element, usually mixed into an otherwise realistic dream. On the other hand, 10 percent of our dreams involve mostly nonsensical story lines, and another 10 percent of dreams are almost completely fantastic and bizarre (Hall, 1951; Strauch & Meier, 1996).

Meaning of Dreams

Why do we dream about the things that fill our heads during sleep? What is the meaning of dreams? A century of research suggests that some of the content of dreams is easy to understand, while the rest remains a mystery.

Day Residue and Stimulus Incorporation A large part of the content of dreams is directly related to things going on in our lives during the day—things that Sigmund Freud called **day residue**. The majority of dreams contain at least one character or event from the preceding day—or less often, from the preceding week or even earlier in the dreamer's life. The most important characters and events are more likely to reflect day residue than are less central parts. One clear demonstration of the importance of day residue in the content of dreams is that half of all dreams reported by research participants in sleep laboratories include the sleep researchers or parts of the laboratory in the dream (Strauch & Meier, 1996).

The role of day-to-day events and people in our dreams also was demonstrated in a well-designed study conducted at the Max Planck Institute of Psychiatry in Munich, Germany (Lauer, Riemann, Lund, & Berger, 1987). Participants slept in the sleep laboratory after being shown either a neutral film or an upsetting film depicting violence, humiliation, and despair. They were awakened during their first REM stage and asked if they were dreaming. After viewing the upsetting film, the participants' REM dreams were rated as containing considerably more aggressive and anxious content than on the night following the neutral film. Furthermore, about one-third of the dreams contained images or themes directly related to the content of the upsetting film.

day residue
Dream content that is similar to events in the person's waking life.

A more naturalistic study of the impact of daytime events on the content of dreams was conducted by Wood, Bootzin, Rosenhan, Nolen-Hoeksema, and Jourdon (1992). On October 17, 1989, a major earthquake that hit the San Francisco area caused more than $5 billion in damage and killed 62 people, including 42 killed when a freeway collapsed on them. The researchers asked students at two universities in the San Francisco area to keep track of the number of upsetting dreams that they had during a 3-week period immediately following the earthquake. As a control group, students at the University of Arizona who had not been near the earthquake did the same thing. Not surprisingly, the students in the area of the earthquake reported more vivid, upsetting dreams than did the students in Arizona. In addition, 40 percent of the students in the San Francisco area reported at least one dream about earthquakes, compared with 5 percent of the students in Arizona (Wood & others, 1992). Persons exposed to highly stressful events, such as wars, sometimes have nightmarish dreams about them for many years afterward (Neyland & others, 1998). Clearly, events and concerns in our daily lives are among the most common things that we dream about.

Sometimes a real-world event included in the dream is something going on while we are asleep. Have you ever had a dream that included a telephone or alarm clock ringing in your ear at the time? This phenomenon is called **stimulus incorporation**. Sometimes the stimulus in the real environment is directly incorporated into the dream, but more often it is transformed somewhat. In a Swiss study, sleep participants were presented with the recorded sound of a jet plane while asleep. About one-third later reported dreaming about flying or reported hearing something that sounded like a jet plane (such as a sputtering gas stove) in their dream, but the sound was usually not heard in the dream exactly as it actually sounded (Strauch & Meier, 1996).

stimulus incorporation Stimuli occurring during sleep that are incorporated into dreams either directly or in altered form.

Dream Interpretation We know that some of the content of dreams simply reflects the events and concerns of daily life, but what about the rest? And what is the meaning of the bizarre and fictional images in dreams? Different psychologists have very different views of the meaning of dreams, ranging from the opinion that they mean virtually nothing to the belief that they provide a rich source of information about hidden aspects of our personalities that cannot be revealed easily in other ways.

To followers of Sigmund Freud, dreams are the "royal road to the unconscious." They allow us to travel deep into the unconscious mind and view hidden conflicts and motives cloaked only by the symbols of dreams. Freud divided the content of dreams into two levels—manifest and latent. The events that we experience in dreams are their **manifest content**. This level held little interest for Freud; he believed it was necessary to get beyond the surface and find out what the manifest content of the dream symbolized to discover its true meaning, or **latent content**. For example, the manifest content of a young woman's dream might involve riding on a train and becoming frightened as it enters a tunnel. On the surface, the dream is about trains and tunnels. But what does the manifest content of the dream symbolize? Freud might see the train as symbolizing a penis and the tunnel as symbolizing a vagina. Hence, the hidden, or latent, content of the dream might concern the young woman's conflicts about having sex.

manifest content According to Freud, the literal meaning of dreams.

latent content According to Freud, the true meaning of dreams that is found in the symbols in their manifest content.

nightmares
Dreams that occur during REM sleep and whose content is exceptionally frightening, sad, angry, or in some other way uncomfortable.

night terrors
Upsetting nocturnal experiences that occur most often in preschool-age children during deep non-REM sleep.

sleepwalking
Waking and carrying on complicated activities during the deepest part of non-REM sleep.

sleeptalking
Talking during any phase of the sleep cycle.

sleep disorders
Disturbances of sleep.

insomnia A disorder in which the person has difficulty falling asleep or staying asleep.

narcolepsy A sleep disorder in which the person suddenly falls asleep during activities usually performed when fully awake, even when the person has had adequate sleep.

Such interpretations are provocative and fascinating, but are they accurate? Psychologists simply do not agree on this issue. Because symbols can be interpreted in infinite ways, we can never be sure that our interpretations are correct. Perhaps as a result, most contemporary psychologists place much less emphasis on dream interpretation than did Freud.

Nightmares and Other Sleep Phenomena

We have all had terrifying dreams known as **nightmares**. The content of these dreams that occur during REM sleep is exceptionally frightening, sad, provoking, or in some other way uncomfortable. They are upsetting enough to wake us up during the dream, so we can vividly remember our nightmares, even though they account for only a small proportion of the dreams most of us have (Hartmann, Russ, Oldfield, Sivian, & Cooper, 1987).

Night terrors are a less common but perhaps even more upsetting nocturnal experience. The individual awakens suddenly in a state of panic, sometimes screaming and usually with no clear recollection of an accompanying dream. A sense of calm usually returns within a few minutes, but these can be terrifying experiences. Unlike nightmares, they do not occur during REM sleep but during the deepest phases of non-REM sleep. Night terrors are most common in preschool-age children, but sometimes adults also experience them (Hartmann & others, 1987).

Sleepwalking is another interesting phenomenon that occurs primarily during the deepest parts of non-REM sleep. Sleepwalkers rise from the bed and carry on complicated activities, such as walking from one room to another, even though they are sound asleep. Sleepwalking is most common in children before the age of puberty but is not particularly unusual in adults. Sleepwalking usually reappears in adults only during periods of stress, but except for the danger of accidents while wandering around in the dark, it's not an abnormal behavior.

Sleeptalking is a fairly common phenomenon that can occur during any phase of the sleep cycle. In this, the soundly sleeping person says words, sometimes making fairly coherent statements for a brief period of time. It's most common in young adults but occurs at all ages.

Sleep Disorders

Although we all sleep, some people sleep more or less than they would prefer or they experience other serious difficulties with the sleep process. The term **sleep disorders** is often used to refer to these troublesome but highly treatable disorders.

Insomnia refers to a variety of difficulties in which individuals report that they sleep less than they wish. There are two major varieties of insomnia. In *sleep-onset insomnia*, individuals have difficulty falling asleep at the hour at which they would like, but sleep is normal after it begins. In contrast, *early-awakening insomnia* is characterized by waking up earlier than desired, either several times in the middle of the night or early in the morning. Both are found in individuals experiencing no other psychological problems but are more common in individuals undergoing periods of stress, anxiety, or depression.

Narcolepsy is a rare sleep disorder, occurring in less than one-half of 1 percent of the general population, but its impact can be quite serious. The narcoleptic often unexpectedly falls into a deep slumber in the middle of work or even during conversations with others, especially when upset or stressed. Often, the individual experiences loss of muscle tone and shows a lack of body movement, as if suddenly falling into dream sleep. However, laboratory studies show that narcoleptic sleep is not REM sleep. Narcolepsy is not just intense sleepiness, because it occurs in individuals who get adequate sleep. Narcolepsy often causes serious difficulties with the use of dangerous machines and other job-related activities.

sleep apnea The sudden interruption of breathing during sleep.

Sleep apnea is the sudden, temporary interruption of breathing during sleep. To qualify as sleep apnea, these interruptions of breathing must be longer than 20 seconds, because brief interruptions are normal. Sleep apnea is common, particularly in older adults who snore. It is caused either by too much relaxation of the muscles of the throat or by a temporary cessation of brain signals for breathing. It is more common in persons who are overweight. Serious sleep apnea can lead to serious medical problems.

REVIEW

Each night, we depart the world of waking consciousness and enter another world that we scarcely remember the next morning. Alternating among periods of sleep that contain no conscious experience, we live a life of dreams. When studied systematically, much of the content of dreams is found to reflect daily events and concerns. Still, the meaning of dreams has long fascinated us and played a major role in Freud's attempts to understand the hidden workings of the mind. Sleep eludes some of us for part of the night, or we are troubled by sleep disorders. The daily rhythm of sleep and wakefulness is only one of numerous natural rhythms that tend to follow daily, weekly, or annual patterns.

CHECK YOUR LEARNING

To be sure that you have learned the key points from the preceding section, cover the list of correct answers and try to answer each question. If you give an incorrect answer to any question, return to the page given next to the correct answer to see why your answer was not correct.

1. Research suggests that _____ may be the most important components of sleep because subjects deprived of them were irritable, inefficient, and fatigued.

   a. hypnagogic sleep
   b. myoclonia and REM sleep
   c. REM sleep and deep sleep
   d. naps

2. According to Freud, the _____ , or true meaning of dreams, reveal(s) hidden conflicts and motives in the unconscious mind.

   a. latent content
   b. manifest content
   c. events
   d. colors

3. _____ is a rare sleep disorder in which the person suddenly falls asleep during activities usually performed when fully awake, such as during conversations with others.
   a. Sleep apnea
   b. Insomnia
   c. Epilepsy
   d. Narcolepsy

4. Body temperature and hormones such as cortisol follow a _____, or daily cycle linked to the sleep cycle.

Correct Answers: 1. c (p. 474), 2. a (p. 477), 3. d (p. 478), 4. circadian rhythm (p. 471).

THINKING CRITICALLY ABOUT PSYCHOLOGY

There are no right or wrong answers to the following questions. They are presented to help you become an active reader and think critically about what you have just read.

1. In your opinion, why do we sleep? Why do we dream?
2. What does research on sleep-wake cycles suggest about being at your best when taking a test?

SUMMARY

Chapter 5 explores human awareness, normal waking consciousness, sleeping and dreaming, and altered states of consciousness. . . .

Approximately one-third of our lives is spent in sleep, but not all of sleep is unconscious.

A. Sleep begins with a semiwakeful, hypnagogic state and moves through stages of progressively deeper sleep.
B. Dreams occur mostly during the phase of sleep known as REM sleep, but dreams that tend to be somewhat less bizarre and emotional often occur in non-REM sleep.
C. Sleeping and dreaming seem important to health, but even brief periods of sleep deprivation cause fatigue, inefficiency, and irritability.
D. Nightmares, night terrors, sleepwalking, and sleeptalking are fairly common sleep phenomena.
E. Some persons suffer from the sleep disorders of insomnia (inability to get sufficient sleep), narcolepsy (falling asleep during daily activities), and sleep apnea (breathing stops briefly during sleep). . . . ✳

39 Race

CONRAD PHILLIP KOTTAK

"Race" is an excerpt from the chapter entitled "Ethnicity and Race," from a leading cultural anthropology textbook.

RACE

Race, like ethnicity in general, is a cultural category rather than a biological reality. That is, ethnic groups, including "races," derive from contrasts perceived and perpetuated in particular societies, such as Ghana, . . . rather than from scientific classifications based on common genes (see Wade 2002).

It is not possible to define human races biologically. Only cultural constructions of race are possible—even though the average person conceptualizes "race" in biological terms. The belief that human races exist and are important is much more common among the public than it is among scientists. Most Americans, for example, believe that their population includes biologically based "races" to which various labels have been applied. These labels include "white," "black," "yellow," "red," "Caucasoid," "Negroid," "Mongoloid," "Amerindian," "Euro-American," "African American," "Asian American," and "Native American."

We hear the words *ethnicity* and *race* frequently, but American culture doesn't draw a very clear line between them. As an illustration, consider two articles in the *New York Times* of May 29, 1992. One, discussing the changing ethnic composition of the United States, states (correctly) that Hispanics "can be of any race" (Barringer 1992, p. A12). In other words, "Hispanic" is an ethnic category that cross-cuts "racial" contrasts such as that between "black" and "white." The other article reports that during the Los Angeles riots of spring 1992, "hundreds of Hispanic residents were interrogated about their immigration status on the basis of their *race* alone [emphasis added]" (Mydans 1992*a*, p. A8). Use of "race" here seems inappropriate because "Hispanic" is usually perceived as referring to a linguistically based (Spanish-speaking) ethnic group, rather than a biologically based race. Since these Los Angeles residents were being interrogated because they were Hispanic, the article is actually reporting on ethnic, not racial, discrimination. However, given the lack of a precise distinction between race and ethnicity, it is probably better to use the term *ethnic group* instead of *race* to describe *any* such social group, for example, African Americans, Asian Americans, Irish Americans, Anglo Americans, or Hispanics.

THE SOCIAL CONSTRUCTION OF RACE

Races are ethnic groups assumed (by members of a particular culture) to have a biological basis, but actually race is socially constructed. The "races" we hear about every day are cultural, or social, rather than biological categories. In Charles Wagley's terms (Wagley 1959/1968), they are social races (groups assumed to have a biological basis but actually defined in a culturally arbitrary, rather than a scientific, manner). Many Americans mistakenly assume that "whites" and "blacks," for example, are biologically distinct and that these terms stand for discrete races. But these labels, like racial terms used in other societies, really designate culturally perceived rather than biologically based groups.

Hypodescent: Race in the United States

How is race culturally constructed in the United States? In American culture, one acquires his or her racial identity at birth, but race isn't based on biology or on simple ancestry. Take the case of the child of a "racially mixed" marriage involving one black and one white parent. We know that 50 percent of the child's genes come from one parent and 50 percent from the other. Still, American culture overlooks heredity and classifies this child as black. This rule is arbitrary. From *genotype* (genetic composition), it would be just as logical to classify the child as white.

American rules for assigning racial status can be even more arbitrary. In some states, anyone known to have any black ancestor, no matter how remote, is classified as a member of the black race. This is a rule of **descent** (it assigns social identity on the basis of ancestry), but of a sort that is rare outside the contemporary United States. It is called **hypodescent** (Harris and Kottak 1963) (*hypo* means "lower") because it automatically places the children of a union or mating between members of different groups in the minority group. Hypodescent helps divide American society into groups that have been unequal in their access to wealth, power, and prestige.

The following case from Louisiana is an excellent illustration of the arbitrariness of the hypodescent rule. It also illustrates the role that governments (federal, or state in this case) play in legalizing, inventing, or eradicating race and ethnicity (Williams 1989). Susie Guillory Phipps, a light-skinned woman with "Caucasian" features and straight black hair, discovered as an adult that she was "black." When Phipps ordered a copy of her birth certificate, she found her race listed as "colored." Since she had been "brought up white and married white twice," Phipps challenged a 1970 Louisiana law declaring anyone with at least one-thirty-second "Negro blood" to be legally black. In other words, having 1 "Negro" great-great-great-grandparent out of 32 is sufficient to make one black. Although the state's lawyer admitted that Phipps "looks like a white person," the state of Louisiana insisted that her racial classification was proper (Yetman 1991, pp. 3–4).

Cases like Phipps's are rare, because "racial" and ethnic identities are usually ascribed at birth and usually don't change. The rule of hypodescent affects blacks, Asians, Native Americans, and Hispanics differently (see Hunter 2005). It's easier to negotiate Indian or Hispanic identity than black identity. The ascription rule isn't as definite, and the assumption of a biological basis isn't as strong.

To be considered "Native American," one ancestor out of eight (great-grandparents) or four (grandparents) may suffice. This depends on whether the assignment is by federal or state law or by an Indian tribal council. The child of a Hispanic may (or may not, depending on context) claim Hispanic identity. Many Americans with an Indian or Latino grandparent consider themselves "white" and lay no claim to minority-group status.

Race in the Census

The U.S. Census Bureau has gathered data by race since 1790. Initially this was done because the Constitution specified that a slave counted as three-fifths of a white person and because Indians were not taxed. The racial categories specified in the U.S. census include White, Black or Negro, Indian (Native American), Eskimo, Aleut or Pacific Islander, and Other. A separate question asks about Spanish-Hispanic heritage. . . .

An attempt by social scientists and interested citizens to add a "multiracial" census category has been opposed by the National Association for the Advancement of Colored People (NAACP) and the National Council of La Raza (a Hispanic advocacy group). Racial classification is a political issue. It involves access to resources, including jobs, voting districts, and federal funding of programs aimed at minorities. The hypodescent rule results in all the population growth being attributed to the minority category. Minorities fear their political clout will decline if their numbers go down.

But things are changing. Choice of "Some other race" in the U.S. Census more than doubled from 1980 (6.8 million) to 2000 (over 15 million)—suggesting imprecision in and dissatisfaction with the existing categories (Mar 1997). In the year 2000, 274.6 million Americans (out of 281.4 million censused) reported they belonged to just one race, as shown in Table 14.3.

Nearly 48 percent of Hispanics identified as White alone, and about 42 percent as "Some other race" alone. In the 2000 census, 2.4 percent of Americans, or 6.8 million people, chose a first-ever option of identifying themselves as belonging to more than one race. About 6 percent of Hispanics reported two or more races, compared with less than 2 percent of non-Hispanics (http://www.census.gov/Press-Release/www/2001/cb01cn61.html).

The number of interracial marriages and children is increasing, with implications for the traditional system of American racial classification. "Interracial," "biracial," or "multiracial" children who grow up with both parents undoubtedly identify with particular qualities of either parent. It is troubling for many of

TABLE 14.3 AMERICANS REPORTING THEY BELONGED TO JUST ONE RACE	
White	75.1%
Black or African-American	12.3%
American Indian and Alaska Native	0.9%
Asian	3.6%
Native Hawaiian and Other Pacific Islander	0.1%
Some other race	5.5%

Source: http://www.census.gov/Press-Release/www/2001/cb01cn61.html.

them to have so important an identity as race dictated by the arbitrary rule of hypodescent. It may be especially discordant when racial identity doesn't parallel gender identity, for example, a boy with a white father and a black mother, or a girl with a white mother and a black father.

How does the Canadian census compare with the American census in its treatment of race? Rather than race, the Canadian census asks about "visible minorities." That country's Employment Equity Act defines such groups as "persons, other than Aboriginal peoples [aka First Nations in Canada, Native Americans in the United States], who are non-Caucasian in race or non-white in colour" (Statistics Canada 2001a). Table 14.4 shows that "Chinese" and "South Asian" are Canada's largest visible minorities. Note that Canada's total visible minority population of 13.4 percent (up from 11.2 percent in 1996) contrasts with a figure of about 25 percent for the United States in the 2000 Census. In particular, Canada's black 2.2 percent population contrasts with the American figure of 12.5 percent for African Americans, while Canada's Asian population is significantly higher than the U.S. figure of 3.7 percent on a percentage basis. Only a tiny fraction of the Canadian population (0.2 percent) claimed multiple visible minority affiliation, compared with 2.4 percent claiming "more than one race" in the United States in 2000.

Canada's visible minority population has been increasing steadily. In 1981, 1.1 million visible minorities accounted for 4.7 percent of the total population, versus more than 13.4 percent today. Visible minorities are growing much faster than is Canada's total population. Between 1996 and 2001, the total population increased 4 percent, while visible minorities rose 25 percent. If recent

TABLE 14.4 VISIBLE MINORITY POPULATION OF CANADA, 2001 CENSUS

	Number	Percent
Total population	**29,639,030**	**100.0**
Total visible minority population	3,983,845	13.4
Chinese	1,029,395	3.5
South Asian	917,075	3.1
Black	662,210	2.2
Arab/West Asian	303,965	1.0
Filipino	308,575	1.0
Southeast Asian	198,880	0.7
Latin American	216,980	0.7
Korean	100,660	0.3
Japanese	73,315	0.2
Other visible minority	98,915	0.3
Multiple visible minority	73,875	0.2
Nonvisible minority	25,655,185	86.6

Source: From Statistics Canada, 2001a, 2001 Census, http://www40.statcan.ca/l01/cst01/demo50a.htm?sdi =visible.

immigration trends continue, by 2016, visible minorities will account for one-fifth of the Canadian population.

Not Us: Race in Japan

American culture ignores considerable diversity in biology, language, and geographic origin as it socially constructs race within the United States. North Americans also overlook diversity by seeing Japan as a nation that is homogeneous in race, ethnicity, language, and culture—an image the Japanese themselves cultivate. Thus in 1986, former Prime Minister Nakasone created an international furor by contrasting his country's supposed homogeneity (responsible, he suggested, for Japan's success in international business) with the ethnically mixed United States. To describe Japanese society, Nakasone used *tan'itsu minzoku*, an expression connoting a single ethnic-racial group (Robertson 1992).

Japan is hardly the uniform entity Nakasone described. Some dialects of the Japanese language are mutually unintelligible. Scholars estimate that 10 percent of Japan's population are minorities of various sorts. These include aboriginal Ainu, annexed Okinawans, outcast *burakumin*, children of mixed marriages, and immigrant nationalities, especially Koreans, who number more than 700,000 (De Vos, Wetherall, and Stearman 1983; Lie 2001).

To describe racial attitudes in Japan, Jennifer Robertson (1992) uses Kwame Anthony Appiah's (1990) term *intrinsic racism*—the belief that a (perceived) racial difference is a sufficient reason to value one person less than another. In Japan, the valued group is majority ("pure") Japanese, who are believed to share "the same blood." Thus, the caption to a printed photo of a Japanese American model reads: "She was born in Japan but raised in Hawaii. Her nationality is American but no foreign blood flows in her veins" (Robertson 1992, p. 5). Something like hypodescent also operates in Japan, but less precisely than in the United States, where mixed offspring automatically become members of the minority group. The children of mixed marriages between majority Japanese and others (including Euro-Americans) may not get the same "racial" label as the minority parent, but they are still stigmatized for their non-Japanese ancestry (De Vos and Wagatsuma 1966).

How is race culturally constructed in Japan? The (majority) Japanese define themselves by opposition to others, whether minority groups in their own nation or outsiders—anyone who is "not us." The "not us" should stay that way; assimilation is generally discouraged. Cultural mechanisms, especially residential segregation and taboos on "interracial" marriage, work to keep minorities "in their place."

In its construction of race, Japanese culture regards certain ethnic groups as having a biological basis, when there is no evidence that they do. The best example is the *burakumin*, a stigmatized group of at least four million outcasts. They are sometimes compared to India's untouchables. The *burakumin* are physically and genetically indistinguishable from other Japanese. Many of them "pass" as (and marry) majority Japanese, but a deceptive marriage can end in divorce if *burakumin* identity is discovered (Aoki and Dardess, eds. 1981).

Burakumin are perceived as standing apart from majority Japanese. Through ancestry and descent (and thus, it is assumed, "blood," or genetics), *burakumin* are "not us." Majority Japanese try to keep their lineage pure by discouraging mixing. The *burakumin* are residentially segregated in neighborhoods (rural or urban) called *buraku,* from which the racial label is derived. Compared with majority Japanese, the *burakumin* are less likely to attend high school and college. When *burakumin* attend the same schools as majority Japanese, they face discrimination. Majority children and teachers may refuse to eat with them because *burakumin* are considered unclean.

In applying for university admission or a job, and in dealing with the government, Japanese must list their address, which becomes part of a household or family registry. This list makes residence in a *buraku,* and likely *burakumin* social status, evident. Schools and companies use this information to discriminate. (The best way to pass is to move so often that the *buraku* address eventually disappears from the registry.) Majority Japanese also limit "race" mixture by hiring marriage mediators to check out the family histories of prospective spouses. They are especially careful to check for *burakumin* ancestry (De Vos et al. 1983).

The origin of the *burakumin* lies in a historic system of stratification (from the Tokugawa period: 1603–1868). The top four ranked categories were warrior-administrators (*samurai*), farmers, artisans, and merchants. The ancestors of the *burakumin* were below this hierarchy. An outcast group, they did unclean jobs, like animal slaughter and disposal of the dead. *Burakumin* still do related jobs, including work with animal products, like leather. The *burakumin* are more likely than majority Japanese to do manual labor (including farm work) and to belong to the national lower class. *Burakumin* and other Japanese minorities are also more likely to have careers in crime, prostitution, entertainment, and sports (De Vos et al. 1983).

Like blacks in the United States, the *burakumin* are class-stratified. Because certain jobs are reserved for the *burakumin,* people who are successful in those occupations (e.g., shoe factory owners) can be wealthy. *Burakumin* also have found jobs as government bureaucrats. Financially successful *burakumin* can temporarily escape their stigmatized status by travel, including foreign travel.

Discrimination against the *burakumin* is strikingly like the discrimination that blacks have faced in the United States. The *burakumin* often live in villages and neighborhoods with poor housing and sanitation. They have limited access to education, jobs, amenities, and health facilities. In response to *burakumin* political mobilization, Japan has dismantled the legal structure of discrimination against *burakumin* and has worked to improve conditions in the *buraku.* Still, Japan has not instituted American-style affirmative action programs for education and jobs. Discrimination against nonmajority Japanese is still the rule in companies. Some employers say that hiring *burakumin* would give their companies an unclean image and thus create a disadvantage in competing with other businesses (De Vos et al. 1983).

Phenotype and Fluidity: Race in Brazil

There are more flexible, less exclusionary ways of constructing social race than those used in the United States and Japan. Along with the rest of Latin America, Brazil has less exclusionary categories, which permit individuals to change their racial classification. Brazil shares a history of slavery with the United States, but it lacks the hypodescent rule. Nor does Brazil have racial aversion of the sort found in Japan.

Brazilians use many more racial labels—over 500 have been reported (Harris 1970)—than Americans or Japanese do. In northeastern Brazil I found 40 different racial terms in use in Arembepe, a village of only 750 people (Kottak 2006). Through their classification system Brazilians recognize and attempt to describe the physical variation that exists in their population. The system used in the United States, by recognizing only three or four races, blinds Americans to an equivalent range of evident physical contrasts. The system Brazilians use to construct social race has other special features. In the United States one's race is an ascribed status; it is assigned automatically by hypodescent and doesn't usually change. In Brazil racial identity is more flexible, more of an achieved status. Brazilian racial classification pays attention to phenotype. **Phenotype** refers to an organism's evident traits, its "manifest biology"—physiology and anatomy, including skin color, hair form, facial features, and eye color. A Brazilian's phenotype and racial label may change because of environmental factors, such as the tanning rays of the sun or the effects of humidity on the hair.

As physical characteristics change (sunlight alters skin color, humidity affects hair form), so do racial terms. Furthermore, racial differences may be so insignificant in structuring community life that people may forget the terms they have applied to others. Sometimes they even forget the ones they've used for themselves. In Arembepe, I made it a habit to ask the same person on different days to tell me the races of others in the village (and my own). In the United States I am always "white" or "Euro-American," but in Arembepe I got lots of terms besides *branco* ("white"). I could be *claro* ("light"), *louro* ("blond"), *sarará* ("light-skinned redhead"), *mulato claro* ("light mulatto"), or *mulato* ("mulatto"). The racial term used to describe me or anyone else varied from person to person, week to week, even day to day. My best informant, a man with very dark skin color, changed the term he used for himself all the time—from *escuro* ("dark") to *preto* ("black") to *moreno escuro* ("dark brunet").

The American and Japanese racial systems are creations of particular cultures, rather than scientific—or even accurate—descriptions of human biological differences. Brazilian racial classification is also a cultural construction, but Brazilians have developed a way of describing human biological diversity that is more detailed, fluid, and flexible than the systems used in most cultures. Brazil lacks Japan's racial aversion, and it also lacks a rule of descent like that which ascribes racial status in the United States (Degler 1970; Harris 1964).

For centuries the United States and Brazil have had mixed populations, with ancestors from Native America, Europe, Africa, and Asia. Although "races" have mixed in both countries, Brazilian and American cultures have constructed the results differently. The historical reasons for this contrast lie mainly in the different characteristics of the settlers of the two countries. The mainly English early settlers of the United States came as women, men, and families, but Brazil's Portuguese colonizers were mainly men—merchants and adventurers. Many of these Portuguese men married Native American women and recognized their "racially mixed" children as their heirs. Like their North American counterparts, Brazilian plantation owners had sexual relations with their slaves. But the Brazilian landlords more often freed the children that resulted—for demographic and economic reasons. (Sometimes these were their only children.) Freed offspring of master and slave became plantation overseers and foremen and filled many intermediate positions in the emerging Brazilian economy. They were not classed with the slaves, but were allowed to join a new intermediate category. No hypodescent rule developed in Brazil to ensure that whites and blacks remained separate (see Degler 1970; Harris 1964).

SUMMARY

1. An "ethnic group" refers to members of a particular culture in a nation or region that contains others. Ethnicity is based on actual, perceived, or assumed cultural similarities (among members of the same ethnic group) and differences (between that group and others). Ethnic distinctions can be based on language, religion, history, geography, kinship, or "race." A race is an ethnic group assumed to have a biological basis. Usually race and ethnicity are ascribed statuses; people are born members of a group and remain so all their lives.

2. Race is a cultural category, not a biological reality. "Races" derive from contrasts perceived in particular societies, rather than from scientific classifications based on common genes. In the United States "racial" labels such as "white" and "black" designate socially constructed races—categories defined by American culture. American racial classification, governed by the rule of hypodescent, is based neither on phenotype nor on genes. Children of mixed unions, no matter what their appearance, are classified with the minority-group parent.

3. Racial attitudes in Japan illustrate "intrinsic racism"—the belief that a perceived racial difference is a sufficient reason to value one person less than another. The valued group is majority ("pure") Japanese, who are believed to share "the same blood." Majority Japanese define themselves by opposition to others, such as Koreans and *burakumin.* These may be minority groups in Japan or outsiders—anyone who is "not us."

4. Such exclusionary racial systems are not inevitable. Although Brazil shares a history of slavery with the United States, it lacks the hypodescent rule. Brazilian racial identity is more of an achieved status. It can change during someone's lifetime, reflecting phenotypical changes. Given the correlation between poverty and dark skin, the class structure affects Brazilian racial classification. Someone with light skin who is poor will be classified as darker than a comparably colored person who is rich.

CRITICAL THINKING QUESTIONS

1. What's the difference between a culture and an ethnic group? In what culture(s) do you participate? To what ethnic group(s) do you belong? What is the basis of your primary cultural identity?

2. Name five social statuses you currently occupy. Which of those statuses are ascribed, and which ones are achieved?

3. What kind of racial classification system operates in the community where you grew up or now live? Does it differ from the racial classification system described for American culture in this chapter?

4. If you had to devise an ideal system of racial categories, would it be more like the North American, the Japanese, or the Brazilian system? Why? ✳

SYLVIA S. MADER

40 Seed Plants, Gymnosperms, and Angiosperms

The final selection in Part Six is an excerpt from a chapter titled "Evolution and Diversity of Plants" from an introductory biology textbook.

24.5 SEED PLANTS

In the first seed plants of the Devonian period, the seeds developed along branches within small, cuplike structures, now called cupules. Following pollination, fertilization of an egg cell occurred within the cupule, prior to seed formation. Were these plants ancestral to both gymnosperms and angiosperms? A fairly good history of gymnosperm evolution is available, but exactly when angiosperms arose is shrouded in mystery. Today, the seed plants—the gymnosperms and angiosperms—are the most plentiful plants in the biosphere.

Seeds contain a sporophyte embryo and stored food within a protective seed coat. The seed coat and stored food allow an embryo to survive harsh conditions during long periods of dormancy (arrested state) until environmental conditions become favorable for growth. Seeds can even remain dormant for hundreds of years. When a seed germinates, the stored food is a source of nutrients for the growing seedling. The survival value of seeds largely accounts for the dominance of seed plants today.

Seed plants are heterosporous (have two types of spores) and produce two kinds of gametophytes—male and female—each of which consists of just a few cells. Pollen grains, which are drought resistant, become a multicellular male gametophyte. **Pollination** occurs when a pollen grain is brought to the vicinity of the female gametophyte by wind or a pollinator. Later, sperm move toward the female gametophyte through a growing pollen tube. *Note that no external water is needed to accomplish fertilization.* The whole male gametophyte, rather than just the sperm as in seedless plants, moves to the female gametophyte. A female gametophyte develops within an ovule, which eventually becomes a seed. In gymnosperms (mostly cone-bearing seed plants), the ovules are not completely enclosed by sporophyte tissue at the time of pollination. In flowering plants (angiosperms), the ovules are completely enclosed within diploid sporophyte tissue (ovaries), which becomes a fruit.

Gymnosperms and angiosperms are the seed plants, which produce pollen grains and seeds. Pollen grains and seeds are well protected from drying out.

24.6 GYMNOSPERMS

The four groups of living **gymnosperms** [Gk. *gymnos*, naked, and *sperma*, seed] are conifers, cycads, ginkgoes, and gnetophytes. All of these plants have ovules and seeds exposed on the surface of sporophylls or analogous structures. (Since the seeds are not enclosed by fruit, gymnosperms have "naked seeds.") Early gymnosperms were present in the swamp forests of the Carboniferous period . . . , and they became dominant during the Triassic period. Today, living gymnosperms are classified into 780 species. The conifers are more plentiful today than other types of gymnosperms.

Conifers

Conifers (phylum **Coniferophyta**) consist of about 575 species of trees, many evergreen, including pines, spruces, firs, cedars, hemlocks, redwoods, cypresses, yews, and junipers. The name *conifers* signifies plants that bear **cones**, but other gymnosperm phyla are also cone-bearing. The coastal redwood *(Sequoia sempervirens)*, a conifer native to northwestern California and southwestern Oregon, is the tallest living vascular plant; it may attain nearly 100 m in height. Another conifer, the bristlecone pine *(Pinus longaeva)* of the White Mountains of California, is the oldest living tree; one is 4,900 years of age.

Vast areas of northern temperate regions are covered in evergreen coniferous forests. . . . The tough, needlelike leaves of pines conserve water because they have a thick cuticle and recessed stomata. Note in the life cycle of the pine . . . that the sporophyte is dominant, pollen grains are windblown, and the seed is the dispersal stage. Conifers are **monoecious** since a tree produces both pollen and seed cones.

Uses of Pines The wood of pines and other conifers is used extensively in construction. The wood consists primarily of xylem tissue that lacks some of the more rigid cell types found in flowering trees. Therefore, it is considered a "soft" rather than a "hard" wood. Although called soft woods, some soft woods such as yellow pine are actually harder than so-called hard woods. The foundations of the 100-year-old Brooklyn Bridge are made of southern yellow pine. Resin, made by pines as an insect and fungal deterrent, is harvested commercially for a derived product called turpentine.

Cycads

Cycads (phylum **Cycadophyta**) include 10 genera and 140 species of distinctive gymnosperms. The cycads are native to tropical and subtropical forests. *Zamia pumila* found in Florida is the only species of cycad native to North America. Cycads are commonly used in landscaping. One species, *Cycas revoluta*, referred to as the sago palm, is a common landscaping plant. Their large, finely divided leaves grow in clusters at the top of the stem, and therefore they resemble palms or ferns, depending on their height. The trunk of a cycad is unbranched, even if it reaches a height of 15–18 m, as is possible in some species.

Cycads have pollen and seed cones on separate plants. The cones, which grow at the top of the stem surrounded by the leaves, can be huge—even more than a meter long with a weight of 40 kg. . . . Cycads have a life cycle similar to that of a pine tree, but they are pollinated not by wind but by insects. Also, the pollen tube bursts in the vicinity of the archegonium, and multiflagellated sperm swim to reach an egg.

Cycads were plentiful in the Mesozoic era at the time of the dinosaurs, and it's likely that dinosaurs fed on cycad seeds. Now cycads are in danger of extinction because they grow very slowly, a distinct disadvantage.

Ginkgoes

Phylum **Ginkgophyta**, although plentiful in the fossil record, is represented today by only one surviving species, *Ginkgo biloba*, the **ginkgo** or maidenhair tree. It is called the maidenhair tree because its leaves resemble those of a maidenhair fern. Ginkgoes are **dioecious**—some trees produce seeds . . . and others produce pollen. The fleshy seeds, which ripen in the fall, give off such a foul odor that male trees are usually preferred for planting. *Ginkgo* trees are resistant to pollution and do well along city streets and in city parks. *Ginkgo* is native to China, and in Asia, *Ginkgo* seeds are considered a delicacy. Extracts from *Ginkgo* trees have been used to improve blood circulation.

Like cycads, the pollen tube of *Gingko* bursts to release multiflagellated sperm that swim to the egg produced by the female gametophyte located within an ovule.

Gnetophytes

Gnetophytes (phylum **Gnetophyta**) are represented by three living genera and 70 species of plants that are very diverse in appearance. In all gnetophytes, xylem is structured similarly, none have archegonia, and their strobili (cones) have a similar construction. Angiosperms don't have archegonia either, and molecular analysis suggests that among gymnosperms, the gnetophytes are most closely related to angiosperms. The reproductive structures of some gnetophyte species produce nectar, and insects play a role in the pollination of these species. *Gnetum*, which occurs in the tropics, consists of trees or climbing vines with broad, leathery leaves arranged in pairs. *Ephedra*, occurring only in southwestern North America and southeast Asia, is a shrub with small, scalelike leaves. . . . Ephedrine, a medicine with serious side effects, is extracted from *Ephedra*. *Welwitschia*, living in the deserts of southwestern Africa, has only two enormous, straplike leaves. . . .

24.7 ANGIOSPERMS

Angiosperms [Gk. *angion*, dim. of *angos*, vessel, and *sperma*, seed] (phylum **Anthophyta**) are the flowering plants. They are an exceptionally large and successful group of plants, with 240,000 known species—six times the number of all other plant groups combined. Angiosperms live in all sorts of habitats, from fresh water to desert, and from the frigid north to the torrid tropics. They range in size from the tiny, almost microscopic duckweed to *Eucalyptus* trees over 100 m tall. It would be impossible to exaggerate the importance of angiosperms in our everyday lives. . . . [T]hey provide us with clothing, food, medicines, and other commercially valuable products.

The flowering plants are called angiosperms because their ovules, unlike those of gymnosperms, are always enclosed within diploid tissues. In the Greek derivation of their name, *angio* ("vessel") refers to the ovary, which develops into a fruit, a unique angiosperm feature.

Origin and Radiation of Angiosperms

Although the first fossils of angiosperms are no older than about 135 million years, the angiosperms probably arose much earlier. Indirect evidence suggests the possible ancestors of angiosperms may have originated as long as 200 million years ago. But their exact ancestral past has remained a mystery since Charles Darwin pondered it.

To find the angiosperm of today that might be most closely related to the first angiosperms, botanists have turned to DNA comparisons. Gene-sequencing data single out *Amborella trichopoda* . . . as having the oldest lineage among today's angiosperms. This small shrub, with small cream-colored flowers, lives only on the island of New Caledonia in the South Pacific.

Although *A. trichopoda* may not be the original angiosperm species, it is sufficiently close that much may be learned from studying its reproductive biology. Botanists hope that this knowledge will help them understand the early adaptive radiation of angiosperms in the late Cretaceous and early Tertiary periods. It could very well be that the rise to dominance of angiosperms is tied to the increasing diversity of flying insects at this time. Insects are significant **pollinators**—animals that carry pollen between flowers.

Monocots and Eudicots

Most flowering plants belong to one of two classes. These classes are the **Monocotyledones (Liliopsida)**, often shortened to simply the **monocots** (about 65,000 species), and the **Eudicotyledones**, shortened to **eudicots** (about 175,000 species). The term *eudicot* (meaning true dicot) is more specific than the term *dicot*. It was discovered that some of the plants formerly classified as dicots diverged before the evolutionary split that gave rise to the two major classes of angiosperms. These earlier evolving plants are not included in the designation eudicots.

Monocots are so called because they have only one cotyledon (seed leaf) in their seeds. Several common monocots include corn, tulips, pineapples, bamboos, and sugarcane. Eudicots are so called because they possess two cotyledons in their seeds. Several common eudicots include cactuses, strawberries, dandelions, poplars, and beans. **Cotyledons** are the seed leaves that contain nutrients that nourish the plant embryo. Table 24.1 lists several fundamental differences between monocots and eudicots.

TABLE 24.1 MONOCOTS AND EUDICOTS

Monocots	Eudicots
One cotyledon	Two cotyledons
Flower parts in threes or multiples of three	Flower parts in fours or fives or multiples of four or five
Usually herbaceous	Woody or herbaceous
Usually parallel venation	Usually net venation
Scattered bundles in stem	Vascular bundles in a ring
Fibrous root system	Taproot system

The Flower

Although flowers vary widely in appearance . . . , most have certain structures in common. The **peduncle**, a flower stalk, expands slightly at the tip into a **receptacle**, which bears the other flower parts. These parts, called sepals, petals, stamens, and carpels, are attached to the receptacle in whorls (circles) (Fig. 24.25).

- The **sepals**, collectively called the calyx, protect the flower bud before it opens. The sepals may drop off or may be colored like the petals. Usually, however, sepals are green and remain attached to the receptacle.
- The **petals,** collectively called the corolla, are quite diverse in size, shape, and color. The petals often attract a particular pollinator.
- Next are the **stamens**. Each stamen consists of two parts: the anther, a saclike container, and the filament, a slender stalk. Pollen grains develop from microspores produced in the anther.
- At the very center of a flower is the **carpel**, a vaselike structure with three major regions: the **stigma**, an enlarged sticky knob; the **style**, a slender stalk; and the **ovary**, an enlarged base that encloses one or more ovules. The ovule becomes the seed, and the ovary becomes the fruit.

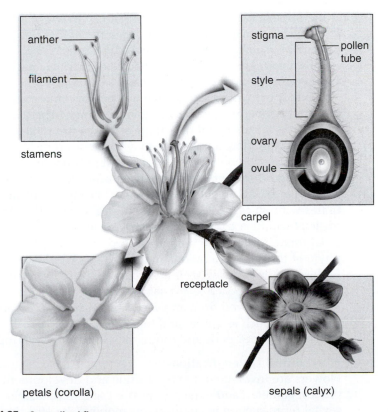

Figure 24.25   Generalized flower.
A flower has four main parts: sepals, petals, stamens, and carpels. A stamen has an anther and filament. A carpel has a stigma, style, and ovary. An ovary contains ovules.

TABLE 24.2 OTHER FLOWER TERMINOLOGY	
Term	**Type of Flower**
Complete	All four parts (sepals, petals, stamens, and carpels) present
Incomplete	Lacks one or more of the four parts
Perfect	Has both stamens and (a) carpel(s)
Imperfect	Has stamens or (a) carpel(s), but not both
Inflorescence	A cluster of flowers
Composite	Appears to be a single flower but consists of a group of tiny flowers

It can be noted that not all flowers have all these parts (Table 24.2). A flower is said to be complete if it has all four parts; otherwise it is incomplete.

Flowering Plant Life Cycle

Figure 24.26 depicts the life cycle of a typical flowering plant. Like the gymnosperms, flowering plants are heterosporous, producing two types of spores. A **megaspore** located in an ovule within an ovary of a carpel develops into an egg-bearing female gametophyte called the embryo sac. In most angiosperms, the embryo sac has seven cells; one of these is an egg, and another contains two polar nuclei. (These two nuclei are called the polar nuclei because they came from opposite ends of the embryo sac.)

Microspores, produced within anthers, become pollen grains that, when mature, are sperm-bearing male gametophytes. The full-fledged mature male gametophyte consists of only three cells: the tube cell and two sperm cells. During pollination, a pollen grain is transported by various means from the anther to the stigma of a carpel, where it germinates. During germination, the tube cell produces a pollen tube. The **pollen tube** carries the two sperm to the micropyle (small opening) of an ovule. During double fertilization, one sperm unites with an egg, forming a diploid zygote, and the other unites with polar nuclei, forming a triploid endosperm nucleus.

Ultimately, the ovule becomes a seed that contains the embryo (the sporophyte of the next generation) and stored food enclosed within a seed coat. Endosperm in some seeds is absorbed by the cotyledons, whereas in other seeds endosperm is digested as the seed matures.

A **fruit** is derived from an ovary and possibly accessory parts of the flower. Some fruits such as apples and tomatoes provide a fleshy covering, and other fruits such as pea pods and acorns provide a dry covering for seeds.

Flowers and Diversification

Flowers are involved in the production and development of spores, gametophytes, gametes, and embryos enclosed within seeds. Successful completion of sexual reproduction in angiosperms requires the effective dispersal of pollen and then seeds. The various ways pollen and seeds can be dispersed have resulted in many different types of flowers.

Wind-pollinated flowers are usually not showy, whereas insect-pollinated flowers and bird-pollinated flowers are often colorful. Night-blooming flowers attract nocturnal mammals or insects; these flowers are usually aromatic and white or cream-colored. Although some flowers disperse their pollen by wind, many are adapted to attract specific pollinators such as bees, wasps, flies, butterflies, moths, and even bats, which carry only particular pollen from flower to flower. For example, glands located in the region of the ovary produce nectar, a nutrient that is gathered by pollinators as they go from flower to flower. Bee-pollinated flowers are usually blue or yellow and have ultraviolet shadings that lead the pollinator to the location of nectar. The mouthparts of bees are fused into a long tube that is able to obtain nectar from the base of the flower.

The fruits of flowers protect and aid in the dispersal of seeds. Dispersal occurs when seeds are transported by wind, gravity, water, and animals to another location. Fleshy fruits may be eaten by animals, which transport the seeds to a new location and then deposit them when they defecate. Because animals live in particular habitats and/or have particular migration patterns, they are apt to deliver the fruit-enclosed seeds to a suitable location for seed germination (when the embryo begins to grow again) and development of the plant.

Angiosperms are the flowering plants. The flower attracts animals (e.g., insects), which aid in pollination, and produces seeds enclosed by fruit, which aids in their dispersal.

SUMMARY

24.5 Seed Plants

Seed plants also have an alternation of generations, but they are heterosporous, producing both microspores and megaspores. Gametophytes are so reduced that the female gametophyte is retained within an ovule. Microspores become the windblown or animal-transported male gametophytes—the pollen grains. Pollen grains carry sperm to the egg-bearing female gametophyte. Following fertilization, the ovule becomes the seed. A seed contains a sporophyte embryo, and therefore seeds disperse the sporophyte generation. Fertilization no longer uses external water, and sexual reproduction is fully adapted to the terrestrial environment.

24.6 Gymnosperms

The four phyla of gymnosperms are cone-bearing plants, but they do not have an immediate common ancestor. The conifers, represented by the pine tree, exemplify the traits of these plants. Gymnosperms have "naked seeds" because the seeds are not enclosed by fruit, as are those of flowering plants.

24.7 Angiosperms

In angiosperms, the reproductive organs are found in flowers; the ovules, which become seeds, are located in the ovary, which becomes the fruit. Therefore, angiosperms have "covered seeds." In many angiosperms, pollen is transported from flower to flower by insects and other animals. Both flowers and fruits are found only in angiosperms and may account for the extensive colonization of terrestrial environments by the flowering plants. ✳

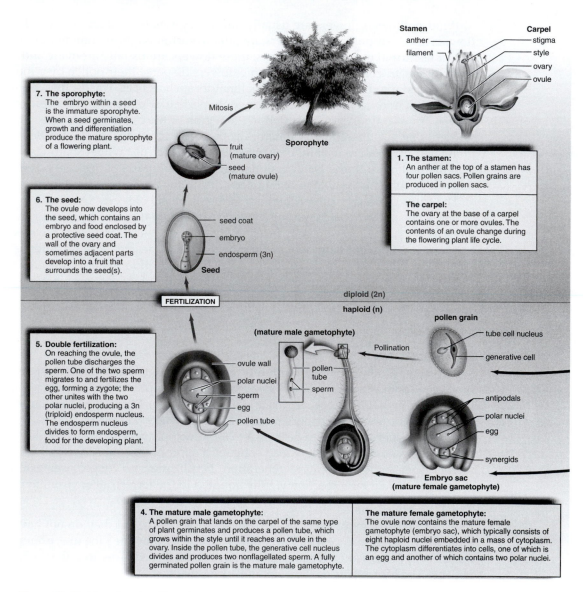

Figure 24.26   Flowering plant life cycle.
The parts of the flower involved in reproduction are the stamens and the carpel. Reproduction has been divided into significant stages of female gametophyte development, male gametophyte development, and also significant stages of sporophyte development.

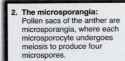

2. The microsporangia:
Pollen sacs of the anther are microsporangia, where each microsporocyte undergoes meiosis to produce four microspores.

The megasporangium:
First, an ovule within an ovary contains a megasporangium, where a megasporocyte undergoes meiosis to produce four megaspores.

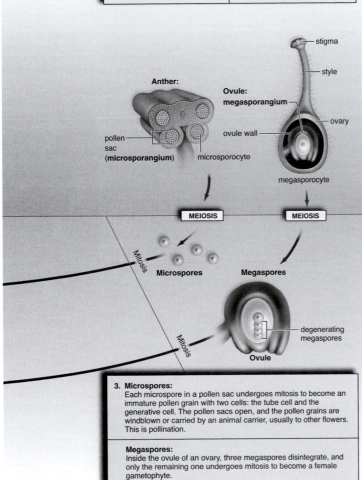

3. Microspores:
Each microspore in a pollen sac undergoes mitosis to become an immature pollen grain with two cells: the tube cell and the generative cell. The pollen sacs open, and the pollen grains are windblown or carried by an animal carrier, usually to other flowers. This is pollination.

Megaspores:
Inside the ovule of an ovary, three megaspores disintegrate, and only the remaining one undergoes mitosis to become a female gametophyte.

Index

Abbott, Joe, "To Kill a Hawk," 3, 5, 8, 67–70
annotating, 116–119
argument, structure of, 400
articles and essays, differences between, 36–37

Bailey, Cornelia, "Still Gullah: A Sea Island Sister Struggles to Preserve the Old Ways," 11, 18, 85–88, 301
Barasch, Marc Ian, "The Bystander's Dilemma: Why Do We Walk On By?" 10, 37, 125–132, 210–211
Barry, Dave, "Tips for Women: How to Have a Relationship with a Guy," 4, 23–26, 45, 307
Bettelheim, Bruno, *The Uses of Enchantment*, 303
bias, 400–401
Blow, Charles M., "Farewell, Fair Weather," 405–406
"Briquette a Day, A," 123–124
Bryson, Bill, "Lonely Planet," 284–289

Coen, Joel and Ethan, 37
context clues, using, 7–10
    antonyms, 9
    emotion, 10
    examples or series of details, 9
    situation, 9–10
    synonyms, 8
Cowley, Geoffrey, "The Language Explosion," 9, 12, 122, 164–169, 213–214, 304

definitions, choosing correct, 16, 18–19
development, patterns of, 298–303
    examples, 299–300
    listing facts or details, 299
    process, 302
    reasons (cause and effect), 300–302
    contrast, 302–303
Diamond, Jared, "Easter's End," 37, 378–387
Dickerson, Debra J., "Raising Cain," 309–313
dictionaries, 14–21
    entry, 14
    etymology, 16
    guide words, 14
    order of definitions, 15–16
    parts of speech, 15
    print vs. online, 19–21
    pronunciation symbols, 15
    sample column in, 17
    stress marks, 15
    variant forms, 16
Dominick, Joseph R., Fritz Messere, and Barry L. Sherman, "The Ratings Process," 460–467
Duke, Lynne, "The Picture of Conformity," 333–339

Electronic spellers, 21

Ferrell, David, "Badwater: The Ultra-Marathon," 347–358
fiction and nonfiction, difference between, 36

Finney, Charles, "The Life and Death of a Western Gladiator," 5, 9, 12, 104–109, 119–120, 212–213, 301, 307

Flora, Carlin, "Hello, My Name Is Unique," 41, 43–44, 367–372

Frazier, Ian, "Dearly Disconnected," 263–267, 306

global warming, 446–447

grades, low (four surefire ways to get), 450–452

Grim, Pamela, "Care in Midair," 3–4, 46–51, 306

Guest, Tim, "Linden Lab's Second Life: Dreamers of the Dream," 13, 251–256, 300–301, 307

Guilbault, Rose, "School Days," 11, 75–79, 120–121, 307

Handelsman, Walt (cartoon), 436

Hunter, Duncan, "Building a Wall Between Worlds" (paired editorial), 437–439

implied main ideas, 42–43

inferences, making, 208–215

Jordan, Pete, "Head Dishwasher?" 11, 56–61

Kottak, Conrad Phillip, "Race," 481–488

Lahey, Benjamin B., "Sleep and Dreams: Conscious While Asleep," 468–480

Lappé, Frances Moore, and Jeffrey Perkins, "The Two Sides of Fear," 7, 12, 152–156

Lewis, Judith, "Walk on the Wilshire Side," 12, 18–19, 94–98, 300

Losco, Joseph, and Ralph Baker, "Measuring Public Opinion," 456–459

Mader, Sylvia S., "Seed Plants, Gymnosperms, and Angiosperms," 489–497

main idea, identifying, 36–43

Mandela, Nelson, "Long Walk to Freedom," 308, 320–325

Margolin, Malcolm, 300

Martin, Courtney E., "Is the American Dream a Delusion?" 415–417

McKibben, Bill, "The Environmental Issue from Hell," 10, 409–412

Morell, Virginia, "Minds of Their Own," 39–40, 118–119, 175–184, 299, 305

Navarrette, Ruben, "Racial Profiling Is Un-American," 421–423

"Paired Web Sites—Two Scientific Views of Global Warming," 446–447

paraphrasing, 119–121

persuasive writing, principles of, 394
    aims of, 394–395
    claims, types of, 396–397
    evidence, kinds of, 397–398
    how to read, 395–396
    opinions, forming, 404
    refutation in, 398–399

Petit-Zerman, Sophie, "No Laughing Matter," 302

Plumwood, Val, "Being Prey: Surviving a Crocodile Attack," 238–244

Pomfret, John, "Two Sides to the Border Fence," 426–429

purpose, identifying, 45

Rose, Chris, "Hell and Back," 12, 138–145, 304

Royte, Elizabeth, "A Fountain on Every Corner," 401–403

Schlosser, Eric, "Fast Food Nation: Behind the Counter," 38–39, 42–43, 216–222

Shames, Lawrence, "The Hunger for More," 13, 274–277

Sipress, David (cartoon), 208

SQ3R study method, 453–455

study time, making the most of, 453

summarizing, 121–124

Terkel, Studs, "Somebody Built the Pyramids," 13, 229–232

thesis statements, in articles and essays, 43–44

transitional elements, 303–308

Turnley, Peter, "The Line—Photographs from the U.S.–Mexican Border" (photo essay), 443–444

Urrea, Luis Alberto, "$1.2 Billion Fence Adds Little or No Security" (paired editorial), 430–434

vocabulary
   acquiring new words, 1–2
   breaking words down, 4–5
   context clues, 7–10
   etymology, 5
   using note cards or notebook, 3
   using the three-dot method, 2
   word-of-the-day sites, 6

Walker, Alice, "The Civil Rights Movement: What Good Was It?" 302

Wolkomir, Richard, "Making Up for Lost Time: The Rewards of Reading at Last," 5, 12–13, 192–201, 305

Index of Vocabulary Preview Words

a-, an-, 333
aboriginal, 239
acronyms, 431
androgynous, 309
animal adjective suffixes, 192
anonymous, 229–230
anti-, 229
aquatic, 238
automated, 216

bene-, 56, 320
bi-, 84

chron-, 175
circulatory, 46
co-, con-, 405
cogn-, recognition, 67
contra-, 85
credentials, 84

de-, 104
demographic, 216
demos, epidemiology, 405
dictatorial, 153

eco-, 430–431
em-, 75, 125
empathy, 138
equi-, 125–126
equivalent, 409
eu-, 347
extra-, 378

-fy, 164

homogeneous, 367

idiosyncratic, 367–368
ignominious, 348
illiteracy, 192–193
indigenous, 239
-ine, 192
initiates, 320
innovations, 252
ir-, irrevocable, 67
-ist, 415
-ity, 238
-ize, 175

linguist, 164

magnitude, 409
mal-, 138
mater-, 263
-meter, 22
micro-, 46
mobility, 415

nano-, 284
numerical prefixes, 84

phobia, 310
potent, 126
pre-, 251
prejudice, 421
primal, 152–153
psychologist, 421

re-, 152
renovation, 252
revive, 378

sensibilities, 56
snafu, 431
somnolent, 104
speculate, 274
sub-, 75
sympathy, 138

tele-, 263
terra, terrestrial, 284

trans-, 334
transmission, 23
tri-, 274

vivid, 86

Reading Comprehension Progress Chart

To calculate your progress, find the number of the selection at the top and the number representing your percentage of correct answers at the left. At the square where the two numbers meet, shade it in with a pencil. This will allow you to keep track of the progress you make during the term. Remember that a score of 70 percent or above is considered acceptable and that since the selections become progressively more difficult, a constant score of 70 percent throughout the text indicates improvement.